TAIWAN
BUSINESS

**World Trade Press
Country Business Guides**

CHINA Business
HONG KONG Business
JAPAN Business
KOREA Business
MEXICO Business
SINGAPORE Business
TAIWAN Business

TAIWAN
BUSINESS

The Portable Encyclopedia
For Doing Business With Taiwan

Christine A. Genzberger   Edward G. Hinkelman
David E. Horovitz   William T. LeGro
Jonathan W. Libbey   Charles Smithson Mills
James L. Nolan   Stacey S. Padrick
Karla C. Shippey, J.D.   Kelly X. Wang
Chansonette Buck Wedemeyer   Alexandra Woznick

Auerbach International • Baker & McKenzie
China External Trade Development Council
CIGNA Property and Casualty • Ernst & Young
Far Eastern Economic Review • Foreign Trade
Reed Publishing (USA) Inc.

Series Editor: Edward G. Hinkelman

WORLD
TRADE
PRESS ®

Resources for International Trade

1505 Fifth Avenue
San Rafael, California 94901
USA

Published by World Trade Press
1505 Fifth Avenue
San Rafael, CA 94901
USA

Cover and book design: Brad Greene
Illustrations: Eli Africa
Color Maps: Gracie Artemis
B&W maps: David Baker
Desktop Publishing: Kelly R. Krill and Gail R. Weisman
Charts and Graphs: David Baker and Kelly R. Krill

Library of Congress Cataloging-in-Publication Data
Taiwan business : the portable encyclopedia for doing business with
  Taiwan / Christine Genzberger . . . [et al.].
    p. cm. — (World Trade Press country business guides)
  Includes bibliographical references and index.
  ISBN 0-9631864-5-0 : $24.95
    1. Taiwan—Economic conditions—1975- 2. Taiwan—Economic
  policy—1975- 3. Investments, Foreign—Government policy—Taiwan.
  4. International business enterprises—Taiwan. I. Genzberger,
  Christine. II. Series.
  HC430.5.T3375 1994   93-45978
  330.95124'9–dc20   CIP

Printed in the United States of America

ACKNOWLEDGMENTS

Contributions of hundreds of trade and reference experts have made possible the extensive coverage of this book.

We are indebted to numerous international business consultants, reference librarians, travel advisors, consulate, embassy, and trade mission officers, bank officers, attorneys, global shippers and insurers, and multinational investment brokers who answered our incessant inquiries and volunteered facts, figures, and expert opinions.

A special note of gratitude is due to those at the U.S. Department of Commerce, the China External Trade Development Council (CETRA), and the Singapore Trade Development Board.

We relied heavily on the reference librarians and resources available at the Marin County Civic Center Library, Marin County Law Library, San Rafael Public Library, San Francisco Public Library, University of California at Berkeley libraries, and U.S. Department of Commerce Library in San Francisco.

Special thanks to attorneys Robert T. Yahng and Anne M. Kelleher, with Baker & McKenzie, San Francisco, who spent precious time in assisting us with the law section. We also extend our sincere appreciation to Barry Tarnef, with CIGNA Property and Casualty Co., who graciously supplied information on world ports, and to Benjamin Hsu, with the Los Angeles office of Taiwan's Commercial Division of the Coordination Council for North American Affairs, who kindly gave us investment information.

We also acknowledge the valuable contributions of Philip B. Auerbach of Auerbach International, San Francisco, for translations; all the patient folks at Desktop Publishing of Larkspur, California; and Krystal Lee, Leslie Endicott, and Susan August for reviewing, proofing, and correcting down to the smallest details.

Our thanks to Elizabeth Karolczak for establishing the World Trade Press Intern Program, and to the Monterey Institute of International Studies for its assistance.

To Jerry and Kathleen Fletcher, we express our deep appreciation for their immeasurable support.

Very special thanks to Mela Hinkelman without whose patience, understanding, generosity and support this project would not have been possible.

DISCLAIMER

We have diligently tried to ensure the accuracy of all of the information in this publication and to present as comprehensive a reference work as space would permit. In determining the contents, we were guided by many experts in the field, extensive hours of research, and our own experience. We did have to make choices in coverage, however, because the inclusion of everything one could ever want to know about international trade would be impossible. The fluidity and fast pace of today's business world makes the task of keeping data current and accurate an extremely difficult one. This publication is intended to give you the information that you need in order to discover the information that is most useful for your particular business. As you contact the resources within this book, you will no doubt learn of new and exciting business opportunities and of additional international trading requirements that have arisen even within the short time since we published this edition. If errors are found, we will strive to correct them in preparing future editions. The publishers take no responsibility for inaccurate or incomplete information that may have been submitted to them in the course of research for this publication. The facts published indicate the result of those inquiries and no warranty as to their accuracy is given.

Contents

Introduction

The Republic of China (ROC), more commonly known as Taiwan, is one of the world's most dynamic economies. An island backwater with few natural resources, it did not exist as a separate entity before it was thrust onto the world scene in 1949. In that year it became the focus of the continuing struggle for control between mainland Communist China and the Chinese Nationalists who fled to its shores.

Since then Taiwan has built a modern, internationally oriented industrial economy largely from scratch. This economy, based on low-cost, high-quality export production, has grown at an average rate of more than 9 percent per year for the past 40 years. Despite its small size, Taiwan is the fourteenth-largest trading economy in the world, its trade having grown at an annual rate of almost 15 percent since the late 1970s. Although Taiwan continues to be politically estranged from mainland China, declaring trade with it to be illegal, activity between the two that accounts for perhaps 10 percent of Taiwan's total trade is an open secret. Taiwan is rapidly becoming a second gateway to markets in China.

Ranked third in the world among newly industrialized countries in the 1993 World Competitive Report, Taiwan is a market well worth investigating from a number of perspectives. For buyers Taiwan can provide a wide range of competitive goods at virtually any level of sophistication. It is a leading producer of electronics and computer products; metal-, wood-, and plastics-fabricating machinery; auto parts; hand tools; textiles, garments, and footwear; and furniture, housewares, and giftware, among many other items. Its businesses can handle anything from the smallest to the largest orders.

From the seller's standpoint Taiwan needs a wide range of agricultural and industrial raw materials, intermediate components, and specialty items to feed its active industry. Both the upgrading of that industry and Taiwan's large public- and private-sector development projects require materials, capital goods, and services. And the rapidly rising demands of its relatively affluent and newly unleashed consumers offer opportunities to place goods in the island's developing consumer market. Taiwan has relied on Japan for many goods, but the strength of the yen has made Japanese products less competitive, opening up opportunities for new suppliers.

For manufacturers Taiwan has a pool of well-educated semi-skilled to highly skilled labor experienced in the areas already noted as well as in many others. In addition to its generally advanced industrial plant, Taiwan has built a variety of special production facilities, including export-processing zones and a high-technology science park. This infrastructure offers a competitive base for a variety of outsourcing needs.

For investors Taiwan is in the process of opening up additional areas of its economy that had previously been off-limits to foreigners, including its growing service and financial sectors. It particularly encourages foreign participation in its emerging high-technology industries and the development of key technologies and targeted product groups, offering tax breaks, exemptions, and incentives.

The Taiwanese miracle is beginning to show signs of both maturity and age. Taiwan is refocusing its economy on high-tech, high-value-added, clean, capital-intensive products as it gives up some of its edge in low-cost, low-technology production. The adaptability of its small- and medium-sized businesses argues that it will successfully make the transition to a new economy. Taiwanese business is generally more entrepreneurial and responsive and less rigidly hierarchical than some other Asian systems, and the absence of the giant corporations that dominate many other Far Eastern economies makes it more accessible to foreigners.

Taiwan is also making the transition to a more open and democratic political system after years of authoritarian rule, although it maintains a core of stability within its pro-business government. The overall pace and level of change are expected to accelerate over the near term, making Taiwan one of the most complex, challenging, and most compelling places on the globe to do business.

TAIWAN Business was designed by business people experienced in international markets to give you an overview of how things actually work and what current conditions are in Taiwan. It will give you the head start you need as a buyer, seller, manufacturer, or investor to evaluate and operate in Taiwanese markets. Further, it tells you where to go to get more specific information in greater depth.

The first chapter discusses the main elements of the country's **Economy** including its development, present situation, and the forces determining its future prospects. **Current Issues** explains the top five concerns affecting the country and its next stage of development. The **Opportunities** chapter presents 11 major areas of interest to importers plus 10 additional hot prospects, and 20 major areas for exporters plus 12 more hot opportunities. Discussions of six major sectoral growth areas and a section on trade zones and other specialized facilities follow. The chapter also clarifies the nature of the government procurement that will drive Taiwan's US$230 billion Six-Year Development Plan with its focus on telecommunications, transportation, construction, environmental, energy, and aerospace projects. **Foreign Investment** details policies, incentives, regulations, procedures, and what is allowed and restricted, with particular reference to Taiwan's drive to develop high-technology enterprises.

Although Taiwan is banking on high technology as the wave of the future, it remains a highly diversified export-oriented economy with many thriving low- and medium-technology operations. The **Foreign Trade**, **Import Policies**, and **Export Policies** chapters delineate the nature of Taiwan's trade, what and with whom it trades, trade policy, and the practical information, including nuts-and-bolts procedural requirements, necessary to trade with it. The **Industry Reviews** chapter outlines Taiwan's 16 most prominent industries and their competitive position from the standpoint of a business person interested in taking advantage of these industries' strengths or in exploiting their competitive weaknesses. **Trade Fairs** provides a comprehensive listing of trade fairs in Taiwan, complete with contact information, and spells out the best ways to maximize the benefits offered by these chances to see and be seen. **Business Travel** offers practical information on how to travel to Taiwan, including travel requirements, resources, internal travel, local customs, and ambiance, as well as comparative information on accommodations and dining in Taipei and Kaoshiung, the two main business markets in Taiwan. **Business Culture** provides a user-friendly primer on local business style, mind-set, negotiating practices, and numerous other tips designed to improve your effectiveness, avoid inadvertent gaffes, and generally smooth the way in doing business with the Taiwan-

ese. **Demographics** presents the basic statistical data needed to assess the Taiwanese market, while **Marketing** outlines resources, approaches, and specific markets on the island, including seven ways to approach Taiwanese markets, seven ways to sell your product, five ways to help your agent serve you better, and five ways to build business relationships.

Business Formation discusses business entities and registration procedures for setting up operations in Taiwan. **Labor** assembles information on the availability, capabilities, costs, terms of employment, and business relations in Taiwan. **Business Law** interprets the structure of the Taiwanese legal system, giving a digest of substantive points of commercial law prepared from Martindale-Hubbell with additional material from the international law firm of Baker & McKenzie. **Financial Institutions** outlines the workings of the financial system, including banking and financial markets, and the availability of financing and services needed by foreign businesses. **Currency and Foreign Exchange** explains the workings of the complicated foreign exchange system. **International Payments** is an illustrated step-by-step guide to using documentary collections and letters of credit in trade with Taiwan. Ernst and Young's **Taxation—Corporate** and **Taxation—Personal** provide the information on tax rates, provisions, and status of foreign operations and individuals needed to evaluate a venture in the country.

Ports and Airports, prepared with the help of CIGNA Property and Casualty Company, gives current information on how to physically access the country. The **Business Dictionary**, a unique resource prepared especially for this volume in conjunction with Auerbach International, consists of more than 425 entries focusing specifically on Taiwanese business and idiomatic usage to provide the business person with the basic means for conducting business in Taiwan. **Important Addresses** lists more than 650 Taiwanese government agencies and international and foreign official representatives; local and international business associations; trade and industry associations; financial, professional, and service firms; transportation and shipping agencies; media outlets; and sources of additional information enable business people to locate the offices and the help they need to operate in Taiwan. Full-color, detailed, up-to-date **Maps** aid the business traveler in getting around the major business venues in Taiwan.

TAIWAN Business gives you the information you need both to evaluate the prospect of doing business in Taiwan and to actually begin doing it. It is your invitation to this fascinating society and market. Welcome.

Economy

The Republic of China (ROC), generally known as Taiwan, is a relatively small island nation that has existed in its current form for fewer than 45 years. During most of that period, it has been threatened to a greater or lesser extent with takeover by the much larger People's Republic of China (PRC), survived the social tensions occasioned by the presence of a subordinate local majority, and struggled to maintain and develop itself as a viable independent entity in a restricted territory that has few available resources.

Taiwan consists of an oblong main island named Formosa by the Portuguese and several considerably smaller islands of limited economic significance, including the Penghu or Pescadores group and the flash point islets of Quemoy and Matsu, located just off the Chinese coast. The country, which lies only about 100 miles from the Chinese mainland, is somewhat smaller than the Netherlands, larger than Belgium, and half the size of Ireland. Its sparsely populated eastern two-thirds are marked by a north-south trending ridge of high mountains, which slopes to a broad, relatively flat plain that covers the western one-third of the island.

Taiwan's 13,885 square miles of territory supported a growing population of 21 million people in 1993, 72 percent of whom lived in urban areas. The resulting population density of more than 1,500 persons per square mile is exceeded only by that of Bangladesh. Although the effective local density varies considerably, 10 percent of the population are concentrated in the capital city of Taipei, and one-third of the population is found in Taiwan's six major cities, which all are located on the western coastal plain. Taiwan's inhabitants are virtually all ethnic Chinese, although there are significant historic and social differences between the 84 percent who are classed as native Taiwanese—including 14 percent Hakka—and the 14 percent who are identified as late 1940s mainland Chinese immigrants. Some 2 percent are classed as non-Chinese aborigines.

Some two-thirds of Taiwan is mountainous, and only 24 percent is arable. About 55 percent is forested, mostly in the upland areas, while 5 percent is grasslands, and 16 percent is classed as "other," which includes developed urban areas, inland waters, and bare ground. The island is poor in natural resources, and the few strategic resources that it does possess are inadequate to meet domestic needs. From its beginnings, Taiwan has focused on value-added trade to secure what it lacks and gain the resources that it needs to develop its economy.

HISTORY OF THE ECONOMY

Premodern Taiwan

Taiwan has been known to the Chinese for at least 2,000 years. However, they did not settle the island until around AD 500, when Hakka refugees moved in from southern China. The island was not officially claimed until 1430, after mainstream migrants from nearby Fujian province began to settle there, partly because of crowding on the mainland and partly to escape official controls. Attempts to exploit the island were sporadic, and its economy remained largely one of subsistence fishing and farming, with a little smuggling and piracy thrown in. The Portuguese explored the island in 1517, and the Dutch settled it in 1624, fending off would-be Spanish colonizers in 1641.

The Manchu conquest of China in the early 1600s resulted in the flight of defeated Taiwan-born Ming admiral Koxinga and 30,000 followers to the island. Koxinga expelled the Dutch in 1661 and set up a Chinese nationalist government-in-exile on Taiwan. The Manchus finally subjugated the Ming loyalists, incorporating Taiwan as a subdivision of adjacent Fujian province in 1684. Over the next 200 years, immigration from China increased steadily, the vast majority of it from Fujian, although the economy developed slowly, and the central government never established very tight control over what it considered to be an unimportant backwater area. Taiwan, with a population of 2.5 million, became a separate province of China in 1887.

The Japanese Period

The island was ceded to Japan in 1895 after China's defeat in the Sino-Japanese war (1894-1895). Japan operated Taiwan as a colony until Japan's defeat in World War II in 1945, when the island reverted to Chinese jurisdiction. During their tenure, the Japanese developed Taiwan's economy, educational system, and infrastructure, although their rule was strict, and their motives were hardly altruistic, because the economy that they constructed was designed to benefit Japan, not the locals. Much of the island's plant and organization had deteriorated by the time the prolonged war ended in 1945. However, exposure to the Japanese system had made the Taiwanese better prepared for future industrialization than they would have been if they had remained within China's sphere.

The Beginning of the Modern Era

While Taiwan was occupied as a Japanese colony, the bankrupt Q'ing dynasty on the mainland collapsed in 1911, giving way to the Republic of China (ROC), founded by Sun Yatsen. China was thrown into chaos as rival factions competed for control. Japan took advantage of this disorganization to seize Manchuria in 1931 and invade China itself in 1937. The situation turned into a three-way struggle among the Japanese, the Chinese Communists, and the nationalist Chinese Kuomintang (KMT) party. With the defeat and withdrawal of the Japanese in 1945, the conflict continued as a civil war between the Communists and the KMT. The nationalists were effectively defeated in 1949, and Mao Zedong proclaimed the Communist People's Republic of China (PRC).

Taiwan took on its modern identity when two million KMT supporters led by Chiang Kai Shek fled mainland China in 1949 and set up a nationalist government-in-exile on Taiwan. This KMT-led ROC government declared martial law; claimed sovereignty over all China, including rights of eminent domain over Taiwan; and set the reconquest of the mainland as its goal. At the same time, the PRC claimed full and exclusive sovereignty over China, citing Taiwan as a rebellious province.

The flight of the KMT increased the population of Taiwan by about one-third to 7.5 million virtually overnight. The KMT refugees—soldiers, bureaucrats, business elites, hangers-on, and their families—commandeered positions of authority and such resources as existed, and tensions between them and the subordinated locals increased. The Taiwanese considered the KMT newcomers to be corrupt and authoritarian carpetbaggers, while the KMT considered the Taiwanese to be untrustworthy and un-Chi-

nese due to their traditional marginality and long exposure to the Japanese. In 1947, the local Taiwanese rebelled against the autocratic exactions of the KMT, an uprising that was crushed quickly and somewhat brutally. The military core of the KMT, which remained on a war footing, had no trouble forcing its rule on the local majority.

A social rift between the locals and the mainlanders remains to this day, although the distinctions are fading. All factions view themselves as Chinese, and the divisions will become even less important as the old-guard dies off and more younger people intermarry and begin to see themselves as native Taiwanese.

From the beginning, the nationalists on Taiwan expected to be attacked by the PRC. However, the Communists needed time to consolidate their hold on the mainland and were distracted from an apparent planned invasion in 1950 by their involvement in the Korean War (1950-1953). This gave the KMT, which was supported by US military forces, time to consolidate its own control. A US-Taiwan defense agreement signed in 1954 helped to forestall the feared Communist invasion. KMT plans for a reconquest of the mainland also languished.

In 1971 Taiwan was expelled from the United Nations and its seat was awarded to the PRC. The ROC was also dropped from many international organizations, and it lost formal diplomatic recognition by all but a few of the smaller nations. Even Taiwan's staunchest international ally, the United States, formalized diplomatic relations with the PRC in 1979, although it has continued to support Taiwan unofficially. Despite the loss of face, the ROC has not seemed to suffer materially from the loss of recognition.

Changing Circumstances and Leadership

KMT leader Generalissimo Chiang Kai Shek ruled autocratically as president until his death in 1975, at which point his son, Chiang Ching-kuo, replaced him. However, the old-guard mainlanders lost control as the economy developed, and the younger Chiang paved the way for a more modern system through small, symbolic steps designed to ease the inevitable opening up of the government and the economy. By 1985 the half of the population that could be considered middle-class was demanding more freedom at home and a greater role in government.

Martial law was lifted in 1987, and the government dropped the permanent state of emergency in 1991. Although the PRC and the ROC continue to refuse to recognize each other and officially remain at war, they have contracted to allow each others' citizens to travel between the territories under their respective control.

The KMT relinquished its official single-party monopoly in 1989, having acquiesced to the formation of the opposition Democratic Progressive Party

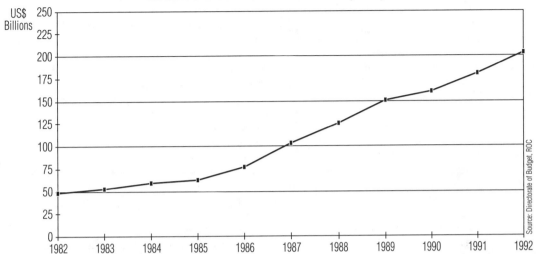

Taiwan's Gross National Product (GNP)

Source: Directorate of Budget, ROC

(DPP) in 1986. Although the KMT retained effective control of the government, it did not disband the DPP, which was illegal at the time, and it has grudgingly seen its single-party majority position erode. The government made an additional significant symbolic step toward the gradual easing of control by allowing Lee Teng-hui to succeed Chiang Ching-kuo as the first native-born Taiwanese president, despite objections fromoold-guard hardliners. It also allowed the first open multiparty open elections in 1989. The Taiwanese government has tentatively pursued greater contacts with the PRC, especially as the economic interests of the two become linked to an increasing extent, although the issue of sovereignty remains unresolved.

Economic Development

The economic development that occurred against this backdrop has been stunning. The single-party authoritarian government that the KMT had set up instituted social and economic planning with such programs as land reform; free, compulsory education; and vast public works projects. These policies, largely funded by government aid and private investment from the United States, have driven the development of Taiwan's economy, which has occurred in three broad stages.

The first phase involved the development of agriculture and basic, local intermediate industries— largely from scratch, following the deterioration of the Japanese-built system during the 1930s and 1940s—in the early 1950s. This effort, designed to increase food production and save foreign exchange through import substitution manufacturing, resulted in the development of a solid base in agriculture and commodity industries, such as cement, paper, and fertilizer production.

During the 1960s and 1970s the focus shifted from import substitution to the export of low-cost, labor-intensive manufactured products in which Taiwan's low wage costs gave it a competitive advantage. These manufactures included toys, apparel, and footwear during the 1960s and electronic consumer goods during the 1970s. During the 1970s Taiwan also concentrated on developing its heavy industrial base and on public infrastructure projects that pumped large infusions of cash into the economy. This government spending helped Taiwan get through the global recession precipitated in the mid-1970s by the surge in oil prices relatively unscathed, despite its dependence on foreign trade and oil imports, and gave its technicians valuable development experience.

As the economy developed during the 1980s, Taiwan's currency appreciated in value, and its labor and overhead costs rose, making its traditional industrial exports increasingly less competitive in world markets. In response, the government instituted programs aimed at upgrading infrastructure and encouraging the development of high-technology, high-value-added, and capital-intensive export-oriented industries.

SIZE OF THE ECONOMY

Known variously as one of the newly industrialized countries (NICs), Asian Tigers, or Little Dragons, Taiwan boasts an economy that is the fourth largest in Asia after Japan, China, and South Korea. This level of gross domestic product (GDP) places Taiwan on a par in absolute terms with the much wealthier Netherlands and the much larger Mexico worldwide. Taiwan's GDP was US$206.5 billion in 1992, up 13 percent in nominal terms and 6.7 percent in real terms from US$183 billion in 1991.

GDP, a modest US$1.2 billion in 1952, had risen to US$156.6 billion in 1990, and it grew at an average annual rate of 9.1 percent between 1950 and 1990. Following the worldwide slowdown in 1984, Taiwan's growth slowed to 4.5 percent in 1985—anemic by its standards—but rebounded in 1986 to an all-time high increase of 12.6 percent in real terms. After that, the real rate of growth slowed to 7.3 percent in 1989, 5.3 percent in 1990, and 7 percent in 1991. Preliminary figures indicate that Taiwan's economy grew at 6 percent in 1993, below the anticipated 6.5 percent rate. The Central Bank of China predicts a 6.1 percent growth rate for 1994.

Per capita gross national product (GNP), which was US$145 in 1951, rose to US$9,895 in 1992, an increase of 12.3 percent over the preceding year in nominal terms. By some measures, per capita income topped the psychologically important threshold of US$10,000 in 1992, and Taiwan's appreciated currency means that the actual purchasing power implied by this figure is even greater than the number would suggest. These numbers, which place Taiwan below Japan, Australia, Hong Kong, and Singapore and above China and South Korea in terms of standard of living among major Pacific Rim countries, are roughly comparable with the per capita incomes found in Southern European countries.

CONTEXT OF THE ECONOMY

The State Sector

Although Taiwan is nominally free market and capitalist, its economy is managed to an extensive degree by a massive state bureaucracy. Taiwan's rigid, authoritarian, single-party system has provided a high degree of stability and allowed the government to advance the standard of living by initiating and funding such social programs as education, public health, family planning, transportation and infra-

structure improvements, and reforestation and environmental protection on a large and continuing scale. All these advantages have enabled its export-oriented economy to flourish.

State-run enterprises account for nearly one-third of Taiwan's GDP. State-owned monopolies control alcohol and tobacco, sugar, telecommunications, petroleum refining, steel, shipbuilding, fertilizer production, transportation, and many areas of banking. During the late 1980s the government initiated an ambitious privatization program that aims to make the economy more efficient by exposing it to market forces as well as to boost Taiwan's stalled stock market by injecting an additional US$20 billion by the end of the decade via sale of stock in privatized firms.

There has been a great deal of bureaucratic foot-dragging in opening up and streamlining the targeted firms for free market operation, and results to date have been poor. Several issues have failed to sell, and others have fallen sharply in price after the initial offering. The stranglehold that bureaucrats exert on the core elements of the official economy and the cozy relationship between big business and government have prevented these behemoths from being opened up for redirection and more efficient operations.

The Private Sector: The Large and, Mostly, the Small of It

Some 97 percent of all Taiwanese firms are small- or medium-sized and privately owned, and about 85 percent of Taiwan's workers are employed by small businesses. Such operations play a correspondingly large role in the nation's economy. One of Taiwan's strengths is its small, usually family-owned and operated businesses. The entrepreneurs who run them have proved to be highly adaptable risk takers ca-

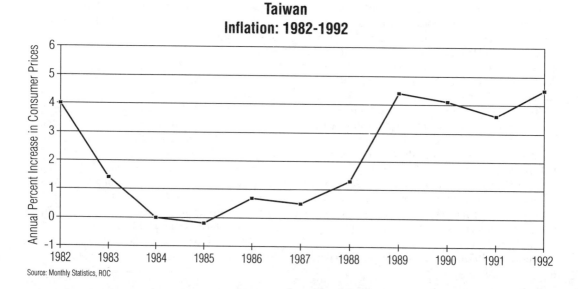

Taiwan
Inflation: 1982-1992

Annual Percent Increase in Consumer Prices

pable of moving quickly to exploit opportunities and niches. Their enterprises have flourished in an environment that, although heavily regulated, still offers a broad range of opportunities. In fact, Taiwan is in some ways as open as other, more laissez-faire Asian economies, such as Hong Kong and Singapore, because in practice many of its regulations and strictures can be routinely ignored.

There is a fairly wide gap between the thousands of small businesses and the few large state monopolies. Taiwan is not known internationally for large, private, big-name firms with recognizable brand names. The small operations that form the base of the economy lack the capital to project an image, while the monopoly poweroof the state-run sector has stunted the development of competing large-scale operations. This has left Taiwan without the large private firms, such as the *zaibatsu* in Japan, the *chaebol* in South Korea, and the *hongs* in Hong Kong, that have influenced the economic development of those Asian countries and allowed them to cast such a large shadow in world commerce.

The China Gap

Taiwan's claim to be the only China has skewed its economic development. Although the ROC and the PRC are linked culturally, they have been involved in a prolonged family feud and effectively have not spoken to each other in forty years, which has cut them off from potential mutually advantageous dealings. This situation is changing rapidly if as yet mostly unofficially. In a grudging bow to the changing reality, Taiwan has recently eased restrictions on indirect dealings and investments in the PRC, investments which until this relaxation could bring stiff fines. Taiwan will gradually allow citizens to open businesses in China, starting with service ventures. Nevertheless, Taiwan has missed out on the economic impetus that Hong Kong has enjoyed as an intermediary between the mainland and the world at large.

The Underground Economy

While single-party rule has allowed for stability in Taiwan, it also has led to stagnation in certain areas, particularly in many state-run enterprises. Although Taiwan is far from having a command economy, heavy central direction at the macro level and lack of responsiveness at the micro level have resulted in a certain degree of systemic inflexibility and misallocation. There is a general perception that the ruling party and its entrenched bureaucrats operate in conjunction with favored contributors and vested interests at the expense of an open, efficient economic system, and that the little guy has been frozen out of the most lucrative and safest deals.

As a result, the island's entrepreneurs have developed a large and pervasive underground economy, which operates in the interstices and evades official controls. Some observers estimate this unofficial economic activity to be as much as 40 percent of the total official economy.

Most business in Taiwan is done on a cash basis, and even bank drafts are considered somewhat exotic. Because many transactions are concluded with a handshake, there is little in the way of documentation or formality and therefore little or no paper trail. Accounting standards are lax, and income often goes unreported. Taiwan's official business operations lack transparency, and its bureaucracy has traditionally been viewed as obstructionist and open to corruption. Licensing, operating regulations, and tax laws are so complex, onerous, and erratically enforced that many small to medium-sized operators take the unofficial route after deciding that paying a fine if they are caught is preferable and an acceptable cost of doing business.

Taiwan
Consumer Price Index (CPI)

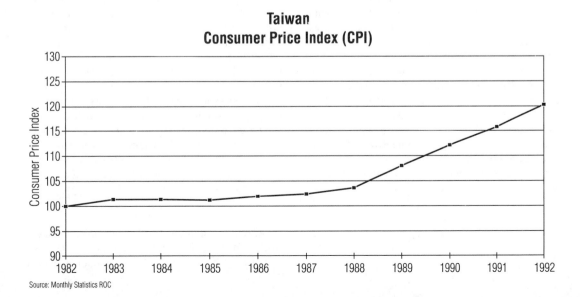

Source: Monthly Statistics ROC

Intellectual Property Rights

Taiwan is a major world source of counterfeit goods. In principle, Taiwan protects copyrights, trademarks, patents, and similar rights, but enforcement, although it has improved since the mid-1980s, continues to be ineffective and has a low priority. Taiwan's entrepreneurial culture and tradition of avoiding regulation have made the country a major center for the production of counterfeit items, to the ire of many of its trading partners.

INFLATION

Given the robust real, sustained growth of Taiwan's economy, inflation historically has remained relatively low, increasing by 4.5 percent in 1992. Consumer inflation was 3 percent in 1972, surged to 19 percent in 1980, and eased to a slightly negative 0.2 percent in 1985. Following the slowdown during the mid-1980s, inflation did not top 1 percent again until 1988, although in 1989 it bumped up to an annual rate of 4.4 percent and then began to slow—4.1 percent in 1990, 3.6 percent in 1991, and 3.3 percent on an annualized basis in June 1993. Forecasters anticipate that inflation will increase at a 4.2 percent annual rate by mid-1994.

Another measure of expectations on inflation is provided by the prime rate, although it is heavily controlled by the government manipulated financial sector. In mid-1993, Taiwan's prime rate stood at 8 percent, high by the standards of developed Asian economies and close to double the 4.5 percent recorded during much of the 1980s. Observers expect it to rise to around 8.5 percent by mid-1994. Adding to inflationary pressures, monetary authorities have allowed the money supply to grow at a rate almost double that of real growth.

Many observers consider these official statistics on inflation to be suspect. Civil service and private sector wages have risen at rates of 7 to 10 percent a year for several years, well above the official inflation figures. Informal consumer surveys indicate a much higher real rise in the cost of living, due partially to the inefficient and restrictive distribution and retail system that keeps consumer choice low and prices high. The much-discussed shortage of unskilled and semi-skilled laborers and of highly skilled personnel in such areas as finance, marketing, and research and development would suggest that upward pressure on prices is a more extensive and long-lived phenomenon than the government seems willing to recognize officially.

LABOR

Taiwan's work force is generally well trained and industrious. School attendance is mandatory for nine years, and under new regulations, mandatory schooling will rise to 12 years over a phase-in period. The Taiwanese educational system has been highly responsive to the needs of business. In fact, the current labor shortage owes much to the fact that the labor force is so well trained and successful that there are relatively few low-level workers available.

The Labor Shortage

High wages and high growth over the last several years have resulted in a shortage of unskilled and semi-skilled workers. Moreover, the shift in Taiwan's economy away from the manufacturing and toward the service sector has produced a need for specialized workers in such areas as finance and marketing. Nevertheless, Taiwan is well supplied with most categories and skill levels of personnel. The clamor for less-skilled workers has made illegal foreign workers an issue. The government has allowed foreign workers in only when officials declare an industry-specific labor shortage, only for a limited period of time and only on payment of a substantial deposit.

Many firms have bypassed these rules by bringing in workers illegally. Conservative estimates at the end of 1992 placed the number of such illegals at around 30,000. Other observers put the total as high as 200,000. The Employment Services Law that was passed in April 1992 requires that work permits for all foreign workers be issued in advance. Such permits could be rationed to control foreign workers. However, the government has not yet decided how to set quotas, issue permits, or enforce the new regulations.

Unemployment

In 1992 the unemployment rate was a low 1.6 percent, and it has not exceeded 2 percent since 1987, although underemployment was a hefty reported 20.5 percent in 1991. Unemployment rose as high as 2.9 percent in 1985 during the recession, but for most of the 1970s and early 1980s, it stayed below 1.5 percent, a figure that indicates essentially no structural unemployment. The shortage of unskilled and low-skilled labor has kept unemployment down, although as high costs cause the traditionally low-wage, labor-intensive industries to move offshore, both the labor shortage and the unemployment situation could be reversed.

Unions

Although about one-third of Taiwan's 8.6 million workers nominally belong to a union—a percentage higher than in any of the Asian economies except

China and higher than in most industrialized Western countries—unions play a minor role in Taiwan's economy. The government has taken a hard line in labor disputes, and as the Taiwanese economy slows and concern over holding onto jobs increases, employers have become increasingly more confrontational. Unions, many of which are more associations than traditional Western-style collective bargaining entities, have behaved circumspectly, and the number of disputes and the number of workers involved in them has fallen substantially in recent years.

Labor Costs

The average weekly wage in Taiwan's manufacturing sector was US$225.69 in 1992, plus mandated benefits of 8.2 percent or US$18.51. Benefits include health, workmen's compensation, disability, unemployment, and death benefits insurance as well as severance and retirement benefits and the employer's contribution to an employee welfare fund. Workers are customarily paid an annual New Year's bonus equal to at least one month's salary, and they get paid holidays, vacation, and overtime, although smaller firms can evade some of these requirements by operating outside the formal economy. Additional benefits can include housing, transportation, and food allowances. In 1991 Taiwan's official minimum weekly wage was US$113.54, but in practice no labor was available at that level. Labor costs vary widely by skill level, with weekly wages ranging from about US$275 for low-level supervisory and technical personnel to around US$1,500 for senior managerial personnel.

Labor costs are broadly comparable to those in South Korea, where average weekly wages are US$295, and Singapore, with US$261. In contrast, average weekly wages, including benefits, in Japan are US$705 and US$7.37 in China.

Workweek

Taiwan's regular workweek is 48 hours for manufacturing personnel and 44 hours for service personnel. Multinational firms are instituting a 40-hour workweek, but it is expected to be some time before the shorter week becomes standard. In 1991 the overall average workweek in Taiwan is 45.5 hours, one of the shortest in Asia. By comparison, the workweek averages 47.9 hours in South Korea, 46.7 in Singapore, 46.1 hours in Japan, and 46 hours in Hong Kong. Among Western industrialized countries, the average workweek is 43.6 hours in the United Kingdom, 39.9 hours in Germany, 39 hours in France, and 34.3 hours in the United States. (Refer to "Labor" chapter.)

SECTORS OF THE ECONOMY

Taiwan's economy relies heavily on its manufacturing and industrial sector, which produced 45.8 percent of GDP in 1991. The service sector, dominated by finance and trade, represented 50.2 percent, while agriculture accounted for 4 percent. At the beginning of 1992 12.9 percent of the work force were employed in agriculture, while 40.2 percent worked in industry and 46.9 percent in services.

In 1983, the agricultural sector accounted for 7.2 percent of GDP, while the industrial sector represented 45 percent and the service sector 47.8 percent. The contribution of agriculture to GDP has dwindled by almost half over the last ten years, while that of the service sector has increased. These trends are expected to continue, with agriculture shrinking in significance both in GDP—to less than 2.5 per-

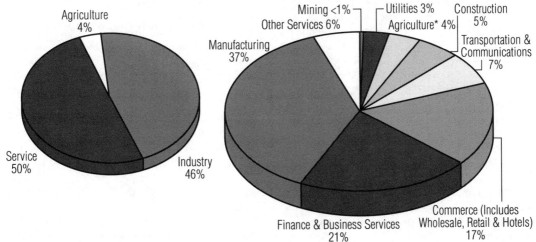

Structure of the Taiwanese Economy - 1991

Agriculture 4%

Service 50%

Industry 46%

Mining <1%
Other Services 6%
Manufacturing 37%
Utilities 3%
Agriculture* 4%
Construction 5%
Transportation & Communications 7%
Commerce (Includes Wholesale, Retail & Hotels) 17%
Finance & Business Services 21%

Note: Figures are rounded to the nearest percentage point. Source: Department General Of Budget, Accounting, and Statistics, ROC

* Includes Forestry & Fishing

cent—and in employment—to less than 7.5 percent—by decade's end. The industrial sector will contract, dropping to 37.5 percent of both GDP and employment, and services will provide almost 55 percent of the jobs and 60 percent of the GDP as Taiwan's economy matures over the remainder of the decade.

In 1990, private consumption in Taiwan represented roughly 54 percent of GDP, with government consumption 17.5 percent and gross domestic capital formation 35 percent, evidence that Taiwan funded a high percentage of its growth from internally generated savings. Both consumption and government spending can be expected to rise, with domestic savings falling as a result. The average annual fixed investment in Taiwan between 1988 and 1992 was around 28 percent of GDP; figures for Japan and the United States during the same period were 33 percent and 15 percent respectively.

As recently as 1990, government debt was a modest 5 percent of GNP. However, by June 1993, it was estimated at US$62 billion, approximately 30 percent of GNP. Although Taiwan has nominal foreign borrowings—foreign debt was US$600 million in 1992—its domestic public debt is growing at a rate that some find alarming, and efforts have been made to rein in government issuance of debt, with anticipated issues in FY1994 expected to be US$5.6 billion, down from US$8 billion in FY1993. These numbers point to potential problems with inflation and a maturing economy in which public debt service could begin to crowd out private investment. Nevertheless, there are few indications that current conditions are preventing private projects from going through in Taiwan.

Agriculture

Prior to the 1940s, the island's economy was based on agriculture, and one of the critical tasks for Taiwan's leadership after 1949 was to increase production to feed the island's augmented population. Nevertheless, the role of agriculture has waned over the last thirty years. The agricultural sector, which includes fisheries and forestry, accounted for 4 percent of GDP in 1991 and employed 12.9 percent of the labor force, primarily on very small family farms.

From 1953 through 1962 overall agricultural production grew by an annual average rate of 3.7 percent; between 1963 and 1972, the rate eased to 2.8 percent, and between 1973 and 1987 it fell to what was effectively a break-even position with a nominal annual growth rate of 0.1 percent. Between 1978 and 1987, output of virtually all major crops showed double-digit percentage contractions, although livestock production has continued to increase steadily over the last 30 years. During the 1980s, as agricultural production plateaued and crop prices stagnated, workers left the farm to seek employment in the fast-growing manufacturing sector. Although the area under cultivation dropped by only 1.4 percent, the population involved in agriculture plummeted by 32.1 percent.

Taiwan's major crops are rice, sugar cane, sweet potatoes, peanuts, asparagus, mushrooms, tea, citrus fruits, pineapples, pears, and bananas. Livestock production has almost doubled over the last ten years, although at the cost of large imports of feed grains. Swine and poultry are Taiwan's major animal products. Although fishing grew during the 1980s, and a significant portion of the catch was exported, catches had stabilized by the early 1990s, and they are unlikely to increase substantially in the future. The insignificant forestry industry has contracted as concerns over conservation issues and a drop in the exploitable timber stock—due to poor accessibility and a failure to reseed—have resulted in a substantial decline in lumbering.

Foreign investment in agriculture is banned, and there is a de facto ban on imports of agricultural products that Taiwan produces, such as rice and sugar—which are overproduced due to guaranteed price subsidies—peanuts, pork, and poultry products. Despite these restrictions, foodstuffs are still one of Taiwan's top ten imports. As with many traditionally agricultural societies in the Far East and elsewhere, Taiwan's farming lobbies continue to wield political influence far out of proportion to their numbers and their contribution to GDP. This situation can be expected to wane—slowly, but faster than it will in some other Asian economies, such as Japan and South Korea—as farming becomes increasingly less important to the economy and rural ties lessen over time.

In November 1993 Taiwan was faced with the prospect of cutting its winter rice planting by 40 percent because of a continuing drought. Farmers who are unable to plant will be given a government subsidy in compensation.

Manufacturing and Industry

More than any other sector, industry—including manufacturing, mining, construction, and utilities—has driven the growth of Taiwan's economy. In 1991 manufacturing and industry accounted for 45.8 percent of its GDP, produced virtually all its exports, and employed 40.2 percent of its total work force. Manufacturing alone contributed 37.1 percent of GDP—the largest single contributor in the entire economy—and employed 32 percent of the work force.

Manufacturing is expected to remain Taiwan's primary focus in the near future. Although Taiwan's traditionally strong lower-end light industrial manufactures, such as apparel, plastic items, footwear, and toys, are being co-opted by lower-cost labor in China and Southeast Asia, they still provide important export products. Taiwan has had problems with heavy industry as a result of environmental difficulties, stumbling privatization efforts, and a lessening of international competitiveness due to increasing costs. Such industries as steel and petroleum refining, which supplies feedstock for the important plastics industry as well as fuels, operate inefficiently at well below capacity.

Taiwan's strength traditionally has been as a low-cost, high-quality manufacturer of existing items. The cliché has it that the United States does the basic research, Japan does the applications research, and Taiwan copies the products, adding bells and whistles, at a low, low price. Now that its low-cost leadership is starting to slip, Taiwan is trying to compensate by adding technological value. Although Taiwan is making an effort to boost high-tech research and development, its record to date in the development of new technologies and applications is unimpressive. However, necessity and the adaptability of Taiwan's entrepreneurs, as much as the government's push for development of high-tech manufactures, should ensure that the country remains competitive.

Currently, the electronics industry is at the forefront of development, shifting from assembly of lower-end consumer and commercial electronics—whose numbers fell by 6.7 percent in 1991—to assembly of higher-end items and production of component subassemblies as both original equipment and replacement parts. Parts represent the most dynamic growth area, as Taiwanese manufacturers work to develop specialties in computer components, telecommunications equipment subassemblies, integrated circuitry, office equipment, and consumer electronics parts. Taiwan is now the fourth largest producer of semiconductors worldwide, after the United States, Japan, and Korea.

Taiwan is also trying to establish an aerospace industry, although the failure to work out deals with McDonnell Douglas to produce wide-body jets and with British Aerospace to produce smaller jets has left it high and dry for the moment. Telecommunications is another targeted area. The Taiwanese presence in this area to date is small and occupies the lower end of the industry with the production of receivers and exchange systems hardware. Medium-tech manufactures include auto parts and metal and woodworking machinery.

The construction industry has grown considerably from a 1.3 percent share of GDP in 1983 to a 4.7 percent share in 1991, and it continues to grow, fueled primarily by public sector infrastructure projects.

Infant industries on Taiwan's research and development and incentive agenda that previous perfor-mance suggests have the potential to be winners include industrial controls, optics, materials science applications, medical equipment, precision and scientific instruments, and information technology and telecommunications equipment. (Refer to "Opportunities" and "Industry Reviews" chapters.)

Services

The service sector—which includes finance, international trade, domestic commerce, transportation and communications, health care, support services, and government services—accounted for 50.2 percent of GDP and employed 46.9 percent of the work force in 1991. It is expected that services will assume an even larger role in coming years, especially as lower-level manufacturing jobs move offshore and rising disposable income increases internal consumption. Personal consumption rose by two-and-one-half times between 1980 and 1991, increasing at an average annual rate of 11 percent, with the majority of the increases coming in discretionary retail spending on goods and services.

Finance, which includes banking, insurance, real estate, and business services, represents 20.9 percent of total GDP, up from a 13.2 percent share in 1983, making it the largest single contributor in the services sector. The wholesale, retail, and restaurant and lodging industries are the next largest service subsector, with a 16.9 percent share of GDP, up from 13.3 percent in 1983. Other services account for 12.4 percent, up from 10.4 percent in 1983.

Financial and Business Services

The government hopes to upgrade its financial capabilities in a bid to take on Hong Kong's role as a world financial center after 1997. Although strides are being made, particularly in upgrading Taiwan's limited business communications infrastructure, many observers remain skeptical that the Taiwanese, who traditionally have kept a tight, exclusionary rein on their financial markets, will be psychologically able to open their system up to the degree needed if it is to be competitive in global financial markets.

Foreigners are still restricted from direct ownership of shares on Taiwan's stock exchange, which at the end of May 1993 had a market capitalization of US$63 billion, larger than Brazil's, but smaller than Malaysia's booming exchange. Attempts to sell shares in state-owned enterprises have fared poorly due to procedural difficulties and the inability of foreign buyers to operate freely. Restrictions on the participation of foreign investors essentially limit such privatization efforts to domestic capital, which is inadequate to absorb the volume of shares to be issued—a volume intended to increase the value of the stock market by 30 to 40 percent. The Taiwan

Taiwan's Foreign Trade

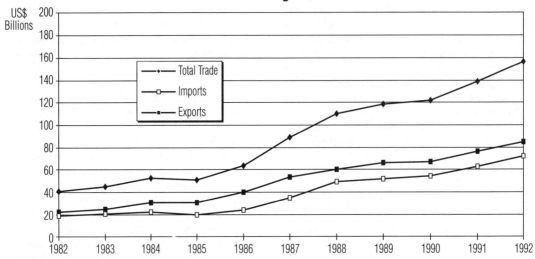

Source: Ministry of Economic Affairs, ROC

Stock Exchange ended 1993 at about 48 percent of the value it had reached at its high point in February 1990, although that peak level reflected the excesses of a speculative market. The year-end close represented an 80 percent gain during 1993. (Refer to "Financial Institutions" chapter.)

TRADE

In 1991, Taiwan was fourteenth among the world's trading nations, a major feat for a country that ranks 46th in the world in population and 134th in land area. In 1992 it racked up total trade of US$156.4 billion, a 12.4 percent increase from the US$139.2 billion registered for 1991 and a figure equivalent to three quarters of its GDP. Figures for mid-1993 suggest that total trade will rise to US$175 billion for all 1993, an increase of 11.9 percent.

Since 1978, Taiwan's total trade has grown at an average annual rate of 14.4 percent, although it seesawed between marginal drops and some major surges. The biggest overall advance has occurred since 1987. When figured in local currency, the increases are somewhat less startling, given the appreciation of the New Taiwan dollar (NT$) since the mid-1980s. Growth in trade has eased in recent years, but the annual increases are still much higher than those in most Western economies.

Exports have grown at an average annual rate of 6.6 percent for the last five years, reaching US$84.4 billion in 1992. Imports increased by an annual 7.8 percent during the same period to US$72 billion in 1992. The easing in the rate of growth of exports coupled with the increase in imports is another indication that Taiwan's economy is maturing. However, it is also an indication that the appreciated NT$ buys more in US$ terms. (Refer to "Foreign Trade" chapter.)

Balance of Trade

Taiwan consistently recorded trade deficits between 1952 and 1970. Since 1971, with the exception of the recessionary oil shock years of 1974 and 1975, Taiwan has racked up increasingly large trade surpluses. Although Taiwan's balance of trade remains highly favorable, both the rate of growth and the actual numbers have shrunk. Over the last 15 years, exports have averaged 55.1 percent of total trade, and imports have averaged 44.9 percent, although the figures have fluctuation by as much as 10.4 percent during the period, ranging from one year in which exports and imports were essentially equal to another year in which exports were more than 60 percent of total trade.

Taiwan's merchandise trade surplus dropped from a high of US$18.7 billion in 1989 to US$12.4 billion in 1992; the figure for 1993 is estimated at US$8 billion. This easing is important, because Taiwan's chronic trade surplus has made it a target of protectionist sentiment abroad. It also has fueled the appreciation of the NT$, weakened Taiwan's international competitive position, and exacerbated domestic inflationary pressures. One of Taiwan's major trade goals is to diversify its products and trade partners to lessen the level of conflict with its primary partners over trade imbalances.

Taiwan's international reserves, which stood at US$84.9 billion in April 1993, surpassed even those of Japan, which generally has maintained the largest reserves in the world in recent years. The reserve figure represents a US$2.1 billion, or 2.6 percent, rise from the previous year. The largest portion of Taiwan's reserves represents trade surpluses with the United States, its main trading partner.

EXPORTS

Taiwan's main exports are machinery and electrical equipment and textiles, which together account for about half of its total exports. Basic metals and metal articles; plastic and rubber products; footwear and related items; transportation equipment; toys, games and sporting goods; precision instruments (including clocks, watches, and musical instruments); animal products; and chemicals account for an additional third of exports. Together, these ten categories account for 86.9 percent of Taiwan's exports. Other export product categories each account for less than 2 percent of the total.

Long-term trends show that labor-intensive products are falling as a percentage of Taiwan's exports. Although products in these categories continue to account for robust sales abroad, the unit volume of apparel exports fell by 35.8 percent between 1986 and 1990, while footwear exports dropped by 51.7 percent, and color television sets, a product that had benefited from cheap assembly labor, fell by 47.6 percent during the same period.

During the 1950s agricultural products accounted for about 92 percent of all exports, with industrial products accounting for the remaining 8 percent. By 1991, this situation had reversed, with industrial goods accounting for 95.3 percent of exports, and agricultural products accounting for 4.7 percent. As an export-driven country, Taiwan has had to be responsive to world markets, producing and selling what those markets demanded. Some of the recent easing in the rate of growth in Taiwan's trade results from slackening demand in developed countries due to the global economic slowdown. Nevertheless, exporting continues to lead Taiwan's economy.

As an intermediate step in its gradual shift away from low-end products, Taiwan is working to add value and move upmarket by producing more expensive and sophisticated consumer goods in electronics, such as monitors and laptop computers, and sporting goods, such as mountain bicycles and tennis rackets. As part of the government's focus on high-technology, high-value-added, and capital-intensive industries, Taiwan's exports of such products as data processing equipment, telecommunications equipment, electrical circuits, and components and subassemblies for office and computer equipment are rising.

IMPORTS

Taiwan's main imports are machinery and electrical equipment, basic metals and metal articles, chemicals, and minerals; together they account for 64.1 percent of the total. Transportation equipment, textiles, precision instruments, foodstuffs, plastics, and gems and jewelry account for an additional 22.2

percent. Products in these ten categories account for 86.3 percent of Taiwan's imports. The other categories each represent less than 2.25 percent of the total. Imports of machinery, which make up nearly 30 percent of all imports, underscore Taiwan's focus on upgrading its industrial capacity, especially in high-tech areas. The remaining major categories underline the country's dependence on imported raw materials and food as well as its growing consumer market.

Although the structure of Taiwan's exports has shifted considerably since the 1950s, its import habits have not changed substantially. In 1952, agricultural products and raw materials accounted for 65 percent of its imports; in 1972, the share was 70 percent. In 1991, 72.4 percent of Taiwan's imports consisted of agricultural products and industrial raw materials, 16.8 percent were capital equipment, and 10.8 percent represented consumer goods. The primary products category probably has peaked, because Taiwan will need to invest in capital equipment to pursue its high-technology export policy, and its strong currency and immense surplus suggest that consumers can be expected to begin spending more on themselves.

TRADING PARTNERS

Taiwan's major trading partners have remained fairly stable in recent years. In 1991 the United States was still Taiwan's primary partner, taking 29.3 percent of its exports and providing 22.4 percent of its imports. Trade between Taiwan and Japan is increasing, and Japan now supplies 30 percent of Taiwan's imports while taking 12.1 percent of its exports. Together, Taiwan's trade with the United States and Japan represented 41.4 percent of its total exports and 52.4 percent of its total imports.

The disparity in the balance of trade between the United States and Taiwan has led US authorities to put pressure on the Asian nation. One of Taiwan's goals for the 1990s is to diversify its trade and decrease its dependence on a few large trading partners. To this end, it has applied for membership in international associations, and it is cultivating trade relationships elsewhere in the world, especially in Southeast Asia and Europe. Trade with these areas represented 44.4 percent of Taiwan's total exports and 26.8 percent of its total imports in 1991. Trade with the Middle East, Latin America, Oceania, and Africa accounts for 8.6 percent of its exports and 13.9 percent of its imports. The remaining 5.7 percent of Taiwan's exports and 6.8 percent of its imports are classed as miscellaneous, much of which represents sub rosa trade with China.

CHINA TRADE

Trade with Hong Kong, most of which is subsumed under the heading of Southeast Asia, is growing, primarily because Hong Kong acts as an entrepôt for Taiwan's trade with China. Although direct trade with China is strictly forbidden, China was estimated in 1991 to be Taiwan's fourth largest trading partner. Such trade is expected to account for an increasing percentage of Taiwan's total foreign trade over time.

Taiwan's stance toward trade with China has been conditioned by the KMT government's traditional fear that intimate dealings with the mainland will weaken Taiwan's bargaining position as it attempts to regain authority over China and maintain its autonomy from China. From this viewpoint, any linkage between the two economies risks giving China leverage that it can use to absorb the smaller Taiwan, despite Taiwan's more highly developed economy. Although China's population is 55 times larger than Taiwan's, and China has vastly greater land area and resources, China's GNP is only twice that of Taiwan, and Taiwan manages to export nearly as much as its giant neighbor.

Taiwan's trade with China has been growing at an annual average of 36 percent since 1987, with the dollar value of that total trade increasing sixfold during this period. Estimates of Taiwan's two-way trade with the mainland in 1992 range from 9 percent to 11 percent of its total foreign trade—a minimum of about US$15 billion. The Taiwanese government's unofficial allowable level of China trade is set at 10 percent of its total foreign trade. That level may already have been reached, if not surpassed.

The strength of Taiwan's currency, its low unemployment rate, and its high labor costs are forcing the country to look abroad for outsourcing sites. The proximity, shared language and culture, and low cost structure of mainland China are proving highly attractive to many Taiwanese business people, despite political and legal restrictions. (Refer to "Current Issues" chapter.)

FOREIGN PARTICIPATION IN THE ECONOMY

Taiwan's trade-oriented economy depends heavily on foreign participation. In 1991, foreign investors produced 14 percent of Taiwan's GNP, employed 12 percent of its manufacturing work force, paid 24 percent of all taxes, and shipped 25 percent of its export goods. For all these reasons, the government has made efforts to accommodate foreign investors. Many barriers to foreign investment have been removed or scaled back. There are virtually no local content rules and few tariff barriers, procedures for necessary permits have been streamlined, and rules governing repatriation of earnings and capital have been liberalized, although foreign exchange controls remain that inhibit the free transfer of funds. In 1989, Taiwan opened to foreign participation all major industries except agriculture, utilities, petroleum refining, transportation, telecommunications, and defense-related industries.

Foreigners may invest in any industry or activity that is not among those prohibited or restricted by government decree. Compliance is important because foreign investment approved (FIA) status is necessary for a foreign firm to repatriate capital and profits. At the end of 1993 the government announced that, as part of its efforts to enter the General Agreement on Tariffs and Trade (GATT), it would open up investment in its financial sector to foreigners.

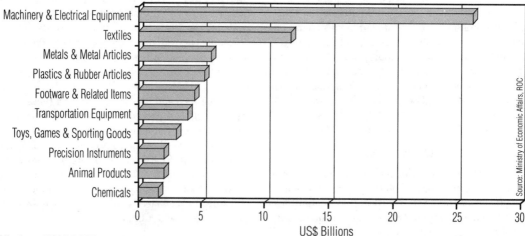

Taiwan's Leading Exports By Commodity - 1991

Machinery & Electrical Equipment
Textiles
Metals & Metal Articles
Plastics & Rubber Articles
Footware & Related Items
Transportation Equipment
Toys, Games & Sporting Goods
Precision Instruments
Animal Products
Chemicals

0   5   10   15   20   25   30
US$ Billions

Source: Ministry of Economic Affairs, ROC

All others: US$9.9 Billion or 13% of total
Total 1991 Exports: US$76.1 Billion

Tax and regulatory treatment is roughly on a par for both foreign and domestic firms, although there are incentives to encourage high-tech investment. Incentives come mainly in the form of tax credits. Taiwan operates a one-stop Industrial Development and Investment Commission (IDIC) for foreign investors.

The government is trying to direct new investment into its preferred high-technology areas, although it does not actively discourage any allowed investments. Most recent investment has avoided labor-intensive areas and gone into high-technology, capital-intensive, and financial services areas. (Refer to "Opportunities" and "Foreign Investments" chapters.)

Size and Nature of Foreign Participation

As of 1991 foreign individuals and firms had invested a cumulative total of US$15.2 billion in more than 6,200 Taiwanese firms. About 60 percent of that sum had been contributed in roughly equal shares by United States and Japanese investors. About 60 percent of all foreign investment has been in manufacturing—electronics, chemical, machinery, and metals industries—and another 25 percent has been in service industries.

However, the rise in the cost of doing business in Taiwan, the development of lower-cost investment alternatives elsewhere in Asia, and the worldwide economic slowdown combined to reduce approved foreign investment in Taiwan in 1993 to an estimated US$950 million, down from the high of almost US$2.2 billion in 1989. Investment fell a whopping 28 percent in 1991, but it still accounted for 11.7 percent of the cumulative total to date, a fact that indicates continuing growth.

Service Sector Investment

In the service sector, foreign commercial banks may operate roughly under the same rules as local banks as far as most commercial transactions are concerned. All financial institutions are hampered by branching limitations and overshadowed by the state-run banks. (Refer to "Financial Institutions" and "Currency & Foreign Exchange" chapters.) Foreign securities firms are gaining a foothold, as are the first foreign (US) insurance companies. Foreign advertising agencies and management consulting firms are also making small inroads. Wholesale, retail, and distribution business is still predominately local, with significant barriers to entry, although companies from Japan and Hong Kong haveoopened supermarkets and department stores.

The government has relaxed official barriers on foreign entry into several service businesses, although access remains largely theoretical to date. Among the areas available are fast food, retailing, trading, leasing, engineering, brokerage and investment services, and inspection services. (Refer to "Marketing" chapter.)

Taiwanese Overseas Investment

Taiwanese investment abroad has been relatively minor, partly as a result of the structure of its economy, which is dominated by state-run industry, and its generally restrictive foreign exchange allowances, which inhibit the flow of capital out of the country. Its major investment target has been China, in which by 1992 an estimated 12,000 Taiwanese companies had already invested an estimated US$13 billion since 1983, either directly or—to maintain the fiction of arm's length dealings—through Hong Kong middlemen. This cumulative figure represents 80

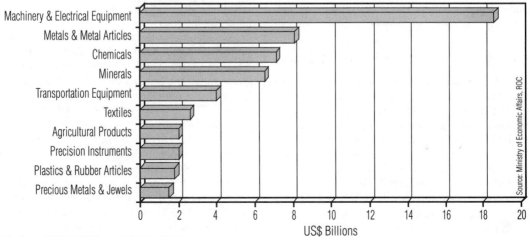

Taiwan's Leading Imports By Commodity - 1991

Source: Ministry of Economic Affairs, ROC

US$ Billions

All others: US$8.7 Billion or 13.8% of total
Total 1991 Imports: US$62.9 Billion

percent of all Taiwanese overseas investment during the period.

The next largest target has been the United States, where Taiwan invested a cumulative US$1.3 billion between 1981 and 1990, primarily to gain access to technology. Taiwan also spent US$366 million in Europe between 1986 and 1990, mostly to buy into distribution chains. Taiwan likes to call attention to its rapidly growing investment in Southeast Asia, where it hopes to get in on the ground floor as local economies develop and where it finds both a cheap source of raw materials and a ready market for its own goods. Taiwan invested US$940 million in Southeast Asia between 1986 and 1990. Taiwan's overseas commitment, except in China, remains small, and it will have to make further investments to ensure its international position over the long haul.

GOVERNMENT ECONOMIC DEVELOPMENT STRATEGY

Taiwan's economic development strategy, laid out in January 1991 in the Statute for Promotion of Industrial Upgrading (SIU), is to encourage export-oriented high-technology, high-value-added, capital-intensive industries, especially electronics manufacturing and assembly. The manufacture of electrical machinery, components, and parts is the fastest growing area. In the government's view, this area, along with precision instrumentation and computers, should assume the importance that more labor-intensive production and assembly of consumer electronics products, such as monitors, television sets, radios, tape recorders, and calculators, once had. Other areas flagged for development include auto parts, aeronautical equipment, and chemicals. The SIU is directed primarily toward foreign investors, indicating that despite Taiwan's talk about increasing domestic research and development and enhancement of its own capabilities, it intends to continue to rely on imported technology, expertise, and capital in managing its economy.

THE SIX-YEAR DEVELOPMENT PLAN

In January 1991 the government also announced a US$303 billion Six-Year Development Plan to upgrade Taiwan's transportation, energy, and communications infrastructure. The 775 projects proposed included construction of a high-speed railway on the island's west coast, expressways, mass transit systems, power plants, and pollution control projects, among others. Concern that the economy was facing a potentially severe slowdown fueled this pump priming public works-oriented program.

In July 1993 Taiwan's cabinet simultaneously approved a three-year US$2.25 billion stimulus package aimed at aiding the private sector and cut back on the government-led Six-Year Development Plan. The core of the new stimulus package was US$1.5 billion in low-cost loans to small- and medium-sized companies and US$750 million in loans to certified high-tech companies. The package also releases 75,000 acres of government land for development, offers tax holidays on some high-technology products, authorizes more foreign workers to enter the country, and eases restrictions on imports from China.

Skeptics have argued that the stimulus package is largely cosmetic in nature and inadequate to address the real needs of small private business. However, analysts note that the shift in emphasis away from the state controlled sector and toward the private sector is significant. The cutbacks associated with the stimulus package chop the budget of the government-led development plan by 22 percent and drop 141 projects, although officials have been somewhat vague about exactly where the cuts will fall. (Refer to "Current Issues" chapter.)

POLITICAL OUTLOOK FOR THE ECONOMY

The Six-Year Development Plan has served to focus public attention on the political situation. Martial law was lifted in 1987 after 38 years; the 43 year long state of emergency came to an end in 1991; and the opposition may now legally form political parties. Taiwan is in the process of adjusting to a radically different environment that includes an unaccustomed level of democracy and participation as the old ways of doing things become less viable. These developments have been accompanied by calls for changes in the way in which business traditionally has been done. In August 1993 10 veteran KMT legislators resigned to form the Chinese New Party, ostensibly dedicated to eliminating corrupt sweetheart deals between big business and Taiwan's authoritarian rulers.

Responding to fears that massive government projects will fuel inflation and crowd out private business while benefiting insiders with links to the government, the Legislative Yuan or congress, led by the main opposition Democratic Progressive Party (DPP), which controls about 20 percent of the seats, symbolically slashed the budget of the Industrial Technology Research Institute (ITRI), seen as a stronghold of old-style political patronage, by 20 percent. The legislature also killed funding for the US$17 billion high-speed train that was to be the centerpiece of the Six-Year Development Plan and canceled a US$2 billion deal to build widebody jet aircraft. A successor deal to develop smaller jet aircraft has foundered in squabbles among competing government entities over turf. The underlying business concerns over technology transfers and guarantees that formed legitimate issues for negotiation were obscured by this infighting.

So far, the rebellion has been aimed at large operations with close government ties that are seen as having prospered at the expense of the small and medium-sized private businesses that make up 97 percent of Taiwan's enterprises. Its leaders are politicians with a strong following among mostly native and middle-class voters, who, they say, run the private businesses and take the risks that drive the economy.

The DPP also has engaged in a debate to drop the ROC's traditional claim to be the sole legitimate government of China and declare the independence of Taiwan as a separate national entity. This proposal has been roundly criticized by the PRC, which has threatened military action if Taiwan tries to secede, and it was soundly defeated at home by the ruling KMT, to which the idea is anathema. So far, the public at large has rejected the proposal, partially because it fears mainland intervention but also because it hopes ultimately to cut a better deal by reconciling with China than by striking out on its own. There is not likely to be any significant movement on these issues over the near term.

Moves toward increased openness and reduced domination of the economy by the government will be slow and halting at best. The entrenched KMT, whose members control patronage through the bureaucracies and state-run enterprises, can be expected to resist major changes in the status quo. The ruling party overwhelmingly reelected President Lee Teng-hui at its August 1993 session, although not by acclamation, as it had in 1988.

In advance of tough local elections in November 1993, the president appointed two critics as party vice-chairmen in an attempt at conciliation. Polls showed that only 25 percent of those interviewed intended to vote for KMT candidates, down from 28 percent a year earlier and 42 percent four years ago. Some 9.5 percent favored the DPP, up from 6 percent a year ago, while the Chinese New Party received a 4.6 percent rating. This also indicates that 60 percent are either undecided or apathetic. However, voters gave the KMT a resounding victory at the polls, apparently falling in line with KMT rhetoric that claimed that its defeat would lead to economic disruption.

Cynics have suggested that opposition activity is designed as much to gain some share of the spoils by breaking the KMT's stranglehold on power as it is to institute real reform. New regulations require Taiwanese officials to disclose assets. Of the 800 who have complied so far, about half have reported net worths of greater than US$1 million each, indicating that political connections are important in accumulating wealth. (Refer to "Current Issues" chapter.)

TAIWAN'S INTERNATIONAL ROLE

Taiwan's expulsion from the United Nations in 1971 and its loss of diplomatic recognition, which left it with embassies in only 28 small nations around the world, plus its continuing expenditure of energies in opposition to the PRC, have left it in an equivocal position in the world: a successful reality but an unrecognized idea. Taiwan has stepped up its efforts to gain independent recognition internationally through the United Nations and among major nations.

As part of Taiwan's efforts to move with the times by developing an increasingly international outlook, the country has applied for membership in the General Agreement on Tariffs and Trade (GATT), which will require it to open closed areas of its economy to outside activity. It has joined Asia Pacific Economic Cooperation, the Central American Bank for Economic Development, and the Southeast Asian Nation Central Bank Governors Conference, and it has established ties with the European Bank for Reconstruction and Development and the Inter-American Development Bank by making contributions. Through its International Economic Cooperation and Development Fund, Taiwan had committed US$138 million to overseas development projects by the middle of 1992.

Current Issues

STRENGTH THROUGH TRADE: TAIWAN'S TRADE SURPLUS

The Republic of China (ROC), once a poor, preindustrialized debtor nation overlooked by the world's major economic players, has become a creditor nation boasting trade surpluses with all the major economic powers of the world except Japan. In the 1960s foreign investment funneled into Taiwan by firms from the United States, Japan, and Europe introduced modern, labor-intensive technology to the island. Throughout the 1970s and 1980s foreign investment—moving to industries producing higher-value-added products for export—triggered Taiwan's export boom and created Taiwan's current trade imbalance with most of its trading partners.

Trade: Taiwan's Economic Power Source Taiwan's development, lit by the match of foreign investment, has been fueled by exports of electronics, textiles, plastics, and sporting goods, among other products. The total value of trade increased nearly five-fold in the 1960s. In the 1970s it increased ten-fold. By 1971 Taiwan was able to say farewell to the trade deficits that had characterized its predevelopment past. The total value of Taiwan's trade tripled in the 1980s, and Taiwan registered six consecutive record high trade surpluses between 1982 and 1987. By 1992 Taiwan had the fourteenth largest trading economy in the world. Because of its strong export market and its trade surpluses, Taiwan continues to reduce its already minimal foreign debt, even while local currency appreciates.

Trade Relations with the United States In 1992 Taiwan ranked as the United States' sixth largest trading partner, with bilateral trade reaching nearly US$40 billion. The US merchandise trade deficit with Taiwan has steadily declined from its peak of US$17 billion in 1987 falling to US$8.2 billion in 1991. During the first eleven months of 1992, US exports to Taiwan reached US$13.8 billion, just shy of US$2 billion more than the $11.9 billion registered for the same period in 1991. Nevertheless, the US was the second largest contributor to Taiwan's trade surplus

in 1992. (Hong Kong was the first.)

The American Perspective If you were to ask an American for the first word that came to mind when hearing the word trade deficit, the most likely response would be Japan. Although America's trade deficit with Japan is a constant point of contention, Taiwan holds the second highest trade surplus with the United States. The United States, therefore, has called for Taiwan to reduce the deficit by eliminating barriers to US exports and investment.

Moves Toward Greater Parity As Taiwan's economic power has increased, rising living standards for Taiwanese have spurred Taiwan's consumers to seek foreign productsoonce considered out of reach. Imports have surged—a sign of good health for the Taiwanese economy—and a hint that Taiwan's trade relationship with America will become more balanced. In 1992 an increase in Taiwan's imports outpaced its export growth and its trade surplus dropped for the first time in several years. Future economic development in Taiwan will stimulate demand for upscale consumer goods and more sophisticated capital goods, markets that the United States is well positioned to serve.

Potential Problems Encouraging news, one might think, but is that the whole story? There is some concern that trade relations might become more contentious as Taiwanese firms become more competent competitors with US firms, particularly in sophisticated products, such as machine tools. Moreover, certain protectionist measures proposed by the US Congress may check those measures aimed at free trade.

Another potential threat to US interests results from Taiwan's maneuvers with Hong Kong and the People's Republic of China (PRC) to form a very competitive export-oriented economic zone, particularly in labor-intensive industries. Cheap labor in mainland China, coupled with capital and management expertise from Taiwan, has created an export machine that in 1992 beat the world economic slowdown by grabbing market share from other newly developed nations. Products exported from the mainland are constructed with components made in Taiwan that have been shipped to the mainland for assembly. Although the US trade deficit with Taiwan is expected to continue to shrink, in fact, it will grow under another name: China.

Among Neighbors As its exports to the US, Japan, and the European Community have slowed, Taiwan has diversified its trade markets by directing exports toward its Asian neighbors. Between 1987 and 1991 Taiwan's exports to Southeast Asian nations doubled. Taiwan's primary new market (unofficially, of course) is its enemy, China. Due to laws against trade with the mainland, most products are shipped to China via Hong Kong. Exports to Hong Kong jumped by 45 percent in 1991 and by 35 percent in the first five months of 1992. Consequently, Hong Kong replaced the United States as the largest source of Taiwan's trade surplus in 1991.

Compared with the other Asian "little dragons" (Hong Kong, Singapore, and South Korea), Taiwan breathes the most fire. In 1992 Taiwan was the only dragon that had a trade surplus with the rest of the world. Also, Taiwan's overall economic growth rate was the highest among the little dragons in 1992.

While the United States continues to lick its wounds from the Vietnam war, tarrying over allowing US investment, Taiwan has jumped on investment opportunity in Vietnam and is now the world's leading investor there. Having lassoed Vietnam, Taiwan continues to round up other Southeast Asian markets by setting up production operations and marketing the output within the producing region. As the interdependency among these nations increases, their ties with traditional markets, such as the United States, loosen. Regional interdependency will make it difficult for America to influence any one of these nations selectively.

Some Good News for the United States Although one can easily list the potential problems with US-Taiwan trade relations, there is some good news, too. As Taiwan grows in economic power and international stature and moves toward entering the General Agreement on Tariffs and Trade (GATT), it will have to bring its regulatory regime more into line with international standards and practices, a development that should eliminate many of the restrictions that American businesses now face. This in turn should expand the opportunities open for American companies. Some growth areas that US companies are in a good position to target are computers and peripherals, electronic laboratory instruments, medical equipment, cosmetics, high-value food products, and refrigeration equipment.

A Continuing Trade Power Given that Taiwan has few natural resources, a small land area, and a high population density, foreign trade will continue

to serve as the guiding principle of Taiwan's economic development as it forges into the future and onto the world stage.

MOVES TOWARD REFORM: POLITICS IN TAIWAN

History Since establishing the new China on the island of Taiwan in 1949, the Kuomintang (KMT), as the followers of Chiang Kai Shek were known, has been the ruling party. Although fiercely anti-Communist, the KMT unmistakably resembled the mainland Communist Party in its authoritarian rule on the island. In fact, martial law remained in effect from 1949 until 1987. The first fully democratic election was not held until December 1992. Although the KMT has consistently held onto a large percentage of the vote, it has become increasingly riven by internal strife.

The Leaders Until recently, the conservative old guard, faithful descendants of those who fought with General Chiang against the Communists on the mainland, dominated the KMT. However, as the political voice of the native Taiwanese—84 percent of the population—grows stronger, the power held by the conservatives has been shifting to the more reform-minded members of the party. Consequently, on the death of former President Chiang Ching-kuo in 1988, Lee Teng-hui, a native Taiwanese, became president. In 1990 President Lee was elected to a six-year term in his own right. Representing the mainstream faction of the KMT, he has sought to open the political process to native Taiwanese.

Since 1990 General Hau Pei-tsun, a staunch conservative who is backed by the New Kuomintang Alliance (a faction to the right of the mainstream KMT) has served as the prime minister. During the December 1992 election, he was the target of demonstrations and unrest among native Taiwanese. Born on the mainland, Hau and his fellow conservatives still envision a China united under the rule of the KMT.

The Opposition Although the KMT emerged from the December 1992 election with a relatively strong victory, its members were alarmed by the one-third rise in votes for the main opposition party, the liberal Democratic Progressive Party (DPP). Formed in 1986, the DPP, a native Taiwanese party, has called for a totally independent Taiwan—one that does not claim sovereignty over the mainland or seek reunification with it. The DPP has been very vocal in elected bodies and often uses public forums to raise controversial or sensitive issues.

A Call for Change On March 1, 1993 due to strong voices of opposition to General Hau from both the DPP and the reform-minded faction of the KMT, President Lee appointed a new prime minister, Lien Chan. For the first time in its history, the Republic of China has both a president and prime minister who were born in Taiwan. Prime Minister Lien, rather than continuing to fight for Taiwan to be recognized at China's expense, has proposed that the international community grant China and Taiwan "dual recognition."

Despite bickering within and between parties, their members all share one concern: Taiwan's autonomy in the face of increasing economic ties with the mainland. Taiwan's leaders hope that dual recognition will protect Taiwan from future political vulnerability to China. If dual recognition is established, doors to international institutions, such as the United Nations and GATT should open more easily.

TRADE AND POLITICAL RELATIONS BETWEEN TAIWAN AND THE PEOPLE'S REPUBLIC OF CHINA

Since the day when the Kuomintang (KMT) government fled the mainland in 1949 to set up headquarters on the island of Taiwan, both the PRC and the ROC have claimed sovereignty over one-fifth of the world's population under the slogan of one China. On Taiwan, the KMT established a policy of no contact, no negotiation, and no compromise regarding the mainland. Mainland leaders, who still consider Taiwan a rebellious province of China, have been equally hostile toward the island.

In the last few years, the relationship between the PRC and ROC has gradually warmed: increasing numbers of Taiwanese—an estimated four million in just the last few years—are crossing the strait to visit their relatives on the mainland. More money is crossing the strait, and more trade is being funneled through Hong Kong. With the deregulation of foreign exchange controls and liberalization of tourist travel to the mainland, the number of Taiwanese firms investing in China has risen dramatically.

Trade Relations In 1987 with unofficial bilateral trade between the PRC and the ROC via Hong Kong totaling approximately US$1.6 billion, both Beijing and Taipei sought to establish more formal relations, particularly in the areas of trade and investment. By 1991 bilateral trade grew to almost US$6 billion (a 43 percent increase over the preceding year. While exports from Taiwan to most destinations grew 7 percent in 1991, exports to China increased by 35 percent. China became Taiwan's fourth largest trading partner, while Taiwan became China's fifth.

Moreover, Taiwan's rate of investment in the PRC has skyrocketed in the last ten years. What was initially the transference of labor-intensive industries to the mainland by Taiwanese investors in search of cheap labor, land, and raw materials has expanded to include increasingly capital-intensive investments in electronics, automobiles and automobile parts, machinery, chemicals, and such services as real es-

tate, tourism, and golf course construction. In fact, there are fears that the flow of capital from Taiwan to the mainland has been excessive, particularly in high-technology industry and property development.

While direct investment into and trade with the mainland are still prohibited in Taiwan by law, unofficial estimates of Taiwanese investment on the mainland range between US$10 billion and US$25 billion. The depletion of Taiwan's capital reservoirs has had detrimental effects on Taiwan's economy: Interest rates have risen, stock prices are falling, and the $300 billion that Taiwan needs for its six-year infrastructure project is getting hard to find.

Time to Talk No longer turning their eyes from their booming trade and investment relationship, representatives of Taiwan and China met in Singapore in 1993—their first quasi-official albeit nongovernmental meeting since the KMT fled the mainland. The talks centered on steps that could be taken to uproot the growing weeds of corruption and piracy in the absence of official relations. Through these talks, the Taiwanese hoped to gain more protection over Taiwan's investment in the mainland, while mainland Chinese sought to facilitate direct trade. At the end of the talks, both sides signed documents (regarding compensation for lost mail, the establishment of mechanisms for future contacts, and verification of official documents) aimed at improving business interactions.

Underneath its agenda to facilitate trade, the PRC has dreams of reunification. By increasing its influence over the ROC through closer trade links, the PRC hopes eventually to reclaim the prodigal province for its own. Fully aware of this intent, the Taiwanese are concerned that increasing financial bonds make them increasingly vulnerable economically (and ultimately politically) to every switch of the dragon's tail. Some believe that within the next 30 years, reunification will naturally follow economic interdependency between the PRC and the ROC.

THE RACE TO ENTER GATT

The Importance of GATT GATT, as the General Agreement on Tariffs and Trade is generally known, is a multilateral trade agreement aimed at expanding international trade. To liberalize world trade and improve access to markets, it seeks to reduce or eliminate tariff and other barriers to trade, such as domestic subsidies and quotas; and to foster an economic climate that will promote investment and job creation, especially in less-developed countries. Through GATT, participating nations have established guidelines to ease commercial transactions across national borders. More than 80 percent of world trade is carried out under GATT guidelines.

The Race for Membership Certainly, Taiwan

would like to be a party to GATT for the increased trading relations that such membership would provide. More important, given that only one China is diplomatically recognized, Taiwan is seeking to obtain membership in preference to the People's Republic of China. As China and Taiwan establish greater unofficial links through increased trade and investment, President Lee Teng-hui has begun to push harder for Taiwan's entrance into GATT as well as the United Nations (UN). Still smarting from having been bumped out of the UN so that the PRC could occupy the "Chinese" seat, Taiwan has stepped up its efforts to become the "Chinese" member of GATT.

Taiwan has an even more pressing reason for its concern about entrance into GATT—a reason which is less political than it is economic. Today, economic trading power is viewed as the ticket to legitimacy on the world stage. If Taiwan has been unrecognized politically, it cannot be ignored economically, especially if it is a member of GATT.

Current Situation in Taiwan Since 1986 Taiwan has sought to reduce and remove many controls and tariffs on imports in response to pressure from its trading partners. Nevertheless, some nontariff barriers remain. Entrance into GATT would help Taiwan to ensure positive long-term trading relationships. Since Taiwan has few natural resources and is extremely economically interdependent with other nations, it views trade as necessary for economic survival.

TAIWAN'S LABOR SHORTAGE: THE UNSKILLED WORKER'S PARADISE

History Taiwan's rapid development in the 1960s and 1970s made "Made in Taiwan" a familiar label on many low-cost products shipped throughout the world. During this period of rapid economic growth, which relied primarily on low-technology and labor-intensive industries, the government focused on educating and training its future work force. The good news is that Taiwan today hosts a wealth of skilled workers, technicians, and managers. The downside is the resultant shortage of unskilled workers.

Today In 1991 the labor force totaled 8.57 million (about 40 percent of the population). The unemployment rate in that year was 1.5 percent, its lowest level since 1981, and one that makes Western nations envious. Today, the Taiwanese economy is shifting toward high-technology and capital-intensive industries. The industries that once fueled its growth and mobilized much of its work force are being sent abroad.

To Meet the Needs Two courses of action have arisen to meet the needs created by changes in industry, rising labor and land costs, and the shortage of unskilled labor. One has been to export Taiwan's traditional labor-intensive industries to the mainland and to its less-developed neighbors in Southeast Asia: Indonesia, the Philippines, Malaysia, and Thailand.

The second, adopted by industries that have not shifted their manufacturing operations elsewhere, has been to import illegal workers from Southeast Asia. This strategy has created problems of its own. In April 1992 the government enacted a law requiring all foreign workers to obtain a work permit before accepting employment in Taiwan. How this law will be implemented has yet to be determined, and the number of workers to allow and their countries of origin are still under debate. The number of foreign workers in Taiwan by the end of 1992 reached 30,000 according to conservation estimates. With labor standards—including insurance, severance pay, retirement pay, and meal and transportation allowances—among the highest in the world, it is no wonder that foreign workers who face minimal employment conditions, underemployment, and high unemployment at home are delighted to help Taiwan solve its labor shortage.

Opportunities

OPPORTUNITIES FOR IMPORTING FROM TAIWAN

Taiwan exports a wide variety of high-quality, competitively priced products to countries all over the world. Products range from electronic and textile goods to furniture and vehicles. The diversity of Taiwan's products gives foreign importers an equally wide variety of opportunities. This section describes Taiwan's most important industries and the opportunities that they offer to foreign importers.

ELECTRONICS & COMPUTERS

Electrical and electronics goods are among Taiwan's leading exports. There are approximately 4,500 manufacturers of electronic goods in Taiwan at the present time. They manufacture not only components but finished products, such as modems, personal computers, workstations, and facsimile machines. Taiwan's electronics industry has four leading product sectors: consumer electronics, electronic components, computer products, and telecommunications equipment.

Consumer Electronics Although the manufacture of consumer electronics will continue to play an important role in Taiwan's economy, rising labor costs have reduced Taiwan's competitiveness in this area. Many manufacturers have either suspended operations entirely or moved production to Southeast

Asia. Nevertheless, exports of TV games continue to grow, and the development of such high-end products as projection and high-definition television sets, and digital radios is beginning to replace exports of audio and video products.

Electronic Components The manufacture of electronic components in Taiwan remains strong, especially for products at the low end of the market, such as capacitors, connectors, coils, resistors, switches, and transformers. Foreign subsidiaries are the most important exporters of electronic components. Exports presently account for more than half of the electronics industry's total output.

Taiwan is now the fourth largest producer in the world of semiconductors behind the United States, Japan, and Korea. The country's semiconductor industry is expected to grow by 19 percent a year through 1996. But unless Taiwan can develop its technological base further in the next couple of years, its production of electronic components will be largely limited to such low- to medium-end items as integrated circuits (ICs), cathode-ray tubes (CRTs), liquid crystal displays (LCDs), and printed circuit boards (PCBs). Manufacture of integrated circuits will benefit over the next several years from the National Science Council's promotion of research and development programs aimed at encouraging the development of key electronic parts and components.

Computer Products Information products have become Taiwan's mainstay in the electronics industry, accounting for nearly one-third of the island's total shipments of electronic products. Personal computers and computer monitors lead, with annual growth in sales exceeding 20 percent in the last couple of years. Exports of personal computers, components, and peripherals include desktops, laptops, notebooks, and palmtops, while Taiwan-made peripherals include mainboards, power switching supplies, image scanners, graphic cards, and network cards.

Telecommunications The gradual opening of Taiwan's closed telecommunications market should provide increased opportunities for domestic and international sales. Presently, telephones make up the bulk of the communications products exported from Taiwan. However, Japanese original equipment manufacturers have recently increased contracts with Taiwanese manufacturers of telephones and answering machines. Production of mobile telephones and fax machines is also increasing. Taiwan also exports radio communication equipment, transmission equipment, and communication parts and components that utilize new technologies.

Some of the HOT electronic items:
- answering machines
- calculators
- computer parts and peripherals
- electronic clocks
- electronic quartz clocks
- electronic spare parts
- electronic wire and telecommunications cables
- facsimile machines
- passive components
- personal computers
- printed circuit boards
- quartz crystal and optic electronic devices
- radios and cassette players
- telecommunications equipment parts
- telephones
- video games and products

MACHINE TOOLS AND METALWORKING MACHINERY

Taiwan ranks as one of the world's top ten producers and exporters of machine tools. Of the almost 300 machine tool factories on the island, most located in its central region, about 40 manufacture computer numerically controlled (CNC) metalworking machines. Most of the components for these machines, including ball screws, hydraulic pumps, and gears, are produced locally. However, controllers are still mostly imported from Japan.

Recent levels of investment in new capital equipment suggest that CNC machines will soon produce 50 percent of all Taiwan-made machine tools. The development of flexible manufacturing systems is also predicted to become a popular trend within the next two years.

Taiwan exports metalworking machinery to Southeast Asia, Europe, and the United States; Thailand, Malaysia, and Indonesia are the largest potential markets, owing in part to recent increases in investment by Taiwanese companies in the region, which has stimulated demand for machine tools. Exports of machine tools to Europe and the United

States are expected to remain steady over the next few years.

Some of the HOT items:
- automatic material-handling systems
- ball screws, hydraulic pumps, gears components
- CNC lathes
- CNC milling machines
- EDM machine tools with CNC controls
- flexible machining cells
- laser cutting units

WOODWORKING MACHINERY

At present, about 200 factories on Taiwan are involved in the production of woodworking machinery. In an effort to remain competitive in this industry, Taiwanese manufacturers have recently developed innovative multispindle shapers, double-spindle dowel cutters, multispindle four-sided planers, and surface spray-painting machines, which all have been patented. Annual exports of woodworking machinery currently exceed US$200 million, and it appears that the prospects for overseas sales will remain bright for the foreseeable future.

Traditionally, Taiwan has produced such woodworking machinery as lathes, milling machines, sanding machines, jointers, sawing machines, and drilling machines. However, in recent years the island's manufacturers have also been successful in developing such automated, high-value-added machinery as edge-banding machines, CNC trimmers, copy shapers, multisurface planers, and CNC routers.

Some of the HOT items:
- CNC cutoff machines
- CNC routers
- double-spindle dowel cutters
- drilling machines
- edge-banding machines
- jointers
- lathes
- milling machines
- multispindle four-sided planers
- multispindle shapers
- multiple-side planers
- sanding machines
- sawing machines
- surface spray-painting machines

PLASTICS-PROCESSING MACHINERY

Fueled by a well-established plastics industry, Taiwanese manufacturers of plastics-processing machinery are now the second largest suppliers in Asia behind Japan. The plastic injection molding machine is the leading export item, with approximately 15 firms accounting for the bulk of production. The most recent statistics place total annual production of injection molding machines at between 5,000 and 6,000 units, a figure that puts Taiwan third in the world behind Japan and Germany. A wide variety of models is available, including horizontal, vertical, thermoset, and double-injection units. Extruders are also important in the export market. Annual production capacity currently stands at over 3,000 single- and double-screw units.

In the years ahead, strong competition between local manufacturers and public sector encouragement of research and development should guarantee that Taiwanese plastics-processing machinery remains competitive in international markets. Buyers can expect to see an expanding range of increasingly sophisticated items, often priced substantially below similar products from Germany and Japan.

Some of the HOT items:
- blow-molding machines
- plastic injection molding machines
- single- and double-screw plastic extruders
- tire and tube-making machines
- vacuum-forming machines

HAND TOOLS

Taiwan currently exports a large variety of manual and electric hand tools. At present, the sector faces heavy competition from other newly industrialized nations. In response, most of Taiwan's 400 hand tool manufacturers have switched from low-end to higher-end items. The United States is the principal market for Taiwan's hand tool exports, but Taiwanese tool manufacturers are increasingly targeting the Asian market, especially Japan, as well as Europe.

Manual Tools Taiwan offers an extensive choice of manual hand tools for a variety of activities, including carpentry, electrical work, plumbing, painting, measuring, automobile repair, and gardening. Socket wrenches are currently the top export item, followed by screwdrivers and jacks.

Electric Tools Exports of Taiwan-made electric tools are aimed primarily at the do-it-yourself (DIY) market. Bestselling items include drills, sanders, saws, soldering irons, and heat guns. The current trend is toward the production of cordless tools that offer multiple functions and longer battery life. Many DIY power tools feature nickel-cadmium batteries and LED indicators and displays.

Pneumatic Tools Air tools are another important category of export products, and manufacturers have increased in recent years the number of models produced for professional and industrial uses. These tools include impact wrenches, air sanders, air grinders, air drills, air screw drivers, air tackers, and air spray guns.

Some of the HOT items:
- air tools
- cordless tools
- impact wrenches
- jacks
- power DIY tools
- screwdrivers
- socket wrenches

PLASTICS AND RUBBER PRODUCTS

The rubber and plastics industry has played an extensive role in Taiwan's economic development. Manufacturers continue to expand their product lines. The principal items produced for export include shoes, imitation leather, adhesive tapes, acrylic sheets, luggage, inflatables, and casings for electronic products. Tires, rubber boots, athletic shoes, air mattresses, rubber boats, gloves, pipes, and a wide range of health and medical products are some of Taiwan's leading exports in this category.

Some of the HOT items:
- acrylic sheets
- adhesive tapes
- electronic casings
- health and medical products
- imitation leather
- inflatables
- luggage
- pipes
- rubber boots
- shoes
- tires

AUTO PARTS

In a relatively short time, Taiwan's auto parts industry has managed a successful shift from primarily low-end to higher-end items. The more important auto parts and components available for export include sheet metal auto body parts, electrical parts, engine parts, transmission parts, tires and wheels, steering parts, and decorative accessories. Overseas sales in many of these categories are substantial. For example, Taiwan's exports of electrical parts in 1991 were valued at US$110 million. The United States has been the leading buyer for most of these items. Other promising areas for exports include Western and Eastern Europe and Southeast Asia.

Some of the HOT items:

* decorative accessories
* electrical and electronic parts
* engine parts
* sheet metal auto body parts
* tires and wheels

GIFTWARE

Taiwan-made giftware can be divided into two categories: decorative items and housewares. Decorative items include Christmas decorations, jewelry boxes, porcelain figurines, flower pots and vases, artificial flowers, and photo frames. Of these, Christmas decorations currently rank as the single most important export product. Housewares include such items as plastic containers and utensils, clocks, hair brushes, and combs, which all depend on Taiwan's well-developed plastics industry and its expertise in mold making.

The rate at which Taiwan's giftware exports have been growing has slowed in recent years as labor has become short in supply, the NT dollar has appreciated, and economic recession has tightened in the large US market. To cope with these developments over the long term, Taiwanese manufacturers are moving their labor-intensive operations to neighboring Southeast Asian countries. At the same time, they are upgrading factories on the island to support the manufacture of higher-value-added products. To the same end, Taiwanese giftware manufacturers have begun to hire substantial numbers of design personnel and promote their own brand names in overseas markets.

Some of the HOT items:

* Christmas decorations
* plastic housewares
* porcelain and ceramic products
* steel housewares

FOOTWEAR

Currently, well over 1,000 active shoe factories in Taiwan manufacture leather, cloth, rubber, and plastic footwear. Taiwan has been particularly successful in its exports of athletic shoes, among them such internationally known brands as Adidas, Nike, and Reebok.

The total export value of Taiwan-made shoes exceeds US$3 billion. The largest markets for these exports are the United States, Japan, Germany, the United Kingdom, Canada, and Hong Kong. The volume of exports to the American market declined in recent years, but increased sales to Japan, Germany, and Hong Kong have largely filled the gap.

At the same time, the shift of many lower-end shoe-manufacturing operations from Taiwan to mainland China and Southeast Asia has resulted in a lively export trade in shoe parts, raw materials, and even machinery. Leading items include uppers, insoles, outersoles, heels, fittings, plastics, and synthesized leather. Relocation of many footwear factories to China and other countries has led Taiwan's domestic footwear industry to focus increasingly on supplying footwear parts and materials.

Someoof the HOT items:

* athletic shoes
* dress shoes
* footwear machinery
* leather and plastic raw materials
* sandals
* shoe parts

FURNITURE

In recent years, Taiwan's furniture industry has been plagued by rising production costs and shortages of raw materials. As a result, a considerable number of the island's furniture makers have established trading partnerships in Southeast Asia or relocated production facilities in order to secure reliable supplies of raw materials and reduce production costs. Nevertheless, many designers of furniture products and marketing representatives have remained in Taiwan, where they work in cooperation with manufacturers in other countries. In this way, Taiwan has been able to remain a participant in the industry.

Some of the HOT items:

* cabinets and shelves
* living room furniture
* medical furniture and parts
* office and computer furniture
* outdoor furniture
* stone and marble goods

TEXTILES AND GARMENTS

Textile manufacturing was one of the first light industries to be established in Taiwan. In 1951, it was the island's largest export industry. Although Taiwan's textile industry currently ranks second to electronics in terms of total value, the country is still one of the world's top ten exporters of textiles. Together, yarns and fabric account for more than half of the country's textile exports.

Apparel turned out by the domestic garment industry consists mainly of woven and knitted garments. But exports of garments are moderate compared with those of yarns and fabrics.

Hong Kong is by far the largest market for Taiwanese fabrics and yarns, while the United States is the main market for Taiwan-made garments. The European Community receives an increasingly large share of Taiwan's textile exports. Taiwanese textile producers are working to establish themselves firmly in Europe, as that market becomes increasingly integrated. Exports to that region are expected to rise.

Some of the HOT items:

- casual wear
- fabrics
- athletic wear
- synthetic fibers
- woven and knitted garments
- yarns

TEN EXTRA PROSPECTS FOR IMPORTING FROM TAIWAN

- clocks and watches
- food and beverages
- home products
- jewelry
- metal products (excluding iron and steel)
- photographic equipment
- sporting goods
- stationery
- toys and games
- transportation equipment

OPPORTUNITIES FOR EXPORTING TO TAIWAN

A multitude of name-brand items produced abroad, including automobiles, housewares, cosmetics, and processed foods, are widely known in the Taiwan market. In addition, demand for such capital-intensive and high-technology goods and services as pollution control equipment, computers and peripherals, scientific instruments, and advanced electronic components is particularly strong. As Taiwan's economy continues to develop, it will remain an attractive market for foreign exporters. Two of the most important considerations for foreign exporters to Taiwan are price competitiveness and solid customer service. This section describes areas of opportunity in Taiwan for foreign exporters.

POLLUTION CONTROL EQUIPMENT

Taiwan's current Six-Year Development Plan places great emphasis on environmental protection, and this emphasis has stimulated rapid growth in the market for pollution control equipment and services. Between 1992 and 1997, 68 public environmental protection projects budgeted at US$37 billion will be initiated. Water quality protection, waste water control, air pollution control, monitoring systems, toxic and solid waste management, and noise-control devices and materials have been highlighted. The growing demand for technologically advanced products means that foreign firms should continue to dominate Taiwan's market for pollution control equipment.

Some of the HOT items:
- compressor parts
- dust analysis apparatus
- fan and blower parts
- filters
- hazardous industrial waste containers
- incinerators
- monitoring and testing devices
- pumps
- skimmers
- sludge-dewatering machines
- solenoid valves

COMPUTERS AND PERIPHERALS

Rapid computerization of the private and public sectors in Taiwan has created a strong demand for sophisticated computers and peripherals. Twenty-nine national computerization projects are now being planned by various public agencies, and several additional projects are envisaged under the 10-year (1991-2000) Information Industry Sector Development Project. These projects as well as private initiatives

have spurred particularly rapid growth in sales of mainframe systems, central processing units (CPUs), minicomputers, workstations, and peripherals. US firms lead in sales of mainframe computers, while Japanese firms lead in sales of peripherals.

Some of the HOT items:
- central processing units
- dot matrix printers
- hard disk drives
- high-performance workstations
- laser printers
- magnetic ink character readers
- magnetic tape devices
- mainframe systems
- optical character readers
- personal computers (386 and 486 models)
- plotters, mice, and digitizers
- professional-use terminals

CAD/CAM/CAE/CIM SYSTEMS AND COMPUTER SOFTWARE

The growing market for computers and peripherals in Taiwan is closely linked to increased demand for computer-aided systems and software, which arises from the push to upgrade product development capability and accelerate the automation of production. Taiwan's 80,000 factories purchase computer-aided design (CAD) and computer-aided manufacturing (CAM) systems from US, Japanese, and European suppliers to enhance design productivity and manufacturing flexibility. Increased use of computer-aided engineering (CAE) technology has been stimulated by extremely tight labor markets and high computer literacy. Sales of computer integrated manufacturing (CIM) equipment and software are also expected to grow in line with continuing upgrades in technology.

Some of the HOT items:
- computer-aided design (CAD)
- computer-aided manufacturing (CAM)
- system software
- tooling applications software
- vertical applications software

LABORATORY SCIENTIFIC INSTRUMENTS

According to the Taiwan National Science Council, total public expenditures for research and development (R&D) in industrial science and technology are projected to reach US$3.3 billion by 1995. In addition, private sector firms involved in R&D programs are to benefit from tax incentives and grants. These efforts should produce a sharp increase in the demand for sophisticated laboratory scientific instruments. Virtually all must be imported. Sales of laboratory instruments could increase by 20 to 25 percent annually through 1995.

Some of the most promising products are analytical instruments, electronic laboratory instruments, medical instruments, optical instruments, clinical treatment equipment, metal-testing equipment, and measuring instruments. US firms currently maintain the largest share of the market, followed by Japanese, German, and UK firms.

Some of the HOT items:

- automatic regulating and controlling instruments
- barometers
- cathode-ray oscilloscopes and oscillographs
- electricity meters
- gas meters
- metal-testing machines and appliances
- PH meters
- speed indicators
- stroboscopes
- tachometers

ELECTRONIC COMPONENTS

The continued rapid growth of Taiwan's electronics industry has resulted in strong demand for sophisticated electronic components. In order to maintain the competitiveness of their assembly operations, Taiwan's computer assembly firms must import a significant percentage of advanced components. For at least the next three years, such items as digital, analog, and monolithic integrated circuits (ICs), diodes, oscillators, capacitors, resistors, and multilayer printed circuit (PC) boards offer excellent sales opportunities. US and Japanese suppliers are the strongest competitors within this market area.

Some of the HOT items:

- digital, analog, and monolithic ICs
- diodes (non-LED and photosensitive)
- fixed resistors (greater than 20 watts)
- high-resolution color CRTs (less than 0.3 mm)
- lead frames for transistors and diodes
- quartz crystal oscillators
- rheostats and potentiometers
- rigid multilayer PC boards
- rigid two-layer PC boards
- tantalum, ceramic dielectric, and multi-layer capacitors
- transistor chips and wafers
- variable or adjustable capacitors

SEMICONDUCTOR MANUFACTURING EQUIPMENT

Several semiconductor firms are now actively upgrading their production and processing capability to enhance their competitiveness in the world market. Because almost all semiconductor manufacturing equipment must be imported, the outlook for future sales of semiconductor manufacturing equipment in Taiwan remains promising.

Some of the HOT items:

- automatic testing equipment
- diffusion furnaces
- etching systems
- ion implanters
- lithography equipment
- molding equipment
- plasma enhanced CVD systems
- probers
- sputtering systems
- steppers
- wire-bonding equipment

TELECOMMUNICATIONS EQUIPMENT

Major efforts to introduce new and upgraded products and services suggest that demand in Taiwan for telecommunications services and equipment will grow rapidly throughout the 1990s. As the dominant public monopoly, the Directorate General of Telecommunications (DGT), is the principal buyer of key technology-based products. DGT purchases, mainly from foreign firms, are estimated to account for approximately 80 percent of the telecommunications products sold to Taiwan. These purchases include network switching systems, local distribution electronics, and long haul transmissions.

The private sector is the largest user of private branch exchange (PBX) systems, facsimile machines, and mobile phones. As the telecommunications market gradually opens to direct sales, foreign exporters can expect many more opportunities in this industry.

Some of the HOT items:

- cellular systems
- customer premises equipment
- facsimile machines
- high-gate PBX systems
- local area networks
- mobile telephones
- modems
- network switching systems
- paging systems
- terminal adapters
- videotapes
- workstations

MEDICAL EQUIPMENT

According to government authorities, Taiwan's National Health Insurance (NHI) program is slated for implementation by 1994. This program, together with the increased number of elderly people in Taiwan, has led to a significant increase in the demand for medical equipment.

At this time, most local demand for advanced equipment is met by foreign firms, particularly those from the United States, Japan, and Germany.

Some of the HOT items:

- artificial hearts, valves, vascular grafts
- cardioscopes
- CT scanners
- electrocardiographs
- electrodiagnostic apparatus
- laser lithotripter impact equipment
- linear accelerators
- MRI scanners
- ophthalmic apparatus
- ozone and aerosol therapy apparatus
- plastic surgery instruments
- ultraviolet or infrared ray apparatus
- ultrasonic scanners
- x-ray plates and film

LASER AND ELECTRO-OPTICS

In response to rising labor costs, Taiwan's firms are making increased use of automated equipment to facilitate information handling and improve productivity. This trend has resulted in strong demand for imports of optical appliances and components. Opportunities exist for such items as laser tools, optoelectronic semiconductors, optical components, and optical communications instruments.

At the same time, rising disposable incomes have resulted in dramatic increases in consumer purchasing power. Demand for high-quality laser-optic audio and video products is rising.

Some of the HOT items:

- contact lenses
- instant print cameras
- laser tools
- medical lasers
- optical components and appliances
- optical fibers and cables
- optoelectronic semiconductors
- precision instruments
- slide projectors
- spectrometers
- telescope parts and accessories
- telescopes

AUTOMOBILES, PARTS, AND ACCESSORIES

Taiwan is one of the best markets for foreign auto manufacturers in the world. Future prospects for automobiles, parts, and accessories should remain positive as proposed tariff reduction programs are implemented.

After a two-year slowdown, US, Japanese, and European manufacturers are currently achieving impressive sales. Small-engine sedans, sports and utility vehicles, light commercial vehicles, and trucks are currently the bestselling motor vehicles. The steady increase in the number of automobiles in Taiwan is bolstering demand for foreign parts and service equipment. Such equipment includes radial tires, diesel engines, fuel nozzles, and compression engine parts as well as computer diagnostics, body repair equipment, and mechanical tools and equipment.

Foreign firms also enjoy a strong market position in the auto accessories market, accounting for about 80 percent of domestic sales. As the automotive market continues to expand, demand for high-quality imported automotive accessories, including high quality car waxes, floor mats, waxing sponges, wipe cloths, and cup holders, will increase.

Some of the HOT items:

- automotive parts and service equipment
- decorative accessories
- floor mats
- light vans and trucks
- lubricants
- sedans and station wagons
- sports and utility vehicles
- waxes and polishes
- waxing sponges and wipe cloths
- wiper blades

HOUSEHOLD CONSUMER GOODS

The dramatic rise in consumer purchasing power, combined with appreciation of the New Taiwan dollar, has made imported household consumer goods, especially home appliances, one of the best export prospects for foreign firms. Many foreign suppliers have already established strong brand name recognition for their products in Taiwan, and most have strong service networks. Imports of such items as garbage disposals, filters, microwave ovens, and washers and dryers are expected to continue to expand by an average 15 percent per year for the next three or four years.

Some of the HOT items:

- color TVs
- electric air filters and purifiers
- electric water filters (household types)

- fully automatic washers and dryers
- immersion heaters
- kitchen garbage disposals
- microwave ovens

INDUSTRIAL PROCESS CONTROLS

Industrial process control (IPC) equipment plays an increasingly vital role in Taiwan as the economy continues to move away from labor-intensive to automated production. Because Taiwanese manufacturers who use IPC technology are primarily assembly operations, most process control systems used locally must be imported. Foreign suppliers are in a strong position to take advantage of IPC imports, which have been projected to reach $1.5 billion by 1995. In particular, suppliers from the US, Japan, and Europe are in a highly competitive position regarding electronic and electric industrial process controls and computer-based control systems.

Some of the HOT items:

- gas analyzers
- gas or liquid chromatographs
- logic analyzers
- measuring instruments
- multimeters
- oscilloscopes
- potentiometers
- pressure, transmissions, and safety valves
- spectroscopic analyzers
- spectrum analyzers

COSMETICS AND TOILETRIES

Changing consumer preferences and rising living standards are expanding the market for imported cosmetics and toiletries. Given a strong preference for foreign products, such international brands as Lancôme, Elizabeth Arden, and Clinique currently enjoy lucrative sales of high-end products, including facial creams, foundation, lipstick, eye makeup, face cleansers, nail polish, and perfumed soaps. Steady growth is also projected for perfumes, shampoos, and powders.

Some of the HOT items:

- cleansing creams
- hair sprays and related care products
- lipstick and eye makeup
- nail polish
- perfumed bath salts
- perfumes and toilet waters
- shampoos and rinses
- shaving products
- skincare products
- toilet soap

BUILDING SUPPLIES

Taiwan's continuous economic growth, along with heavy infrastructure investment under the Six-Year Development Plan, is bringing impressive sales of construction-related products. The outlook for sales of imported building supplies is especially promising. Both consumer preference for high-quality renovation products as well as increased commercial construction are stimulating demand for such items as prefabricated structures, water heaters, plaster materials, particle board, adhesives, insulating products and door locks. Firms from Japan and the United States are leading exporters, followed by firms from Germany, Korea, and Malaysia.

Some of the HOT items:

- anti-corrosives
- coniferous woods
- flooring plates, titles or strips (plastics)
- glues and adhesives
- heat-insulating or sound-absorbing materials
- locks (base metal)
- other paints or enamels
- prefabricated buildings
- tubes, pipes and hoses (plastics and aluminum)
- veneer and plywood sheets

AIR-CONDITIONING AND REFRIGERATION EQUIPMENT

Ten years ago, air-conditioning was rare in Taiwan. At present, few private, commercial, or industrial buildings in urban areas are built without it. Taiwan manufacturers are fairly competitive in wall and window units, but lack of appropriate technology and capital equipment compels Taiwan to import most of its large-scale central air-conditioning equipment.

Demand for refrigeration has undergone a similar transformation, driven by the emergence of wholesale discount stores, department stores, supermarkets, and convenience stores. In addition to household refrigerators, foreign firms are highly competitive in industrial refrigeration.

Some of the HOT items:

- air-conditioning compressors
- air-conditioning machine parts
- centrifugal pumps
- chilling and condensing equipment
- cold drink machines
- coolers, refrigeration devices
- freezer parts and equipment
- freezers
- household refrigerators
- ice-making machines
- window or wall type air-conditioning machines

CHEMICAL PRODUCTION MACHINERY

Increased demand for chemical intermediates means that midstream chemical producers in Taiwan are continually expanding their plant facilities, and the need for sophisticated chemical production machinery has increased. Mounting investment, particularly in the petrochemical industry, is expected to stimulate sales of such items as agitators, dryers, filters, and heat exchangers. Demand should remain strong through 1994.

Some of the HOT items:
- auxiliary plant parts and condensers
- chlorinators
- filtering and purifying machinery and apparatus
- gas recoverers
- heat exchange units
- pressure-reducing valves
- water tube boilers

INDUSTRIAL ORGANIC CHEMICALS

Although Taiwan is capable of producing industrial organic chemicals, many local manufacturers find it more cost effective to import them, a preference that presents numerous opportunities for foreign producers and exporters of chemicals.

Some of the HOT items:
- acetic acid
- acetone
- acrylonitrile
- ethylene glycol
- propylenes
- purified terephthalic acid
- styrene
- vinyl acetate
- vinyl chloride

ENGINEERING PLASTICS

With its large-scale industrial development and expanding foreign trade, Taiwan is buying increasing quantities of engineering plastics. There is strong competition from local manufacturers of polybutylene terephthalate and polyacetal, while competition is moderate among local suppliers of polyamide 6 and polyethlene terephthalate. Because it lacks the technology needed to produce other engineering plastics, Taiwan depends heavily on Japanese, US, and German suppliers for other polyamides, polyoxylene oxide, and polycarbonates.

Some of the HOT items:
- polyacetals in primary forms
- polyamide -11, -12, -6.9, -6, 10, or -6, 12
- polyamide 6 (nylon 6)
- polyamide 6,6 (nylon 6,6)
- polybutylene terphthalate
- polycarbonates in primary forms
- polyoxylene oxide

HIGH-VALUE FOOD AND BEVERAGE PRODUCTS

Taiwanese authorities have set a zero-growth target for the island's agricultural sector. This policy, coupled with ever-increasing production costs and rising consumer income, are likely to boost Taiwan's imports of high-value food and beverage products during this decade. Demand in Taiwan for fruit, dairy products, beef, and other agricultural and beverage items should expand significantly in the years ahead.

Some of the HOT items:
beverages
- beer
- champagnes
- cognacs, armagnacs, and brandies
- red wines
- sparkling wines

canned foods
- canned fruits
- high-value canned vegetables
- quality Western-style canned meats

confectionery products
- chewing gum
- chocolate
- other candies

dairy products
- cheese
- frozen dairy products and yogurt
- ice cream
- milk- and cream-based fluid products

fresh vegetables
- celery
- leeks
- lettuce
- potatoes
- radishes

meats
- beef
- ham
- sausage
- shredded pork and pork jerky

fresh fruit
- apples
- cherries
- grapefruit
- grapes
- kiwis
- nectarines
- peaches

- pears
- sugar plums

nuts and dried fruit

- almonds
- cashews
- chestnuts
- pistachios
- walnuts

TOYS, GAMES, AND SPORTING GOODS

Once a major exporter of toys, games, and sporting goods, Taiwan has become a large importer in recent years. The local market for toys, games, and sporting goods amounts to US$300 million, with imported products now accounting for 51 percent of all sales on the island.

Several factors have contributed to the growing market for foreign-made products in this sector, including the increased spending on recreational activities by more affluent Taiwanese consumers, the growing competitiveness of foreign producers, appreciation of the New Taiwan dollar, and labor shortages in Taiwan, which have driven more than 70 toy and sporting goods makers to mainland China and other countries in Southeast Asia.

Some of the HOT items:

- baseball equipment
- board games
- bowling equipment
- toy cars and trucks

TWELVE EXTRA PROSPECTS FOR EXPORTING TO TAIWAN

- aircraft and parts
- avionics and ground support equipment
- base metals, minerals
- composite materials
- construction equipment
- electrical power systems
- electronics production and test equipment
- food processing and packaging equipment
- garments and clothing accessories
- hotel and restaurant equipment
- railroad equipment
- travel security and safety equipment

OPPORTUNITIES FOR GROWTH

REAL ESTATE

The real estate market in Taiwan boomed in the early 1990s. The export-led economic prosperity of recent years has been followed by sustained growth in private sector construction projects to meet the demand for new office space and residential housing, and new domestic building projects have now become a significant component of Taiwan's economic growth. While construction of large-scale projects appears not to be financially feasible for overseas businesses, architectural design, engineering services, residential remodeling, industrial land and factory acquisition, and leasing are opportunity areas.

Commercial

The land that can be used for building is very limited, and it must be utilized efficiently. The level of new building has been especially strong in the south, because the lack of space has forced companies to look outside of the northern city of Taipei.

Demand for high-rise buildings is increasing. One of the more notable examples is the 126-story building planned for Kaohsiung. New technology and new materials will be needed. This field affords excellent opportunities to overseas companies that provide architectural design and engineering services or that supply building materials. Specialty architectural services, such as aerial photography could also be especially profitable.

Many industry sources, including the International Engineering and Construction Corporation, have stated that it is generally difficult for overseas companies to obtain commercial construction contracts.

Residential

While overall commercial building has slowed, the residential market remains robust, with some US$42 billion allocated for investment between 1991 and 1996. The steady increase in disposable income has made renovation of middle-income homes common.

Industrial

Foreign manufacturers are permitted to own land and factories in Taiwan, and certain kinds of service organizations may own offices. Land experts at the Industrial Development and Investment Commission (IDIC) can assist investors in locating plant sites and negotiating the purchase of private land.

IDIC, Ministry of Economic Affairs
10/F., 7 Roosevelt Rd.
Sec. 1, Taipei, Taiwan
Tel: [886] (2) 3947213 Fax: [886] (2) 3926835

In order to simplify the acquisition of land for industrial development, Taiwanese authorities have designated more than 74 sites throughout the island for use as industrial land. Selection criteria for these sites include easy access to rail and highway transportation, ample supplies of water and electricity, and an adequate local labor force. Investors may purchase land from the private owners of these designated sites or, in publicly developed industrial estates, from local authorities. Investors may purchase land within these estates in seven- to 15-year installments. The authorities offer financing for 75 to 80 percent of the purchase price.

Leasing

Land in Taiwan's three export-processing zones (EPZs) and the Hsinchu Science-Based Industrial Park is not for sale but leased to investors by the authorities. Standard factory buildings are available for purchase in the EPZs and three industrial estates. Aside from some buildings in the Science Park, few factories that meet Western standards are available for lease in Taiwan.

Modern offices are readily available for lease or purchase in most metropolitan areas of Taiwan. For leasing, landlords usually require three to six months' rent as a security deposit and three to twelve months' rent in advance. Offices can be leased for one to five years. Leases can be renewed subject to rate increases. Leases with an option to buy are not uncommon.

FINANCIAL SERVICES

Taiwan's financial services market is slowly being liberalized. In 1992, 15 new private domestic banks were allowed to begin operations in Taiwan. At least a dozen American insurance firms have established operations there. The policy of liberalization has created many opportunities for foreign firms either as direct participants or as service providers to other firms. Software, management, analytical, and technical consulting services; equipment provision; offshore liaison; publishing; and information services are all subsectors that may interest overseas firms.

Insurance

In June 1992 the Ministry of Finance (MOF) announced the new Criteria for Establishment of Insurance Companies as part of the Amended Insurance Law. The new law allowed foreign firms to participate in new domestic insurance companies; however, it stipulated that a qualified foreign insurance company that has no branch office in Taiwan may only own up to 30 percent of a new insurance company and that aggregate foreign ownership in a new company may not exceed 49 percent. At the end of 1993 the government further eased its policy on foreign participation, announcing that it would remove all caps on foreign ownership in the insurance industry.

Recent liberalization has greatly increased foreign access to Taiwan's insurance market. However, since the insurance business is domestically oriented and is intimately related to the country's culture, society, and customs, it is vital for an overseas insurer to design new products tailored to the needs of its new foreign clients. Do not rely on country-of-origin policies.

The potential for life insurance providers in Taiwan is large, but competition is growing as foreign firms enter the market. High demand for family protection, adolescent educational funds, and retirement plans makes individual life and accident insurance the major areas of growth. Health insurance will continue to grow as per capita income and living standards increase. Demand for health care and cancer victim insurance has been increasing, particularly in the medium- and high-income groups.

To meet the requirements of emerging single-parent and double-income families, foreign insurance firms may want to introduce disability income insurance, such as variable life and universal life insurance. Although few foreign firms have shown an interest in the casualty insurance market, foreign insurance providers that support the industry with analytical or other services may do well.

Banking Automation and Security Systems

Taiwan is making an effort to enhance its financial services, the goal being to become one of Asia's largest financial centers, especially after Hong Kong reverts to Chinese rule in 1997. Taiwan hopes to take important steps toward the realization of that goal by increasing the automation of banking functions and introducing advanced security systems.

Taiwan's nationwide project for banking automation began in 1984. Demand for banking automation systems has increased by an average of 10 to 12 percent a year for the past three years. The pace is expected to pick up 15 to 25 percent a year for the next three years. Demand for automated teller machines (ATMs) is particularly strong.

AVIONICS

Dramatic growth in the number of domestic and international passenger airlines and air freight services has made existing facilities in Taiwan inadequate. The situation is likely to become even more acute if direct flights to the PRC are approved. Five major airport expansions are planned before 1996. In addition, the Civil Aeronautics Administration (CAA) will coordinate several regional projects for

navigation radar and meteorology. Training, software, and services are also in great demand. Aviation ground support equipment is one of the most promising subsectors. (*See* Aerospace in the Public Procurement Opportunities section.)

ADVANCED MATERIALS

Taiwanese authorities have designated the advanced materials industry as a strategic industry. Public financing is available for local firms that wish to enter this field. Industries that use advanced materials include aerospace, machine tools, precision instruments, and automotive engineering. Moreover, many of Taiwan's traditional export-oriented industries, such as sporting goods, plastic products, and electronics, are using increasing amounts of advanced, composite materials, many of which must be imported.

BIOTECHNOLOGY

Biotechnology has recently been designated a strategic industry, and it is thus eligible for various types of public support. R&D will be subsidized through semigovernmental organizations and consortia of private companies. Improvements in the protection afforded intellectual property have made Taiwan more attractive to overseas biotech companies as well as to companies in the pharmaceutical and agricultural industries. This market is expected to become significant in the short- and medium-term. Long-term prospects are especially promising given stronger enforcement of intellectual property rights.

FRANCHISING

Franchising is a rapidly growing industry. US companies lead the market, followed by firms from Japan and Hong Kong. Fast food, convenience store, and automated servicing franchises have proliferated. US companies have opened new markets with Western-style bar franchises and retail music outlets. While the market for franchises is generally attractive, lack of suitable space and trained personnel are stumbling blocks for foreign companies.

PUBLIC PROCUREMENT OPPORTUNITIES

Taiwan authorities are active participants in the island's economy. They develop and administer centralized economic plans, use foreign investment incentives to promote specific industries, make low-interest loans available to strategic sectors, and use Taiwan's flexible tax system to advance economic objectives. In addition, the state owns a substantial portion of Taiwan's financial institutions and heavy industry.

State-owned enterprises have historically been a major factor in the Taiwanese economy. It has been estimated that as much as one-third of Taiwan's GDP is generated by state-owned enterprises. The Ministry of Economic Affairs supervises the operations of all public corporations. (By law, a firm is considered a public corporation if the authorities hold more than 50 percent of its equity.) Products and services that are wholly or partly controlled by the Taiwanese government include power generation, water, petroleum products, banking, insurance, steel, fertilizer, salt, sugar, tobacco, beer, and wine.

Although the authorities have stated their intention to privatize most of these operations, little progress has been made to date. Moreover, there is no timetable for the privatization program, and trade and investment in many of these sectors remain severely restricted.

MAJOR PROJECTS AND THE SIX-YEAR DEVELOPMENT PLAN

Although Taiwan possesses a modern infrastructure, transportation, energy, and communications facilities have not kept pace with the island's rapid economic expansion. In an effort to upgrade infrastructure, encourage investment, and improve the quality of life, Taiwan's cabinet approved an ambitious Six-Year Development Plan (1991-1996).

The plan targets investment in such major areas of Taiwan's infrastructure as expressways, power plants, railways, and petrochemical facilities. Although many projects in the plan preexist it, it still provides overseas firms with vast export opportunities. Moreover, few people expect the plan to be completed in six years.

Realistically, the Taiwan authorities have stated that some projects in the plan may not be implemented according to schedule. They have also cut the number of projects by almost 20 percent from 775 to 634, a move that lowers the projected cost by 22 percent. As an additional cost-cutting measure, the government is encouraging involvement by the private sector.

A list of all major projects open to foreign participation is available from:

American Institute in Taiwan
7, Lane 134, Hsin Yi Road
Section 3, Taipei, Taiwan
Tel: [886] (2) 7092000 Fax: [886] (2) 7014216

Other agencies and organizations in Taiwan that can provide information about public procurement projects include the Ministry of Economic Affairs, Taiwan Power Company, Chinese Petroleum Corporation (CPC), China Steel Corporation, Taiwan Tobacco and Wine Monopoly Bureau (TTWMB), Taiwan Sugar Corporation (TSC), and the Industrial Development Bureau (IDB). (Refer to "Important Addresses" chapter.)

This section describes some of the major projects to be conducted under the Six-Year Development Plan. Projects are arranged by industry.

TELECOMMUNICATIONS

The Directorate General of Telecommunications (DGT) continues to provide basic services, and it has made efforts to introduce new and upgraded services. Along with implementation of data and cellular services, it plans to introduce an integrated service digital network (ISDN), an intelligent network, and fiber optic local loops in this decade. By the year 2000, the switching network will be completely digital, and almost every household is expected to have a telephone.

The efforts of the DGT and expected purchases by the private sector will increase local demand for telecommunications services and equipment, and rapid growth is projected for the remainder of the decade. The Six-Year Development Plan targets the total number of ISDN subscribers at 25,000 by 1996, about 500 times the figure for 1990. Telephone density will increase from 30 subscribers per 100 in 1990 to 39 subscribers per 100 in 1996. Since the DGT introduced cellular mobile telephone service in July 1989, about 65,000 lines have been connected. By the end of 1996, it is estimated that phone subscribers will total 370,000, up 861 percent from the level of 1990.

A proposed telecommunications law that will deregulate the telecommunications industry and allow the private sector to provide services is presently in the legislature. Regulations governing foreign investment in telecommunications services have yet to be finalized, but it is likely that liberalization will be gradual. Some investment restrictions, including equity requirements, are likely to remain in place for the foreseeable future.

A proposed cable television law may give foreign firms other opportunities. Most hardware meets international standards, which would enable foreign suppliers of cable television equipment, software, and services to enter the market.

Finally, in an attempt to keep Taiwan competitive and enter the 21st century as an advanced industrialized country, the Ministry of Transportation and Communications (MOTC) announced a US$7.3 billion budget for telecommunications projects as part of the Six-Year Development Plan. Large state-owned corporations and military organizations may issue independent bids for telecommunications goods and services.

Telecommunications projects under MOTC for 1991-1997 include: a city telephone project for central Taiwan, a long distance communication project, an international communications project, and a city telephone project for southern Taiwan.

Additional information can be obtained from:

Ministry of Transportation and Communications
(MOTC)
2 Changsha St.
Sec. 1, Taipei, Taiwan
Tel: [886] (2) 3112661 Fax: [886] (2) 3812260

TRANSPORTATION

The Six-Year Development Plan includes harbor improvements, construction of the West Coast Highway and the Northern Freeway, completion of the second segment of the north-south expressway, and construction of metro systems in Taipei and Kaohsiung.

Here are the budgets, projected date of completion, and contacts for the MOTC's current projects:

- Construction of four underground rail lines between Wanhua and Panchiao: US$1.5 billion; 1999; Taipei Railway Underground Project Office, MOTC
- Improvement of the Eastern Taiwan Railway: US$1.6 billion; 1998; Taiwan Provincial Department of Communication
- Cross-Island Express Highway: US$1.4 billion; 1997; Institute of Transportation, MOTC
- West Coast Express Highway: US$2.0 billion; 1996; Highway Bureau, MOTC
- Southern Cross-Island Freeway: US$4.9 billion; 1993; Taiwan Area National Freeway Bureau, MOTC
- Preliminary Mass Rapid Transit (MRT) Project, Taipei: US$11.1 billion, 1998; Department of Mass Rapid Transit System (DORTS), Taipei Municipal Authorities, and MOTC
- Kaohsiung MRT System: US$4.9 billion; 2000; Department of Kaohsiung MRT, Kaohsiung Municipal Authorities, and MOTC
- MRT Systems for Taoyuan, Hsinchu, Taichung,

and Tainan cities: US$7.4 billion; Taiwan Housing and Development Bureau.

Additional assistance regarding the Cross-Harbor Bridge project can be obtained from:

Chen Chi-Ju, Project Manager
Kaohsiung City Public Works
New Construction and Engineering Department
6/F., 2 Si Wei 3rd Rd.
Kaohsiung City, Taiwan
Tel: [886] (7) 3373287, 3314316
Fax: [886] (7) 3314169

Cross-Harbor Bridge Project
Liu Chiu-Ping, Project Manager
Kaohsiung City Public Works
New Construction and Engineering Department
6/F., 2 Si Wei 3rd Rd.
Kaohsiung City, Taiwan
Tel: [886] (7) 3373266, 3373000 x2306
Fax: [886] (7) 3314169

CONSTRUCTION

Construction and such related services as engineering, have expanded rapidly in Taiwan since the Six-Year Development Plan was initiated. More than US$40 billion has been allocated for public investment between 1991 and 1996. Demand is likely to remain strong, because the government is committed to a series of major infrastructure projects in transportation, telecommunications, public utilities, and environmental protection.

Taiwan's imports of building supplies should expand by approximately 10 percent in 1993, with the total between US$1 and US$2 billion. All segments of this market have great potential. Taiwan design, architectural, and construction firms are actively looking for durable, high-quality building materials. In the longer term, the demand for high-rise buildings, the growing use of air-conditioning and automobiles, and the need for energy conservation are all likely to create a need for changes in building design and materials, which means new opportunities for foreign experts and suppliers.

ENVIRONMENT

The environmental protection field is another area that overseas companies should find attractive. The most important factor underlying Taiwan's environmental problem is the island's population density. There are an average of 571 people per square km in Taiwan, and only 3.5 percent of Taiwan's residential units are hooked up to a sewage treatment system. There are also a good number of automobiles—283 motor vehicles per square km. Taiwan's authorities estimate that they will need to spend approximately US$40 billion over the next ten years to clean up the island's environment.

Demand for air and water pollution control equipment and solid waste treatment equipment is likely to be strong. Sales of such equipment reached US$940 million in 1992, and they are expected to increase at an annual rate of 20 to 25 percent through 1995.

These are some of the projects that fall under the jurisdiction of Taiwan's Environmental Protection Administration: a US$1.3 billion industrial pollution control project (1990-1994); a US$1.9 billion project for construction of sewerage systems (1991-2001; contact Taiwan Provincial Authorities for information); a US$1 billion construction in Taipei City (1991-2001; contact the Taipei City authorities for details); a US$856 million Phase Two Garbage Disposal project for Taiwan province (1991-1996); and a US$707 million ocean pollution control project (1992-2001).

Additional information can be obtained from:

Environmental Protection Administration
1 Hsiang Yang Road
Taipei, Taiwan
Tel: [886] (2) 3117722 Fax: [886] (2) 3116071

ENERGY

Taiwan's rapid economic development strains its energy-producing capabilities. The situation is most acute during periods of peak demand in the summer months. In summer 1991, Taipei City experienced a record number of brownouts.

To deal with the problem, the Ministry of Economic Affairs included five projects in the Six-Year Development Plan: a fourth nuclear power plant estimated to cost US$6 billion (US$4.2 billion is to be spent on foreign procurement), thermal power plants at Taichung (budgeted at US$3 billion, is to be spent on foreign procurement); six Mingtan pumped storage facilities worth US$1.88 billion; the US$422 million Maan Project; and the US$440 million Liyutan Reservoir Project.

Additional information is available from:

Ministry of Economic Affairs
15 Fu Chou Street
Taipei, Taiwan
Tel: [886] (2) 3212200 Fax: [886] (2) 3919398

Taiwan Power Company (Taipower)
242 Roosevelt Rd.
Sec. 3, Taipei, Taiwan
Tel: [886] (2) 3651234 Fax: [886] (2) 3561509

AEROSPACE

Taiwan announced the Aeronautics and Space Industries Development Program in August 1990. In addition to promoting the development of aeronautics and space industries, the program aims to stimulate parallel development of parts and components industries, improve the integration of national defense industries, and increase the use of advanced technologies. In pursuing these objectives, Taiwan will seek to encourage foreign aeronautics and space companies as well as parts manufacturers to transfer and license advanced technologies to local firms.

Over the next few years, Taiwan's aerospace firms are expected to concentrate on manufacturing and supplying parts to large US and European aerospace firms. Southern Taiwan's Tainan area has the potential to emerge as a center for Taiwan's aerospace industry. The area is home to the National Chang Kung University's Institute of Aeronautics and Astronautics as well as to firms with experience in parts manufacturing and in aircraft maintenance and repair.

A number of public agencies, including the Ministry of National Defense, Ministry of Economic Affairs, and the Bank of Communications, will offer incentives aimed at developing the aerospace industry. These incentives include low-interest credit facilities and tax breaks. The Ministry of Economic Affairs also plans to establish an aeronautics and space industrial park specifically for the development of the aerospace industry.

The Aeronautics and Space Industries Development Program requires significant procurement of foreign aerospace products by state-owned entities. Such procurement can include such previously negotiated transactions as counterpurchases of aerospace products or technology transfers. In addition, when private companies, including airlines, make large purchases of foreign aerospace products, reciprocal transactions are required if the companies want to obtain preferential financing.

Two large-scale projects now under way and a large private aerospace firm should fuel growth in this industry. The Industrial Cooperation Program is a 10-year (1988-1998), US$340 million offset program between China Air Lines (CAL) and three US companies.

Phase One (1988-1992) allocated US$74.8 million for technology transfers and technician training and US$30.6 million for the purchase of airplane parts. In Phase Two (1992-1995), US$34 million will be spent on technology transfers and personnel training and US$61.2 million on the purchase of airplane parts.

Phase Three (1995-1998) schedules US$27.2 million for technology transfers and personnel training and US$112.2 million for the purchase of airplane parts. The Indigenous Defense Fighter (IDF) program (1990-1997) budgets US$6.3 billion for aircraft production and US$285 million for the manufacture of aircraft components, engines, and electronic parts. The private project centers on an agreement between Taihsiang Aerospace and Pratt and Whitney to develop the JT8D-290 engine in cooperation with European companies.

Additional projects include expanding five airports and developing navigation radar, which the Civil Aeronautics Administration will coordinate.

Additional information is available from:

Ministry of Economic Affairs (MOEA)
15 Fu Chou Street
Taipei, Taiwan
Tel: [886] (2) 3212200 Fax: [886] (2) 3919398

Industrial Development Bureau, MOEA
41-3 Hsin Yi Road
Sec. 3, Taipei, Taiwan
Tel: [886] (2) 7541255 Fax: [886] (2) 7030160

PUBLIC PROCUREMENT PROCESS

REGULATIONS

Public procurement that exceeds NT$50 million (US$1.87 million) must be handled by the state-owned Central Trust of China (CTC). CTC purchases most capital equipment and industrial raw materials required by Taiwan's administrative and educational institutions, military organizations, and publicly owned commercial enterprises. Other official procurement bodies, such as military services organizations and the Taiwan Supply Bureau, which imports goods for Taiwan's provincial authorities, play an additional but relatively minor role in commercial purchasing abroad.

In fiscal year 1991, the CTC procured more than US$839 million in foreign goods and services on behalf of Taiwanese organizations. Approximately 9.5 percent of its purchases were for machinery and tools, 12.5 percent for telecommunications equipment, 10.2 percent for electric equipment, 9.3 percent for transportation equipment, 40 percent for pollution control equipment, 3.3 percent for steel and metals, 5.2 percent for fertilizer and raw materials, and 3.6 percent for agricultural, fishery, animal, and mineral products.

To regulate procurement, the authorities require all public administrative agencies and commercial enterprises to file detailed estimates of their import needs. Foreign exchange for purchases of imported products is approved if the products are not available locally in adequate quantity or quality or if the price of the goods produced locally is substantially higher (usually 15 percent) than the import's landed cost, which includes the costs of insurance and freight. Public organizations do not need CTC bids to purchase routine items, but all equipment and supplies with a purchase price exceeding the designated audit ceiling (approximately NT$50 million) must be purchased through CTC tenders.

EXCEPTIONS

Purchases by state-run enterprises that fall below the designated audit ceiling can be handled directly by the end user. In some cases, the central authorities grant certain end users special permission to handle overseas procurement by themselves or through a foreign consulting firm. The exceptions include crude oil, complete refining units, petroleum cracking units of the Chinese Petroleum Corporation, mass rapid transit systems of the Taipei municipal authorities, nuclear power plants, and the Taichung thermal power plant of the Taiwan Power Company. China Steel Corporation and China Shipbuilding also may handle their own overseas procurement.

GENERAL PROCEDURES

The CTC uses open tender methods to solicit foreign bids. At least three firms must make bid offers before a contract can be awarded. In some cases, the CTC may request special permission from the Ministry of Audit to hold a *restricted tender*. In a restricted tender, bids are limited to prequalified foreign suppliers. The authorities occasionally grant special authorization for negotiated purchases if there is only a single supplier or if rapid procurement is necessary.

The CTC announces scheduled procurement in local newspapers, on CTC bulletin boards, and in a local English-language newspaper devoted solely to public tenders. When open bids call for supplies from a specific country, the CTC sometimes issues notices through its foreign branches.

A firm must have its own copy of the invitation to bid, which is available at a nominal fee from CTC Taipei. The CTC also mails invitations to bid to interested parties. A bid bond of 1 percent is required at the time of submission. The bond is refunded if the bid is unsuccessful. The CTC considers fax, cable, and telex bids to have been submitted officially if they are accompanied by all required attachments and if they are forwarded to the CTC prior to the bidding deadline. Many open tenders limit bidding to North American and European Community firms. In addition, many invitations to bid now request an alternative price quotation on a free on board (FOB) basis. This provision benefits foreign suppliers by removing the price disadvantages associated with high transportation and insurance costs in the standard cost, insurance, freight (CIF) quotation.

OBSTACLES AND BARRIERS

Overseas firms have cited three aspects of the Taiwanese procurement process as potential obstacles or barriers to bidding on CTC or other publicly procured projects. First, lead times for major tenders are short. Bids may be required to be submitted as little as 30 to 60 days after publication. Second, a 5 percent price preference is given to domestic bidders. This preference gives them an unfair advantage when price is the primary consideration in award of the contract. Third, public works contracts require the contractor to assume an excessive level of risk. This requirement can cause them to inflate their prices to a level that puts them out of the running. Moreover, some of Taiwan's tax policies inhibit foreign firms from bidding on certain contracts. For example, Taiwan classifies engineering or management consulting fees as royalties subject to a 20 percent withholding tax rather than as technical service fees subject to a 3.75 percent tax. It also classifies engineering or designing work done abroad as having been performed locally and therefore subject to local taxation.

For more detailed information on the procurement process, contact:

Central Trust of China
49 Wu Chang Street
Section 1, Taipei, Taiwan
Tel: [886] (2) 3111151 Fax: [886] (2) 3118107

Industrial Parks

Taoyuan
Northern Taiwan Petrochemical
Tayuan

Neili
Chungli
Yushih
Hukou
Lungtan
Pingchen
Toufen
Tunglow
Taichung Yushih
Taichung Harbor
Taichung EPZ
Taichung
Fuhsing
Nankang

Pitou
Chushan
Fengtien
Yuanchang
Chiaotou
Chiatai

Penghu

Yichu

Kuantien
Hsinshih
Tainan Shin
Anping
Lungchi
Yungan
Tashe
Nantze EPZ
Jenwu

Kaohsiung Chuan-Shih

Kaohsiung EPZ
Linhao
Fengshan
Taliao
Linyuan Petrochemical
Pingtung

Taishan
Shulin
Kueishan

Tuchen
Tingkein

Taipei Chuan-Shih

Tawulun
Chilung Shih
Liu T

Taoyuan

Taipei

Taipei

Hsinchu Shih

Hsinchu

Ilan

Miaoli

Taichung

Taichung Shih

Changhua

Meilun

Nantou

Yunlin

Chiayi

Chiayi Shih

Hualien

T'ainan

Chilshang

Kaohsiung

Taitung

Pingtung

0   25   50 km
0   25 mi

EPZ: Export Processing Zone

SPECIAL TRADE ZONES

EXPORT PROCESSING ZONES

The ROC's export-processing zones (EPZs) have been designed to meet the needs of foreign and domestic investors, as well as to encourage the introduction of new technologies into Taiwan, and expand the export of products and services. There are three EPZs in Taiwan: Kaohsiung EPZ, established in 1966, is located in the southern port of Kaohsiung County; Nantze EPZ, established in 1969, is located near Kaohsiung; and Taichung EPZ, established in 1969, is located in Taichung County. All three operate under the authority of the Export Processing Zone Administration (EPZA).

Major Investors by Country Among the more than 240 enterprises that have been authorized for operation in the three EPZs, Japanese investment has generally predominated. However, the United States, Western Europe, and Hong Kong also account for significant percentages of foreign investment.

EPZA Duties The EPZA and its supporting agencies are authorized to act for government authorities in handling operations within the zones. They take care of such matters as the processing and approval of investment applications, import and export licensing, foreign exchange settlement, company registration, construction licensing, labor administration, and customs clearance.

EPZ Facilities and Services Taiwan's EPZs offer a complete range of facilities and services. Standard factory buildings and comprehensive water, power, waste disposal, warehousing, and transportation facilities are available at competitive rates. Such ancillary services as banking and shipping are also provided in order to facilitate the full range of manufacturing and commercial operations.

Criteria The basic criteria that potential investors must meet in order to establish facilities in an EPZ cover a number of areas. Among other things, EPZ production may not have adverse effects on factories outside the zone, nor may it cause pollution. There are also minimum requirements governing the lease of land in the zones and the amount of initial investment.

Eligibility At present, manufacturers of the following products are eligible to set up operations in the EPZs:

- biscuits and confectioneries
- chemical products
- communications equipment
- cosmetics
- educational materials and equipment
- electrical appliances and products
- electrical products
- furniture and decorative wooden items
- garments
- handicraft products
- knitted and woven goods
- leather products, excluding tanning operations
- machinery
- medical instruments and appliances
- metal products
- musical instruments
- optical products
- plastic products
- precision machinery and instruments
- printed matter and office equipment
- rubber products
- sports gear
- toys
- yachts and mobile homes

Benefits For foreign and domestic companies that manufacture any of the products just listed, Taiwan's EPZs offer enormous advantages. Companies currently located in Taiwan's EPZs are entitled to many of the following benefits:

- Exemption from customs duties on the importation of raw materials, parts, and machinery for the company's own use;
- Duty-free export of finished products (this exemption does not include a harbor construction fee of 0.5 percent that must be paid for all imports and exports shipped by ocean carrier);
- Exemption from commodity taxes;
- Exemption from business taxes;
- Freedom to repatriate all after-tax profits and all invested capital after one year of operation;
- Exemption from the deed tax on factory buildings;
- Availability of loans at attractive rates to build factories;
- Reduced taxes on profits made in high-tech industries;
- Permission to sell certain items produced in the zones on Taiwan's domestic market;
- Permission to subcontract work to factories outside the zones—in fact, the government is encouraging subcontracting because it helps to enhance the overall efficiency and competitiveness of EPZ-based operations.

Application Procedure The application procedure for investing in the three EPZs is relatively easy. Potential investors will find that they are able to take care of everything from the initial application to final start-up authorization through the Export Processing Zone Administration. Detailed information about procedures and costs and other relevant information can be obtained by contacting the EPZA directly.

Kaohsiung Export Processing Zone Administration
Ministry of Economic Affairs
600 Chiachang Road, Nantze
Kaohsiung, Taiwan
Tel: [886] (7) 3611212 Fax: [886] (7) 3614348

Taipei Export Processing Zone Administration
Ministry of Economic Affairs
7/F., 90 NanYang Street
Taipei, Taiwan
Tel: [886] (2) 3310012 Fax: [886] (2) 3314520

HSINCHU SCIENCE-BASED INDUSTRIAL PARK

The Hsinchu Science-Based Industrial Park is situated some 70 km south of Taipei. It was established in 1980 to encourage both foreign and domestic firms to set up R&D and manufacturing facilities in Taiwan. Under the Six-Year Development Plan, the park should triple in size by 1996 to accommodate at least 500 high-technology firms and more than 100,000 workers. Another park similar to the one in Hsinchu is being planned for another region of Taiwan.

The Hsinchu park, which covers 2,100 hectares (approximately 5,190 acres), includes industrial, research, and residential zones. It has grown steadily over the years, and it is currently home to more than 140 high-tech companies engaged in the research or manufacture of electronics and information products; precision instruments and equipment; computers and semiconductors; and materials science, energy science, and biochemical engineering products. Estimates place the number of firms in the park by 1996 at around 250 and the value of their total annual output at about US$6 billion.

Facilities and Services The park offers excellent support facilities and services, including schools that teach in both English and Mandarin, high-quality apartments and townhouses at modest rents, and recreational facilities. The existence of such facilities and services makes it relatively easy for companies in the park to attract and keep qualified personnel in virtually any field. In fact, thanks at least in part to the quality of this living and working environment, many companies have been able to persuade overseas Taiwanese in a variety of fields to return to Taiwan.

Another advantage for companies with operations in the park is the number of research institutes and colleges in the surrounding area. This concentration of intellectual and scientific resources gives them ready access to a huge pool of talent, from which it is easy to recruit personnel for research and consulting work. It also facilitates productive interaction and cooperation among business, the academic community, and government. A large number of special training programs and projects have grown out of such

cooperation. Innovative matching-grant programs as well as strategic alliances between firms in the park have helped many companies to achieve maximum effectiveness in the allocation of resources.

Benefits Firms investing in the Hsinchu Science-Based Industrial Park enjoy substantial tax benefits, concessionaire public financing, low land costs, and such support services as warehousing, factories, and telecommunications facilities. Customs duties must generally be paid if the finished product is sold domestically. Overall, the Hsinchu Science-Based Industrial Park provides one of the best packages of tax and investment benefits available in Taiwan. Like the EPZs, it essentially operates as a bonded, duty-free area. Foreign companies located in the park are entitled not only to most of the benefits that accompany foreign investment approved (FIA) status but also to additional benefits:

- Special low-interest loans; assistance with start-up financing and rental of facilities; government venture capital; five-year tax holiday with a four-year deferral provision, or five-year period of accelerated depreciation on production equipment; a four-year tax holiday with deferral provisions on expansion projects, or a 15 percent investment credit on such projects; and equity capitalization of investors' patents or know-how.
- Land in the park is available for lease only. Rates for standard 400- to 900-square-meter factory buildings run at US$2.50-US$3.40 per square meter per month. Sites for custom-built factories are also available at US$0.50 per square meter per month. Normally, construction costs run in the neighborhood of US$200 per square meter.

Space in the park is currently at a premium, and priority is given to high-tech investment. The park administration also considers the potential for technology transfer, the impact of an investment on Taiwan's overall economic and industrial development, the quantity and quality of the R&D to be undertaken, and its impact on training and utilization of the domestic work force. Factors of more immediate concern, such as probable pollution levels and the quality of management teams, financial plans, and marketing strategies also receive close attention.

The Future Plans for the development of a vast Hsinchu Science City are included in the ROC's Six-Year Development Plan. The project is designed to make Hsinchu a modern metropolitan city suitable for the expansion of high-tech industries of all kinds. As part of this effort, a third-phase expansion of the Hsinchu Science-Based Industrial Park will be undertaken to establish a secondary park occupying approximately 600 hectares (1,483 acres) of land in the vicinity. These new facilities, together with the second science park of some 300 hectares (740 acres) mentioned earlier, are intended to enhance Taiwan's high-tech potential and help transform Hsinchu into an international center for science and technology equal to Japan's Tsukuba Science City.

INDUSTRIAL PARKS

Taiwan has 83 privately and publicly managed industrial parks; 73 are fully operational, and 10 are partially completed. These parks feature complete road and transportation facilities, sewage and industrial waste-water disposal systems, and all the other utilities necessary for industrial operations of almost any kind. Rates for these services are low, and factory buildings and land in these parks can either be rented or purchased at reasonable prices.

Requirements The primary requirement for location in such a park is that the applicant is a productive (manufacturing) enterprise. Some parks are designed for specialized industries. For example, firms in the petrochemical industry are currently concentrated near the facilities of the government-operated China Petroleum Corporation.

Advantages Two practical advantages of the parks are the availability of existing buildings and facilities and the ample supply of labor. There are also special tax and investment incentives, although they are generally somewhat less extensive than those offered to firms locating in the EPZs or the Hsinchu Science-Based Industrial Park.

Those interested in making industrial investments in Taiwan should also be aware that a number of new parks are either in the planning stage or already under construction. Such efforts reflect the desire on the part of both the government and the private sector to create more advanced high-value-added industries, increase the amount of land available for industrial use, and distribute manufacturing facilities more evenly across the island.

To achieve these goals, the Industrial Development Bureau of the Ministry of Economic Affairs has established the National Industrial Zone Development Corporation. This organism, which has substantial capital contributions from various state-run enterprises, is designed to provide at least partial funding for basic park development.

New Projects and Future Plan Two of the most important new projects are to be located in Changhua and Yunlin counties in central Taiwan. Construction of the former, which will be known as the Changhua Coastal Industrial Zone, began in mid-1990. It will have an area of some 3,643 hectares (9,000 acres) and state-of-the-art facilities, including schools, a cultural center, and parks as well as other public amenities. According to current projections, sites in the park should sell for approximately US$110 per square meter.

Construction of the Yunlin complex is slated to begin soon. This park, covering some 10,000 hectares (24,700 acres), will be the largest in Taiwan. Targeted at firms engaged in the production of high-end petrochemical items, it will offer a full range of quality facilities. There are also tentative plans for a high-tech industrial zone in Yunlin, which would be located near the petrochemical park.

Between NT$4 and NT$6 billion (US$105 and US$160 million) will be invested in a 12-hectare (30 acre) software industrial park in the Taipei suburbs. Scheduled to open in the near future, it will serve as an extension of the Hsinchu Science-Based Industrial Park. With room for up to 1,000 firms, the software park should help to enhance the overall efficiency of the industry by promoting the concentration of manpower and equipment.

The park will contain several so-called intelligent buildings, and companies that locate there will profit from exposure to the latest research and development advances and enjoy access to mainframe computers, data banks, and marketing information systems. Other services will include a software quality control center and a training facility for engineers. Such advantages should not only benefit firms in the park but also help to speed the internationalization of Taiwan's information industry as a whole.

Additional information about publicly and privately managed parks can be obtained from:

Industrial Development and Investment Commission (IDIC)
10/F., 7 Roosevelt Road
Sec. 1, Taipei, Taiwan
Tel: [886] (2) 3947213 Fax: [886] (2) 3926835

Industrial Development Bureau (IDB)
41-3 Hsin Yi Road
Sec. 3, Taipei, Taiwan
Tel: [886] (2) 7541255 Fax: [886] (2) 7030160

Foreign Investment

INVESTMENT CLIMATE AND TRENDS

Taiwan has a history of offering attractive investment opportunities to foreigners. In past decades overseas investors could take advantage of inexpensive labor and a business environment largely free from government regulation. In the 1980s and 1990s rising labor costs and increasingly strict regulations have made Taiwan somewhat less competitive than such countries as China, Malaysia, and Thailand. Between these factors and the international economic slowdown, approved foreign investment in Taiwan declined steadily from 1989 through the beginning of 1993. However, recognizing that foreign investment continues to play a significant role in Taiwan's economic development, government authorities are now looking at new ways of promoting and maintaining an attractive investment climate.

Toward this end, Taiwan has removed or scaled back many barriers to foreign investment. There are now virtually no export performance or local content requirements, and rules on earnings and capital repatriation have been liberalized. Measures implemented in 1989 further opened to outside investors all major industries except agriculture, power generation, oil refining, transportation, telecommunications, and those directly relating to national defense.

Nearly 60 percent of all foreign investment in Taiwan since the 1950s has been in the electronics, chemical, machinery, and metal products industries. In 1991 foreign invested firms produced about 14 percent of Taiwan's gross national product (GNP), hired 12 percent of its manufacturing work force, paid 24 percent of all corporate taxes, and shipped 25 percent of all export goods.

In light of changing economic conditions, the Taiwan government is encouraging a fundamental reorientation from traditional labor-intensive industries such as electronics assembly, to increasingly capital-intensive, high-technology industries both in the industrial and service sectors. Foreign invest-ment is now permitted in such services as fast food, retailing, trading, securities consulting, software consulting, and inspection. Foreign investors are still subject to equity restrictions in shipping, securities trading, and leasing.

Since the mid-1980s the government has sought to increase foreign investment in the following ten industries and eight technologies:

Industries
- advanced materials
- aeronautics
- consumer electronics
- environmental protection equipment and technologies
- information products
- medical care and hygiene products and services
- precision and automation equipment
- semiconductors
- special chemicals and medicines
- telecommunications

Technologies
- advanced detection
- applications of new materials
- biotechnology
- computer software
- energy conservation
- industrial automation
- natural resource application
- optical electronics

Overall, Taiwan is an attractive place in which to invest. Factors that make Taiwan especially favorable to investment include generous tax credits, a modern infrastructure, established industrial districts and export processing zones, easy credit availability, a growing domestic market, a well-educated and productive labor force, an absence of labor strife, and political and economic stability.

Foreign Investment Approved (FIA) Status

As an inducement to overseas investment, Taiwan grants foreign investment approved (FIA) status to companies limited by shares and to branch offices engaged in manufacturing or production. No other type of business entity is eligible for FIA status. Eligible investments include establishment of new enterprises or the expansion of existing ones; acquisition of ownership in existing firms via securities purchases to the extent allowed by Taiwanese securities law; investment in existing firms via loans, machinery and equipment, or raw materials; and investment of technical know-how or patent rights as capital stock.

Foreign and overseas Chinese investors who do not qualify for or desire FIA or Statute for Investment by Overseas Chinese (SIOC) status are still permitted to invest in regular domestic firms organized by ROC nationals. Such investments are eligible for some benefits under the Statute for Promotion of Industrial Upgrading (SIU). However, a number of FIA incentives are not available, and foreign participation and operating freedom are restricted under the SIU if the entity does not have FIA status. Many foreign investors consider the benefits available with FIA status to be indispensable to profitable operations in Taiwan. Most important of all, an entity must have FIA status in order to purchase the foreign exchange necessary to make payments and remittances overseas.

Benefits of FIA Status FIA status confers the following major benefits:

- Annual net operating and interest income and initial invested capital may be repatriated starting one year after business operations begin; profits from land sales are excluded.
- The entity is exempted from standard nationality and residency requirements. Such exemption is necessary for 100 percent foreign ownership, management, and board membership. Restrictions on employment of foreign technical and professional personnel are also waived.
- The withholding tax on dividends drops from 35 percent to 20 percent.
- As long as foreign investment represents 45 percent or more of the company's total capital, the firm is exempted from requirements that it offer its stock to the public or to its employees.
- Firms with 45 percent or more foreign investment are free

from official requisition or nationalization for a period of 20 years. Taiwan has never taken over foreign firms.
- The entity is entitled to the same rights and privileges as a domestic company.

Obtaining FIA Status An entity that wants to obtain FIA status applies to the Investment Commission of the MOEA. FIA status cannot be granted retroactively. Investors wishing to locate in one of the Export Processing Zones or the Hsinchu Science-Based Industrial Park may apply through those administrations.

Specific investments are usually approved provided that the investors supply the appropriate documentation and the proposed business raises no regulatory or policy issues. However, if you contemplate investment in restricted areas, you must obtain all necessary permissions from the authorities governing those specific business areas before you can apply for FIA status.

Applicants must be recognized as a foreign business by the MOEA, or its designate. This procedure is similar to that involved in gaining recognition to form a company or branch. Applicants must submit an application form, certified copies of documents confirming the nationality and legal status of the foreign investors, credit references, and detailed business plans. These plans should include data on the investors; the proposed scope of business; the entity's legal form; the intended locations of operation; staffing; amount and nature of capital contribution; production and sales plans; and, if applicable, real estate, construction, and development plans, needs for power, equipment, and raw or intermediate materials, and domestic and import procurement plans. Approval usually takes about two months.

When approval has been received, the investors must open an account with a local bank and transfer to it the working capital contribution that they have agreed on. After these funds have been deposited and certified, all the investors must make the capital contributions they have agreed on and ratify the articles of incorporation. The board must certify ratification, elect the corporate officers, and make other such arrangements necessary for operation of the business. The company then completes its registration by obtaining a company license from the MOEA and obtaining a business license and taxpayer identification number from local tax authorities.

LEADING FOREIGN INVESTORS

Cumulative foreign investment in Taiwan since the early 1950s totaled US$15.2 billion at the end of 1991. Fifty-eight percent of that sum came from Japan and the United States. Japanese and US investment accounted for 29 percent and 28 percent of total foreign investment approvals. Among overseas Chinese investors, Hong Kong residents have the greatest presence in Taiwan. Much of the drop in foreign investment in recent years is due to the pullback of Japanese investors who are focusing on their own domestic situation.

INVESTMENT POLICY

Taiwan permits foreign direct investment through new investments, acquisitions, mergers, and takeovers. But foreign individuals are prohibited from directly acquiring shares of companies listed on the Taiwan Stock Exchange. Foreign institutional investors are permitted to acquire shares as long as foreign ownership in a listed company does not exceed 10 percent for each foreign investor and total foreign ownership is limited to between 20 and 30 percent depending on the type of company. One-hundred percent foreign ownership is generally allowed for firms not listed on the Taiwan Stock Exchange.

Investors with foreign investment approval are permitted to repatriate capital and profits provided that their initial investment was approved by Taiwan authorities, particularly the Central Bank of China (CBC) (see below for information on foreign investment approval). Transactions involving outward or inward remittances are limited to US$5 million per account per year. Remittances of US$1 million or more must be approved by the CBC. These regulations apply both to individual and corporate accounts.

Prohibited and Restricted Areas A negative list adopted in July 1990 designates specific economic activities closed to foreign investment or in which investment is restricted. The list contains 54 prohibited and 55 restricted activities. Prohibited activities are not open to overseas Chinese and foreign nationals, and include such things as poultry farming, weapons manufacturing, power generation, telecommunications, and real estate. Restricted activities are open to overseas Chinese and foreign nationals who meet certain requirements prescribed by the regulatory authorities. Some of these include coal mining, and the operation of shipping agencies, life insurance companies, and investment companies. Most foreign investment applications in activities not on the negative list receive approval. (For the complete negative list, *see* table at end of this chapter.)

Technical Cooperation Foreign nationals who do not wish to make substantial investments in Taiwan may still want to license specific technologies, trademarks, or patents to Taiwanese firms or individuals. Most of the licensing agreements involve an agreement by Taiwanese firms or individuals to pay royalties or technical service fees in exchange for the right to use the particular technologies, trademarks, or patents. Although it is not required, investors normally obtain a Technical Cooperation Approval from the Investment Commission of the Ministry of Economic Affairs (MOEA). Such approval allows foreign firms to receive royalties tax free. Foreign investors should consider licensing technologies even if they have already established a company in Taiwan.

Most royalties obtained under the terms of such agreements are subject to a 20 percent withholding tax. Certain technologies deemed by the government to be of strategic importance are exempted from this requirement.

Outward Investment All outward investment must be approved by the Investment Commission if it exceeds US$5 million. Taiwan nationals and all firms located in Taiwan are prohibited from investing directly in the People's Republic of China, although indirect investment is permitted in certain sectors with prior approval.

Foreign Investment Approval An application for foreign investment approval (FIA) is screened by the Investment Commission (IC) of the MOEA to determine whether the investment project is subject to restriction. The time needed to obtain an approval has been shortened considerably since new procedures went into effect in June 1992. It normally takes two months from the date of filing for an FIA application to be processed and approved. Domestic legal representation is usually necessary. Prospective investors should work through legal counsel in their own country or contact a Taiwan-based law firm. (For a list of Taiwan-based law firms, refer to "Important Addresses" chapter.)

Companies wishing to obtain FIA status must apply to the MOEA for approval before forming a new company or investing in an existing firm. The Export Processing Zone Administration and the Hsinchu Science-Based Industrial Park Administration review applications for investment in their respective industrial districts. (Refer to "Business Formation" chapter for detailed information on applying for FIA status and establishing a business.)

Investment applications should include a detailed description of the project, plant construction specifications, a projection of future production and sales, raw material and capital equipment needs (both imports and domestic purchases), a certificate of incorporation, and credit references for the investor firm.

If the application if approved, foreign investors must fulfill the following requirements:

- Remit capital into Taiwan and notify the IC of the remittance.
- Apply to the IC for company registration.
- Apply to local authorities for registration as a profit- seeking enterprise.
- Purchase or lease land for plant site, if appropriate. (Assistance can be provided by the Industrial Development and Investment Commission of the Ministry of Economic Affairs. Refer to "Important Addresses" chapter.)
- Apply to the local authorities for licenses to establish and construct a factory building, if appropriate.
- Apply to Taipower's regional office for supply of electricity, if appropriate.

INVESTMENT INCENTIVES

Investment incentives usually take the form of tax concessions, which are available to foreign and local investors without discrimination. Most foreign companies will find it advantageous to have FIA, although such approval is not required in order to operate or invest in a business in Taiwan. FIA has some important benefits:

- The firm may obtain foreign exchange for repatriation of invested capital, net profits, or interest earned from equity and loan investments.
- The firm is exempt from the requirement that stock be offered to the public or employees, provided that the investor owns at least 45 percent of the company.
- The firm is exempt from nationalization or expropriation within twenty years of the start of business operations, provided that the investor owns at least 45 percent of the company.
- The income tax payable by foreign investors who derive dividends from a such a firm is withheld at a rate of 20 percent.
- The firm receives a waiver of the normal domicile, nationality, and capital stock requirements for shareholders and officers (the invested firm may be 100 percent owned).
- The firm receives treatment and protection equal to that extended to domestic firms.

Industrial Upgrading On January 1, 1991 the Statute for Promotion of Industrial Upgrading (SIU) replaced the Statute for Encouragement of Investment. The SIU is intended to move Taiwan from low- to high-value-added production and transform it into an exporter of high-technology products, particularly in such fields as information services, electronic components, telecommunications, auto parts, aeronautical equipment, and chemicals.

Under the SIU, reinvestment of earnings is encouraged, although repatriation of earnings and capital from FIA investments is also permitted. Earnings can be repatriated six months after they are declared to the authorities. There are no limitations on the transfer of investment capital out of Taiwan and no restrictions on repatriation of capital gains derived from increased land value.

Qualified domestic and foreign investors (with FIA) will find a broad range of incentives. Eligibility criteria are often updated to reflect changes in Taiwan's industrial policy. Tax credits equaling 5 to 20 percent of the cost of automation equipment, pollution control equipment, research and development, personnel training, and international marketing are available under the SIU. Firms spending more than NT$3 million per year on research and development receive a 15 percent tax deduction, while those investing at least NT$600,000 in personnel training or NT$3 million on promotions overseas receive a 5 percent deduction. The SIU also allows investors who have been present for more than two years in certain enterprises in underdeveloped regions to credit 20 percent of their investments toward business or personal income taxes.

The SIU no longer automatically gives enterprises in export-oriented industries tax holidays and duty-free treatment. However, qualified investors are granted tax credits of up to 20 percent for venture capital investments and research and development expenditures in such fields as production, marketing, management, antipollution technology, and automation.

For example, research and development expenses can be fully deducted from annual taxable income, and imported research and development equipment can qualify for duty-free treatment. The SIU also permits approved companies to depreciate equipment related to research and development projects over two years.

Other incentives available under the SIU include exemption from personal income tax for earnings derived from patented or copyrighted computer software developed locally, exemption from stamp and deed taxes, and deferred payment of the land value increment tax for acquisitions and mergers.

Incentives for Small- and Medium-Sized Businesses Effective in February 1991, the Statute for Development of Small- and Medium-Sized Enterprises encourages growth of small- and medium-sized firms. Offering most of the incentives available under the SIU, it is the government's response to criticism by small business owners that the SIU only benefits large enterprises.

Industry Incentives Under the Establishment and Expansion of Industrial and Mining Enterprises Act, manufacturing, mining, and construction firms in specified industries may qualify for duty exemptions when importing machinery and equipment. Fields include aluminum, base metals, ceramics, chemicals, copper, electrical appliances, fishing equipment, food, handicrafts, iron, machinery manufacturing, medical equipment, nonmetallic products, organic fertilizers, paper, plastics, shipbuilding, steel, textiles, transportation facilities, warehousing, and wood processing.

Venture Capital Investment Enterprises A venture capital investment enterprise (VCIE) is a company or partnership that specializes in making direct investment in technology companies. The Ministry of Finance determines which enterprises qualify as technology companies. Three special incentives are available to VCIEs:

- If a company limited by shares invests in a VCIE, 80 percent of the income derived from the investment is excluded from the company's taxable income.
- The income tax on registered stock dividends of a VCIE is deferred until the stocks are sold, bestowed, or distributed.
- An individual or profit-seeking enterprise that invests in a VCIE may be entitled to a credit of up to 20 percent of the value of the VCIE's stocks, provided the credit is used toward income tax owed. The unused investment credit can be carried forward for four years.

NATIONALIZATION POLICY

Firms with 45 percent or more foreign investment are free from nationalization for twenty years. Potential foreign investors should be aware that no foreign-invested firm regardless of percentage of ownership has ever been nationalized or expropriated.

REGULATORY AGENCIES

The principal government agencies with jurisdiction over business affairs are the Ministry of Economic Affairs (MOEA), the Central Bank of China (CBC), and the Ministry of Finance (MOF).

The MOEA is responsible for promulgating and implementing business laws and regulations. Various agencies within the ministry handle specialized areas. Two handle many issues related to foreign investment.

- The Investment Commission (IC) reviews applications for foreign investment and determines whether they meet official requirements.
- The Industrial Development and Investment Commission (IDIC) promotes foreign investment by providing prospective investors with information, assisting them in making local contacts, and helping to implement their investment plans.

The CBC operates as an agency of the Executive Yuan and as a government bank. It manages foreign exchange, regulates the money supply and credit, issues currency, sets policy on interest rates, engages in open market operations, and acts as the government's fiscal agent. The CBC also has jurisdiction over financial institutions, and its approval is required for certain inward and outward remittances.

All financial matters with the exception of foreign exchange and offshore banking are under the jurisdiction of the MOF. The principal agencies under the MOF are:

- The National Tax Administration, which collects corporate and individual income taxes,
- And the Securities and Exchange Commission, which oversees the Taiwan Stock Exchange and regulates brokers, dealers, underwriters, and others involved with the stock market.

Taiwan has a relatively comprehensive set of laws and regulations governing most aspects of business transactions and business relations. Although the laws and regulations are meant to facilitate the mobilization and allocation of investment resources, foreign investors and others active in commerce complain that they are not enforced consistently. In this sense, complying with official rules and regulations can at times seem an unnecessary burden especially when many local firms selectively comply with many regulations.

Additional measures have been introduced in recent years to simplify existing investment procedures. It remains to be seen whether these steps will produce a significant improvement. These measures include the formation of the Fair Trade Commission in January 1992, enactment of the Fair Trade Law in February 1991, and appointment of the IDIC as coordinator between investors and all agencies involved in investment approvals. To further streamline the investment application process the IC was authorized in July 1992 to make final decisions on investment applications involving new investment of no more than NT$50 million (about US$1.875 million) or acquisition of an existing firm worth no more than NT$100 million (about US$3.75 million).

Central Bank of China
2 Roosevelt Road
Sec. 1, Taipei, Taiwan
Tel: [886] (2) 3936161 Fax: [886] (2) 3973750
Tlx: 21532 GOVTBANK

Investment Commission, MOEA
8/F., 7 Roosevelt Road
Sec. 1, Taipei, Taiwan
Tel: [886] (2) 3513151 Fax: [886] (2) 3963970

Industrial Development and Investment
Commission, MOEA
10/F., 7 Roosevelt Road
Sec. 1, Taipei, Taiwan
Tel: [886] (2) 3947213 Fax: [886] (2) 3926835

Ministry of Economic Affairs
15 Fu Chou Street
Taipei, Taiwan
Tel: [886] (2) 3212200 Fax: [886] (2) 3919398

Ministry of Finance
2 Ai Kuo West Road
Taipei, Taiwan
Tel: [886] (2) 3228000 Fax: [886] (2) 3965829

National Tax Administration, MOF
547 Chung Hsiao East Road
Sec. 4, Taipei, Taiwan
Tel: [886] (2) 7631313 Fax: [886] (2) 7617698

Securities and Exchange Commission, MOF
12/F., 3 Nan Hai Road
Taipei, Taiwan
Tel: [886] (2) 3928572 Fax: [886] (2) 3948249

LOANS AND CREDIT AVAILABILITY

Firms in Taiwan with either full or partial foreign ownership are permitted access to bank credits and loans. The Central Bank of China has established a NT$20 billion (about US$750 million) credit facility to assist companies planning new investments. Loans are meant to encourage investment in information technology, machinery, electronics, textiles, pollution control equipment, the purchase of automated equipment, among other government-targeted areas. The Central Bank of China offers loans at preferential interest rates for imports of machinery for the ten key industries and eight technologies listed earlier.

Taiwanese policy generally encourages the free flow of financial resources and the efficient allocation of credit. Legal, regulatory, and accounting systems are transparent and consistent with international norms. Monetary authorities exercise a good deal of control over banking operations. However, banking regulations have been liberalized in recent years. (Refer to "Financial Institutions" chapter).

ECONOMIC DEVELOPMENT PROGRAMS

As part of its effort to attract investment, the Taiwan government instituted the Ten-Year Science and Technology Development Program in 1986. This wide-ranging program has four objectives: enhance overall public knowledge of science and technology, raise research and development spending, promote environmentally safe methods of sustainable growth, and facilitate the conversion of defense industries to civilian use. Annual research and development expenditure is expected to reach NT$93 billion (about US$3.5 billion) by 1995, a figure equal to roughly 2 percent of projected GNP. The private sector contribution to research and development is expected to account for at least 60 percent of total outlays.

A more controversial program, known as the Six-Year Development Plan, was announced in 1991. Expected to run through June 1997, it is designed to improve Taiwan's infrastructure. Although infrastructure is already fairly well developed, the island's major transportation, energy, and communication facilities have not kept pace with the rapid economic expansion of recent years. In addition to concern over Taiwan's infrastructure, the plan was motivated by fears that Taiwan's economy faced a serious slowdown. Growth slowed to 5 percent in 1990 (low by Taiwan's standards), and hundreds of manufacturers had already abandoned the island for lower-cost China and Southeast Asia.

But fears that the government is borrowing too much and thus crowding out private borrowing have led to substantial reductions in the overall plan. In July 1993, the Taiwan Cabinet approved a 22 percent reduction that brought the plan's cost to NT$6.4 trillion. The number of projects was also cut from 775 to 634.

Ironically, economic conditions improved shortly before these modifications were made. Private sector investment grew by 18 percent in 1992, and growth in GNP exceeded 6 percent in 1992 and the first quarter of 1993. Perhaps as a way of prolonging this recent upturn, the Cabinet approved a three-year economic stimulus package on July 1, 1993. The package has five main features:

- NT$40 billion (about US$1.5 billion) are earmarked for small- and medium-sized businesses.
- NT$20 billion (about US$750 million) are designated for high-technology enterprises.
- 30,000 hectares of government-owned land are made available for private commercial use.
- A five-year tax holiday is offered to selected high-tech industries.
- To relieve labor shortages in manufacturing and construction, the number of foreign workers who could be admitted into the country was increased.
- The list of semifinished industrial goods that may be imported from China for processing in Taiwan was increased.

Observers note that the three-year stimulus package represents a fundamental shift in emphasis toward the private sector. They hope that the government's chief planning agency, the Council for Economic Planning and Development, has realized that incentives can make private business more effective in furthering economic development than any public works program.

COMMERCIAL AND INDUSTRIAL SPACE

Commercial and industrial space is very limited in Taiwan, since only 2 percent of the island's total land area is devoted to these functions. However, the government has established more than sixty industrial parks, with land available for purchase or lease. Companies with FIA status have the option of either purchasing or leasing space for their operations in Taiwan. Other foreign firms may only rent facilities. Eligible companies may also construct factory facilities of their own.

Purchases cannot be made for the purpose of speculation in land or real estate. To guard against speculation, a provision in the SIU permits Taiwanese authorities to buy back unused land at a greatly reduced price (in some cases as little as 10 percent of the purchase price). At present, this provision has been applied only to one foreign firm.

Choosing a Site In selecting a commercial or industrial site, investors should look for easy access to rail and highway transportation, ample supplies of water and electricity, telecommunications facilities, and an adequate local labor force. There are industrial parks that include all of these features, but investors are not limited to these parks. Investors may purchase land within commercial and industrial sites on an installment basis over seven to 15 years. Taiwan authorities usually offer financing for 75 to 80 percent of the purchase price. Experts on land ownership at the Industrial Development and Investment Commission can help investors to locate plant sites and negotiate the purchase of private land.

Land in Taiwan's three export processing zones (EPZs) and the Hsinchu Science-Based Industrial Park is leased to investors by the authorities. Standard factory buildings are available for purchase in the EPZs and three industrial parks. Aside from some buildings in the Hsinchu park, few factories that meet Western standards are available for lease in Taiwan.

Modern offices are readily available for lease or purchase in most metropolitan areas of Taiwan. Leases usually run for a period of three to five years, with options for extension. Rents are generally adjusted annually, either by a set percentage or in accordance with the Consumer Price Index (CPI). Since the CPI has risen only slightly in the last few years, CPI-based adjustments are preferable to fixed increases.

Terms of Lease Leases vary widely in content and degree of detail. However, the majority address the following points:

- responsibilities of the tenant
- responsibilities of the landlord
- definition of the premises
- duration of the lease
- rental amount
- method of payment
- conditions of termination
- conditions of renewal
- management of public space
- maintenance and repair
- default
- parking
- jurisdiction and governing laws
- force majeure (event or effect that cannot be reasonably anticipated or controlled).

Lease agreements are domestic contracts and therefore fall under Taiwan's civil code. English versions of agreements are often provided for foreign tenants, but, in the event of questions or disputes, the text of the Chinese version is binding.

After signing a lease, the tenant is usually required to pay a deposit amounting to four to six times the monthly rent in the case of office space and to six to 12 times the monthly rent in the case of retail space. In some instances, the tenant can pay one year's rent in advance in lieu of a deposit.

Responsibility of the Landlord The landlord of an office building is generally responsible for supplying central air conditioning, elevators, finished ceilings, curtains, and rest rooms. The landlord is also obligated to provide maintenance and to repair any damage resulting from force majeure during the term of the lease. In addition, all property taxes and fire insurance are covered by the landlord.

Responsibility of the Tenant In most cases, all interior decorations, carpeting, light fixtures, and partitions are installed, maintained, and repaired at the tenant's expense. Any insurance covering these interior furnishings against loss or fire must also be borne by the tenant.

Real Estate Market and Prices As a result of the real estate boom in Taiwan in recent years, prices for factories, industrial sites, and commercial office space have increased rapidly in recent years. The increases for factories and industrial sites have been fueled by a shortage of suitably zoned land, and by purchases by existing manufacturers in anticipation of future price rises. Strong overall demand and lack of available land in major urban centers are primarily responsible for the high prices of office space.

The unit used in Taiwan for measuring area is the Chinese *ping*, which is equivalent to 3.3 square meters (35.3 square feet). Total rental space is calculated in *ping* and includes usable business space as well as certain common areas, such as hallways.

Purchase prices for industrial land and factory buildings vary greatly depending on location, support facilities, and other factors. Prices in the range from NT$10,000 to NT$20,000 per *ping* (about US$375 to US$750) are common, with prime locations in some industrial parks going for as much as NT$50,000 to NT$70,000 per *ping* (about US$1,875 to US$2,625). Rental costs are equally variable. Quality factory buildings on privately owned sites in northern Taiwan usually run between NT$1,000 and NT$3,000 per *ping* per month (about US$37.50 to US$112.50).

Office space in Taipei rents for an average of NT$1,000 to NT$3,000 per *ping* per month (about US$37.50 to US$112.50). Retail store space is available for monthly rates between NT$3,000 and NT$20,000 per *ping* (US$112.50 to US$750).

The rental market for both office and retail space in Taipei is relatively tight, with occupancy rates well above 95 percent at one point recently. However, the market appears to be easing slightly as the result of an additional 63,000 *ping* of office space completed at the end of 1992. Although this development helped to cut rental rates by more than 5 percent, no dramatic long-term fall in rates is expected. As a result, an increasing number of major domestic companies have begun to relocate to suburban areas, where prices tend to be lower and the ability to expand is greater.

The Taiwan real estate market is complex and continuously changing, and success in negotiating its complexities requires a great deal of knowledge of the island's culture and economy. Therefore, foreign investors interested in purchasing or leasing real estate are well advised to seek out a corporate real estate consultant or reliable agent as well as an independent property valuation service.

INVESTMENT ASSISTANCE

Several government and quasi-government offices in Taiwan offer assistance to investors. The Industrial Development and Investment Commission (IDIC) serves as a central information source for investors seeking to establish operations in Taiwan. (Refer to "Important Addresses" chapter.) It operates through the following four divisions, all of which can be reached through the IDIC:

- The Investment Promotion Division provides investment consultation and other services.
- The Coordination Division arranges meetings between investors and government officials and helps investors to locate and acquire commercial land and facilities.
- The Investment Research Division identifies attractive investment opportunities.
- The Information Division publishes information relating to investment in Taiwan.

The Investment Commission of the Ministry of Economic Affairs is the starting point for most foreign investors. (Refer to "Important Addresses" chapter.) It provides the required application forms and evaluates investment proposals.

The China External Trade Development Council (CETRA) sponsors exhibitions, promotes activities to open foreign markets for domestic products, administers a computerized foreign trade information system, and operates foreign trade information libraries.

China External Trade Development Council
4-8/F., 333 Keelung Road
Sec. 1, Taipei 10548, Taiwan
Tel: [886] (2) 7255200 Fax: [886] (2) 7576653
Tlx: 21676 CETRA

Negative List for Investment by Overseas Chinese and Foreign Nationals

The following list is current as of April 1993. The codes are a Taiwanese system of industrial codes, and may be useful if you are trying to gather further information about prohibitions and restrictions. You may also want to contact the responsible authority. (Refer to "Important Addresses" for address and telephone information.) Abbreviations for various government agencies have been used. (COA = Council of Agriculture; DOH = Department of Health; EPA = Environmental Protection Administration; GIO = Government Information Office; MOC = Ministry of Communications; MOE = Ministry of Education; MOEA = Ministry of Economic Affairs; MOF = Ministry of Finance; MOND = Ministry of National Defense.)

Prohibited industries

Code	Industry	Authority
0111	Growing of rice	COA
0112	Growing of dryland food crops	COA
0113	Growing of specialty crops	COA
0114	Growing of vegetables	COA
0115	Growing of fruit	COA
0116	Growing of mushrooms	COA
0117	Growing of sugar cane	COA
0118	Growing of flowers*	COA
0119	Growing of other crops	COA
0121	Raising of dairy and beef cattle	COA
0122	Raising of hogs	COA
0123	Raising of other livestock	COA
0124	Raising of chickens	COA
0125	Raising of ducks	COA
0126	Raising of other poultry	COA
0129	Raising of other animals	COA
0140	Hunting, trapping, game propagation	COA
0211	Reforestation*	COA
0212	Forestation of specialty trees	COA
0321	Brackish water culture	COA
0322	Freshwater culture	COA
2701	Manufacure of basic chemicals, including: Nitroglycerine, Soda-chloride factories operating withmercuric electrolyzers, Sodium cyanide, Potassium cyanide	MOND; MOEA; EPA
2804	Manufacture of pesticides and herbicides, including: Dieldrin, DDT, Toxaphene, Methylmercury, Endrin, Septachlor, Hexachlorocyclohexane, Aldrin, DBCP, Chlordane, Leptophose, Chlorobezilate, Nitrofen, Dinoseb, Lindane	EPA

* Indicates industries not restricted for overseas Chinese.

Source: Ministry of Economic Affairs, Industrial Development and Investment Commission, 10/F., 7 Roosevelt Rd., Sec.1, Taipei, Taiwan; Tel: [886] (2) 3947213 Fax: [886] (2) 3926835.

Code	Industry	Authority
2809	Manufacture of other chemical products, including: Dulcin, MSG factories using fermentation method, Yellow phosphate match, Benzidine and its salts, 4-Amino diphnyl and its salts, 4-Nitro diphenyl and its salts, B-Naphthylamine, Manufacture and use of polychlorinated biphenyl, Gun powder, fuse agents for fire, fulminating mercury, pentachlorophenol and its salts	MOEA
2910	Petroleum refineries, including: Refining gasoline and diesel fuel	MOEA
2990	Other oil and coal industries, including: Coking	EPA
3314	Steel forging, including: Gun barrel forging	MOND
3329	Other basic industry of non-ferric metal, including: Asbestos and its related products, Refining metalline cadmium and stearic acid, etc., made with cadmium as a main raw material Recycling industries of waste metals	EPA
3401	Manufacture of cutlery hand tools and general hardware, including: Saber manufacturing	EPA
3590	Manufacture and repair of other machinery, including: Firearms, weapon manufacture, arms repair	EPA
3802	Manufacture of photographic and optical instruments, including: Military instrument equipment	EPA
3901	Manufacture of jewelery and related articles, including: Processing	COA
4100	Electric light and power supply, including: Electricity supply, Categories prescribed by the Electricity Business Law	MOEA
4200	Gas supply, including: Fuel gas supplied by pipe lines	MOEA
4400	Water works and supply Provincial or city government	
5101	Construction of basic civil structure, including: Military engineering and construction	MOND
5102	Construction of houses	MOTI
7111	Railway transport	MOC
7113	Passenger bus service*, including: Highway passenger bus service, City passenger bus service	MOC
7114	Taxi transport*	MOC
7115	Tour bus services	MOC
7116	Car rental services	MOC
7118	Truck freight transport	MOC

Code	Industry	Authority
7133	Harbor services	MOC
7134	Supporting services of water transports	MOC
7143	Airport ground transportation	MOC
7310	Postal services	MOC
7320	Telecommunications*	MOC
8104	Postal saving and remittance services	MOC
8311	Real estate trading, leasing, and brokerage	MOTI
9120	National defense, including:	MOND
	Military production institution, Military hospital, Affiliate agency of dissemination	
9322	Radio and television broadcasting	GIO
9409	Other culture and recreational services, including:	GIO
	Coffee shop with waitress, bar, tea shop with waitress, tavern and dance halls	

Restricted industries

Code	Industry	Authority
1100	Mining of coal	MOEA
1201	Mining of crude petroleum and natural gas	MOEA
1202	Mining of geothermal energy	MOEA
1301	Mining of iron ore	MOEA
1302	Mining of non-ferrous ore	MOEA
1400	Mining of salt	MOEA
1501	Mining of clay	MOEA
1502	Mining of stone	MOEA
1600	Mining of chemical and fertilizer mineral	MOEA
1701	Mining of precious stones	MOEA
1709	Mining of other materials not elsewhere classified	MOEA
1811	On-land clay quarrying	MOEA
1812	On-land stone quarrying	MOEA
1821	River gravel quarrying	MOEA
1822	Coastal gravel quarrying	MOEA
1890	Other quarrying	MOEA
2070	Manufacture of prepared feed, including:	COA
	Feed additive	
2401	Leather finishing	COA
2704	Manufacture of chemical fertilizers	COA
2802	Manufacture of medicine, including:	MOEA, COA, DOH
	Medical materials medicine for animal and human being	
2803	Manufacture of Chinese medicines	DOH

Indicates industries not restricted for overseas Chinese.

Code	Industry	Authority
2804	Manufacture of Pesticides and Herbicides	COA
3624	Manufacture of communication equipment and apparatus, including:	MOEA
	Office digital electric switching system	
6206	Retail of general chemical products, including:	MOEA
	Gas stations	
7132	Inland and coastal water transport	MOC
7134	Supporting services to water transports	MOC
7141	Civil air transport*	MOC
7142	General aviation	MOC
7151	Travel agency services*	MOC
7153	Shipping agency services*	MOC
7155	Water freight transport forwarding services*	MOC
7156	Air cargo agency services*	MOC
7157	Container terminal operation*	MOC
7158	Ship leasing services*	MOC
7169	Services incidental to other shipping transport	MOC
7200	Warehouses, including:	MOC
	Air cargo terminal business	
7320	Telecommunications, including:	MOC
	CPE (customer premises equipment)	
	PBX (private branch exchange)	
8102	Domestic banking	MOF
8103	Foreign banks	MOF
8105	Credit cooperatives*	MOF
8107	Trust and investment	MOF
8111	Securities	MOF
8119	Other financing	MOF
8201	Personal insurance	MOF
8202	Property and liability insurance	MOF
8204	Foreign insurance	MOF
8205	Auxiliary insurance services	MOF
8209	Other insurance	MOF
8412	Accounting services	MOF
9319	Other education and training services, including:	MOE
	Short-term supplementary classes	
9321	Journalism	GIO
9324	Audio tape and record publishing	GIO
9344	Medical test and examination services	DOH
9345	Midwife services	DOH
9349	Other medical services	DOH

* Indicates industries not restricted for overseas Chinese.

Foreign Trade

Foreign trade is of vital importance to Taiwan's economic development, health, and status in the international community. The island's few natural resources are insufficient to meet domestic demand, and densely populated Taiwan is more dependent than most nations on imports. Almost all of the raw materials needed for industry and energy generation, as well as a significant percentage of the country's foodstuffs, must come from abroad, a reality that has helped spur the development of the island's export-led economy.

The strong performance of its exports over the last two decades has given Taiwan one of the world's most rapid economic growth rates. The Republic of China (ROC) has official relations with 28 mostly smaller countries and maintains trade offices in a total of 58 countries, enjoying less formal trade relationships with scores of others. Because of its anomalous status as the "other" China, Taiwan depends on its commercial and economic ties with its trading partners to shore up its international political position, as well as to support its economic development.

The composition of Taiwan's exports has been determined primarily by overseas demand. As a result, the growth of most of its industries was affected more by the economic conditions of other countries than by the demands of domestic markets. In the 1950's when Taiwan was still basically a subsistence economy, raw and processed agricultural and related products accounted for nearly 92 percent of total exports, with industrial products accounting for the remaining 8.1 percent. This situation shifted dramatically during the period of focused industrial development from the late 1950s through the 1980s.

In the 1980s the government began actively to promote more capital-intensive and high-value-added industries. High-technology industries have received special attention and support. Measures to promote this development included the establishment of the Hsinchu Science-Based Industrial Park to provide an environment for scientific innovation and a dramatic increase in appropriations for research and development activities. At the same time, joint ventures in strategic high-technology industries were encouraged in order to help Taiwanese firms gain access to the latest technologies from around the world. By 1990 the composition of Taiwan's exports had been reversed: industrial goods accounted for 95.6 percent of total exports, while raw and processed agricultural products accounted for only 4.4 percent. Agricultural exports continue to fall in value and importance.

EXPORTS AND IMPORTS

In 1992 Taiwan's total exports were US$84.4 billion, equal to 41.5 percent of its gross national product (GNP) of US$203.4 billion. By comparison, exports represent only about 9 percent of Japan's economy and 8 percent of that of the United States (however, exports represent 121 percent of Hong Kong's truly trade-dependent economy). Exports have grown steadily at an average rate of 6.6 percent since the late 1980s. Imports rose to US$72 billion in 1992, 35.4 percent of GNP, having grown at an average annual rate of 7.8 percent since the late 1980s. Imports account for about 6.2 percent of the economy of Japan, about 9.5 percent of that of the United States, and 125 percent of that of Hong Kong, which conducts trade worth far more than the total value of its economy.

These trade successes have not come without problems. Taiwan's remarkable export performance has generated huge trade surpluses that help to fuel protectionist sentiment abroad, increase pressure for the further appreciation of the NT$, and worsen domestic inflation. To resolve these potential economic difficulties the government has committed itself to a policy geared toward making Taiwan a fully developed nation by the year 2000.

The Six-Year Development Plan and the Statute for Industrial Upgrading (SIU) contain the general outline for the future direction of Taiwan's economic and trade policy. During the 1990s the emphasis will be on restructuring the economy with a focus on the development of high-technology, high-value-added, capital-intensive, clean and energy-efficient, export-oriented industries. Given its desire to join the General Agreement on Tariffs and Trade (GATT), Taiwan is expected to expand the scope and speed up the implementation schedule of its market liberalization programs in virtually all areas of industry. Taiwan's trade policy increasingly encourages imports, and both tariff and nontariff barriers have been eased substantially during the past decade. This policy and the robust domestic demand for both consumer and capital goods have resulted in a surge in imports in recent years. The growth rate of imports now exceeds that of exports, although exports are still 15 percent greater than imports by value. At current rates Taiwan could expect to continue recording trade surpluses for another 15 years before imports balance exports.

Labor-intensive manufacturing will likely continue to move offshore, primarily to Southeast Asia and the People's Republic of China (PRC), while high-technology products such as electronics and other sophisticated goods will likely increase from a 40 percent share of total exports in 1991 to more than 50 percent of total exports by the year 2000.

In 1991 Taiwan's leading exports were machinery and electrical equipment which accounted for 34.6 percent, slightly more than one-third, of all exports. This category was followed by textiles (15.8 percent); metals and metal articles (7.6 percent); plastics and rubber articles (6.8 percent); footwear and related items (5.8 percent); transportation equipment (5.1 percent); toys, games, and sporting goods (3.9 percent); precision instruments (2.6 percent), animal products (2.6 percent), and chemicals (2.1

percent). Together these top ten categories accounted for 86.9 percent of exports, with remaining categories each representing less than 2 percent of the total.

Items within the machinery and electrical equipment category also represented Taiwan's primary imports, accounting for 29.6 percent of imports in 1991. Metals and metal articles (12.9 percent), chemicals (11.3 percent), minerals (10.3 percent), transportation equipment (6.4 percent), textiles (4.1 percent), precision instruments (3.2 percent), agricultural products (3.2 percent), plastics and rubber articles (2.9 percent), and precious metals and jewels (2.4 percent) made up the next highest import categories. Together these top ten categories accounted for 86.3 percent of all imports, with remaining categories each representing less than 2.25 percent of the total.

TRADING PARTNERS

In 1991 the United States took 29.3 percent of total exports, followed by Hong Kong (16.3 percent), Japan (12.1 percent), Germany (5.1 percent), Singapore (3.2 percent), the Netherlands (2.9 percent), and the United Kingdom (2.8 percent). Together these seven main partners accounted for 71.7 percent of all exports, with remaining countries each accounting for less than 2.75 percent of the total. The majority of items exported to Hong Kong are destined for the PRC, with which it is illegal to conduct direct trade.

In 1991 Taiwan's leading supplier of imports was Japan, which provided 30 percent of the total, followed by the United States (22.4 percent), Germany (4.8 percent), Australia (3.2 percent), Hong Kong (3 percent—again mostly acting as an intermediary for

Taiwan's Leading Trade Partners

Exports - 1991

United States 29%
Other 29%
United Kingdom 3%
Netherlands 3%
Singapore 3%
Germany 5%
Japan 12%
Hong Kong 16%

Total 1991 Exports: US$ 76.1 Billion

Imports - 1991

Japan 30%
Other 31%
South Korea 3%
Saudi Arabia 3%
Hong Kong 3%
Australia 3%
Germany 5%
United States 22%

Total 1991 Imports: US$ 62.9 Billion

Taiwanese Imports by Country
(in millions of US dollars)

Country	1990	% Change from 1989
Japan	16,000	0
United States	12,612	5
Germany	2,668	3
Australia	1,660	2
Saudi Arabia	1,539	11
Hong Kong	1,446	-34
Singapore	1,406	58
Korea	1,344	8
Switzerland	1,201	45
United Kingdom	1,154	24
France	1,132	42
Malaysia	1,003	13
Indonesia	922	31
Canada	839	-16
Italy	817	4
Netherlands	729	10
Thailand	448	15
Belgium	393	31
Kuwait	369	-15
Eastern Europe, including former East Germany	307	24

Source: Foreign Trade Magazine

Taiwanese Exports by Country
(in millions of US dollars)

Country	1990	% Change from 1989
United States	21,746	-9
Hong Kong	8,557	22
Japan	8,338	-8
Germany	3,183	24
Singapore	2,204	12
United Kingdom	1,979	-6
Netherlands	1,856	18
Canada	1,559	-11
Thailand	1,424	29
Australia	1,279	-17
Indonesia	1,246	34
Korea	1,213	7
France	1,132	4
Malaysia	1,104	59
Italy	985	13
Philippines	811	4
Belgium	487	6
Saudi Arabia	459	-17
Switzerland	370	21
Eastern Europe, including former East Germany	210	81

Source: Foreign Trade Magazine

Chinese goods), South Korea (2.7 percent), and Saudi Arabia (2.7 percent). Together these top seven countries accounted for 68.8 percent of all imports, with remaining countries each supplying less than 2.5 percent of the total.

One of Taiwan's principal policy goals for the 1990s is to diversify its export markets, reducing its reliance on large trading partners. Concerned over Taiwan's traditional dependence on the United States, which has been the most vocal among the island's trading partners in trying to get it to reduce its trade surplus, policymakers have focused on boosting exports to Southeast Asia, Hong Kong (a proxy for trade with the PRC), and the European Community (EC).

Although Taiwan relies heavily on the United States, Japan, and Europe for technical know-how and capital goods, its economy is increasingly integrated with that of the surrounding region, especially China. The Taiwanese government now grudgingly acknowledges reality by permitting indirect trade with China via Hong Kong. It is also planning to lift trade bans on Cuba and North Korea and is targeting Eastern European and former Soviet countries as potential new markets and low-cost suppliers.

INTERNATIONAL TRADE ORGANIZATION MEMBERSHIP

Taiwan's status as a political orphan has led it to place great emphasis on gaining economic recognition, and recently it has stepped up its efforts to be included in several international trade-based organizations. Taiwan is not a party to GATT, but in September 1992 a working party was set up to consider Taiwan's application for membership. This application is expected to be approved soon, at which point Taiwan will be required to reduce import barriers even further (under GATT regulations tariffs must be negotiated bilaterally rather than imposed uni-

Top 10 Taiwanese Imports by % Change

Commodity	% Change
Transmission & broadcasting equipment	225
Oils from the distillation of coal & tar	186
Petroleum gases & other gaseous carbons	178
Aircraft & spacecraft	121
Acyclic hydrocarbons	104
Derricks, cranes & mobile lifting frames	79
Wood fuel, logs, twigs, wood chips, particles, sawdust & wood waste	79
New pneumatic rubber tires	66
Electrical switching & connecting equipment	63
Specialized electrical machinery	57

Source: Foreign Trade Magazine

laterally). In its negotiations to join GATT, Taiwan has agreed to abide by accepted developed country standards, and foreign traders can expect that many of its remaining official nontariff restrictions will be eliminated.

In addition to being a potential party to GATT, Taiwan is a nonregional full member of the Central American Bank for Economic Development, and a full member of the Asia Pacific Economic Cooperation group. It has also tried to gain some influence or presence in such regional bodies as the European Bank for Reconstruction and Development and the Inter-American Development Bank through its financial contributions.

Taiwan has used some of its massive foreign exchange reserves to promote bilateral relations and insinuate itself into accepted status. The island's International Economic Cooperation and Development Fund, which was established in 1988 with a capitalization of US$1.2 billion, has so far committed US$130 million in low-interest loans and technical assistance grants to 10 nations, most of them in Latin America.

MAJOR PROJECTS AND THE SIX-YEAR DEVELOPMENT PLAN

Although Taiwan possesses a generally modern infrastructure, its transportation, energy, and communications facilities have not kept pace with its rapid economic expansion. In an effort to upgrade the island's business infrastructure, encourage investment, and improve its overall quality of life, the cabinet approved an ambitious US$303 billion Six-Year Development Plan to run from 1991 through 1996. Although the legislature trimmed the budget

by around US$73 billion in spring 1993, the plan will still make Taiwan the world's largest market for major projects, particularly infrastructure development, during coming years. In addition to rail and highway construction, projects also include power plants and petrochemical facilities. Although much of the plan consists of projects previously conceived or actually under way, it still provides vast export opportunities for foreign firms and is expected to dominate Taiwan's import markets for some years. Few people expect the plan to be finished in the six years allotted for its completion.

CROSS-STRAITS ECONOMIC RELATIONS

In 1949 when the nationalist Kuomintang (KMT) party established itself on Taiwan, it instituted the so-called Three No's policy toward the mainland: no contact, no negotiation, and no compromise. Since 1987 both Beijing and Taipei have begun to establish more formal, albeit still officially deniable, relations. These began with humanitarian and educational issues, such as reunification of families, travel, and cultural exchanges, but are rapidly spreading to encompass areas of trade and investment. Taiwan has established a number of public organizations to handle its burgeoning relationship with the mainland. These include the National Reunification Committee, the Mainland Affairs Council, and a nominally private, quasi-official organization, the Straits Exchange Foundation (SEF), which monitors and develops policy on such contacts on behalf of the government.

In July 1988 Beijing published its Regulations on

Top 10 Taiwanese Exports by % Change

Commodity	% Change
Machinery	24
Chemicals	21
Prepared foodstuffs, beverages & tobacco products	20
Transportation equipment	15
Fiber, yarn, linen & fabric	14
Information & communications products	14
Clocks & watches	3
Plastic & rubber articles	2
Optical, photographic, measuring, medical instruments	2
Metal products (excluding iron & steel)	1

Source: Foreign Trade Magazine

Top 10 Taiwanese Exports by Commodity (in millions of US dollars)

Commodity	1990	% Change from 1989
Machinery & electrical equipment	23,130	6
Textile products	10,285	0
Basic metals & articles thereof	5,215	-1
Plastic & rubber articles	4,430	2
Footwear, headgear, umbrellas	4,116	-8
Transport equipment	3,450	15
Toys, games & sports products	2,906	-4
Precision instruments, clocks & watches, musical instruments	1,721	3
Animals & animal products	1,653	-8
Leather & fur products	1,316	-12

Source: Foreign Trade Magazine

Encouraging the Investment of Taiwanese. The PRC, however, did not officially approve the indirect trade, investment, and technical cooperation to be carried out with Taiwan until October 1989 and in 1993 guaranteed Taiwanese investments based on the theory that Taiwanese investors were really Chinese. The PRC has established another nominally unofficial body, the Association for Relations Across the Straits, as its counterpart to Taiwan's SEF. Additional contacts on an increasingly official basis were being instituted as of the end of 1993, although both parties continued to maintain their hard line official positions.

In 1991 Taiwan became China's fifth-largest trading partner, while China probably accounted for as much if not more of Taiwan's trade than Germany, making the PRC Taiwan's fourth largest trading partner. In 1987 unofficial bilateral trade between Taiwan and China via Hong Kong (Taiwan law prohibits direct trade with and investment in the PRC) totaled approximately US$1.6 billion. By 1991 bilateral trade had grown to almost US$6 billion, a 43 percent increase over 1990. Bilateral trade reached an estimated $7.5 billion in 1992, up 28 percent from 1991. Taiwanese exports to the PRC rose 35 percent in 1991 (exports to all other destinations grew by only 7 percent), and making up 7.7 percent of its total exports. Products included synthetic fabrics, plastic raw materials, electronic components, raw and semifinished manufactures (such as yarn), PVC, leather, and a variety of machinery and equipment for new factories. China, in turn, has become an important exporter of intermediate products to many of Taiwan's textile and petrochemical companies.

Leading Exporters to Taiwan (in millions of US dollars)

Country	1990 Value	% Market Share
Electric Machinery		
Japan	4,282	47.4
United States	2,127	23.6
Hong Kong	415	4.6
Transportation Equipment/Parts		
Japan	1,141	40.1
United States	695	24.4
Germany	463	16.3
Scientific Measuring/Precision Instruments		
Japan	572	43.3
United States	410	31.0
Germany	105	7.9
Iron and Steel		
Japan	1,081	38.2
South Africa	336	11.9
Brazil	253	9.0
Plastics and Articles Thereof		
Japan	569	39.6
United States	370	25.7
Germany	102	7.1

Source: Foreign Trade Magazine

Top Import Commodities to Taiwan (in millions of US dollars)

Commodity	1990	% Change from 1989
Crude oil	3,180	22
Integrated circuits & electronic microassemblies	2,745	17
Motor vehicles	1,361	-21
Gold, including unwrought or in semi-manufactured or powered forms	1,289	-33
Oils obtained from bituminous materials other than crude	1,265	80
Automated data processing machines	1,017	12
Coal briquettes & other coal products	1,007	13
Specialized machinery	904	14
Thermionic, cold cathode or photo cathode valves & tubes	802	15
Motor vehicle parts	721	20
Maize	705	15
Refined copper & alloys	692	-13
Cyclic hydrocarbons	660	9
Iron or non-alloy steel semi-finished products	625	-2
Semiconductors & other electronic parts	568	10
Aircraft & spacecraft	529	121
Soybeans	513	-5
Telephone & telegraph equipment	498	50
Electric switching devices	492	-1
Chemicals & other acids	444	-9
Unwrought aluminum	434	-10
Automated data processing parts & accessories	431	23
Wood	426	-10
Electric motors & generators	416	69
Cotton, not carded or combed	408	-3
Motorcycles & parts	386	44
Acyclic alcohols & their derivatives	381	-27
Chemicals for use in electronics	353	-4
Flat-rolled iron or non-alloy steel	342	-7
Petroleum gases & other gaseous hydrocarbons	318	178
Vessels, incl. warships & other boats	287	-30
Meat & fish products not for human consumption	272	-4
Spinning, doubling or twisting machines	260	-7
Television, radio, radar, radar navigation & remote control equipment	255	-6
Metal scrap & waste	244	-25
Electrical capacitors	243	4
Television receivers	239	16
Air or vacuum pumps, other gas compressors, fans & equipment	237	-10
Wood scraps	237	18

Commodity	1990	% Change from 1989
Refrigerators, freezers, heat pumps & equipment	237	8
Transmission & broadcast equipment	235	225
Synthetic dyes & agents	232	12
Halogenated derivatives of hydrocarbons	229	-20
Iron ores & concentrates	223	6
Flat rolled steel products	221	-3
Electrical transformers, static converters & inductors	212	19
Iron or steel bars & rods	201	42
Milk or cream containing sugar or sweeteners	197	-4
Sound & video recording & reproduction equipment	196	-41
Raw hides & skins	193	3
Resins & textile fibers	192	9
Chemical wood pulp & like materials	187	-1
Bovine or equine leather	186	16
Printing machinery	186	7
Bulldozers & other earth-moving machinery	177	21
Ethylene polymers	176	1
Non-electric machinery & equipment	173	-4
Heterocyclic compounds, nucleic acids & salts	173	-7
Taps, cocks, calves, etc.	172	4
Equipment for the chemical industry	169	10
Rubber or plastic making machinery	168	35
Air conditioners & machinery	168	-8
Motor vehicles to transport goods	163	-2
Bars & rods of iron or non-alloy steel	163	-18
Wheat & meslin	163	-7
Paper or paperboard waste & scrap	162	-5
Regulation & controlling instruments	155	-22
Synthetic filaments & yarns	148	13
Pumps for liquids	146	8
Zinc waste & scrap	142	-9
Insulated wires & cable	141	31
Electrical measuring & calibrating instruments & meters	140	20
Frozen bovine meat	140	-4
Chemical analysis instruments	140	32
Piston engine parts	139	12
Paper, paperboard, cellulose wadding, etc.	139	22
TOTAL including others	**$57,665**	**N/A**

Source: Foreign Trade Magazine

GEOGRAPHIC AREAS OF TRADE FOCUS

Taiwan's overall trade with Southeast Asia amounted to US$2.4 billion in 1991. The island's current sizable trade surplus with countries in the region is due primarily to technology transfers and exports of capital goods for which it receives lower-value raw and intermediate materials. To minimize trade friction and enhance greater regional prosperity, the ROC government is considering numerous measures to open its markets more widely to the products of its regional neighbors.

Total trade between the ROC and the EC has shown steady growth since the mid-1980s, rising from US$4.8 billion in 1985 to US$20.1 billion in 1991, an increase of some 319 percent overall and an average of nearly 23 percent per year. The dramatic expansion in trade with EC nations reflects both Taiwan's efforts to establish a presence in Europe and Europe's growing awareness of Taiwan as a market for high-quality consumer goods. A number of European firms have contracted to work on projects under the Six-Year Development Plan. Despite the absence of formal diplomatic relations, 18 European countries maintain trade representatives on the island. These offices have already done a great deal to facilitate increased Taiwanese purchases of European goods, as well as to strengthen commercial and investment ties.

In 1991 Taiwan's exports to Eastern Europe amounted to a mere US$240 million, up 15 percent over the previous year. Imports of Eastern European goods rose to US$467 million—a gain of 56 percent. Widespread political changes combined with the ROC government's relaxation of restrictions on trade with former Soviet bloc countries have cast Eastern Europe in the role of a growth market for Taiwanese imports and exports. Public- and private-sector organizations in the ROC are confident that markets in Eastern Europe and the nations that have emerged as a result of the breakup of the Soviet Union offer immense long-term potential. These organizations are encouraging the Taiwan's business community to increase its trade and investment ties with Eastern Europe and the Commonwealth of Independent States to capitalize on the region as a source of raw materials and expedite the diversification of Taiwan's export markets.

Taiwan's bilateral trade with Latin America should continue to expand rapidly in the coming years as a result of ongoing economic reforms in Latin American countries. Although the total volume of trade with these nations was only US$3.6 billion in 1991, that figure represented an increase of about 35 percent from the previous year. Currently, Brazil, Chile, Argentina, and Mexico are the ROC's major trading partners in Latin America. Public and private organizations in Taiwan are working to develop a stronger presence in the region. In 1991 the Ministry of Economic Affairs launched a wide-ranging trade program to enhance Taiwan's commercial and trade ties throughout Latin America. Taiwanese companies are being urged to step up exports of machinery and turnkey processing and manufacturing operations to the region, as well as to establish factories, warehousing facilities, and sales outlets as direct investments in Latin American venues.

Import Policy & Procedures

As a result of major changes in Taiwan's import policies since the late 1980s, Taiwan has become one of the world's top twenty importers. Many protectionist tarriff and non-tariff barriers have been dismantled, foreign exchange controls have been relaxed, and restrictions on the importation of many services have been eliminated. And in a significant break with past policies, the Taiwan government now officially encourages imports from both the advanced, industrialized countries and the newly industrialized countries.

If anything, Taiwan has been compelled to import more foreign goods and services to support the rapid expansion of its manufacturing industries—continued restrictions would soon starve industries of necessary industrial materials, heavy machinery, and transportation equipment. Other items high in demand include electronic products, electrical machinery, base metals, chemicals, and pollution control equipment. Finally, in the early 1990s, import tariffs and other restrictions on many foreign consumer goods, foodstuffs, and services were either lifted or eased. (Refer to "Opportunities" chapter for more information on imports and exports.)

The following section discusses Taiwan's import policy and the procedures for importing into the country. This information is useful for people who want to sell goods and services to Taiwan, for those who establish manufacturing facilities or other operations in Taiwan, and for foreign investors. (Refer to "Marketing" chapter for information on selling in Taiwan.)

REGULATORY AGENCY

The administration of foreign trade is primarily the responsibility of the Board of Foreign Trade (BOFT), an agency of the Ministry of Economic Affairs (MOEA). In addition to a broad range of functions vis-à-vis international trade policy, the BOFT administers imports and exports, issues licenses, conducts inspections, monitors the operations of registered importers and exporters, and classifies products.

Board of Foreign Trade
Ministry of Economic Affairs
1 Hu Kou Street
Taipei, Taiwan
Tel: [886] (2) 3510271, 3510286
Fax: [886] (2) 3311587, 3513603, 3517080

IMPORT POLICY

Authorization of Importer

Products are imported into Taiwan through three channels: public trading agencies; end-users, such as manufacturers and public utilities; and private traders operating on commission. Private traders wishing to import are required to register with the BOFT and to have minimum paid-in capital of NT$5 million. Foreign firms may employ registered Taiwan firms or foreign branches in Taiwan as commercial agents. Commercial agents are not required to register with the BOFT. End-users and manufacturers are permitted to import raw materials, machinery, and replacement equipment.

Import Licensing

Taiwan regulates imports under a licensing system. The BOFT classifies import products into three categories: permissible, controlled, and prohibited. Controlled imports are subject to restrictive licensing, and prohibited imports may not normally be imported. Permissible imports are divided into those that require an import license and those that do not. Of the 9,153 items listed in Taiwan's tariff schedule, 97.3 percent are currently permitted for importation. Among them, 5,918 items can be imported without any permit or license; 699 items require a permit from the BOFT; and the remaining 2,194 items require specific licenses from units authorized by the BOFT, such as the Export Processing Zone Administration, the

Science-Based Industrial Park Administration, and licensed banks.

Licenses for permissible imports are normally issued automatically, and they can usually be obtained within 24 hours of filing the application. An import license is valid for six months. If the licensed shipment cannot be completed within that period of time, the importer can apply to the original licensing agency either for an extension or for a new license.

Licenses for controlled imports are restrictive, and they are usually granted only to government trading agencies or end-users. Taiwan is expected to adopt a negative list system soon to expedite review of import approvals. According to Taiwanese authorities, this system will function like the licensing systems of most developed countries: Products not on the negative list can be freely imported.

FIA Exemptions and Benefits

It is possible for a foreign firm to import machinery and other capital equipment duty free if Foreign Investment Approval (FIA) is obtained. (Refer to "Foreign Investment" chapter.) Moreover, raw materials, equipment, and semi-finished items can be imported duty free, provided they are used or processed for reexport in a factory located in an export processing zone, in an independent bonded factory, or in the Hsinchu Science-Based Industrial Park. There are also special provisions that allow for the importation of leased capital equipment. A Taiwan agent or law firm is the best source of information about eligibility under these special provisions.

Restrictions

Although Taiwan has already deregulated much of the import process, certain restrictions still apply. This section identifies some of the restrictions that still remain.

- As of June 1992, six industrial and 123 agricultural products were still subject to import control. For example, animal offals, herring, mackerel, squid, liquid milk, wheat flour, and waste plastics cannot normally be imported.
- Certain imports, such as narcotics, arms, and munitions, are prohibited or controlled on the grounds of national security, maintaining the public order, or preserving human, animal, or plant health. All such items require a prior import permit issued by the Board of Foreign Trade.
- Four industrial and 77 agricultural products are subject to discretionary licensing. These include rice, chicken meat, red beans, peanuts, potatoes, and rubber accelerators.
- Area restrictions on 35 industrial and 19 agricultural goods limit the places from which such goods can be imported.

- In some cases, the importer must obtain prior authorization from other agencies before applying to the BOFT for the import license. For instance, the Department of Health must approve imports of cosmetics, and the Council of Agriculture must approve imports of food products.
- Taiwan prohibits all direct imports from mainland China. Permissible products originating in China must be imported through a third country.
- Quotas and special shipping regulations apply to some agricultural commodities normally imported in bulk.
- Some commodities, such as gasoline, are covered under government monopolies, and they may not be imported by private companies without special permission.
- Live animals and plants and plant products require certificates of inspection and quarantine.
- Old newspapers require sanitation certificates.
- Cotton rags, old jute, and feather waste require fumigation certificates.
- All cosmetics must be registered with the Department of Health. Inspection and permit are required for cosmetics containing toxic or medicinal ingredients.
- Tobacco, spirits and cigarettes are subject to a very high tax and require documentary approval by the Taiwan Tobacco and Wine Monopoly Bureau.
- Seeds and shoots are controlled by the Council of Agriculture.
- Animal fodder or additives must be registered for inspection prior to import.
- Pesticides require inspection and a permit from the Council of Agriculture.
- Grain imports require a license.
- Fertilizer imports require a permit from the county authorities of the county of destination.
- Nuclear materials, nuclear fuels, radioactive materials, and machinery that produces radiation require prior approval from the Atomic Energy Council.
- Telecommunications equipment requires licensing by the Ministry of Communications.
- Energy-consuming equipment, appliances, and vehicles must comply with MOEA regulations on energy consumption.
- Medicines and medical equipment may only be imported under permit by importers who have registered with the Department of Health. If the shipment is for resale, the importer must also obtain a sales permit from provincial or municipal authorities.
- All chemicals damaging to the environment and toxic chemicals listed by the Environmental Protection Administration, must be inspected, registered, and licensed by that agency before they are imported.

- Imports used in or in conjunction with foods, such as additives, cleaning agents, appliances, containers, and packaging, must be inspected and licensed by the Department of Health.
- Quarantine regulations pertain to imports of animals and vegetables.
- Cholera quarantine procedures must be followed for certain animal and vegetable products and for all marine products, and no marine products may be imported from the following cholera-endemic areas: Algeria, Angola, Bangladesh, Benin, Brunei, Burma, China, South Yemen, Ghana, Equatorial Guinea, Hong Kong, India, Indonesia, Iraq, Ivory Coast, Macao, Malaysia, Mozambique, Nigeria, Nepal, the Philippines, Singapore, Sri Lanka, Sudan, Tanzania, Thailand, Uganda, and Vietnam.

Restrictions on Transport

Imports to Taiwan should be carried by ship. Commodities may be imported by air if they are of high value relative to weight or if they are in urgent demand. Imports must usually be shipped directly from the producing country. With prior approval from the BOFT, goods may be shipped from a free port or entrepôt outside the producing country. Priority must be given to Taiwan shippers for the importation of soybeans and soybean flower, wheat, barley, corn, sorghum, rape seed, and raw cotton. Foreign goods may not be repackaged in Taiwan harbors for transshipment to third countries.

Import Duties

In November 1988, Taiwan authorities announced a four-year (1989-1992) tariff reduction plan designed to cut the effective duty rate to 3.5 percent (the average for the industrialized countries that make up the Organization for Economic Cooperation and Development) and the average nominal duty rate to 7 percent by 1992. Even so, tariffs on agricultural and some industrial products remain relatively high, and the 1992 round of tariff reductions was postponed. To be admitted to the General Agreement on Tariffs and Trade (GATT), Taiwan will have to reduce its tariff rates significantly and across the board.

Valuation

Taiwan revised its customs law in July 1986 in order to adopt procedures consistent with the Agreement on Implementation of Article VII of the GATT, which sets standards for the valuation of all imports pursuant to the assessment of duties. Taiwanese authorities have stated that Taiwan will fully adhere to the customs valuation code when it is admitted to GATT. The dutiable value of an import into Taiwan is currently defined as the value of its cost, insurance, and freight (CIF) value as reflected in the invoice. If the customs official handling the entry process deems that the transaction value on an invoice is too low, he or she will employ alternate methods of valuation listed in the GATT customs valuation code. Duty must be paid no more than 14 days after customs issues the duty statement.

Classification Before Shipment

When a firm cannot identify the tariff classification of an article or is in doubt about the proper classification, it can write to the Inspectorate General of Customs in advance of shipment to request a ruling regarding the applicable classification and import duty. A sample should be submitted with the written request for information. When it is not feasible to send a sample, a complete description of the article, accompanied by specifications and photographs, is an acceptable substitute.

Additional Charges

In addition to duty, a number of other charges apply to imports: harbor dues, a commodity tax, and a value-added tax. Harbor dues are charged on every import arriving by sea. They are calculated as a percentage of the dutiable value. The equivalent for air shipments, called the airport construction fee, is determined by weight. Some products are subject to a domestic excise or commodity tax, which is due when duty is paid. A value-added tax (VAT) is levied on many products. Exports and reexports as well as goods brought into bonded factories and warehouses, the Hsinchu Science-Based Industrial Park, and Taiwan's three export-processing zones are all exempt from any VAT. (Refer to the "Taxation" chapters for more information on the VAT.)

Unfair Competition

Countervailing duties or antidumping duties can be levied on imported goods that have been found to be subsidized or dumped into the Taiwan market (sold at less than the local market value) and that threaten domestic industries.

Countertrade

Taiwan has no specific government regulations or requirements governing countertrade transactions. An importer wishing to engage in such commerce can request a ruling for a specific transaction.

Samples and Advertising Materials

Customs clearance of advertising materials can be a lengthy process. The Taiwanese customs official handling the importation determines whether a sample has commercial value and then assigns duty status accordingly. His determination of commercial value is based on the product's duty-paying value and point of origin. Determinations of dutiable value can be appealed, but customs can hold the goods until final decision is reached. Dutiable samples are exempted from customs duties when they are to be reexported abroad within six months of importation.

IMPORT PROCEDURES

In order to import into Taiwan, a private trader must be registered as an importer with the BOFT and comply with a number of legal requirements. Besides registering with the BOFT, the importer must apply for the necessary import licenses. When licensing is required, the importer should submit a completed application form, a copy of the firm's approved registration form, the original of the foreign exporter's price quote clearly indicating the exporter's name and address, date of quotation, and all details relevant to the shipment; and any other pertinent documentation, such as special permits. Whether or not a license is required, the importer must present a completed import declaration form along with all other necessary documents to customs. This declaration must be made by the duty payer within 15 days of the shipment's arrival date.

MARKING, LABELING, AND PACKING REQUIREMENTS

The Commodity Labeling Law governs the labeling of all commodities in Taiwan. It is aimed at assuring accurate labeling, protecting producers' reputations, and safeguarding the interests of consumers.

Marking

All imported cargo must bear a mark of distinctive design, a set of three or more letters, or a combination of design and letters indelibly stenciled, stamped, or burned on the packing or on the cargo itself. For cargo packed in cases, boxes, crates, casks, drums, or cylinders, each container should bear a separate number. A number cannot be repeated within a period of two years. Bags or bales must also bear a nonrecurring number, date, or set of three or more letters. In addition, each package in a consignment must be numbered consecutively. Numbering is not essential for large lots of cargo except when it is packaged in cases, boxes, or crates, provided that each package in the consignment contains cargo of identical weight.

Labeling

The net contents of packaged goods must be shown in metric units. Dual labeling in metric and nonmetric units is permitted. Measuring instruments calibrated in nonmetric units must show metric equivalents. It is recommended that labels on containers of prepared foods and pharmaceuticals include a quantitative analysis of the contents. Although Taiwanese law generally leaves the choice of marking the origin of an imported product to the producer, it is strongly recommended that products exported to Taiwan be clearly marked with their country of origin. Mark of origin is required for imports of certain textile and garment products.

Packaging

There are no general packaging requirements for shipments to Taiwan. It is advisable to take precautions against rough handling, pilferage, water seepage, high heat, and humidity. Packaging requirements for shipments of hazardous materials should be ascertained on a case-by-case basis. In addition to UN recommendations for the handling of these materials, Taiwan may have specific regulations of its own.

DOCUMENTATION

It is essential when importing to Taiwan to be sure that all documents agree and that they comply with the requirements of the Taiwanese government. Even small irregularities, such as typographical errors, can create a discrepancy that protracts the import process and increases its cost. Accompanying documents necessary for customs clearance vary with the type of goods, the exporting country, and the nature of the business in which the applicant is engaged. A general discharge permit secured by the shipping agent prior to the arrival of the cargo authorizes the discharge of cargo from the vessel. The importer may request a survey at the port of export and a certificate stating that the goods meet the specifications of the order. This section reviews the necessary import documentation.

Import License

When a commodity is imported under license, the license number must appear on all documents required for customs clearance. The license is valid for six months.

Commercial Invoice

The accompanying commercial invoice must include the import license number, if any; the names of the buyer and seller; the number of packages; a description of contents, including gross and net weights; quantity; dimensions; price per unit; FOB value; freight, insurance, and other charges; the shipping mark and number on each package; and any other information required for the particular type of import. The value and the commodity description on the invoice must be identical to those on the import license. Any goods covered under a different license or not licensed must appear separately. The exporter's signature should appear on the invoice to certify that the information supplied is accurate.

Pro Forma Invoice

The pro forma invoice must include the following information: a full description of the goods, including brand names; packing method; quantity; unit price, total cost, freight, insurance, and any other charges; method, date, and port of shipment; port of destination; terms of payment; validity of offer; name and address of the letter of credit beneficiary; and any other details requested by the importer.

Bill of Lading

There are no requirements regarding the form of a bill of lading, but all marks and case numbers appearing on the packages in the shipment must appear on it. Grouping of marks or numbers on shipments of mixed commodities is not permitted. For shipments coming by air, air waybills replace bills of lading. Bills of lading and air waybills must conform strictly to the conditions and terms of the buyer's letter of credit.

Packing List

Two copies of the packing list are required for customs clearance. The information on the packing list must match that on other documents.

Certificates of Origin

According to the BOFT, imports of tea, apparel classified under Harmonized System categories 61 and 62, and partial fishery products require a certificate of origin. A certificate of origin must be issued by the original manufacturer and notarized. If the ROC has a commercial agency in the country of origin, it also must certify the document. Although the vast majority of imports no longer require a certificate of origin, it can be requested as part of the agreement between supplier and buyer. In that case, the standard form available from commercial stationers will suffice. The authorizing signature does not need to be that of the original manufacturer as long as a responsible official of the exporting firm signs it, and the document can be certified by a chamber of commerce.

Other Documents

Any other documents required depend on the nature of the shipment. These other documents can include special permits as well as certificates of inspection, quarantine, fumigation, or sanitation.

STANDARDS AND INSPECTIONS

The Chinese National Standards (CNS), written and published by the MOEA's National Bureau of Standards (NBS), list the standards required for products imported into Taiwan. The CNS are similar or identical to such international standards as ISO and

IEC. The Bureau of Commodity Inspection and Quarantine (BCIQ) carries out inspections of commodities necessitated by the Commodity Inspection Law. Inspection is intended to promote the quality of commodities, safeguard product safety, and protect the interests of consumers, and inspection methods generally conform to international standards. Most applications for any required inspections and/or quarantine clearance can be made either before the shipment is unloaded or when the customs declaration is presented. Application should be made to the BCIQ at the port of entry. A certificate of inspection and/or a quarantine certificate will be issued if the goods pass inspection.

Bureau of Commodity Inspection and Quarantine
Ministry of Economic Affairs
4 Tsi Nan Road
Sec. 1, Taipei, Taiwan
Tel: [886] (2) 3511241 Fax: [886] (2) 3932324
Tlx: 27247 BCIBCIQ

National Bureau of Standards
Ministry of Economic Affairs
3/F., 185 Hsin Hai Road
Sec. 2, Taipei, Taiwan
Tel: [886] (2) 7380007

Electric Current

The electric current used in Taiwan is AC 60 cycle, 110/220 volts, 1, 3 phases, 2, 3, and 4 wires.

IMPORT FACILITATORS

Local customs brokers can be very useful in navigating Taiwanese licensing and documentation requirements. Consignees who entrust the clearance of goods having an import value exceeding US$5,000 to a customs brokerage company will need to establish a power of attorney. Power of attorney is also required when special documents are needed for customs clearance.

METHODS OF SETTLEMENT

Present practice dictates two methods of settlement for the sale of imports into Taiwan. Most payments are made by letter of credit in a foreign currency. Banks require a deposit of 10 percent when opening a letter of credit; the balance is paid when the goods arrive. Payment can also be made by a document against payment (D/P) or a document against acceptance (D/A). The importer settles in foreign currency at maturity or when the goods or the relative shipping documents are received.

PORTS OF ENTRY AND INLAND TRANSPORT

Taiwan has five international seaports: Keelung, Kaohsiung, Hualien, Suao, and Taichung. Its international airports are in Taipei and Kaohsiung. All the ports have adequate customs and storage facilities, including customs-supervised bonded warehouses. The island's infrastructure is extensive. Highways, freeways, and railways provide access to all areas. (Refer to "Ports & Airports" chapter for details.)

REEXPORTS AND BONDED FACTORIES

Reexports

Under Taiwan's present duty rebate system, the import duties levied on raw materials destined for local processing and reexport are comparable with duties levied on general imports. When these materials have been reprocessed and shipped, you can ask the government to refund the duties paid. The percentage of duty refunded to exporters will be reduced gradually and offset by continuing reductions in tariff rates. At the same time, the authorities have accelerated tariff reductions on raw materials, auto parts and accessories, and semifinished products to lessen the impact on export industries.

Bonded Factories and Warehouses

Bonded factories may be established anywhere in Taiwan. They are not restricted to designated industrial or export processing zones. Bonded factories produce primarily for export markets, and they may import their manufacturing components and raw materials duty free. They may sell a designated percentage of their production on the Taiwan market. Taiwanese authorities recently raised the paid-in capital requirement for companies wishing to establish bonded factories from NT$6 million to NT$20 million. Licenses are granted only to companies that have had no operating losses for the preceding three years and no record of tax evasion, document falsification, or other illegal activity for the same time period. Taiwan no longer extends duty-free treatment to items whose duty rate is already considered minimal, materials known to pollute the environment, or items for which a domestic source is readily available.

Adequate bonded storage facilities are available in Taiwan. They are limited almost entirely to warehouses under the direct supervision of the Directorate General of Customs. Goods can be entered into bonded warehouses on arrival in Taiwan provided the consignee applied to customs for such entry. Within prescribed time limits, the products may be reexported duty free.

Export Policy & Procedures

Although Taiwan's trade policy has long been oriented toward export promotion, a vast amount of regulations and paperwork has typically made the export process cumbersome and confusing. This has been especially true for foreign firms with Taiwan-based manufacturing operations that wish to export their products. The opening of export processing zones and the Hsinchu Science-Based Industrial Park in the early 1980s helped to simplify the export process, but the export of many categories of products still remained tightly controlled. In the late 1980s and early 1990s, Taiwan began lifting many more export restrictions and simplified the export process even further, classifying all controlled and permissible exports into one of two categories: those requiring an export license and those that can be exported without one. Currently, 6,200 products, or nearly 70 percent of all products designated as permissible for export, require no export license.

The following section discusses Taiwan's export policy and the procedures for exporting from the country. This information is useful for people who want to purchase goods and services from Taiwan, for those who establish manufacturing facilities or other operations in Taiwan, and for foreign investors.

REGULATORY AGENCY

The administration of foreign trade is primarily the responsibility of the Board of Foreign Trade (BOFT), an agency of the Ministry of Economic Affairs (MOEA). In addition to a broad range of functions vis-à-vis international trade policy, the BOFT administers imports and exports, issues licenses, conducts inspections, monitors the operations of registered importers and exporters, and classifies products.

Board of Foreign Trade
Ministry of Economic Affairs
1 Hu Kou Street
Taipei, Taiwan
Tel: [886] (2) 3510271, 3510286
Fax: [886] (2) 3311587, 3513603, 3517080

EXPORT INCENTIVES

Reexports

Under Taiwan's duty rebate system, the import duties levied on raw materials destined for local processing and reexport are refunded when these materials have been reprocessed and shipped. Duties can also be refunded when goods are imported and then reexported within one year, provided that you have secured prior approval from the Ministry of Finance. No duty is charged on goods imported for storage in a local bonded warehouse that are reexported within two years. Moreover, if the foreign seller of such goods has appointed a local agent to handle the storage and reexport, no income tax is levied on the foreign enterprise.

Export Processing Zones

To encourage investments and expand exports of products and services, Taiwan has established export processing zones (EPZs). Three EPZs in Kaohsiung and Taichung house more than 200 manufacturers and generated US$4 billion in exports in 1991. Because existing space is considered insufficient to meet future industrial goals, the MOEA is considering such sites as industrial parks in Changpin and Kuanyin and land near Taichung Harbor as possible future EPZs. Enterprises located in EPZs are exempt from commodity and business taxes, and the products that they import for their own use enter duty free. The export process is facilitated because all export procedures are handled within the zone.

Hsinchu Science-Based Industrial Park

Opened in 1980, the Hsinchu Science-Based Industrial Park is Taiwan's most visible attempt to move into technology-intensive industries. By the end of 1990, the park's administrators had approved 139 investment applications. Of these, 121 companies are already in operation. Together, they employ 22,360 workers. According to the Six-Year Development Plan, the authorities will triple the park's size by 1996 to accommodate at least 500 high-technology firms and more than 100,000 workers. A park similar to the one in Hsinchu is planned for another region in Taiwan in the near future. Firms investing in the Hsinchu Science-Based Industrial Park enjoy substantial tax benefits, concessionary public financing, low land costs, and such support services as warehousing, factories, and telecommunications facilities. Customs duties must be paid on any finished product that is sold domestically, thus giving an incentive to produce goods for export.

EXPORT POLICY

Export Authorization

Private traders and manufacturing enterprises wishing to export are required to register with the BOFT and have minimum paid-in capital of NT$5 million (about US$188,000). The BOFT can suspend or revoke permission to export. For instance, once a company registers, BOFT begins recording its annual export volume. If the record shows zero in any year, the BOFT may revoke the company's registration. Export licenses can also be revoked for counterfeiting, disregarding export quotas, or losing a judgment in a trade dispute involving a foreign firm.

Export Licensing

Goods exported from Taiwan are classified into three categories: permissible, controlled, and prohibited. Prohibited goods may not be exported under any circumstances. Licenses are required for export of controlled goods. Applications for these licenses must be submitted to the BOFT, and they are approved on a case-by-case basis. Of the 9,011 items listed in Taiwan's current tariff schedule, 8,907 items (98.9 percent) may be exported. As of June 1992, 2,707 (30 percent) of those items require export licenses. A permissible item requires an export license for one of six reasons:

* Implementation of quantitative restriction arrangements and voluntary restraint arrangements (VRA), voluntary export restrictions (VER), or orderly marketing arrangements (OMA)—for the export of textile and garment products to the United States (since 1972),

Canada (since 1975), the European Community (since 1977); of silk cloth to Japan (since 1980); of footwear to the European Community (since July 1990); and of machine tools and steel to the United States (both since 1987);
* National security—Taiwan is concerned about ensuring its supply of such daily necessities and important industrial materials as rice, salt, coal, and uranium;
* Social and financial policies involving such commodities as gold, gold ores and concentrates, and narcotics;
* Protection of endangered species of wild fauna and flora, such as grouper fry, Formosan landlocked salmon, and white-skin sugarcane;
* Concern over hygiene and health of certain products, such as puffer fish, turtles, prawns, and pork;
* Concern over agricultural development of certain products, such as bananas, seedless watermelons, onions, eels, and raw sugar.

Countertrade

Taiwan has no specific regulations or requirements governing countertrade transactions. Persons wishing to engage in such commerce can request a ruling for a specific transaction.

EXPORT PROCEDURES

The exporter is responsible for registering with the BOFT and for obtaining any necessary export license. If the exporter is seeking a license for a shipment of permissible goods, he can usually apply for it at any authorized foreign exchange bank. If the exporter is seeking a license for a controlled product or product restricted by quotas, he should apply for the license directly to the BOFT. The exporter will be expected to supply such details about the shipment as a description of goods, including its Harmonized System classification, product specifications, unit price, shipping port, transshipment port, and the names of the buyer and consignee. The nature of the export will determine whether additional documents are required. These additional documents can include a certificate of inspection, a trade association export endorsement form, and permission letters from designated government agencies. Applications for export licenses are normally processed within a few hours. Licenses are valid for 30 days from the date of issue. Shipment must take place during that time. If the shipment is delayed, the exporter must apply for a new license.

Inspection

Certain categories of export goods listed by the Ministry of Economic Affairs are subject to mandatory inspection by the Bureau of Commodity Inspection and Quarantine (BCIQ). Inspection is intended to promote the quality of commodities, ensure product safety, and protect the interests of consumers, and inspection methods generally conform to international standards. Some categories of products are inspected by organizations that BCIQ has authorized for that purpose.

- For electronics, the Electronics Testing Center of Taiwan
- For machinery and metals products, the Taiwan Metal Industry Development Center
- For rice, the Taiwan Food Bureau
- For rubber products, the Taiwan Rubber Industry Research and Testing Center
- For air conditioners, the Taiwan Electric Research and Testing Center, Inc.

Bureau of Commodity Inspection and Quarantine
Ministry of Economic Affairs (BCIQ)
4 Tsi Nan Road
Sec. 1, Taipei, Taiwan
Tel: [886] (2) 3511241 Fax: [886] (2) 3932324
Tlx: 27247 BCIBCI

All inspections are performed as prescribed by the Chinese National Standards (CNS), written and published by the MOEA's National Bureau of Standards (NBS), which list the standards required for various products. The CNS are similar or identical to such international standards as ISO and IEC. When the CNS do not prescribe inspection standards for a product, the MOEA develops temporary standards. If the foreign buyer stipulates individual standards of inspection that fall below the CNS, the exporter must provide the BCIQ with documentation showing that the BOFT has approved those standards. When the BCIQ finds that samples meet legal requirements, it issues a certificate of inspection. This document must be presented at the shipping port when the BCIQ's port staff rechecks the export products for packaging and appearance. If the products conform to the certificate of inspection, the goods proceed to customs for clearance.

Documentation

When you export from Taiwan, it is absolutely crucial that you present all documentation in the proper form and in the specified number of copies and that you obtain all approvals at the proper time. Missing approvals and/or missing documents can delay departure of a shipment or impede payment. The documents needed for customs clearance include the export license, the certificate of inspection, the customs declaration form, a letter of attorney to the customs broker, the commercial invoice, the bill of lading, and the packing list. The packing list specifies the type of packing, cubic measurement, and number of packages. It is prepared by the supplier or by the freight forwarder or consolidator. It can also appear as part of the commercial invoice.

Bill of Lading

The bill of lading is considered the most important document in a transaction involving transport by sea or by air, and is usually called an air waybill for air shipments. It is your document of title to the merchandise, and as such, must conform strictly with the terms in your letter of credit. When shipping under CIF, CFR, CIP, EXS, or DDP terms, your supplier contracts and pays for the freight. However, many buyers prefer to arrange for the shipment themselves in cooperation with a local freight forwarder, consolidator, or shipping line. In this case, payment is made under EXW, FRC, FAS, FOB, or FOA terms. Make certain that the shipping agent is aware of the correct terms and how the freight charges will be paid. This will help ensure that the carrier prepares the bill of lading in accordance with the conditions of the letter of credit, purchase contract, and other documents.

The bill of lading lists the port of departure, port of discharge, name of the carrying vessel, and date of issue. The date of issue is very important because it indicates whether goods have been shipped within the time period required in your letter of credit. The supplier must therefore submit all required documents on time to receive payment under the terms of the credit.

Bills of lading can be either negotiable or nonnegotiable. A negotiable bill of lading is made to the order of the shipper, who makes a blank endorsement on the back, or it is endorsed to the order of the bank that issues your letter of credit. A nonnegotiable bill of lading is consigned to a specific party (to you or your representative) and endorsement by the shipper is not required. In this case, the consignee must produce the original bill of lading in order to take delivery.

Customs Clearance

Once the BCIQ has completed the port inspection, the goods are placed in a bonded area, and documents are submitted to customs. Customs then checks the goods against conditions laid down in the export license, comparing the shipment with the invoices, permits, and approvals that you have submitted before issuing an export declaration for customs clearance. As soon as you have obtained approval for export from customs, the goods are free for loading and shipping.

Exports Restricted by Quota

The BOFT quota allocation and an endorsed export license obtained from the BOFT or the Bank of Taiwan are required for customs clearance of goods restricted by quota. Taiwan has bilateral agreements with countries that import quota goods under which the importing country issues import permits only to importers who submit a certificate of origin and other special quota-related documentation that the exporter has obtained in Taiwan. To obtain these documents, the exporter must submit copies of the relevant export license with the customs stamp to the appropriate organization:

- For textiles:

  Taiwan Textile Federation
  22 A Kuo E. Rd.
  Taipei, Taiwan
  Tel: [886] (2) 3417251 Fax: [886] (2) 3923855

- For all other goods restricted by quota:

  Bank of Taiwan
  120 Chungking S. Road
  Sec. 1, Taipei 10036, Taiwan
  Tel: [886] (2) 3147377/88 Fax: [886] (2) 3814139
  Tlx: 11201 TAIWANBK

Marking

It is essential that goods intended for export from Taiwan be properly marked. Noncomplying shipments can be detained. With certain exceptions, all items, including packaging, should be marked "Made in Taiwan, Republic of China" or "Made in Taiwan, ROC." Products too small to carry such a mark and components to be assembled in a finished product are exempt from this requirement. Goods destined for countries that do not officially recognize the Republic of China can be marked "Made in Taiwan."

Fees

All products leaving Taiwan by sea are subject to a harbor construction fee that is 0.5 percent of the product's value.

Export Facilitators

Local customs brokers can be very useful in navigating the Taiwanese licensing and documentation requirements. Exporters who use a customs brokerage company to clear goods may need to establish a power of attorney. (Refer to "Important Addresses" chapter for a listing of shipping agents and customs brokers in Taiwan.)

Industry Reviews

This chapter describes the status of and trends in major Taiwan industries. It also lists key contacts for finding sources of supply, developing sales leads and conducting economic research. We have grouped industries into 17 categories, which are listed below. Some smaller sectors of commerce are not detailed here, while others may overlap into more than one area. If your business even remotely fits into a category don't hesitate to contact several of the organizations listed; they should be able to assist you further in gathering the information you need. We have included industry-specific contacts only. General trade organizations, which may also be very helpful, particularly if your business is in an industry not covered here, are listed in the "Important Addresses" section at the end of this book.

Each section has two segments: an industry summary and a list of useful contacts. The summary gives an overview of the range of products available in a certain industry and that industry's ability to compete in worldwide markets. The contacts listed are government departments, trade associations, publications, and trade fairs which can provide information specific to the industry. An entire volume could likely be devoted to each area, but such in-depth coverage is beyond the scope of this book. Our intent is to give you a basis for your own research.

All addresses and telephone numbers given are located in Taiwan, Republic of China, unless otherwise noted. The telephone country code for Taiwan is [886]; other telephone country codes are shown in square brackets where appropriate. Telephone city codes, if needed, appear in parentheses.

We highly recommend that you peruse the chapters on Trade Fairs and Important Addresses, where you will find additional resources including a variety of trade promotion organizations, chambers of commerce, business services, and media.

COMPUTER AND OTHER INFORMATION PRODUCTS

Taiwan is one of the world's top ten producers of computer-related products. Although the United States has long been Taiwan's major export market, Taiwan's manufacturers are diversifying with particular emphasis on European markets. Exports to the Netherlands, England, and Germany have increased dramatically.

Computer manufacturers in Taiwan focus primarily on hardware. Only a small number of firms produce software.

Hardware Products Major exports are color and monochrome monitors. IBM-compatible personal computers (PCs) and computer parts are other leading export items. The computer parts exported include motherboards, switching power supplies, image scanners, graphic cards, computer mice, and

Key Industries

Hsinchu Science Park
Biochemical Products
Computers
Electronics
Precision Machinery/
    Instruments
Semiconductors
Telecom Products

Taoyuan County
Chemicals
Electronics
Plastic Goods
Umbrellas

Taipei City/County
Chemicals
Chemical Products
Ceramics
Electronics
Leather Goods
Machinery
Plastic Goods
Textiles

Taichung City/County
Food-processing
Footwear
Furniture
Hardware
Machinery
Paper/Printing
Plastic Goods
Textiles
Umbrellas
Wood/Bamboo Goods

Miaoli County
Ceramics
Minerals

Changhua County
Food-processing
Footwear
Hardware
Textiles
Umbrellas

Hualien County
Cement
Handicrafts
Wood/Bamboo Goods
Marble Products

Tainan City/County
Chemicals
Chemical Products
Electronics
Hardware
Leather Goods
Machinery
Plastic Goods
Textiles and Garments
Wood/Bamboo Goods

EPZs
Electronics
Food-processing
Garments
Hardware
Household Appliances
Leather Goods
Machinery
Optical Goods
Plastic Goods

Kaohsiung City/County
Chemicals
Food-processing
Hardware
Machinery
Shipbuilding
Shrimp Culture
Steel

Pingtung County
Food-processing
Shrimp Culture
Wood/Bamboo Goods

network cards. Taiwan's computer firms also export disk drives, printers, terminals, and keyboards; production of these items has decreased slightly from past levels.

Software Approximately 125 Taiwan firms are specializing in development of computer software. A majority produce applications software, but the absence of state-of-the art technology prevents all but a few from developing systems software. Most Taiwan software producers are small-sized firms with fewer than 20 employees, little capital, and minimal R&D efforts. Production is primarily limited to personal computer software products for computer-aided design and manufacturing (CAD/CAM) applications. Exports account for only about one-sixth the value of Taiwan's total software production. Taiwan's largest export markets for software are Western Europe and the United States.

Competitive Situation

Exports of computer hardware have been affected by global recession, rapid decline in retail prices for computer products, and lagging competitiveness. Overexpansion has slowed increases in the production value of motherboards. To remain competitive, Taiwan's computer firms are shifting to high-end laser printers and high-performance workstations and PCs. Most major computer manufacturers are concentrating on high-resolution color monitors, microcomputers with faster processing capacities, and minicomputers, including laptops and notebooks. In an effort to decrease their reliance on foreign sources for the components used in their products, Taiwan's computer firms are increasing their R&D for systems software and upgrading their technology for production of floppy and hard disk drives.

Taiwan's production and exports of software have been severely curtailed by growing worldwide awareness and enforcement of intellectual property rights. Nevertheless, Taiwanese authorities are actively encouraging local software firms to upgrade development technology through the five-year Software Industry Development Plan, which includes establishment of a software industry park to assist software companies in developing products for export. In addition, many Taiwanese software firms are emphasizing customized products and aftersale service for customers.

Government Agencies

Hsinchu Science-Based Industrial Park
3 Shing An Rd.
Hsinchu
Tel: (35) 773310 Fax: (35) 776222
Tlx: 32188 NSCSITA

Ministry of the Interior
Copyright Committee
107 Roosevelt Rd.
Sec. 4, Taipei
Tel: (2) 3625241 Fax: (2) 3634950, 3628354

Trade Associations

Taipei Computer Association
3/F., 2, Pa Teh Rd.
Sec. 3, Taipei
Tel: (2) 7764249 Fax: (2) 7764410

Taiwan Science-based Industrial Park
Manufacturers Association
7/F., 2 Hsin An Rd.
Hsinchu City
Tel: (35) 775996

Directories & Publications

Asia Computer Weekly
(Bimonthly)
Asian Business Press Pte., Ltd.
100 Beach Rd., #26-00 Shaw Towers
Singapore 0718
Tel: [65] 2943366 Fax: [65] 2985534

Asian Computer Directory
(Monthly)
Washington Plaza
1/F., 230 Wanchai Road
Wanchai, Hong Kong
Tel: [852] 8327123 Fax: [852] 8329208

Asian Computer Monthly
(Monthly)
Computer Publications Ltd.
Washington Plaza, 1/F.
230 Wanchai Road
Wanchai, Hong Kong
Tel: [852] 9327123 Fax: [852] 8329208

Asian Sources: Computer Products
(Monthly)
Asian Sources Media Group
22/F., Vita Tower
29 Wong Chuk Hang Road
Wong Chuk Hang, Hong Kong
Tel: [852] 5554777 Fax: [852] 8730488

Asiatechnology
(Monthly)
Review Publishing Company Ltd.
6-7/F., 181-185 Gloucester Road
GPO Box 160
Hong Kong
Tel: [852] 8328381 Fax: [852] 8345571

Computerworld Hong Kong
(Weekly)
Asia Computerworld Communications, Ltd.
701-4 Kam Chung Bldg., 54 Jaffe Rd.
Wanchai, Hong Kong
Tel: [852] 86132258 Fax: [852] 8610953

Information and Computer
(Monthly; Chinese)
116 Nanking E. Rd
Sec. 2, Taipei
Tel: (2) 5422540 Fax: (2) 5310760

Taiwan Computer
(Monthly)
United Pacific International, Inc
PO Box 81-417
Taipei
Tel: (2) 7150751 Fax: (2) 7125591 Tlx: 28784

Trade Winners, Computers & Communications:
Including Electronics & Components Information
(Weekly)
PO Box 7-250
Taipei
Tel: (2) 7333988 Fax: (2) 7333990

What's New in Computing
(Monthly)
Asian Business Press Pte., Ltd.
100 Beach Rd., #26-00 Shaw Towers
Singapore 0718
Tel: [65] 2943366 Fax: [65] 2985534

Trade Fairs

Refer to the "Trade Fairs" chapter for complete listings, including contact information, dates, and venues. Trade fairs with particular relevance to this industry include the following, which are listed in that chapter under the heading given below:

Computer & Information Industries
- Business Computerizing Fair
- Information Month - Taichung Show
- Taipei Computer Applications Show
- Taipei International Computer Show (COMPUTEX)
- Taipei International Information Services Show

For other events listed in the "Trade Fairs" chapter that may be of interest, we recommend that you also consult the heading Electronic, Electric & Communications Equipment.

ELECTRONICS PRODUCTS

Electronics products are one of Taiwan's top three exports. More than 4,500 Taiwan manufacturers are producing electronics-related products. Almost all these products are for export.

Major export items can be grouped into two categories: consumer electronics (for example, calculators, audio and video equipment, cassette recorders) and electronic parts and components (for example, resistors, capacitors, diodes, connectors, micro motors, semiconductors, switches, wires and cables, transformers).

Consumer Electronics Exports of consumer electronics have decreased since 1985, although the decline began to slow in 1991. Many Taiwanese electronic firms have moved their operations to Southeast Asian countries and China for low-cost production. Others have shifted to manufacturing more profitable items, such as computer monitors. Investment in R&D is negligible, and many important components, such as cathode-ray tubes (CRTs), are imported from Japan. To encourage the upgrading of this industry's technological capability, Taiwan authorities have initiated several product development programs and have allocated R&D funds to the Electronic Research and Service Organization for the development of high-value products, such as projection televisions, digital radios, and high-definition televisions. With these efforts, annual production and export of consumer electronics are expected to increase.

Electronic Components Taiwan is the world's foremost supplier of many electronic components, and its exports of electronic components continue to expand rapidly. Exports of electronic components from Taiwan can be grouped in three categories: display and electronic tubes, semiconductors, and passive components. In terms of value, CRTs accounted for more than half of the tubes exported, and annual production capacity of monochrome CRTs is nearly two times that of color units. Efforts to develop computer displays, especially liquid crystal displays (LCDs), are growing. In comparison, output of light-emitting diodes (LEDs) has decreased.

Semiconductors rank second in value among Taiwan's exports of electronic components. The products in this category include integrated circuits (ICs), diodes, and transistors. Major IC producers are circuit design companies, IC manufacturers, IC packaging firms, and photo-masking companies. Taiwan's semiconductor industry is shifting its focus from consumer electronics to information products—computers and peripherals. The lack of state-of-the art technology has limited Taiwan-produced semiconductors to low- and medium-range items.

Exports of passive components from Taiwan continue to increase gradually. Taiwan-made passive components include printed circuit boards (PCBs), capacitors, resistors, and transformers. Taiwan imports most of the raw materials needed to produce passive components from Japan, and this industry has therefore lost much of its competitiveness. However, Taiwanese firms are upgrading their technology to improve the quality of their products and diversify their product lines.

The largest number of Taiwan's exports of passive component are PCBs. Taiwan firms that produce PCBs are expanding their existing plants and constructing new ones. Most PCB producers are now making high-density perforated double-layer boards, multilayer boards, and flexible PCBs instead of single-layer boards.

In terms of production value and export sales, capacitors rank second among passive components shipped overseas by Taiwan companies. These firms produce manufactured electrolytic, ceramic, metal-lized plastic film, plastic film, chip, tantalum, vari-able, and mica capacitors. Most capacitor firms are small to medium in size.

Other major Taiwan-made passive components include resistors, micro motors, transformers, and connectors. Exports of resistors, including fixed car-bon film and variable resistors, rank first within this group.

Government Agencies

Hsinchu Science-Based Industrial Park
3 Shing An Rd.
Hsinchu
Tel: (35) 773310 Fax. (35) 776222
Tlx: 32188 NSCSITA

Ministry of Transportation and Communications (MOTC)
2 Changsha St.
Sec. 1, Taipei
Tel: (2) 3112661, 3492900 Fax: (2) 3118587

Trade Associations

Taiwan Electric Appliance Manufacturers Association
6/F., 6 Chung Hsiao W. Rd.
Sec. 1, Taipei 10012
Tel: (2) 3718371 Fax: (2) 3312917

Taiwan Electric Engineering Association
11/F., 76 Sung Chiang Rd.
Taipei 10428
Tel: (2) 5719238/9 Fax: (2) 5232996

Taiwan Electric Wire & Cable Industries Association
11/F.-1, 2 Fu Chin St.
Taipei
Tel: (2) 7151784/5 Fax: (2) 7182307

Taiwan Export Processing Zone Electronics Manufacturers Association
600-6 Chia Chang Rd., K.E.P.Z.
Kaohsiung 81120
Tel: (7) 3632250 Fax: (7) 3636050

Taiwan Regional Association of Ceramic Industries
124 Lane 27, Chung Shan N. Rd.
Sec. 2, Taipei 10419
Tel: (2) 5616536, 5712395

Taiwan Science-based Industrial Park Manufacturers Association
7/F., 2 Hsin An Rd.
Hsinchu City
Tel: (35) 775996

Directories & Publications

Asian Electricity
(11 per year)
Reed Business Publishing Ltd.
5001 Beach Rd., #06-12 Golden Mile Complex
Singapore 0719
Tel: [65] 2913188 Fax: [65] 2913180

Asian Electronics Engineer
(Monthly)
Trade Media Ltd.
29 Wong Chuck Hang Rd.
Hong Kong5
Tel: [852] 5554777 Fax: [852] 8700816

Asian Sources: Electronic Components
(Monthly)
Asian Sources Media Group
22/F., Vita Tower
29 Wong Chuk Hang Road
Wong Chuk Hang, Hong Kong
Tel: [852] 5554777 Fax: [852] 8730488

Electronic Business Asia
(Monthly)
Cahners Publishing Company
275 Washington St.
Newton, MA 02158, USA
Tel: [1] (617) 964-3030 Fax: [1] (617) 558-4506

Trade Winners, Computers & Communications: Including Electronics & Components Information
(Weekly)
PO Box 7-250
Taipei
Tel: (2) 7333988 Fax: (2) 7333990

Trade Fairs

Refer to the Trade Fair chapter for complete list-ings, including contact information, dates, and ven-ues. Trade fairs with particular relevance to this in-dustry include the following, which are listed in that chapter under the heading given below:

Electronic, Electrical & Communication Equipment
- International Electronics & Electrical Show (Taipei ELEC)
- Taichung Domestic Electronic & Furniture Show
- Taipei International Electronics Show
- Taipei International Nepcon-Semiconductor Exhibition (INTERNEPCON-SEMI Taipei)
- Taipei International Telecommunications Show (TAIPEI TELECOM)

For other events listed in the "Trade Fairs" chap-ter that may be of interest, we recommend that you also consult the heading Computer & Information Industries.

FOOD AND BEVERAGE PRODUCTS

Taiwan's agricultural sector is small but productive. Although only about one-quarter of Taiwan's land is arable, domestically produced foods constitute about 6 percent of the island's gross national product. Nearly one-third of Taiwan's processed foods are exported, and food exports, particularly of frozen products, are gradually increasing. Major markets for Taiwan's exports of food are Japan and other nearby Asian countries.

Taiwan's food industry consists of more than 5,600 firms, approximately 3,000 of which are engaged in food processing. Exports are varied, with emphasis on Chinese prepared foods, seafood, fruits, vegetables, sugar, and teas. Most food products are still low-value-added items.

Chinese Prepared Foods Taiwan offers Chinese prepared foods in frozen, canned, and pouch forms. In the face of stiff competition from China, Taiwan's prepared-food firms have shifted to high-value goods. They are concentrating on developing microwaveable frozen Chinese foods, such as prepared dumplings, fried rice meals, sticky rice dumplings, noodle dishes, and desserts. These food products are sold primarily to Japanese customers and overseas Chinese. Taiwan's prepared-food firms are seeking to expand their export markets by making their products more appealing to Western tastes.

Seafood Foremost among Taiwan's seafood exports are prawns and shrimp. Black tiger prawns, striped shrimp, and peeled prawns are major exports. Taiwan's deep-sea and inshore fisheries are noted for their exports of tuna and eel as well as a variety of other fish. Exports of seaweed and seaweed products are also significant.

Fruits and Vegetables Taiwan ships fresh tropical fruits, particularly bananas, to nearby countries. Canned, preserved, and dehydrated fruits and vegetables are exported worldwide.

Beverages Taiwan has seven major soft drink firms, which produce carbonated water, fruit and vegetable juices, tea, coffee, sport drinks, and mineral water. Fruit juices are the most significant export. Competition from China in the tea market, combined with increasing domestic consumption, has caused a decline in tea exports. A small percentage of domestically produced beer is exported.

Competitive Situation

In an effort to become more competitive in domestic and overseas markets, Taiwan's food producers have begun to upgrade their production facilities and make higher-quality products. Foreign imports currently account for a substantial and rapidly increasing share of Taiwan's domestic market, particularly in dairy products, frozen meats, convenience foods, edible oils, and dehydrated, canned, and preserved foods. Taiwan's food industry is shifting to Western-style products to meet changes in local patterns of consumption. Many firms have invested heavily in plant expansion for processed foods, including frozen, convenience, dairy, and beverage products, and some have moved their production of traditional Chinese foods to overseas locations, primarily in China. Taiwan food firms are also creating increasingly elaborate packaging materials to enhance the value of their products.

Government Agency

Council of Agriculture, Executive Yuan
37 Nan Hai Rd.
Taipei
Tel: (2) 3812997 Fax: (2) 3812991

Government Run Corporations

Taiwan Sugar Corporation
25 Paoching Rd.
Taipei
Tel: (2) 3110521 Fax: (2) 3817049

Taiwan Tobacco and Wine Monopoly Bureau
4 Nanchang St.
Sec. 1, Taipei
Tel: (2) 3214567 Fax: (2) 3972086

Trade Associations

Taiwan Agricultural Machinery Manufacturers Association
57 Chung Hus Rd.
Sec. 2, Taipei 10731
Tel: (2) 3813789 Fax: (2) 3821409

Taiwan Association of Barley Industry
6/F., 6 Tun Hua N. Rd.
Taipei 10390
Tel: (2) 7412093

Taiwan Association of Frozen Vegetable & Fruit Manufacturers
Rm. 6, 11/F., 103 Chung Cheng 4th Rd.
Kaohsiung
Tel: (7) 2015694, 2517317 Fax: (7) 2210471

Taiwan Bakery Association
2/F., Lane 96, Kun Ming St.
Taipei
Tel: (2) 3314741 Fax: (2) 3611285

Taiwan Brown Sugar Association
3/F., 62 Hsi Ning N. Rd.
Taipei
Tel: (2) 5522021 Fax: (2) 5522776

Taiwan Canners Association
7/F., 170 Min Sheng E. Rd.
Sec. 2, Taipei 10444
Tel: (2) 5022660/9 Fax: (2) 5022667

Taiwan Confectionery Biscuit and Floury Food Association
9/F.-1, 390 Fu Hsing S. Rd.
Sec. 1, Taipei 10640
Tel: (2) 7041662 Fax: (2) 7084429

Taiwan Corn Industry Association
B1, 3 Alley 42, Lane 78, Fu Hsing S. Rd.
Sec. 2, Taipei
Tel: (2) 7553353 Fax: (2) 7840128

Taiwan Deep Sea Tuna Boatowners and Exporters
Association
4/F., 40-42 Chungking S. Rd.
Sec. 3, Taipei 10742
Tel: (2) 3037189, 3016554 Fax: (2) 3095495

Taiwan Eel Exporters Association
8/F., 24 Chilin Rd.
Taipei 10424
Tel: (2) 5711254, 5711255 Fax: (2) 5635752

Taiwan Feed Industry Association
Rm. C, 9/F., 368 Fu Hsing S. Rd.
Sec 1, Taipei
Tel: (2) 7028070 Fax: (2) 7028073

Taiwan Flour Mills Association
6/F., 6 Tun Hwa N. Rd.
Taipei
Tel: (2) 7512181 Fax: (2) 7410803

Taiwan Food Industrial Association
6/F., 10 Chungking S. Rd.
Sec. 1, Taipei 10036
Tel: (2) 3719848 Fax: (2) 3817084

Taiwan Frozen Meat Industry Association
4/F., 19 Lane 118, An Chu St.
Taipei 10675
Tel: (2) 7339112, 7335351 Fax: (2) 7354155

Taiwan Frozen Seafood Exporters Association
3/F., 29 Lane 30, Yung Chi Rd.
Taipei 10541
Tel: (2) 7657157 Fax: (2) 7634259

Taiwan Frozen Seafood Industries Association
8/F.-6, 103 Chung Cheng 4th Rd.
Kaohsiung 80-113
Tel: (7) 2411894 Fax: (7) 2519603

Taiwan Fruit & Vegetable Juice Manufacturers
Association
3/F., 6 Lare 59, Yi Tung St.
Taipei 10431
Tel: (2) 5070830 Fax: (2) 5080516

Taiwan Fruit Exporters Association
12/F.-3, 31-1, Hsin Sheng N. Rd.
Sec. 2, Taipei 10423
Tel: (2) 5715191 Fax: (2) 5628411

Taiwan Margarine Industries Association
9/F., 390 Fu Hsing S. Rd.
Sec. 1, Taipei 10640
Tel: (2) 7060839 Fax: (2) 7085979

Taiwan Monosodium Glutamate Manufacturers
Association
4/F., 6 Chang-chun Rd.
Taipei 10413
Tel: (2) 5414313, 5119540 Fax: (2) 5414313

Taiwan Provincial Federation of Tobacco and Wine
Industry
2/F., 1, Nan Chang Rd.
Sec. 1, Taipei
Tel: (2) 3212096

Taiwan Province Rice & Cereals Association
Rm. 9, 4/F., 18 Chung Cheng N. Rd.
Sanchung City, Taipei Hsien 24103
Tel: (2) 9867375 Fax: (2) 9867375

Taiwan Regional Association of Preserved Fruits
6/F.-4, 36-1 San Ming St., Yuan Lin
Chang Hua Hsien 51001
Tel: (2) 8321006 Fax: (2) 8321280

Taiwan Salt Trade Federation
297 Chien Kang Rd.
Sec. 1, Tainan 70203
Tel: (6) 2652238

Taiwan Soy Sauce & Fermenting Industry
Association
4/F.-3, 24 Peiping E. Rd.
Taipei 10026
Tel: (2) 3410739 Fax: (2) 3518475

Taiwan Tea Manufacturers Association
Rm. 9, 10/F., 165 Nanking W. Rd.
Taipei 10102
Tel: (2) 5417251 Fax: (2) 5416601

Taiwan Vegetable Oil Manufacturers Association
6/F., 27 Chang An E. Rd.
Sec. 1, Taipei 10404
Tel: (2) 5616351 Fax: (2) 5621745

Taiwan Vegetable Processing Association
15/F., 125 Nan King E. Rd.
Sec. 2, Taipei
Tel: (2) 5616351 Fax: (2) 5074012

Taiwan Vegetables Exporters Association
12/F.-3, 31-1 Hsin Sheng N. Rd.
Sec. 2, Taipei 10473
Tel: (2) 5316517, 5715191

Directories & Publications

Agricultural Association Of China Journal
(Quarterly; in Chinese, with summaries, added
table of contents, and some articles in English)
Taiwan Agricultural Research Institute
189 Chungcheng Rd
Wufeng
Taichung, Taiwan
Fax: (4) 3338162

Asia Pacific Food Industry
(Monthly)
Asia Pacific Food Industry Publications
24 Peck Sea St., #03-00 Nehsons Building
Singapore 0207
Tel: [65] 2223422 Fax: [65] 2225587

Asia Pacific Food Industry Business Report
(Monthly)
Asia Pacific Food Industry Publications
24 Peck Sea St., #03-00 Nehsons Building
Singapore 0207
Tel: [65] 2223422 Fax: [65] 2225587

Asian And Pacific Council Food And Fertilizer
Technology Center Technical Bulletin
(Semi-monthly)
5/F., 14 Wenchow St
Taipei
Fax: (2) 3620478

Taiwan Sugar
(Bimonthly)
Taiwan Sugar Corporation
Rm. 606, 25 Pao Ching Rd
Taipei 100

Trade Fairs

Refer to the "Trade Fairs" chapter for complete
listings, including contact information, dates, and
venues. Trade fairs with particular relevance to this
industry include the following, which are listed in
that chapter under the headings given below:

Food, Beverages & Food Processing
• Taipei International Food Industry Show
• Food Industry & Packing Exhibition
• Taichung International Food Industry Fair
Machines & Instruments
• Taipei International Food Industry Show

FOOTWEAR

Footwear is one of Taiwan's top five exports. The
leading markets for Taiwan-made footwear are the
UK, France, and the United States.

Major Taiwan footwear exports are shoes, sandals,
and slippers. All are produced in a variety of materials, including leather, textiles, rubber, and plastic.

Footwear More than 1,000 manufacturers are
producing footwear in Taiwan. Rubber and plastic
footwear, primarily sports shoes, constitute more
than half of Taiwan's footwear exports. Taiwan-made
athletic shoes are particularly outstanding. Taiwan
is a renowned source for internationally famous
brands, such as Adidas, Nike, Puma, and Reebok.
Leather and textile shoes also have significant shares
of Taiwan's footwear export market, with dress shoes
ranking second in value. Most production is on an
original equipment manufacturer (OEM) basis.

Footwear Parts Exports of Taiwan-made footwear
parts and raw materials are gradually increasing, primarily to China and Southeast Asia. Leading products
include uppers, insoles, outersoles, heels, fittings,
molded plastic sections, and artificial leather pieces.

Competitive Situation

Taiwan's footwear industry has maintained its
competitive edge in world markets because most raw
materials critical to shoe manufacturing, including
rubber, plastic, and textiles, are produced domestically. However, rising domestic labor costs and competition from developing countries, where wages are
lower, have forced footwear firms to shift production from low-end labor-intensive products to increasingly sophisticated high-end products. Many of
Taiwan's footwear producers have moved their labor-intensive shoe operations offshore, particularly
to Indonesia, Malaysia, and China. Taiwan-based facilities continue to upgrade the industry's technology; emphasis is on automated production systems
and computer-aided design (CAD). In an effort to
support the domestic footwear industry, Taiwanese
authorities have given shoe producers incentives to
upgrade design and manufacturing capabilities. They
have also established educational programs to improve the skills of the work force.

Trade Associations

Taiwan Export Processing Zone Leather Industries
Association
1 West 17th St., K.E.P.Z.
Kaohsiung 80681
Tel: (7) 8216862

Taiwan Footwear Exporters Association
13/F., 131 Sung Chiang Rd.
Taipei 10429
Tel: (2) 5066190 Fax: (2) 5081489

Taiwan Leather Manufacturers Association
4/F., 7 Chung Hwa Rd.
Sec. 1, Taichung 40302
Tel: (4) 2238725 Fax: (4) 2204904

Taiwan Regional Association of Leather Goods
Manufacturers
6/F.-1, 5-1 Nanking W. Rd.
Taipei 10403
Tel: (2) 5210090 Fax: (2) 5210090

Taiwan Regional Association of Synthetic Leather
Industries
5/F., 30 Nanking W. Rd.
Taipei 10410
Tel: (2) 5219204 Fax: (2) 5415823

Taiwan Regional Association of Tanneries
6/F.-1, 5-1 Nanking W. Rd.
Taipei
Tel: (2) 5413472 Fax: (2) 5210090

Taiwan Shoe Industry Association
13/F., 131 Sung Chiang Rd.
Taipei
Tel: (2) 5066191/4 Fax: (2) 5081489

Directories & Publications

Asia Pacific Leather Directory
(Annual)
Asia Pacific Leather Yearbook
(Annual)
Asia Pacific Directories, Ltd.
6/F., Wah Hen Commercial Centre
381 Hennessy Rd.
Hong Kong
Tel: 8936377 Fax: 8935752

Asian Plastic News
(Quarterly)
Reed Asian Publishing Pte., Ltd.
5001 Beach Rd.
#06-12 Golden Mile Complex
Singapore 0719
Tel: [65] 2913188 Fax: [65] 2913180

Trade Fairs

Refer to the "Trade Fairs" chapter for complete listings, including contact information, dates, and venues. Trade fairs with particular relevance to this industry include the following, which are listed in that chapter under the heading given below:

Textiles & Apparel
• Beowulf Shoes Exhibition
• Taipei International Leather Goods Show

For other events listed in the "Trade Fairs" chapter that may be of interest, we recommend that you also consult the heading Hobbies & Recreation.

FURNITURE

Taiwan's furniture industry has become one of the nation's most important manufacturing sectors. Taiwan ranks as one of the world's top five producers of furniture. Major export markets for Taiwan furniture include Japan and the United States, although exports to the United States have declined since Taiwan lost status in the US Generalized System of Preferences (GSP) program; the appreciating NT dollar and sluggish US economy have also adversely affected Taiwan's furniture industry.

Products Taiwan's furniture manufacturers use a wide assortment of materials, ranging from wood, rattan, and bamboo to marble, plastic, and metal. Chinese- and Western-style furniture is produced for living room, dining room, office, computer, medical, nursery, and outdoor use. Wood living room furniture is the top export. Exports of stone and marble goods are growing rapidly.

Competitive Situation

Taiwan's furniture industry has been affected by unfavorable exchange rates, rising production costs, and global recession. In addition, it must rely heavily on imports of natural products, except for marble and dolomite, which are mined in Taiwan. Many import sources of raw material have become unreliable, particularly since Southeast Asian countries have begun to restrict their exports of such materials to foster development of indigenous industries using domestic raw materials.

To remain competitive in world markets, Taiwan's furniture manufacturers are improving their quality standards. Many Taiwan furniture-manufacturing firms are also improving their marketing channels, for example, by creating their own brand names and by establishing overseas warehouse and branch office operations. Taiwan's furniture producers are also seeking to diversify into other markets in Europe. A considerable number of furniture makers have established trading partnerships in Southeast Asia or have moved their production facilities there to secure reliable supplies of raw material and reduce labor costs. These firms have kept their design, technology development, and marketing operations in Taiwan.

Trade Associations

Taiwan Export Processing Zone Furniture & Handicraft Products Manufacturers Association
1 West 17th St., K.E.P.Z.
Kaohsiung 80681
Tel: (7) 8319394

Taiwan Wooden Furniture Industrial Association
Rm. 905 100 Chung Hsiao E. Rd.
Sec. 2, Taipei
Tel: (2) 3215791, 3215811 Fax: (2) 3951754

Directories & Publications

Taiwan Furniture
(3 per year)
China Economic News Service
555 Chunghsiao East Road
Section 4, Taipei
Tel: (2) 7681234 Fax: (2) 7632303

Taiwan Gifts & Housewares
(Annual)
Trade Winds, Inc
No. 7, Lane 75, Yungkang St.
Postal address: PO Box 7-179, Taipei
Tel: (2) 3932718 Fax: (2) 3964022 Tlx: 24177

Trade Fairs

Refer to the "Trade Fairs" chapter for complete listings, including contact information, dates, and venues. Trade fairs with particular relevance to this industry include the following, which are listed in that chapter under the heading given below:

Furniture & Housewares
• Taichung Domestic Electronic & Furniture Show
• Taipei International Furniture Show
• Taipei International Hardware, Houseware and Building Materials Show

For other events listed in the "Trade Fairs" chapter that may be of interest, we recommend that you also consult the headings Construction & Housing; and Gifts, Jewelry & Stationery.

HAND TOOLS

Taiwan is one of the world's top suppliers of hand tools. In terms of value, hand tools rank as one of Taiwan's ten largest exports. Taiwan's three largest export markets for hand tools are England, Canada, and the United States. Although Taiwan firms still rely heavily on exports to the United States, they have successfully diversified their markets to include additional European countries, particularly Germany, France, and the Netherlands. Exports to Japan and Australia have also increased significantly.

Taiwan's manufacturers produce a wide variety of hand tools, which can be classified as manual, hydraulic, electric power, and pneumatic. Most exported items are sold on an original equipment manufacturer (OEM) basis.

Manual Tools Taiwan's tool firms manufacture manual hand tools for such varied trades as carpentry, electrical work, plumbing, painting, plastering, measuring, automotive repair, and gardening. Socket wrenches and screwdrivers are top export items. Other major export goods include scissors, pliers, nose pliers, vices, and hammers.

Electric Power Tools Most exports of electric tools are do-it-yourself (DIY) power tools. Bestselling items include drills, sanders, saws, soldering irons, and heat guns. Current trends in production are toward cordless tools with multiple functions and longer battery life.

Pneumatic Tools Taiwan exports impact wrenches, air sanders, air grinders, air drills, air screw drivers, air tackers, and air spray guns. After a slight downturn in the export market, the makers of pneumatic tools have targeted models for professional, industrial, and automotive repair uses.

Competitive Situation

Taiwan's tool makers remain competitive by producing a large variety of tools for export and by maintaining their reputation for reliable delivery times. As competition with developing countries increases, Taiwanese manufacturers are creating more high-value-added professional and industrial tools. Additional features, such as nickel-cadmium batteries, light-emitting diode (LED) microcomputer reserve power indicators, displays, and oil pressure button devices, are being added to DIY power tools. Taiwan's tool firms continue to improve the quality and durability of their basic products by using better materials, automating production, and focusing on quality control. In many kinds of hand tools, Taiwan's firms have replaced carbon steel with chrome-vanadium and chrome-molybdenum. Taiwan's tool firms are using computer-aided design and manufacturing (CAD/CAM) programs extensively in the development and manufacture of new products, and some are adopting flexible manufacturing systems.

Trade Associations

Taipei Instruments Commercial Association
3/F., 20, Lane 16, An Tong St.
Taipei
Tel: (2) 7111300 Fax: (2) 7753434

Taiwan Regional Hand Tools Association
3/F., 687-1 Min Tsu E. Rd.
Taipei 10488
Tel: (2) 7152250, 7130667 Fax: (2) 7152617

Taiwan Screw Industrial Association
4/F.-1, 71 Sung Chiang Rd.
Taipei
Tel: (2) 5060918 Fax: (2) 5072429

Government Run Corporation

Taiwan Machinery Manufacturing Corporation
3 Taichi Rd., Hsiao-kang
Kaohsiung
Tel: (7) 8020111 Fax: (7) 8022129

Directories & Publications

Asian Sources: Hardware
(Monthly)
Asian Sources Media Group
22/F., Vita Tower
29 Wong Chuk Hang Road
Wong Chuk Hang, Hong Kong
Tel: [852] 5554777 Fax: [852] 8730488

China Sources : Hardware
(Monthly)
Sino Comm Company Ltd
B1K B 5/F Vita TWR
29 Wong Chuk Hang Road
Hong Kong

Taiwan Buyer's Guide: Hardware
(Annual)
Trade Winds, Inc
No. 7, Lane 75, Yungkang St
Postal address: PO Box 7-179
Taipei
Tel: (2) 3932718 Fax: (2) 3964022 Tlx: 24177

Target Machinery & Hardware (TMH)
(Monthly)
United Pacific International, Inc
PO Box 81-417
Taipei
Tel: (2) 7150751 Fax: (2) 7169493 Tlx: 28784

Trade Fairs

Refer to the "Trade Fairs" chapter for complete listings, including contact information, dates, and venues. Trade fairs with particular relevance to this industry include the following, which are listed in that chapter under the heading given below:

Machines & Instruments
- Industrial Technology Exhibition
- Taipei International Automation & Precision Machinery Show

- Taipei International Hardware, Houseware and Building Materials Show
- Taipei International Machine Tool Show (TIMTOS)
- Taipei International Woodworking Machinery Show
- Taiwan Precision Machinery Fair

For other events listed in the "Trade Fairs" chapter that may be of interest, we recommend that you also consult the headings Construction & Housing; Electronic, Electric & Communication Equipment; and Medicine & Pharmaceuticals.

HOUSEWARES AND APPLIANCES

Taiwan's exporters of household products have a small but growing share of world markets, supplying primarily household appliances and a vast array of housewares.

Taiwan's major market for exports of household products is the United States. Exports to other markets, primarily Japan, are increasing rapidly as manufacturers improve the quality of their goods and intensify their marketing efforts.

Household Appliances A variety of small and large household appliances are manufactured in Taiwan. Most items are medium- to low-end products. Small appliances include irons, food processors, hair dryers, space heaters, vacuum cleaners, and coffee grinders. Ceiling, decorative, and standing fans are other notable exports. Taiwan appliance firms also produce many large appliances, including microwave ovens, stoves, washers, dryers, refrigerators, and sewing machines. Although Taiwan's appliance manufacturers lack the technology needed to produce large-scale air-conditioning equipment, they offer competitively priced nonducted mini spit air conditioners and window- and wall-style air conditioners.

Housewares Taiwan exports a broad spectrum of housewares, including kitchenware, tableware, china and bone china dishes, clocks, hairbrushes, and combs. Most exports in this category are made of plastic or stainless steel. Taiwan's houseware manufacturers depend heavily on Taiwan's plastics industry and its mold-making capabilities. Items made of bamboo, rattan, and porcelain also have a significant share of the housewares export market.

Lighting Light bulbs have become one of Taiwan's major export items. Standard bulbs and fluorescent tubes are foremost among its lighting exports. Taiwanese firms also export Christmas lights, miniature watch lights, and tungsten filament bulbs for flashlights, reflection lamps, and cars.

Competitive Situation

Despite worldwide recession and increasing domestic labor shortages, Taiwan's exports of household products have remained competitive in world markets, in part because the majority of Taiwan's manufacturers of household goods are small to medium in size. They are therefore highly flexible and able to respond rapidly to changing market trends and emerging opportunities. These firms also have a well-organized satellite factory system, which enables them to provide samples, quote prices, and deliver almost any item in a short time.

Many Taiwan manufacturers of household goods have taken additional steps to remain competitive. Some have moved their labor-intensive operations to Southeast Asia. Many have upgraded their factories on Taiwan to make higher-end products and have begun to concentrate on designing and developing innovative products. A few firms have expanded their marketing activities, such as by promoting their own brand names. Original equipment manufacturer (OEM) orders still predominate.

Trading houses continue to handle most exports of household goods, because orders are generally small and diverse. Trading houses not only act as liaison between overseas buyers and domestic firms but also help to inform Taiwan's producers of international developments in design and materials.

Trade Associations

Taiwan Electric Appliance Manufacturers Association
6/F., 6 Chung Hsiao W. Rd.
Sec. 1, Taipei 10012
Tel: (2) 3718371 Fax: (2) 3312917

Taiwan Gas Appliance Manufacturers Association
5/F., 3 Lane 328, Lang Chiang Rd.
Taipei 10482
Tel: (2) 5038831, 5032704 Fax: (2) 5044842

Taiwan Gifts & Housewares Exporters Association
6/F., 28 Alley 2, Lane 250, Nanking E. Rd.
Sec. 5, Taipei 10571
Tel: (2) 7697303 Fax: (2) 7615942

Taiwan Refrigerating and Air-conditioning Engineering Association of ROC
2/F., Fu-lo Mansion
2 Lane 995, Min Sheng E. Rd.
Taipei 10581
Tel: (2) 7685423/4 Fax: (2) 7685424

Taiwan Refrigeration Industry Association
3/F., 29 Lane 30, Yung Chi Rd.
Taipei 10550
Tel: (2) 7657152 Fax: (2) 7634259

Taiwan Soap and Detergent Manufacturers Association
64 Kai-feng St.
Sec. 2, Taipei 10011
Tel: (2) 3610611/2

Taiwan Tableware Manufacturing & Export
Association
20 Lane 131, Hangchow S. Rd.
Sec. 1, Taipei 10044
Tel: (2) 3419342 Fax: (2) 3948980

Taiwan Towel Industry Association
12/F., 22 Ai Kuo E. Rd.
Taipei 10726
Tel: (2) 3210866, 3410435 Fax: (2) 3410434

Directories & Publications

Asian Sources: Gifts & Home Products
(Monthly)
Asian Sources Media Group
22/F., Vita Tower
29 Wong Chuk Hang Road
Wong Chuk Hang, Hong Kong
Tel: [852] 5554777 Fax: [852] 8730488

Taiwan Gifts & Housewares
(Annual)
Trade Winds, Inc
No. 7, Lane 75, Yungkang St
Postal address: PO Box 7-179
Taipei
Tel: (2) 3932718 Fax: (2) 3964022 Tlx: 24177

Trade Fairs

Refer to the "Trade Fairs" chapter for complete listings, including contact information, dates, and venues. Trade fairs with particular relevance to this industry include the following, which are listed in that chapter under the headings given below:

Construction & Housing
• "Home" Show
• Taipei International Hardware, Houseware and Building Materials Show
Furniture & Housewares
• Taichung Domestic Electronic & Furniture Show

For other events listed in the "Trade Fairs" chapter that may be of interest, we recommend that you also consult the heading Gifts, Jewelry & Stationery.

JEWELRY, TIMEPIECES, GIFTS, STATIONERY, AND FASHION ACCESSORIES

Taiwan is a leading exporter of jewelry, gifts, stationery, and fashion accessories to world markets. Major export markets include many European countries, Japan, and the United States.

Decorative and Gift Items More than half of the decorative and gift items exported by Taiwan firms are holiday products, particularly for Christmas. Exports of decorations for Easter, Halloween, and Thanksgiving are increasing dramatically. Other decorative and gift exports include keychains, jewelry boxes, music boxes, figurines, perfume bottles, flower pots, vases, artificial flowers, and photograph frames. These items are available in a great variety of materials, including brass, ceramic, porcelain, glass, and paper; brass products are the top gift export.

Leading export markets for Taiwan's decorative and gift items are Japan and the United States.

Jewelry Taiwan's jewelry firms offer a broad array of items, including costume jewelry, copper imitation jewelry, and coral, pearl, and precious stone items. In recent years, Taiwan's jewelry industry has been affected adversely by rising domestic wages and depletion of domestic stocks of jade and coral. To remain competitive in world markets, Taiwan's jewelry makers are creating innovative and higher-quality designs. To encourage this industry, Taiwanese authorities have cut import tariffs on precious and semiprecious stones and have allowed jewelry makers to import such raw materials as pearls, jade, gold, and crystal directly from China.

Watches and Clocks More than 300 firms in Taiwan make timepieces. These companies supply both finished products and parts. Of finished products, quartz timepieces are major exports. Domestically produced quartz movements were developed through Taiwan's Industry Technology Research Institute, making Taiwan's timepiece firms less dependent on imports from Switzerland, France, and Japan.

However, the majority of Taiwan's timepiece-related exports are watch and clock parts. Taiwan is one of the largest suppliers of watch dials in the world. Other major exports include quartz movements, cases, bands, hands, batteries, and liquid crystal display panels. Most part exports are produced on an original equipment manufacturer (OEM) basis.

Handicrafts Taiwan's major exports of handicrafts include woodcarvings, pottery, and bamboo goods. Most of Taiwan's handicraft makers are small-sized operations. Taiwan's Chinese handicraft exports have declined slightly, primarily because Taiwanese firms increased the mass production of products based on designs requested by foreign buyers and neglected their own traditional and innovative designs. However, Taiwan's handicraft firms have moved away from mass production in recent years, and they are regaining a substantial share in world markets.

Stationery Taiwan's stationery industry is supported by more than 300 firms that supply paper stationery, writing utensils, and office and computer desk accessories. Major exports are plastic products, such as pencil cases, tape dispensers, and file and diskette organizers. Exports of brass items, including letter openers, hole punchers, and desk set accessories, are also significant. Faced with stiff competition from Hong Kong, Korea, China, Thailand, and Malaysia, Taiwan's stationery manufacturers are concentrating on producing goods with innovative designs and high-quality materials. Many firms are now offering multiuse products, such as pen flashlights and keychains.

Accessories Taiwan exports a tremendous variety of fashion accessories. It ranks first in the world in the export of umbrellas, most of which are produced by small-sized family operations. Leather and imitation leather products are other notable exports. Taiwan produces purses, wallets, and a variety of luggage goods on an original equipment manufacturer (OEM) basis for world-renowned designers, such as Pierre Cardin and Christian Dior. It is also one of the world's largest exporters of hats and caps. Several cap makers have established their own outlets and brand names in the United States.

Competitive Situation

Taiwan's producers of jewelry, gifts, stationery, and accessories have remained competitive in world markets partly because most are small to medium in size and can respond quickly to emerging market trends and opportunities. Most firms can create samples, quote prices, and deliver goods within a short time. Trading houses still handle most of these exports, because orders are generally small and diverse.

Government Run Corporation

Taiwan Chung Hsing Paper Corporation
10/F., 35 Kuanfu S. Rd.
Taipei
Tel: (2) 7673171 Fax: (2) 7659026

Trade Associations

Taiwan Bags Association
12/F., 22 Ai Kuo E. Rd.
Taipei 10726
Tel: (2) 3925310, 3925305 Fax: (2) 3979253

Taipei Clock, Watch & Glasses Association
3/F., 210 Chung Hwa Rd.
Sec. 2, Taipei
Tel: (2) 3063634

Taiwan Decorative Pottery Exporters Association
13/F., 25 Min Sheng E. Rd.
Taipei 10448
Tel: (2) 5639171, 5435343 Fax: (2) 5639171

Taiwan Export Processing Zone Furniture & Handicraft Products Manufacturers Association
1 West 17th St., K.E.P.Z.
Kaohsiung 80681
Tel: (7) 8319394

Taiwan Export Processing Zone Leather Industries Association
1 West 17th St., K.E.P.Z.
Kaohsiung 80681
Tel: (7) 8216862

Taiwan Feather Export Association
Rm. 711, 7/F., 27 Chung Shan N. Rd.
Sec. 3, Taipei 10451
Tel: (2) 5954983 Fax: (2) 5918702

Taiwan Flower Export Association
Rm. 901, 41 Chung Hsiao W. Rd.
Sec. 1, Taipei
Tel: (2) 3313146 Fax: (2) 3119336

Taiwan Gifts & Housewares Exporters Association
6/F., 28 Alley 2, Lane 250, Nanking E. Rd.
Sec. 5, Taipei 10571
Tel: (2) 7697303 Fax: (2) 7615942

Taiwan Glass Industry Association
12/F.-3, 22 Chungking N. Rd.
Sec. 1, Taipei 10206
Tel: (2) 5376018 Fax: (2) 5376765

Taiwan Glove Manufacturers Association
12/F., 22 Ai Kuo E. Rd.
Taipei
Tel: (2) 3918396 Fax: (2) 3951532

Taiwan Handbags Export Trade Association
12/F., 22 Ai Kuo E. Rd.
Taipei
Tel: (2) 3925305, 3925310 Fax: (2) 3949253

Taipei Handicraft Association
2/F., 18-1 Hsining S. Rd.
Taipei 10448
Tel: (2) 3810306 Fax: (2) 3818605

Taiwan Hat Exporters Association
6/F., 22 Ai Kuo E. Rd.
Taipei 10726
Tel: (2) 3937892, 3937894 Fax: (2) 3963842

Taiwan Hosiery Manufacturers Association
6/F., 22 Ai Kuo E. Rd.
Taipei 10726
Tel: (2) 3913709, 3921483 Fax: (2) 3221744

Taiwan Jewelry Industry Association
Rm. 11, 6/F., 41 Chung Hsiso W. Rd.
Sec. 1, Taipei 10012
Tel: (2) 3610108 Fax: (2) 3615033

Taiwan Leather Manufacturers Association
4/F., 7 Chung Hwa Rd.
Sec. 1, Taichung 40302
Tel: (4) 2238725 Fax: (4) 2204904

Taiwan Precious Stones Manufacturing Association
Rm. 611, 6/F., 41 Chung Hsiao W. Rd.
Sec. 1, Taipei
Tel: (2) 3610108 Fax: (2) 3615033

Taiwan Regional Association of Leather Goods Manufacturers
6/F.-1, 5-1 Nanking W. Rd.
Taipei 10403
Tel: (2) 5210090 Fax: (2) 5210090

Taiwan Regional Association of Synthetic Leather Industries
5/F., 30 Nanking W. Rd.
Taipei 10410
Tel: (2) 5219204 Fax: (2) 5415823

Taiwan Regional Association of Tanneries
6/F.-1, 5-1 Nanking W. Rd.
Taipei
Tel: (2) 5413472 Fax: (2) 5210090

Taiwan Umbrella Manufacturers Association
6/F.-4, 149 Ho Ping W. Rd.
Sec. 2, Taipei 10721
Tel: (2) 3117557 Fax: (2) 3119162

Directories & Publications

Asian Sources: Timepieces
Asian Sources: Gifts & Home Products
(Monthly)
Asian Sources Media Group
22/F., Vita Tower
29 Wong Chuk Hang Road
Wong Chuk Hang, Hong Kong
Tel: [852] 5554777 Fax: [852] 8730488

Taiwan Gifts & Housewares
(Annual)
Trade Winds, Inc
No. 7, Lane 75, Yungkang St
Postal address: PO Box 7-179
Taipei
Tel: (2) 3932718 Fax: (2) 3964022 Tlx: 24177

World Jewelogue
(Annual)
Headway International Publications Co.
907 Great Eagle Center
23 Harbour Rd.
Hong Kong
Tel: [852] 8275121 Fax: [852] 8277064

Trade Fairs

Refer to the "Trade Fairs" chapter for complete listings, including contact information, dates, and venues. Trade fairs with particular relevance to this industry include the following, which are listed in that chapter under the headings given below:

Gifts, Jewelry & Stationery
- Art Fair Taiwan
- Art Galleries Fair ROC
- Taipei International Gift & Stationery Show
- Taipei International Jewelry & Timepiece Show

Hobbies & Recreation
- Asian Floral Design Exhibition & Greater Flower Designing Competition of ROC
- Taipei International Flower Show
- Taiwan Amusement Exhibition
- World of Women Beauty Wares Show

Textiles & Apparel
- Taipei International Leather Goods Show

For other events listed in the "Trade Fairs" chapter that may be of interest, we recommend that you also consult the heading Furniture & Housewares.

MEDICAL AND
HEALTH-RELATED PRODUCTS

Taiwan's exports of medical and health-related products are still relatively small, with the exception of a few product lines. Taiwan exports medical products primarily to the United States.

Taiwan's medical products industry consists of about 800 firms, one-fifth of which manufacture medical devices. The remainder produce Western and Chinese herbal medicines. Most firms are small- to medium-sized, and 80 percent of their products are of low value. Taiwan's most significant medical exports are disposable latex gloves, bandages, and pharmaceuticals.

Pharmaceuticals Nearly 640 Taiwan firms make pharmaceuticals, and their production is gradually but steadily growing. Approximately 380 firms are producing western medicines, and about 260 are making Chinese herbal drugs. Products available include antibiotics, vitamins, gastric and intestinal drugs, hormones, sulfa drugs, and nutrition supplements.

Most Taiwan pharmaceutical firms are very small-scale operations. Production technology remains at a low and inconsistent level, and quoted prices vary widely from one producer to another. Taiwanese authorities have instituted a Good Manufacturing Practices program to monitor the quality of pharmaceuticals, but only program members are inspected, which means that most smaller producers are not.

Cosmetics About 415 registered Taiwan firms are engaged in manufacturing cosmetics, and their production has increased dramatically in recent years. Major Taiwan cosmetics suppliers are outlets for exports and imports, and many are foreign invested. Some larger companies, such as the Taiwan Kiss Me Cosmetics, Co., have established their own brand names. Several firms have begun to shift product lines away from middle-aged customers and instead are targeting younger groups, where a greater potential exists for product growth.

Medical Equipment Approximately 135 manufacturers in Taiwan offer low-end medical devices. Only about 40 percent of all Taiwan-made medical equipment is exported. Major products are disposable hospital appliances and supplies. Taiwan has become a major world supplier of latex gloves, particularly since the spread of AIDS. Other significant exports include adhesive bandages, blood donor sets, blood pressure units, artificial limbs, wheelchairs, crutches, scales, catheters, clinical thermometers, ear plugs, contact lenses, medical office furnishings, hearing aids, infant incubators, laboratory equipment, mechanotherapy appliances, needles and syringes, operating scissors, operating lamps, oxygen masks and connecting tubes, medical instrument and appliance parts, percussion hammers, physical therapy appliances, scalp view infusion sets, electrosphygmomanometers and pacemakers, stethoscopes, suture silk, tape measures, and ultrasonic medical analyzers. Several types of electrodiagnostic equipment are made in Taiwan, including ultraviolet, infrared, and medical x-ray apparatus. Taiwan's medical equipment producers also manufacture items for dental practice, such as dental instruments, appliances, x-ray apparatus, and patient units and chairs.

Competitive Situation

Taiwanese medical products have a minimal share of world markets, and a significant improvement in international exports is not expected for the immediate future. Most suppliers lack the capital needed to expand production or upgrade technology.

Government Agencies

Council of Agriculture, Executive Yuan
37 Nan Hai Rd.
Taipei
Tel: (2) 3812997 Fax: (2) 3812991

Department of Health
100 Aikuo E. Rd.
Taipei
Tel: (2) 3210151 Fax: (2) 3122907

Trade Associations

Taiwan Export Processing Zone Optical & Precision Instrument Industries Association
18 Chien Kuo Rd., Tantzu Hsiang
Taichung Export Processing Zone
Taichung Hsien
Tel: (4) 5322123, 5322127

Taiwan Eyeglass Industry Association
2/F., 406 Min Chuan E. Rd.
Taipei
Tel: (2) 5057583 Fax: (2) 5070260

Taiwan Pharmaceutical Industry Association
6/F., 8 Cheng Teh Rd.
Sec. 1, Taipei
Tel: (2) 5511890, 5511671 Fax: (2) 5239936

Taiwan Surgical Dressings & Medical Instruments Industrial Association
3/F., 85 Chien Kuo S. Rd.
Sec. 2, Taipei 10633
Tel: (2) 7071856 Fax: (2) 3250286

Directories & Publications

Asian Hospital
(Quarterly)
Techni-Press Asia Ltd.
PO Box 20494
Hennessy Road
Hong Kong
Tel: [852] 5278682 Fax: [852] 5278399

Asian Medical News
(Bimonthly)
MediMedia Pacific Ltd.
Unit 1216, Seaview Estate, 2-8 Watson Rd.
North Point, Hong Kong
Tel: [852] 5700708 Fax: [852] 5705076

Asia-Pacific Dental News
(Quarterly)
Adrienne Yo Publishing Ltd.
4/F., Vogue Building
67 Wyndham Street
Central, Hong Kong
Tel: [852] 5253133 Fax: [852] 8106512

Far East Health
(10 per year)
Update-Siebert Publications
Reed Asian Publishing Pte
5001 Beach Rd.
#06-12 Golden Mile Complex
Singapore 0719
Tel: [65] 2913188 Fax: [65] 2913180

Medicine Digest Asia
(Monthly)
Rm. 1903, Tung Sun Commercial Centre
194-200 Lockhart Rd.
Wanchai, Hong Kong
Tel: [852] 8939303 Fax: [852] 8912591

Trade Fairs

Refer to the "Trade Fairs" chapter for complete listings, including contact information, dates, and venues. Trade fairs with particular relevance to this industry include the following, which are listed in that chapter under the heading given below:

Medicine & Pharmaceuticals
- Taipei International Medical Equipment & Pharmaceuticals Show
- Taiwan International Medical Equipment & Pharmaceuticals Show

For other events listed in the "Trade Fairs" chapter that may be of interest, we recommend that you also consult the heading Food, Beverages & Food Processing.

METALWORKING MACHINERY

Taiwan ranks among the world's top ten producers of machine tools. Approximately 300 such factories are operating in Taiwan.

Products Only about 40 of Taiwan's machine tool firms produce computer numerically controlled (CNC) metalworking machines. Exported CNC machines include lathes and milling machines, machining centers, and other boring, drilling, and grinding machine tools. Taiwan's machine tool firms produce most components for these machines, including ball screws, hydraulic pumps, and gears. However, controllers are still imported from Japan.

Competitive Situation

Taiwan's machine tools have remained competitive in price and quality on the world market because of a stable division of labor, convenient transport, steady improvements in production, and enhanced product standardization. Machine tool firms continue to invest heavily in improving their technological capabilities, and they have emphasized the development of numerically controlled tools, flexible manufacturing systems, laser cutting units, and automatic material handling systems. Some of Taiwan's machine tool makers have also undertaken new marketing strategies by creating their own brand names (for example, Leadwell, YAM, Kingston, Victor, Dah Lih, FEMCO). A number of larger concerns have established overseas branches, but Taiwan's smaller makers still rely on machinery traders for their marketing.

A 1986 voluntary restraint agreement between the United States and Taiwan limited Taiwan's exports to the United States of machine tools to a market share under 5 percent and a zero growth rate. As a result, Taiwan's manufacturers have sought other markets, particularly in Southeast Asia. Taiwan's machine tool firms have also been successful in diversifying sales to European markets, particularly Britain, Italy, Germany, and France.

Government Run Corporation

Taiwan Machinery Manufacturing Corporation
3 Taichi Rd., Hsiao-kang
Kaohsiung
Tel: (7) 8020111 Fax: (7) 8022129

Trade Associations

Taiwan Association of Machinery Industry
2/F., 110 Huaning St.
Taipei 11037
Tel: (2) 3813722, 3813724 Fax: (2) 3813711

Taiwan Manufacturers Industrial Association
Rm. 905, 100 Chung Hsiao E. Rd.
Sec. 2, Taipei
Tel: (2) 3215791 Fax: (2) 3951754

Taiwan Steel & Iron Industries Association
10/F., 9 Chang An E. Rd.
Sec. 1, Taipei 10404
Tel: (2) 5427900, 5427903 Fax: (2) 5316708

Taiwan Steel Wire & Wire Rope Industries Association
5/F., 369 Fu Hsing N. Rd.
Taipei 10483
Tel: (2) 7155032 Tlx: 26155

Directories & Publications

Asiamac Journal: The Machine-Building and Metal Working Journal for the Asia Pacific Region
(Quarterly; English, Chinese)
Adsale Publishing Company
21/F., Tung Wai Commercial Building

109-111 Gloucester Road
Hong Kong
Tel: [852] 8920511 Fax: [852] 8384119, 8345014
Tlx: 63109 ADSAP HX

Asian Manufacturing
Far East Trade Press Ltd.
2/F., Kai Tak Commercial Building
317 Des Voeux Road
Central, Hong Kong
Tel: [852] 5453028 Fax: [852] 5446979

Directory of Turn-Key in Taiwan
Taiwan Association of Machinery Industry
2/F., 110 Huaining St
Taipei
Tel: (2) 3813722 Fax: (2) 3813711

Taiwan Machinery
(Semi-annual)
China Economic News Service
555 Chunghsiao East Road
Sec. 4, Taipei
Tel: (2) 7681234 Fax: (2) 7632303

Target Machinery & Hardware (TMH)
(Monthly)
United Pacific International, Inc
PO Box 81-417
Taipei
Tel: (2) 7150751 Fax: (2) 7169493 Tlx: 28784

Who Makes Machinery in Taiwan
(Annual)
Taiwan Association of Machinery Industry
2/F., 110 Huaining St
Taipei
Tel: (2) 3813722 Fax: (2) 3813711

Trade Fairs

Refer to the "Trade Fairs" chapter for complete listings, including contact information, dates, and venues. Trade fairs with particular relevance to this industry include the following, which are listed in that chapter under the headings given below:

Industrial Materials, Chemicals & Metal
• Taichung International Metal Casing, Forging, Welding & Treating Show

Machines & Instruments
• Industrial Technology Exhibition
• Taipei International Automation & Precision Machinery Show
• Taipei International Machine Tool Show (TIMTOS)
• Taipei International Textile Machinery Show
• Taiwan Precision Machinery Fair

For other events listed in the "Trade Fairs" chapter that may be of interest, we recommend that you also consult the heading Construction & Housing.

PLASTIC/RUBBER-PROCESSING MACHINERY

Taiwan is Asia's second largest supplier of plastic- and rubber-processing machinery. Most Taiwanese firms that produce this type of machinery are small- to medium-sized enterprises and export primarily to Southeast Asia and the Middle East.

Products Leading export items are plastic injection-molding machines and single- and double-screw extruders. Other items include machinery for tubular film making, blow molding, crushing, vacuum forming, pelletizing, recycling, compression molding, making rubber latex gloves, vulcanizing, and making tires and tubes.

Available models of plastic injection-molding machines include horizontal, vertical, thermoset, and double-injection units. Taiwan's firms currently produce machines ranging in clamping force from 5 to 2000 tons and in injection quantities from 1 to 350 ounces. Significant exports also include rubber and plastic machinery for shoe manufacturing.

Competitive Situation

Taiwan's manufacturers of plastic- and rubber-processing machinery have maintained their competitiveness in world markets by their success in meeting buyers' specifications and the use of a satellite factory system that integrates the operations of many factories into one network. In terms of price, quality, and innovation, Taiwan's plastic- and rubber-processing machinery continues to be highly competitive as new manufacturers keep entering the field. Encouraged by public sector assistance, Taiwan's manufacturers of plastic- and rubber-processing machinery have upgraded their technology and increased their R&D efforts.

Government Run Corporation

Taiwan Machinery Manufacturing Corporation
3 Taichi Rd., Hsiao-kang
Kaohsiung
Tel: (7) 8020111 Fax: (7) 8022129

Trade Associations

Taiwan Plastic Bags Exporters Association
4/F., 140 Chung Hsiao E. Rd.
Sec. 1, Taipei 10023
Tel: (2) 3917604 Fax: (2) 3932714

Taiwan Plastic Christmas Tree Manufacturers & Exporters Association
10/F., 320 Chung Hsiao E. Rd.
Sec. 4, Taipei
Tel: (2) 7312063 Fax: (2) 7711036

Taiwan Plastics Industry Association
8/F., 162 Chang An E. Rd.
Sec. 2, Taipei 10406
Tel: (2) 7719111/3 Fax: (2) 7315020

Taiwan Regional Association of Rubber Industry
7 Ning Po E. St.
Taipei 10767
Tel: (2) 3512261 Fax: (2) 3412691

Directories & Publications

Asian Plastic News
(Quarterly)
Reed Asian Publishing Pte., Ltd.
5001 Beach Rd.
#06-12 Golden Mile Complex
Signapore 0719
Tel: [65] 2913188 Fax: [65] 2913180

Directory of Turn-Key in Taiwan
Taiwan Association of Machinery Industry
2/F., 110 Huaining St
Taipei
Tel: (2) 3813722 Fax: (2) 3813711

Trade Fairs

Refer to the "Trade Fairs" chapter for complete listings, including contact information, dates, and venues. Trade fairs with particular relevance to this industry include the following, which are listed in that chapter under the headings given below:

Industrial Materials, Chemicals & Metal
• Taipei International Plastics & Rubber Industry Show (Taipei PLAS)

Machines & Instruments
• Industrial Technology Exhibition
• Taipei International Automation & Precision Machinery Show
• Taiwan Precision Machinery Fair

For other events listed in the "Trade Fairs" chapter that may be of interest, we recommend that you also consult the heading Packaging, Printing & Graphic Design.

SPORTING GOODS

Sporting goods are one of Taiwan's top ten exports, and Taiwan is now a major world supplier of sports-related products. Nearly all sporting goods produced in Taiwan are exported, with the United States its major market. To increase exports of sporting goods, Taiwan's firms have made efforts to diversify to other markets. Sales to Japan are growing rapidly, particularly of golf and tennis equipment. Exports to European countries, particularly England, Germany, France, and Spain, have also increased dramatically.

Significant exports include bicycles, golf, tennis, and billiards equipment; sporting balls; indoor games; exercise apparatus; water sports items; and sports accessories. Athletic footwear and sports clothing are excluded from this category. (*See* Footwear; Textiles and Garments.)

Golf Equipment Exports of Taiwan-made golf

equipment have surged in recent years. Taiwan's sports manufacturers produce a variety of golf-related products, including clubs, club heads, and golf bags.

Racket Sports Taiwan ranks within the top five exporters of tennis rackets in the world. Squash, racquetball, and badminton rackets are also notable exports. Production is still on an original equipment manufacturer (OEM) basis.

Bicycles Taiwan is currently the world's leading supplier of bicycles and bicycle parts. Bicycle manufacturers in Taiwan have been innovative in their use of high-quality materials, including aluminum alloy and carbon fibers, to improve their products while keeping prices competitive. Popular exports include racing, foldable, and mountain bicycles. Taiwan's bicycle firms produce such parts as brakes, frames, and wheel hubs as well as a variety of other accessories.

Competitive Situation

Production of Taiwan sporting goods is still largely on an original equipment manufacturer (OEM) basis. To remain competitive in world markets, Taiwan sporting good firms are experimenting with the use of high-tech materials, such as graphite, fiberglass, boron, carbon fibers, and polyethylene. Larger firms are moving to higher-end products and are promoting their own brand names (for example, Rox, Victor, Mitsushiba, Pro-Kennex).

Trade Association

Taiwan Sporting Goods Manufacturers Association
8/F., 22 Teh Huei St.
Taipei 10469
Tel: (2) 5941864 Fax: (2) 5919396

Directories & Publications

Taiwan Bicycles & Parts Buyer's Guide
(Annual)
Trade Winds, Inc
No. 7, Lane 75, Yungkang St
Postal address: PO Box 7-179
Taipei
Tel: (2) 3932718 Fax: (2) 3964022 Tlx: 24177

Trade Fairs

Refer to the "Trade Fairs" chapter for complete listings, including contact information, dates, and venues. Trade fairs with particular relevance to this industry include the following, which are listed in that chapter under the heading given below:

Hobbies & Recreation
• Taipei International Cycle Show
• Taipei International Sporting Goods Show
• World Fishing Exhibition Taipei

For other events listed in the "Trade Fairs" chapter that may be of interest, we recommend that you also consult the heading Automobiles & Automotive Parts.

TELECOMMUNICATION PRODUCTS

Taiwan's telecommunication industry has a large number of small producers of customer premises equipment. These companies have little international recognition and produce primarily low-end goods.

Approximately 170 Taiwan firms are producing corded and cordless telephones, which are Taiwan's major export in this category. Retail prices of Taiwan-made telephones are generally lower than those of competing equipment. Other major exports include modems, key-telephone systems, exchanges, and fax machines. Many Taiwan telecommunication products manufacturers have moved production of traditional telephone product lines to China and Southeast Asia to take advantage of low-cost labor there.

Competitive Situation

Through joint development programs with the Industrial Technology Research Institute (ITRI) of Taiwan, larger communications firms are now actively developing radio communication equipment, transmission equipment, and key communication parts and components. However, investment in R&D is still minimal, and production technology for radio communication and transmission equipment is unsophisticated. Nevertheless, several large firms are actively upgrading their production technologies through joint development programs with ITRI. Products under development include radio communication equipment, transmission equipment, and key communication parts and components.

Government Agencies

Directorate General of Telecommunications
31 Aikuo E. Rd.
Taipei
Tel: (2) 3443601 Fax: (2) 3223738

Ministry of Transportation and Communications
2 Changsha St.
Sec. 1, Taipei
Tel: (2) 3112661, 3492900 Fax: (2) 3118587

Trade Associations

Taiwan Electric Wire & Cable Industries
Association
11/F.-1, 2 Fu Chin St.
Taipei
Tel: (2) 7151784/5 Fax: (2) 7182307

Taiwan Export Processing Zone Electronics
Manufacturers Association
600-6 Chia Chang Rd., K.E.P.Z.
Kaohsiung 81120
Tel: (7) 3632250 Fax: (7) 3636050

Directories & Publications

Asia Pacific Brodcasting & Telecommunications
(Monthly)
Asian Business Press Pte., Ltd.
100 Beach Rd., #26-00 Shaw Towers
Singapore 0718
Tel: [65] 2943366 Fax: [65] 2985534

Asiatechnology
(Monthly)
Review Publishing Company Ltd.
6-7/F., 181-185 Gloucester Road
GPO Box 160
Hong Kong
Tel: [852] 8328381 Fax: [852] 8345571

Tien Hsin Chi Shu
(Quarterly; Chinese, with summaries in English)
Directorate General of Telecommunications
31 Aikuo East Road
Taipei 106
Tel: (2) 3443601 Fax: (2) 3223738

Trade Winners, Computers & Communications:
Including Electronics & Components Information
(Weekly)
PO Box 7-250
Taipei
Tel: (2) 7333988 Fax: (2) 7333990

Trade Fairs

Refer to the "Trade Fairs" chapter for complete listings, including contact information, dates, and venues. Trade fairs with particular relevance to this industry include the following, which are listed in that chapter under the heading given below:

Electronics, Electrical & Communications Equipment
- International Electronics & Electrical Show (Taipei ELEC)
- Taipei International Electronics Show
- Taipei International Telecommunications Show (Taipei Telecom)

For other events listed in the "Trade Fairs" chapter that may be of interest, we recommend that you also consult the heading Computer & Information Industries.

TEXTILES & GARMENTS

Taiwan is one of the world's five largest exporters of textiles, which are one of its top five exports, although their export value has declined slightly in recent years. Most textiles produced in Taiwan are exported. Taiwan's three largest markets for textiles are Japan, Hong Kong, and the United States.

Taiwan's textile production can be divided into four sectors: man-made fiber, yarn, fabric, and apparel and accessories.

Man-Made Fiber Taiwan ranks first in the world in the production of man-made fiber (MMF). Taiwan's 20 MMF firms produce nearly three-quarters of the raw materials used in Taiwan's textile production. These firms depend heavily on Taiwan's petrochemical industry. To meet strong export demands, MMF firms have expanded their production capacities and upgraded their facilities. Products include polyester filament, polyester staple, nylon filament, acrylic staple, rayon staple, rayon filament, and nylon staple.

Yarn Yarn-spinning firms can be divided into two sectors: spinners of cotton, blended cotton, and MMF spun yarns; and spinners of woolen, worsted woolen, and worsted MMF yarns. Cotton spinners constitute the largest sector, with more than 200 firms. There are fewer than 80 wool-spinning firms. Faced with strong competition from other countries, Taiwan's larger cotton-spinning firms have invested heavily in new computer-controlled autodoffing or semiautodoffing equipment. Smaller firms that cannot afford to replace their older machinery may not be able to remain competitive and therefore may be forced to close.

Fabric Most of Taiwan's producers of fabric are small to medium-sized operations. They include weavers, knitters, and nonwoven fabric firms. More than 70 percent of all woven fabric produced is MMF fabric. In recent years, Taiwan's weaving firms have invested heavily in upgrading their plants to remain competitive in world markets.

Nonwoven Fabric Taiwan has become the second largest producer of nonwoven fabrics in Asia. Approximately 100 firms are currently producing nonwoven fabric. In general, nonwoven fabric is destined for applications in apparel rather than in industrial manufacturing. Nonwoven fabrics are commonly used for apparel interlinings. To produce higher-value-added products, several major firms are creating high-end products by advanced meltblown and spun-laced technology. Sales of nonwoven fabrics have been hindered because downstream processors are not aware of their potential applications. Industrial usage is increasing dramatically. Nonwoven fabrics are now being used in health care products, automotive parts, air cleaner and air-conditioning filters, baby diapers, and disposable coverings. Use of geotextiles for civil engineering projects and hazardous waste management is also growing.

Apparel Taiwan ranks as one of the world's ten largest exporters of apparel and accessories. More than 2,800 firms are registered as manufacturers of apparel and accessories. Major exports include woven garments, knitwear, and sweaters. To remain competitive, these firms have shifted from mass production of low-quality goods to high-value-added products featuring complex designs and requiring the use of computerized cutting equipment, computer-aided design and manufacturing (CAD/CAM) equipment in quick-response production systems, and flexible manufacturing systems.

Strict measures imposed by Taiwan and US authorities to curb illegal transshipment of semifinished goods and final products from offshore to Taiwan for reexport have affected apparel. In February 1992, the United States cut Taiwan's apparel quotas by an average 6.5 percent. Taiwanese authorities have adopted several administrative measures, including regulations on overseas processing of textile exports to restricted areas and mandatory certification and origin labels for textile imports. Taiwan firms must also obtain licenses to import textiles from Hong Kong, Macao, and Vietnam.

Competitive Situation

Taiwan's textile industry is heavily influenced by rising domestic labor costs and appreciation of the NT dollar. As a result, textile exports have been declining slightly since 1990. To become more competitive, Taiwan's textile industry has shifted its emphasis from apparel, which is labor-intensive, to the capital-intensive production of yarn and fabric products. Exports have since rebounded. With this shift, Hong Kong has become Taiwan's largest market for exported fabric and yarn, most of which is directly transshipped to China. The United States remains Taiwan's largest buyer of apparel and accessories.

Trade Associations

Kaohsiung Export Processing Zone Knitting & Woven Manufacturers Association
1 West 17th St., K.E.P.Z.
Kaohsiung 80681
Tel: (7) 8218524, 8216770

Taiwan Association of Synthetic Stretch Yarn
12/F., 22 Ai Kuo E. Rd.
Taipei 10726
Tel: (2) 3410571 Fax: (2) 3218793

Taiwan Carpet Manufacturers Association
Rm. 207, 2/F., 25 Pao Ai Rd.
Taipei 10035
Tel: (2) 3810660 Fax: (2) 3831802

Taiwan Clothing Manufacturers Association
8/F.-3, 202 Nanking E. Rd.
Sec. 5, Taipei 10573
Tel: (2) 7666661/2 Fax: (2) 7625722

Taiwan Cotton Spinners Association
11/F., 22 Ai Kuo E. Rd.
Taipei 10726
Tel: (2) 3916445 Fax: (2) 3916449

Taiwan Dyestuff & Pigment
Industrial Association
7/F., 137 Fu Hsing S. Rd.
Sec. 1, Taipei
Tel: (2) 7318131, 7412802 Fax: (2) 7318132

Taiwan Export Processing Zone Garment Industry
Association
3 E. 1st Rd., K.E.P.Z.
Kaohsiung 80681
Tel: (7) 8215066, 8413957 Fax: (7) 8418542

Taiwan Export Processing Zone Leather Industries
Association
1 West 17th St., K.E.P.Z.
Kaohsiung 80681
Tel: (7) 8216862

Taiwan Knitting Industry Association
7/F., 22 Ai Kuo E. Rd.
Taipei 10726
Tel: (2) 3945121 Fax: (2) 3971356

Taiwan Leather Manufacturers Association
4/F., 7 Chung Hwa Rd.
Sec. 1, Taichung 40302
Tel: (4) 2238725 Fax: (4) 2204904

Taiwan Man-Made Fiber Industries Association
9/F., 22 Ai Kuo E. Rd.
Taipei
Tel: (2) 3914151 Fax: (2) 3947327

Taiwan Non-Woven Fabrics Industry Association
4/F., 51 Min Sheng E. Rd.
Sec. 3, Taipei
Tel: (2) 5019010 Fax: (2) 5059791

Taiwan Regional Association of Leather Goods
Manufacturers
6/F.-1, 5-1 Nanking W. Rd.
Taipei 10403
Tel: (2) 5210090 Fax: (2) 5210090

Taiwan Regional Association of Synthetic Leather
Industries
5/F., 30 Nanking W. Rd.
Taipei 10410
Tel: (2) 5219204 Fax: (2) 5415823

Taiwan Regional Associationoof Tanneries
6/F.-1, 5-1 Nanking W. Rd.
Taipei
Tel: (2) 5413472 Fax: (2) 5210090

Taipei Sewing Machine Association
2/F., 46, Chin Hsi St.
Taipei
Tel: (2) 5620687

Taiwan Sewing Machine Exporters Association
Rm. 1, 12/F., 185 Ming-chuan Rd.
Taichung 40301
Tel: (4) 2245712 Fax: (4) 2239042

Taiwan Silk & Filament Weaving Industrial
Association
6/F., 22 Ai Kuo E. Rd.
Taipei 10736
Tel: (2) 3917815, 3917817 Fax: (2) 3973225

Taiwan Sweater Industry Association
9/F.-1, 22 Ai Kuo E. Rd.
Taipei 10726
Tel: (2) 3945216 Fax: (2) 3945270

Taiwan Textile Federation
22 Ai Kuo E. Rd.
Taipei
Tel: (2) 3417251 Fax: (2) 3923855

Taiwan Textile Printing Dyeing & Finishing
Industrial Association
12/F., 22 Ai Kuo E. Rd.
Taipei 10726
Tel: (2) 3211095/7 Fax: (2) 3223522

Taiwan Weaving Industry Association
10/F., 22 Ai Kuo E. Rd.
Taipei 10726
Tel: (2) 3911317/9 Fax: (2) 3929413

Taiwan Wool Textile Industrial Association
6/F., 22 Ai Kuo E. Rd.
Taipei
Tel: (2) 3913544 Fax: (2) 3518771

Taiwan Zippers Manufacturers Association
3/F., 9-3 Lane 174, Pa Teh Rd.
Sec. 2, Taipei 10401
Tel: (2) 7310638, 7400692 Fax: (2) 7401109

Directories & Publications

Asia Pacific Leather Directory
(Annual)
Asia Pacific Leather Yearbook
(Annual)
Asia Pacific Directories, Ltd.
6/F., Wah Hen Commercial Centre
381 Hennessy Rd.
Hong Kong
Tel: [852] 8936377 Fax: [852] 8935752

ATA Journal: Journal for Asia on Textile & Apparel
(Bimonthly)
Adsale Publishing Company
Tung Wai Commercial Building, 21st Fl.
109-111 Gloucester Road
Wanchai, Hong Kong
Tel: [852] 8920511 Fax: [852] 8384119

Trade Fairs

Refer to the "Trade Fairs" chapter for complete listings, including contact information, dates, and venues. Trade fairs with particular relevance to this industry include the following, which are listed in that chapter under the heading given below:

Textiles & Apparel
• Beowulf Shoes Exhibition
• Taipei International Leather Goods Show
• Taipei International Textile Machinery Show

For other events listed in the "Trade Fairs" chapter that may be of interest, we recommend that you also consult the headings Hobbies & Recreation; Furniture & Housewares; and Gifts, Jewelry & Stationery.

TOYS

Taiwan is one of the world's foremost suppliers of toys, ranking as one of the top five exporters. Its primary markets are Japan, Europe, and the United States.

Products More than 1,300 Taiwan companies are producing a wide array of toys. Most toy makers are small. Major exports include inflatable plastic toys, dolls, baby carriages, indoor games, toys with wheels, and electronic, radio-controlled, remote-controlled, and battery-operated toys. Stuffed animals are a large share of Taiwan's toy exports.

Competitive Situation

Exports of toys from Taiwan plunged in 1988, when Japan introduced home electronic video games. In an effort to increase and stabilize toy exports, Taiwan's toy makers have shifted from heavy dependence on US markets, and have increased their exports to Europe and Japan. Taiwan's toy makers are also striving to remain competitive despite rising domestic wages and appreciation of the NT dollar. Larger toy makers have invested in R&D programs, and many have moved production offshore, particularly to Thailand and the Philippines. Taiwanese investments in toy factories located in China has also increased. An increasing number of smaller toy makers, who lack funds to undertake adequate R&D programs, have gone out of business.

Trade Associations

Taiwan Gifts & Housewares Exporters Association
6/F., 28 Alley 2, Lane 250, Nanking E. Rd.
Sec. 5, Taipei 10571
Tel: (2) 7697303 Fax: (2) 7615942

Taiwan Plastics Industry Association
8/F., 162 Chang An E. Rd.
Sec. 2, Taipei 10406
Tel: (2) 7719111/3 Fax: (2) 7315020

Taiwan Regional Association of Rubber Industry
7 Ning Po E. St.
Taipei 10767
Tel: (2) 3512261 Fax: (2) 3412691

Taiwan Toy Manufacturers Association
6/F., 42 Min Sheng E. Rd.
Sec. 1, Taipei 10443
Tel: (2) 5711264, 5711266, 5362107 Fax: (2) 5411061

Directories & Publications

Taiwan Bicycles & Parts Buyer's Guide
(Annual)
Trade Winds, Inc
No. 7, Lane 75, Yungkang St
Postal address: PO Box 7-179
Taipei
Tel: (2) 3932718 Fax: (2) 3964022 Tlx: 24177

Taiwan Gifts & Housewares
(Annual)
Trade Winds, Inc
No. 7, Lane 75, Yungkang St
Postal address: PO Box 7-179
Taipei
Tel: (2) 3932718 Fax: (2) 3964022 Tlx: 24177

Trade Fairs

Refer to the "Trade Fairs" chapter for complete listings, including contact information, dates, and venues. Trade fairs with particular relevance to this industry include the following, which are listed in that chapter under the heading given below:

Hobbies & Recreation
- Taipei International Toy Show
- Taiwan Amusement Exhibition

For other events listed in the "Trade Fairs" chapter that may be of interest, we recommend that you also consult the headings Automobiles & Automotive Parts; Computer & Information Industries; and Gifts, Jewelry & Stationery.

VEHICLE PARTS

Taiwan is a prime supplier of low-end vehicle parts worldwide. In terms of gross production value, vehicle parts are one of the top five categories of Taiwan's manufactured products. Nearly 80 percent of the vehicle parts produced in Taiwan are exported. Japan and the United States are the largest markets.

Taiwan has about 2,000 manufacturers of vehicle parts, which concentrate production in two areas: vehicle body parts and low-end decorative accessories. Most of these firms are small, with fewer than 20 employees.

Vehicle Body Parts The vehicle parts produced in Taiwan include sheet metal body parts, electronic parts, engine parts, transmission parts, tires, tire tubes, and wheels, brake parts, steering parts, and such decorative accessories as seat cushions, sun roofs, and wheel covers. Exports of crash parts to the United States, which are significant, have been spurred by demands from insurance companies for low-cost repair parts. Most of the Taiwanese firms that produce major vehicle parts are joint ventures with Japanese investors. In addition, more than 60 such companies have entered into technical cooperation arrangements with overseas manufacturers.

Vehicle Accessories Taiwan's exports of vehicle accessories include decorative items, simple car chemicals, and disposable goods. Approximately 250 small firms are currently producing such items. These firms specialize in a limited line of low-tech parts or components and concentrate on products for the aftersales market. By keeping their operations small and specialized, these firms have been able to adapt easily to market trends and move into new markets with exceptional speed and efficiency. Many are shifting to the manufacture of higher-end items, with an emphasis on R&D of new products and quality control of existing lines.

Competitive Situation

Many of Taiwan's vehicle parts suppliers have shifted to original equipment manufacturer (OEM) production and contract manufacturing for other brand name firms. Taiwan authorities are encouraging local manufacturers to focus on OEM production with a long-term objective of using electronic control devices and flexible manufacturing systems to develop new products for worldwide markets. Local Taiwan production of automobile parts is growing rapidly, stimulated by joint ventures with overseas automobile manufacturers, who are using Taiwan as a center for a parts procurement network.

A significant number of firms are foreign invested, particularly with Japan. The Industrial Development Board has announced plans to offer conditional concessions for Japanese automobile imports into local Taiwan markets in exchange for Japanese assistance in improving production technology for vehicle parts.

To improve marketing channels, some Taiwan vehicle part firms are selling products under their own brand names. They have also begun to diversify into export markets in new areas, such as the Middle East, Africa, Southeast Asia, and Western Europe.

Government Agency

Ministry of Transportation and Communications
2 Changsha St.
Sec. 1, Taipei
Tel: (2) 3112661, 3492900 Fax: (2) 3118587

Trade Associations

Taiwan Automobile Repair Industries Association
3/F., 4-1 Fu Shun St.
Taipei 10453
Tel: (2) 5966965 Fax: (2) 5966965

Taiwan Transportation Vehicle Manufacturers Association
9/F., 390 Fu Hsing S. Rd.
Sec. 1, Taipei
Tel: (2) 7051101 Fax: (2) 7066440

Publication

Taiwan Bicycles & Parts Buyer's Guide
(Annual)
Trade Winds, Inc.
No. 7, Lane 75, Yungkang St.
Taipei
Postal address: PO Box 7-179, Taipei
Tel: (2) 3932718 Fax: (2) 3964022 Tlx: 24177

Trade Fairs

Refer to the "Trade Fairs" chapter for complete listings, including contact information, dates, and venues. Trade fairs with particular relevance to this industry include the following, which are listed in that chapter under the heading given below:

Automobiles & Automotive Parts
- Marlboro Super Bike Show
- Taichung International Auto Show
- Taichung International Auto Machinery
- Taipei International Auto & Motorcycle Parts & Accessories Show

WOODWORKING MACHINERY

Taiwan is one of the world's major supplier of woodworking machinery and turnkey plant packages, ranking third among the exporters of such products in 1991. Approximately 200 Taiwan factories produce a wide variety of woodworking machinery. The United States is Taiwan's largest market, but exports to Southeast Asia are increasing rapidly as some of those countries, particularly Malaysia and Indonesia, restrict their exports of unprocessed woods in an effort to strengthen their own furniture industries.

Most of Taiwan's woodworking machinery is produced on an original equipment manufacturer (OEM) basis. Taiwan producers of woodworking machinery still rely heavily on exhibitions and trading companies for promotion and sale of their products.

Taiwan's woodworking machinery can be classified into two groups: traditional tools and do-it-yourself (DIY) tools. Major exports of traditional machinery include sawing, milling, shaping, and drilling machines; sanders; lathes; and lumber-processing equipment. Two types of DIY tools are available: hand tools and workshop machinery. DIY hand tools include circular saws, jigsaws, drills, planers, routers, and sanders. DIY workshop tools include radial arm saws, table saws, jointers, lathes, planers, and shapers.

Competitive Situation

Taiwan's factories that produce woodworking machinery face growing competition from makers in developing nations. They have also been adversely affected by domestic labor shortages and the appreciation of the NT dollar. To remain competitive, most firms are creating high-end, high-value-added, multipurpose machinery. Such items include edge-banding machines, numerically controlled (NC) trimmers, copy shapers, multisurface planners, and routing, cut-off, and computerized numerically controlled (CNC) copy machines. They have also developed innovative multispindle shapers, double-spindle dowel cutters, multispindle four-sided planers, and surface spray-painting machines. In addition, Taiwan's firms are exporting an increasing number of entire turnkey plants.

Government Run Corporation

Taiwan Machinery Manufacturing Corporation
3 Taichi Rd., Hsiao-kang
Kaohsiung
Tel: (7) 8020111 Fax: (7) 8022129

Trade Associations

Taiwan Plywood Manufacturers & Exporters Association
9/F., 82 Chung Shan N. Rd.
Sec. 1, Taipei 10417
Tel: (2) 5212548, 5212551 Fax: (2) 5626290

Taiwan Wooden Furniture Industrial Association
Rm. 905 100 Chung Hsiao E. Rd.
Sec. 2, Taipei
Tel: (2) 3215791, 3215811 Fax: (2) 3951754

Directories & Publications

Asian Architect And Contractor
(Monthly)
Thompson Press Hong Kong Ltd.
Tai Sang Commercial Building, 19th Fl.
24-34 Hennessy Road
Hong Kong

Building & Construction News
(Weekly)
Al Hilal Publishing (FE) Ltd.
50 Jalan Sultan, #20-06, Jalan Sultan Centre
Singapore 0719
Tel: [65] 2939233 Fax: [65] 2970862

International Construction
(Monthly)
Reed Business Publishing, Ltd.
Reed Asian Publishing Pte
5001 Beach Rd.
#06-12 Golden Mile Complex
Singapore 0719
Tel: [65] 2913188 Fax: [65] 2913180

Southeast Asia Building Magazine
(Monthly)
Safan Publishing Pte.
510 Thomson Rd.
Block A, #08-01 SLF Complex
Singapore 1129
Tel: [65] 2586988 Fax: [65] 2589945

Taiwan Machinery
(Semi-annual)
China Economic News Service
555 Chunghsiao East Road
Section 4, Taipei
Tel: (2) 7681234 Fax: (2) 7632303

Who Makes Machinery in Taiwan
(Annual)
Taiwan Association of Machinery Industry
2/F., 110 Huaining St
Taipei
Tel: (2) 3813722 Fax: (2) 3813711

Trade Fairs

Refer to the "Trade Fairs" chapter for complete listings, including contact information, dates, and venues. Trade fairs with particular relevance to this industry include the following, which are listed in that chapter under the headings given below:

Construction & Housing
- "Home" Show
- Taichung Architecture Show
- Taichung Building Material Show
- Taipei International Construction Show
- Taipei International Hardware, Houseware and Building Materials Show

Machines & Instruments
- Industrial Technology Exhibition
- Taipei International Automation & Precision Machinery Show
- Taipei International Woodworking Machinery Show

For other events listed in the "Trade Fairs" chapter that may be of interest, we recommend that you also consult the headings Furniture & Housewares; Industrial Materials, Chemicals & Metal; and Electronic, Electric & Communications Equipment.

Trade Fairs

Taiwan hosts a wide range of trade fairs and expositions that should interest anyone who seeks to do business in this dynamic and expanding economy. Whether you want to buy Taiwanese goods or exhibit your own goods and services for sale to the Taiwanese market, you will almost undoubtedly find one or more trade fairs to suit your purposes.

The listing of trade fairs in this section is designed to acquaint you with the scope, size, frequency, and length of the events held in Taiwan and to give you contact information for the organizers. While every effort has been made to ensure that this information is correct and complete as of press time, the scheduling of such events is in constant flux. Announced exhibitions can be canceled; dates and venues are often shifted. If you are interested in attending or exhibiting at a show listed here, we urge you to contact the organizer well in advance to confirm the venue and dates and to ascertain whether it is appropriate for you. (*See* Tips for Attending a Trade Fair, following this introduction, for further suggestions on selecting, attending, and exhibiting at trade fairs.) The information in this chapter will give a significant head start to anyone who has considered participating in a trade fair as an exhibitor or attendee.

In order to make access to this information as easy as possible, fairs have been grouped alphabetically by product category and within product category, alphabetically by name. Product categories, with cross references, are given following this introduction in a table of contents. Note that the first heading, *Comprehensive*, is out of alphabetical order. The trade fairs listed under *Comprehensive* do not focus on a single type of product but instead show a broad range of goods that may be from one geographic area or centered around a particular theme. When appropriate, fairs have been listed in more than one category. The breadth of products on display at a given fair means that you may want to investigate categories that are not immediately obvious. Many exhibits include the machinery, tools, and raw materials used to produce the products associated with the central theme of a fair; anyone interested in such items should consider a wide range of the listings.

The list gives the names and dates of both recent and upcoming events, together with site and contact information; for some fairs, the listing also describes the products to be exhibited. Many shows take place on a regular basis. Annual or biennial schedules are common. When we were able to confirm the frequency of a show through independent sources, it has been indicated. Many others on the list may also be regular events. Some are one-time events. Because specifics on frequency are sometimes difficult to come by and because schedules for some 1994 and many 1995 shows were not available at press time, we have given both recent and future dates. It is quite possible that a fair listed for 1993 will be held again in 1994 or 1995, so it would be worthwhile getting in touch with the contact listed for *any* show that looks interesting. Even if we were not able to confirm the frequency, you can infer a likely time cycle if several dates are given for a fair.

As you gather further information on fairs that appeal to you, do not be surprised if the names are slightly different from those listed here. Some large trade fairs include several smaller exhibits, some use short names or acronyms, and Chinese names can be translated in a variety of ways. Dates and venues, of course, are always subject to change.

For further information Most international trade fairs in Taiwan are organized by the China External Trade Development Council (CETRA) and held at the Taipei World Trade Center. For Taipei World Trade Center trade show listings, contact CETRA or the Taipei World Trade Center. (Refer to "Important Addresses" for worldwide addresses of CETRA and its sister organization, Far East Trade Service (FETS)). The World Trade Center Taichung also hosts trade fairs, although they are less publicized and generally smaller. Contact the World Trade Center Taichung directly for listings. A third site in Taiwan

The International Trade Mart

While the number of significant trade fairs in Taiwan is relatively small, the Taipei World Trade Center offers for both importers and exporters an additional means of displaying wares. The International Trade Mart (located in World Trade Center Exhibition Hall, the venue used for the Taipei International Trade Shows) includes the Import Mart and Import Products Display Center and the Export Mart and Export Products Display Center. The Export Mart occupies the second through sixth floors. Its 900 showrooms, divided into 14 categories, are staffed by sales-people looking to do business with foreign buyers. The Import Mart, on the seventh floor, has showrooms and offices for the use of representatives of foreign private companies and public sector organizations. CETRA has multilingual staff on call to aid in negotiations if need be.

The Export and Import Marts have unmanned permanent Product Display Centers on the second and seventh floors. Professed to constitute the largest collection in Asia of sample products displayed under one roof, the center displays are organized around booths; each is one square meter in size. Approximately 800 booths are available in the Import Mart and 1500 in the Export Mart. Individual booths are arranged by product group, and displays remain in place for an 11-1/2 month period running from early January to mid December. CETRA has staff on site to respond to buyers' inquiries and distribute catalogs and business cards. Information collected from prospective buyers is passed along to the displaying companies.

For more information on the International Trade Mart, contact any CETRA or FETS office. (Refer to "Important Addresses" chapter for CETRA and FETS offices.)

---

for trade fairs is the Sungshan Airport Exhibition Hall. Sungshan Airport is a small domestic airport located 8 km (5 miles) north of Taipei. Because most of the exhibitions held there are oriented toward the domestic market, English-language brochures are not prepared, and the shows are relatively unpublicized. Contact the CETRA Design Promotion Center at the Sungshan Airport for listings.

CETRA (Head office)
4-8/F., CETRA Tower
333 Keelung Rd.
Sec. 1, Taipei 10548, Taiwan
Tel: [886] (2) 7255200 Fax: [886] (2) 7576653

Taipei World Trade Center
5 Hsinyi Road
Sec. 5, Taipei, Taiwan
Tel: [886] (2) 7251111 Fax: [886] (2) 7251314

World Trade Center Taichung
60 Tienpao Street
Taichung 40706, Taiwan
Tel: [886] (4) 2542271 Fax: [886] (4) 2542341

CETRA Design Promotion Center
2/F., CETRA Exhibition Hall, Sungshan Airport
340 Tun Hwa N. Rd.
Taipei, Taiwan
Tel: [886] (2) 7151551 Fax: [886] (2) 7168783

Other valuable sources of information include chambers of commerce and other business organizations dedicated to trade between your country and Taiwan. Professional and trade organizations in Taiwan involved in your area of interest may also be worth contacting. (Refer to "Important Addresses" chapter for Taiwanese chambers of commerce and business organizations, and trade organizations.)

While the annual directory *Trade Shows Worldwide* (Gale Research Inc., Detroit, Michigan) is far from comprehensive, it may provide further information on some trade fairs in Taiwan, and it is worth seeking out at your local business library.

TRADE FAIRS
TABLE OF CONTENTS

Tips for Attending a Trade Fair

Overseas trade fairs can be extremely effective for making face-to-face contacts and sales or purchases, identifying suppliers, checking out competitors, and finding out how business really works in the host country. However, the cost of attending such fairs can be high. To maximize the return on your investment of time and money, you should be very clear about your goals for the trip and give yourself plenty of time for advance research and preparation. You should also make sure that you are aware of the limitations of trade fairs. The products on display probably do not represent the full range of goods available on the market. In fact, some of the latest product designs may still be under wraps. And while trade fairs give you an opportunity to make face-to-face contact with many people, both exhibitors and buyers are rushed, which makes meaningful discussions and negotiations difficult. These drawbacks can easily be minimized if you have sufficient preparation and background information. Allow at least three months for preparation—more if you also need to identify the fair that you will attend. Under ideal circumstances, you should begin laying the groundwork nine to 12 months in advance.

Tips for Attending a Trade Fair (cont.)

Selecting an appropriate trade fair

Consult the listings of trade fairs here to find some that interest you. Note the suggestions for finding the most current calendars of upcoming fairs. Once you have identified some fairs, contact their organizers for literature, including show prospectus, attendee list, and exhibitor list. Ask plenty of questions. Do not neglect trade organizations in the host country, independent show-auditing firms, and recent attendees. Find out whether there are "must attend" fairs for your particular product group. Fairs that concentrate on other, but related, commodities might also be a good match. Be aware that there may be preferred seasons for trade in certain products. Your research needs to consider a number of points.

Audience • Who is the intended audience? Is the fair open to the public or only to trade professionals? Are the exhibitors primarily foreigners looking for local buyers or locals looking for foreign buyers? Many trade fairs are heavily weighted to one or the other. Decide whether you are looking for an exposition of general merchandise produced in one region, a commodity-specific trade show, or both.

Statistics • How many people attended the fair the last time it was held? What were the demographics? What volume of business was done? How many exhibitors were there? How big is the exhibition space? What was the ratio of foreign to domestic attendees and exhibitors?

Specifics • Who are the major exhibitors? Are particular publications or organizations associated with the fair? On what categories of products does the fair focus? Are there any special programs, and do they require additional fees? Does the fair have particular themes that change each time? How long has the fair been in existence? How often is it held? Is it always in the same location, or does it move each time? How much does it cost to attend? To rent space?

Before you go

- If you have not already spoken with someone who attended the fair in the past, make sure to seek someone out for advice, tips, and general information.
- Make your reservations and travel arrangements well in advance, and figure out how you are going to get around once you get there. Even if the fair takes place in a large city, do not assume that getting around will be easy during a major trade fair. If the site is a small city or less-developed area, the transportation and accommodation systems are likely to be saturated even sooner than they can be in metropolitan areas.
- Will you need an interpreter for face-to-face business negotiations? A translation service to handle documents? Try to line up providers well in advance of your need for their services.
- Do you need hospitality suites and/or conference rooms? Reserve them as soon as you can.
- Contact people you'd like to meet before you go. Organize your appointments around the fair.
- Familiarize yourself with the show hours, locations (if exhibits and events are staged at several different venues), and schedule of events. Then prioritize.

While you are there

- Wear business like clothes that are comfortable.
- Immediately after each contact, write down as much information as you can. Do not depend on remembering it .

After the fair

- Within a week after the conclusion of the fair, write letters to new contacts and follow up on requests for literature. If you have press releases and questionnaires, send them out quickly as well.
- Write a report evaluating the experience while it is still fresh in your mind. Even if you don't have to prepare a formal report, spend some time organizing your thoughts on paper for future reference and to quantify the results. Did you meet your goals? Why or why not? What would you do differently? What unforeseen costs arose?
- With your new contacts and your experience in mind, start preparing for your next trade fair.

If you are selling _____

- Set specific goals for sales leads, developing product awareness, selling and positioning current customers, and gathering industry information; for example, number of contacts made, orders written, leads converted into sales, visitors at presentations, brochures or samples distributed, customers entertained, seminars attended. You can also set goals for total revenue from sales, cost-to-return benefit ratio, amount of media coverage, and amount of competitor information obtained.

- Review your exhibitor kit, paying particular attention to show hours and regulations, payment policies, shipping instructions and dates, telephone installation, security, fire regulations, union regulations, and extra-cost services. Is there a show theme that you can tie into?

- Gear your advertising and product demonstrations to the audience. Should you stress certain aspects of your product line? Will you need brochures and banners in different languages? Even if you do not need to translate the materials currently in use into another language, do you need to re-write them for a different culture? Consider advertising in publications that will be distributed at the fair.

- Plan the display in your booth carefully; you will have only a few seconds to grab the viewer's attention. Secure a location in a high-traffic area—for example, near a door, restroom, refreshment area, or major exhibitor. Use banner copy that is brief and effective. Focus on the product and its benefits. Place promotional materials and giveaways near the back wall so that people have to enter your area, but make sure that they do not feel trapped. If you plan to use videotapes or other multimedia, make sure that you have enough space. Such presentations are often better suited to hospitality suites, because lights are bright and noise levels high in exhibition halls.

- Do not forget about the details. Order office supplies and printed materials that you will need for the booth. If you ordered a telephone line, bring your own telephone or arrange to rent one. Have all your paperwork—order forms, business cards, exhibitor kit and contract, copies of advance orders and checks, travel documents, and so on—in order and at hand. Draw up a schedule for staffing the booth.

- Plan and rehearse your sales pitch in advance, preferably in a space similar to the size of your booth.

- Do not sit, eat, drink, or smoke while you are in the booth.

- If you plan to return to the next show, reserve space while you're still at the fair.

- Familiarize yourself with import regulations for products that you wish to exhibit at the fair.

If you are buying _____

- Set specific goals for supplier leads and for gathering industry information; for example, number of contacts made, leads converted to purchases, seminars and presentations attended, booths visited. Other goals might be cost-to-return benefit ratio, amount of competitor information gathered, and percentage of projected purchases actually made.

- List all the products that you seek to purchase, their specifications, and the number of units you plan to purchase of each.

- Know the retail and wholesale market prices for the goods in your home country and in the country where you will be buying. List the highest price you can afford to pay for each item and still get a worthwhile return.

- List the established and probable suppliers for each of the products or product lines that you plan to import. Include their addresses and telephone numbers and your source for the information. Contact suppliers before you go to confirm who will attend and to make appointments.

- Familiarize yourself with customs regulations on the products that you seek to purchase and import into your own country or elsewhere. Be sure to include any products that you might be interested in.

Trade Fair	Site	Exhibition Profile	Organizer
COMPREHENSIVE **Trade fairs exhibiting a wide range of goods**			
A Celebration of Excellence: Showcase of Taiwan Products January 12-17, 1993 April 2-6, 1994	Taipei World Trade Center	Highlighting Taiwan products of outstanding quality and design, as well as Taiwan brand names with an international reputation.	CETRA Exhibition Department 4-8 Fls., 333 Keelung Rd. Sec. 1, Taipei 10548 Tel: (2) 7251111 Fax: (2) 7251314
ENEX Taipei Annual (Dates not available)	Taipei	Power generation, transmission and distribution equipment and systems and related devices.	Cahners Exhibitions 2808 Office Tower Convention Plaza, 1 Harbour Rd. Wanchai, Hong Kong Tel: [852] 8240330 Fax: [852] 8240246 Tlx: 62270 CEG HX
Expo Vietnam Last held: July 24-August 1, 1993	Taichung World Trade Center		Trade Winds Inc. Tel: (2) 3932718
AEROSPACE & OCEANIC			
Russia Aerospace Science Fair February 20-April 10, 1994	Taichung World Trade Center		Exhibition Business Dept., WTC Taichung 60 Tienpao Street Taichung 40706 Tel: (4) 2551118 Fax: (4) 2542341
Taipei Aerospace Technology Exhibition Every 2 years August 19-22, 1993 August, 1995	Taipei World Trade Center	Satellites, aerospace components and parts, ground equipment, engines, control and navigation equipment, airport equipment, ground and traffic control, manufacturing equipment and technology, defense equipment and technology.	CETRA Exhibition Department 4-8 Fls., 333 Keelung Rd. Sec. 1, Taipei 10548 Tel: (2) 7251111 Fax: (2) 7251314
World Fishing Exhibition Taipei Every 2 years Last held: August 30-September 3, 1993	Taipei World Trade Center	Shipbuilding, commercial fishing, fishing electronics, deck machinery, navigational aids, radar and loran, sonar and echosounders, marine engines, net-making equipment, ornamental fish and related equipment, seafood and seafood processing, aquaculture.	CETRA Exhibition Department 4-8 Fls., 333 Keelung Rd. Sec. 1, Taipei 10548 Tel: (2) 7251111 Fax: (2) 7251314

AUTOMOBILES & AUTOMOTIVE PARTS

Event	Venue	Description	Contact
Marlboro Super Bike Show Last held: August 14-17, 1993	Taichung World Trade Center		Tait Marketing & Distribution Co. Tel: (2) 4518401
Taichung International Auto Show Last held: December 30, 1993-Jan. 3, 1994	Taichung World Trade Center		Exhibition Business Dept., WTC Taichung 60 Tienpao Street Taichung 40706 Tel: (4) 2551118 Fax: (4) 2542341
Taichung International Auto Machinery February 25-March 1, 1994	Taichung World Trade Center		Exhibition Business Dept., WTC Taichung 60 Tienpao Street Taichung 40706 Tel: (4) 2551118 Fax: (4) 2542341
Taipei International Auto & Motorcycle Parts & Accessories Show Annual May 6-9, 1993 May 17-20, 1994	Taipei World Trade Center	Auto parts, motorcycle parts, accessories.	CETRA Exhibition Department 4-8 Fls., 333 Keelung Rd. Sec. 1, Taipei 10548 Tel: (2) 7251111 Fax: (2) 7251314

COMPUTER & INFORMATION INDUSTRIES
SEE ALSO Electronic, Electric & Communication Equipment

Event	Venue	Description	Contact
Business Computerizing Fair Last held: July 16-20, 1993	Taichung World Trade Center		Taichung Computer Association Tel: (4) 2130243
Information Month - Taichung Show Last held: December 17-22, 1993	Taichung World Trade Center		Feng Chia University Tel: (4) 2525773
Taipei Computer Applications Show Annual August 7-11, 1993 August 13-17, 1994	Taipei World Trade Center	Local market oriented show. Computers, peripherals, system software, factory and office automation software, image processing systems, value added networks, point of sale systems.	CETRA Exhibition Department 4-8 Fls., 333 Keelung Rd. Sec. 1, Taipei 10548 Tel: (2) 7251111 Fax: (2) 7251314
Taipei International Computer Show (COMPUTEX) Annual June 1-5, 1993 June 2-6, 1994	Taipei World Trade Center	Computers, peripherals, software, components, office automation systems, data communications.	CETRA Exhibition Department 4-8 Fls., 333 Keelung Rd. Sec. 1, Taipei 10548 Tel: (2) 7251111 Fax: (2) 7251314

Note: Country codes for telephone and fax numbers are not displayed unless they are *outside* of Taiwan. All country codes have square brackets around them, while city codes have parentheses. The country code for Taiwan is [886].

Trade Fair	Site	Exhibition Profile	Organizer
Taipei International Information Services Show (Dates not available)	Taipei		International Information Service Industry Association 8F, 111 Chung Shan North Road Sec. 2, Taipei Tel. (2) 522-1350 Fax: (2) 511-8234

CONSTRUCTION & HOUSING
SEE ALSO **Furniture & Housewares**

Trade Fair	Site	Exhibition Profile	Organizer
"Home" Show January 27-31, 1994	Taichung World Trade Center		Economic Daily News Tel: (4) 2310122
Taichung Architecture Show Last held: Aug. 25-29, 1993	Taichung World Trade Center		Commercial Times 132 Da Li Street, Taipei Tel: (2) 3818720, 3816208 Fax: (2) 3048138
Taichung Building Material Show Last held: December 25-29, 1993	Taichung World Trade Center		Supperline International Co. Tel: (2) 7588173
Taipei International Construction Show Every 2 years Last held: March 17-21, 1993	Taipei World Trade Center	Building materials, equipment, machinery, vehicles, automation and maintenance systems, fire/security systems, technology transfer packages, consulting services.	CETRA Exhibition Department 4-8 Fls., 333 Keelung Rd. Sec. 1, Taipei 10548 Tel: (2) 7251111 Fax: (2) 7251314
Taipei International Hardware, Houseware and Building Materials Show Last held: 1993 (Dates not available)	Taipei World Trade Center	Hardware, housewares, building materials and related equipment, supplies and services.	CETRA Exhibition Department 4-8 Fls., 333 Keelung Rd. Sec. 1, Taipei 10548 Tel: (2) 7251111 Fax: (2) 7251314

ELECTRONIC, ELECTRIC & COMMUNICATION EQUIPMENT
SEE ALSO **Computer & Information Industries**

Trade Fair	Site	Exhibition Profile	Organizer
International Electronics & Electrical Show (Taipei ELEC) Annual February 20-24, 1993 March 25-29, 1994	Taipei World Trade Center	Electronic parts and components, meters and instruments, electronic manufacturing equipment, electrical machinery and apparatus, consumer electronics, illumination devices, telecommunications, cable television.	CETRA Exhibition Department 4-8 Fls., 333 Keelung Rd. Sec. 1, Taipei 10548 Tel: (2) 7251111 Fax: (2) 7251314

Event	Location	Description	Contact
Taichung Domestic Electronic & Furniture Show Last held: November 6-14, 1993	Taichung World Trade Center		Exhibition Business Dept., WTC Taichung 60 Tienpao Street Taichung 40706 Tel: (4) 2551118 Fax: (4) 2542341
Taipei International Electronics Show Annual October 5-10, 1993 October 6-11, 1994	Taipei World Trade Center	Consumer electronics, meters, instruments, electronic components and parts, communications equipment, computers and peripherals, satellite TV reception products.	CETRA Exhibition Department 4-8 Fls., 333 Keelung Rd. Sec. 1, Taipei 10548 Tel: (2) 7251111 Fax: (2) 7251314
Taipei International Nepcon-Semiconductor Exhibition (INTERNEPCON -SEMI Taipei) Every 2 years Last held: November 23-26, 1993	Taipei World Trade Center	Components, equipment and systems for PCB, semiconductor and microelectronics design, production, processing testing and packaging with concurrent industry conference.	CETRA Exhibition Department 4-8 Fls., 333 Keelung Rd. Sec. 1, Taipei 10548 Tel: (2) 7251111 Fax: (2) 7251314
Taipei International Telecommunications Show (TAIPEI TELECOM) Every 2 years September 27-30, 1994	Taipei World Trade Center	Antenna systems, data communications, data processing equipment, ISDN, networks, power suppliers, mobile communications, public telephones, satellite communications, security equipment, submarine cables, telephones, test and measurement equipment, transmission.	CETRA Exhibition Department 4-8 Fls., 333 Keelung Rd. Sec. 1, Taipei 10548 Tel: (2) 7251111 Fax: (2) 7251314

ENVIRONMENTAL INDUSTRIES

Event	Location	Description	Contact
International Environment Control and Protection Technology Exhibition (ENPROTECH) Every 2 years Last held: February 6-9, 1993	Taipei World Trade Center	Environmental control and protection equipment, supplies and services.	ENPROTECH Postbus 10 NL-2501 The Hague Netherlands Tel: [31] (70) 3441521 Fax: [31] (70) 3853531 Tlx: 32306
Taichung International Energy Use Saving & Environmental Control Protection Technology Show Last held: October 15-19, 1993	Taichung World Trade Center		Exhibition Business Dept., WTC Taichung 60 Tienpao Street Taichung 40706 Tel: (4) 2551118 Fax: (4) 2542341

Note: Country codes for telephone and fax numbers are not displayed unless they are *outside* of Taiwan. All country codes have square brackets around them, while city codes have parentheses. The country code for Taiwan is [886].

Trade Fair	Site	Exhibition Profile	Organizer
FOOD, BEVERAGES & FOOD PROCESSING			
Food Industry & Packing Exhibition March 18-22, 1994	Taichung World Trade Center		Taiwan Packing Industry Magazine Tel: (2) 8315385
Taichung International Food Industry Fair Last held: September 3-7, 1993	Taichung World Trade Center		Taichung Visitors Association Tel: (2) 7641007
Taipei International Food Industry Show Every 2 years June 22-26, 1994	Taipei World Trade Center	Vegetables and fruits, cereals, meat products, candies and biscuits, dairy products, health products, beverages, wines and liquors, condiments, refrigeration equipment, frozen foods, hotel catering equipment, food preparation equipment, food packaging equipment and machinery, food processing machinery, vending machines.	CETRA Exhibition Department 4-8 Fls., 333 Keelung Rd. Sec. 1, Taipei 10548 Tel: (2) 7251111 Fax: (2) 7251314
FURNITURE & HOUSEWARES *SEE ALSO* **Construction & Housing**			
Taichung Domestic Electronic & Furniture Show Last held: November 6-14, 1993	Taichung World Trade Center		Exhibition Business Dept., WTC Taichung 60 Tienpao Street Taichung 40706 Tel: (4) 2551118 Fax: (4) 2542341
Taipei International Furniture Show Annual March 9-12, 1993 March 9-12, 1994	Taipei World Trade Center	Indoor, outdoor and office furniture. Furniture parts and accessories, home decorations.	CETRA Exhibition Department 4-8 Fls., 333 Keelung Rd. Sec. 1, Taipei 10548 Tel: (2) 7251111 Fax: (2) 7251314
Taipei International Hardware, Houseware and Building Materials Show Last held: 1993 (Dates not available)	Taipei World Trade Center	Hardware, housewares, building materials and related equipment, supplies and services.	CETRA Exhibition Department 4-8 Fls., 333 Keelung Rd. Sec. 1, Taipei 10548 Tel: (2) 7251111 Fax: (2) 7251314
GIFTS, JEWELRY & STATIONERY **Includes art, timepieces**			
Art Fair Taiwan Last held: October 23-November 1, 1993	Taichung World Trade Center		Exhibition Business Dept., WTC Taichung 60 Tienpao Street Taichung 40706 Tel: (4) 2551118 Fax: (4) 2542341

Art Galleries Fair R.O.C. Last held: October 7-11, 1993	Taichung World Trade Center		Art Galleries Association R.O.C. Tel: (2) 3256575
Taipei International Gift & Stationery Show Twice a year (Spring & Autumn) March 1-4, 1993; November 4-7, 1993 April 27-30, 1994; November 4-7, 1994	Taipei World Trade Center	Seasonal gifts. Souvenir, premium, incentive items. Glassware, ceramics, electronic novelties, housewares, handicrafts, school and office supplies.	CETRA Exhibition Department 4-8 Fls., 333 Keelung Rd. Sec. 1, Taipei 10548 Tel: (2) 7251111 Fax: (2) 7251314
Taipei International Jewelry & Timepiece Show Annual September 17-20, 1993 September 8-11, 1994	Taipei World Trade Center	Costume jewelry, semi-precious stones, fine jewelry, watches, clocks, components, parts, manufacturing equipment.	CETRA Exhibition Department 4-8 Fls., 333 Keelung Rd. Sec. 1, Taipei 10548 Tel: (2) 7251111 Fax: (2) 7251314

HOBBIES & RECREATION
Includes flower shows, sporting goods, toys

Asian Floral Design Exhibition & Greater Flower Designing Competition of R.O.C. Last held: September 26-30, 1993	Taichung World Trade Center		Tai Chan International Enterprise Co. Tel: (2) 5883099
Taipei International Cycle Show Annual April 28-May 1, 1993 April 11-14, 1994	Taipei World Trade Center	Complete bicycles, bicycle parts and accessories.	CETRA Exhibition Department 4-8 Fls., 333 Keelung Rd. Sec. 1, Taipei 10548 Tel: (2) 7251111 Fax: (2) 7251314
Taipei International Flower Show Every 2 years Last held: April 10-14, 1993	Taipei World Trade Center	Cut flowers, potted plants, bonsai, floral design/supplies, seeds, bulbs, cuttings, plugs, seedlings, saplings, garden tools, greenhouse technology, landscaping materials, artificial flowers and plants, dried flowers.	CETRA Exhibition Department 4-8 Fls., 333 Keelung Rd. Sec. 1, Taipei 10548 Tel: (2) 7251111 Fax: (2) 7251314
Taipei International Sporting Goods Show Annual April 20-23, 1993 April 19-22, 1994	Taipei World Trade Center	Equipment for ball games, water sports, martial arts, skiing, skating, camping, fishing, indoor games. Also golf equipment, exercise equipment, billiards, tennis and badminton rackets, sports bags, covers, garments, shoes.	CETRA Exhibition Department 4-8 Fls., 333 Keelung Rd. Sec. 1, Taipei 10548 Tel: (2) 7251111 Fax: (2) 7251314
Taipei International Toy Show Annual September 26-29, 1993 October 27-30, 1994	Taipei World Trade Center	Toys, games, hobbies, amusements, Christmas items.	CETRA Exhibition Department 4-8 Fls., 333 Keelung Rd. Sec. 1, Taipei 10548 Tel: (2) 7251111 Fax: (2) 7251314

Note: Country codes for telephone and fax numbers are not displayed unless they are *outside* of Taiwan. All country codes have square brackets around them, while city codes have parentheses. The country code for Taiwan is [886].

Trade Fair	Site	Exhibition Profile	Organizer
Taiwan Amusement Exhibition September 17-21, 1993 March 4-13, 1994	Taichung World Trade Center		Creative International Public Relations Consultants Tel: (2) 3215101
World Fishing Exhibition Taipei Every 2 years Last held: August 30-September 3, 1993	Taipei World Trade Center	Shipbuilding, commercial fishing, fishing electronics, deck machinery, navigational aids, radar and loran, sonar and echosounders, marine engines, net-making equipment, ornamental fish and related equipment, seafood and seafood processing, aquaculture.	CETRA Exhibition Department 4-8 Fls., 333 Keelung Rd. Sec. 1, Taipei 10548 Tel: (2) 7251111 Fax: (2) 7251314
World of Women Beauty Wares Show January 17-21, 1994	Taichung World Trade Center		Lo Tin Co., Ltd. Tel: (4) 2551833

INDUSTRIAL MATERIALS, CHEMICALS & METAL

Trade Fair	Site	Exhibition Profile	Organizer
Taichung International Metal Casing, Forging, Welding & Treating Show Last held: October 15-19, 1993	Taichung World Trade Center		Exhibition Business Dept., WTC Taichung 60 Tienpao Street Taichung 40706 Tel: (4) 2551118 Fax: (4) 2542341
Taipei International Chemical Industry Show (Taipei CHEM) Dates not available	Taipei World Trade Center	Equipment, supplies and services for the chemical industry.	
Taipei International Plastics & Rubber Industry Show (Taipei PLAS) Every 2 years Last held: October 25-29, 1993	Taipei World Trade Center	Raw materials, molds, machinery, engineering components, semifinished and finished products, auxiliaries, equipment.	CETRA Exhibition Department 4-8 Fls., 333 Keelung Rd. Sec. 1, Taipei 10548 Tel: (2) 7251111 Fax: (2) 7251314
Taipei International Woodworking Machinery Show Every 2 years Last held: October 15-19, 1993	Taipei World Trade Center	General machinery for plywood working, rattan processing, bamboo processing. DIY machinery, raw materials, parts, accessories.	CETRA Exhibition Department 4-8 Fls., 333 Keelung Rd. Sec. 1, Taipei 10548 Tel: (2) 7251111 Fax: (2) 7251314

INVESTMENT

Trade Fair	Site	Exhibition Profile	Organizer
Taipei International Fair (TIF) Every 2 years October 18-23, 1994	Taipei World Trade Center	Showcasing countries which intend to develop trade, investment and economic partnerships with one another. Group registration only.	CETRA Exhibition Department 4-8 Fls., 333 Keelung Rd. Sec. 1, Taipei 10548 Tel: (2) 7251111 Fax: (2) 7251314

MACHINES & INSTRUMENTS
Includes tools
SEE ALSO other categories which may include exhibitions with machines and tools specific to those industries

Event	Venue	Description	Contact
Industrial Technology Exhibition Last held: September 11-13, 1993	Taichung World Trade Center		Ministry of Economic Affairs 15 Fu Chou Street Taipei Tel: (2) 5422540, 5422105 Fax: (2) 3919398
Taipei International Automation & Precision Machinery Show Every 2 years May 7-11, 1994	Taipei World Trade Center	Metal working machinery, CNC machine tools and industrial machinery (for textiles, plastic processing, woodworking, shoe making, electronic processing, packaging, and material handling). Automation machinery and FMC/FMS, control units, computer systems, software and CAD/CAM, automatic machinery parts, components and auxiliary equipment, inspection, measuring and testing equipment, service.	CETRA Exhibition Department 4-8 Fls., 333 Keelung Rd. Sec. 1, Taipei 10548 Tel: (2) 7251111 Fax: (2) 7251314
Taipei International Food Industry Show Every 2 years June 22-26, 1994	Taipei World Trade Center	Vegetables and fruits, cereals, meat products, candies and biscuits, dairy products, health products, beverages, wines and liquors, condiments, refrigeration equipment, frozen foods, hotel catering equipment, food preparation equipment, food packaging equipment and machinery, food processing machinery, vending machines.	CETRA Exhibition Department 4-8 Fls., 333 Keelung Rd. Sec. 1, Taipei 10548 Tel: (2) 7251111 Fax: (2) 7251314
Taipei International Jewelry & Timepiece Show Annual September 17-20, 1993 September 8-11, 1994	Taipei World Trade Center	Costume jewelry, semi-precious stones, fine jewelry, watches, clocks, components, parts, manufacturing equipment.	CETRA Exhibition Department 4-8 Fls., 333 Keelung Rd. Sec. 1, Taipei 10548 Tel: (2) 7251111 Fax: (2) 7251314
Taipei International Machine Tool Show (TIMTOS) Every 2 years Last held: March 27-April 1, 1993	Taipei World Trade Center	Metal cutting machine tools, metal forming machine tools, cutting tools and measuring equipment, machine tool accessories, machine tool parts and other related items.	CETRA Exhibition Department 4-8 Fls., 333 Keelung Rd. Sec. 1, Taipei 10548 Tel: (2) 7251111 Fax: (2) 7251314

Note: Country codes for telephone and fax numbers are not displayed unless they are outside of Taiwan. All country codes have square brackets around them, while city codes have parentheses. The country code for Taiwan is [886].

Trade Fair	Site	Exhibition Profile	Organizer
Taipei International Textile Machinery Show November 19-23, 1994	Taipei World Trade Center	Textile, fiber and yarn preparing machines, weaving machines, knitting machines, dyeing and finishing machines.	CETRA Exhibition Department 4-8 Fls., 333 Keelung Rd. Sec. 1, Taipei 10548 Tel: (2) 7251111 Fax: (2) 7251314
Taipei International Woodworking Machinery Show Every 2 years Last held: October 15-19, 1993	Taipei World Trade Center	General machinery for plywood working, rattan processing, bamboo processing. DIY machinery, raw materials, parts, accessories.	CETRA Exhibition Department 4-8 Fls., 333 Keelung Rd. Sec. 1, Taipei 10548 Tel: (2) 7251111 Fax: (2) 7251314
Taiwan Precision Machinery Fair Last held: August 5-9, 1993	Taichung World Trade Center		Chan Chao International Co. Tel: (2) 5230130

MEDICINE & PHARMACEUTICALS

Trade Fair	Site	Exhibition Profile	Organizer
Taipei International Medical Equipment & Pharmaceuticals Show Annual November 12-14, 1993 November 11-13, 1994	Taipei World Trade Center	Medical materials and instruments, hospital supplies, pharmaceuticals, computer systems, publications, biotech products, educational items, diagnostics.	CETRA Exhibition Department 4-8 Fls., 333 Keelung Rd. Sec. 1, Taipei 10548 Tel: (2) 7251111 Fax: (2) 7251314
Taiwan International Medical Equipment & Pharmaceuticals Show May 7-11, 1994	Taichung World Trade Center		Exhibition Business Dept., WTC Taichung 60 Tienpao Street Taichung 40706 Tel: (4) 2551118 Fax: (4) 2542341

PACKAGING, PRINTING & GRAPHIC DESIGN
SEE ALSO Computer & Information Industries

Trade Fair	Site	Exhibition Profile	Organizer
Food Industry & Packing Exhibition March 18-22, 1994	Taichung World Trade Center		Taiwan Packing Industry Magazine Tel: (2) 8315385
Taipei International Design Exhibition (TIDEX) Every 2 years Last held: May 23-26, 1993	Taipei World Trade Center	Products/packaging/graphic design from Taiwan and abroad, corporate identity systems, design companies, displays from emerging young designers.	CETRA Exhibition Department 4-8 Fls., 333 Keelung Rd. Sec. 1, Taipei 10548 Tel: (2) 7251111 Fax: (2) 7251314
Taipei International Nepcon-Semiconductor Exhibition (INTERNEPCON-SEMI Taipei) Every 2 years Last held: November 23-26, 1993	Taipei World Trade Center	Components, equipment and systems for PCB, semiconductor and microelectronics design, production, processing testing and packaging with concurrent industry conference.	CETRA Exhibition Department 4-8 Fls., 333 Keelung Rd. Sec. 1, Taipei 10548 Tel: (2) 7251111 Fax: (2) 7251314

Taipei International Packaging Machinery & Materials Show (Taipei PACK) Every 2 years Last held: September 9-13, 1993	Taipei World Trade Center	Packaging machinery and materials, converting machinery, printing machinery, physical distribution, materials handling and warehouse equipment.	CETRA Exhibition Department 4-8 Fls., 333 Keelung Rd. Sec. 1, Taipei 10548 Tel: (2) 7251111 Fax: (2) 7251314

TEXTILES & APPAREL

Beowulf Shoes Exhibition January 27-31, 1994	Taichung World Trade Center		Beowulf Exhibition Design Co. Tel: (4) 7367036
Taipei International Leather Goods Show Annual April 20-23, 1993 April 19-22, 1994	Taipei World Trade Center	Travelware, handbags, garments, small leather items, materials, accessories.	CETRA Exhibition Department 4-8 Fls., 333 Keelung Rd. Sec. 1, Taipei 10548 Tel: (2) 7251111 Fax: (2) 7251314
Taipei International Textile Machinery Show November 19-23, 1994	Taipei World Trade Center	Textile, fiber and yarn preparing machines, weaving machines, knitting machines, dyeing and finishing machines.	CETRA Exhibition Department 4-8 Fls., 333 Keelung Rd. Sec. 1, Taipei 10548 Tel: (2) 7251111 Fax: (2) 7251314

Note: Country codes for telephone and fax numbers are not displayed unless they are *outside* of Taiwan.
All country codes have square brackets around them, while city codes have parentheses. The country code for Taiwan is [886].

Business Travel

Taiwan is smaller than China and not as rough, bigger than Hong Kong and not as rich or modern, more fun than Singapore and less predictable. If you're going to travel and do business in Asia, Taiwan is a good place to start. Especially to the traveler of European descent, it is foreign enough to amaze, please, excite, shock, frustrate, and disillusion, but Western enough to ease the rigors of it all. Business is work, after all, even when it's fun, and traveling in a very foreign land while you're trying to master a whole new style of business can make your work all the more challenging.

Taiwan's Confucian culture is very alien to Western minds. Its people may seem rude and abrupt on the impersonal level and overly polite, formal and humble in your personal dealings with them. But Taiwan also has state-of-the-art telecommunications, first-class hotels replete with amenities ranging from saunas to business centers, advanced medical technology, good roads, and efficient if sometimes hair-raising transportation systems—and peaceful mountain resorts when it all gets to be a bit too much.

NATIONAL TRAVEL OFFICES WORLDWIDE

The Taiwan Visitors Association provides information on what to see and where to go as well as referrals to government agencies and trade offices. The Taiwan Visitors Association has offices worldwide, a few of which are listed below. In Taipei, you can contact:

Ministry of Communications, Tourism Bureau
280 Chunghsiao Road
Sec. 4, Taipei, Taiwan
Tel: (2) 7218541 Fax: (2) 7735487 Tlx: 26408

North America

Chicago 333 North Michigan Avenue, Suite 2329, Chicago, IL 60601; Tel: (312) 346-1037/8 Fax: (312) 346-1037. (Canadian residents of Saskatchewan, Manitoba and western Ontario can contact this office.)

New York 1 World Trade Center, Suite 7953, New York, NY 10048; Tel: (212) 466-0691 Fax: (212) 432-6436. (Canadian residents of eastern Ontario, Quebec and the Maritimes can contact this office.)

San Francisco 166 Geary Street, Suite 1605, San Francisco, CA 94108; Tel: (415) 989-8677 Fax: (415) 989-7242. (Canadian residents of Alberta and British Columbia and Mexican residents can contact this office.)

Asia

Seoul Marine Center Building, 118 Namdaemoon Road, 2-ka, Chong-ku, Room 1901, Seoul, Rep. of Korea; Tel: (2) 721-8541 Fax: (2) 775-4729.

Singapore 14-07, UIC Building, 5 Shenton Way, Singapore 0106; Tel: 223-6546/7 Fax: (2) 225-4616.

Tokyo Imperial Hotel, Uchisaiwai-cho 1-1-1, Chiyoda-ku, Tokyo 100, Japan; Tel: (3) 3501-3591/2 Fax: (3) 3501-3586.

Australia

Sydney MLC Building, Suite 1904, Sydney, NSW 2000; Tel: (2) 231-6942, 231-6973 Fax: (2) 233-7752.

Europe

Frankfurt Dreieichstr. 59, 6000 Frankfurt/Main 70, Germany; Tel: (69) 610743 Fax: (69) 624518 Tlx: 414460.

VISA AND PASSPORT REQUIREMENTS

As of January 1994, citizens of 12 countries (the US, Canada, the UK, France, Germany, the Netherlands, Belgium, Austria, Luxembourg, Australia, New Zealand, and Japan) are permitted to enter Taiwan for visits of five days or less without a visa, provided they hold a round-trip ticket. A valid visa is an absolute necessity for all other travelers to Taiwan. Without a visa, you won't even be able to get on the plane. Since few countries have diplomatic relations with

Taiwan, you'll probably have to go through Taiwan's "quasi-embassies" in whatever country you happen to be in at the time. (Refer to the CETRA, FETS & Ministry of Economic Affairs Representative Offices Overseas section in "Important Addresses" for a listing of Taiwan's appropriate offices worldwide.)

To obtain a visa, you'll need your passport and three passport photos, and an onward plane ticket. You'll receive the visa in a day. The typical 60-day visitor visa is good for tourism, business, training, study, and several other purposes. You can extend it twice for 60 days each time. If you want to stay longer than six months—for business, employment, study, research, investment, or other purposes— you'll need a resident visa. Whatever you do, don't overstay your visa: the punishment is endless explaining and paperwork, plus a fine depending on how long you overstayed, how well you explain and fill out forms, and the mood of the Foreign Affairs Police that day.

IMMUNIZATION

Required Cholera if arriving from an infected area (South America); yellow fever if arriving from an infected area (tropical Africa or South America).

Strongly advised Hepatitis B (as many as 20 percent of Taiwan's people are carriers); gamma globulin for hepatitis A (endemic); tetanus booster.

Recommended Flu vaccination (most flus begin in this region of the world).

CLIMATE

When you pack for your trip to Taiwan, don't forget a good raincoat—one that goes with the "dress-for-success" business suit that the Taiwanese will expect you to wear. Taiwan's climate is sub-tropical in the island's northern half and tropical in the southern, giving the island only two seasons—a warm summer and a cool winter—both of them wet. Taipei's winter temperatures range from 12°C to 19°C (54°F to 66°F), with occasional dips to freezing, and in the summer from 25°C to 34°C (76°F to 92°F). Kaohsiung's temperatures are slightly milder in the winter and just as warm in the summer.

The rain is not only plentiful—221 cm (83 inches) annually in Taipei—but dirty: The major cities are heavily polluted, and the rain spatters particulates all over your formal businesswear. Summer brings occasional typhoons, the western Pacific's version of hurricanes. You'll find the best weather in October and November.

BUSINESS ATTIRE

Except for formal situations, Taiwanese business people don't put a lot of emphasis on dress, which sets them apart from other East Asians who share their Confucian heritage. They will expect you to wear a business suit appropriate to your status, a suit conservatively cut and of darker hues (which help hide the sooty spatter of raindrops!). But they won't mind at all if you strip down to your tie and short-sleeve dress shirt when you're working in the summer heat and humidity. Factory managers and workers alike often wear short-sleeve pullover company shirts with the company logo.

While you'll need tropical-weight attire during the summer, you'll need heavier-weight clothing to get through the winter. Many buildings don't have central heating, so you may find you have to dress warmly indoors as well as outdoors.

Businesswomen are expected to dress somewhat more formally than men, and certainly should avoid exposing too much skin.

Raincoats and umbrellas are a necessity year-round. Worn in moderation, fine gold jewelry and accessories are a good way to display your status without overdressing. Don't even pack black clothes unless you plan on attending funerals or making the Taiwanese think about death. (Refer to "Business Culture" chapter.)

AIRLINES

Taipei Taiwan's capital, major trade and financial center and largest city is served by, among others, Air New Zealand, British Airways, Canadian Airlines International, Cathay Pacific, China Airlines, Continental, Delta, Far Eastern Air, Great China Airlines, Japan Asia, KLM, Korean Air, Lufthansa, Northwest, Philippine Airlines, Singapore Airlines, South African Airways, Taiwan Airlines, Thai Airways, and United.

Kaohsiung Most visitors fly into Taipei, but the business traveler may want to consider entering Taiwan through the nation's second-largest city, Kaohsiung, a large industrial and shipping center on the southwest coast, especially if their business contacts are in that part of the island. Arrival and departure flights are few compared to Taipei, but the airport is well served internationally and domestically by, among others, Cathay Pacific, China Airlines, Far Eastern Air, Japan Asia, Malaysia Airlines, Taiwan Airlines, Thai Airways, and Transasia Airways.

AIR TRAVEL TIME TO TAIPEI

Here is a small sampling of the airlines and flights available from cities around the world to Taipei. In airline-speak, "direct" means that you have to stop over in another city along the way but you don't have to change planes. The direct flight times given here include time on the ground in the stopover cities.

- From Auckland nonstop on Air New Zealand: 11 hours, 30 min.
- From Bangkok nonstop on Thai Airways: 3 hours, 30 min.
- From Beijing am nonstop on Air China or Dragonair to Hong Kong, pm nonstop on China Airlines: 5 hours, 30 min., including 1-hour layover in Hong Kong
- From Frankfurt direct on Lufthansa via Bangkok: 15 hours
- From Hong Kong nonstop on British Airways: 1 hour, 30 min.
- From Jakarta nonstop on Garuda Indonesia: 5 hours
- From Kuala Lumpur nonstop on Malaysian Airlines: 4 hours, 15 min.
- From London direct on British Airways via Hong Kong: 16 hours
- From Manila nonstop on Philippine Airlines: 1 hour, 50 min.
- From New York City direct on United via San Francisco: 21 hours
- From San Francisco nonstop on United: 13 hours
- From Seoul nonstop on Korean Airlines: 2 hours
- From Singapore nonstop on Singapore Airlines: 4 hours
- From Sydney nonstop on Air New Zealand: 9 hours, 20 min.
- From Tokyo nonstop on Japan Airlines: 3 hours, 25 min.

TIME CHANGES

Auckland	+4
Bangkok	-1
Beijing	0
Frankfurt	-7
Hong Kong	0
Jakarta	-1
Kuala Lumpur	0
London	-8
Manila	0
New York City	-13
San Francisco	-16
Seoul	+1
Sydney	+2
Tokyo	+1

TIME CHANGES

Taiwan shares its time zone—8 hours ahead of Greenwich Mean Time—with China, the Philippines, Malaysia, Singapore, central Indonesia, and the state of Western Australia. When you're in Taiwan, you can determine the time in any of the cities listed in the table on this page by adding to or subtracting from Taiwan time the numbers shown.

CUSTOMS ENTRY (PERSONAL)

Taiwan allows foreigners to bring in most personal items undeclared and duty-free. You can also bring in up to NT$12,000 (about US$450) in professional samples duty-free, but be aware that (as of fall 1993) Taiwan does not honor the ATA carnet system for temporary duty-free imports. Certain items—electric appliances, cameras, tape recorders, computers, and similar items—must be declared and are subject to duties if you can't prove that they're for your own personal use. If you bring such items into Taiwan, make sure that they look used, aren't in their original boxes, and preferably have a sales receipt showing that you bought them a long time ago.

Cash You can bring any amount of foreign cash into the country, but you must declare it. If it's more than US$5,000 or the equivalent in any foreign currency—and you haven't spent it all by the time you leave—you may take it out of the country only if you declared it and received a customs certificate when you arrived. Otherwise, when you leave, customs can confiscate the amount in excess of US$5,000. These rules apply only to cash: there's no restriction on traveler's checks, personal checks or bank orders.

Other You can bring in one bottle (1,000 cc or less) of an alcoholic beverage, or 10 sample bottles (100 cc each or less); 25 cigars, 200 cigarettes or 500 grams (about 1 pound) of tobacco; and up to 62.5 grams (about 2 ounces) of gold in any form, including jewelry and art. Taiwan will charge you duties on any more than that, and you'll also have to store it with customs until you leave the country.

Prohibited You cannot bring in: anything made or originating in mainland China—it will have to be stored with customs; arms and ammunition; toy guns or gun-shaped appliances; pro-Communist publications; narcotics and other illegal drugs; pornography or indecent literature (including Playboy magazine); or gambling items.

Traveling in some foreign countries may have left you doubting the honesty of customs officials. You don't have to worry about Taiwan: its customs officers have a reputation for scrupulous honesty and fairness. (For information about commercial imports, please refer to "Import Policy & Procedures" chapter.)

FOREIGN EXCHANGE

The New Taiwan dollar (NT$) is comprised of 100 cents; coins come in denominations of NT$0.5, NT$1, NT$5, and NT$10, while notes come in denominations of NT$50, NT$100, NT$500, and NT$1,000. At the end of 1993 the US dollar was worth NT$26.65. Because the Taiwan dollar is a controlled currency and not freely traded, it's not easily convertible outside Taiwan except in Hong Kong, nor do Taiwan hotels and businesses accept foreign currencies. This means you must convert your currency into Taiwan dollars when you arrive, and reconvert when you leave.

The first place to change money is at either of the two international airports, Taipei and Kaohsiung. Elsewhere, the best place to convert and reconvert currency is the International Commercial Bank of China, which has branches everywhere and takes any kind of traveler's check. Most banks readily exchange US cash dollars. You can also change money at hotels (for a premium, and traveler's checks only if you're a guest) and at the Bank of Taiwan, Changhua Commercial Bank, First Commercial Bank and Hua Nan Commercial Bank; foreign-owned banks change only their own traveler's checks. You may not be able to cash traveler's checks in small towns or rural areas, so change them before you leave the cities. (Refer to "Important Addresses" chapter for addresses of listed banks in Taipei.)

Taiwan tightly controls its currency. Be sure to keep your receipts so you can reconvert your excess Taiwan dollars when you leave, which you can do at any bank when you present your passport. If the amount you wish to reconvert is small, you may be able to do it without a receipt. Banks give very good money-changing rates, so you should shun black-market money-changers.

Large hotels, restaurants and stores honor most major credit cards.

TIPPING

Tipping isn't yet the norm in Taiwan unless you're granted extra service—delivery of a message to your hotel room, for example, or the taxi driver helping with your luggage (NT$10 or so is appropriate). While service workers in Taiwan aren't always standing about with their palms outstretched, it's customary to leave the taxi driver the small change from the fare, while porters and hotel bellhops should be tipped from as little as NT$10 per bag in a budget hotel to NT$50 in a top-end hotel. Hotels and restaurants typically add 10 percent service charges to your bills, but still it's common practice to leave the small change when you pay. Chinese New Year, however, can be more expensive; if you can even find a needed service worker—taxi driver, hairdresser, barber—expect to pay double the usual fee.

ACCESS TO CITY FROM AIRPORT

Taipei Chiang Kai Shek Airport is in Taoyuan, about 40 km (25 miles) west of the city. Buses run every 15 to 20 minutes to city center. The first-class Chunghsing Line costs NT$72 (about US$2.75), while the Express Bus Line costs NT$34 (about US$1.25). Take the first-class line: it's less crowded, has bigger luggage racks and is just as fast as the Express—about an hour. From city center, you can take a taxi to your hotel.

Hundreds of taxis will be at the airport to greet you, so many that the supply-and-demand theory of capitalism is turned on its head. Taiwanese taxis are metered, but rides from the airport to Taipei include a 50 percent surcharge on the meter fare because there's too much competition; the drivers have to wait an hour or more to get a fare and so make up for the lost time by charging more. You can expect to pay NT$1,000 (about US$37.50) for your ride. The ride to the airport, however, is the meter fare—usually about NT$650 (about US$24.50)—plus a NT$5 surcharge. If you have any problem with an airport taxi driver, report it to the airport police (Tel: (3) 3982242).

Your hotel may provide a limousine or shuttle service for airport transfers if you make these arrangements ahead of time by telephone, fax or letter. Someone will be there to greet you outside customs, holding up a sign imprinted with your name. This service will cost about NT$1,000.

Kaohsiung The airport is 11 km (7 miles) southeast of the city, and you can take a taxi or bus to your hotel. The airport taxi fare is usually a flat fee of at least NT$200 (about US$7.50), but you can get a metered taxi just outside the airport, and the fare is likely to be lower. The bus runs every half-hour to the city center for about NT$10.

ACCOMMODATIONS

Taiwanese place great emphasis on face, so stay in the best hotel that you can afford. That may present a problem because Taiwan hotels are generally expensive. Most hotels have bars, restaurants, meeting rooms, air conditioning, telephones, and TV, while many have health clubs, conference facilities, and shops. The Taiwan Visitors Association publishes an excellent list, Taiwan Hotel and Restaurant Guide, which is available at the Taipei airport.

Taipei—Top-end

Grand Hotel 1 Chung Shan Road North, Section 4; isolated site in northern Taipei on Keelung River overlooking city. Distinctive architecture and atmosphere, excellent view, conference facilities, bowling alley. Rates: NT$3,800 to NT$5,000; Tel: (2) 5965565 Fax: (2) 5948243 Tlx: 11646.

Taiwan

Republic of China

- ✪ National Capital
- ◉ County Capital
- ● City
- Primary Road
- Railroad
- Regional Boundary
- International Border

0   25   50 km
0   25 mi

Vuchiu Hsu

Formosa Strait

Taipei Chuan-Shih

Tanshui

Chilung Shih

Chilung

Taoyuan

Yangmingshan

Taoyuan

Tao-shui Ho

✪ Taipei

Panchiao

Taipei

Ilan

Hsinchu Shih

Hsinchu

Cho-shui Hsi

Suao

Hsinchu

Ilan

Miaoli

Miaoli

Cho-shui Hsi

Taichung Shih

Fengyuan

Taichung

Taichung

Changhua

Hualien

Chunghsinghsintsun

Nantou

Penghu

Changhua

Nantou

Fenglin

Yunlin

Touliu

Penghu Shuitao

Makung

Pescadore Islands

Chiayi

Chiayi

Chiayi Shih

Hsinying

Hualien

Tainan

Kuanshan

Pacific

Ocean

Tainan Shin

Tainan

Kaohsiung

Taitung

Pingtung

Pingtung

Taitung

Kaohsiung Chuan-Shih

Kaohsiung

Fengshan

Lu Tao

Fangliao

Liuchlu Yu

Lu Yu

Hengchun

120°   122°

Kaohsiung

1 Railway Station	**10** Post Office	**19** City Government Building
2 Bus Station	**11** President Department Store	**20** Literary/Martial Temple
3 Royal Hotel	**12** Central Park	**21** City Council and Police Bureau
4 Union Hotel	**13** American Institute	**22** Ambassador Hotel
5 Taiwan Hotel	**14** Export Processing Zone	**23** Holiday Inn
6 Prince Hotel	**15** Far Eastern Department Store	**24** Chenghuang Temple
7 Sanhua Hotel	**16** Hsi Tuu Bay Beach	**25** Sanfeng Temple
8 El Sol Plaza Hotel	**17** Chung Shan National University	**26** Kingdom Hotel
9 Empire Hotel	**18** Martyr's Shrine	

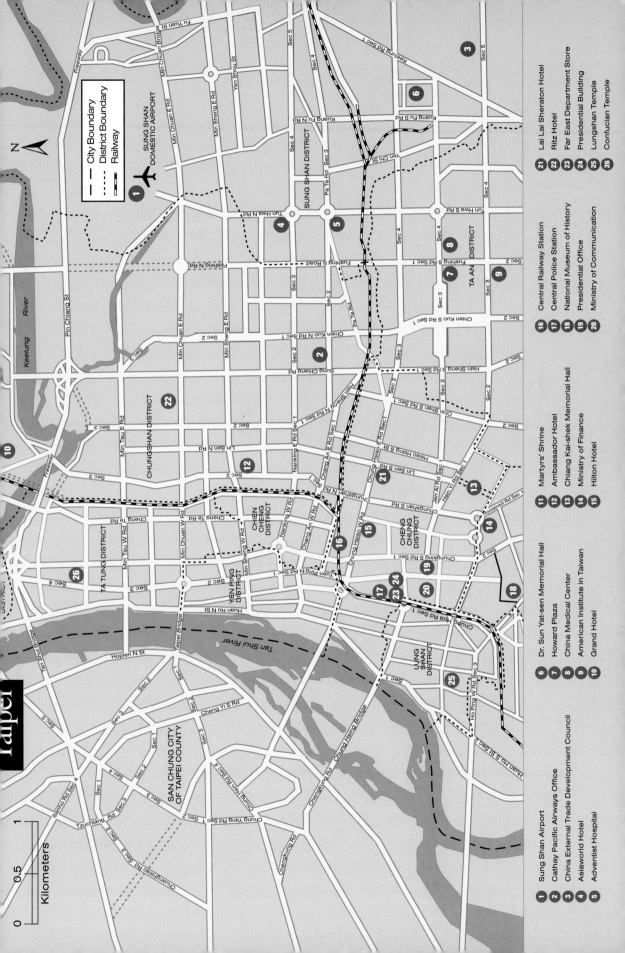

Taipei

Kilometers
0   0.5   1

Legend
- City Boundary
- District Boundary
- Railway

SUNG SHAN
DOMESTIC AIRPORT

1

Districts
- SUNG SHAN DISTRICT
- TA AN DISTRICT
- CHUNGSHAN DISTRICT
- CHIEN CHENG DISTRICT
- CHENG CHUNG DISTRICT
- YEN PING DISTRICT
- TA TUNG DISTRICT
- LUNG SHAN DISTRICT

Keelung River
Tan Shui River

SAN CHUNG CITY
OF TAIPEI COUNTY

1 Sung Shan Airport
2 Cathay Pacific Airways Office
3 China External Trade Development Council
4 Asiaworld Hotel
5 Adventist Hospital
6 Dr. Sun Yat-sen Memorial Hall
7 Howard Plaza
8 China Medical Center
9 American Institute in Taiwan
10 Grand Hotel
11 Martyrs' Shrine
12 Ambassador Hotel
13 Chiang Kai-shek Memorial Hall
14 Ministry of Finance
15 Hilton Hotel
16 Central Railway Station
17 Central Police Station
18 National Museum of History
19 Presidential Office
20 Ministry of Communication
21 Lai Lai Sheraton Hotel
22 Ritz Hotel
23 Far East Department Store
24 Presidential Building
25 Lungshan Temple
26 Confucian Temple

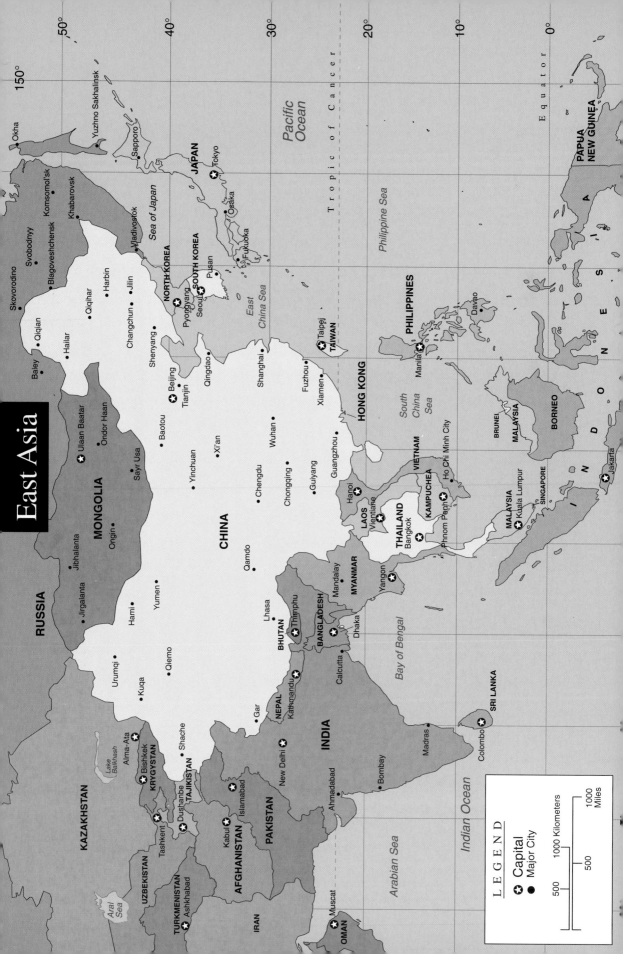

East Asia

Grand Hyatt 2 Sung Shou Road; far eastern part of city next to World Trade Center. New, expensive, glitzy; health club, conference facilities, meeting rooms. Rates: NT$5,500 to NT$6,125; Tel: (2) 7201234 Fax: (2) 7201111 Tlx: 12738.

The Regent 41 Chungshan Road North, Section 2; city center, important shopping and business district. Executive Travel Magazine's Best New Hotel of 1991; super-deluxe; top-of-the-line for business travelers; conference facilities, health club, meeting rooms. Rates: NT$5,800 to NT$7,000; Tel: (2) 5238000 Fax: (2) 5232828 Tlx: 20385.

Sherwood Taipei Hotel 637 Minsheng East Road; financial district. Elegant, European-style; business travelers only; health club, conference facilities, meeting rooms. Rates: NT$5,825 to NT$6,825; Tel: (2) 7181188 Fax: (2) 7130707.

Moderate

China Hotel Taipei 14 Kuanchien Road; near city center, bus and train stations, Post Office, New Park, Provincial Taiwan Museum. Rates: NT$2,300 to NT$2,500; Tel: (2) 3319521 Fax: (2) 3812349 Tlx: 21757.

Gala Hotel 186 Sungchiang Road; in business district. Meeting rooms, business center. Rates: NT$3,000 to NT$4,825; Tel: (2) 5415511 Fax: (2) 5313831 Tlx: 28453.

Golden China Hotel 306 Sungchiang Road; in business district. Meeting rooms, shops. Rates: NT$3,125 to NT$3,500; Tel: (2) 5215151 Fax: (2) 5312914 Tlx: 19550.

Budget

Leofoo Inn 168 Changchun Road; in business district. Meeting rooms, shops. Rates: NT$1,700 to NT$2,100; Tel: (2) 5073211 Fax: (2) 5082070 Tlx: 11182.

Miramar Hotel 3 Nanking East Road, Section 2; near business district. Conference facilities, shops. Rates: NT$900 to NT$1,600; Tel: (2) 5111241 Fax: (2) 5415571 Tlx: 25483.

Paradise Hotel 24 Hsining South Road; in city center, near bus and train stations, New Park, Provincial Taiwan Museum, Post Office. Business center, meeting rooms. Rates: NT$1,900 to NT$4,000; Tel: (2) 3141181 Fax: (2) 3147873 Tlx: 26972.

Kaohsiung Top-end

Ambassador Hotel 202 Minsheng 2nd Road; in city center. Conference facilities, health club, shops. Rates: NT$3,300 to NT$5,625; Tel: (7) 2115211 Fax: (7) 2811115 Tlx: 72105.

Grand Hotel 2 Yuanshan Road; on Chengching Lake 6 km (4 miles) from city center; Imperial Palace architecture, most beautiful hotel in Kaohsiung, world-famous. Conference facilities, health club, tennis, driving range, shops. Rates: NT$2,200 to NT$5,000; Tel: (7) 3835911 Fax: (7) 3814889 Tlx: 71231.

Kingdom Hotel 42 Wufu 4th Road; in city center. Conference facilities, meeting rooms, shops. Rates: NT$3,200 to NT$3,800; Tel: (7) 5518211 Fax: (7) 5210403 Tlx: 81938.

Moderate

Buckingham Hotel 394 Chihsien 2nd Road; in city center. Conference facilities, meeting rooms. Rates: NT$1,700 to NT$2,400; Tel: (7) 2822151 Fax: (7) 2814540 Tlx: 71500.

Summit Hotel 426 Chiuju 1st Road; near city center. Conference facilities, health club. Rates: NT$2,300 to NT$2,500; Tel: (7) 3845526 Fax: (7) 3844739 Tlx: 72423.

Budget

Duke Hotel 233 Linsen 1st Road; near city center, Post Office. Rates: NT$400 to NT$625; Tel: (7) 2312111 Fax: (7) 2118224.

Hungpin Hotel 40 Chienkuo 3rd Road; near city center, train station. Rates: NT$400 to NT$600; Tel: (7) 2913173.

EATING

Food in Taiwan is delicious and varied, with every mainland regional and ethnic style represented—Canton, Sichuan, Hakka, Hunan, Beijing, and Mongolia—as well as native Taiwan, Indian, Japanese, Indonesian, Thai, French, Italian, German, and American, and even American fast-food. The excellent Chinese vegetarian restaurants generally have a swastika sign outside to identify them—it's an ancient Buddhist symbol that tells prospective diners that the food is prepared according to strict Buddhist practices.

With so many exotic possibilities just in Chinese restaurants, it's a good idea to dine out with your Chinese contacts and let them order for you without asking them what you're getting. Something that sounds unappetizing may turn out to be your favorite dish. Take care when ordering—prices for certain specialty items may astound you. The hotels just named generally have very good Chinese restaurants. The restaurants listed below are non-hotel establishments, are either moderately-priced or expensive, and have received excellent reviews. Budget restaurants abound, as do street vendors.

Taipei

This city is Singapore's stiffest competition in Chinese cuisine. These restaurants come highly recommended:

Tu I Chu, the best Beijing food; 506 Jenai Road,

Section 4, opposite Sun Yat-sen Memorial Hall; Tel: (2) 7297853.

An Lo Yuan, one of the best Cantonese menus; 232 Tunhua North Road; Tel: (2) 7154929.

Fa Hua, fine vegetarian; 132 Minchuan East Rd., Section 3; Tel: (2) 7175305.

Ploughman's Inn, best Mongolian barbeque; 8, Lane 460, Tunhua South Road; Tel: (2) 7733268.

Shih Tou Chi (Jane's Bungalow), menu modeled after dishes served in a famous Chinese novel; 87 Juian St.; Tel: (2) 7025465.

Kaohsiung

Chuan Wei Sichuan, Sichuan cuisine; 226 Tatun 1st Road.

Liu Jia Xiao Guan, Sichuan cuisine; 52 Minsheng 1st Road.

Wu's Chao Shou, 148 Chihsien 3rd Road; Tel: (7) 5612276.

Hai Pa Wang (Sea King), seafood, 2 Hsingchung 2nd Road; Tel: (7) 3334486.

Twin Oaks, western and Chinese, 147 Peimen 2nd Road; Tel: (7) 2267001.

LOCAL CUSTOMS OVERVIEW

If any people in the world could be said to have invented business, surely it must be the Chinese. They're among the world's hardest workers and most adventurous entrepreneurs. Yet their culture is anything but Western. There are several important facets of Chinese culture that you must keep in mind if you want your business trip to Taiwan to have the highest possible potential for success.

- You are entering a Confucian society, which prizes dignity, mutual respect, humility, courtesy, and deference. It's all part of "face," as in having, creating or losing face. Face applies to greetings, conversations and leave-taking, to every facet of human interaction. It means that you must never criticize your Chinese acquaintances directly, especially in frontoof others, because that makes them lose face. To help them gain or maintain face, you should take care to praise or thank them when appropriate, especially in front of others but never effusively.
- Confucian society is paternalistic. You will deal with business people and managers who are benevolent despots, whose every word is law, and who care about the most personal details of their workers' lives as if they were family. To break into this circle, you will need an intermediary.
- You will have to learn to read between the lines. Chinese avoid the word "no" like the plague. Western-style directness can seem hostile or disrespectful.

- Shake hands and exchange business cards when you meet someone. Use both hands to present and receive cards. Make a point to read the card presented to you; then place it in a pocket above your waist.
- Be prepared to banquet.

(Refer to "Business Culture" chapter for an in-depth discussion.)

DOMESTIC TRANSPORTATION

Air On an island only 395 km (245 miles) long and 130 km (70 miles) across, there's not much need to take a plane anywhere, especially not when such easy and fast bus and train service is available. However, China Airlines, Far Eastern Air Transport, Taiwan Airlines, Transasia Airways, and Makung Airlines provide domestic flights to most of the country's dozen or more airports. For ease of refund, buy your ticket from the airline, not a travel agent. Be sure to check in at least one hour before your flight, or you may find your seat has been given to someone else.

Train There are five classes of train travel, from luxury to common. West coast trains are electric, while east coast trains are diesel. A first-class ticket from Taipei to Kaohsiung costs about NT$600 (about US$22.50) for the 5-hour trip. Taiwanese pack the trains on weekends and holidays, so it's a good idea to buy your ticket a few days ahead of time. Always keep your ticket: At the end of your trip when you leave the station, you must present it at the gate or pay a penalty equal to the ticket price.

Bus Long-distance bus travel comes in two classes, first and second. First-class has a restroom (which comes in handy if you have traveler's diarrhea) and a smoother ride, but isn't any faster than second-class. The first-class fare between Taipei and Kaohsiung is about NT$425 (about US$18.75). Save your ticket to present to the driver when you get off, or face having to pay the full fare again. It's always wise to buy a reserved-seat ticket in advance, especially for Sunday travel, when every Taiwanese on the island seems to want to ride a bus. Without that reservation, you'll find yourself in the middle of a very non-Confucian shoving match where face gets thoroughly ground into the dust.

That's the official, boring, nonsmoking, nondrinking, government-run bus line. If you want to live a little dangerously, you can hop on board a "wild chicken" bus, a fast, extremely luxurious, somewhat top-heavy wheeled party complete with video movies, lower prices, and dubious brakes and engine (but the horn always works)—and a cabin full of tobacco-smoking, beer-drinking Chinese and foreigners on the road for some long-distance festivities. It's definitely the most fun way to travel in Taiwan, if you can handle the smoke. The government keeps threatening to chop off the wild chickens' heads, but it will have to catch them first, and that doesn't seem very likely—and meanwhile the wild chickens are running off with all the eggs. Their depots are usually right next to government depots. However, since the wild chicken lines are illegal, their depots tend to move more often than you might expect of the typical, rather sedentary bus terminal: a depot may be in one place one day and a block down the street the next. So keep your eyes open for your missing depot.

Local buses cover the cities admirably and are very economical, but because their drivers rarely speak English or any language but Chinese, getting on the right bus and getting off at the right place present problems for foreigners. If you travel on a local bus, take along a Chinese-speaking friend, or have your hotel write down your destination to show to the drivers.

Taxi It's the most convenient way for a short-term foreign visitor to get around the cities. Taipei alone has almost 70,000 taxis, which do their part to jam up traffic, so you often sit in gridlock as the fare mounts. When traffic is actually moving, a Taiwan taxi ride can be a little hair-raising. Many drivers apparently imagine that they're world-class racers. If you want a more sedate trip, simply refuse to get in a taxi that has Christmas lights and racing stripes.

Taxis in major cities must use meters; make sure the driver resets the meter when you get in. Drivers rarely speak any language but Chinese, so go with a Chinese-speaking friend; or have your hotel write down your destination, hotel name and address, and expected fare on a card to present to the driver. If the driver tells you—whether in broken English or sign language—that your destination has moved or is much farther away than the map shows, don't believe him. If you're traveling in a rural area, bargain with the driver for a flat fare, because drivers aren't required to use meters in these areas.

"Wild chicken" taxis are not a smaller counterpart of wild chicken buses. Even among Taiwanese they have a shady reputation, although they may be legal. Often bigger than regular taxis and equipped with diesel engines, they're designed for longer trips, and are usually painted red or black. The driver often will approach you, saying that your bus or train has just left so you'd better take his taxi at some absurdly low price—which gets doubled or tripled once you're at his mercy somewhere between Taipei and Lion's Head Mountain.

HOLIDAYS/BANK HOLIDAYS

A national holiday that falls on a Sunday is observed the following Monday. Businesses, schools and government agencies generally shut down, although shops and stores may remain open, especially on Sundays. And many people take an entire week off for Chinese New Year, which often closely follows extended days taken off for Constitution Day and Founding Day.

BUSINESS HOURS

Most Taiwan businesses and government agencies are open six days a week: Monday through Friday from 8:30 am to 5:30 pm, with lunch from noon to 1:30 pm; and Saturday from 8:30 am to noon. Banking hours are 9 am to 3:30 pm Monday through Friday and 9 to noon on Saturdays. In contrast to citizens in less-evolved cultures, Taiwanese are smart enough to nap an hour or two after lunch, right at their desks. The big shopping day is Sunday. Shopping hours are 9 am to 10 pm daily. Smaller shops and restaurants open at dawn and close near midnight.

COMMUNICATIONS

Taiwan's telecommunications system is among the best in Asia, while its postal system ranks among the world's best.

Telephones Taiwan's telephone system is run by the International Telecommunications Administration

---

National Holidays

Founding Day–January 1-2

Chinese New Year–End of January

Spring Festival*–early March

China Youth Day–March 29

Children's and Women's Day–April 4

Tomb-Sweeping Day–April 5

Labor Day–May 1

Dragon-Boat Festival*–Early May

Mid-Autumn Festival*–August

Teacher's Day–September 28

National Day–October 10

Taiwan Restoration Day–October 25

Chiang Kai Shek's Birthday–October 31

Dr. Sun Yat-Sen's Birthday–November 12

Constitution Day–December 25

*A lunar calendar-based holiday whose date differs each year.

(ITA), a government monopoly. International calls to and from Taiwan are often as clear as calls next door. You can make international calls either from your hotel or from the ITA office at 28 Hangchou South Road, Section 1, Taipei. Taiwan's country code is 886. Among the area codes within Taiwan are: Hualien, 038; Kaohsiung, 07; Taichung, 04; Tainan, 06; Taitung, 05; Taipei, 02. Omit the "0" in the area code when you call Taiwan from outside the country, but use it when calling from another area code within Taiwan. When you're in Taiwan, dial "100" to reach an international operator; however, direct-dialing is reliable and much cheaper. You can direct-dial mainland China from Taiwan, but there is a special and rather arcane routing.

Local service is generally good, but not always as reliable as international. Lines seem to go dead when you dial, and you can get a busy signals when the line isn't actually busy. You can have your own phone installed within two weeks for about NT$6,800 (about US$255); the business line monthly rate is NT$300 (about US$11.25) for the first 250 calls and NT$1 per call thereafter.

The blue public pay phones are everywhere, but it's best to use the digital-display models, which are newer and more reliable. A 3 minute call costs NT$1; you can put in as much money as you want and the display will tick off the time that you've used—the phone beeps at you when your time is nearly up, when you'll be abruptly cut off unless you put in more money. A more convenient version of this phone uses a magnetic card, which you can buy for NT$100 in shops where you see these phones—ask for a dianhua ka.

To direct dial internationally If you're calling from your hotel room, first ask the hotel operator how much the hotel surcharge is. You may decide you want to call Country Direct, which is cheaper (see below). Otherwise, dial the international access code—002—the country code, the area or city code (if any), and the local phone number.

To use Country Direct dialing A cooperative effort among several large telephone systems, including AT&T, Country Direct enables you to bypass the local telephone system (in this case, Taiwan) and reach the US or another country directly on that country's system. First dial the access code—0080-1-288-0; a recording or an operator will offer you the option of using your home country calling card or a credit card (except US), or making a collect call.

USEFUL TELEPHONE NUMBERS

- ITA general information: (2) 3975811
- ITA international direct-dial information: (2) 3212535
- Taipei Foreign Affairs Police (English-speaking):

COUNTRY CODES OF MAJOR COUNTRIES			
Australia	61	Malaysia	60
Brazil	55	Mexico	52
Canada	1	New Zealand	64
China	86	Pakistan	92
France	33	Philippines	63
Germany	49	Russia	7
Hong Kong	852	Singapore	65
India	91	South Africa	27
Indonesia	62	Spain	34
Italy	39	Thailand	66
Japan	81	United Kingdom	44
Korea	82	United States	1

(2) 3817475
- Overseas operator: 100
- English directory assistance: (2) 3116796
- Tourist Information Hotline: (2) 7253737
- Taiwan Visitors Association: (2) 5943261
- Travel Information Service Center, Sungshan Domestic Airport: (2) 5142688
- Government Information Office: (2) 3228888

English-Language Yellow Pages The Trade Pages Group publishes the *Trade Yellow Pages* (PO Box 72-50, Taipei, Taiwan; Tel: (2) 3050803 Fax: (2) 3071000 Tlx: 24838 TRADEPAG). The Trade Pages Group includes the Taiwan Yellow Pages Corp., which, with the Taiwan Visitors Association, publishes the *Taiwan Yellow Pages* (PO Box 81-02, Taipei, Taiwan; Tel: (2) 7715995, (2) 7313069 Fax: (2) 7818982 Tlx: 14300 TYPAGES). Each book lists tens of thousands of trade, industrial, professional, and service companies.

Fax and telex Because they're the only fast way to transmit Chinese-language messages, pictures and graphics, fax machines are everywhere in Taiwan cities. Hotels and businesses have fax services, as do the ITA offices and many post offices.

You can send telegrams and telexes from the main ITA office in Taipei and its branches, and from hotels.

Videoconference The ITA runs an extensive international videoconferencing service out of its Taipei Communications Building, 28 Hangchou South Road, Section 1, Taipei. This two-way audiovisual system can also transmit documents. Call ITA's International Videoconference Operation Center for details: (2) 3975811.

Post Office Taiwan's mail service is cheap, reliable, fast, and efficient. Not only are post offices open six days a week from 8 am to 5 pm, but some are open 24 hours a day. Workers collect mail several times a day from branch post offices and street mailboxes. Domestic regular mail (NT$5) takes one to two days, while domestic express letters (NT$7 plus the regular rate) arrive within 24 hours. Mail to Asia and Oceania arrives in three to five days; to Europe, Africa and the Americas in seven to 10 days; and to Hong Kong and Macao in two days. Travelers can receive mail by general delivery at any post office.

English-language media The *China News* and *China Post* are daily newspapers; *Business Taiwan* is a weekly newspaper. The monthly magazine *Free China Review* covers Taiwanese politics, society and culture, while the free magazine *This Month in Taiwan* targets business travelers. You can also find the *Asian Wall Street Journal,* the *International Herald-Tribune, USA Today, Financial, Times, The Economist,* the top-rated weekly magazine *Far Eastern Economic Review, Time,* and *Newsweek.*

So many satellite dishes have sprouted on rooftops all over Taiwan that the government has just about decided to legalize them. Foreigners can tune in to CNN and BBC, among many other foreign networks and programs. The sole English-language radio station is 24-hour-a-day ICRT at FM 100 and AM 576.

Courier Services Most of the large international courier services operate in Taiwan.

Federal Express 361 Da Nan Road, Shih Lin, Taipei (next to the Grand Hotel); Tel: (toll-free) 080-251080, or (2) 7883535

TNT 3rd Floor, 207 Tun Hua North Road, Taipei; Tel: (2) 7132345, Pick-up Hotline: (2) 7127700 Fax: (2) 7122234 Tlx: 25062 TNTPAC

UPS Basement Level, 361 Da Nan Road, Shih Lin, Taipei (next to the Grand Hotel); Tel: (2) 8833868 Fax: (2) 8833890 Tlx: 17669 UPSTWN

LOCAL SERVICES

Taiwan has every kind of business service that you'd expect in a thriving capitalist economy: printers, lawyers, secretaries, interpreters, translators, publicists, computer services, accountants, advertising agencies, freight forwarders, consultants of every stripe, and a myriad host of others, listed in the English-language *Trade Yellow Pages* and *Taiwan Yellow Pages.* Following is a cursory listing of a few of the most basic services you're likely to need soon after you arrive.

Business centers

The big hotels often have business centers with computer, typing, fax, and secretarial services available. Among them are:

Taipei Ambassador, Asiaworld Plaza, Fortune Dai-

Ichi, Gala, Howard Plaza, Lai-Lai Sheraton, Paradise, Rebar Hotel Crown.

Kaohsiung Holiday Garden.

Taichung Plaza International.

Printers

You simply cannot do business in Taiwan without business cards—lots of them. And there are lots of printing companies in Taiwan that specialize in business cards, delivering accurate work within a few days at reasonable prices, complete with Chinese character translations on the reverse. The concierge or reception staff at the better hotels can give you the names and addresses of local printers. Here are three suggestions:

Ann Kung Printing Company, Ltd.: Number 1, Alley 5, Lane 70, Yen Chi Street, Taipei; Tel/Fax: (2) 7729792.

Dixon Press, Ltd.: 1st Floor, Number 52, Pao Ai Road, Taipei; Tel: (2) 3615281 Fax: (2) 3314375.

Sung Fong Printing Company, Ltd.: 1st Floor, Number 346, Keelung Road, Section 1, Taipei; Tel: (2) 7230097 Fax: (2) 7230107.

Translation and Typing Agencies

Some companies provide translators and secretaries as a package. A sampling includes:

ABC, 1 Fu Shing N. Road, Taipei; Tel: (2) 7312483 or 8739601.

Pristine Translation and Language Consultants, 2nd Floor, 5 Lane 734, Ting Chou Road, Taipei; Tel: (2) 3947640 Fax: (2) 3947640.

Shakespeare, 3rd Floor, 190 Nanking E. Road, Section 2, Taipei; Tel: (2) 5066401.

(Refer to "Important Addresses" chapter for a more complete listing of these local business services.)

STAYING SAFE AND HEALTHY

Taiwan is an advanced society with high standards of health, hygiene, and public safety. Yet any foreigner anywhere is bound to encounter some problems, frustrations and fears. In Taiwan, all can be surmounted, and only one could truly be called life-threatening.

Traffic That one is the traffic, especially in the cities. Traffic accidents are the leading cause of death for Taiwanese under age 50. To be outside a car but too close to one is to be in the most dangerous place on the island. It's not that Taiwanese drivers don't see pedestrians; it's just that they don't much care. Don't expect anyone to stop for you merely because you're crossing the street, in a crosswalk or not. Drivers do stop at red lights, but only at major intersections. Be extremely careful, and whenever possible use the many pedestrian underpasses.

The second most unsafe place to be in Taiwan is inside a car. Taiwanese drive extremely aggressively. You're pretty safe in a bus, but a taxi is another matter. If your driver is scaring you, tell him to slow down—*kai man yidian, hao bu hao!*

Bronchitis The number-one disabling illness for travelers in Taiwan is also traffic related: bronchitis. Not what you expected? Each year's new strain of influenza begins in this region of the world. Lowered resistance from the flu plus the world-class smog and dust in Taiwan's large cities often adds up to bronchitis, which can be either viral or bacterial. The main danger of bronchitis is that it can set you up for pneumonia. You can protect yourself by getting a flu shot before you leave for Taiwan or as soon as you arrive. (Be aware, however, that your immunity doesn't reach its peak for a few weeks after the shot.)

If you get the flu anyway, you can fend off bronchitis by getting out of the city to a place with fresh air and a relaxing pace: the mountain resort of Alishan, for example, or the peaceful east coast town of Hualien, or the hot springs of Peitou just outside Taipei. If you can't get away, don't hang around the streets too much, always travel in air-conditioned taxis and buses, and avoid cigarette smoke (and thus wild chicken buses). Treatment includes steam inhalation and hot drinks to loosen the thick phlegm that you will be coughing up, plus a balanced and varied diet with plenty of liquids. If it's a severe case of bacterial bronchitis, you may need to see a doctor for antibiotics.

Diarrhea Traveler's diarrhea is as common for foreigners in Taiwan as it is for foreigners in the United States or anywhere else. Your digestive system isn't ready for the strange intestinal flora it encounters and tries to expel them, at great inconvenience and occasional embarrassment but with slight risk to you and your busy schedule.

Taiwanese generally boil their tap water when they prepare tea or cook, and boiled or bottled water is available everywhere. Precautions are wise. Don't drink tap water or use it to brush your teeth; don't use ice cubes, since they may be made from tap water; don't eat raw fruits or vegetables unless you can wash them in boiled or bottled water and peel them yourself. If you're traveling for three weeks or less, you may want to take Pepto-Bismol or an antibiotic (doxycycline or trimethoprim/ sulfamethoxazole) as a preventive, but be careful. Sometimes there are side-effects, and antibiotics in particular increase the risk that your body will develop resistant bacteria.

Even with precautions, it's likely that you'll have a bout of diarrhea. The best treatment is to ride it out as your body adapts and heals itself. The main danger is dehydration, especially in a warm climate like Taiwan's. Keep yourself well hydrated by drinking plenty of water (boiled or bottled is best, but any is better than none), carbonated drinks, herbal teas, fruit juices, and clear broth soups. Drink at least two glasses of liquid after each trip to the bathroom. Avoid solid foods for the first 24 hours, and then begin eating bland foods—bananas, rice, crackers, potatoes, fish, lean meat, beans, lentils. Avoid dairy products, raw fruits (except bananas) and vegetables, fats, greasy foods, colas, and spicy foods. Also avoid caffeine and alcohol: both are diuretics, which cause your body to lose water.

If severe nausea or vomiting accompanies your diarrhea, don't try to eat anything, but focus on rehydration. Take small, frequent sips of liquid. If the vomiting doesn't stop within a day, take an antinausea drug such as promethizine, which you can get from your hotel doctor or a pharmacy without a prescription.

If you must travel with traveler's diarrhea, take the train or the Kuokuang bus—both have bathrooms. If the bathroom just can't meet your needs, Pepto-Bismol can usually handle mild or moderate diarrhea. If you have heavy-duty diarrhea, you'll need over-the-counter Immodium or Lomotil. Be aware, though, that while these drugs are very good at stopping you up, they treat only the symptoms, not the cause, so take them only when absolutely necessary. Otherwise, follow the treatment regimen above and allow your body to heal itself.

Hepatitis Hepatitis isn't common in Taiwan, but it isn't uncommon, either. This liver infection comes in two main forms—A and B. You can prevent both varieties by getting vaccinated. For extra protection against hepatitis A, use disposable chopsticks in restaurants and at street vendors, or bring your own chopsticks—the disease is spread through contamination of food, water, and cooking and eating utensils. The main avenues of transmission for hepatitis B are sex and non-disposable needles (whether used for intravenous drugs, tattooing, or acupuncture).

Crime Taiwan is a fairly safe place, especially compared with some Western cities, and you probably have more chance of being struck by lightning than of being mugged on the street. But there are precautions that you should take to avoid becoming a statistic.

- Check in with your embassy or consulate upon your arrival, both to let them know that you're there and to ask about crime conditions.
- Avoid displays of flashy jewelry and watches; dress and behave conservatively.
- Be aware that pickpockets like crowds, and don't give them a chance. Don't carry much cash, and do carry it in a money belt. Conduct most of your transactions with credit cards or traveler's checks.
- Ask at your hotel about the safety of the surrounding streets.

- Behave and walk as if you know where you are and where you're going. Muggers are as drawn to the lost and confused as they are to Rolex watches and rolls of cash.
- To keep bicycling or motorcycling thieves from grabbing your briefcase or shoulder bag, carry it on the side away from the street.

Personal-Care Products Most of the personal-care products you're accustomed to can be found in Taiwan, but bring your own shaving lotion, dental floss, vitamins, deodorant, sunscreen, cosmetics, and mosquito repellent—these are either unavailable or horrendously expensive. You should also bring a sufficient supply of your prescription medications. And while toilet paper is readily available in stores and hotels, most public restrooms don't have it, so take a supply of your own when you're out and about.

EMERGENCY INFORMATION

In a medical or fire emergency dial 119 anywhere in Taiwan. In a police emergency, dial 110. However, it's not likely that dispatchers speak English, so you may need assistance from passersby or shopkeepers.

Doctors If you need a doctor, your hotel will be able to refer you to one. Taiwanese doctors are first-rate.

Hospitals

Hospitals in Taiwan expect to be paid a deposit before they treat you, so always bring cash or a credit card to the hospital.

Taipei *Adventist Hospital*, 424 Pateh Road, Section 2; Tel: (2) 7718151.
Mackay Memorial Hospital, 92 Chungshan North Road, Section 2; Tel: (2) 5433535.
National Taiwan University Hospital, 1 Changteh Street; Tel: (2) 3123456.
Taipei Municipal Chunghsin Hospital, 145 Chengchou Road; Tel: (2) 5213801.
Veterans General Hospital, 201 Shihpai Road, Section 2; Tel: (2) 8712121 (English information: extension 3530).
Kaohsiung *Kaohsiung City Tatung Hospital*, 68 Chunghua 3rd Road; Tel: (7) 2618131.
Kaohsiung Veterans General Hospital, 386 Tachung 1st Road, Tsoying; Tel: (7) 3422121.
Taichung *Taichung Veterans General Hospital,* 160 Chungkang Road, Section 3; Tel: (4) 3592525.
Tainan *Father Fox Memorial Hospital,* 901 Chunghua Road; (6) 2521176.
Taitung *Taiwan Provincial Taitung Hospital,* 1 Wuchuan St.: Tel: (5) 324112.

DEPARTURE FORMALITIES

Your ease of leaving Taiwan depends partly on how thoroughly you declared at customs when you entered the country and partly on what you're taking with you—how much gold, New Taiwan dollars, antiques, guns, opium, counterfeit money, endangered species, fruit sprouts, or other restricted or prohibited items that you've packed in your luggage. You're limited on the first two items, while the following six are flatly prohibited and will give you a lot of explaining to do to Customs police (who have seen everything and heard every excuse). (Refer to "Export Policy & Procedure" chapter for information about commercial exports.)

Customs requires departing travelers to make declarations when they are taking out of the country the following items:

- foreign currency
- New Taiwan dollars
- gold or silver ornaments
- computer media (tapes, disks).

You can't leave Taiwan with more than US$5,000 in currency or its foreign equivalent unless you declared it upon arrival. You can't leave with more than 62.5 ounces of gold or 625 ounces of silver, in any form, unless you had it with you when you arrived, declared it then, and stored it with customs, or unless you get a Ministry of Finance permit in advance. You're allowed to take up to NT$40,000 in notes and up to 20 circulating coins out of Taiwan without a permit—more if you've gotten a Ministry of Finance permit in advance.

BEST TRAVEL BOOKS

Travel books won't prevent culture shock, but they can help to cushion it. The best thing you can do before you embark on any foreign travel, be it for business or pleasure, is to read as much as you can about the people whose country you're going to visit. This is even more important if you're a Westerner traveling in Asia. It's often hard for a traveler of European descent to believe that these countries, these peoples, these cultures inhabit the same planet as his or her own. It's easier if the traveler has first studied some good travel books.

Three books stand out from the rest by virtue of their comprehensiveness, organization, perspective, good tables of contents, and depth. All are available in well-stocked bookstores. Don't be surprised if prices, addresses and phone numbers noted in the books are different than what you find in reality. Things change, books take time to produce, and people make mistakes, especially in travel books. Forgive them.

Four Dragons Guidebook: Hong Kong, Singapore, Thailand, Taiwan, by Fredric M. Kaplan. Houghton Mifflin Company, Boston, 1991. ISBN 0-395-58577-5; 688 pages; US$18.95. A lot of detail and scope in a mere 144-page section; strong on trip planning, visas, touring, lodging, dining; has a valuable chapter called "Doing Business in Taiwan"; still manages to squeeze in five decent maps; has the only good index of the three.

Taiwan: a travel survival kit, by Robert Story. Lonely Planet Publications, Hawthorn, Victoria, Australia, 1990. ISBN 0-86442-100-1; 290 pages, US$11.95. The typical alternative Lonely Planet guide—irreverent and mildly cynical, chatty, funny, very much geared to the independent traveler, good maps, highly informative, clearly a labor of love based on much personal experience.

Taiwan: Treasure Island, by Paul Mooney, photography by Nigel Hicks. Passport Books, NTC Publishing Group, Lincolnwood, Illinois, 1993. ISBN 0-8442-9824-7; 360 pages, US$15.95. Strong on history, religion, legends, culture, and the arts; very good background information on specific sights; the most literate of the three books; striking photography and special essays; hard information (lodging, dining) sparse and less up-to-date than you'd expect but made up for by a true feel for the island, its people and society.

Typical Daily Expenses in Taiwan

Expense	TAIPEI LOW	MOD	HIGH
Hotel	NT$1,650	NT$3,300	NT$6,600
Local transportation*	20	200	500
Food	400	2,000	3,300
Local telephone†	5	20	40
Tips	30	150	300
Personal entertainment#	150	400	700
TOTAL	**NT$2,255**	**NT$6,070**	**NT$11,440**
One-way airport transport	35	800	1,000

US Government per diem allowance as of December, 1993 was US$128 for hotels (approximately NT$3,410) and US$81 for meals and incidentals (approximately NT$2,160). **(NT$26.65=US$1 year-end 1993)**

Expense	KAOHSIUNG LOW	MOD	HIGH
Hotel	550	2,230	4,400
Local transportation*	18	200	500
Food	400	2,000	3,300
Local telephone†	5	20	40
Tips	30	150	300
Personal entertainment#	150	350	600
TOTAL	**NT$1,153**	**NT$4,950**	**NT$9,140**
One-way airport transport	10	150	250

US Government per diem allowance as of December, 1993 was US$97 for hotels (approximately NT$2,585) and US$82 for meals and incidentals (approximately NT$2,185). **(NT$26.65=US$1 year-end 1993)**

* Based on 2 bus rides for low cost, 2 medium length taxi rides for moderate cost and 4 longer taxi rides for high cost.
† Based on 2 telephone calls from pay phones for low cost, 4 calls from the hotel room for moderate cost and 6 calls from the hotel room for high cost.
 # Based on a visit to a museum and a coffee shop for low cost, a visit to a disco with a drink for moderate cost and a live floor show for high cost.

Business Culture

Business is the life blood of modern Taiwan. For both economic and political reasons, the Taiwanese view business with the outside world as the key to their country's growth and stability. In the 1970s the Republic of China (ROC) government in Taiwan, which claims to be the legitimate government of all China, faced a crisis that threatened its very existence. In 1971, the ROC was expelled from the United Nations, and the People's Republic of China (PRC) government in Beijing joined the UN Security Council. Richard Nixon's visit to the mainland in 1972 signaled the beginning of the end of official recognition of the ROC by the United States, and in 1979 the US switched diplomatic recognition to Beijing.

To maintain de facto legitimacy and real economic importance to Western governments, Taiwan adopted a strategy of increasing export trade with the world. The strategy worked. Although very few nations officially recognize the ROC government, almost every Western government today maintains a trade mission or institute in Taiwan that serves as a de facto embassy. The key to Taiwan's success has been trade. As Taiwanese imports pour into the Western world, governments have needed to maintain quasi-official contacts with Taipei in order to ensure smooth trade relations. The importance of Taiwanese trade and investment has even allowed the ROC government to maintain official diplomatic relations with some small countries, mostly countries in Latin America.

The Taiwan Miracle Economically, Taiwan's burgeoning trade with the world has brought new prosperity to its people. Standards of living have steadily increased, and today Taiwan is classified as a newly industrialized country (NIC). Businessmen and ordinary people in Taiwan are aware of the importance of trade and contact with the outside world, and they are proud of their country's achievements in the face of opposition and hostility from the PRC government on the mainland. The ROC refers to this success as the Taiwan Miracle, and its leaders point to increased levels of production and improved standards of liv-

ing as concrete proof that their free market system is superior to Communism. This combination of economic and political concerns has made business and trade more important in Taiwan than they are perhaps anywhere else in the world.

THE TAIWANESE BUSINESS MIND

Style is Conservative The typical Taiwanese businessman can be noted for his down-to-earth practicality, the relative simplicity of his work style, and his shrewdness in negotiations. Most businessmen grew up in poverty under a totalitarian sociopolitical system, and their business styles were shaped by these experiences. The affluence evident in Taiwan today is a new phenomenon that is hardly more than a decade old. Company executives are often in their forties or fifties, and many come from peasant backgrounds in Taiwan or fled from the mainland with ROC forces in 1949. They often remain cautious about their wealth, and they are uncertain about the future. Their attitudes are somewhat similar to those of Americans who grew up in the Great Depression or Europeans who lived through World War II and the subsequent reconstruction. They enjoy the fruits of economic success, but they are skeptical of the new generation of Taiwanese who have never experienced real hardship. Older Taiwanese complain that the young have never "eaten bitter" and that they are lazy, selfish, and too influenced by Western culture. Many of them still cannot believe they are really well-off, although that mentality is changing.

Work is Not Just a Means For the Taiwanese, work is one of the highest virtues. Most businessmen and workers jump at the chance to work longer hours and earn more money. Although the standard workweek is five and a half days (8:30 am to 5 pm on weekdays, 8:30 am to noon on Saturdays), it is common for people to work ten or more hours every day, especially if they are self-employed. In business environments, there is usually one boss, *lao ban* in

Chinese, who commands absolute respect and obedience from his employees. He makes all the key decisions and expects his subordinates to follow his commands to the letter. In return, he plays the role of a father figure to his employees, concerning himself with their personal as well as their professional lives. Indeed, Taiwanese businesses can be viewed in the context of the traditional Confucian family, which is organized in a hierarchical structure with clear orders of seniority and status.

Business is Small-Scale Company loyalty in Taiwan has its limits. Unlike the Japanese, Taiwanese generally do not like to work for large companies, and skilled and resourceful people often aspire to establish their own small businesses. There is a saying in Taiwan that it is better to be the head of a chicken than the tail of an ox, meaning that it is better to work for one's own benefit than for a large organization. The result is that small-scale capitalism is the norm in Taiwan. Thousands of small family-operated companies produce everything from umbrellas to car parts, almost exclusively for export. This can be an advantage for foreign businesspeople in Taiwan looking for Taiwanese partners in a start-up business. Many skilled junior or mid-level company employees are happy to quit their job and, Rolodex in hand, move to a new company that may ultimately compete with their former employer. The negative side is that business rivalries in Taiwan can be personal and even vicious in nature, not unlike family vendettas.

Small scale is also the norm for businesses in the service sector. Every neighborhood or community in Taiwan has a small family-operated grocery store. Meats and vegetables are bought in large open-air markets where individual families operate counters specializing in pork, chicken, eggs, greens, or other foodstuffs. Although Western-style supermarkets have appeared in recent years, the majority of Taiwanese still prefer to shop at the traditional morning markets where produce is fresher and often cheaper. The prevalence of small shops in Taiwan complicates the logistics of selling and marketing products. Distribution networks are complex, and products can change hands several times before they reach store shelves. Any foreign businessman who wishes to market goods directly in Taiwan must work hard to understand its distribution systems.

CONFUCIANISM: THE BASIS OF SUCCESS

The mentality of modern Taiwanese is still shaped largely by the teachings of Confucius, who lived more than 2,500 years ago. The basic tenets of Confucian thought are obedience and respect for superiors and parents, duty to family, loyalty to

friends, humility, sincerity, and courtesy.

Age and rank are respected in Taiwan, and young people are expected to obey their elders unquestioningly. In the workplace, respect and status increase with age. Older foreign businesspeople have an advantage in this regard, and they are likely to receive more serious attention than younger people.

The family is by far the preeminent institution in Taiwanese society. One's first duty is to the welfare of one's family, and working family members often pool their financial resources. In many ways, Taiwanese view themselves more as parts of the family unit than as free individuals. Most small factories are family-run operations, and the top executives in large companies may all be related through blood or marriage.

Humility and courtesy are respected traits among the Taiwanese. You will seldom hear a Taiwanese be overly boastful or self-satisfied, even if his accomplishments are laudable. In some cases, Taiwanese can be downright self-deprecating.

Taiwanese are among the most courteous people in the world, especially toward foreigners. Every detail of a guest's stay with a Taiwanese friend may be prearranged, and the guest may not be allowed to spend his own money on even the smallest items. For individualists from the West, this form of courtesy may be overwhelming.

Never Say Never Another aspect of Taiwanese courtesy that can cause problems for Westerners is the general reluctance to say anything that can be construed as negative or as not meeting another's expectations. Taiwanese will often say what they think a person wants to hear, whether it is true or not. Almost always, they do this to prevent the hearer from being disappointed, not with malicious intent. Likewise, Taiwanese will almost always avoid saying no to a request. Instead of refusing outright, they may say that something is inconvenient or suggest an alternative. In such situations, pressing the issue is likely to cause embarrassment.

The Price of Culture The general effect of Confucianism on the Taiwanese people has been to homogenize their culture and eradicate many traits of individuality. Unquestioning acceptance of the status quo is the norm, and people are not known for their creativity or inventiveness. On the positive side, Confucianism has instilled a humaneness, geniality, and sense of honor that any visitor can appreciate.

FACE VALUE

No understanding of the mind-set of Taiwanese businessmen is complete without a grasp of the concept of face, *mianzi* in Chinese. Having face means having a high status in the eyes of one's peers, and it is a mark of personal dignity. Taiwanese are acutely sensitive to having and maintaining face in all aspects of social and business life. Face can be likened to a prized commodity: it can be given, lost, taken away, or earned. You should always be aware of the face factor in your dealings with Taiwanese and never do or say anything that could cause someone to lose face. Doing so could ruin business prospects and even invite recrimination.

The easiest way to cause someone to lose face is to insult the individual or to criticize him or her harshly in front of others. Westerners can offend Taiwanese unintentionally by making fun of them in the good-natured way that is common among friends in the West. Another way to cause someone to lose face is to treat him or her as an underling when his or her official status in an organization is high. People must always be treated with proper respect. Failure to do so makes them and the transgressor lose face for all others aware of the situation.

Just as face can be lost, it can also be given by praising someone for good work in front of peers or superiors or by thanking someone for doing a good job. Giving someone face earns respect and loyalty, and it should be done whenever the situation warrants. However, it is not a good idea to praise others too much, as it can make you appear to be insincere.

You can also save someone's face by helping him to avoid an embarrassing situation. For example, in playing a game you can allow your opponent to win even if you are clearly the better player. The person whose face you save will not forget the favor, and he will be in your debt.

A person can lose face on his own by not living up to other's expectations, by failing to keep a promise, or by behaving disreputably. Remember in business interactions that a person's face is not only his own but that of the entire organization that he represents. Your relationship with the individual and the respect accorded him is probably the key to your business success in Taiwan.

IT'S NOT WHAT YOU KNOW...

Personal connections are the key element of doing business in Taiwan. As in China and Hong Kong, little or no distinction is made between business and personal relationships. This point cannot be overemphasized. To succeed in Taiwan, you must cultivate close personal ties with business associates and earn their respect and trust. Attempts to establish long-term businesses in the country have often failed because foreigners did not recognize that business relationships were also personal relationships.

Money Talks The one area of business in Taiwan where the importance of personal connections is minimal is export trade. Because Taiwan has been exporting to the West for decades, Taiwanese businessmen understand that foreigners have little understanding of their society and traditions. Selling goods to foreigners is now itself a tradition, and since it usually does not involve close cooperation between the two sides, it can be conducted impersonally. But to market products or engage in cooperative ventures in Taiwan, foreign businessmen must cultivate connections.

Guanxi and Clans The importance of personal connections—guanxi in Chinese—has its roots in the traditional Chinese concept of family. For the Chinese, individuals are parts of the collective family whole. The family is the source of identity, protection, and strength. In times of famine or war, the Chinese family structure was a bastion against the outside world, where no one and nothing could be trusted. As a result, trust was reserved for family members and extremely close friends. Through arranged marriages or other means, heads of families could establish connections with other households, thereby strengthening the support system. New connections incorporated psychologically into the family, and they gained (and gave) unequivocal loyalty. Today, Taiwanese are safe from the dangers that their ancestors faced, but the tradition of personal connections is as strong as ever. In essence, the Taiwanese possess a clan mentality under which those inside the clan work cooperatively and view those outside the clan either as inconsequential or as potential threats. To be accepted into a network of personal or business relations in Taiwan is an honor for foreigners. It entails responsibility and commitment to the members of the network.

Guanxi for Profit In the business world of Taiwan, executives work constantly to maintain and extend their networks of connections. Largely through school or family associations, networks extend to other companies and individuals. While the purpose of such contacts is mutual financial profit, the criteria are the same as those for personal networks. Cultivating friendships in business circles is an art learned through practice and close attention to the needs and expectations of others. You form such relations by doing favors and demonstrating your integrity and sincerity.

CULTIVATING RELATIONSHIPS

For the foreign businessman, the difficulties in cultivating solid relationships can be the biggest obstacle to success in Taiwan. A Taiwanese who does not already know a potential business associate will hesitate to do business with him until he has had time to get acquainted and size up his associate's character and intentions.

Find a Matchmaker The best way to make contact with potential Taiwanese business associates is to have a mutual friend serve as an intermediary and introducer. If the third party has close relationships with both sides, that alone may constitute solid grounds for the conduct of business. Finding a third party may be as simple as asking an overseas Chinese if he or she has any family members in Taiwan who could be potential associates. Anyone who has worked in Taiwan or who has cooperated with Taiwanese in the past could be a key source of business contacts. There are also many business consultants who can provide assistance for a fee. Chambers of commerce, small business associations, and ROC international trade offices may also help you to find contacts.

Go to the Source If finding a third party for introductions in your home country proves impossible, consider making a fact-finding trip to Taiwan. A trade show in Taipei that would allow you to display your goods or services gives you a good opportunity to gauge your business prospects, or you could spend time meeting people in your area of business. Before leaving for Taiwan, send faxes to businesses with which you would be interested in working in to set up appointments. However, don't be surprised if some businesses ignore your request: they do not know you, and therefore may consider you to be a non-entity.

Patience On your first and perhaps even your second trip to Taiwan, you may accomplish nothing more than getting to know several possible candidates for business relationships. Rushing into business before you have established a personal relationship is an invitation to failure. After drawing up a list of possible candidates, take time to evaluate each person carefully. Weigh his or her strengths and weaknesses before you decide who to follow up with. In future visits, you will learn more about these and other people and gain valuable firsthand experience in the country.

After making your first contacts with businessmen in Taiwan, be prepared to spend a lot of time deepening and strengthening relationships through visits, dinners, gift giving, and many small favors. While this can be costly and time-consuming, Taiwanese appreciate all sincere efforts in this area, and no favor done goes unnoticed. Likewise, keep a running account of all favors done for you, all small gifts received, and the like. The odds are good that you will be expected to reciprocate in the future. Remember this aspect of Taiwanese business culture whenever someone offers you a favor, dinner, or gift. If you absolutely do not want to be in the person's debt, be creative and find some polite excuse for declining the offer. And decline it only if you have no intention of having a relationship, because declining offers can be insulting to Taiwanese.

Maintain Your Perspective Finally, foreign businesspeople will benefit from the process of cultivating personal connections by keeping in mind that it gives them an opportunity to learn about the people with whom they are dealing. Getting to know your business associates is practical regardless of your culture. Learning about the personality of an associate can make communication and understanding smoother, and the resulting knowledge can be critical when it comes time to decide how far to take the business relationship.

The Company Face A foreign business should designate a personable member of the company to act as the face man for the organization in Taiwan, and that individual should continue to represent the business on a long-term basis. Whether they are dealing with a large foreign company or an individual, Taiwanese like to deal with the same individual, and they treat every interaction as a personal one. Over time, if the business relationship is a success, Taiwanese may come to regard the face man as a close personal friend. Replacing that individual could jeopardize the business relationship, unless the current representative introduces the new representative and spends some time bringing him closer to the Taiwanese.

MEETING THE TAIWANESE

When meeting Taiwanese businessmen, foreigners should display sincerity and respect. Shaking hands is the accepted form of salutation. An exchange of business cards should follow. If at all possible, cards should have English text on one side and Chinese text on the other. Names can be transliterated into Chinese. Seek the advice of a knowledgeable person on the characters used for transliteration. Some characters have better connotations than others.

When exchanging business cards, the proper procedure is to give and receive cards with both hands. Hold the card by the corners between thumb and forefinger. On receiving a card, do not simply pocket it immediately, but take a few moments to study the card and what it says. The card represents the person who presents it, and it should be given the respect that he or she is due.

Presenting letters of introduction from well-known business leaders, overseas Chinese, or former government officials who have dealt with Taiwan is an excellent way of showing both that you are a person of high standing and that you mean business. Taiwanese are very concerned about social status, and anything that you can do to enhance their regard for you is a plus. But be careful not to appear arrogant or haughty, as Confucian morality condemns such behavior.

While Taiwanese are not overly concerned about styles of dress, they will probably expect you to wear a Western business suit. In the factory, both managers and workers often wear company shirts with the company logo. Similar to short-sleeved pullover golf shirts, they are practical in Taiwan's hot, humid summer weather. However, in meetings with foreigners, Taiwanese are likely to adopt Western business wear.

GIVING AND RECEIVING GIFTS

Taiwanese are inveterate gift givers. Gifts express friendship, and they can symbolize hopes for good future business, the successful conclusion of an endeavor, or appreciation for a favor done. Foreign businesspeople should spend some time choosing appropriate presents before embarking on a trip to Taiwan. The Taiwanese consider the Western habit of simply saying thank you for a favor glib and perhaps less than sincere. Favors should be rewarded materially, although gifts can have more symbolic than monetary value. Avoid very expensive gifts unless the recipient is an old associate who has proved to be particularly important in business dealings. Gifts are not expected on the first visit, but they can be given if you feel that the beginnings of a relationship have been established.

In an office or business environment, it is best to present business-related gifts, such as pens or paperweights with your company logo. If only one gift is to be given, it should be presented to the head of the Taiwanese group at a dinner or on the conclusion of a successful meeting. If gifts are to be given to several individuals, be sure that each person receives a gift of roughly equal value or else that the chief executive receives a gift of greater value. Omit no one with whom you have a relationship when giving several gifts at the same time.

If you are invited to a Taiwanese person's home, it is courteous to arrive with a small gift. Suitable presents include a basket of fruit, tea, flowers, or any memento from your home country that the Taiwanese can associate with you. Picture books of your home area make good presents. Presenting a wife with perfume or children with toys is likely to be appreciated. Such presents show that you are concerned about the welfare of the entire family, not just the business relationship. Foreign liquor is another gift that is much appreciated. French cognac is the most prized, although it can be rather expensive, and it should only be given to those with whom you already have a personal relationship.

As in the case of business cards, the polite way to present and receive gifts is with both hands outstretched.

It is polite for the recipient to refuse a gift two or three times before finally accepting it. For Westerners, the process can be tricky. If the Taiwanese appears embarrassed when he refuses your gift and says that he cannot possibly receive such a nice item,

the proper thing to do is to insist that your gift is only a small token and to add that you would be honored if it were accepted. As a rule, after some hemming and hawing, the Taiwanese will accept the present graciously. If your attempts to give a present are rejected several times and it is evident that the intended recipient is serious about not wishing to accept it, it may be that he is sincere and that your offer should be withdrawn. He may refuse your gift because he does not want to be in your debt or because he has no intentions of having a relationship with you.

When a gift is offered to you, it is not necessary for you to refuse it ceremonially as the Taiwanese do. Humble acceptance and a few choice words of appreciation are enough. A gift from a Taiwanese businessperson may simply be a courtesy that he accords to all visitors, but it can also be an acknowledgment that a relationship with you exists. Or, it may indicate that you will be asked for a favor. In any case, if someone presents you with a gift, you are expected to reciprocate in kind or through a favor.

If the gift is wrapped, it is considered impolite to open it in front of the giver unless he or she encourages you to do so. Tearing the wrappings off hastily is a sign of greediness. Any gift that you give wrapped to an individual should be wrapped in the traditional lucky colors of gold or red. White and black are considered colors of mourning.

CONVERSATION

Cultural and linguistic differences can cause trouble for Taiwanese and foreigners over the simple matter of small talk. Expect people whom you do not know well to ask questions that you consider to be of a personal nature, such as your age, the amount of money you make, or the number of people in your family. It is not polite to tell people that these matters are none of their business, and to give frank answers is a sign of familiarity and trust. Taiwanese are curious about foreigners and their habits, and their questions are related to what they themselves consider to be important in life; money and family are among them.

Family matters Family members can be an important topic of conversation, because Taiwanese who are getting to know you may be as interested in you as the member of a family as much as they are in you as an individual. Asking Taiwanese about their families is readily acceptable, and they can go into great detail about the lives of brothers, sisters, parents, spouses, and children. If you are divorced or unmarried, the topic of family may be uncomfortable to you. It is an unfortunate fact that some Taiwanese regard the West as morally loose and full of homosexuals, both of which they regard as unacceptable. In a tense situation, it may be better to lie than to be open about something that could jeopardize a relationship.

Money Matters The subject of money often comes up in conversation. For example, a Taiwanese may ask you how much your watch cost or what kind of car you have and how much it is worth. If people ask you about your income, it is fine to tell them the truth. Remember that Taiwan is not a poor country, and the fact that you report a decent income will not be resented. If you are really uncomfortable about this topic, you can give a figure that is neither too high nor too low, or you can simply laugh and say that you don't make as much as you would like to.

Chinese Politics One area of conversation about which you need to be careful is Chinese-Taiwanese relations. Though Taiwan is for all practical purposes an independent country, the official ROC line is that Taiwan is part of China and that the ROC is the legitimate government of all China. However, a sizable minority of Taiwanese advocates official independence from China, and you can seldom be sure of the political opinions of the people with whom you are talking. Also, you should never refer to the Communist People's Republic of China on the mainland, although the discussion of mainland China as a cultural or economic entity is fine. In conversation, you may find that some people refer to themselves as Taiwanese and that others refer to themselves as Chinese. The individual preference may or may not have political implications. About 15 percent of the people on Taiwan today fled mainland China in 1949 or are descendants of those who did. Children of mainlanders who were born and raised on Taiwan can tell you that their home is in Beijing, Shanghai, or some other place on the mainland although they have never been there. To avoid offense on this sensitive subject, it is best to simply call Taiwan what it is: Taiwan. The rest of China should be called mainland China.

Avoid criticism of Taiwan's society or its obviously polluted environment. The people there are acutely aware of the problems on their island, but they do not appreciate foreigners' opinions on such subjects. And say nothing that could in any way be construed as critical of your host's hospitality.

The Language Barrier Language differences can pose problems for meaningful dialogue between Taiwanese and foreigners. Few people in Taiwan speak English well, but in the business community many speak broken English, and some who have been educated in the West speak English quite fluently. Most likely, you will have to pay close attention to the person with whom you are communicating if an interpreter is not present. When speaking to Taiwanese, use short, simple sentences, and refrain from using colloquialisms and slang. The Taiwanese are most familiar with American-style English, so speakers of British or Australian English should try to use American equivalents of words like lorry (truck) and lift (elevator).

It is an immense asset to learn some Mandarin Chinese before you visit Taiwan. Spoken Chinese is actually quite simple grammatically, and a few hours of study each week for a couple of months can prepare you for simple conversation and survival communication in Chinese. Also, Taiwanese are more likely to warm up to a foreigner who has taken the trouble to learn their language. If you are planning to stay in Taiwan for an extended period of time, by all means take Chinese classes, or hire a private instructor.

BODY LANGUAGE

Taiwanese often use body language that can be incomprehensible to Westerners, and some Western body language or positions can be misunderstood. This section reviews a few issues that you need to keep in mind when you visit Taiwan.

- When Taiwanese want someone to come approach, they extend the hand palm down and curl the fingers as if scratching an imaginary surface.
- Holding one's hand up near the face and slightly waving means no, or it can be a mild rebuke.
- Pointing at a person is considered accusatory, rude, or hostile.
- The meaning of laughter and smiles among Taiwanese depends on the situation. When Taiwanese are nervous or embarrassed, they often smile or laugh nervously. They may be responding to an inconvenient request, or to a sensitive issue that has been brought up in conversation. Another possible explanation is that the smiler or another person near by has committed a faux pas.
- While shaking hands is now the standard form of greeting, traditional etiquette calls for making a fist with the left hand, covering it with the right palm, and shaking the hands up and down. Some Taiwanese still do this, especially with close friends. It is also a formal way of saying thank you and a sign of reverence.
- When Taiwanese are embarrassed, they cover their faces with their hands.
- When Taiwanese yawn, cough, or use a toothpick, they cover their mouths.
- It is impolite to point one's feet at another person. Taiwanese sit upright in chairs with both feet on the floor.
- In Taiwanese homes, shoes are removed at the

entrance. Be sure to wear clean socks!

- In public, Taiwanese rarely hug or display emotion through physical contact. Lightly touching another person's arm when speaking is a sign of close familiarity. Men and women rarely hold hands in public, but it is not uncommon for friends of the same sex to hold hands or to clasp each other by the shoulders. This is especially true of young people.

NAMES AND FORMS OF ADDRESS

In Chinese, an individual's family name precedes his or her personal name. The family name is almost always monosyllabic, and the personal name usually has two syllables, although one-syllable personal names are not uncommon. For example, Lee Teng-hui's family name is Lee, and his personal name is Teng-hui. Lu Hsun, a famous author of the early 20th century, has a one-syllable personal name: Hsun. Each syllable is represented by one written character.

Taiwanese who deal with Westerners often adopt English names, since they know it is difficult for foreigners to remember Chinese names. Sometimes they invert their names so that the family name follows the personal name. This can prove very confusing, since it is difficult to know whether a name has been inverted. As a general rule, assume that a name has not been inverted.

People outside the family rarely address each other by their personal names, even if they are very close. The exception exists, especially if a Taiwanese uses an English name. Westerners are expected to use Mister, Miss, or Mrs. when addressing Chinese. Although a woman does not take her husband's family name when she marries, it is acceptable for Westerners to use the Western form to address a married woman, such as Mrs. Hu if the woman's husband is Mr. Hu.

Another common form of address is to use a person's designated position in society. For example, a teacher with the last name Yuan can be referred to as Teacher Yuan. This form of address also applies to company managers, directors, and higher-ranking officials.

TRADE DELEGATIONS

There are a few important points to remember when you send a trade delegation to Taiwan. First, keep in mind that the Taiwanese are a group-oriented people and that they are more comfortable functioning as members of a group than as individuals. Generally, they assume that this is true of all people. They are confused when members of a visiting group speak as individuals and make statements that are contradictory or inconsistent with the stated views of the group as a whole. Individual opinions are not wanted.

Therefore, every trade delegation should have a designated speaker, who is also its most senior member. The Taiwanese will look to that member for all major communication and accept his words as the words of the entire organization.

The Importance of Status Taiwanese are really concerned about the status that an individual holds in a company or organization. They will evaluate the seriousness of a trade delegation by the rank of its members, and a delegation is not likely to succeed if the Taiwanese know that its head is a junior executive. Likewise, they will wish to match your delegation with executives of similar status from their own organization. It is wise to send them a list of the delegates who will attend that gives their ranks in the company and to request that they do the same. If the Taiwanese company sends someone to a meeting who is obviously of lower rank, the chances are that it is not particularly interested in you or that it is unaware of the status of the members of your delegation.

Delegation Leaders A trade delegation should be led by older members of the company who have at least middle-level executive rank. They should be patient, genial, and persistent, and have extensive cross-cultural experience. Ideally, they have already had some experience in Taiwan or Asia, and they have enough rank to make decisions on the spot without fear of repercussions from the home office.

Foreign Businesswomen In contrast to many other cultures, Taiwan accepts doing business with foreign women, and a trade delegation should have no problem having women members. However, women have not traditionally headed trade delegations. Outside of the cosmetic and fashion industries, companies should consider balancing delegations with men if the leader is a woman.

Interpreters The interpreter is an important member of any trade delegation . While the study of English is mandatory in schools, few Taiwanese speak much English. Even those who do speak English are not likely to put themselves at the disadvantage of having to speak a foreign language in negotiations. One member of the Taiwanese delegation will be their interpreter, but it is not wise to depend on that person for communication. Having an interpreter of your own can be costly, but it is a real advantage. In Taipei there are services that can provide you with an interpreter for the length of your stay. Look for an interpreter who is fluent in both Mandarin Chinese and Taiwanese. Although the official language of Taiwan is Mandarin, 85 percent of the people speak Taiwanese as their mother tongue, and more than half of Taiwan's businesses use Taiwanese in the office. You can assist your interpreter by thoroughly briefing him or her in advance of negotiations and providing as much written material as possible.

First Day Protocol Little in the way of serious business will be accomplished on the first day of a delegation's visit to Taiwan. This is a time for getting to know one another and for feeling out the personalities who will be involved in later negotiations. Use this time to get to know the Taiwanese side, and try to determine the status of all the members and their likely relations with one other. Because most Taiwanese companies are small, the person who heads the Taiwanese delegation may be the company's senior executive. He will be the only spokesman for the group on substantive issues, but other members will probably have some say in decision making. Taiwanese place great stock in consensus. Most likely they will debate their position on the business at hand among themselves, but never in front of the foreign delegation.

As hosts, the Taiwanese will have an itinerary of events for your delegation, and most of your time will be taken up doing what they have planned. The first day may include a factory tour or visits to cultural landmarks, followed in the evening by a traditional Chinese banquet, which may be followed by a trip to a popular karaoke club.

BANQUETING: A NATIONAL SPORT

It is fair to say that the number one pastime in Taiwan is eating. As one Taiwanese said, "When foreigners are happy, they dance. When we're happy, we eat!" If you like Chinese food, going to a traditional banquet may be your most pleasant experience in Taiwan. The form of the meal is ancient, and thus there are rules of etiquette which should be followed. Although your Taiwanese host will not expect you to know everything about proper banquet behavior, he will greatly appreciate your displaying some knowledge of the subject, because it shows that you have respect for Taiwanese culture and traditions.

Arrival Banquets are usually held in restaurants in private rooms that have been reserved for the purpose. All members of your delegation should arrive together and on time. You will be met at the door and escorted to the banquet room, where the hosts are likely to have assembled. Traditionally, and as in all situations, the head of your delegation should enter the room first. Do not be surprised if your hosts greet you with a loud round of applause. The proper response is to applaud back.

Seating and Settings The banquet table is large and round and can seat up to twelve people. If there are more than twelve people, guests and hosts will have been divided equally among tables. Seating arrangements, which are based on rank, are stricter than in the West. This is another reason why you should give your host a list of delegation members that clearly identifies their rank. The principal host

is seated facing the entrance and farthest from the door, usually with his back to the wall. The principal guest sits to the host's immediate right. If there are two tables, the second-ranking host and guest sit at the other table facing the principal host and guest. Interpreters sit to the right of the principal and second-ranking guests if there are two tables. Lower-ranking delegation members are seated in descending order around the tables, alternating with Taiwanese hosts. Guests should never assume that they may sit where they please and should wait for hosts to guide them to their places.

Each place setting at the table contains a rice bowl, a dish for main courses, a dessert dish, a spoon, and chopsticks on a chopstick rest; usually there is a napkin. Two glasses are customary: a larger glass for beer or soda and a small thin glass for hard liquor. In the middle of the table is a revolving tray on which entrees are placed. During the meal it can be spun at will to gain access to the dishes that it holds.

Chopsticks Your host may politely ask if you are able to use chopsticksoor if silverware would be more convenient. It is advisable to learn how to use chopsticks before you come to Taiwan. One good method of learning is to practice picking up peanuts from a bowl. If you are able to pick up a bowlful of peanuts with relative ease, then you should have no trouble at a banquet. If you absolutely cannot master chopsticks, silverware will be provided.

Smoking and Drinking It is probable that your host will offer cigarettes throughout the banquet. Most Taiwanese men smoke, but it is perfectly acceptable to decline the invitation to light up. It is rude to light a cigarette without first offering cigarettes to others. If at all possible, bear with the secondhand smoke. It would be rude in the extreme to ask the host not to smoke while enjoying a banquet.

Beer is the standard drink of choice at banquets, but you may feel free to substitute soda. Hard liquor, usually rice wine or perhaps brandy, is served ceremonially and reserved for toasts. It is impolite to drink liquor alone.

Beginning the Feast The first round of food at a banquet consists of small plates of coldcuts. They may already be on the revolving tray when you sit down. The dishes may contain pork, chicken, pickled vegetables, codfish, scallops, tofu, or any number of different foods. It is polite, but certainly not mandatory, to try a taste of each dish. It is better not to partake of foods that you cannot eat than to gag at the table, but if you find something on your plate that you dislike, you may simply push it around on your plate to make it look as if you have at least tasted it.

It is the host's responsibility to serve the guests, and at very formal banquets people do not begin to eat until the principal host has broken into the dishes by serving a portion to the principal guest. Or, the host may simply raise his chopsticks and announce that eating has begun. After this point, one may serve oneself any food in any amount, although it is rude to dig around in a dish in search of choice morsels. Proper etiquette requires that serving spoons or a set of large chopsticks be used to transport food to one's dish, but in fact many Taiwanese use their eating chopsticks for this purpose. Watch your host to determine which procedure to use.

After the first course of coldcuts comes a succession of delicacies. Waiters will constantly remove and replace dishes as they are soiled or emptied, so that it is hard to tell exactly how many courses are served through the event. Some banquets can include more than twelve courses, but ten are more likely. Remember to go slow on eating. Don't fill yourself up when five courses are left to go. To stop eating in the middle of a banquet is rude, and your host may incorrectly think that something has been done to offend you.

Manners Table manners in Taiwan often have no relation to manners in the West. There are no prohibitions on putting one's elbows on the table, reaching across the table for food, or making loud noises when eating. Usually it is impolite to touch one's food with anything except chopsticks, but when eating chicken, shrimp, or other hard-to-handle food, Taiwanese use their hands. Bones and shells are usually placed directly on the tablecloth next to the eating dish. Waiters periodically come around and unceremoniously rake the debris into a bowl or small bucket. Although banquets have their prescribed methods for behavior, manners conform more to practicality than they do in the West. In fact, banquet time is when businesspeople tend to be the most relaxed and comfortable.

Liquor and Toasts The practice of drinking figures prominently in Taiwanese banquets. Toasting is mandatory, and the drinking of spirits commences only after the host has made a toast at the beginning of the meal. It is likely that he will stand and hold his glass out with both hands while saying a few words to welcome the guests. When he says the words *gan bei*, which means bottoms up (literally, dry glass), all present should drain their glasses. After this initial toast, drinking and toasting are open to all, but the head of the visiting group will be expected to toast the well-being of his hosts in return. Subsequent toasts can be made from person to person or to the group as a whole. No words are needed to make a toast, and it is not necessary to drain your glass, although to do so is more respectful.

Remember that hard liquor should never be drunk alone. If you are thirsty, you can sip beer or a soft drink individually, but if you prefer to drink hard liquor, be sure to catch the eye of someone at your table, smile and raise your glass, and drink in unison. Beer or soft drinks can also be used for toasting, but do not switch from alcohol to a soft drink in the middle of the banquet lest the host think that something has offended you.

Also, it is impolite to fill your own glass without first filling glasses of all others. This applies to all drinks and not just to alcohol. If your glass becomes empty and your host is observant, it is likely that he will fill it for you immediately. When filling another's glass, it is polite to fill it as full as you can without having the liquid spill over the rim. This symbolizes full respect and friendship.

It is a matter of courtesy for the host to try to get his guests drunk. If you do not intend to drink alcohol, make it known at the very beginning of the meal to prevent embarrassment. Even then, the host may good-naturedly try to goad you into drinking. One way to eliminate this pressure is to tell your host that you are allergic to alcohol.

In the course of drinking at banquets, it is not unusual for some Taiwanese to become quite inebriated, although vomiting or falling down in public entails loss of face. After a few rounds of heavy drinking, you may notice your hosts excusing themselves to the bathroom, from whence they often return a bit lighter and rejuvenated for more toasting! Also, many Asians are unable to metabolize alcohol as fast as Westerners do. The result is that they often get drunk sooner, and their faces turn crimson, as if they were blushing.

The Main Dish The high point of a Taiwanese banquet is often the presentation of a large whole cooked fish. In formal situations, the fish is placed on the revolving tray with its head pointing toward the principal guest. The guest should accept the first serving, after which everyone helps himself.

The final rounds of food follow, usually a soup followed by rice, concluding with fresh fruit. Taiwanese consider soup to be conducive to digestion. Rice is served at the end so that guests can eat their fill, as if the preceding courses had not been enough. It is polite to leave some rice and other food on your plate; to finish everything implies that you are still hungry and that you did not have enough to eat. Fruit is served to cleanse the palate.

Concluding the Banquet When the fruit is finished, the banquet has officially ended. There is little ceremony involved with its conclusion. The host may ask if you have eaten your fill, which you undoubtedly will have done. Then, without further ado, the principal host will rise, signaling that the banquet has ended. Generally, the principal host will bid good evening to everyone at the door and stay behind to settle the bill with the restaurateur. Other hosts may accompany guests to their vehicles and remain outside waving until the cars have left the premises.

RECIPROCITY

After you have been entertained by your Taiwanese associates, it is proper to return the favor unless time or other constraints make it impossible. A good time to have a return banquet is on the eve of your departure from Taiwan or at the conclusion of the business at hand.

If possible, a third party should relay your invitations to the Taiwanese. If for some reason the Taiwanese must refuse the invitation, they will feel more comfortable telling the third party than speaking directly to you.

While Taiwan has some adequate Western restaurants, it is advisable to make reservations at a Chinese restaurant where you are sure to get good service and food. Your Taiwanese guests are likely to appreciate it more than Western fare. Banquets are priced per person and cover all expenses except alcohol. There is no need to order specific dishes, although you may do so. Good restaurateurs know how to prepare adequately for a banquet.

KARAOKE

After a banquet, a hardy Taiwanese host may invite you to go singing at a karaoke club (pronounced kala-okay in Chinese). Karaoke clubs began in Japan, but in recent years the craze has spread to all other countries in East Asia. For Taiwanese, the karaoke phenomenon is a technological extension of their natural propensity to sing with close friends.

Karaoke clubs feature a raised platform with a microphone above which is a monitor. The monitor displays preselected music videos with accompanying music but without vocals. The words of the song are displayed at the bottom of the screen. The designated singer will then sing the words. Most karaoke clubs in Taiwan have Chinese, Japanese, and English songs. Expect to be forced to sing at least one song when you visit a karaoke. For Taiwanese, being a competent singer enhances face, because one's close friends will be watching. Foreign guests are not expected to sing proficiently, and any attempt to sing will be greeted with much praise and applause. In higher-class karaoke clubs, large private rooms with big-screen television sets are the norm. Groups of friends can use these rooms to sing and drink until the sun comes up, attended the while by beautiful hostesses. It is an experience that you are not likely have in the West, although some foreigners find it rather boring unless they are drunk.

Many observers have wondered why karaoke has become so popular in the collectivist cultures of Asia. One answer is that singing in front of one's peers is one of the very few socially acceptable ways in which an individual can display his or her talent without being branded arrogant or self-centered. It fulfills the latent desire to gain credit as an individual without jeopardizing the need to be accepted by the whole group. Of course, no one goes to a karaoke club individually, and it usually is a meeting place for the closest of friends. If you wish to establish close relations with Taiwanese, going to karaoke is one of the best ways of doing it. However, some Taiwanese regard karaoke as somewhat low-class, so you should avoid mention of karaoke unless you are invited to go.

BRING YOUR CLUBS

Besides eating, drinking, smoking, and singing, Taiwanese businessmen also like to get some exercise on the golf course. Golf, a relatively recent import from the West, is a high-status game in Taiwan, as it is in all Asian countries. Visiting foreign businesspeople may be invited to a round of golf, so it can be a definite asset to know how to play and have access to golf clubs. Golfing with a Taiwanese associate has the advantage of being an activity that can be shared without the need for strong verbal communication. Membership in golf courses is prohibitively expensive in Taiwan, but urban driving ranges are popping up all over the island. For a reasonable rate, people can go to these ranges in the evening with a few friends and practice driving a bucket or two of balls.

BUSINESS NEGOTIATIONS

After banqueting, singing, or golfing with Taiwanese businesspeople, foreigners may begin to believe that their business dealings will be equally smooth. This is possible but not likely. Taiwanese can be tough negotiators. Most every aspect of a business deal between Taiwanese and foreigners is subject to the give-and-take of the negotiating process. Before going into negotiations, foreigners must be prepared for subtle and aggressive tactics. In fact, the lavish entertainment heaped on foreign businesspeople before everyone sits down at the negotiating table is partly an attempt to soften up the delegation psychologically and gain maximum advantage in the process that arrives at a business agreement.

Negotiation Etiquette When arranging for negotiations with Taiwanese it is customary to give them as much detail on the issue to be discussed as reasonable, plus notice of all delegation members who will be present. The team leader's name should be listed first. Other members should be listed in order of seniority or importance for the deal. The number of negotiation members can vary from two to ten, depending on the nature of the business. The Taiwanese side will try to match their team members with the visiting team.

Beginning the Meeting Negotiations are often held in meeting rooms at the Taiwanese place of business. A functionary escorts the members of the visiting delegation to the meeting room as soon as they arrive. The Taiwanese team is already there. The head of the visiting delegation should enter the meeting room first. This is Taiwanese custom, and not to observe it could confuse the Taiwanese about the identity of the delegation leader. If an interpreter escorts the visiting team, he or she should enter close behind the leader and remain by the leader's side throughout the negotiations.

After a round of handshaking and smiles, the visitors are seated at the negotiation table. The table is usually rectangular, and teams sit opposite each other, with the heads of delegations sitting eye to eye. Other team members are arrayed next to delegation heads, often in descending order of importance. Most likely, the guest delegation will be seated facing the door, a common Taiwanese courtesy. Tea or other drinks are provided.

Taiwanese are patient people and do not expect to jump into substantive negotiations right away. Some small talk is usually necessary in order to get the ball rolling, and this time can also be used to get a feel for those present. Taiwanese like to know with whom they are dealing. The subject of business usually comes up naturally after the participants feel comfortable enough to begin.

Entering Substantive Talks After initial courtesies, the head of the host delegation usually delivers a short welcoming speech and then turns the floor over to the head of the guest delegation. Taiwanese customarily allow visitors to speak first in negotiations. In some ways, this can be to their advantage, but participants usually know enough about each other's positions through prior communication that there are few surprises. As noted earlier of trade delegations, Taiwanese look to the senior leader for all meaningful dialogue. Conflicting statements from different team members are to be avoided, and team members should speak only when they are asked to do so.

When speaking, the visiting delegation leader should look toward the head of the Taiwanese team, not at the interpreter. For clarity, he should speak slowly and not say too much before allowing the interpreter to speak. A couple of sentences at a time is enough. Interpreters need to rest at least every two hours. If negotiations are to continue for more than a day, you may need two interpreters. Using an interpreter can stretch a meetings to three times its normal length, so be patient with the flow of discussion.

The Taiwanese do not like surprises in negotiations, so it may be wise to lay out your basic position at this time. It can also be useful to distribute sheets stating your main points in Chinese. When tackling a business issue at the appropriate time,

Taiwanese appreciate directness. Anything that you can do to clarify their understanding of your position is fine, but in the initial stage, your presentation may need to involve only the big picture. Details can be saved for later. However, in some forms of negotiations, the Taiwanese will expect a very serious and in-depth presentation, covering all the major details and answering all foreseeable questions at the very outset of talks. A typical opening statement highlighting the major topics that need to be discussed can last between five and ten minutes.

After the visitor outlines his team's position, the Taiwanese team leader takes the floor and answers point by point, remedying any perceived omissions. From this point on, the negotiation process runs with the rhythm of a controlled conversation, not an open-ended chat. The Taiwanese approach is often first to gain a holistic view of the entire proposal, then to break it down into specific chunks, at which time concrete issues and problems can be discussed. Use your own judgment in the talks, and adopt methods that are naturally suitable for your particular subject.

TYPES OF NEGOTIATIONS

Foreigners may encounter a few unfamiliar negotiating scenarios when dealing with Taiwanese. As already noted, one of the easiest and quickest kinds of business that a foreigner can do with Taiwan is to import goods produced there into another country. Negotiations of this type aim to arrive at a straight purchasing agreement. Issues of quality control and time and method of payment and shipment will be discussed. Negotiations for such an agreement can be concluded within a matter of hours if both sides have prepared adequately before the meeting. It is not unusual to hit a snag over price. The Taiwanese are increasingly seen as having unreasonable prices for goods. They may be trying to squeeze as much profit as possible, although the phenomenal rise in the cost of labor over the last few years means that export prices must be higher. Made in Taiwan, once a symbol of low price and doubtful quality, now often means good quality at a relatively high price.

A very different type of business relationship is one between the ROC government and a foreign company. The ROC has launched a multi-billion-dollar six-year development project in which foreign companies are involved for special goods and services. Good personal connections can be useful when dealing with the ROC government. However, the factor that has the most weight is quality that your side can bring into a project. Taiwan holds more foreign reserves than any country in the world, and the government can afford to expect the very best when contracting for foreign expertise. Foreign businesspeople will do well to develop an excellent presentation and make sure that they have a thorough knowledge of every detail of the project being negotiated.

In other negotiations, such as those for cooperative efforts between companies or for marketing to Taiwan, personal relationships remain the preeminent factor. But the Taiwanese play hardball in negotiations, even when there is a personal relationship. They may even try to use the relationship as leverage in the business negotiation.

TAIWANESE NEGOTIATING TACTICS

Taiwanese negotiators are shrewd and use many tactics. This section reviews some of the most common ones.

- Controlling the schedule and location. Negotiations with Taiwanese businesspeople are often held in Taiwan. Taiwanese are aware that foreigners must spend a good deal of time and money to come to Taiwan, and that they do not want to go away empty-handed. The Taiwanese may appear at the negotiating table seemingly indifferent to the success or failure of the meeting, and then make excessive demands on the foreign side.
- Threatening to do business elsewhere. Taiwanese may tell you that they can easily do business with someone else, for example, the Japanese or the Germans, if their demands are not met.
- Using friendship as a way of gaining concessions. Taiwanese who have established relations with foreigners may remind them that true friends would aim to hammer out an agreement of maximum mutual benefit. Be sure that the benefits in your agreement are not one-way.
- Showing anger. Although the display of anger is not acceptable under Confucian morality, Taiwanese may show calculated anger to put pressure on the opposite side, which may be afraid of losing the contract.
- Sensing the foreigner's fear of failure. If the Taiwanese know that you are committed 100 percent to procuring a contract and that you are fearful of not succeeding, they are likely to increase their demands for concessions.
- Flattery. Taiwanese are not above heaping praise on foreigners either for personal attributes or business acumen. Don't let their skill at stroking your ego give them an advantage.
- Knowing when you need to leave. If the Taiwanese know the date of your departure, they may delay substantive negotiations until the day before you plan to leave in order to

pressure you into a hasty agreement. If possible, make departure reservations for several different dates, and be willing to stay longer than anticipated if there is a real chance for success.
- Attrition. Taiwanese negotiators are patient and can stretch out the negotiations in order to wear you down. Excessive entertaining in the evening can also take the edge off a foreign negotiator's attentiveness.
- Using your own words and looking for inconsistencies. Taiwanese take careful notes at discussions and they have been known to quote a foreigner's own words in order to refute his current position.
- Playing off competitors. Taiwanese may invite several competing companies to negotiate at the same time, and they will tell you about it to apply pressure.
- Inflating prices and hiding the real bottom line. Taiwanese may appear to give in to your demand for lower prices, but their original stated price may have been abnormally high.

TIPS FOR FOREIGN NEGOTIATORS

A number of tactics may be helpful for foreign negotiators dealing with the Taiwanese.

- Be absolutely prepared. The effective negotiator has a thorough knowledge of every aspect of the business deal. At least one member of your negotiating team should have an in-depth technical knowledge of your product and be able to display it to the Taiwanese. Be prepared to give a lengthy and detailed presentation on your side of the deal.
- Play off competitors. If the going gets tough, you may let the Taiwanese know that they are not the only game in town. Competition is cutthroat among Taiwan producers, and you can probably find other sources in the country for what your counterpart has to offer. Also, if price is the problem, you may be able to strike a cheaper deal in China or Southeast Asia. If quality is the concern, Japanese companies may be able to outdo the Taiwanese.
- Be willing to cut your losses and go home. Let the Taiwanese know that failure to agree is an acceptable alternative to a bad deal.
- Cover every detail of the contract before you sign it. Talk over the entire contract with the Taiwanese side. Be sure that your interpretations are consistent and that everyone understands his duties and obligations.
- Take copious and careful notes. Review what the Taiwanese side has said, and ask for

clarification on any possible ambiguities.

- Pad your price. Do as the Taiwanese do. Start out high, and be willing to give a little from there.
- Remain calm and impersonal during negotiations. Don't show your agitation, lest the Taiwanese know your sensitive areas. Even if you were good buddies the night before, a standoffish personal attitude in negotiations lets the Taiwanese know that your first priority is good business.
- Be patient. Taiwanese believe that Westerners are always in a hurry, and they may try to get you to sign an agreement before you have adequate time to review the details.
- State your commitment to work toward a fair deal. Tell the Taiwanese that your relationship can only be strengthened by a mutually beneficial arrangement.
- Be willing to compromise, but don't give anything away easily.

THE TAIWANESE APPROACH TO CONTRACTS

A few years ago, many Taiwanese viewed written contracts as virtually meaningless compared to personal commitments between associates. This view still causes problem in mainland China, but Taiwan is rapidly evolving into a full democracy based on the rule of law, and the Taiwanese now accept that a contract is a legally binding document. Such a view is especially prevalent among people who have had experience with the West. (Refer to "Business Law" chapter.)

In contrast to the Western view, some Taiwanese still consider a contract to be a loose commitment to do business, not a document outlining every aspect of the business relationship. Some head executives would rather sign a short agreement on the principle of doing business and allow subordinates to work out the details at a later time. Avoid this situation if you can, because it increases the chance of misunderstanding on both sides and necessitates further negotiations, which can be costly.

While negotiating a detailed contract is important, understand that the Taiwanese often view any deal with foreigners as only one component of a larger, ongoing relationship. The Taiwanese see the immediate issue as a sort of building block that allows them to measure and strengthen reliability and cooperation. This is a practical and realistic philosophy that any Westerner who wants to do business in Taiwan over the long term should appreciate and adopt for his own ventures.

FURTHER READING

The preceding discussion of Taiwanese business culture and etiquette is by no means complete. The books listed here can give the reader additional insight. While some of these titles focus mainly on business in mainland China, many of the customs discussed are equally applicable to Taiwan.

Dealing With the Chinese, by Scott D. Seligman. New York : Warner Books, 1989. ISBN 0-446-38994-3. $12.95. A detailed examination of business relationships and etiquette between Chinese and foreigners whose author has extensive experience in mainland China and uses personal stories and examples to illustrate Chinese behavior and etiquette.

Chinese Etiquette and Ethics in Business, by Boye De Mente. Lincolnwood, Ill : NTC Business Books, 1989. ISBN 0-8442-8525-0. $14.95. A broad cultural survey of Chinese morals and values related to business interaction, mostly in mainland China.

Do's and Taboos Around the World, edited by Roger Axtell. New York : John Wiley and Sons, 1990. ISBN 0-471-52119-1. $10.95. A humorous and insightful bestseller compiled by the Parker Pen Company on different customs around the world that contains information on Taiwan, China, and Hong Kong.

Gestures: The Do's and Taboos of Body Language Around the World, by Roger Axtell. New York: John Wiley and Sons, 1991. ISBN 0-471-53672-5. $9.95. A follow-up to the preceding book focused on body languages of different cultures.

Demographics

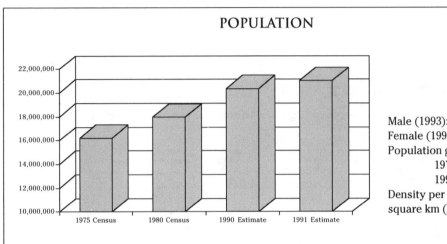

POPULATION

22,000,000			
20,000,000			
18,000,000			
16,000,000			
14,000,000			
12,000,000			
10,000,000			
1975 Census	1980 Census	1990 Estimate	1991 Estimate

Male (1993): 10.9 million
Female (1993): 10.1 million
Population growth rate
       1978-79 2.00%
       1990-91 0.96%
Density per
square km (1991) : 571.0

1991 POPULATION BY SEX AND AGE

Age Group	Total	Male	Female
0-4	1,619,000	842,000	778,000
5-9	1,789,000	922,000	867,000
10-14	2,004,000	1,031,000	973,000
15-19	1,835,000	840,000	895,000
20-24	1,869,000	957,000	911,000
25-29	1,963,000	1,005,000	958,000
30-34	1,886,000	963,000	958,000
35-39	1,717,000	877,000	840,000
40-44	1,297,000	663,000	634,000
45-49	871,000	443,000	428,000
50-54	871,000	437,000	434,000
55-59	758,000	390,000	368,000
60-64	737,000	422,000	315,000
65-69	570,000	327,000	242,000
70-74	375,000	205,000	170,000
75-79	232,000	120,000	112,000
80 and over	164,000	71,000	94,000
TOTAL	**20,557,000**	**10,615,000**	**9,942,000**

BIRTHS, MARRIAGES AND DEATHS; RATES PER THOUSAND

YEAR	BIRTHS		MARRIAGES		DEATHS	
	Number	Rate	Number	Rate	Number	Rate
1986	308,187	15.9	145,591	7.5	94,711	4.9
1987	313,062	16.0	146,076	7.5	96,033	4.9
1988	341,054	17.2	155,321	7.9	101,786	5.1
1989	314,553	15.7	158,015	7.9	102,975	5.2
1990	334,872	16.6	142,753	7.1	105,322	5.2
1991	321,276	15.7	162,766	8.0	105,933	5.2

THE GRAYING OF TAIWAN

Percentage of population aged over 65

1992	2000
6.5%	8.4%

COST OF LIVING INDEX

(1986 = 100)

ITEM	1989	1990	1991
Food	109	113	114
Clothing	99	99	99
Housing	106	112	118
Transport and communications	98	100	106
Medical care	107	111	116
Education and entertainment	113	121	131
All items, incl. others	106	111	115

HOW TAIWANESE SPEND THEIR MONEY (1979-1991)

Total and percentage of national consumption

YEAR	Total (US$ million)	Food Beverages & Tobacco	Clothing & Footwear	Rent, Water Charge, Fuel Electricity*	Medical Care & Health	Transport & Communications	Recreation, Education & Cultural Services
1979	16,425	43.67	5.36	20.76	4.79	7.35	11.29
1985	30,207	37.17	5.04	22.83	5.28	8.20	14.56
1991	98,625	29.48	4.63	18.72	4.85	13.46	17.27

*includes household equipment and operation

Taiwan
Consumer Price Index (CPI)

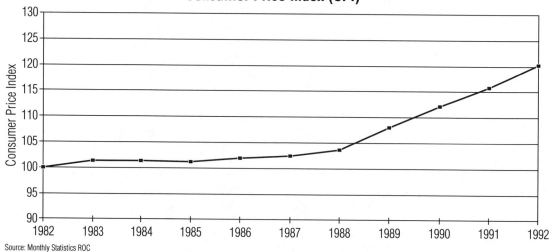

Source: Monthly Statistics ROC

1990 PER FAMILY INCOME, CONSUMPTION EXPENDITURES AND SAVINGS

	Per Family Income (US$)	Percent of national total income	Per Family Consumption Expenditures (US$)	Per Family Savings (US$)
Average Total	**19,187**		**13,655**	**5,532**
1. 1st quintile	7,144	7.4	6,561	583
2. 2nd quintile	12,681	13.2	10,581	2,100
3. 3rd quintile	16,799	17.5	13,076	3,723
4. 4th quintile	22,276	23.2	15,894	6,382
5. 5th quintile	37,032	38.6	22,163	14,869
Ratio of 5:1	5.18		3.38	25.5

TAIWANESE PLASTIC

Major Credit Cards	New Accounts in 1992 (first 11 months)
National Credit Card:	880,000
Visa:	830,000
Mastercard:	120,000
Average Purchase:	US$160.00

PER CAPITA PRIVATE CONSUMPTION

(current prices)

1980	1991
US$1,290	US$4,545

TAIWAN'S CITIES

Largest Cities	*(1991 Estimate)*
Taipei	2,717,992
Kaohsiung	1,396,425
Taichung	774,197
Tainan	689,541
Panchiao	542,924
Chungho	379,968
Shanchung	378,397
Keelung	355,894
Hsinchu	328,911
Hsinchuang	308,293
Fengshan	293,522
Chungli	276,878
Chiayi	258,468
Yungho	247,473
Taoyuan	246,056
Hsintien	233,277
Changhwa	217,328
Pingtung	212,335

STANDARD OF LIVING

Living Standard & Quality (1984-1990)	1984	1987	1990
Food intake per capita per day:			
Energy (calories)	2,810.9	2,999.0	3,019.52
Protein (grams)	80.2	88.4	90.37
Average life span (years)			
Male	70.5	71.1	71.5
Female	75.5	76.3	76.7
Percentage of households that have electricity	99.7	99.7	99.7
Telephones (per 100 persons)	27.8	33.2	41.33
Motor vehicles (per 1,000 persons)	64.6	87.8	147.65
TV Sets (per 100 households)	100.8	107.6	98.26
Enrollment rate of school-age children	99.8	99.7	99.9
Ratio of income of the richest 20% and the poorest 20% of the population	4.4	4.69	5.18
Physicians (per 10,000 population)	7.99	9.85	10.95
Hospital beds (per 10,000 population)	32.86	43.88	43.8

PER CAPITA NATIONAL INCOME

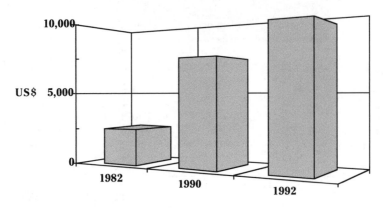

EDUCATION 1991-92

Institution	Schools	Enrollment	Teachers
Preschool	2,495	235,099	14,852
Primary	2,495	2,293,444	84,304
Secondary & vocational	1,095	1,870,315	87,206
Higher	123	613,376	29,444
Special	11	3,620	972
Supplementary	567	292,436	2,951
TOTAL (incl. others)	6,787	5,223,715	219,788

Students as percentage of total population: 25.9

RELIGION

FAITH	ADHERENTS*
Buddhism	4,860,000
Taoism I-kuan Tao†	880,000
Protestants	422,000
Roman Catholic	304,000
Islam	52,000

* Some people adhere to more than one faith, especially followers of Taoism and I-kuan Tao.
† Universal religion of principles common to Taoism, Buddhism, Christianity, Islam, Judaism, and Hinduism

HOW TAIWANESE SPEND THEIR FREE TIME

(average minutes per day)

ACTIVITY	1987	1990
Shopping	21	24
Studying, research, preparing for tests	38	30
Watching TV or videotapes	121	131
Reading	22	25
Visiting friends and relatives	44	46
Goingoon outings	11	11
Watching movies	14	19
Exercising	12	12
Attending parties or dinners	2	4
Attending religious activities	2	3
Going to the doctor, recuperating from illness	7	7
Resting and relaxing	65	58
Other	6	5

MOTOR VEHICLES

CATEGORY	1989	1990	1991
Passenger cars	1,969,291	2,328,439	2,636,228
Buses	21,852	21,357	20,765
Commercial	573,576	632,512	660,548
Motorcycles	7,619,038	8,460,138	9,232,889

Marketing

What's true for the rest of East Asia is true for Taiwan: selling your product isn't all that difficult. There's no import barrier, no language barrier, no obtuse bureaucrat, no law hidden from foreign exporters in case they're thinking of violating it, no octopus-like all-controlling state-run conglomerate—and Taiwan has all these—that can stop a committed salesperson from bringing in a needed, quality product. All along the way, you'll find knowledgeable, experienced people whose job it is to help you wend your way through the mazes constructed by knowledgeable, experienced people whose job it is to get you lost. You don't need to spend a fortune on marketing to learn if there is a market. You can find that out easily from a variety of sources; this book is one, your own embassy's commercial service and Taiwan's trade agencies are others. You don't need to learn a foreign language; you just need to take into account the cultural nuances that make one country a little different than another.

You do need to keep your initial costs as low as possible—probably through direct sales—until you have a toehold. You must go overboard to service your orders *immediately*, you must answer your faxes *immediately*. And above all, your company must make the commitment to export, because otherwise your worst problems will come from within, not without. Export sales generate a momentum of their own that is actually hard to stop, and they pull along with them repeat business, new accounts, and offers from people eager to be your agent or partner.

Beyond a few details, that's all there is to it. Now let's get to the details.

Getting a Toehold

Three major channels dominate distribution in Taiwan, and it's through them that you'll get your foot in the door:

- private traders—importers and wholesalers who buy and sell for their own accounts;
- end users, such as manufacturers, public

utilities, hospitals, schools and other public institutional buyers;
- public trading agencies—Central Trust of China and Taiwan Supply Bureau.

These channels either import directly or through supplier-appointed local agents. All seven methods listed in the next section employ one of these channels at some stage of importing, distribution or marketing. The channel you choose depends on the product you want to bring to Taiwan. Most exporters of consumer goods and light industrial equipment usually start with a local, nonexclusive distributor who directly handles the first few orders from end users. Later, the exporter often appoints a local, exclusive agent to handle distribution and marketing.

Once you've established a presence in Taiwan, you may want to set up your own sales office, but even then you'll absolutely need a local sales agent to increase your long-term chances for finding large institutional buyers. Foreign manufacturers, excluding the Japanese, have long assumed that Taiwan was strictly an exporting nation and so have neglected its huge import needs. Thus, Taiwan buyers are often completely unaware that nations other than Japan can provide products that may meet their needs, and award contracts to Japanese firms largely by default. A good local agent can enlarge the Taiwanese perspective by making personal sales calls to potential and existing customers.

There are no special laws in Taiwan regulating distributorship agreements. As long as neither you nor your agent breaches the contract, there are no penalties for ending the relationship. However, there are cultural penalties for causing your agent, distributor or representative to lose face—and so, in Taiwan as in all of East Asia, breaking a relationship is sometimes harder than beginning one.

SEVEN WAYS TO APPROACH THE TAIWAN MARKET

1. Establish a representative office

Preferred for products needing heavy after-sales service and cultivation of close relationships with clients: for example, software, computers, appliances, sophisticated or large-scale equipment.

Advantages: Allows you to retain a competitive edge in prompt service, customer commitment, and consulting aspects of a sale; suggests to your buyers that you have a permanent presence in domestic markets, giving the appearance of stability and long-term availability.

Disadvantages: Cost of office, plus added costs for specializing for customer's needs.

2. Exhibit at trade fairs

Preferred for product and new product promotion; available only if trade fair includes your product.

Advantages: Allows for contacts with major and smaller buyers and foreign and local industry representatives; facilities for hands-on demonstration techniques increase product awareness.

Disadvantages: Market limited to attendees; competition with other products targeted for same industry may be intense.

3. Get a distributor or agent

Preferred for consumer products with well-established competitors or for nonconsumer products (business and vertical market applications software, industrial machinery, electronic parts) aimed at government or commercial institutions.

Advantages: Removes need for you to create your own marketing structure; knows local needs and customs; often aware of opportunities before bids are announced; knows ins and outs of bidding; monitors and promotes smaller sales, which can add up over time.

Disadvantages: Middleman fees raise cost of product in market; marketing is limited by agent's preferences and biases.

4. Do direct marketing

Preferred for consumer products (auto parts and accessories, small appliances, consumer electronic products) but also common among industries, including factories, that want to avoid middleman costs.

Contact local importers who market through warehouse stores, hypermarkets, or other retail outlets.

Advantages: direct access to large consumer market.

Disadvantages: extreme competition with other producers because such stores market a large number of products.

Advertise in industry-specific trade journals or magazines.

Advantages: Economical and effective means to increase product awareness among large number of consumers; good for testing the market.

Disadvantages: Limited time; costs of extended advertising can be high.

5. Open your own distributorship or retail stores

Preferred for companies with a large array of products to offer (for example, auto accessories).

Advantages: Direct market access, which allows you to keep prices low and competitive by eliminating middlemen, control sales environment type of building, training of sales personnel, and improves quality and service by reducing the gap between you and the end user.

Disadvantages: High cost to establish, maintain, and staff; need to overcome bias of consumers towards already established local merchants; language and cultural barriers.

6. Negotiate a joint arrangement with a local company

Preferred for high-tech products such as high-tech software that must be modified for sale in local market, that are in growing international demand, and that are protected by copyright, patent, or similar intellectual property laws.

Advantages: Direct resource for creating specialized products aimed at particular needs of consumers in domestic market; allows use of local company's marketing and other contacts.

Disadvantages: Allows for technology transfer, potential infringement on design and technology rights, and resulting enforcement problems—a real problem in Taiwan.

7. Enter a bid on projects

Primarily for sales to public organizations.

Advantages: Successful bid may further your product's reputation in domestic markets.

Disadvantages: Price concessions may be needed for success; often obstructionist, obfuscatory regulations for foreign firms.

ADVERTISING

Foreign businesses exporting to Taiwan are becoming increasingly aware of the growing importance of media advertising in promoting their products. Despite the country's leading role in the manufacture of telecommunications equipment, and its position second only to Japan's in the region's telecommunications systems, Taiwan is not as dependent on radio and television advertising as are Western economies.

Print media

Newspapers are the leading avenue of advertising in Taiwan, accounting for almost 40 percent of all advertising spending. The 31 daily newspapers and more than 200 other newspapers combine for a daily circulation of about 4 million, a significant increase in recent years as disposable income, literacy, news coverage, and promotion have all risen dramatically.

Taiwan's three major dailies are *Central Daily News*, *China Times* and *United Daily News*. Many of the papers feature color advertisements.

Magazines are responsible for more than 7 percent of all advertising spending in Taiwan. The island's publishers churn out more than 3,000 consumer, trade and technical periodicals, including the *Reader's Digest* Chinese-language edition, which, at more than 200,000 copies per issue, has the largest circulation in the republic. The top magazine advertisers are invariably cosmetics and household products manufacturers.

Television

Television accounts for almost 33 percent of all advertising spending in Taiwan (it's 52 percent in the US.), and is growing fast. Televisions aren't as omnipresent in Taiwan as they are in Japan or Western countries, but that is changing. Currently there are more than 6 million sets, and advertising revenue is crucial to the operations of the nation's three networks—Taiwan Television Enterprise (TTV), China Television Company (CTV) and China Television Service (CTS). The Government Information Office regulates the three networks, creating guidelines for programming and advertising and supervising the amount of time allocated to commercials. The major advertisers are food and beverage manufacturers.

Radio

Most of Taiwan's 178 radio stations, which are owned by 33 radio broadcasting companies, have shifted from entertainment to professional services and now focus on news, agriculture and traffic reports. Many stations specialize in one field, and their advertising, almost 7 percent of all advertising spending in the country, reflects their audiences, which tune in on more than 15 million radios.

CHECKLIST FOR CHOOSING AN AGENT OR A DISTRIBUTOR

In many ways Taiwan's business practices are less than efficient and reliable by Western standards. This is especially true of agents and distributors. Many Taiwanese agents and distributors don't care much for the lower profit margins and relatively few after-sales services offered by foreign suppliers. The suppliers, in turn, recount nightmare stories of late deliveries, nondeliveries, slipshod sales and service, short-term profit making instead of long-term investment, inadequate experience and financing, and blatant misrepresentation of abilities and commitment. Honor-bound Confucian ethics dominate Taiwanese business, and Western-style iron-clad contract law is still largely unknown and underappreciated, so what you may consider to be clearly understood, the Taiwanese may see as wide open to interpretation—in their favor.

Don't be scared off by the tales of woe. Sometimes true, sometimes apocryphal, they can serve as guidelines in selecting a competent, committed agent or distributor. Investigate your prospective partner's:

√ **experience**—in distributing, selling or servicing foreign goods in general and your product line in particular;

√ **financial status**—get an independant analysis

√ **reputation**—with other clients and his bankers;

√ **strength**—many Taiwanese companies with impressive names are only mom-and-pop operations;

√ **goals**—you want someone who has long-term objectives, not a grab-the-money-and-run type;

√**conflicts of interest**—you want someone who isn't involved with other companies or organizations whose interests compete with yours.

Other

Cinema, outdoor advertising and direct mail advertising are three other marketing options in Taiwan. Moviegoers are treated to advertising strips or stills before the film is shown, although spending in this category is less than 1 percent of the total. Billboards and posters also account for slightly less than 1 percent of the total, while direct mail advertising amounts to about 5 percent.

Advertising Agencies

There are more than two dozen advertising agencies in Taiwan that can help to prepare and place advertisements in the various media. However, these agencies predominantly serve as managers of local campaigns developed by foreign parent companies and rarely do any creative work on their own. A number of US and European advertising agencies have offices in Taiwan.

Public Relations Firms

These are often overlooked marketing resources that, used properly, can give more bang for the buck than advertising. Decent television commercials or four-color advertisements in newspapers, magazines or billboards cost thousands of dollars, while a skillful PR agency can turn a US$10,000 investment into US$1 million worth of publicity. Sometimes all it takes is a well-timed, well-placed news release. If your budget is limited, a PR agency may be the best way to go. A number of Taiwan agencies have sprung up in recent years to take advantage of the increasing import market. They can help establish your company's name in that competitive market, build your reputation through such means as corporate sponsorships and community betterment projects, spread the word about your product, help with labor relations, and lay the groundwork for financial assistance. However, be sure to check the agencies credentials and past performance: bad PR is worse than none.

MAJOR MARKETS OF TAIWAN

There's no doubt about Taipei's importance in Taiwan's economy, but any supplier of foreign goods to Taiwan's market also needs to get out of the city and into the other five major centers of activity. After all, Taiwan didn't become the world's 14th largest trading economy solely on the basis of Taipei's industrial, financial and commercial prowess. Japan and increasingly France and Germany have a strong presence in these cities: Kaohsiung, Taichung, Tainan, Hsinchu, and Keelung. To have any hope of meeting the competitive challenge, a marketer will have to visit these commercial and industrial centers and their formidable factories.

Taipei

The capital and largest city of Taiwan, and a bona fide boomtown, Taipei has a population of nearly 3 million, twice the size of its nearest rival, and new residents continue to flow in from other parts of the island. Taipei is also the country's wealthiest and most cosmopolitan city, replete with international airport, many corporate headquarters, industries, financial and educational institutions, and foreign embassies and businesses.

On the financial scene, Taipei is the site of the Taiwan Stock Exchange (TAIEX), the Import-Export Bank of the Republic of China, The First Commercial Bank, the Bank of Taiwan, several major international banks, and local offices of several of the Big Six international accounting firms. Commercially, Taipei hosts the World Trade Center, the headquarters of many import-export companies, and 18 major department stores.

Taipei City's and Taipei County's leading industries include chemicals, ceramics, electronics, leather goods, machinery, plastics, and textiles. The county region contains four times more plants than the city it surrounds.

As people and industry flock to the metropolitan area, Taipei is in the throes of a years-long building boom. The result is a revitalized downtown and an entirely new section of the city in the eastern section. In addition, the city of Keelung, 30 km (19 miles) northeast of Taipei and part of Taipei County, adds its 360,000 people and number-two port city status to Taipei's metropolitan market, as do the giant suburbs of Panchiao, Chungho, Taoyuan, and Hsintien. Keelung is also the home of the West Coast Railway Truck Line, which serves cities from Keelung to Kaohsiung. Keelung's environmental claims to fame center on its coastal location and its 214 days of rain annually. Taoyuan is the site of Chiang Kai Shek Airport, Taiwan's largest, the 12th largest air cargo airport in the world, and the entry point for more than 90 percent of all visitors to the island.

Kaohsiung

Kaohsiung ranks second to Taipei in population, trade, finances, shopping, and education. Located on the southwest coast, it is the nation's leading port and manufacturing center, and in wealth it runs a close second to Taipei. Possessing the island's largest harbor, the city of 1.5 million is the world's third-largest container shipping port after Hong Kong and Singapore, and its second-largest dry dock. (Taiwan ranks third in the world in cargo loading and unloading, following only the US and Japan.) The government is embarking on a 30-year, US$12-billion project to build the island's only deepwater harbor in Kaohsiung to serve the heavy industry of the area. Another veritable Taiwanese boomtown, Kaohsiung and its environs have the island's only international airport outside Taipei, two huge export processing zones, aluminum-processing plants, oil refineries (including China Petroleum), sugar refineries, Taiwan Machinery Manufacturing, Tang Eng Iron Works, China Shipbuilding, and China Steel Corporation.

Kaohsiung and its county are the site of several large chemicals and plastics plants, food processors, hardware manufacturers, and tool and machinery makers, and the region is the island's leading shrimp cultivator. Like Taipei 300 km (186 miles) to the north, Kaohsiung has the building boom and snarled traffic to go with its rapidly growing economy.

Taichung

Located on the west-central plain about 150 km (93 miles) southwest of Taipei, Taichung is the nation's third-largest city, with about 775,000 residents, and serves as the economic and communications center of central Taiwan. Known more for its educational and cultural facilities, the city and its surrounding county nevertheless comprise a major manufacturing zone, with thousands of plants churning out processed foods, footwear, furniture, hardware, machinery, paper, plastics, rubber goods, textiles, umbrellas, and wood and bamboo products. Taichung is the center of the nation's machine tool industry.

Taichung also has an international seaport 25 km (16 miles) west of the city and one of the country's three major export-processing zones in a nearby suburb. Although Taipei generates by far the greatest amount of wealth in the country, the people of Taichung enjoy the highest per capita income and rank second in per capita consumer spending.

Tainan

Located in southwestern Taiwan, 10 km (6 miles) from the coast and about 50 km (31 miles) north of Kaohsiung, Tainan is the oldest city on the island and was the capital of Taiwan for more than 200 years. Tainan is Taiwan's center of history, religion, culture, and tradition. With nearly 700,000 residents it is also the country's fourth-largest city. Along with its surrounding county, Tainan is a manufacturing center for clothing, fashion accessories, chemicals, electronics, hardware, leather goods, machinery, plastics, textiles, and wood and bamboo products.

Hsinchu

This city of northwest Taiwan, about 75 km (47 miles) southwest of Taipei, is the nation's high-tech center and a thriving example of Taiwan's future. Most of Taiwan's technology-oriented companies are headquartered in Hsinchu's 2,100-hectare (approximately 5,200 acres) Science-Based Industrial Park, which has given this city of 330,000 the nickname Taiwan's Silicon Valley. The park is a totally planned business and residential community, and it's seen

FIVE WAYS TO HELP YOUR LOCAL AGENT

1. Make frequent visits to Taiwan to support your agent's efforts. They help to build the relationship, without which no amount of effort can succeed in Taiwan. Keep in mind that your competitors are also paying personal visits to their agents and customers. And invite your agent to your country to reciprocate his hospitality and to familiarize him with your country and your company.

2. Hold many demonstrations and exhibits of your products. If you're a supplier to Taiwanese manufacturers, the value of sales presentations at factories cannot be overemphasized. Factory engineers and managers are directly responsible for the equipment and machinery to be purchased, and they have much influence over the decision to buy. This is so highly effective—and so cheap—a sales booster that it's irresponsible for an exporter to ignore it.

3. Increase the distribution of promotional brochures and technical data to potential buyers, libraries and industry associations. When your agent makes personal sales calls, your potential customers won't be completely in the dark.

4. Improve follow-up on initial sales leads. Let your agent know you're backing him or her up with whatever it takes to pursue the lead. "All our foreign partners know that they have the support of a large system behind them," McDonald's spokesman Brad Trask says. "The support system is available on request."

5. Deliver on time. If you don't, you can believe that someone else will. Failure to deliver on time not only makes your agent lose face and thereby undermines your relationship, but it jeopardizes your sales. There's not much you can do to make ships go faster or airlines schedule more flights, but you can stockpile your products in Taiwan to ensure that your agent has a steady supply. When you have to (and it's possible) forget the expense and airfreight the product for two-day delivery: The extra effort will go a long way in establishing and fortifying your reputation.

as the linchpin to Taiwan's necessary move from low-end, labor-intensive manufacturing to high-end, cleaner, and more profitable industries. Here, an hour's drive from the smog and congestion of Taipei—and only 40 minutes from Chiang Kai Shek Airport—are research, development and manufacturing facilities for more than 140 firms: biochemical companies, computer and semiconductor makers, electronics and telecommunications companies, and precision-instrument makers. Together, they employ more than 26,000 workers. Among these companies are 37 from the US and other foreign countries, as well as Taiwan's largest computer maker, Acer, and Taiwan Semiconductor, whose profitability in 1993 may have exceeded that of US giant Intel. The park's companies had 1992 sales of US$3.3 billion, up 15 percent over 1991, while semiconductor sales soared 50 percent. Twenty-three new projects valued at more than $170 million began construction in 1992 alone, while current firms added $276 million worth of expansion.

Taiwan's two best technical schools, Chiaotung University and Tsinghua University, along with the Industrial Technology Research Institute, are appropriately located in Hsinchu. Farther down the line is Hsinchu Science City, planned for an eventual 1.2 million people.

The high educational status and high-paying jobs of Hsinchu's residents, along with housing costs one-fifth those in Taipei, have made them the biggest per capita spenders in the country, major-league consumers who are especially attuned to Western products and culture.

HELPING YOUR COMPANY LEARN TO LOVE EXPORTING

Five In-House Rules

1. Eliminate as much guesswork as you can

Expert export consultation is usually time and money well spent. You need a well thought out marketing plan. You cannot get into successful exporting by accident. It's not a simple matter of saying, "Let's sell our product in Taiwan." You need to know that your product will, in fact, sell and how you're going to sell it. First, do you need to do anything obvious to your product? Who is your buyer? How are you going to find him? How is he going to find you? Do you need to advertise? Exhibit at a trade fair? How much can you expect to sell? Can you sell more than one product? A plan may be the only way you can begin to uncover hidden traps and costs before you get overly involved in a fiasco. While you may be able to see an opportunity, knowing how to exploit it isn't necessarily a simple matter. You must plot and plan and prepare.

2. Just go for it

We're not suggesting you throw caution to the winds, but sometimes your "plan" may be to use a shotgun approach - rather than the more tightly targeted rifle approach - and just blast away to see if you hit anything. You can narrow things down later. If your product is new to the market, there may be precious little marketing information, and you may have essentially no other choice. Two scenarios illustrate these points: Two companies decide to begin selling similar products in East Asia, which has never seen such products before. Company A hires a market research firm, which spends six months and US$50,000 to come up with a detailed plan. Company Z sends its president to a trade fair — not to exhibit but just to look around and meet people. He follows that trip up with two others. On the last one his new associates present him with his first order. Company Z also spent six months and US$50,000 investigating doing export business, but it has an order to show for it, while Company A only has an unproven plan.

3. Get your bosses to stick with the program

Whether your company consists of 10, 50, 500, or 5,000 people — or just you — and whether you're the head of the company, the chief financial officer, or the person leading the exporting charge, there must be an explicit commitment to sustain the initial setbacks and financial requirements of export marketing. You must be sure that the firm is committed to the long-term: Don't waste money by abandoning the project too early.

International marketing consultants report that because results don't show up in the first few months, the international marketing and advertising budget is *invariably* the first to be cut in any company that doesn't have money to burn. Such short-sighted budgetary decisions are responsible for innumerable premature failures in exporting.

The hard fact is that exports don't bring in money as quickly as domestic sales. It takes time and persistence for an international marketing effort to succeed. There are many hurdles to overcome — personal, political, cultural, and legal, among others. It will be at least 6 to 9 months before you and your overseas associates can even begin to expect to see glimmers of success. And it may be even longer. Be patient, keep a close but not a suffocating watch on your international marketing efforts, and give the venture a chance to develop.

4. Avoid an internal tug-of-war

Consultants report that one of the biggest obstacles to successful export marketing in larger companies is internal conflict between divisions within a company. Domestic marketing battles international marketing while each is also warring with engineering, and everybody fights with the bean counters. All the complex strategies, relationship building, and legal and cultural accommodations that export marketing requires mean that support and teamwork are crucial to the success of the venture.

5. Stick with export marketing even when business booms at home

Exporting isn't something to fall back on when your domestic market falters. Nor is it something to put on the back burner when business is booming at home. It is difficult to ease your way into exporting. All the complex strategies, relationship-building, legal and cultural accommodations, and financial and management investment, and blood, sweat, and tears that export marketing requires means that a clear commitment is necessary from the beginning. Any other attitude as good as dooms the venture from the start, and you may as well forget it. We can't overstress this aspect: Take the long-range view or don't play at all. Decide that you're going to export and that you're in it for the long haul as a viable money-making full-fledged division within your company.

McDonald's Corporation spokesperson Brad Trask, commenting on his company's overwhelming international success, notes, "We're a very long-term focused company. We do things with patience; we're very deliberate. We're there to stay, not to take the money and run." And Texas Instruments, which has suffered recent losses in its semiconductor business, has made a considered move into long-term joint ventures in East Asia, banking that these investments will provide a big payoff five years down the road.

FIVE WAYS TO BUILD A GOOD OVERSEAS RELATIONSHIP

1. Be careful in choosing overseas distributors

This is crucial. Whether you choose to go with a subsidiary, agent, export trading company, export management company, dealer, distributor, or your own setup, you must investigate the potential and pitfalls of each. Pay personal visits to potential partners to assure yourself of their long-term commitment to you and your product, and their experience, ability, reputation, and financial stability. Many Taiwanese trading companies are relatively small, and, while they are often reputable and competent on their own level, they may not measure up to your needs. Rather than relying on bank or credit sources for information on a prospective distributor's financial stability and resources, hire an independent expert to advise you.

The keys to the McDonald's Corporation's foreign success, says spokesman Brad Trask, is a search for partners that focuses on "shared philosophies, past business conduct, and dedication. After all,

we're asking a businessman to give up two years to be absorbed into the McDonald's way of business. We want to be sure we're right for each other."

2. Treat your overseas distributors as equals of their domestic counterparts

Your overseas distributors aren't some poor family relations entitled only to crumbs and handouts. They are part of your company's future success, a division equal to any domestic division. Offer them advertising campaigns, discount programs, sales incentives, special credit terms, warranty deals, and service programs that are equivalent to those you offer your domestic distributors and tailored to meet the special needs of that country.

Also take into account the fact that distributors of export goods need to act more independently of manufacturers and marketers than do domestic distributors because of the differences in trade laws and practices, and the vagaries of international communications and transportation.

McDonald's partners in Taiwan adhere to the company's overall standards of consistency and quality, Trask says, but in all other ways, the McDonald's restaurants in Taiwan are thoroughly Taiwanese—owned, staffed and operated. "We're not operational police," Trask says. "Those partners have purchased the rights to a formula for proven success. We've never found anyone foolish enough to fly in the face of success. Instead, they've adapted the formula to suit their needs." Kentucky Fried Chicken sees things the same way. "We mandate that our partners or licensees have the Colonel up on the logo, and they have to serve original recipe chicken and cole slaw," says Steve Provost, KFC's vice president of International Public Affairs. "Beyond that it's up to them."

3. Learn the dos and taboos

Each country does business in its own way, a process developed over years to match the history, culture and precepts of the people. Ignore these practices and you lose. "McDonald's system has enough leeway in it to allow the local businessmen to do what they have to do to succeed," Trask says. Thus every new McDonald's in Thailand holds a "staff night" just before the grand opening. The families of the youthful employees descend *en masse* to be served McDonald's meals in an atmosphere that they can see for themselves is clean and wholesome. (Refer to "Business Culture" chapter.)

4. Be flexible in forming partnerships

American companies in particular are notoriously obsessed with gaining a majority share of a joint venture, the type of partnership most favored by East Asian governments. One reason is accounting. Revenue can show up on the books at home only when the stake is more than 50 percent. Another reason is the US Foreign Corrupt Practices Act, which makes US citizens and companies liable for the conduct of their overseas partners; the idea, presumptuous at best, is that majority control translates into control of the minority partner.

Here, again, Japanese practices are illuminating. Ownership is yet another area where the Japanese have succeeded; they see a two-sided relationship where Americans see themselves as the superior partner in knowledge, finances, technology, and culture—in other words, know-it-alls. Westerners, and Americans in particular, have a lot to learn about flexibility in business relationships. McDonald's Corporation has chosen the 50-50 joint-venture route, with great profitability—more than half its income now comes from outside the US. KFC is another American company that has found enormous success by being flexible. "We have a philosophy of relying heavily on our joint venture or franchise partners to guide us," says KFC's Trask. "We'd never dream of trying to impose our attitudes on them."

Finally, keep in mind that there is more than one way to do business overseas and that changing laws or market conditions will often force you to consider other options. Where a distributorship may be best at first, a joint venture or a licensing agreement may be the way to go later.

5. Concentrate on the relationship

We cannot emphasize this point too greatly. The Confucian culture of East Asia emphasizes personal relationships above all else. Building a good relationship takes time, patience, courtesy, reliability, dignity, honorable conduct, and farsightedness; a poorly developed relationship dooms even your best marketing efforts to failure. One US computer maker made a great mistake when it fired its Asian distributor after a falling-out. The dismissal, handled in a typically abrupt American way, caused the man to lose face, and ruined all the relationships the company had built through this man. For three years afterward, company executives couldn't find another distributor because no one would talk to them. Not only did the company lose untold millions of dollars in sales, but it took US$40 million in advertising to create enough consumer-driven demand for local distributors to even consider meeting with the firm.

So do your very best to build a sound, trusting and profitable relationship with your overseas partners. They are putting themselves on the line for you, spending time, money and energy in hopes of future rewards and a solid, long-term relationship.

Also, don't expect your foreign distributors to jump through hoops on a moment's notice. For example, they need price protection so they don't lose money on your price changes. If they buy your product for US$100 and a month later you cut your price to US$90, you have to give them credit so they don't get stuck with inventory at the higher price. If you raise your price, you have to honor your prior commitment while you give ample notice of the increase.

With their focus on long-term relationships and on mutual respect and trust, East Asians, in particular, make honorable partners once you have gained their confidence by showing them they have yours.

Seven Rules for Selling Your Product

Respect the individuality of each market

The profit motive generally operates cross-culturally and the nationals of most countries, especially within a given region, will have much in common with one another. However, there will also be substantial differences, enough to cause a generic marketing program to fall flat on its face and even build ill-will in the process. You may have some success with this sort of one-size-fits-all approach, but you won't be able to build a solid operation or maximize profits this way. "Japan proves this point phenomenally," says Steve Provost, KFC's vice president of International Public Affairs. "Our first three restaurants in Tokyo were modeled after our American restaurants, and all three failed within six months. Then we listened to our Japanese partner, who suggested we open smaller restaurants. We've never looked back." What works in Japan doesn't necessarily work in Taiwan. Taiwanese tastes may be more similar to US tastes than to Japanese or may differ in other ways.

Adapt your product to the foreign market

Markets are individual, and you may well need to tailor your products to suit individual needs. As the United States' Big Three automakers have yet to learn, it's hard to sell a left-hand-drive car in a right-hand-drive country. White may be a popular color in your country, but may also be seen as the color of death in your foreign market. Dress, styles, and designs considered fashionably tasteful at home can cause offense abroad. One major US computer manufacturer endured years of costly marketing miscalculations before it realized that the US

Seven Rules (cont'd.)

is only one-third of its market, and that the other two-thirds required somewhat different products as well as different approaches.

You can avoid this company's multi-million dollar mistakes by avoiding lazy and culturally-biased thinking. A foreign country has official regulations and cultural preferences that differ from those of your own. Learn about these differences, respect them, and adapt your product accordingly. Often it won't even take that much thought, money, or effort. Kentucky Fried Chickenooffers a salmon sandwich in Japan, fried plantains in Mexico, and tabouleh in the Middle East — and 450 other locally specific menu items worldwide. And even the highly standardized McDonald's serves pineapple pie in Thailand, teriyaki burgers and tatsuda sandwiches (chicken with ginger and soy) in Japan, spicy sauces with burgers in Malaysia (prepared according to Muslim guidelines), and a seasonal durian fruit shake in Singapore.

Don't get greedy

Price your product to match the market you're entering. Don't try to take maximum profits in the first year. Take the long-term view. It's what your competitors are doing, and they're in it for the long haul. The Taiwanese are very price-conscious. When you're pricing your product, include in your calculations the demand for spare parts, components, and auxiliary equipment. Add-on profits from these sources can help keep the primary product price down and therefore more competitive.

Demand quality

A poor-quality product can ambush the best-laid marketing plans. The Taiwanese may look at price first, but they also want value and won't buy junk no matter how cheap. And there's just too much competition to make it worth your while to put this adage to the test. Whatever market you gain initially will rapidly fall apart if you have a casual attitude towards quality. And it is hard to come back from an initial quality-based flop. On then other hand, a product with a justified reputation for high quality and good value creates its own potential for market and price expansions.

Back up your sales with service

Some products demand more work than others — more sales effort, more after-sales service, more hand-hold-ing of the distributor, and more contact with the end user. The channel you select is crucial here. Paradoxically in this age of ubiquitous and lightning-fast communications and saturation advertising, people rely more than ever on word of mouth to sort out the truth from hyperbole. Nothing will sink your product faster than a reputation for poor or nonexistent service and after-sales support. US firms in particular need to do some serious reputation building for such after-sales service. Although the Taiwanese see US products as generally superior in quality and performance, they rate Japanese after-sales service as vastly better. And guess whose products they buy.

Consider setting up your own service facility. If you're looking for a Taiwanese agent to handle your product, look for one who has qualified maintenance people already familiar with your type of product or who can handle your service needs with a little judicious training. And make sure that this partner understands how important service and support are to you and to your future relationship with him.

Notice that foreigners speak a different language

Your sales, service, and warranty information may contain a wealth of information but if it's not in their language, you leave the foreign distributors, sales and service personnel, and consumers out in the cold. It's expensive to translate everything into Chinese, but it's absolutely necessary.

Focus on specific geographic areas and markets

To avoid wasteful spending, focus your marketing efforts. A lack of focus means that you're wasting your money, time, and energies. A lack of specificity means that your foreign operations may get too big too fast. Not only does this cost more than the local business can justify or support, it also can translate into an impersonal attitude towards sales and service and the relationships you've working so hard to build. Instead concentrate your time, money, and efforts on a specific market or region, and work on building the all-important business relationships that will carry you over the many obstacles to successful export marketing.

Business Entities & Formation

FORMS OF BUSINESS ORGANIZATION

The Republic of China (ROC) offers Taiwanese and foreign nationals a fairly wide range of recognized options for establishing a business. These include several different types of companies, as well as branches and representative or liaison offices. Investors also can form agent, distributor, and cooperative agreements. The specific type of business entity that an investor selects will be determined by the objectives, circumstances, degree of control desired, and the anticipated duration of the investment. However, the range of likely solutions to most business needs is fairly narrow.

Of particular interest to foreign investors are the company limited by shares and the branch office. Taiwanese law grants incentives to entities using these forms. Although businesses structured in other ways are legal, they are not generally recognized in Taiwan as appropriate vehicles for serious foreign investment. Moreover, they are ineligible for foreign investment approved (FIA) status and incentives offered under this and other official programs, they could leave the investor open to substantial personal liability, and they could have difficulty in gaining acceptance within the local business community.

Companies

A company is a legal enterprise organized and registered for profit-seeking purposes. Taiwanese law recognizes four types of companies: unlimited companies, limited companies, unlimited companies with limited-liability shareholders, and companies limited by shares. All four types can be established for the purpose of conducting business in the ROC. The company limited by shares is the most suitable type for foreign investors, although other types could be advantageous under special circumstances.

Company Limited by Shares The company limited by shares closely resembles a US corporation. It is the accepted, standard structure for serious commercial and industrial firms operating in Taiwan,

both foreign and domestic. A foreign investment approved company limited by shares is generally deemed to be the most practical and beneficial form of entity for foreign investment. Moreover, it is the only type of company that can receive the preferential tax and investment incentives provided under the Statute for Promotion of Industrial Upgrading (SIU).

This type of company requires a minimum of seven shareholders, more than half of whom, including management, must be nationals domiciled in Taiwan. This requirement can be circumvented by seeking FIA status, which allows companies limited by shares to be 100 percent foreign owned, staffed, and managed. There is no upper limit on the number of shareholders. Theoretically, if the authorized capital is not fully subscribed, the outstanding shares must be offered to the public, but this issue is usually moot, because those planning the business arrange to provide the full investment amount.

The total capital must be divided into shares of equal value having a stated par value. As in Western law, the liability of individual shareholders is limited to the value of the portion of the business represented by shares owned. Once shares have been issued, they may not be retired unless paid-in capital is reduced by a proportional amount.

The company may be established as either a publicly held or a privately held enterprise, unless its capital is greater than NT$200 million (about US$7.5 million), in which case it must be a public company regulated by Taiwan's Securities and Exchange Commission (SEC.) Being a public company means that the firm must produce public financial statements and other filings, although the company's shares do not have to be listed on the stock exchange. An FIA status company can remain private and does not have to submit to SEC regulation or disclose information publicly.

A company limited by shares can issue preferred shares as well as common shares. It may also issue registered as well as bearer shares, although at least

50 percent of all shares must be in bearer form. The company's articles of incorporation specify the composition of types of shares to be issued within these parameters.

Investors who wish to maintain absolute control can set up a wholly-owned foreign subsidiary as a company limited by shares. To set up such an entity, they must obtain FIA status, which allows 100 percent foreign ownership and management.

Unlimited Company An unlimited company has two or more shareholders bearing both unlimited and joint and several liability for the company's obligations. The managing shareholder and at least half of all shareholders must be resident ROC nationals. This form is used primarily by small, local family enterprises or by investors who want above all to minimize potential liability. The unlimited company is not eligible for FIA status, does not qualify for the investment incentives extended under the SIU, and it is usually not an appropriate format for foreign investors doing business in Taiwan.

Limited Company A limited company must have at least five and may have no more than 21 shareholders. Their liability is limited to the amount of their capital contribution. More than 50 percent of the shareholders as well as the managing director or directors must be resident ROC nationals, and more than 50 percent of the capital must come from resident ROC nationals.

The limited company resembles a closely held US corporation. It is not eligible for FIA status and does not qualify for incentives under the SIU, and so it is generally not attractive to foreign investors doing business in Taiwan. However, a limited company could be appropriate in cases where there were a small number of investors, the majority of whom were locals, and limitation of liability was a primary consideration.

Unlimited Company with Limited-Liability Shareholders The unlimited company with limited-liability requires one or more shareholders whose liability with regard to company obligations is unlimited and one or more shareholders whose liability is limited to the amount of their capital contribution. The managing shareholders, whom all must bear unlimited liability, must be resident ROC nationals.

The unlimited company with limited-liability shareholders resembles a US limited partnership. It is not eligible for FIA status or for SIU incentives, and the unequal apportionment of liability and the requirements for local participation make this model unlikely to be of interest to foreign investors.

Company Capital Requirements In general, a minimum paid-in capital of NT$1 million (about US$37,500) is necessary to form a company in Taiwan. Import-export operations must have capital of at least NT$5 million (about US$188,000). Companies involved in such activities as construction, offshore fishing, automotive production, tourist hotels, mining, investment management, and waste management, among others, are subject to larger minimum capital requirements.

Paid-in capital must be at least 25 percent of authorized capital. Capital can be increased or decreased only with approval of the shareholders, and any change requires the company to reregister with the authorities. A decrease requires public notification and a comment period. Increases can be made by capitalization of retained earnings without specific shareholder approval if the articles of incorporation allow it. However, excessive retained earnings—those greater than 50 percent of paid-in capital—are subject to taxation.

Companies must set aside 10 percent of their annual net income, less losses carried forward, as a reserve against potential legal liabilities, until the legal reserve is equal to the company's total capitalization. Additional financial items, such as share premiums above par, certain surpluses, gains from consolidations, donations received, and gains on disposal of assets, must be carried as capital reserves.

Shareholders, Directors, and Officers Unless otherwise specified by the laws covering specific types of companies, every company has broad authority to define the rights and responsibilities of its shareholders and officers in its articles of incorporation. However, the adoption or amendment of articles of incorporation must have the unanimous approval of the company's shareholders. Companies limited by shares must issue stock certificates to shareholders within three months of incorporation or of any increase in capital. The other types of companies issue certificates of ownership detailing the allocation of profits, losses, and liabilities.

A meeting of shareholders must be held at least once a year no later than six months after the fiscal year ends. A minimum of 50 percent of the voting shares must be represented to establish a legal quorum. Directors and other officers must be registered with government authorities within 15 days of their election or appointment.

A limited company must have at least one and no more than three directors. A company limited by shares must have a board of directors with a minimum of three members elected from among and by its shareholders. Directors can serve a maximum term of three years, but directors can be reelected to additional terms. Activities of executives are limited: they may not engage in any other business activities of a similar nature without board approval.

A company limited by shares must elect at least one outside supervisor who is a shareholder but not a director, officer, or staff member to function as an independent auditor. This supervisor is charged with assessing the company's business and financial condition. He acts as an ombudsman to the shareholders at large, reviewing the decisions of management and the board, and he has full authority to examine the company's books, records, and documents and to retain outside auditors and other professional personnel on behalf of the company.

Dissolution A company can be dissolved under any of the following circumstances: the criteria for dissolution are specified in the company's articles of incorporation; the company has achieved, or failed to achieve, its organizational objectives as defined in its articles of incorporation; all those with an ownership interest in the company agree to dissolve it; a change in the number of shareholders has left it with fewer shareholders than the law requires it to have; the company has merged or been consolidated with another company; the company is bankrupt; or a court decree or judgment mandates its dissolution.

Branch Offices

A branch office is any office in Taiwan that is authorized, managed and administered, and paid for by the company's principal office. Because a branch office is seen as fully subordinate to its parent firm, a branch is not considered a separate legal entity, and the parent company must assume full liability for the operations of its branch. A foreign company that wants to set up a branch office in Taiwan must formally be recognized by the ROC government as a legal business entity that is registered as such in its designated country of origin.

Besides the company limited by shares, the branch office is the type of business entity that foreign investors most commonly use in Taiwan. Branch offices are specifically authorized by law, and they are well defined by usage. As a legal extension of its parent firm, a branch office can conduct virtually any kind of business activity within Taiwan. However, the broad range of allowable activity means that a branch office is subject to virtually all the regulations and registration and licensing requirements that apply to an independent company.

A branch office must also obtain local business registration and licenses. As permanent resident business entities, foreign branch offices are subject to the same laws and regulations as domestic companies. Branch offices do not require foreign investment approval to operate. However, a branch office engaged in production or manufacturing can apply for FIA status. Branch offices that do not produce a tangible product cannot receive FIA status.

A branch office, which is relatively easy to set up, is a practical way to manage some production activities and to run service and trade operations. It is not subject to withholding taxes on earnings remitted, although such remittances—except for trade-related earnings, which are unrestricted—are limited to US$5 million per year in outward remittances and US$50,000 per year in inward remittances. A branch office cannot remit working capital, because in theory it is permanent.

A branch office must have a branch manager and a designated legally responsible person to be the official respondent in lawsuits and other official business. The same individual may hold both positions; however, all but the smallest branch offices assign these roles to separate persons. These officials must be either resident ROC nationals or resident foreigners with an alien resident certificate. Alien resident certification is generally granted as a courtesy to key foreign branch personnel in recognition of the officeholders' status as representatives of a recognized foreign entity.

All funds for a branch office must be channeled through the entity's overseas headquarters. A branch office requires a minimum working capital of NT$1 million (about US$37,500) for registration. Branches engaged in import-export operations must have available capital of at least NT$5 million (about US$188,000).

Representative Offices

Representative offices are allowed under Taiwanese law, although their legal status is somewhat marginal. A representative office is any office operating in Taiwan with the authorization of the company's main office. In contrast to branch offices, which can conduct actual business operations, representative offices may not engage in commercial activities or act as principal in any domestic commercial transaction. Their primary function is to act as an authorized representative and local facilitator for the home company in such areas as inspection of goods, procurement, bidding, sign-off on the execution of contracts, and in legal and other matters for which it is convenient to have a local presence.

The individual who operates a representative office must be either a resident ROC national or a foreigner holding an alien resident certificate. The government does not automatically grant an alien resident certificate to a foreigner managing a representative office as it does for branch office personnel. A representative office should register with the Commercial Division of Taiwan's Ministry of Economic Affairs (MOEA) and local tax authorities. FIA status is not available for representative offices. A firm that wants to open a representative office should have a local attorney draw up a letter of appointment—the equivalent of a company's articles of incorporation—formally defining the intended activities of the office.

Although representative offices may engage only in narrowly delimited operations, they have the advantage of being free of income taxes because they generate no income on their own, and their operating expenses are paid by the headquarters office. And because the head office is directly liable for all expenses, there is no registered capital requirement.

Liaison Offices

Liaison offices have no specific authorization in law. However they are common and well defined in practice. A liaison office differs from a representative office in that it cannot conduct commercial or legal activities, it cannot enter into any agreement whereby it earns income, and it cannot maintain an inventory of goods or merchandise. Basically, a liaison office is restricted to handling local communications and providing information, although it may engage in ancillary activities as long as it can convince the government that such activities are not binding on the parent organization and that they are not directly profit-making in nature. A liaison office can be a useful vehicle for a foreign firm that is interested in exploring opportunities, developing relationships, and gaining name recognition in Taiwan.

Because liaison offices lack legal status, there are no specific requirements regarding personnel. However, foreign personnel must have the alien residential certificate required for anything but a short visit to Taiwan. Appointment to operate a liaison office is not sufficient to gain an alien resident certificate for the appointee. Because a liaison office generates no income and its expenses are paid by its home office, it has no income tax liability and no minimum capital requirement.

It is unnecessary to register a liaison office with the MOEA, although approved offices are given a Taiwanese company registration number. However, even a registered liaison office is not allowed to carry out foreign exchange operations. Registration is more an expression of bona fides than a matter of legal necessity or practical benefit.

Technical Cooperation Agreements

Technical cooperation agreements usually refer to agreements under which a foreign business licenses specific technologies, trademarks, or patents to ROC firms or individuals. In exchange for use of the technology or patent rights, the Taiwanese entity pays the foreigners technical service fees or fixed royalty payments. Approval can be obtained from the MOEA for such arrangements, but it is not mandatory.

Taiwanese authorities strongly encourage the licensing of advanced industrial technology. They have not looked with favor on the licensing of consumer products or labor-intensive manufactures.

Both foreign businesses with no Taiwanese presence and previously established FIA companies or branches are eligible to engage in technological licensing agreements.

Royalties payable under the terms of licensing agreements are subject to a 20 percent withholding tax, but exemptions can be allowed for operations using patents that have been registered in the ROC as part of the technology transfer and for technologies classified as strategic. Under the terms of the Statute for Technical Cooperation (STC), entities may apply to the Investments Commission of the MOEA for approval of technical cooperation agreements. Such approval allows them to receive royalties tax free. The procedure involves giving all agencies potentially involved in any aspect of the technologies and industries involved in the transfer a chance to intervene, and it can delay and complicate the deal for the contracting parties.

Commercial Agents and Distributorships

Commercial agents and distributorships are individuals or firms that contract to provide local representation for a foreign enterprise that wants to sell its products in Taiwan. Domestic agents or distributorships are usually responsible for day-to-day operations, such as sales functions, on-site storage, order processing, and delivery of goods. They can, to some extent, also provide customer service and handle customer inquiries. They cannot serve as proxy business entities, and they are not involved in production, planning, negotiation of contracts, or other management functions.

Besides providing the simplest form of organization from the legal point of view, such relationships also can be the most cost-effective. Under the ROC Civil Code, foreign investors do not need to establish a physical presence in Taiwan or submit to local regulation if their legal presence exists exclusively of contracts with domestic agents or distributors. Moreover, either party can terminate the agency agreement without incurring liability, provided that termination of the agreement involves no breach of contract.

Difficulties can arise if an agent accepts direct payments from local customers on behalf of the foreign firm for sales or the provision of services. Such income is taxable. However, no tax is due if an agent provides quotations, bids on contracts, or executes contracts negotiated by other, but does not accept payment for the company's goods. Thus, billing and payment procedures are important considerations when such arrangements are made.

Joint Ventures

As in much of the rest of Asia, a joint venture in Taiwan is a vague description that refers to a wide range of mutual agreements between contracting parties, often—but not always—of different nationalities. It is not a specific type of business structure with legal standing as it is in most Western legal practice. ROC law provides no precise legal definition for a joint venture, and joint ventures are not recognized as legal entities in Taiwan. For this reason, unless it is carefully structured within the accepted framework of Taiwanese company law, a joint venture can cause difficulties for the foreign partner in such areas as obtaining foreign exchange, repatriating funds, paying taxes, and resolving disputes.

Any of the four types of companies described earlier can be structured to accomplish the intent of a joint venture. Or, if appropriate, a joint enterprise

and operating as sole proprietors, such businesses are ineligible for FIA status or for SIU incentives.

Sole proprietorship must have a minimum capital of NT$3,000 (about US$115) although participation in certain areas of business may require larger minimum levels. Proprietorship may dissolve essentially at will because there are no interested parties other than the individual owner to consider. However, the proprietor retains unlimited liability to creditors and other parties with potential claims even after dissolution.

Despite the regulatory ease and low initial cost of doing business as an individual, the sole proprietorship is not a recognized vehicle for serious business in Taiwan, especially for foreign investment, and

Small- to Medium-Sized Business Enterprises

It is not necessary to be a huge, multinational corporation with international name recognition in order to operate a successful business venture in Taiwan. The vast majority of businesses operating in Taiwan are small- to medium-sized entities, and small, entrepreneurial firms are the engine that drives Taiwan's economy. Such firms are comfortable dealing with foreign counterparts. To encourage foreign investment, the 1991 Statute for Promotion of Industrial Upgrading (SIU) abolished restrictions on the scale of production in the Statute for Encouragement of Investment that it replaced. Small and medium-sized domestic and foreign companies are now eligible for many incentives once available only to large businesses. The Statute for Development of Small- and Medium-Sized Enterprises, which became effective on February 6, 1991, grants SIU-like incentives specifically to small- and medium-sized enterprises. To learn more about the benefits and privileges extended under this legislation, foreign investors should contact the Industrial Development and Investment Commission (IDIC) at the Ministry of Economic Affairs (MOEA).

Finally, foreign investors may wish to investigate the advantages of forming a joint venture or strategic alliance with ROC nationals. In addition to minimizing risk and optimizing relationships, having local partners with established contacts can be an effective market penetration strategy. Foreign investors can contact the IDIC for assistance with introductions to potential Taiwanese business partners. Thorough independent investigation and careful selection of such partners or representatives are keys to success.

can be structured as a technical cooperation agreement in which the foreign partner provides the technology. Most joint ventures are organized as a company limited by shares. Such companies are eligible to obtain FIA status, and they are eligible for SIU incentives. If all parties to a joint venture operating in Taiwan are foreign, the government considers the entity to be the equivalent of a subsidiary of a foreign corporation.

Sole Proprietorship

A sole proprietorship generally refers to an individual engaged in a profit-seeking venture. Taiwanese law does not recognize sole proprietorship as legal persons, and sole proprietors thus have unlimited personal liability. Although there are no specific legal barriers to prevent foreign investors from registering

investors attempting to do business in this way may have difficulty gaining local acceptance.

Partnerships

According to ROC civil law, partnerships are entities in which contributions and assets under contract are agreed on and jointly held by two or more individuals. Unless otherwise specified, accounts must be reconciled and profits must be distributed annually. Although companies can be accorded the status of legal persons, they are not individuals and they may not form partnerships.

In a general partnership, two or more individuals are responsible both for joint capital contributions and for management of business operations. In general partnerships, all partners have unlimited liability. A limited partnership encompasses both participating and nonparticipating individuals, with those who actively manage the business bearing joint and several liability, while nonparticipating partners have no managerial responsibility, and their liability is limited to their capital contribution.

Partnerships must have at least NT$3,000 (about US$115) in capital. Minimum capital requirements can be higher for entities involved in certain areas of business. Because liability is unlimited, the capital potentially at risk is unlimited, although the initial capital requirements are negligible. A partnership may dissolve if the time duration specified for it has expired; if all partners have agreed to dissolve the relationship; or if the partnership has achieved, or failed to achieve, its stated objectives.

Although foreigners can legally form partnerships, partnerships cannot obtain FIA status and they are not eligible for SIU incentives. Because partnerships are not legal persons, they generally fail to offer legal standing and protection from unlimited liability to the partners. Moreover, local practice does not consider partnerships to be an appropriate vehicle for foreign investment, and investors attempting to do business as a partnership may have difficulty dealing with local firms.

REGISTERING A BUSINESS

With the exception of only the smallest, most informal local entities, every business must register with the government and obtain authorization before starting operations. Moreover, no entity may conduct business in areas or activities not specifically authorized in the terms of its registration. Registration procedures call for a relatively specific and narrow definition of the scope of the proposed business, and any significant changes in business goals, methods, or operations are likely to require an entity to reregister.

Although it is theoretically possible for individuals to navigate the shoals of business formation procedures on their own, most investors who want to set up a business in Taiwan turn the applications procedure over to professionals, such as accounting or legal firms with expertise in such matters. Many of these firms maintain specialized staff to handle this type of activity, which is a significant part of their business. Because virtually all foreign and domestic enterprises operating in Taiwan are governed by ROC company or civil law, both local and home country legal and tax and accounting assistance should be sought to ensure that individual and corporate enterprises comply with all regulatory requirements and procedures. (Refer to "Important Addresses" for names and addresses of law firms and CPA firms dealing with Taiwanese business issues.)

Licensing Most forms of business require registration with the MOEA or the appropriate provincial or municipal authorities. An entity must also obtain a business license and a taxpayer identification number by registering with the local tax authorities.

Special Registration for Businesses In addition to observing all laws governing the particular business structure under which an entity has been organized, activity in certain areas requires a business to obtain additional special authorization or licensing. Such businesses can be registered only after they have received such approvals. The areas affected include: banking, insurance, insurance brokerage, stock brokerage, trust operations, investment management and consulting, venture capital and investment banking, customs brokerage, construction, publishing, shipping, airlines, transportation, travel, hotels, restaurants, theaters, pharmaceuticals, and electronics products manufacturing. This list is not exhaustive and is subject to modification.

Restrictions Taiwan has placed restrictions on foreign investment and operations in such areas as agriculture, power generation, and mining. After reviewing the Negative List for Investment by Overseas Chinese and Foreign Nationals, investors should contact the appropriate government office for further details regarding their specific proposal.

Fees Registration fees are set according to the level of capital required for the business to be registered. Fees generally involve small amounts that can be characterized as nominal processing fees: the registration fee is 1/4000 of the registered capital amount. For a company with the minimum capital amount of NT$1 million, this fee is about US$10; for a large company with a capitalization of NT$200 million, the registration fee would still be under US$2,000. Business licenses generally cost NT$2,000—about US$75.

Basic Authorizations Needed and Application Procedures

Although each kind of business organization has its own specific requirements for the formation and registration of new entities, every entity must fulfill three basic requirements. First, it must be officially recognized by the MOEA. Second, it must register and obtain necessary permissions from the MOEA and its various agencies. Third, it must apply to the appropriate tax authorities in the jurisdiction where it is located to obtain a business license and receive a tax identification number. Each subsequent step requires submission of authorizations received in the preceding step.

The reader should note that while general application procedures and the types of information and documentation needed to obtain various approvals, registrations, and licenses are fairly well

Foreign Investment Approved (FIA) Status

As an inducement to overseas investment, Taiwan grants foreign investment approved (FIA) status to companies limited by shares and to branch offices engaged in manufacturing or production. No other type of business entity is eligible for FIA status. Eligible investments include establishment of new enterprises or the expansion of existing ones; acquisition of ownership in existing firms via securities purchases to the extent allowed by Taiwanese securities law; investment in existing firms via loans, machinery and equipment, or raw materials; and investment of technical know-how or patent rights as capital stock.

Foreign and overseas Chinese investors who do not qualify for or desire FIA or Statute for Investment by Overseas Chinese (SIOC) status are still permitted to invest in regular domestic firms organized by ROC nationals. Such investments are eligible for some benefits under the Statute for Promotion of Industrial Upgrading (SIU.) However, a number of FIA incentives are not available, and foreign participation and operating freedom are restricted under the SIU if the entity does not have FIA status. Many foreign investors consider the benefits available with FIA status to be indispensable to profitable operations in Taiwan. Most important of all, an entity must have FIA status in order to purchase the foreign exchange necessary to make payments and remittances overseas.

Benefits of FIA Status FIA status confers the following major benefits:

- Annual net operating and interest income and initial invested capital may be repatriated starting one year after business operations begin; profits from land sales are excluded.
- The entity is exempted from standard nationality and residency requirements. Such exemption is necessary for 100 percent foreign ownership, management, and board membership. Restrictions on employment of foreign technical and professional personnel are also waived.
- The withholding tax on dividends drops from 35 percent to 20 percent.
- As long as foreign investment represents 45 percent or more of the company's total capital, the firm is exempted from requirements that it offer its stock to the public or to its employees.
- Firms with 45 percent or more foreign investment are free

from official requisition or nationalization for a period of 20 years. Taiwan has never taken over foreign firms.
- The entity is entitled to the same rights and privileges as a domestic company.

Obtaining FIA Status An entity that wants to obtain FIA status applies to the Investment Commission of the MOEA. FIA status cannot be granted retroactively. Investors wishing to locate in one of the Export Processing Zones or the Hsinchu Science-Based Industrial Park may apply through those administrations.

Specific investments are usually approved provided that the investors supply the appropriate documentation and the proposed business raises no regulatory or policy issues. However, if you contemplate investment in restricted areas, you must obtain necessary permissions from the authorities governing those specific business areas before you can apply for FIA status.

Applicants must be recognized as a foreign business by the MOEA, or its designate. This procedure is similar to that involved in gaining recognition to form a company or branch. Applicants must submit an application form, certified copies of documents confirming the nationality and legal status of the foreign investors, credit references, and detailed business plans. These plans should include data on the investors; the proposed scope of business; the entity's legal form; the intended locations of operation; staffing; amount and nature of capital contribution; production and sales plans; and, if applicable, real estate, construction, and development plans, needs for power, equipment, and raw or intermediate materials, and domestic and import procurement plans. Approval usually takes about two months.

When approval has been received, the investors must open an account with a local bank and transfer to it the working capital contribution that they have agreed on. After these funds have been deposited and certified, all the investors must make the capital contributions they have agreed on and ratify the articles of incorporation. The board must certify ratification, elect the corporate officers, and make other such arrangements necessary for operation of the business. The company then completes its registration by obtaining a company license from the MOEA and obtaining a business license and taxpayer identification number from local tax authorities.

established, specific requirements and policies are subject to change and variations. Therefore, all applicants should check with the appropriate agencies of the MOEA and with experienced local professionals to confirm the requirements for their specific circumstances.

Summary of Approval Procedures by Type of Entity

Companies Companies cannot be incorporated unless they have been recognized by and properly registered with the appropriate branch of the MOEA, which will issue a license to operate. Companies must also apply to the appropriate tax authorities for a business license and taxpayer identification number.

Foreign Investment Approved (FIA) Status To apply for FIA status, a company must submit an application, certified copies of documents confirming the nationality and legal status of foreign investors, and detailed business plans. Such plans include data on the investors, business scope, legal form, intended locations, staffing, amount and natureoof capital contribution, production and sales plans, real estate, construction, and development plans, where applicable, equipment and raw materials needed, domestic and import procurement plans, and credit references. When approval has been received, the investors must open an account with a local bank and transfer to it the working capital that they have agreed on.

When these funds have been deposited and certified by accountants, the company must have its articles of incorporation ratified by all investors, with the board certifying the result. The board must also certify that shareholders have made their agreed capital contributions. The board must elect corporate officers and make other arrangements necessary for operation of the business. The company then completes its registration by certifying its incorporation and obtaining a company license from the MOEA and obtaining a business license and taxpayer identification number from local tax authorities.

Branch Offices A branch office must apply for investment approval in accordance with ROC company law. To receive a certificate of recognition, the parent company must submit an application form and documentation through its local agent describing itself and its plans for operations in Taiwan. It must also designate a local manager and legally responsible agent. The parent company must open a local bank account and transfer to it the working capital contribution that it has agreed to in order to obtain recognition. When recognition has been granted, the parent company must then obtain a branch office license from the Bureau of Reconstruction office that has jurisdiction over its business location. It also must register with tax authorities to obtain a business license and a tax identification number.

Representative Offices A representative office does not need investment approval, but it must register with the Commercial Division of the MOEA and with the local tax office and receive a tax number. To register with the MOEA, it submits certified documents demonstrating that the parent is incorporated in its home country and that it has appointed a representative. The documents must include business plans for the Taiwan office.

Liaison Offices A liaison office does not have to have investment approval or to register with the MOEA, but it should register with the local tax office and receive a tax number. To register with the local tax office, the parent company submits a certified letter of appointment for its liaison officer, identity documents for the officer, and evidence, such as lease documents, of its right to occupy office space.

Specific Procedures

Applying for Recognition Registration is usually a formality, because recognition is granted as a matter of course once the required documentation has been submitted. However, registration can be denied in cases involving the national interest, in cases where the applicant's home country does not recognize ROC entities, or in cases where there are problems with the proposed investment.

As a general rule, the following certified documents should be submitted to the MOEA:

- Application form (and proxy letter appointing an agent and executed by an attorney, if the application is filed by an agent rather than a principal); and
- Application form for preinvestigation of proposed corporate name.

Recognition Registration Card A1 and A2 and Itemized Recognition Card

The application form for foreign entities asks for the following information:

- Name, type, and nationality of the company;
- Scope of the business to be conducted in the ROC;
- Authorized capital stock and amount of paid-in capital;
- Amount of working capital for operations in the ROC;
- Location of the overseas head office and location of branch office or other offices within the ROC;
- Date of incorporation and anticipated beginning date of business operations;

- Names, addresses, and nationalities of directors, other authorized representatives, managing shareholders, and board members;
- Proxy letter to the local authorized representative responsible for operations in Taiwan who has been authorized to receive legal andoother notices, inclusive of power of attorney;
- Approval from assigned representatives with names, nationalities, addresses, and qualifications. (Foreign nationals should enclose a copy of their ROC Alien Residential Certificate. Taiwanese nationals should enclose a copy of their personal ID or Household Register Record);
- Name, address, nationality, number of shares purchased, and amount paid for each unlimited liability shareholder of an unlimited company and each shareholder of an unlimited company with limited-liability shareholders;
- Copy or photocopy of the articles of incorporation issued by the government of the company's country of origin or other proof of authorization;
- Copy or photocopy of the business license and registration record issued to the company by its country of origin;
- Authorization by the parent company for the formation of the entity in Taiwan that is to be registered under the laws of the ROC; this authorization should consist of the minutes of the meeting of the parent company's shareholders or directors at which the motion to apply for recognition was adopted.

Companies may be authorized without desiring or being eligible for FIA Status. However, obtaining recognition is also the first step in filing for FIA status. Requesting FIA Status involves the filing of a different application form which requires much of the same information.

Registration Procedures After the entity has been recognized, it must register with the appropriate authorities. The procedure is the same regardless of the governmental level to which application is made. To obtain a company license from the MOEA or local government authorities:

- Companies limited by shares and branch offices involved in production can obtain FIA status if they desire it. Requirements, applications, and information on FIA status can be obtained from the Investment Commission of the Ministry of Economic Affairs. Potential investors should seek appropriate legal assistance. Entities with FIA status must obtain a business license, as must all legally registered firms.
- When recognition or FIA approval has been obtained, the entity opens a local bank account and deposits the required working capital.
- When this deposit has been certified, the company follows incorporation procedures in accordance with Taiwanese company law and furnishes proof thereof. No company may be formed before incorporation procedures have been carried out and government authorities have granted a certificate of incorporation. A foreign company must keep a copy of its articles of incorporation and a register of shareholders with unlimited liability in its branch office or in the office of its registered agent for legal and other matters.
- Companies that do not have FIA status, including trading branch offices, liaison offices, and representative offices, must apply to the Department of Commerce of the MOEA or to the relevant municipal or provincial authorities for a business license.
- Every business entity must also register with the local tax authorities to obtain a business license and a tax identification number.

Applicants must check with the office of the MOEA or other agency to confirm the number of copies of each document that are required. Relevant documents must be certified by official agencies in the country of origin and in some cases by Taiwanese authorities as well. Applicants must submit a certified translation into Chinese of all documentation in a language other than Chinese along with originals or copies of the documents required. Applications may be made by a principal or an appointed agent, who may apply in person or by mail.

TEN REMINDERS, RECOMMENDATIONS, AND RULES

1. The company limited by shares and the branch office are the types of entity that foreign investors in Taiwan most often use. They also are the only types favored by ROC authorities with eligibility for FIA status and SIU incentives. Domestic Taiwanese businesses also prefer dealing with these types of businesses.
2. Allow adequate time for the investment approval and application process. It usually takes a minimum of two months, and can take four months or longer, depending on the complexity of the business operations proposed, the quality of the documentation supplied, and on whether the proposed investment raises any regulatory or policy questions.
3. A company or branch office should not open a local bank account or deposit funds until investment approval has been obtained from authorities. It must, however, do so as soon as authorization is received.
4. FIA status guarantees the right to remit profits and repatriate capital. Obtaining foreign ex-

change for the remission of such funds may be difficult to impossible without FIA status.

5. If the enterprise is to be established in an export-processing zone, the application for approval must be submitted to the Export Processing Zone Administration. If the enterprise is to be established in the Hsinchu Science-Based Industrial Park (SBIP), the application must be submitted to the SBIP administration.

6. If plans involve the operation of a factory, additional approvals are needed, including permits from the Department of Reconstruction for construction and operation of a manufacturing facility and for authorization of power allocations from Taipower. If operations are to be conducted in the Hsinchu Science-Based Industrial Park, application is made to the SBIP administration.

7. If the enterprise is involved in importing or exporting, it must obtain an import-export permit from the Board of Foreign Trade (BOFT) of the MOEA. If its operations are to be conducted in the Hsinchu Science-Based Industrial Park, application is made to the SBIP administration.

8. A company must file for registration with the MOEA within 15 days of its incorporation or no more than 15 days after its branch or representative office has been established. A local or foreign business must apply to the MOEA or the appropriate local authority for reregistration no more than 15 days after any changes are made that alter the substance of the registrations on file. A business that fails to do so is subject to a fine.

9. Regarding issues of jurisdiction, refer to the Ministry of Economic Affairs at the central government level, the Department of Reconstruction at the provincial government level, and the Bureau of Reconstruction at the municipal government level. Companies with FIA status generally will deal with the MOEA at the national level. Companies with paid-up capital of NT$30 million (about US$1.15 million) that do not have FIA status will deal with the MOEA on the national level. Companies with capitalization of less than NT$30 million that do not have FIA status will deal with the Bureau of Reconstruction in the municipalities of Taipei or Kaoshiung, and with the provincial Department of Reconstruction in the rest of the country.

10. Companies may not use identical or similar names. This restriction applies no matter where the business is located, regardless of what kind of business structure is utilized, and whether they are in the same line of business. Similar names are allowed if wording is used to make the names distinguishable.

USEFUL ADDRESSES

In addition to the government agencies listed here, individuals or firms should contact chambers of commerce, embassies, banks and financial service firms, local consultants, lawyers, and resident foreign businesses for assistance and information. (Refer to "Important Addresses" for a more complete listing.)

China External Trade Development Council (CETRA)
4-8/F., 333 Keelung Road
Sec. 1, Taipei, Taiwan
Tel: [886] (2) 7255200 Fax: [886] (2) 7576653

Ministry of Economic Affairs
15 Fu Chou Street
Taipei, Taiwan
Tel: [886] (2) 3212200 Fax: [886] (2) 3919398

Industrial Development and Investment Commission (IDIC)
Ministry of Economic Affairs
10/F., 7 Roosevelt Road
Sec. 1, Taipei, Taiwan
Tel: [886] (2) 3947213 Fax: [886] (2) 3926835

Investment Commission
Ministry of Economic Affairs
8/F., 7 Roosevelt Road
Sec. 1, Taipei, Taiwan
Tel: [886] (2) 3513151 Fax: [886] (2) 3963970

Medium and Small Business Administration
Ministry of Economic Affairs
3/F., 368 Fu Hsing N. Road
Sec. 1, Taipei, Taiwan
Tel: [886] (2) 704-9470 Fax: [886] (2) 705-4409

FURTHER READING

The preceding discussion is provided as a basic guide for individuals interested in doing business in Taiwan. The resources listed in this section provide additional information on company law, investment, taxation and accounting requirements, and procedural requirements.

Company Law translated by Baker and McKenzie. Taipei, Taiwan: Industrial Development and Investment Commission, 1988. Available in Taiwan from the Industrial Development and Investment Commission, 10/F., 7 Roosevelt Road, Taipei, Taiwan; Tel: [886] (2) 3947213. An English translation of provisions and articles of Taiwan company law.

Doing Business with Taiwan R.O.C. Taipei, Taiwan: China External Trade Development Council (CETRA), 1992. A comprehensive how-to book that covers such topics as trade, investment, importing and exporting, financial services, intellectual property rights, and human resources, plus general business information and useful contact addresses

Doing Business in Taiwan by Ernst & Young. New York: Ernst & Young International, 1988. Available in the United States from Ernst & Young, 787 Seventh Avenue, New York, NY, Tel: (212) 773-3000. Available in Taiwan from Solomon & Chang, CPAs & Attorneys, 4th Floor, 9 Chingtao Road, Taipei 10022, Taiwan; Tel: [886] (2) 3415151/3. Provides an overview of the investment environment, taxation, business organizational structures, business practices, and accounting requirements in Taiwan.

Doing Business in Taiwan by Price Waterhouse. Los Angeles: Price Waterhouse World Firm Limited, 1991. Available in the United States from Price Waterhouse, 400 South Hope Street, Los Angeles, CA 90071-2889; Tel: (213) 236-3000. Available in Taiwan from Price Waterhouse, 27th Floor, 333 Keelung Road, Section 1, Taipei 110, Taiwan; Tel: [886] (2) 7296666. Covers the investment and business environment in Taiwan as well as audit, accounting, and taxation requirements.

Information for Foreign Companies Applying for Establishment of Branch Office/Liaison Office in the Republic of China. Taipei, Taiwan: Industrial Development and Investment Commission, 1989. Information in question-and-answer format about the specific issues and requirements for establishing a branch or liaison office in Taiwan or amending the registration of such offices.

Marketing in Taiwan Washington, DC: US-D.O.C. Overseas Business Reports, International Trade Administration, US Department of Commerce, 1993. Available from the United States from the Government Printing Office, Washington, DC 20402. Further information: Office of the Pacific Basin; Tel: (202) 482-3877 or 482-2522. An annual overseas business report with general information and brief overviews of foreign trade, economic and industry trends, marketing, transportation, trade regulations, and investment in Taiwan.

GLOSSARY

Bureau of Reconstruction The primary government agency responsible for overseeing foreign investment at the municipal level.

Department of Reconstruction The primary government agency responsible for overseeing foreign investment at the provincial level.

Foreign Investment Approved (FIA) Status Official recognition by the Ministry of Economic Affairs that makes foreign investors eligible for incentives, including tax benefits and relief from certain restrictions on business operations, and that allows 100 percent foreign control of operations. Only companies limited by shares and branch offices involved in production are eligible for FIA status. Foreign operations in Taiwan do not require FIA status, but it is highly desirable.

Ministry of Economic Affairs (MOEA) The primary government agency responsible for overseeing foreign investment.

Statute for Investment by Foreign Nationals (SIFN) The statute that offers enterprises involved in manufacturing, service, export-oriented production, import-export, and other businesses deemed advantageous to the development of targeted sectors of the economy non-tax related benefits in addition to those offered with FIA status. FIA status is a prerequisite for SIFN benefits. Interested parties should refer to specific SIFN provisions for further information about pertinent investment criteria, application procedures, and incentives.

Statute for Investment by Overseas Chinese (SIOC) The statute entitling overseas Chinese investors as a class to incentive rights and benefits similar to those offered under the SIFN.

Statute for Promotion of Industrial Upgrading (SIU) The statute that directs investment in Taiwan by providing incentives to promote high technology and environmentally sound industries. The SIU governs foreign and domestic firms, replacing the Statute for Encouragement of Investment. On January 1, 1991, the SIU replaced the more restrictive Statute for Encouragement of Investment. Benefits include investment incentives, accelerated depreciation for investment in research and development, machinery, and equipment, and the extension of limits for retained earnings. Incentives are based on broad functional criteria, rather than by industry.

Statute for Technical Cooperation (STC) The statute governing the licensing of technology by a foreign firm to a Taiwanese firm. Approval is obtained through the Investment Commission of the MOEA. Such approval is not obligatory, but clarifies the standing of such agreements and entitles the foreign firm to benefits, including tax free repatriation of payments.

Labor

THE LABOR ECONOMY

Many of Taiwan's fast-growing traditional manufacturing and assembly industries have been hit hard by shortages of unskilled labor. While some firms have moved operations abroad, others have been able to fill the gap with foreign workers, many of them illegal. Skilled laborers and professional workers in most occupations are widely available, but specialists are scarce in certain newer fields, such as marketing and investment analysis.

Due in part to tough tactics by employers and government authorities, labor unions have tended to avoid confrontation. Although the number of unionized employees continues to rise, it is primarily because self-employed workers, such as taxi drivers and food vendors, have organized in order to participate in publicly subsidized insurance programs. The lack of appropriate laws, regulations, and effective enforcement poses a continuing problem in the handling of labor disputes. However, new legislation is aimed at creating a more stable regulatory environment.

Population

The population of Taiwan in 1991 was 20.56 million. For the last five years, the number has grown at an annual rate of 1 percent. Taiwanese make up the major ethnic group, accounting for 84 percent of the population. Other ethnic groups include mainland Chinese (14 percent) and Aborigines (2 percent).

Labor Force

The civilian labor force totaled 8.57 million people in 1991, an increase of 1.8 percent over the previous year. Men and women make up 62.5 percent and 37.5 percent of the work force, respectively.

Labor Availability and Distribution by Sector

In recent years rising labor costs, currency appreciation, and increasing land prices have prompted many labor-intensive businesses to move to Southeast Asia or mainland China. Nevertheless, Taiwan's more traditional industries, such as dyeing and the manufacturing of textiles, garments, and footwear, have suffered from worsening shortages of unskilled labor.

In general, it is possible to find competent personnel to fill almost any professional level or skilled labor position. For example, there is abundant talent in engineering, computer science, and nearly all export-related businesses, such as banking, shipping, and manufacturing. However, qualified employees are in short supply in consumer retailing and marketing, research and development, and investment analysis. These shortages have perhaps more to do with recent growth in these fields than with any inability of Taiwan's educational system to produce such specialists.

At the beginning of 1992 46.9 percent of the civilian work force was employed in the service sector, 40.2 percent in industry, and 12.9 percent in agriculture. Some 32 percent of the total working population is employed in manufacturing industries. This figure is expected to decline sharply in the future, and the service sector is expected to employ more than 50 percent of the labor force by the end of the century.

Sensing a structural shift in Taiwan's economy, government officials have introduced legislation to provide incentives for investment in high-technology industries. The Taiwan government's Department of Labor Affairs has initiated a program with measures to assist small- and medium-sized businesses in production automation, encourage people to take part-time jobs, and expand existing cooperative arrangements between educational institutions and private firms.

Department of Labor Affairs
Taiwan Provincial Government
Liming New Village
Taichung, Taiwan
Tel: [886] (4) 2515120

Foreign Workers

Taiwan's shortage of workers has created a need for outside labor. The late 1980s and early 1990s saw a significant influx of foreign workers, most of whom entered the country illegally. Estimates of the number of illegal foreign laborers range between 30,000 and 200,000. The majority of these immigrants come from Thailand, Malaysia, the Philippines, and Indonesia.

Since 1989 Taiwan's Council of Labor Affairs (CLA) has issued occasional administrative orders permitting foreign labor to be used in certain industries. Employers in textiles, metalworking, machinery, electrical products, electronics assembly, and construction can apply to import foreign labor after depositing a sum equal to five months' pay for the intended worker with the CLA. (*See* address below.) The number of foreign workers is limited to less than one-third of a factory's work force. A foreign worker may stay in Taiwan for no more than two years.

Council of Labor Affairs (CLA)
5-15/F., 232 Minsheng E. Road
Sec. 3, Taipei, Taiwan
Tel: [886] (2) 7182512
Fax: [886] (2) 5149240, 5149242

In April 1992 Taiwan's Legislative Yuan passed the controversial Employment Services Law (ESL). The ESL authorizes the importation of labor as needed, although specific implementing regulations have yet to be settled. Intense debate continues over enforcement of the ESL and over the number and national origin of the foreign workers who will be admitted. Police manpower and other resources required for enforcement are inadequate.

Arguments against the use of foreign labor include its possible downward pressure on wages; its negative impact on benefits and working conditions; Taiwan's increased dependence on foreigners for the maintenance of infrastructure; and the threat of increased crime and social unrest.

Taiwan has begun to open its labor market on a tightly controlled basis. A dispute between Thailand's Overseas Employment Promotion Committee and the Taiwan authorities over new wage scales early in 1992 prompted Taiwan to place a temporary ban on further importation of labor from Thailand. A similar incident involved employment brokers from Malaysia.

Unemployment Trends

Taiwan's unemployment rate for 1992 was 1.6 percent, the lowest since 1981. However, unemployment has not exceeded 2 percent since 1987. Reasons for the low levels include an especially strong demand for labor in the service sector, shorter working hours, and new construction projects associated with the six-year national development plan initiated in 1991. Increases in per capita income (US$9,895 in 1992) and wages made it possible for workers to enjoy more leisure time, while creating more positions for additional workers.

HUMAN RESOURCES

Like other Asian countries, Taiwan views its people as the country's most valuable resource. The traditional Chinese work ethic and constant efforts to raise educational levels have produced one of the world's most highly educated work forces: the adult literacy rate in 1991 was 92 percent. Taiwan invests substantial sums in worker training. This investment enables Taiwan to adapt quickly to technological advances.

Comparative Unemployment 1990-1991

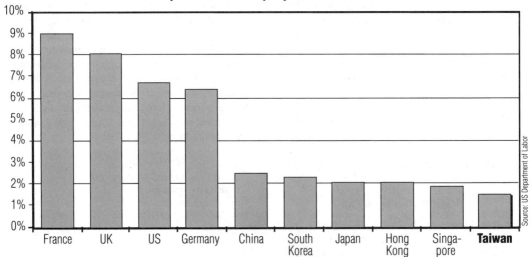

Source: US Department of Labor

Education and Attitudes Toward Learning

Children in Taiwan receive nine years of compulsory education running from primary through junior high school. New regulations aim to phase in compulsory education through high school. Currently, individual interests and success in highly competitive entrance exams determine whether students next enter a senior high school or a vocational school.

On graduation from a senior high school, students take another entrance exam to win admission to one of the 21 universities, 25 colleges, and 75 junior colleges that make up Taiwan's system of higher education. Domestic universities award almost 100,000 baccalaureate degrees annually, including about 40,000 in the natural sciences and 24,000 in business administration. Graduate schools also offer advanced degree programs in a broad range of disciplines. Increasing numbers of Taiwan university and college graduates pursue advanced degrees abroad.

Most of Taiwan's professional employees in both multinational and large domestic firms are college graduates. Mid- and upper-level managers typically have spent at least some time abroad. They are usually capable of understanding written English, and they are familiar with Western management styles.

Workers at all levels seek to upgrade their skills and capabilities through self-education, often long after they have completed their formal studies. For example, many study a foreign language or learn to apply a new technology in the workplace. Still others take advantage of the educational opportunities offered by their companies or the government.

The effort to expand educational opportunities in the information industry illustrates the extent to which individuals, organizations, and institutions are committed to raising overall skill levels. Universities and colleges have increased their offerings in the computer and information sciences. Private computer companies, along with the China Productivity Center, now provide numerous specialized courses in information technology. Taiwan's government has set a goal of computerizing the entire country by the year 2000. Among other aims, this initiative proposes to equip schoolteachers with detailed knowledge of the information industry, familiarize government employees with computerized office systems, and promote the application of advanced information technologies in everyday life.

Training

Taiwan has an extensive system of vocational and technical training in both the public and private sectors. The government has long maintained a consistent policy of assisting those who enter vocational fields to develop their skills and realize their full potential, and it has either established or subsidized 11 public vocational training centers. The Ministry

of Education instituted a six-point plan in 1973 designed to meet the nation's needs for skilled industrial workers. One of its provisions—that of establishing a 40-60 ratio between senior high schools and vocational schools—has been met.

Vocational training programs are usually conducted under auspices of the Vocational Training Bureau of the Executive Yuan. (*See* address below.) Besides providing training facilities, the bureau offers three meals a day and lodging for a monthly fee of US$50 per trainee. The Ministry of the Interior awards a certificate to trainees who complete the program and pass a skills examination and undertakes to introduce them to potential employers. The bureau also offers employee training programs for private enterprises that pay all expenses.

Vocational Training Bureau
Government Information Office, Executive Yuan
2 Tien Chin Street
Taipei, Taiwan
Tel: [886] (2) 3419211 Fax: [886] (2) 3920923

The country also has an informal apprenticeship system, in which private firms cooperate with vocational schools. Students are hired part-time by enterprises that provide on-the-job training. In many cases, students become full-time employees after graduation.

These efforts and others allow workers in Taiwan to move fairly easily into new high-technology manufacturing and service sector occupations. Moreover, the emphasis on continued training is at least partially responsible for Taiwan's significant growth in industrial capacity: the annual per capita productivity in the manufacturing sector in 1991 was roughly twice that recorded in 1986.

Women in the Work Force

Women account for an especially large percentage of university graduates in Taiwan, reflecting the prevailing tendency toward equal opportunity and the government's emphasis on using all the nation's available human resources. A recent United Nations survey ranked Taiwan first in Asia and twelfth in the world in the number and percentage of women with undergraduate and graduate degrees. This suggests that approximately 46 percent of all women in Taiwan have received some form of higher education.

While gender has no limiting effect on school admission, women are still uncommon in management positions. Women in these positions usually have important connections. For example, the husband of a high-ranking woman is the company's president. At the same time, many women in low-profile positions possess influence in day-to-day business operations, having control over financial management, hiring, and firing.

As part of the government's campaign to ease labor shortages, Taiwan's Department of Labor Affairs is encouraging women to work by helping to establish additional nursery schools and day-care centers.

CONDITIONS OF EMPLOYMENT

When Taiwan is measured against other countries in the region, its standards for the workplace are relatively high. However, levels of compliance with official regulations are often low. Some explain this tendency by saying that standards are too high. Others see a lack of effective enforcement as the main problem.

Cost of Living

People who have spent extended periods of time in Taiwan in recent years say that current average monthly salaries in most industries are adequate to support a comfortable, albeit modest, life-style. Moreover, it is common for the members of extended families to live together or at least to pool their resources. There is seldom only one income earner per household. Instead, several individuals contribute by working part-time or second jobs. Bonuses are a regular and important supplement to personal income. It is common to pay employees at least one month's salary at the Chinese New Year.

Working Hours, Overtime, and Vacations

The Labor Standards Law (LSL), which was enacted in 1984, sets standards for certain major industries and any others that the central government may see fit to include. The LSL covers the following industries:

- agriculture, forestry, fisheries, and animal husbandry
- construction
- manufacturing
- mass communications
- mining and quarrying
- transportation, warehousing, and communications
- water, electricity, coal, and gas

Under the LSL, individuals work eight hours a day and 48 hours per week. Employers may ask men to work an additional 46 hours a month as overtime. Women may be asked to work 32 hours in overtime. Permission to ask workers for overtime requires prior consent from the labor union or the workers themselves and the approval of local labor authorities. For overtime work of two hours or less, workers are usually paid 1.33 times the regular hourly wage. For all additional hours, the rate is 1.67 times the regular hourly rate.

LSL rules governing the employment of women and minors are somewhat more restrictive than they are for men. Female employees may work between 10 pm and 6 am only under special circumstances and with official approval. Women who have been employed for at least six months receive eight weeks of maternity leave at full pay. If they have been employed for less than six months, they receive half pay. Children under 15 years of age are not permitted to work. Children between 15 and 16 may not work more than eight hours a day, on legal holidays, or between the hours of 8 pm and 6 am.

Employees receive at least one day off every seven days. They receive paid leave normally totaling 18 days a year on national holidays, such as Labor Day, and other specified holidays. After full-time employment of at least one year, workers are also entitled to paid vacations ranging from seven to 30 days, depending on the number of years worked.

Special Leave

The LSL includes guidelines for the granting of special leave:

- For marriage, eight days with full pay
- For the death of a parent, adoptive parent, stepparent, or spouse, eight days with full pay; for the death of a grandparent, son- or daughter-in-law, parent-in-law, adoptive parent-in-law, or stepparent-in-law, six days with full pay.
- For the death of a brother or sister, three days with full pay.
- For sickness or injury other than occupational accidents, outpatient leave may not exceed 30 days in one year, hospitalization leave is not to exceed one year, and combined outpatient and hospitalization leave may not exceed one year. Sickness and injury leave that does not exceed 30 days in one year is paid at 50 percent of the ordinary wage or salary.
- Leave for medical care and recovery from occupational accidents is granted on a case-by-case basis.
- Casual leave without pay can be granted to settle personal affairs, but may not exceed 14 days in one year.
- For participation in public service in accordance with certain laws, leave can be granted on a case-by-case basis.
- To encourage workers not to request leave, employers may establish rules under which a worker who does not request leave during the month is compensated with additional pay. Leave taken for marriage, funeral, occupational accident, or public service reasons does not effect eligibility for such additional pay.

Termination of Employment

Workers and employees covered by the LSL have well-defined rights regarding termination of employment. An employer who terminates a labor contact must give 10 days advance notice to an employee who has worked at least three months but less than one year for the company. An employee who has worked for one to three years must have 20 days notice, and someone who has been employed for three years or more must receive 30 days notice. An employee who has worked for at least one year is entitled to severance pay equaling one month's average wage or salary for each year worked. For example, a worker who has been employed for seven years and six months by the same employer receives one month's notice and severance pay equaling 7.5 times his or her average hourly wage or monthly salary. Average wage or salary is computed on the basis of the total compensation received by a worker during the six months before the date on which he or she was dismissed.

Under the following circumstances, the employer may dismiss an employee immediately without advance notice or severance pay:

• The worker made a false statement at the time when the employee's labor contract was negotiated and the employer suffers harm as a result.
• The worker violates or violently abuses the employer, the employer's family, or fellow workers.
• A court sentences the worker to prison.
• The worker violates the labor contract or work rules.
• The worker maliciously and intentionally damages machinery and equipment, tools, material,

products, or any other property of the employer. The worker intentionally divulges secrets relating to production technology or business from which the employer suffers harm.
• The worker is absent from work for three consecutive days or six days within one month without good reason.

The Council of Labor Affairs is currently attempting to extend the LSL's regulations in the areas of labor insurance and social security to cover the industries of commerce, finance, insurance, real estate, and social, business, and individual personal services. In practice, many businesses in these industries already follow LSL guidelines. Nevertheless, the expansion would increase the number of workers in Taiwan covered by the law from the present 3.5 million to approximately 4.5 million.

WAGES AND BENEFITS

The Labor Standards Law and the Council of Labor Affairs are both relatively new, and both labor and management have been critical of many of their pronouncements. The council has proposed a number of changes intended to remove existing ambiguities and help improve understanding between employers and employees. Taiwan provides no government medical, unemployment, disability, retirement, or death benefits other than those described in this section.

Wages and Salaries

Wages and salaries in Taiwan are generally higher than in the less-industrialized countries in the region and compare favorably with those in the region's other top economies. In most instances, the skill and

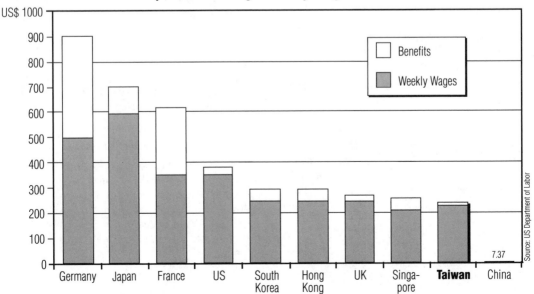

Comparative Average Weekly Wages - 1991

Source: US Department of Labor

productivity of Taiwan's workers offset the differential in the direct costs of their labor. In 1991 the actual average monthly salary varied by industry from a low of NT$24,609 (about US$980) in the manufacturing to a high of NT$55,664 (about US$2,218) in the utilities industry (gas, water, and electricity).

Monthly salaries in major industries almost doubled–and in the case of utilities more than doubled–between 1987 and 1991. These increases reflect the rapid growth in Taiwan's industrial capacity, which has had the combined effect of raising both living standards and the cost of living.

Earnings by occupation also vary considerably. For 1991 the range extends from a low of NT$20,015 (US$797) per month for laborers to a high of NT$43,732 (US$1,742) for administrative workers.

Unskilled and semiskilled workers in manufacturing industries are often paid on a piecework basis, although daily rates of pay are also encountered. Men and women generally receive the same pay for piecework, but women do not fare as well on an hourly basis. Workers are paid at least twice a month on fixed dates.

In addition to salaries and wages, employers are required to pay 80 percent of a worker's insurance costs, and they contribute to welfare association funds, severance and retirement pay, and meal and transportation allowances. In 1991 these additional labor costs amounted to 8.2 percent of a worker's monthly salary or wage.

Average Monthly Earnings by Industry - 1991

Industry	NT$	US$*	% Change from 1990
Manufacturing	24,609	980	11.0
Mining	28,139	1,121	8.2
Utilities	55,664	2,218	20.4
Construction	28,128	1,121	13.7
Commerce	25,287	1,007	8.2
Transportation	33,581	1,338	15.3
Finance	40,138	1,599	7.9
Other Service	26,145	1,042	10.8

Sources: Directorate General of Budget, Accounting, and Statistics ROC; US Department of Labor
* US$1.00 = NT$25.

Average Monthly Earnings by Occupation - 1991

Occupation	NT$	US$*	% Change from 1990
Laborer	20,015	797	12.3
Clerical	23,876	951	11.7
Technician	30,138	1,201	13.1
Administrator	43,732	1,742	3.3
Trader	23,076	919	10.1

Source: US Department of Labor
* US$1.00 = NT$25.1

Minimum Wage

The minimum monthly wage in Taiwan in 1991 was NT$11,040 (US$440), an increase of 13.2 percent over the preceding year. While labor leaders and some scholars argue that the minimum wage is too low to support a single individual, let alone a family, it is also true that because of the shortage of unskilled labor very few workers are paid the minimum allowable under the law. Even in the worst-paid occupation, that of laborer, the average wage is almost twice the minimum wage.

Labor Insurance

The Labor Insurance Act requires firms with six or more employees to apply for labor insurance through the Labor Insurance Commission of the Executive Yuan. Firms with five or fewer employees may also apply. Coverage and premium payments are currently divided into ordinary risk and occupational risk insurance. The premium for ordinary risk insurance amounts to 7 percent of the employee's monthly wage or salary; the employer pays 80 percent, and the employee pays 20 percent. The employer pays the entire cost of occupational risk insurance. The Labor Insurance Commission decides what type of insurance is appropriate.

The difference in coverage between the two types of insurance is minimal, with the exception of maternity benefits for female workers and the wives of insured male workers and the unemployment benefits available under ordinary risk insurance:

- Ordinary risk includes maternity benefits for female workers and the wives of insured male workers, hospitalization and medical expenses for injuries and sickness, disability payments; and unemployment, old age, and death benefits.
- Occupational risk includes hospitalization and medical expenses for injuries and sickness, disability benefits, and death benefits.

All local and foreign workers, including executive and administrative staff, but not the person(s) responsible for an enterprise, are covered by provisions of the Labor Insurance Act concerning labor insurance. No worker of an insured business may decline coverage.

Expansion of Coverage

Changes in labor laws proposed by the Council of Labor Affairs would also affect the Labor Insurance Act. The Executive Yuan approved a comprehensive national insurance program in 1991, but it remains under consideration in the Legislative Yuan. Scheduled to take effect in 1994, the national program would:

- Expand coverage to all employed workers regardless of industry;
- Gradually expand medical coverage to include spouses, children, and dependent parents;
- Increase the premium to between 9.5 and 16.5 percent of salaries and wages;
- Change the relative contributions to 30 percent for the worker and 70 percent for the employer;
- Introduce partial payment for medical benefits;
- Adopt an annuity-based retirement benefit financed by an additional premium of 4 to 7 percent of salaries and wages.

Employee Welfare Fund

The Statute on Employee Welfare Funds stipulates that any business with 50 or more workers must set up a welfare fund. An employees' welfare committee established by the employer administers contributions made to the fund. Contributions are determined as follows:

- 1 to 5 percent of the business's total paid-in capital;
- An allocation each month of 0.05 to 0.15 percent of the firm's total sales;
- A monthly payment of 20 to 40 percent of the selling price of scrap or waste materials;
- A monthly deduction of 0.5 percent from the salary or wage of each employee.

The employees' welfare committee is responsible for approving allocations from the fund and ensuring that the money in it is used to improve the welfare and morale of employees.

Retirement Plan

An employee in Taiwan may voluntarily retire at age 55 after 15 years of service or at any time after 25 years of service with the same employer. Retirement payments are calculated at a rate of two months of the average wage for each of the first 15 years of service and one month of the average wage for each year thereafter up to a maximum of 45 months.

Under the Labor Standards Law, employers must establish a fund to cover the required retirement payments. The employer's contributions to the fund amount to 2 to 15 percent of the total salaries and wages paid to employees. The fund's moneys must be deposited in a special account, and cannot be transferred, attached, or used as collateral.

An employee cannot be compelled to retire unless he or she has reached 60 years of age or is unable to perform a job due to mental or physical disability. An employee forced into retirement by a work-related disability is entitled to an additional 20 percent above and beyond the normal retirement payment.

LABOR RELATIONS

Organized labor in Taiwan has been and continues to be fairly weak. A drive for independent labor unions in the 1980s lost momentum in the face of tough tactics on the part of employers and government authorities. Even well-established unions have sought to avoid confrontation. Although membership in unions is increasing slightly, this is mainly because self-employed workers, such as taxi drivers and food vendors, are organizing to participate in group insurance plans.

Unions and the Labor Movement

Unions in Taiwan are relatively weak because they remain small and isolated. In many cases, they are attractive solely for the group insurance benefits that they provide. Aside from the strong stance against labor activism that prevails among employers and government officials, Taiwan's ongoing labor shortage has undermined unionism: A worker who is unhappy with conditions at his or her place of employment can easily find another job.

The Ministry of the Interior is the government agency that monitors the activities of unions. At the end of 1991 there were 3,564 unions in Taiwan, their membership totalling 2.94 million. Thirty-four percent of all persons employed in Taiwan in that year belonged to a union up from 32.9 percent in the preceding year. So-called craft unions are in the majority (76 percent), because industrial unions are open only to workers in specific factories or industries. Any group of at least 30 workers engaged in the same occupation can establish a craft union. Occupations are loosely classified by the Council of Labor Affairs, which is also responsible for recognizing new unions.

Taiwanese law permits unions to form federations. However, no administrative district, a term that includes cities, counties, and provinces, can have competing labor federations. In practice, this makes it difficult to have more than one countrywide labor federation. The Chinese Federation of Labor, which is closely associated with the ruling Kuomintang (KMT) party, is also affiliated with the International Confederation of Free Trade Unions. Although some workers have formed independent unions and federations under such names as friendship organizations or brotherhood alliances, such groups are technically illegal under current law and exercise little influence.

Taiwan's Labor Union Law states that employers may not refuse employment to, dismiss, or otherwise unfairly treat a worker because he or she is a union member. Even so, workers at textile, shipbuilding, and bus driving companies in 1991 and 1992 were laid off for alleged participation in labor union activities. Rather than provoking unions to retaliate by organizing work stoppages, such actions seem to have led unions to adopt less radical forms of protest. In a November 1991 dispute with the Penghu Bus Transportation Company, drivers maintained service but refused to collect fares from passengers.

Strikes and Disputes

According to the CLA, less than one workday was lost to industrial disputes in 1991. The number was higher in previous years, ranging from 828 workdays in 1990 to 24,157 workdays in 1989. There were 1,810 labor disputes in Taiwan in 1991 involving 12,696 workers, 63 percent fewer workers than in the year before. Of all recorded disputes, 836 related to labor contracts, 528 dealt with wages, 233 concerned occupational safety, and the remainder involved benefits, such as insurance. The CLA reported that only one-quarter of the cases were resolved in favor of workers.

After martial law was lifted in 1987, labor activism came to a head in 1989 with a strike at the Far Eastern Textile Company resulting in the arrest of Worker's Party chairman Lo Mei-Wen and seven other activists. In a demonstration of power over organized labor, the government brought charges against the labor leaders under an obscure 1938 statute covering agricultural, mining, industrial, and commercial sectors during the period of mobilization for the suppression of Communist rebellion. The law prohibited organizing strikes among workers in enterprises making designated products such as cotton, fiber, and wool.

Collective Bargaining

The Bureau of Social Affairs oversees the handling of labor disputes. Lockouts, strikes, and picketing are prohibited in certain vital industries. As soon as a decision between an employer and a union is reached, the result is considered final and binding.

Since the majority of cases involving collective bargaining between labor and management have been decided in favor of employers, critics accuse the Taiwanese authorities of siding with management. They point toward a series of legal precedents set in 1991 under which union leaders and other participants were required to compensate their employers as demonstrating official favoritism for management.

LABOR-RELATED AGENCIES AND ORGANIZATIONS IN TAIWAN

Council for Labor Affairs
5-15/F., 232 Minsheng E. Road
Sec. 3, Taipei, Taiwan
Tel: [886] (2) 7182512 Fax: [886] (2) 5149240, 5149242

Department of Labor Affairs, Taiwan Provincial Government
Liming New Village
Taichung, Taiwan
Tel: [886] (4) 2515120

Bureau of Labor Affairs, Taipei City Government
8/F., 21 Di Hua Street
Sec. 1, Taipei, Taiwan
Tel: [886] (2) 5210506 Fax: [886] (2) 5429331

Bureau of Labor Affairs, Kaohsiung City Government
132, Chungshang 3rd. Road
Kaohsiung, Taiwan
Tel: [886] (7) 3312872 Fax: [886] (7) 3330377

Manpower Planning Department
Council for Economic Planning and Development, Executive Yuan
9-14/F., 87 Nanking E. Road
Sec. 2, Taipei, Taiwan
Tel: [886] (2) 5513522 Fax: [886] (2) 5519011

Chinese Federation of Labor
11/F., 201-18, Tun Hua N. Road
Taipei, Taiwan
Tel: [886] (2) 7135111 Fax: [886] (2) 7135116

China External Trade Development Council
4-8/F., 333 Keelung Road
Sec. 1, Taipei 10548, Taiwan
Tel: [886] (2) 7382345 Fax: [886] (2) 7576653 Tlx: 21676

China Productivity Center
2/F. 340 Tun Hua North Road
Taipei 10592, Taiwan
Tel: [886] (2) 7137731 Fax: [886] (2) 7120650 Tlx: 22954

Taiwan Federation of Textile and Dyeing Industry Workers' Unions
2 Lane 64
Chung Hsiao East Road
Sec. 2 , Taipei, Taiwan
Tel: [886] (2) 3415627

Taiwan Provincial Federation of Labor
11/F., 44 Roosevelt Road
Sec. 2, Taipei, Taiwan
Tel: [886] (2) 3916241 Fax: [886] (2) 3916243

Government Information Office, Executive Yuan
2 Tien Chin Street
Taipei, Taiwan
Tel: [886] (2) 3419211 Fax: [886] (2) 3920923

Business Law

INTRODUCTION

Taiwan is reforming its business laws, particularly as they relate to the activities of foreign businesses. Changes are frequent, and the trend is to improve the climate for foreign investment. In addition, many rules and regulations that significantly affect foreign businesses are in unpublished government advisories and internal policy statements, rather than in the statutes. You should investigate the status of the legal requirements that may affect your particular business activities. The information in this chapter is intended to emphasize the important issues in commercial law, but it should not replace legal advice or council. You should be certain to review your business activities with an attorney familiar with international transactions, the laws of Taiwan, and the laws of your own country. (Refer to "Important Addresses" chapter for a list of attorneys in Taiwan.)

BASIS OF TAIWAN'S LEGAL SYSTEM

Taiwan is a civil code country, which means that its legal system is based on codified laws. Except in criminal cases, trials are nonjury, and judicial decisions are based directly on code provisions, not on precedent set by past decisions.

Taiwan's legal system is similar in many respects to Western law. Based on Germany's legal tradition, Taiwan's legal system has been influenced by other Asian countries, most of which also derived their legal systems from Germany. Taiwan's shift to capitalism and its increasing industrialization created a need for highly developed commercial law, a need met largely by adoption of Western laws.

STRUCTURE OF GOVERNMENT & LAWS

Under Taiwan's constitution, which became effective in 1947, Taiwan's national government, the Central Government of Republic of China, is organized into five yuans or councils: executive, legislative, judicial, examination, and control. Taiwan's constitution specifies the legal rights of Taiwanese citizens and defines the powers, functions, and duties of Taiwan's government.

Taiwan's supreme law is its constitution, pursuant to which the legislative yuan enacts and amends Taiwan's Civil Code, which governs a wide range of legal relationships. The legislative yuan also adopts statutes and regulations that control specific situations. Finally, Taiwan has ratified many international treaties and conventions, such as the Convention on Settlement of Investment Disputes between States and Nationals of Other States.

Taiwan's constitution provides that a treaty must be respected (Constitution 141). A treaty that the national government has ratified is usually valid and enforceable in domestic courts. If a treaty conflicts with domestic law, the treaty prevails, provided that it was ratified after, or on the same date that, the domestic law was promulgated. Enactment of a domestic law does not automatically override a conflicting provision of a treaty that is already in effect, but domestic courts must resolve this issue on a case-by-case basis (see Decree of Judicial Yuan, July 27, 1931, no. 459; Appeal Case no. 1074, Sup. Ct. 1934). Recent cases indicate that domestic courts will hold treaties controlling over domestic laws.

LAWS GOVERNING BUSINESS

Business transactions are governed primarily by the general contract, agency, and remedy laws contained in the Civil Code. (*See* Contracts, Principal and Agent.) Financial aspects of a transaction are also regulated by the Civil Code, and by such specific laws as the Negotiable Instruments Law and the Statute for Governing Foreign Exchange. (*See* Bills and Notes, Foreign Exchange, Foreign Trade.) Foreign investment is covered by the Statute for Investment by Foreign Nationals. (*See* Foreign Investment.)

Individuals and entities that do business in Tai-

BUSINESS LAW
TABLE OF CONTENTS

wan may be required to be licensed or registered under the Commercial Registration Act. (*See* Commercial Register.) Formation and operation of business entities in Taiwan are controlled by Taiwan's Civil Code, and by statutes related to specific organizations, such as the Business Associations Law and the Company Law. (*See* Corporations.) Certain industries are also subject to specific laws, such as the Mining Law, the Land Law, and the Merchant Marine and Civil Aviation Law. (*See* Foreign Investment.) Mergers and combinations of companies are governed by Taiwan's Fair Trade Law, which also covers monopolies, cartels, restraint of trade, and unfair business practices.(*See* Monopolies and Restraint of Trade.)

Taiwan protects intellectual property and trademark rights under its Copyright Law, Patent Law and Enforcement Rules, and Trademark Law. (*See* Copyright, Patents, Trademarks.) Labor relations for most businesses operating in Taiwan are controlled by the Basic Labor Standards Law, and labor unions are regulated by Taiwan's Labor Union Law. (*See* Labor Relations.) Businesses that operate in Taiwan are also subject to environmental laws, such as the Water Pollution Control Statute, the Public Nuisance Dispute Resolution Law, and various other statutes, regulations, and guidelines related to pollution, recycling, and waste disposal. (*See* Environment.)

GEOGRAPHICAL SCOPE OF LAWS

Laws digested in this section are in effect in all areas under the control of Taiwan's national government.

PRACTICAL APPLICATION OF LAWS

Translation of Law Many terms and expressions in the text of Taiwan's laws have no exact English equivalents, and different translators have interpreted the same Chinese characters in different ways. Before you do business with Taiwan merchants, you should seek advice on legal requirements for Taiwan and for each of the other countries connected with the transaction.

Renching The concepts of renching and honor have a significant effect on the legal aspects of business practice in Taiwan. The term renching refers to a relationship characterized by trust and sympathy between the parties. Honor is a similar principle, meaning that both parties are true to their word. Although extremely important in social relations, renching and honor are arguably the most important aspects of business relations as well. That is, the effect of legal requirements on parties

---

Introduction based on interview with Robert S. Yahng, Baker & McKenzie, San Francisco, California.

FOREIGN CORRUPT PRACTICES ACT

United States business owners are subject to the Foreign Corrupt Practices Act (FCPA). The FCPA makes it unlawful for any United States citizen or firm (or any person who acts on behalf of a US citizen or firm) to use a means of US interstate commerce (examples: mail, telephone, telegram, or electronic mail) to offer, pay, transfer, promise to pay or transfer, or authorize a payment, transfer, or promiseoof money or anything of value to any foreign appointed or elected government official, foreign political party, or candidate for a foreign political office for a corrupt purpose (that is, to influence a discretionary act or decision of the official) and for the purpose of obtaining or retaining business.

It is also unlawful for a US business owner to make such an offer, promise, payment, or transfer to any person if the US business owner knows, or has reason to know, that the person will offer, give, or promise directly or indirectly all or any part of the payment to a foreign government official, political party, or candidate. For purposes of the FCPA, the term *knowledge* means *actual knowledge* — the business owner in fact knew that the offer, payment, or transfer was included in the transaction — and *implied knowledge* — the business owner should have known from the facts and circumstances of a transaction that the agent paid a bribe but failed to carry out a reasonable investigation into the transaction. A business owner should make a reasonable investigation into a transaction if, for example, the sales representative requests a higher commission on a particular sale for no apparent reason, the buyer is a foreign government, the product has a military use, or the buyer's country is one in which bribes are considered customary in business relationships.

The FCPA also contains provisions applicable to US publicly held companies concerning financial record keeping and internal accounting controls.

Legal Payments

The provisions of the FCPA do not prohibit payments made to *facilitate* a routine government action. A facilitating payment is one made in connection with an action that a foreign official must perform as part of the job. In comparison, a corrupt payment is made to influence an official's discretionary decision. For example, payments are not generally considered corrupt if made to cover an official's overtime required to expedite the processing of export documentation for a legal shipment of merchandise or to cover the expense of additional crew to handle a shipment.

A person charged with violating FCPA provisions may assert as a defense that the payment was lawful under the written laws and regulations of the foreign country and therefore was not for a corrupt purpose. Alternatively, a person may contend that the payment was associated with demonstrating a product or performing a preexisting contractual obligation and therefore was not for obtaining or retaining business.

Enforcing Agencies and Penalties

Criminal Proceedings The Department of Justice prosecutes criminal proceedings for FCPA violations. Firms are subject to a fine of up to US$2 million. Officers, directors, employees, agents, and stockholders are subject to fines of up to US$100,000, imprisonment for up to five years, or both.

A US business owner may also be charged under other federal criminal laws, and on conviction may be liable for fines of up to US$250,000 or up to twice the amount of the gross gain or gross loss, provided the defendant derived pecuniary gain from the offense or caused pecuniary loss to another person.

Civil Proceedings Two agencies are responsible for enforcing civil provisions of the FCPA: The Department of Justice handles actions against domestic concerns, and the Securities and Exchange Commission (SEC) files actions against issuers. Civil fines of up to US$100,000 may be imposed on a firm; any officer, director, employee, or agent of a firm; or any stockholder acting for a firm. In addition, the appropriate government agency may seek an injunction against a person or firm that has violated or is about to violate FCPA provisions.

Conduct that constitutes a violation of FCPA provisions may also give rise to a cause of action under the federal Racketeer-Influenced and Corrupt Organizations Act, as well as under a similar state statute if enacted in the state with jurisdiction over the US business owner.

Administrative Penalties A person or firm that is held to have violated any FCPA provisions may be barred from doing business with the US government. Indictment alone may result in suspension of the right to do business with the government.

Department of Justice Opinion Procedure

Any person may request the Department of Justice to issue a statement of opinion on whether specific proposed business conduct would be considered a violation of the FCPA. The opinion procedure is detailed in 28 C.F.R. Part 77. If the Department of Justice issues an opinion stating that certain conduct conforms with current enforcement policy, conduct in accordance with that opinion is presumed to comply with FCPA provisions.

to a business transaction is determined by the manner in the parties implement the law, not necessarily by the terms of the law. Thus, technical legal difficulties and minor contract breaches can be overlooked or settled amicably if, by renching and honor, the parties merely choose not to enforce the letter of the law so as to continue their business relationship.

With modernization and Westernization of Taiwan business practices, reliance on renching and honor to remedy breaches of contract may be decreasing. Taiwanese are becoming more willing to sue, lawsuits are no longer regarded as akin to declarations of war, and parties may even continue to do business after concluding a lawsuit. As companies become larger, they not only need, but can also afford, lawyers. Increased reliance on lawyers may tend further to reduce the importance of renching. However, any person who wants to do business in Taiwan must still find ways of creating goodwill with Taiwanese companies, and contract clauses for presenting gifts or other inducements to a Taiwanese business partner may be as important in ensuring that the contract will be performed as the clauses that set forth remedies for breach.

Dispute Resolution Parties involved in business dealings in Taiwan should avoid bringing lawsuits whenever possible if disagreements arise. Despite increasing reliance on Taiwan's legal system to settle disputes, the judicial system remains susceptible to corruption. Civil trials have no juries, and as a result, Taiwan's judges wield enormous power. Bribery and friendships are said to influence many judicial decisions. Lawsuits can drag on and on, and appeals give parties additional opportunities to come before judges who are sympathetic to them. Moreover, many Taiwanese consider a lawsuit to be an insult. If possible, a dispute should be negotiated to resolution.

Property Infringement Concerns Despite new laws, protection of trademarks and intellectual property rights remains a difficult issue in Taiwan. (*See* Copyright, Patents, and Trademarks.) Renching is still one of the best ways of protecting intellectual property rights. That is, developing trust in a personal relationship with a Taiwanese business may lessen the risk that your Taiwanese partner may infringe on your intellectual property rights.

If you have one or more trademarks, you should be certain to register them in Taiwan. Do not rely on international treaties to protect them. (*See* Trademarks.) Moreover, you should register them at the earliest time possible, because the person who registers first owns the mark. Transliteration of a trademark is considered to be a separate mark, and you should therefore register it, too.

RELATED SECTIONS

Refer to the "Taxation" chapters for discussion of tax issues in Taiwan, and to "Business Travel" chapter for details on immigration and visas.

LEGAL GLOSSARY

Agent The person authorized to act on behalf of another person (the principal). Example: A sales representative is an agent of the seller.

Agent ad Litem An agent who acts on behalf of a principal in prosecuting or defending a lawsuit.

Attachment The legal process for seizing property before a judgment to secure payment of damages if awarded. This process is also referred to as sequestration. Example: A party who claims damages for breach of contract may request a court to issue an order freezing all transfers of specific property owned by the breaching party pending resolution of the dispute.

Attorney-in-fact An attorney who is authorized to transact business generally or to perform a designated task of a nonlegal nature on behalf of another person. This authority usually must be conferred by a written power of attorney. Example: If a foreign company buys goods from a Taiwan firm and agrees to place sufficient funds for the purchase in an escrow account, the foreign buyer may authorize a Taiwanese attorney to disburse the escrow funds on receiving verification from the foreign company that the goods are satisfactory. A foreign business owner may also authorize an attorney-in-fact to testify to facts on the company's behalf in arbitration or legal proceedings.

Authentication The act of conferring legal authenticity on a written document, typically made by a notary public who attests and certifies that the document is in proper legal form and that it is executed by a person identified as having authority to do so.

Bill of exchange A written instrument signed by a person (the drawer) and addressed to another person (the drawee), typically a bank, ordering the drawee to pay unconditionally a stated sum of money to yet another person (the payee) on demand or at a future time.

LEGAL GLOSSARY (cont'd.)

Bona fide In or with good faith, honesty, and sincerity. Example: A bona fide purchaser is one who buys goods for value and without knowledge of fraud or unfair dealing in the transaction. Knowledge of fraud or unfair dealing may be implied if the facts are such that the purchaser should have reasonably known that the transaction involved deceit, such as when goods that are susceptible to piracy are provided without documentation of their origin.

Composition with creditors An agreement between an insolvent debtor and one or more creditors under which the creditors consent to accept less than the total amount of their claims in order to secure immediate payment.

Execution The legal process for enforcing a judgment for damages, usually by seizure and sale of the debtor's personal property. Example: If a court awards damages in a breach of contract action and the breaching party has failed to remit the sum due, the party awarded damages may request the court to order seizure and sale of the breaching party's inventory to the extent necessary to satisfy the award.

Force majeure clause A superior force clause. A contract clause that excuses a party who breaches the contract because performance is prevented by the occurrence of an event that is beyond the party's reasonable control. Example: A force majeure clause in a contract may excuse performance on occurrence of such events as natural disasters, labor strikes, bankruptcy, or failure of subcontractors to perform.

Inter absentee Among absent parties. Example: An inter absentee contract is made between parties who do not meet face to face.

Juristic act An action intended to, and capable of having, a legal effect, such as the creation, termination, or modification of a legal right. Example: Signing a power of attorney is a juristic act because it gives legal authority to an agent.

Juristic person An individual or entity recognized under law as having legal rights and obligations. Example: Limited liability companies, unlimited liability companies, corporations, and partnerships are entities that are recognized as juristic persons.

Lex loci actus The law of the place where a wrongful act occurred is applied in a legal action if the laws of more than one jurisdiction could apply.

Lex loci solutionis The law of the place where payment is to be made or a contract is to be performed is applied in a legal action if the laws of more than one jurisdiction could apply

Negotiable instrument A written document that can be transferred merely by endorsement or delivery. Example: A check or bill of exchange is a negotiable instrument.

Power of attorney A written document by which one person (the principal) authorizes another person (the agent) to perform stated acts on the principal's behalf. Example: A principal may execute a special power of attorney authorizing an agent to sign a specific contract or a general power of attorney authorizing the agent to sign all contracts for the principal.

Prima facie Presumption of fact as true unless contradicted by other evidence. Example: Unless an agreement assigning contract rights clearly states that outstanding interest payments are retained by the assignor, the right to collect the payments is deemed transferred prima facie to the assignee.

Principal A person who authorizes another party (the agent) to act on the principal's behalf.

Promoter of corporation The individual or entity that organizes a corporation.

Rescind A contracting party's right to cancel the contract. Example: A contract may give one party a right to rescind if the other party fails to perform within a reasonable time.

Rescission *See* Rescind.

Sequestration *See* Attachment.

Statute of Frauds A law that requires designated documents to be in writing in order to be enforced by a court. Example: Contracting parties may agree orally to transfer ownership of immovable property, but a court may not enforce that contract, and may not award damages for breach, unless the contract was written.

Third-party beneficiary A person who benefits from, but is not a contracting party of, a contract between two or more other persons. Example: A bank that loans a business owner funds to purchase specific property is a third-party beneficiary to the sales contract between the business owner and the seller.

Ultra vires An act performed without the authority to do so. Example: If a contract provision requires both parties to approve an assignment of the contract but one party agrees to an assignment without obtaining the other's consent, the assignment is ultra vires.

INTERNATIONAL SALES CONTRACT PROVISIONS

When dealing internationally, you must consider the business practices and legal requirements of the country where the buyer or seller is located. For a small, one-time sale, an invoice may be commonly accepted. For a more involved business transaction, a formal written contract may be preferable to define clearly the rights, responsibilities, and remedies of all parties. The laws of your country or the foreign country may require a written contract and may even specify all or some of the contract terms. *See* Contracts and Sales for specific laws on contracts and the sale of goods.

Parties generally have freedom to agree to any contract terms that they desire. Whether a contract term is valid in a particular country is of concern only if you have to seek enforcement. Thus, you have fairly broad flexibility in negotiating contract terms. However, you should always be certain to come to a definite understanding on four issues: the goods (quantity, type, quality); the time of delivery; the price; and the time of payment.

You need to consider the following clauses when you negotiate an international sales contract.

Contract date

State the date when the contract is signed. This date is particularly important if payment or delivery times are fixed in reference to it — for example, "shipment within 30 days of the contract date."

Identification of parties

Designate the names of the parties, and describe their relation to each other.

Goods

Description Describe the type and quality of the goods. You may simply indicate a model number, or you may have to attach detailed lists, plans, or drawings. This clause should be clear enough that both parties fully understand the specifications and have no discretion in interpreting them.

Quantity Specify the number of units, or other measure of quantity, of the goods. If the goods are measured by weight, you should specify net weight, dry weight, or drained weight. If the goods are prepack-aged and are subject to weight restrictions in the end market, you may want to provide that the seller will ensure that the goods delivered will comply with those restrictions.

Price Indicate the price per unit or other measure, such as per pound or ton, and the extended price.

Packaging arrangements

Set forth packaging specifications, especially for goods that can be damaged in transit. At a minimum, this provision should require the seller to package the goods in such a way as to withstand transportation. If special packaging requirements are necessary to meet consumer and product liability standards in the end market, you should specify them also.

Transportation arrangements

Carrier Name a preferred carrier for transporting the goods. You should designate a particular carrier if, for example, a carrier offers you special pricing or is better able than others to transport the product.

Storage Specify any particular requirements for storage of the goods before or during shipment, such as security arrangements, special climate demands, and weather protection needs.

Notice provisions Require the seller to notify the buyer when the goods are ready for delivery or pickup, particularly if the goods are perishable or fluctuate in value. If your transaction is time-sensitive, you could even provide for several notices to allow the buyer to track the goods and take steps to minimize damages if delivery is delayed.

Shipping time State the exact date for shipping or provide for shipment within a reasonable time from the contract date. If this clause is included and the seller fails to ship on time, the buyer may claim a right to cancel the contract, even if the goods have been shipped, provided that the buyer has not yet accepted delivery.

Costs and charges

Specify which party is to pay the additional costs and charges related to the sale.

Duties and taxes Designate the party that will be responsible for import, export, and other fees and taxes and for obtaining all required licenses. For example, a party may be made responsible for paying the duties, taxes, and charges imposed by that party's own country, since that party is best situated to know the legal requirements of that country.

Insurance costs Identify the party that will pay costs of insuring the goods in transit. This is a critical provision because the party responsible bears the risk if the goods are lost during transit. A seller is typically responsible for insurance until title to the goods passes to the buyer, at which time the buyer becomes responsible for insurance or becomes the named beneficiary under the seller's insurance policy.

Handling and transport Specify the party that will pay shipping, handling, packaging, security, and any other costs related to transportation, which should be specified.

Terms defined Explain the meaning of all abbreviations — for example, FAS (free alongside ship), FOB (free on board), CIF (cost, insurance, and freight) — used in your contract to assign responsibility and costs for goods, transportation, and insurance. If you define your own terms, you can make the definitions specific to your own circumstances and needs. As an alternative, you may agree to adopt a particular standard, such as the Revised American Foreign Trade Definitions or Incoterms 1990. In either case, this clause should be clear enough that both parties understand when each is responsible for insuring the goods.

Insurance or risk of loss protection

Specify the insurance required, the beneficiary of the policy, the party who will obtain the insurance, and the date by which it will have been obtained.

Payment provisions

Provisions for payment vary with such factors as the length of the relationship between the contracting parties, the extent of trust between them, and the availability of certain forms of payment within a particular country. A seller

will typically seek the most secure form of payment before committing to shipment, while a buyer wants the goods cleared through customs and delivered in satisfactory condition before remitting full payment.

Method of payment State the means by which payment will be tendered — for example, prepayment in cash, traveler's checks, or bank check; delivery of a documentary letter of credit or documents against payment; credit card, credit on open account, or credit for a specified number of days.

Medium of exchange Designate the currency to be used — for example, US currency, currency of the country of origin, currency of a third country.

Exchange rate Specify a fixed exchange rate for the price stated in the contract. You may use this clause to lock in a specific price and ensure against fluctuating currency values.

Import documentation

Require that the seller be responsible for presenting to customs all required documentation for the shipment.

Inspection rights

Provide that the buyer has a right to inspect goods before taking delivery to determine whether the goods meet the contract specifications. This clause should specify the person who will do the inspection — for example, the buyer, a third party, a licensed inspector; the location where the inspection will occur — for example at the seller's plant, the buyer's warehouse, a receiving dock; the time at which the inspection will occur; the need for a certified document of inspection; and any requirements related to the return of nonconforming goods, such as payment of return freight by the seller.

Warranty provisions

Limit or extend any implied warranties, and define any express warranties on property fitness and quality. The contract may, for example, state that the seller warrants that the goods are of merchantable quality, are fit for any purpose for which they would ordinarily be used,

INTERNATIONAL SALES CONTRACT PROVISIONS (cont'd.)

or are fit for a particular purpose requested by the buyer. The seller may also warrant that the goods will be of the same quality as any sample or model that the seller has furnished as representative of the goods. Finally, the seller may warrant that the goods will be packaged in a specific way or in a way that will adequately preserve and protect the goods.

Indemnity

Agree that one party will hold the other harmless from damages that arise from specific causes, such as the design or manufacture of a product.

Enforcement and Remedies

Time is of the essence Provide that timely performance of the contract is essential. The inclusion of this clause allows a party to claim breach merely because the other party fails to perform within the time prescribed in the contract. Common in United States contracts, a clause of this type is considered less important in other countries.

Modification Require the parties to make all changes to the contract in advance and in a signed written modification.

Cancellation State the reasons for which either party may cancel the contract and the notice required for cancellation.

Contingencies Specify any events that must occur before a party is obligated to perform the contract. For example, you may agree that the seller has no duty to ship goods until the buyer forwards documents that secure the payment for the goods.

Governing law Choose the law of a specific jurisdiction to control any interpretation of the contract terms. The law that you choose will usually affect where you can sue or enforce a judgment and what rules and procedures will be applied.

Choice of forum Identify the place where a dispute may be settled — for example, the country of origin of the goods, the country of destination, a third country that is convenient to both parties.

Arbitration provisions Agree to arbitration as an alternative to litigation for the resolution of any disputes that arise. You should agree to arbitrate only if you seriously intend to settle disputes in this way. If you agree to arbitrate but later file suit, the court is likely to uphold the arbitration clause and force you to settle your dispute as you agreed under the contract.

An arbitration clause should specify whether arbitration is binding or nonbinding on the parties; the place where arbitration will be conducted (which should be a country that has adopted a convention for enforcing arbitration awards, such as the United Nations Convention on Recognition and Enforcement of Foreign Awards); the procedure by which an arbitration award may be enforced; the rules governing the arbitration, such as the United Nations Commission on International Trade Law Model Rules; the institute that will administer the arbitration, such as the International Chamber of Commerce (Paris), the American Arbitration Association (New York), the Japan Commercial Arbitration Association, the United Nations Economic and Social Commission for Asia and the Pacific, the London Court of Arbitration, or the United Nations Commission International Trade Law; the law that will govern procedural issues or the merits of the dispute; any limitations on the selection of arbitrators (for example, a national of a disputing party may be excluded from being an arbitrator); the qualifications or expertise of the arbitrators; the language in which the arbitration will be conducted; and the availability of translations and translators if needed.

Severability Provide that individual clauses can be removed from the contract without affecting the validity of the contract as a whole. This clause is important because it provides that, if one clause is declared invalid and unenforceable for any reason, the rest of the contract remains in force.

Copyright Amendment

The ROC Copyright Act has been amended in accordance with the US-ROC Copyright Amendment Agreement.

On April 23, 1993, the Republic of China ("ROC") Legislative Yuan ratified the US-ROC Copyright Agreement as well as amended the Copyright Act ("the Act"). Under the amended Act, importers of any goods bearing intellectual property rights, including compact and laser discs, books, audio and video tapes, computer software and art works, would be subject to two-year prison terms unless consent of the copyright holders or authorised agent was obtained in advance. Furthermore, transplanted from Article 602 of the US Act, the ROC government amended the Copyright Act allowing parallel imports of copyrighted works only for use by government units, academic, religious and non-profit organisations, and for personal use. However, parallel importation of operation manuals for machinery equipment, and usage instructions for products, will be permitted. The amendment becomes effective immediately upon promulgation by the President of the ROC.

Reprinted from Asia Pacific Legal Developments Bulletin, vol. 8, no. 3, Baker & McKenzie, Sept. 1993, with permission of the author, Jeff C.Y. Young, Taipei, and the law firm of Baker & McKenzie, Taipei.

LAW DIGEST

(Abbreviations used are: C.C. for Civil Code; C.C.P. for Civil Code Procedure; B.L.S.L. for Basic Labor Standards Law; Sup. Ct. for Supreme Court.)

ABSENTEES

Generally speaking, an absentee may be represented by an attorney-in-fact. Yet, court may by ruling prohibit person other than lawyer from acting as agent ad litem. (C. C. P. 68). Action against absentee whose whereabouts are unknown may be effected by publication of service. (C. C. P. 149).

ACKNOWLEDGMENTS

Ordinarily the form of acknowledgment in use in the country where the acknowledgment is taken, may be employed. Occasionally, in practice, an acknowledgment to be used in the ROC should be legalized by Chinese Consular or authorized representative. Acknowledgments to be used in USA may be taken before officials of American Institute in ROC. Same usually applies respecting other countries maintaining Consular or authorized representative offices in ROC Office of notary public in ROC is branch of court and obtaining acknowledgments before Chinese notary public must undergo formal official procedure.

ALIENS

Regulations Governing Immigration and Residence of Foreigners in Domain of ROC were promulgated on May 20,1948, and last amended on Jan. 6,1989. Nationals of countries which confer privileges of immigration and residence to Chinese nationals will have similar privileges of immigration and residence in ROC. Aliens residing in ROC must register with local Police Bureau within 15 days of their arrival and obtain resident certificate. Changes of residence and all changes in personal status must be reported to Police within 15 days.

Any alien wishing to leave ROC must report to Police at his place of residence three days before, to obtain multiple exit permit which is valid for six months. Aliens who want to do business in ROC should obtain special permission. *See* Corporations; Partnership.

Acquisition of land rights by aliens may be enjoyed by aliens whose own countries have entered into equal and reciprocal treaty with ROC such as treaty of Friendship, Commerce and Navigation between US and ROC. For US nationals, reciprocity is determined by laws of their State. Aliens may lease or purchase land for following purposes only: (1) Residence, (2) business premises or factories, (3) churches, (4) hospitals, (5) schools for foreign children, (6) diplomatic and consular establishments, premises for public welfare organizations, and (7) cemeteries. Ownership of and claims over real property located within domain of ROC is solely governed by Chinese laws.

Corporations Owned or Controlled by Aliens.— *See* Corporations.

ASSIGNMENTS

Claim may be assigned unless: (1) Nature thereof prevents assignment; (2) there is agreement that claim shall not be assigned; or (3) claim is not subject to judicial attachment. Agreement mentioned in (2) cannot be set up against bona fide third party.

Collaterals and ancillary rights shall be transferred to assignee concurrently with assignment, except for those which are inseparable from and personal to assignor. Outstanding interest payment is transferred prima facie to assignee along with assignment of principal.

Unless otherwise provided by law, assignment will not be binding on debtor unless and until he is notified of assignment by assignor or assignee. Tendering assignment document to debtor has same effect of notification.

Upon notification of assignment or other conduct with equivalent effect, debtor may extend to original assignor his defenses which were originally enforceable against assignee.

Ultra vires assignment refers to assignment in which assignment has not been concluded or effected but debtor has been informed of assignment by assignor. Debtor under ultra vires assignment may extend to original assignor his defenses which were enforceable against assignee.

Assignor should deliver to assignee upon assignment all documentation requisite to verify assigned claim and should provide assignee information with respect to enforcement of assigned claim.

Delegation of obligation, if concluded between third party and obligee (creditor), becomes effective upon conclusion of delegation agreement and obligation in question transfers to third party immediately.

Delegation, if concluded between third party and obligor (debtor), becomes binding on obligee (creditor) upon obligee's consent to delegation. Obligor or third party may ask obligee to respond within certain period to proposed delegation. Obligee's inaction or lack of response should be deemed as his refusal to accept delegation, which would allow either party to delegation right to withdraw their respective promises for delegation.

ASSOCIATIONS

ROC Civil Code (C. C. Art. 45 and 46) distinguishes between associations whose object is to make profits and associations whose object is promotion of public welfare. Associations whose object is promotion of public welfare must, prior to registration, be approved by competent authorities.

In order to form association, articles of association must be drawn up. (C. C. Art. 47). General meeting of members of association is organ in which supreme power of association is vested. (C. C. Art. 50). Decisions are taken by simple majority. (C. C. Art. 52). All changes in articles of association for promotion of public welfare must be approved by competent authorities. (C. C. Art. 53).

Chambers of Commerce and Guilds are nonprofit seeking associations in ROC.

Industrial guilds representing manufacturing concerns are governed by "The Industrial Association Law" promulgated on Dec. 28, 1974 and "The Industrial Guild Law" promulgated on Oct. 21,1929 as last amended on May 2l, 1975. Business associations are governed by "Business Associations Law" promulgated on July 26,1972 as last amended on Dec. 15, 1982.

Most profit-seeking associations are termed "companies" and governed by Company Law (*see* Corporations).

ATTACHMENT

Before judgment, an order for provisional seizure may be obtained. Property provisionallly seized may not be transferred, sold or in any other way disposed of by debtor, nor may it be auctioned by court for time being, except that movables may be sold by court upon request by debtor or creditor and money deposited with court if continued custody would lower their value or involve unreasonable expenses. Notice of sequestration of immovable property must show that it is case of provisional seizure.

BANKRUPTCY

ROC Bankruptcy Law provides two proceedings applicable for situation under which debtor is unable to pay off his debts or debtor has ceased to make repayment, namely: (1) Composition through Court or Chamber of Commerce, and (2) bankruptcy. Both proceedings aim at distribution of debtor's properties among creditors.

Composition through Court or Chamber of Commerce is privilege offered to debtor who applies to court or Chamber of Commerce, subsequent to suspension of payment and prior to application for bankruptcy. Composition through Chamber of Commerce may be applied only by debtor who is merchant. It is similar to bankruptcy, except that only debtor can ask for it and control of debtor's property is not entirely divested. Proceedings must be carried out under supervision of court or local Chamber of Commerce and debtor's business may be continued. However, debtor, after applying for composition, may not perform any gratuitous act prejudicial to rights of creditors, nor any onerous acts beyond scope of normal managerial acts or of ordinary business.

Bankruptcy proceedings may be commenced in case of insolvency or when application for composition or composition proposal is denied by court or when composition through court or Chamber of Commerce fails to reach results. Application for bankruptcy may be filed by debtor or his creditors. Application for bankruptcy proceedings may be denied if it appears to court that composition is still possible or debtor has no property, or debtor only has one creditor. Provisions are made for meeting of creditors to pass resolution on certain matters. Bankrupt cannot leave his residence without court's permission and court may summon or detain bankrupt if this is deemed necessary. If bankrupt, within six months prior to bankruptcy, furnishes security on existing debts or makes payment of obligation not yet due, such transactions may be cancelled, and other acts prejudicial to creditors' rights which are cancellable under Civil Code may be cancelled on application to court.

Creditors must present claims within time fixed by published notice of court. Secured creditors may obtain satisfaction out of their security and if such is insufficient, they may participate with general creditors for balance.

Bankruptcy decree divests bankrupt of control of his present property and such as he may acquire during pendency of bankruptcy.

Certain fraudulent acts of a bankrupt or debtor under composition aiming to prejudice creditors' rights, are punishable by imprisonment, detention and/or fines.

Composition or bankruptcy effected in a foreign country has no effect on the debtor's or bankrupt's property in ROC.

BILLS AND NOTES

Bills of exchange, promissory notes and checks are negotiable instruments within meaning of Chinese Negotiable Instruments Law, promulgated in 1929 and last amended June 29, 1986. Person signing negotiable instrument is liable according to tenor thereof. Seal may be affixed to negotiable instrument in lieu of signature. In case of variation between words and figures with respect to amount of instrument, words prevail. Unless otherwise provided in Negotiable Instruments Law, instrument is invalid as negotiable instrument unless it contains following particulars required by said law.

Bills of exchange must be signed by drawer and contain: (1) Words indicating that instrument is bill of exchange; (2) statement of certain sum of money; (3) unconditional order to pay; and (4) date of issue.

Promissory notes must be signed by maker and contain: (1) Words indicating that instrument is promissory note; (2) statement of certain sum of money; (3) unconditional promise to pay; and (4) date of issue.

Checks must be signed by drawer and contain: (1) Words indicating that instrument is check; (2) statement of certain sum of money; (3) name of drawee; (4) unconditional order to pay; (5) date of issue; and (6) place of payment.

COMMERCIAL REGISTER

Commercial Registration Act was promulgated and enforced as of June 28, 1937 and amended Nov. 28, 1967. Commercial Registration shall be handled in accordance with said Act and, if no applicable stipulation provided therein, shall be subject to regulations of other laws. Any firm including its branch in sole proprietorship or partnership shall not start operation before registration. (Art. 3 of Commercial Registration Act). As for company, it may not be formed until it is incorporated and has obtained certificate of incorporation pursuant to Company Law. Firm or company shall not engage in any business outside of scope of business for which it has been registered. (Art. 8 of Commercial Registration Act & Art. 15 of Company Law). If business of firm or company should require special permission or license of Government, such business can be registered only after such special permission or license is obtained. Businesses requiring special permission include but not limited to following: Banking, insurance, insurance brokerage, customs broker, construction, stock dealer, trust and investment company, venture capital company, securities investment consulting company, travel agent, securities house, shipping, shipping agent, transportation, publisher, drug dealer, air freight forwarder, pharmaceutical company, etc.

In addition, foreign company that desires to transact business and establish branch office within territory of ROC shall apply for recognition pursuant to Company Law. *See* Corporations.

CONTRACTS

Contracts are generally regulated by Civil Code. With few exceptions, most principles concerning contracts are consistent with Anglo-American law. Offer made during face-to-face negotiation ceases to be binding if not accepted at once. Offer made inter absentee ceases to be binding if not accepted by offeree within reasonable period under ordinary circumstances. If offeror specifies period for acceptance, acceptance must reach him within such period.

Oral contracts are legally valid, with a few exceptions, such as real estate lease over a year; contract of mandate under which mandatory has to enter into juristic acts which are required by law to be in writing; contract of life interests; transfer or creation of rights over immovables, and other special cases.

Contracts creating third-party beneficiaries are legally enforceable unless beneficiaries express to either party to contracts their intention not to receive benefits so created under contracts. Moreover, parties to contracts may also modify or cancel contracts before third-party beneficiaries express intention to receive such benefits. Like creditor, third-party beneficiaries have right to enforce contracts against debtor.

Excuses for Nonperformance Party to contract may be excused from performance if such performance becomes impossible due to cause for which he is not responsible, such as force majeure, due to nonperformance of other party who is obligated to perform first, or due to cause for which other party is responsible.

Applicable Law Validity and effectiveness of contract involving foreign elements are determined by law agreed upon by parties to contract. Where parties intention is not ascertainable, applicable law shall be law of country of which both parties are nationals. If parties do not hold same nationality, applicable law shall be lex loci actus. If act is carried out at different places, place where offer is sent shall be deemed as place of act. If place where offer is sent is unknown to other party when making acceptance, domicile of offeror shall be deemed as place of act. If place of act spans more than two countries or does not belong to any country, lex loci solutionis shall apply. (6, Law Governing Choice of Law in Civil Cases involving Foreign Elements).

Government Contracts While law has not expressly specified status of government contracts, an established case law indicates that government contracts are governed by same body of law that regulates nongovernment contracts (see Appeal Case No. 1838, Sup. Ct. 1930).

COPYRIGHT

ROC nationals will acquire copyright upon completion in respect of: (1) Literary works; (2) oral works; (3) translations of literary works; (4) translations of oral works; (5) compilations; (6) artistic works; (7) pictorial works; (8) musical works; (9) motion pictures; (10) sound recordings; (11) video tapes; (12) photographic works; (13) lectures, musical performances, stage presentations, choreography; (14) computer programs; (15) maps; (16) scientific-technical or engineering design drawings; (17) other intellectual works. Copyright owner has exclusive right to reproduce, publicly recite, publicly broadcast, publicly present, publicly perform, publicly exhibit, compile, translate, lease and adapt intellectual work in accordance with nature of work. Copyright may be assigned in whole or in part and may be owned by co-owners. Assignment. succession or pledge of copyright should be registered, otherwise, such copyright cannot be set up against others. Copyright is issued to author for duration of his/her life from date of completion of intellectual work or, when date of completion is unknown, from date of first publication and it may be inherited by his/her heir for 30 years. However, in each of following cases term of copyright is only for 30 years: (1) Where work is copyrighted in name of government agency, school, corporation or other juristic person or organization; (2) where works are motion pictures, video tapes, sound recordings (permitted to be shown and broadcast by separate laws and regulations), compilation, photographic works, computer programs and translation of literary works. Copyright on photographs (included as part of literary work) belongs to author of such literary work. Copyright on translations of literary works does not exclude others from making original translation. To translate intellectual work owned by ROC national, translator shall obtain consent of copyright owner of original work. However, consent of foreign copyright owner of work is not required for translating such work.

In case of infringement, copyright owner may prosecute infringers under penalty clause of ROC Copyright Law and may also recover damages from such infringers. Unrecognized foreign juristic person in ROC may still be qualified in filing criminal complaint or private prosecution against offenses stipulated in ROC Copyright Law, provided that reciprocal rights exist in country of foreign juristic person. Remedies available to copyright owner of infringement include damages, removal of infringement and publication for final court judgment. Copyright owner may claim damages equivalent to sum of profit obtained by infringer and loss suffered by copyright owner, and in any event, is entitled to damages not less than 500 times actual retail price of infringed work. In absence of such retail price, court shall determine amount of damages according to seriousness of infringement. Unregistered intellectual works, printed with word "registered" or synonym thereof, shall be imposed with fine not exceeding NT$24,000 and sale of said intellectual work will be prohibited. If case amounts to criminal offense, offender will be punished accordingly.

Copyright on Foreign Intellectual Works ROC Copyright Law provides that foreigners acquire copyright upon registration of their intellectual works with Ministry of Interior. To qualify for copyright registration, foreign copyright owners must meet either one of two requirements: (1) Work is published for first time in ROC; or (2) according to treaty or law and regulations or custom of copyright owner's country, intellectual works produced by ROC nationals are entitled to equivalent rights in that country. Duly registered foreign copyright owners have equivalent right stipulated in ROC Copyright Law, not including translation right of any intellectual work other than specially produced music, technical and engineering design drawings or art collections. Treaty between US and ROC provides for reciprocal copyright privileges.

CORPORATIONS

Chinese Company Law provides for four kinds of companies: (1) Unlimited company; (2) unlimited company with limited liability shareholders; (3) limited company; and (4) company limited by shares. Unlimited company is company organized by two or more shareholders who bear unlimited joint liability for obligations of company. Unlimited company with limited liability shareholders is one organized by one or more shareholders of unlimited liability and one or more shareholders of limited liability. In such company, shareholders of limited liability are liable only to extent of capital contributed or subscribed by them. Limited company is one organized by not less than five nor more than 21 shareholders who are liable to extent of capital subscribed by them. Company limited by shares is one organized by seven or more shareholders and capital of company is divided into shares and each shareholder is liable to extent of shares subscribed by him.

See also topic Commercial Register.

Special Permission If the business of a company should require special permission by Government, such business can be undertaken only after such special permission shall have been obtained. *See* topic Commercial Register.

Foreign corporations are governed by Company Law of China as amended Nov. 12, 1990, and references herein are to articles of this law.

Foreign corporations desiring to do business in ROC through branch office must first be recognized by ROC government as foreign corporate entity duly registered in country of its origin. Foreign company may or may not be recognized in case country of its origin does not recognize Chinese companies. After being recognized and certificate of recognition is issued, foreign corporation shall then apply for branch license in order to operate business within ROC through branch. (Art. 371). Application for recognition is made to Ministry of Economic Affairs. Application for branch license is made to municipal or provincial government in district where branch is located.

Foreign company shall state following particulars and submit following documents when applying for recognition: (I) Name, class and nationality of company; (2) business of company and business to be undertaken within territory of ROC; (3) total amount of capital and, in case shares are issued, total number of shares, kinds of shares, par value of each share and paid up amount; (4) amount of funds to be used for operation within territory of ROC; (5) location of its head office and location of branch office to be established in territory of ROC; (6) date of incorporation in its own country and date on which it began to operate business; (7) names, nationalities and domiciles of directors and other responsible persons of company; (8) names, nationalities and domiciles or residences of its representative in litigious and nonlitigious matters within territory of ROC and his/her power of attorney; (9) names, nationalities and domiciles of all unlimited liability shareholders of unlimited company, unlimited company with limited liability shareholders or other companies, and number of shares subscribed to and amount paid on such shares by each of them; (10) copies or photostat copies of its articles of incorporation and other certificates of registration in its own country; in absence of articles of incorporation or other certificates of registration, documents issued by competent authority in its own country to prove that it is company; (11) copy or photostat copy of franchise granted by competent authority in its own country, if established under such franchise; (12) copy or photostat copy of franchise, if its business requires franchise according to law or ordinance of ROC; (13) business plan for operation ROC; and (14) minutes of meeting of shareholders or board of directors relating to application for recognition. (Art. 435). In addition, information on introduction of parent company, annual revenue of parent company for past three years, estimated annual revenue of branch for next three years and commencement date of fiscal year for branch should also be provided.

Upon issuance of certificate of recognition, foreign company must apply to local competent authorities for registration of its branch offices. (Arts. 436, 437). In case of any amendment in record of registration, application must be filed with local competent authority for change of record within 15 days after such amendment. Foreign corporation complying with legal formalities has same legal position as Chinese corporation. However, foreign company may not solicit shares or bonds from public in ROC provided laws of its mother state forbids Chinese company to solicit same in her territory, but sale or purchase of shares or bonds of individual shareholders is permitted. (Art. 383).

Prior to any substitution or departure of its designated agent foreign company must designate another agent and file report with competent authority for record. (Art. 385).

Foreign company must keep copy of its articles of incorporation and register of shareholders of unlimited liability in its branch office or in office of its agent in litigious and non-litigious matters in ROC (Art. 374).

Foreign company which does not wish to operate business in ROC through branch but wishes to send its representative to ROC to do juristic acts related to its business may apply to government for establishment of representative office. (Art. 386).

ENVIRONMENT

Environment Authority In reaction to widespread, serious and steadily growing environmental degradation, Environmental Protection Administration (EPA) was founded under Executive Yuan on Aug. 22, 1987 in replacement of former Bureau of Environmental Protection under Department of Health.

Pre-screening of New Factories New factory falling in Category B industries is required to submit Pollution Control Plan and also Environment Analysis Statement if such factory falls in Category A industries, for review and approval by EPA before it purchases factory site (Key Point for Screening and Approval of Pollution Control Plan of New Factories promulgated by Ministry of Economic Affairs on Aug. 11, 1988). If EPA deems necessary, additional Environmental Impact Assessment Report (EIA Report) will be required and factory establishment permit will not be granted before EPA is satisfied with such EIA Report.

Same criteria applies to expansion projects of existing factories.

Water Pollution Water Pollution Control Statute (promulgated on July 11, 1974 and last amended on May 6, 1991) authorizes EPA to set forth, standards for controlling effluent water. EPA promulgated Effluent Water Standards in three staged (last amended on Jan. 16, 1991), of which standards of initial stage will be enforced until Dec. 31, 1992, more strict standards for second stage will be enforced from Jan. 1. 1993 for period of six years and last stage's standards will be started on Jan. 1, 1998. Failure to meet with standards will be subject to penalty of up to NT$600,000, and failure to correct such default within period ordered by competent authority will be given same penalty for each day it is not correct, and, if event is substantially serious, competent authority

may order postponement of business, or, if necessary, effluent permit may be cancelled or business may be forced to cease permanently. (Water Pollution Control Statute, Art. 38).

Permit will be required for discharging waste or (sewage) water in any manner, other than to sewerage system. (Water Pollution Control Statute, Arts. 14, 30).

Water Pollution Control Statute also regulates sewerage systems and deals with waste water containing hazardous substances and other substances harmful to humans, farming and fishing or drinking water resources, etc. (Water Pollution Control Statute, Arts. 26, 34).

Others Various statutes, regulations, guidelines and requirements were implemented or are going to be implemented to regulate and control air pollution, noise, vibration, ocean pollution, waste disposal and recycling, soil pollution, public environmental sanitation, toxic chemicals, and drinking water, etc. Administrative and criminal punishment are or will be imposed on owners, responsible persons of industries and industries themselves.

EXCHANGE CONTROL
See Foreign Exchange and Foreign Trade.

EXECUTIONS

In general creditor may, unless otherwise prohibited by relevant laws, after favorable judgment, secure compulsory execution on any of property of debtor. Compulsory execution may also be obtained against debtor in respect of: (1) His money claims against third persons; (2) claims based on his rights to delivery of some movable or immovable property by third person; (3) claims other than those cited in (1) and (2) above, which debtor has over some property but constituting something other than ownership, such as claim for performance of some service. Court may issue necessary orders or restraining orders against debtor and/or against third persons to effect compulsory execution.

FOREIGN EXCHANGE AND FOREIGN TRADE

Foreign exchange and foreign trade are controlled by Government under Statute for Governing Foreign Exchange promulgated in 1970 as last amended on June 26, 1987 and other relevant regulations. Said Statute and regulations are presently enforced by Foreign Exchange Department of Central Bank of China (in respect of foreign exchange), Ministry of Finance (in respect of foreign exchange-related administration) and Board of Foreign Trade of Ministry of Economic Affairs (in respect of foreign trade). 1987 amendment of Statute made major liberalization of foreign exchange control. Guiding principles thereof are to: (1) Permit private sectors to freely own and use trade-related (i.e., non-capital transfer) foreign exchange, (2) properly regulate inward and outward remittance of funds not related to trade (i.e., capital transfer), (3) permit appointed foreign exchange business banks to freely set conversion rate of forward foreign exchange.

Effective on July 15, 1987, foreign exchange earnings resulting from goods exported or services rendered can be freely converted into NT dollars without limitation on amount. Any resident individual over 20 years of age who is holder of ROC National I.D. Card or alien residency certificate can remit US$2,000,000 (or equivalent in other foreign currencies) each year for conversion into NT dollars since July 18, 1990. However, each remittance exceeding US$1,000,000 will be effected after waiting period of ten business days from application date. Inward remittance representing repatriation of capital and profits of offshore investment or representing investment in ROC by foreign investors or overseas Chinese must be approved in advance by relevant government agencies.

Outward remittance in foreign exchange, as payment for imported goods or services by properly established ROC enterprises can be freely made without any limitation on amount. Any ROC enterprise (including branches of foreign corporations) and resident individual over 20 years of age who is holder of ROC National I.D. Card or alien residency certificate can make outward remittance in foreign exchange up to US$5,000,000 (or its equivalent in other foreign currencies) per year, except that each remittance exceeding US$1,000,000 or its equivalent in other foreign currencies is subject to ten-day waiting period. Other types of outward remittance require prior approval from relevant government agencies.

All private importers and exporters must register themselves before engaging in trading businesses and must have paid-in capital of no less than NT$5,000,000.

FOREIGN INVESTMENT

Government has adopted various measures to encourage foreign investments in ROC and promulgated on July 14, 1954, Statute for Investment by Foreign Nationals; which was last amended May 26, 1989. Under this Statute, foreign investment may consist of inward remittance of foreign exchange; machinery and supplies required for domestic use; techniques or patent rights, and such portions of principal, capital gain, net profit, interest or other income from investments that has been approved in, or for, settlement of foreign exchange. Farms of investment may be: (1) to invest alone or jointly with Government or with Chinese nationals or juristic persons, in establishing new enterprises or in expanding old ones; (2) to purchase, stocks or debentures of existing enterprises, or to extend loans of cash, machinery or supplies to same; (3) to furnish techniques or patent rights as capital stock for joint operation of enterprises with Government or with Chinese nationals or juristic persons.

Investments in following businesses, however, are prohibited: (1) Businesses which are in conflict with public safety; (2) businesses which are in conflict with good morals; (3) businesses which are not opened to foreign investment; and (4) businesses with nature of monopolization or in which foreign investments are prohibited according to laws.

Investments in following businesses are subject to special approval from relevant authorities-in-charge: (1) public utilities; (2) financing and insurance businesses; (3) news and publication businesses; and (4) businesses in which foreign investment is restricted according to laws and regulations. Foreign investment in service industries is being allowed by government, such as advertisement, department store, chain stores, financial consulting services, securities-related business (generally on joint venture basis) and export/import trading.

In 1988 ROC government also promulgated set of guidelines called "Negative Listings" (as last amended on July 11, 1990). These guidelines set forth sectors of R.O.C.'s economy in which foreign investment is either restricted or prohibited. Those sectors not on Negative List are then open to foreign investment without any restriction.

Techniques and patent rights to be recognized as items of foreign investments must be those rights or patents which have been approved by Chinese Government.

Foreign investor is entitled to remit entire annual profits of his investment. After one year from time when enterprise invested in commences its business operation, if investor shall transfer its investment upon government approval, capital of enterprise invested shall be decreased or enterprise invested shall be liquidated, investor is legally permitted to repatriate 100% of his total equity investment. Privilege of remitting profits or repatriating capital is not transferable except to investor's heirs, or to transferee who has status of foreign national.

Enterprises in which foreign capital has been invested are treated on equal footing, with those of same nature, operated by Chinese. Restrictions that (i) Chairman and vice chairman of board of directors must be Chinese and that half of incorporators and at least one supervisor must be domiciled in

ROC, (ii) shares of enterprise invested must be publicly issued and (iii) 10 to 15% of newly issued shares must be reserved for subscription by employees of enterprise invested are exempted in case of duly approved and qualified foreign invested enterprise. Subject to Statute for Investment by Foreign Nationals, foreign investors may also be exempted from certain restrictions in Company Law, Mining Law, Land Law, Merchant Marine and Civil Aviation Law so that they can be on equal footing with Chinese investor.

Specific protection is accorded foreign investors against requisition, or expropriation for period of 20 years so long as foreign capital comprises 45% or more of total capital of enterprise from commencement of business.

Government has definite policy of encouraging private investment and enterprise including foreign. Statute for Encouragement of Investment was promulgated on Sept. 10, 1960 and expired on Dec. 31, 1990 to provide qualified enterprises with certain tax incentives, such as five-year corporate income tax holiday, duty-free importation of machinery and equipment, investment credit on new machinery and equipment, etc. New legislation, Statute for Promotion of Industrial Upgrading (SIU), took effect on Jan. 1, 1991 and provides companies in form of company limited by shares with some investment incentives, such as accelerated depreciation of equipment and instruments for R and D, pollution control, energy conservation purposes, reduced withholding income tax rate on dividends received by foreign investors whose investments have been duly approved under Statute for Investment by Foreign Nationals, etc.

ROC and US Governments have concluded agreement whereby US Government guarantees US investors in ROC against nonconvertibility in remittance of profits or repatriation of capital and against expropriation of investments.

ROC Government has also promulgated a separate but similar law to the above affording encouragement, protection and privileges to Overseas Chinese investors.

FOREIGN TRADE REGULATIONS

See Foreign Exchange and Foreign Trade.

FRAUDS, STATUTE OF

There is no statute of frauds as such, but certain agreements are required to be in writing such as transfer of title of ownership of immovable property.

FRAUDULENT SALES AND CONVEYANCES

Creditor or trustee in bankruptcy may apply to court for invalidation of debtor's gratuitous act if such act is detrimental to creditor's right; while nongratuitous act of debtor may be invalidated only if party receiving benefits of act had knowledge of circumstances at time he received such benefits. If debtor, within six months prior to adjudication of bankruptcy, provides security for outstanding debts (except in cases where commitment of providing security was made prior to expiration of six month period before adjudication of bankruptcy) or repays debts before its maturity, such act may be invalidated by trustee in bankruptcy.

GARNISHMENT

See Attachment.

INSOLVENCY

See Bankruptcy.

INTEREST

Debtors and creditors may agree on interest rate, subject to maximum rate specified in Civil Code, i.e. 20% per annum. In absence of any interest rate being agreed upon, creditors may demand 5% per annum, unless otherwise stipulated by law. If interest rate agreed upon exceeds ceiling provided for by Civil Code, creditor is not entitled to claim portion of interest over ceiling. Agreement for interest on interest is, in principle, not permitted, except when it is made in writing with respect to accrued interest which has not been paid for period of over one year from due date or there shall be commercial usage that indicates otherwise.

JOINT STOCK COMPANIES

See Corporations.

LABOR RELATIONS

Basic Labor Standard Law was promulgated on July 30,1984 and effective on Aug. 1 of same year, which applies to following industries: (1) Agricultural, forestry, fishing and pasturage; (2) mining and quarrying; (3) manufacturing; (4) construction; (5) water, power and gas supplying; (6) transportation, warehousing and communication; (7) mass media; and (8) other industries designated by central authority-in-charge. Such basic working conditions as labor agreements, wages, work hours, rest periods and vacations, child and female workers, retirement, compensation for occupational hazards, apprentices, work rules, etc. are included in Law.

Labor Agreements Job of temporary, short-term,

seasonal or specific nature may be covered by fixed-term agreement. Joboof on-going nature must be subject to non-fixed-term agreement. While fixed-term agreement can be terminated without advance notice and severance pay upon expiration of agreement, non-fixed-term agreement can be terminated only if any of following events occurs and advance notice and, severance pay are granted: (1) Business is closed or transferred; (2) business suffers losses or retrenchment; (3) business is suspended for over a month due to force majeure; (4) reduction of workers becomes necessary because nature of business has changed and there is no appropriate job available for worker; or (5) it is ascertained that worker is not capable of performing work assigned by employer. Of course, worker who commits wrongdoing can be dismissed at any time without advance notice and severance pay being granted. (B.L.S.L. 9.11.12).

Hours of Work Adult workers' hours of work shall, in principle, be limited to an eight hour day. Under special circumstances, working hours may be extended to a 12 hour day, provided that total hours extended in a month shall not exceed 46 hours. (B.L.S.L. 30.32).

Statutory Basic Wage Prevailing minimum wage for adult worker is NT$9,750 per month.

As for child worker which refers to one who has reached his 15th but not 16th year of age, his work time shall not exceed an eight hour day, and he shall not be employed to work between hours of 8 p. m. and 6 a. m. in ensuing morning and shall not be employed to perform any heavy and/or dangerous work. (B.L.S.L. 44, 47, 48).

Female worker shall not be employed to work between hours of 10 pm and 6 am in ensuing morning unless three-shift system is adopted and certain requirements are met. (B.L.S.L. 49).

Worker is entitled to take half hour break with pay after having worked for four consecutive hours and to have one day as holiday in every seven days. Worker shall be granted leave for rest with pay on all public holidays ordained by laws or regulations. In addition to official holidays, worker who has been employed continuously for specific period shall be entitled to special vacation (ranging from 7-30 days per year). If worker does not take his vacation he shall be paid additional wages due for period of such vacation. (B.L.S.L. 35-39).

In case of maternity, female laborer shall be given leave for rest before and after childbirth up to total of eight weeks; she shall receive full pay during such periods if she has been employed for more than six months. (B.L.S.L. 50).

Labor Insurance Labor Insurance Act specifies that all factories, mines and any enterprises having five or more employees are obligated to apply for insurance coverage with Labor Insurance Bureau (LIB) for their employees. 80% of insurance premium is to be paid up by employer and rest by insured employee.

Insured employee is entitled to receive following major benefits: (a) Death payment; (b) old age retirement payment; (c) sickness and injury payment; (d) medical care payment; (e) disability payment; and (f) maternity payment.

Severance Pay Employees who are terminated according to Art. 11 or 13 of B.L.S.L. shall be given severance pay at rate of one month wage for one full year of service. (B.L.S.L. 17).

Retirement Benefits Employees who qualify for voluntary or compulsory retirement shall be granted retirement benefit at rate of two-month wage for one full year of service during initial 15 years and one-month wage for one full year of service in subsequent years, subject to maximum of 45-month wage. (B.L.S.L. 53, 54, 55).

Labor Unions According to Labor Union Law, industrial or craft union shall be organized when in one and same area, or when in one and same industry or workshop, number of workers above full 20 years of age in one and same factory or in one and same area is over 30. There are six national unions, viz., Chinese Federation of Labor Unions, National Union of Railway Workers, National Union of Seamen, National Union of Mailmen, National Union of Mine Workers and National Union of Salt Mine Workers. In addition, there exist many unions on provincial as well as municipal levels. Union organizations became very aggressive in past two years.

The Law Governing, the Handling of Labor Disputes provides mediation and/or arbitration proceedings on labor-management disputes. Union may go out for strike if its, disputes with management fail to be resolved in mediation and majority of its members vote for strike.

LICENSES

Practically, most of business activities, professions and means of transportation as well as all copyrights trademark and patent rights will need license or certificate from authority. (*See* Commercial Register, Copyright, Corporations, Motor Vehicles, Patents, Shipping, and Trademarks.)

LIENS

Law relative to liens is found under title "Right of Retention" in ROC Civil Code. Creditor in possession of personal property belonging to his debtor may retain same: (1) Where his obligation has matured; (2) where there is some connection between obligation and personal property; and (3) where possession of personal property is legal. If debtor is insolvent, creditor may exercise his right of retention before obligation matures. Creditor must exercise due care over property retained and may claim reimbursement for expenses incurred in connection with custody thereof. If debtor has given proper security for performance of obligation, right of retention by creditor is extinguished. Right of retention is also extinguished by loss of possession of property. Lessor of real estate has right of retention over personal property of lessee in/on real estate, to cover damages which he is entitled to recover and rent in arrears.

Innkeeper may retain luggage or other property of guest pending payment for lodging, food or disbursements.

Carrier may retain sufficient goods to secure payment of freight and other expenses. Last carrier may exercise such right of retention for benefit of all.

Forwarding agent likewise has right of retention.

LIMITATION OF ACTIONS

Claim is barred by limitation if not exercised within 15 years, unless shorter periods are provided by law.

Claims for each successive payment falling due at intervals of one year or less are barred by limitation if not exercised within five years.

Claims in respect of following are barred by limitation if not exercised within two years: charges for lodging, food, amusements, or for price of goods for consumption, and for disbursements made by inns, restaurants and places of amusement; cost of transportation and disbursements by carriers; rent due to person who carries on business of letting movables; remuneration of attorneys, public accountants and notaries and their disbursements; restoration of things received from clients by attorneys, public accountants and notaries; remuneration of technical experts, contractors and their disbursements; claims of merchants, manufacturers and craftsmen for price of goods or products supplied.

Extinctive limitation begins to run from time when claim can be exercised, but is interrupted by: (1) Demand; (2) acknowledgment of claim; or (3) initiation of legal action. Limitation which has been interrupted recommences to run from moment when cause of interruption ceases. Interruption of limitation takes effect only as between parties and their successors and assignees.

Limitation of claim for which there is mortgage or pledge or right of retention does not prevent creditor from satisfying himself out of things mortgaged, pledged or retained.

Period of limitation cannot be altered by juristic acts.

Benefit of limitation cannot be waived beforehand.

MONOPOLIES AND RESTRAINT OF TRADE

Fair Trade Law ("FTL") was promulgated on Feb. 4, 1991 and will become effective on Feb. 4, 1992, which would be administered by Fair Trade Commission ("FTC") under Executive Yuan.

Monopolization Monopoly is prohibited from unfairly excluding others from market, maintaining and/or modifying prices unjustifiably, requesting favored treatment unjustifiably, and otherwise abusing its dominant market position. Oligopolistic firms will be treated as monopolies on collective basis without need to prove any anticompetitive agreement. Conceivably, predatory and monopolistic pricing will constitute act of monopolization.

Merger Prior report to FTC and its approval will be required for combination of enterprises where (1) surviving enterprise will have one-third of market share; (2) one of constituent enterprises has one-fourth of market share; or (3) one of constituent enterprises has amount of sales for previous accounting year that exceeds sales criteria publicly announced by FTC.

"Combination" is broadly defined to include mergers, acquisitions of more than one-third of voting stock of or interest in another enterprise, transfer or lease in whole or major part of enterprise's business or property, exercise of effective control over personnel employment of another enterprise, and regular operation of another enterprise or joint operation. FTC has to determine whether combination approval should be granted under economic cost-benefit analysis. Failure to file for FTC's approval may result in divestiture, compulsory disposition of assets, cessation of business and fines.

Cartel Concerted actions to restrict prices, quantities, customers, territories or otherwise restrict each other's commercial activities are not allowed. Accordingly, enterprises in Taiwan would be prohibited from engaging in horizontal price-fixing, horizontal territorial allocation and output restrictions. Several exceptions will be approved if they are found to increase efficiency, unify standards, increase joint research and development, maintain orderly import and export, or avoid bankruptcy.

Restraint of Trade Resale price maintenance will be nullified, with exception of daily consumption goods as published by FTC. FTL will also prohibit certain exclusionary practices such as boycott, discrimination, unfair inducement, tying arrangements and breaches of confidence, if they are found to be unreasonable.

Unfair Practices FTL will also prohibit other means of unfair competition such as trademark infringement, passing off, intentional mislabeling and other acts that may confuse consumers, trade libel, misappropriation of trade secrets, and other deceptive and unfair practices. In addition, pyramid sales plan in which commissions, bonuses or other economic gains are principally derived from recruiting others to join plan will be challenged.

Liabilities and Remedies FTC will have power to investigate possible violations and to impose administrative sanctions. Any person injured by any anticompetitive act or unfair methods of competition could seek injunctive relief, and treble damages may be awarded at discretion of court. Court may use unfair advantage gained by such unlawful act as measure of compensation. Violation of FTL will result in criminal liability, including imprisonment up to three years and fine up to NT$1 million. Criminal sanctions also apply to individuals working for entities engaging in such anticompetitive activities. Importantly, unrecognized foreign legal persons and entities may bring action under FTL if reciprocity exists.

Exemptions from FTL FTL recognizes that patents, trademarks and copyrights are legal monopolies granted by government, if such rights are exercised properly. For five years from its promulgation, FTL exempts acts of public utilities, government owned enterprises, transportation enterprises, if approved by Executive Yuan.

NEGOTIABLE INSTRUMENTS

See Bills and Notes.

NOTARIES PUBLIC

Regulations establishing notary public offices have been promulgated and applied in many localities with object of eventual uniform application throughout ROC. Such offices are established as special division of various local district courts, where notary public assigned to such duties may, on application of parties or other interested persons, issue notary public certificates concerning juristic acts or acts relating to private rights, or give authentication to private documents. Applicants must be properly identified. Fees vary in relation to values involved.

PARTNERSHIP

ROC Civil Code provides that partnership is contract whereby two or more persons agree to make contributions in common for collective purpose. Contributions of members of such partnership and all other properties of partnership are held in common by all of members. Unless otherwise provided for by contract, accounts of partnership must be settled and its profits distributed at end of each business year. If assets of partnership are not sufficient to cover liabilities, partners are liable as joint debtors for deficit.

Dissolution Partnership is dissolved in any of following cases: (1) Where period agreed upon for its duration has expired; (2) when partners unanimously decide to dissolve it; (3) when undertaking which forms its object is accomplished, or when it is impossible to accomplish it.

PATENTS

ROC Patent Law and Enforcement Rules thereof were first put into effect Jan. 1, 1949 and last revised Dec. 24, 1986.

Patent applications filed by foreigners may be accepted if their home country has concluded treaty with ROC or agreement for reciprocal protection of patent rights, or if patent protection agreement has been concluded by and between related organization or institutions and approved by Ministry of Economic Affairs, or if law of above foreign country permits patent protection for nationals of ROC.

Patent is granted for new inventions having utilization value in production, practicable creations relating to form, construction or fitting of any object as well as new designs relating to shape, pattern or color of any article which may evoke sense of beauty.

Patent will be denied for new invention or new utility model if, before filing for patent, invention or new utility model has been published or put to public use anywhere in world therefore making imitation by others possible, or if patent has previously been granted to same invention or new utility model, or if invention or new utility model has been displayed in exhibition, government sponsored or approved, and patent application is filed more than six months from opening date of such exhibition, or if invention or new utility model has been mass produced other than for experimental purposes, or if invention or new utility model utilizes conventional techniques and know-how and is obvious and makes no improvement in effectiveness. For new design applications, novelty will be ruined if, before filing for patent, same or similar design has been published or put to public use anywhere in world, or if patent has previously been granted to same or similar new design or new utility model. Patent is generally not granted for foods, habit-forming articles, new species of animal, plant and microorganism, diagnostic, curing or operative methods for diseases of human body or animals, scientific principles or art of mathematics, rules or methods of games and sports, methods or plans which can be carried out only by means of reasoning and memory of human beings, discovery of new use of article, or any article detrimental to public order, good morals, public health or use of which is contrary to law, or shape of which is identical or similar to party, national or military flag, national emblem, government medal, portrait of National Father Dr. Sun Yat-Sen or official seal.

Patent matters are administered by Ministry of Economic Affairs. Application for patent should be filed by inventor, his assignees or successors, with National Bureau of Standards, by submitting written application, detailed specification and drawings together with oath and/or assignment, as case may be.

All approved patent applications and other patent-related matters will be published in Patent Gazettes published by National Bureau of Standards. Patent rights commence from date of publication, for duration of 15, 10 and 5 years respectively for new invention, new utility model and new design patent; nevertheless, rights shall not exceed 18, 12 and 6 years from filing dates of new invention, new utility model and new design patent applications respectively.

PLEDGES

Pledge can be created on movables and rights. Possession by pledgee of thing pledged is necessary to validity of pledge on movable. Pledge secures principal debt, interest and cost of executing pledge and any damages arising from latent defects in thing pledged, except as otherwise provided for in agreement. Pledgee must exercise good care over thing pledged. Pledgee may make sub-pledge. Chose in action may be subject of pledge.

On default, pledgee may sell thing pledged at auction and pay himself out of proceeds. Agreement that on default ownership of thing pledged shall pass to pledgee is void; but after maturity of obligation pledgee may, by agreement, acquire ownership of thing pledged in order to satisfy his claim.

Pledge is extinguished through return of thing pledged by pledgee to pledger. Upon return of thing pledged, any reservation made in regard to continuance of pledge is void. Pledge is extinguished when pledgee loses possession of thing pledged and cannot demand return of it, or when thing pledged is lost. If compensation can be obtained for loss of thing pledged, pledgee is entitled to be paid out of compensation.

PRINCIPAL AND AGENT

If any authority of agency is conferred by juristic act, act of conferring must be made by manifestation of intention to agent or to third party with whom business delegated is transacted. (C. C. 167). Manifestation of intention which agent makes in name of principal within scope of his delegated authority takes effect directly both in favor of or against principal. (C. C. Art. 103). No limitation or revocation of power conferred on agent can be set up against bona fide third party, unless ignorance of third party is

due to his fault. (C. C. Art. 107). At termination or revocation of power of agency agent has to return written power of agency to party who gave it; he has no right of retention to it. (C. C. Art. 109). Person, who by his own acts represents that he has conferred authority of agency to another person, or who knowing that another person declares himself to be his agent fails to express contrary intention, is liable to third parties in same way as person who confers that authority, unless third parties knew, or ought to have known of absence of authority. (C.C. Art. 169). Juristic act done by person having no authority to act as agent is ineffective against principal unless ratified by principal. (C.C. Art. 170).

SALES

Contract of sale is consummated when parties mutually agree on object to be sold and price to be paid. Vendor is bound to deliver thing sold to buyer and see that he acquires its ownership. Vendor of claim or of right must warrant existence of claim or right, but not in respect of defect in right sold, existence of which was known to buyer at time of concluding contract. Vendor of claim does not warrant solvency of debtor. Vendor warrants that thing sold is free from defect in quality which would render it unfit for ordinary purposes or for purpose of resale, or which would impair or destroy its value. If buyer declines to accept thing forwarded from another place because of defect he is bound to preserve it in his custody temporarily and to prove existence of defect immediately. He may also sell thing forwarded if it is perishable or easily deteriorates, having first acquired permission therefore of authorities, chamber of commerce, or notary of place where thing is. In case of nonperformance by vendor of his duties concerning defect of thing sold, buyer has option to rescind contract or to ask for reduction of price. Rescission of contract on account of defect in principal thing extends to its accessory. Right of rescission of contract or reduction of price of thing sold in case of defect is extinguished if not exercised within six months after delivery, unless defect was intentionally concealed.

Unless otherwise provided by law, by contract or by custom, delivery of object sold and payment of price must take place simultaneously. Profits and risks of object sold pass to buyer at time of delivery, unless otherwise provided by contract. Right of redemption may be exercised if contract so provides, but such right must be exercised within five years. Cost of redemption must be borne by person who redeems.

Particular kinds of sales are: Sale on approval, sale by sample, sale by installments, and sale by auction. In sale by sample, vendor warrants that object sold will conform to sample.

Notices Required. — In case party to sales contract is in default, other party may specify reasonable period of time for him to perform, If party in default does not perform his obligation within such period, other party may rescind contract. In this connection, exercise of right of rescission will not affect right of party not in default to claim for damage. (C. C. 254 & 260). If according to nature of contract or expression of parties, object of contract cannot be fulfilled if performance is not effected within specific period of time, and if said period of time elapses without effectuation of performance by one party, other party may rescind contract without having to give notice required in C. C. Art. 254. Yet notice of rescission must reach other party and is irrevocable. (C. C. 258).

Applicable Law.—*See* Contracts, subhead Applicable Law.

SECURITIES

Unless otherwise stated, articles cited are those of Securities and Exchange Law ("SEL"), which was promulgated on Apr. 30, 1958 and last amended on Jan. 29, 1988.

Regulatory Powers of Supervising Authority Securities and Exchange Commission ("SEC") established under Ministry of Finance ("MOF") is authorized by SEL to administer within comprehensive regulatory framework provided by SEL. (Art. 3).

Definition of "Security" under SEL Under SEL, term "security" includes government bonds, corporate stocks and corporate bonds publicly offered or issued, and any other securities approved by Ministry of Finance. In addition, any stock warrant certificate, certificate of payment or any document of title to any of foregoing securities are deemed as securities. (Art. 6).

Catch-all wording of this article is intended to cover interim securities or other documents that would otherwise escape being governed by SEL. Under authority granted by article, MOF has ruled that beneficial certificates issued by securities investment trust companies are type of "Security."

In addition, MOF also ruled that "the offering and sale of foreign stocks, bonds, government bonds, beneficial certificates or other securities in the nature of investment vehicles, shall be regulated by the ROC securities regulations," without actually defining them as securities, and that conclusion of certain "investment contracts" by overseas Chinese or foreigners for purpose of raising funds in Taiwan is equivalent to issuance of securities. However, criteria for determining whether any particular contract is investment contract has yet to be further defined under SEL.

Subscription, Issuance and Public Offering Subscription, and issuance of securities arc subject to prior SEC review and approval. (Art. 22). In addition to approval system, SEL adopted registration system whereby certain public offerings would become effective upon registration with SEC. Securities exempt from such approval or registration requirements include government bonds, securities issued by special-purpose companies (e.g. government-owned enterprises) and other securities specifically authorized by government.

SEL defines "Public Offering" to mean offer of stocks and bonds to "nonspecific persons" by promoters prior to incorporation, of company, or by issuer prior to issuance of definitive securities. However SEC has yet to define and determine what would constitute "nonspecific persons."

Employees of companies limited by shares generally have preemptive rights on l0 to 15% of their company's new share issues. In addition, existing shareholders have preemptive rights over balance of newly issued shares after employees have exercised their preemptive rights. However, shareholders' preemptive rights are limited by SEL so that when listed company issues new shares to be sold on Taiwan Stock Exchange ("TSE") or over-the-counter market ("OTC"), at, least 10% of such new issuance must be set aside to be subscribed by public at same price offered to existing share-holders. Furthermore. public companies, whose shares are traded neither on TSE nor OTC markets but are subject to disclosure requirements under SEL, must meet shareholder diversification requirements. Unless specific exemption from SEC is obtained, public company failing to meet diversification requirements must set aside for public offering at least 10% of new shares offered for cash.

Disclosure and Reporting Requirements Offering of securities must be made through prospectus containing information required by SEC. (Art. 30). Failure to tender prospectus to subscribers, making materially false statements, or omitting required material statements from prospectus, will lead to liability of issuer, related professionals, certain insiders, and underwriters. (Art. 31 and 32). In addition, "due diligence" defense to false or omitted statement in prospectus to insiders and other persons involved in drafting prospectus is also specified in SEL.

Public companies are required to submit and publish audited annual and semi-annual financial reports as well as first and third quarter financial reports that have been reviewed by their respective independent auditors. Public companies are also required to submit and publish monthly operating statement before tenth of following month. In addition, Art. 36 of SEL provides that all public, companies shall file and publish additional information which will, keep reasonably current all statements filed with SEC. Events that may have significant impact on financial condition of issuer also trigger financial reporting requirement under, 1988 SEL amendment.

Art. 25 of SEL imposes certain public disclosure and reporting requirements regarding share ownership of their managerial personnel, directors, supervisors and holders of more than, 10% of their shares on public companies. These reports must include class, number and par value of issuer's equity securities. Holders of more than 10% of shares of public companies must also file and publish monthly reports with issuer itemizing changes in number of shares they held during preceding month. Issuer is required to consolidate such reports and file them with SEC. Calculation of such holdings includes shares held by another on behalf of shareholder (e.g., spouse, minor child).

Art. 22-2 of SEL also provides that transfer of shares by director, supervisor, manager or holder of more than 10% of shares of issuer may only be effected in accordance with any of following methods: (1) by transfer to nonspecific person following approval by, or registration with, SEC: (2) by transfer of over 10,000 shares which are to be traded in one day on TSE or in OTC and which have been held for period prescribed by SEC, within three days following registration with SEC, or (3) transfer within three days following registration with SEC, by means of private placement to specific persons who meet certain qualifications prescribed by SEC.

Tender Offers Art. 43-1 of SEL requires any person acquiring, individually or jointly with other persons, more than 10% of the total issued and outstanding shares of public company to file with SEC report within ten days after such acquisition. Such report has to disclose purpose and funding source of shares acquisition and any other matters as required by SEC. Unless approved by SEC, tender offers to public may not be made outside of TSE or OTC. SEL authorizes SEC to promulgate relevant regulations intended to govern and regulate tender offers.

Insider Trading Art. 157 of SEL is designed to prohibit corporate "insiders" from taking advantage of their access to information by engaging in short-term trading in securities held by them. This article permits issuer to recover within six months trading profits made by directors, managerial personnel, supervisors and 10% shareholders of issuer.

1988 amendment of SEL contains new Art. 157-1 which requires certain insiders to either disclose confidential material information before they trade on affected securities or refrain from such trading activities. For any violation, person will be liable for damages to any person engaging in transactions on opposite side in good faith. Measure of damages will be limited by difference between purchase (or sale) price prior to disclosure and average of last reported sale price for ten business days after disclosure. In case of any egregious violation, court may award damages up to three times amount of actual damages.

Anti-fraud Provisions and Civil Liabilities Art. 155 of SEL outlaws manipulative practices it; securities trading, and provides private remedy for investors injured by'manipulative conduct prohibited by SEL. In effort to cover fraudulent and manipulative conduct that takes place in OTC markets, article was amended in 1988 to encompass manipulative conducts on TSE and OTC markets. Amended article also modifies language of previous article in order to ensure effective enforcement. In contrast to previous article, which only provided criminal sanctions, new article provides civil remedies to bona fide purchasers or sellers of securities. Art. 155, as amended, prohibits "wash sales" or any transactions entered into simultaneously with purpose of creating misleading appearance of trading. This article also prohibits transactions entered into for purpose of depressing or raising security prices as well as spreading of rumors or misleading information for purpose of manipulating such prices. In addition, Art. 155 contains comprehensive provision intended to prohibit any direct or indirect manipulative conduct aimed at affecting price.

Under general anti-fraud provision contained in Art. 20 of SEL, fraudulent conduct in connection with offering and sale of securities is prohibited. In addition, misrepresentation or omission is prohibited in financial reports or any other relevant documents filed or published by issuer. Violation, of either of these two prohibitions may result in both criminal and civil sanctions. Art. 20 of SEL creates and expresses right of action in hands of bona fide buyers or sellers.

Establishment of Securities Firms SEC promulgated Criteria for the Establishment of Securities Firms ("Establishment Criteria") on May 17, 1988. Under Establishment Criteria, minimum paid-in, capital for underwriting, dealing and brokerage operations is NT$400 million, NT$400 million, and NT$200 million, respectively. Therefore, integrated securities house operation will require total paid-in capital of NT$1 billion.

Foreign access to securities firms can be made in any one of three following ways: First, any foreign investor or overseas Chinese may invest in securities operation by joint venturing with ROC investors. Total amount of foreign and overseas Chinese ownership, however, may not exceed 40% of paid-in capital of entity engaging in securities business, and each foreign or overseas Chinese investor may invest not more than 10% of total paid-in capital of securities entity. Moreover, once foreign or overseas Chinese investor invests in securities entity, it may not invest in any other securities entity. Second, foreign securities firms may set up branch operation; to date, SEC has only allowed foreign securities firms meeting certain requirements to set up branch offices in ROC to engage in securities brokerage business. Third, ROC branches of foreign banks may qualify as financial institutions and set up securities operation. SEC has discretion to limit number and business scope of foreign securities firms setting up branch operations or ROC branches of foreign banks setting up securities operations.

SHIPPING

Chinese vessels are subject to provisions of Admiralty Law promulgated on Dec. 30, 1929 and became effective on Jan. 1, 1931 as last amended on July 25, 1962 and Vessel Law promulgated on Dec. 4, 1930 and became effective on July 1, 1931 as last amended on Dec. 28, 1983. As provided in Art. 1 of Admiralty Law, term "vessel," where used in this Law, refers to oceangoing vessels and vessels navigating on or in waters or waters intercommunicating with sea. Provisions of this Law are not applicable to following classes of vessel, save in case of collision: (1) Motor driven vessels whose gross tonnage is less than 20 tons or nonmotor driven vessels whose gross tonnage is less than 50 tons, (2) military vessels, (3) vessels solely used on public business, (4) vessels not belonging to those provided in Art. 1 of Admiralty Law.

Assignment of whole or part of vessel is void unless made in writing and in accordance with following provisions: (1) In ROC, application must be made to governing authority at place of assignment or place where vessel is lying, and latter must seal and certify assignment; (2) abroad, application must be made to Chinese Consulate, which must seal and certify assignment.

Transfer of ownership of vessel may not be pleaded against third party unless it has been registered.

As provided in Art. 2 of Vessel Law, vessels owned by: (i) Chinese Government (ii) Chinese nationals, (iii) Chinese companies, or (iv) Chinese juristic persons are Chinese flag vessels. Unless otherwise approved by Chinese Government pursuant to Statute for Investment by Foreign Nationals, no foreigner may own Chinese flag vessel.

Foreign Shipping Since abolition of extraterritoriality foreign shipping is excluded from all river and coastal traffic. Foreign shipping companies or their agents must register with Ministry of Communications and Ministry of Economic Affairs. American ships are governed by Art. 22 of Treaty of Friendship, Commerce and Navigation between USA and ROC which has been ratified by both countries. This treaty is based on reciprocity and thus duties, charges or conditions which are not imposed on Chinese ships will not be imposed on American ships.

Shipping Act, promulgated on June 3, 1981, governs all shipping enterprises and shipping industries including carriers, agents, sea cargo forwarders, vessel charters, ship leasing and charter operation, container terminals and leasing operations and employment of sailors. Foreign ships may not solicit or receive passengers or goods for transportation in ROC unless ROC shipping agent has been engaged to execute or handle matters related to carriage of passengers or goods. Such restriction is not applicable to foreign shipping carriers having branch office in ROC

TRADEMARKS

Trademark shall be defined by device. Any word, drawing, symbol, or combination thereof used in trademark shall be markedly distinctive. Colors employed shall be designated. Name of trademark may be entered in device only when name of trademark is registrable as trademark under requirements of Trademark Law. Pronunciation of word is included in word used as trademark.

According to Trademark Law of ROC, trademark design having any one of following features may not be applied for registration: (1) Being identical with or similar to national flag, national emblem, State seal, any military flag, military insignia, official seal or decoration of ROC, or national flag of any other nation; (2) being identical with or similar to image or name of late Dr. Sun Yat-sen or of Chief of State; (3) being identical with or similar to red cross sign, or name or emblem of other famous international organizations; (4) being identical with or similar to Chinese "Standard Quality" label or any local or foreign label of certification nature; (5) being likely to disturb public order or corrupt good morals; (6) being likely to deceive public or cause public to have misbelief; (7) being identical with or similar to world famous mark or symbol owned by another person and used on same goods or goods in same class; (8) being identical with or similar to mark or symbol generally used according to customs on same goods; (9) being identical with or similar to any prize medal or citation awarded by Government of ROC or by authorities of exhibition or to mark of such government offices or authorities of exhibition; (10) containing words, drawing, symbols, or any combination thereof, which are generally used according to customs to indicate name, shape, quality or utility of commodity, or other descriptions of commodity, for which trademark is applied for registration; (11) containing image of another person, or name or tradename of any corporate body or other organization or of famous firm known throughout nation, or name of another person, without obtaining their previous consent; provided that this provision shall not apply if goods covered by scope of business of such firm or corporate body are not same goods or goods in same class as those designated in application for registration of mark sought for registration; (12) being identical with or similar to another person's registered trademark used for same goods or for goods in same class, or being identical with or similar to such registered trademark, registration of which has expired less than two years; provided, however, that this provision shall not apply in case where registered trademark has not been used for two years or more before registration loses its validity; (13) using another person's registered trademark as portion of his own mark to cover same goods or goods in same class.

All Chinese and foreigners of countries which have treaties with ROC for mutual protection of trademarks have right to register trademarks and acquire right of exclusive use thereof for period of ten years commencing from date of registration. With regard to foreigners of countries which have no reciprocal treaties with ROC, they can obtain trademark protection by registration if their countries are deemed friendly to ROC. Under current practice of National Bureau of Standards, no country is prohibited from obtaining protection of trademarks in ROC. This period of exclusive use may, on application, be renewed indefinitely but only for ten years at one time. Applicants for registration must reside or have resident representatives in ROC In case of conflict, first applicant in ROC and not first user is entitled to registration. If two or more such applications are filed on same date and there is no way of ascertaining who is first applicant, applicants shall come to agreement to let one of them enjoy exclusive use. If no agreement can be reached, it shall be determined by lot drawing.

Exclusive right of use of trademark may be cancelled at any time upon application by its owner. In any of following cases occurring after registration of trademark, National Bureau of Standards shall, on its own initiative or upon application by interested party cancel registration: (1) If registered trademark has been used with unauthorized alteration or addition whereby mark is made similar to registered trademark of another person used on same goods or on goods in same class; (2) if trademark has not been put into use, without good cause, for two years after registration, or has been continuously suspended from use for two years; (provisions of this item shall not apply to cases, in which, defensive or

associated trademarks are registered where one of them is still in use); (3) if no application for recordal of assignment has been filed within one year following assignment of trademark rights; (4) if trademark owner authorizes use of his trademark by another person in way contrary to provisions of Art. 26 of Trademark Law or knowingly acquiesces in violation by another person of conditions for licensed, use of mark and has taken no rectifying action.

Under prevailing Trademark Law, one and same person may apply for registration, as associated trademarks, of similar marks for designated use on same goods or on goods in same class; he may also apply for registration, as defensive trademarks, of same mark for designated use on goods which are not in same class but which are of same or similar nature. Service marks are now registrable in ROC Penalty is provided in Trademark Law against malicious use of other person's trademark as part of his own tradename. In addition to criminal liability, infringers are liable to pay for damages. Under Art. 64, trademark owner may claim against infringer any of following damages: (1) Actual injury sustained and actual loss of profit; (2) profit gained by infringer as result of infringement; or (3) amount equivalent to 500 to 1,500 times unit retail price of seized commodities constituting trademark infringement, provided that if commodities under seizure exceed 1,500 pieces, amount of compensation for damages shall be total selling price. Art. 61 provides injunction remedy.

Registered trademarks may be transferred to another, but such transfer must be registered with National Bureau of Standards within one year from effective date of transfer agreement to be effective against third persons.

Arts. 62, 62-1, 62-2, and 63 of Trademark Law and Arts. 253, 254 and 255 of Criminal Code provide for punishment by fine and/or imprisonment for: counterfeiting or imitating registered trademark or tradename with intent to defraud; importing, selling or exposing for sale any article known to bear counterfeit or imitative trademark or tradename; using false marking or other expression concerning quality or country of origin of goods; or knowingly importing, selling or exposing for sale any goods bearing false marks as to quality or country of origin. Under Art. 62-3 of Trademark Law, goods which are manufactured, sold, displayed, exported or imported in violation of any of provisions specified in Arts. 62, 62-1 and 62-2 of Trademark Law are subject to confiscation, regardless of whether they belong to offender or not.

Treaty of Friendship, Commerce and Navigation between US and ROC provides for reciprocal trademark privileges. According to FCN Treaty, nationals, corporations and associations of either country shall be accorded within territory of other country effective protection in exclusive use of trademarks and tradenames upon compliance with applicable laws and regulations, if any, respecting registration and other formalities which are or may hereafter be enforced by duly constituted authorities. Nevertheless, foreign juristic persons or entities. not limited to those recognized by government of ROC, may also file criminal complaint, initiate private prosecution or institute civil suit for trademark infringement under Art. 66-1 of Trademark Law.

Trademark matters are handled by National Bureau of Standards. All approved trademark applications and other trademark matters are published in Trademark Gazette of National Bureau of Standards.

Financial Institutions

Taiwan's financial institutions are relatively diversified and fairly modern and sophisticated, offering many of the services and opportunities found in Western economies. Various kinds of banks, cooperatives, investment and trust companies, insurers, leasing companies, and venture capital firms are available in numbers adequate to handle most of the funding and operational needs that domestic and foreign businesses might have. Offshore banks are also available to finance investment by foreign entities, although the government prefers that necessary financing be obtained through domestically licensed institutions.

Money markets, securities markets, and to a lesser extent foreign exchange markets are developing rapidly, although it is still difficult for foreigners to manage or invest funds locally. Nevertheless, foreign operators should be able to work within the framework of the existing system to fill virtually all their needs, and the system is improving steadily as the Taiwanese gain experience with the operations, standards, and requirements of world financial markets today.

At present, Taiwan's financial ambiance is still somewhat rudimentary and restrictive by international standards. The economy operates on a cash basis to an extent that is astonishing for a relatively developed country in the late 20th century. Because conditions are onerous and funding often difficult to secure, a great deal of financing is carried out through informal arrangements. The general ethos is one of short- to medium-term horizons, and there is little concern for long-term implications. Many of the formal institutions that in other parts of the world are devoted to longer term financing, such as the stock market and insurance companies, are viewed primarily as short-term speculative vehicles in Taiwan.

The financial sector is still dominated by the government, which owns most of the major banks and maintains tight controls over policy and operational issues. Taiwan currently lacks the expertise and infrastructure to provide state-of-the-art financial services. Even more important, to date Taiwan has lacked the will to open up its financial businesses to market forces and outside participation.

Barriers to outward investment by Taiwanese were only recently lifted, and capital transfers are still subject to limitations. Outsiders are still prohibited from free and direct participation in many onshore financial activities, including open trading in securities markets. Because of this nontransparent, exclusionary, and control-oriented heritage, official announcements of massive reform ring hollow for most observers.

Nevertheless, Taiwan has made significant progress in upgrading and modernizing its financial environment. Further exposure to contemporary standards, demands for openness from trading partners, and calls for better service and increased opportunities from both foreign and domestic businesses should ensure that improvements continue.

Taiwan is currently engaged in major reform efforts in banking and related industries. The goal of these reforms is to increase the efficiency of capital allocation and move toward the free flow of funds domestically and internationally. The ROC government hopes to take advantage of the uncertainty over Hong Kong's future to make a bid for some of the colony's financing business in the era after 1997 and transform Taipei into a regional financial center on a par with Singapore, Hong Kong, and Tokyo.

Recent legislation has eased some restrictions on foreign bank branching, deregulated interest rates, and cracked down on underground investment companies. In accord with this and other government initiatives designed to push industry development, banks spent nearly US$400 million on computerization, systems, and security upgrades in 1991. Expenditures on banking systems and infrastructure are expected to increase at an annual rate of 8 to 10 percent over the next several years. The government has also undertaken a privatization program, albeit with limited success to date.

THE BANKING SYSTEM

Taiwan has a central bank and more than 760 domestic banking institutions. Some 38 foreign banks operate authorized branches in Taiwan, and 21 others maintain representative offices. In addition, there are 74 registered credit cooperatives, 285 agricultural credit unions, and 27 fishery credit unions. (Refer to "Important Addresses" chapter for a list of major domestic and foreign banking institutions operating in Taiwan.)

Central Bank of China

The Central Bank of China (CBC) performs most of the functions associated with central banks in other countries. The CBC issues currency; manages foreign exchange and international reserves; handles treasury finances and issues public debt; sets deposit reserve rates and conducts open market operations to manage the money supply; and maintains the discount window, serving as the lender of last resort. The CBC regulates the foreign exchange operations of banks and handles applications by foreign banks wishing to open offshore banking facilities in Taiwan. It does not directly regulate domestic commercial banks, which are subject to Ministry of Finance authority. The CBC controls about 19 percent of financial system assets.

The CBC sets the discount rate, but it does not officially set other interest rates. Nevertheless, it exerts considerable influence in this area. It also has authority to determine foreign exchange rates within a range established by market activity. Individual banks are allowed to set their own interest rates, which stood at slightly over 8 percent for the prime rate in mid-1993.

Domestic Commercial Banks

Commercial banks dominate Taiwan's financial system. The country has 41 domestic commercial banks—also known as national banks, not because of charter requirements but because they operate nationwide—with 1,260 branches offering services that include taking deposits; making personal, mortgage, and business loans; handling trade financing and providing guarantees; and discounting bills and notes. Domestic commercial banks are allowed to lend to foreign business entities operating in Taiwan. Domestic commercial banks control about 49 percent of financial system assets.

There are no separate savings banks in Taiwan, but most commercial banks have separate savings and trust operations. Most are also involved in the securities market in some way, ranging from trading securities to underwriting equity and debt issues. Although securities operations are usually conducted through nominally separate subsidiaries, Taiwanese law does not recognize the split between commercial and investment banking to the degree maintained by many other countries.

Of these commercial banks, 13 are owned and run, totally or in part, by national, provincial, or municipal government entities. These institutions are the main focus of current reform efforts. In style, they are closer to hidebound, entrenched, bureaucratic government agencies than they are to modern, professional financial institutions elsewhere.

Taiwanese banking is something of an anomaly in that the country still has basically a cash economy. Checking accounts and credit cards are still considered novelties, and customers generally must establish a relationship with a bank for six months before they are allowed to open a checking account. As a result, the traditional payments system function of commercial banks is somewhat attenuated in the ROC. The government relaxed regulations on checking accounts in 1992 to encourage their use. Checking accounts represented only 2.7 percent of total deposits in 1993.

Although commercial banks account for 78.4 percent of the formal lending in Taiwan's economy—informal lending being the norm for a great deal of business—lending practices are somewhat bizarre by modern international banking standards. Most commercial banks require borrowers to put up collateral to obtain a loan, and even for large, established entities this collateral usually must equal 100 percent of the loan amount. This requirement stems from the fact that lending officers have traditionally been held personally responsible for the loans that they make. Such standards of doing business have impeded the development of lending and other banking services, especially to small firms and start-up companies. Because of these obstacles, domestic private sector companies have often relied on supplier credits and other informal financing arrangements to meet their needs for working capital, while foreign businesses have often used parent company credits. Foreign businesses selling in Taiwan often find that they are expected to finance the purchases of thinly capitalized buyers who, due to the way the system has traditionally operated, have little access to working capital loans.

New Banks on the Scene

Authorities approved applications for 15 new domestic banks in 1991—the first such approvals in decades and a development that increased the number of commercial banks in Taiwan by nearly 40 percent and more than doubled the number of private banks. This opening up of the banking system to new blood has already resulted in some changes. Competition by these newcomers for market share has forced banks nationwide to drop their interest rates on loans and raise the interest paid on deposits, and customer service has generally improved. New banks are also offering innovative financial products and at least talking about easing loan requirements to serve the small business market.

Given this new, more competitive climate, many banks are moving to broaden their scope of business. Such financial products as gold deposit services, two-generation mortgages, and instant or preapproved line of credit loans are being introduced. The traditionally sleepy trust and long-term savings business is also receiving renewed attention at many institutions. In addition, a number of domestic banks are turning to automation in attempts to improve efficiency and customer service.

The upstarts have a long way to go to overtake the established outlets. Existing banks have large nationwide branch networks, while newly established banks can set up a maximum of five branches during their first year of operations and no more than three additional branches in subsequent years. The newcomers also cannot apply to deal in foreign exchange until they can demonstrate that they have participated in foreign exchange transactions totaling NT$400 million in the preceding year in conjunction with existing licensed foreign exchange banks. Existing banks have generally denied the new players the opportunity of participating in deals in this market, and CBC ceilings on foreign exchange transactions have further reduced the opportunities for developing new business, especially among foreign businesses that require this service.

The new entrants in the Taiwan banking industry have been backed by domestic business groups. The new banks are focusing on the domestic retail market, but they expect ultimately to expand into commercial operations and the international arena. A number have already entered into cooperative ventures with overseas banks. There is concern that more liberal lending policies will result in more bad loans (the old stodgy banks hardly ever had a loss on a loan); that the reduced spreads will mean marginal profitability; and that the initial investment in equipment, facilities, and personnel will mean long payback periods for investors, whose commitment could flag if expected returns fail to materialize.

Privatization

There are plans to sell stakes in government-controlled banks, but actual efforts and results to date have been uninspiring. Offerings to sell small portions—less than 5 percent of equity—of three provincial government-controlled banks in April 1990 failed when less than 1 percent of the shares offered were sold. The situation is gradually improving, and some 15 percent of the International Commercial Bank of China was successfully privatized in January 1992, although the price dropped after the sale,

which bodes ill for future sales. Additional bank offerings are planned, although terms are still under discussion. To date, foreign investors have been barred from participating in these sales, although at the end of 1993, authorities announced their intention to allow foreigners to buy into banks and other financial institutions.

So far the stakes offered have been negligible, and the prices asked have been unrealistically high. Moreover, officials of the banks to be privatized have been reluctant participants in the exercise. There are doubts that Taiwan's internal capital market can successfully absorb the massive privatizations proposed, of which the bank segment is only a small part.

Internationalization

Taiwan's financial institutions have opened a number of overseas branches to assist the surge in outward investment by Taiwan businesses. At the end of 1992 14 domestic banks operated 28 branches, 24 representative offices, and 10 subsidiaries overseas. Currently the most popular areas for such operations are the United States, Southeast Asia, and Europe.

In the United States, branches of Taiwanese banks are designed primarily to serve Taiwanese high-tech companies and trading concerns that have set up operations there in recent years. Interest in Europe stems from attempts to support ROC firms that are seeking to gain a foothold in European Community markets. Branches in Southeast Asia exist to serve the financing requirements of Taiwan-invested manufacturing facilities that have been set up in that region to take advantage of lower labor and production costs.

Taiwanese banks were recently given the right to deal with Chinese banks and third-party banks dealing with China, provided that the transactions occur outside Taiwan.

Some of the island's private sector banks are reportedly looking into the acquisition of banks overseas. The main focus of their attention is currently the western United States, where these Taiwanese banks are seeking to establish footholds. Other countries that are of interest include Singapore and the Philippines, both of which are centers of financial activity conducted by large ethnic Chinese populations.

Foreign Banks

Foreign commercial banks have operated as minor players in Taiwan for more than 30 years. Some 38 foreign banks from 14 countries operate 53 branch offices, most of which are located in Taipei. There are also representative offices of banks from some 20 countries. Although they make only about 3.5

percent of loans in Taiwan, a marginal share figure and hold only about 2 percent of all financial system assets, foreign banks are now playing an increasingly important role in Taiwan's banking system. Their technical expertise and generally more aggressive approach to the Taiwanese market are serving to stir the entire industry to become somewhat more dynamic and efficient. Foreign branches are authorized to provide loans to foreign entities operating in Taiwan.

Foreign banks can engage in trade financing, including accepting commercial drafts and issuing letters of credit; foreign exchange dealings, including payments, remittances, and foreign currency deposit accounts; individual and corporate short- and medium-term lending; and trust account operations. They can make minority investments in domestic leasing and investment and trust companies.

Although they are nominally treated the same as domestic commercial banks, foreign banks can only operate in Taiwan as branches of their parent entities, not as separate companies in their own right, which prevents them from offering a full range of services. There are stringent limits for such banks on maximum allowed foreign exchange liability, processing of credit card transactions, and many commercial dealings. In addition, there are strict limits on amounts they can accept in local currency deposits—limits that are not imposed on domestic banks—which hampers their operations in most domestic commercial and retail markets. Many foreign banks are working to develop consumer loan and credit card services to enlarge their generally limited presence in domestic retail markets.

A prohibition against the operation by foreign banks of subsidiaries precludes them from establishing a presence in the Taiwanese securities markets. Prior to 1990, foreign banks were allowed to have only two branch offices, one in Taipei and one in Kaohsiung. Since then, they have technically been allowed to open up to three branches a year, as are domestic banks. However, as of early 1993, only one foreign bank had been approved to operate more than two branches in Taiwan. At the end of 1993 authorities proposed to relax all limits on the number and location of new foreign bank branches.

The Credit Card Industry

The origins of the charge card business in Taiwan date back to the 1960s, when tourism first began to flourish on the island. At that time, a number of foreign credit and charge cards were introduced. However, it was not until the mid-1970s that domestic financial firms initiated their own system, which ultimately took the form of a centralized facility run as a national monopoly and entrusted with the responsibility for the issuance and processing of debit cards.

In the late 1980s, this debit card facility was converted into the National Credit Card Center, and existing debit cards were superseded by new credit cards. At the same time, the center began to issue various international credit cards, a step that has helped to boost acceptance and bring practices in Taiwan more into line with those abroad.

In Taiwan's predominately cash economy, the credit card has had some difficulty in gaining a foothold for domestic use. Merchants have complained about the fees, payment delays, and processing difficulties. If the idea is to take off, issuers will have to sign up enough outlets to be able to offer ready acceptance of their cards. However, card use among Taiwanese who have taken out credit cards has been remarkable, with usage, per usage amount, and total amounts charged rising rapidly and already outpacing those in other Asian countries where card use is far better established. As of mid-1993 there were 2.7 million credit cards outstanding in Taiwan, and about 28,000 outlets accepted various cards.

Taiwanese institutions, including the post office savings system, are also experimenting with so-called smart cards that allow preauthorization, account debiting, and several other high-tech features.

Further revisions in existing credit card regulations are currently under consideration, with a preliminary decision having already been reached to decentralize the current system. This move would make it possible for banks either to issue their own cards or to take part in an existing credit card group. Other anticipated changes include permission for credit card issuers to offer such services as emergency cash advances and travel accident insurance through their cards. Cash advances could be offered through the system of nearly 6,000 automated teller machines (ATMs) already operating within the financial system.

A foreign bank recently announced plans to set up an Asian regional credit card processing center in Taipei. This center would be responsible for issuing and servicing the institution's credit cards throughout Northern Asia, and it could raise Taiwan's standing in this sector of the international financial arena.

Since January 1989 foreign charge and credit cards denominated in New Taiwan dollars can be issued on Taiwan, but issuing companies are required to have their card activity processed by the National Credit Card Center, which is relatively inefficient and expensive to use. This requirement raises the costs and reduces the competitiveness of foreign card issuers, especially those that possess in-house processing capabilities.

Offshore Banking

The ROC created the legal framework for offshore banking in 1983. Such entities operate in Taiwan, but they are treated as if they were foreign entities operating elsewhere, and thus they are exempt from certain regulations that apply to domestic entities. The main advantages available to such offshore banking units (OBUs) are relief from the need to maintain deposit and loan loss reserves and specific financial ratios as well as exemption from stamp and business income taxes.

Offshore banking is designed to make Taiwan attractive as an international free banking zone separate from the heavily regulated domestic market. OBUs can extend largely unregulated foreign currency loans to resident entities and individuals as well as offer unregulated loans to foreign borrowers through international funding sources. These institutions can make loans to foreign businesses operating in Taiwan, although the government prefers that domestic projects be funded from onshore sources.

To date, 35 domestic and international banks have established OBUs in the ROC. The Ministry of Finance gives preferential consideration to foreign banks wishing to open branches in Taiwan if they also agree to establish OBUs. The CBC limits its consideration to applications from the world's top 500 banks.

So far, the separation of offshore from domestic operations and services has been so effective that it has limited the growth of such operations. Accordingly, the government is considering regulations that would enhance the scope of OBU business activities. Under these proposed regulations, ROC residents would be allowed to open tax-exempt savings accounts, and OBUs would be allowed to expand their activities in areas of export remittances, deposit taking, foreign currency deposits, and financing. This regulatory easing could enable OBUs to contribute more to the internationalization of ROC banking industry as well as to provide additional sources of financing and investment opportunities. However, OBUs are likely to remain of small overall importance unless and until foreign exchange restrictions are lifted and the government revises its strongly stated preference that entities do their borrowing for domestic projects from domestic banks.

OTHER FINANCIAL INSTITUTIONS

Specialized Banks

Other domestic financial institutions include the so-called specialized banks, each of which has been established to serve a specific functional area and clientele. The Chiao Tung Bank, the Export-Import Bank, and the Farmers Bank of China are examples of three such institutions. Mainstream commercial banks can also lend in areas served by the specialized banks, and some have developed a reputation for expertise in certain areas.

The Chiao Tung Bank, also known as the Bank of Communications, assists with long-term financing for communications projects. The Export-Import Bank offers trade financing to domestic importers and exporters, although it also has lent funds to US banks on concessionary terms for relending to foreign exporters to Taiwan. This arrangement was part of a special one-time deal as part of an effort to reduce the Taiwan-US trade imbalance. The Farmers Bank and other institutions, such as the Land Bank and the Cooperative Bank, focus on agricultural development. The China Development Corporation focuses on equity lending and loan guarantees to private Taiwanese firms in high-technology fields.

There are also eight specialized regional banks with 290 branches that are designed to provide financing for small and medium-sized domestic businesses. These institutions represent local mutual loan companies that converted to specialized bank status in the late 1970s. They are sometimes referred to as regional banks—as opposed to the large national commercial banks. Most have savings and trust operations, which allows them to operate effectively as full-service banks. Although they can raise funds by selling bonds, most remain quasi-cooperative in nature, getting their operating funds from deposits. Only one of these banks is government owned. Together they have about a 10 percent share of the official lending market.

These specialized institutions usually will not be in a position to consider funding foreign entities. However, the domestic firms with which foreign businesses deal are often able to obtain financing from these specialized bank sources.

Cooperative Financial Institutions

These member-owned regional and industry-based institutions have a 18.1 percent market share of formal lending in Taiwan. Broken down officially into credit cooperatives of which there are 74, operating 448 branches, and farmers' and fishermen's cooperative associations, of which there are 312, operating 810 branches, these cooperatives take deposits from members and lend them out. Together, these cooperative institutions control about 13.7 percent of assets in the financial system. By definition, they are not sources of funds for foreign businesses, but the substantial role that they play in Taiwan's financial system needs to be noted. The government has recognized their importance by ruling that the larger cooperatives can convert to specialized regional banks.

Investment and Trust Companies

Investment and trust companies (ITCs) play a significant role in the Taiwanese financial system. These entities are designed to make medium- and long-term loans, manage trust deposits and retirement funds, and offer various kinds of custodial and trustee services as investment companies. However, they have come to operate as de facto commercial banks in many respects, and trust accounts are often used functionally as deposit transaction accounts. There are seven ITCs with 59 branches. Foreign investors own significant interests in four of these entities, but ITCs generally are not a source of financing for foreign entities operating in Taiwan. ITCs control about 2.5 percent of the assets in the financial system.

ITCs are permitted to invest for their own account and for customer accounts in the securities markets; underwrite, manage, and guarantee securities; act as custodial agents; operate mutual funds; administer estates; and serve as trustees in bankruptcy proceedings. Some even engage in credit card operations, commercial and personal lending, and mortgage lending and serve as guarantors in domestic and foreign transactions, most of which activities are forbidden to mainstream commercial banks. ITCs also have been known to make equity investments and develop land and real estate. The main areas in which the ITCs have been unable to operate are foreign exchange transactions and overseas branching operations, both of which are reserved for commercial banks.

The Ministry of Finance and the Ministry of Justice are both drafting new trust laws that would define and limit the scope of operations of the island's free-wheeling ITCs. The proposed law includes provisions to strengthen management and clarify the legal status of various activities currently undertaken by these entities without specific official authority. It also defines the rights and obligations of various concerned parties, the volume of capital that can be held by trust companies, the amount of funds that can be guaranteed, the kinds of the property in which trusts may invest, and the terms of trust contracts. The ITCs are trying to play the regulators against each other in an effort to retain their autonomy as long as possible and gain the best deal when regulation does come.

As something of a stopgap measure, the Ministry of Finance has offered to allow ITCs to convert to commercial banks. To comply, most ITCs would have to give up much of their current privileged autonomy, and most are expected to resist conversion. As of 1993 only one ITC had converted to commercial bank status.

Postal Savings System

Taiwan has a well-developed postal savings system. This system enables account holders to make deposits or withdrawals at virtually any post office in the country. It has traditionally enjoyed wide popularity because of its simplicity, convenience, and government backing. It offers competitive interest rates that are usually slightly higher than those offered by banks. The 1,240 branch postal savings system with its 348 special savings agency offices is the main competitor of commercial banks for basic domestic retail deposit, savings, and payments business. It does not lend, depositing most of its funds with the CBC for placement. The postal savings system controls about 9.5 percent of assets in the financial system.

The Directorate General of Posts has developed plans to issue debit cards that postal savings depositors can use to make purchases in retail outlets around the island. This service should enhance the convenience and popularity of the postal savings system and become an increasingly accepted means of handling transactions in coming years.

Insurance Companies

The 196 insurance companies in Taiwan are major intermediaries handling a high volumeoof funds but somewhat ineffective players in the financial markets because of strict limitations on how their funds can be used and invested. They are also restricted in the scope of their operations, because insurance laws stipulate that life and property and casualty business lines cannot be operated within a single company. Insurance firms control about 4 percent of assets in the financial system. Such firms are not currently a source of funding for foreign entities operating in Taiwan.

Most insurance companies are heavily invested in the domestic real estate market, and in an attempt to reduce their risks a draft revision of the insurance law includes a provision lowering the amount of real estate that insurance companies may own. At the same time, the companies themselves are beginning to make investments overseas in an effort to diversify their financial risks and enhance their investment returns.

Recent modifications of regulations have enabled several foreign insurers to begin operating in Taiwan. The foreign firms authorized to do business are all large companies from the United States, primarily because the US government has been so insistent in pressuring Taiwan to make concessions because of the trade imbalance between the two nations.

The presence of these foreign firms should encourage long-term change and facilitate improvements in the training of sales and service personnel. In turn, such advances should further enhance public awareness of the role of insurance in modern economies. Traditionally, the extended family has been responsible for the functions served by insurers, and in general Asians have not responded strongly to the idea of insurance either as an indemnity or an investment product. Products offered to date have been fairly basic. However, sales have increased substantially from a low base in recent years.

Nevertheless, the Taiwanese insurance market is one of the most promising in Asia. There is still considerable room for expansion in terms of the somewhat narrow range of products available and the limited market penetration achieved to date. Most observers believe that, once the still heavily restricted market is fully opened, the number of both foreign and domestic companies will increase and that the industry will become a more significant factor in the island's financial system.

Leasing Companies

There are 16 registered leasing companies in Taiwan, although half are inactive. Two of the largest and most active have substantial foreign ownership positions. Most active leasing firms specialize in such areas as machinery, motor vehicles, computers, tools, transportation equipment, communications equipment, and various other kinds of equipment and instruments. Their customers tend to be growing small- and medium-sized domestic companies that find it difficult to obtain access to adequate bank financing at acceptable rates and purchase assets outright.

Venture Capital Companies

Venture capital companies are relatively new on the Taiwanese financial scene. Under existing regulations, they can make direct investments only in high-technology and certain other defined strategic enterprises. They are allowed to offer a wide range of ancillary services in the areas of business planning and consulting in addition to their traditional financing role. These companies assist with mergers and acquisitions; arrange stock market listings; engage in financial consulting; provide advice related to production technologies, marketing, and management; and handle personnel recruitment assignments. At present, they are prohibited from making loans or accepting deposits. They generally fund domestic projects, however some foreign-Taiwanese high-tech joint ventures could be eligible for funding through such firms.

There were 24 venture capital companies operating in Taiwan at the end of 1991. These firms boasted a total capitalization of nearly NT$16 billion (about US$60 million) in mid-1991, and their cumulative investments in some 294 domestic and foreign entities were estimated at NT$6.35 billion (about US$235 million). More than 80 percent of the total

funds placed by these firms have gone into electronics-based industries. About 43 percent of this investment was in the information industry, while the electronics industry accounted for 27 percent.

Venture capital firms obtain capital from and include both domestic and foreign investors. They are playing an increasingly important role in providing funds and expertise to upgrade industry and globalize Taiwan's still rather insular economy. In addition to providing funding for smaller firms that have difficulty obtaining financing from more conventional lenders, venture capital firms also offer a way for companies to break into industries that the government has designated as essential for the nation's economic development. Access to funding, plus the relatively sophisticated services available from many of Taiwan's venture capital firms, has also enabled companies of all sizes to establish marketing and production facilities abroad.

Most venture capital firms on the island are enjoying substantial growth, albeit from a relatively low base, owing to their success in identifying promising new projects in a rapidly changing economic environment. They are also profiting from the growing tendency of investors to look beyond the island's highly volatile stock market for investment opportunities. Some companies are beginning to tap overseas markets, and there are plans to establish a 100 percent Taiwan-funded venture capital offshore facility under the auspicesof a large US bank.

Financial Management Firms

Financial management consulting firms are beginning to make significant contributions to the growth and development of local enterprises. Many of these firms represent joint ventures with or subsidiaries of international consulting groups. They provide advice on outward investment, listing companies on the stock exchange, mergers and acquisitions, project financing, financial restructuring, privatization of public sector companies, underwriting of securities, and private placements—all areas that are relatively new to financial operations in Taiwan.

Underground Lenders

Mounting evidence suggests that a significant portion of domestic financing in Taiwan, especially lending, comes from unlicensed individuals and loan agencies. Some reports claim that more than half of all loans on the island are made by unregulated secret societies in the informal lending market. As a result, these transactions are missing from official economic statistics, biasing the analysis of Taiwan's economic situation.

These often highly-organized informal and illicit operations grew up over decades to fill needs unserved by the heavily regulated and largely unaccommodating formal sector. During the 1980s, the size, organizational level, and influence of the informal market became a political scandal, and officials were accused of complicity and taking payoffs to allow it to operate.

In 1989 the authorities imposed mechanisms designed to prevent these entities from taking new deposits, and in 1990 they began moving against some of the most blatant operators. The most notable example of these illegal but highly organized operations was the Hung Yuan firm. This operation had deposits of more than NT$100 billion (about US$3.7 billion), which would have made it the ninth largest bank in Taiwan, and hard asset holdings—including a major interest in one of Taipei's biggest department stores—of NT$10 billion (about US$3.7 billion) when it was liquidated. Despite these crackdowns, the underground financial economy persists because the needs that it fills have yet to be served through legitimate channels.

Foreign businesses would be well advised to avoid any dealings with such operations. They should also be aware that many of the local firms with which they deal may have obligations to underground financiers that their financial statements do not reflect. Such obligations could leave a foreign firm in the lurch if the local firm could not meet both its official and unofficial obligations.

FINANCIAL MARKETS IN TAIWAN

Money Markets

Taiwan's first money market was organized in 1976. The Ministry of Finance designated the Bank of Taiwan, the International Commercial Bank of China, and the Chiao Tung Bank to organize three corporations to act as money market dealers and brokers. The first of these, Chung Hsing Bills Finance Corporation, was formed in 1976. The other two, International Bills Finance Corporation and Chung Hwa Bills Finance Corporation, entered the market somewhat later. The shareholders of these three corporations consist of banks and various large public and private enterprises.

The bills finance companies underwrite commercial paper for private sector businesses, act as brokers and intermediaries for government securities and interbank loans, and buy and sell government securities, commercial paper, bankers' acceptances, and bank-issued negotiable certificates of deposit.

Despite the relatively small scale of operations and a shortage of trading instruments, Taiwan's money market has become increasingly active in recent years. By the end of 1992 there were about US$37 billion in money market instruments outstanding. Of these, negotiable CDs accounted for 49.4 percent, commercial paper for 36.2 percent, treasury bills for 8.5 percent, and bankers' acceptances for 5.9 percent. Total transaction value doubled between 1987 and 1992 to more than US$549 billion.

The Fair Trade Commission has been investigating the bills finance companies for collusion and price-fixing. These companies deny the charges and have resisted attempts to loosen their oligopolistic grip on the business. Nevertheless, in 1992, the Ministry of Finance opened up the money markets by allowing banks to act as dealers. By the end of 1992 35 banks had been authorized to serve as brokers, breaking the monopoly of the bills finance companies.

To reach the threshold at which it can function as a going concern, the money market really needs a greater volume of instruments, more than additional broker-dealers, although more participants should increase competition and lower costs and increase efficiency. The government has so far delayed action on schemes to broaden the authority of firms to issue commercial paper, and it has balked at proposals to allow firms to borrow abroad and remit the funds to cover local paper issues.

Private sector enterprises have turned to the money market as a way of obtaining short-term funds, and investors are beginning to see it as a more stable alternative to the volatile stock market. Both trading value in the money market and commercial paper issuance have been increasing rapidly. The opening of new private banks on the island should give the bills finance companies additional paper to trade in, as will the enormous volume of government instruments expected to be issued in connection with the six-year national development plan.

Taiwan's money market is still in its infancy. Foreign firms cannot issue negotiable paper that can be traded in this market and they are prohibited from speculating in it. To date, it has provided financing for relatively few domestic firms. It should become a more efficient and broader market as Taiwan's financial markets in general become more open and sophisticated, but that lies in the future.

The Securities Industry

At the end of 1992 listed Taiwanese securities outstanding were valued at NT$3.252 trillion (about U$127.75 billion). Listed stocks accounted for 78.3 percent, government bonds for 21.7 percent, bank debentures for 3.5 percent, and corporate bonds for 2.5 percent.

The Stock Exchange The Taiwan Stock Exchange or TAIEX was established in 1961. This exchange is subject to regulation by the Securities and Exchange Commission of the Ministry of Finance, as are brokers, dealers, underwriters, and other related entities. The quasi private Fuh Hwa Securities Finance Company was set up under government rules in 1980 to provide credit, make markets, and provide liquidity for the securities markets. Foreign companies are currently prohibited from listing their securities on the TAIEX, although domestic companies with foreign shareholders can be listed. Domestic firms prefer debt financing—most have a debt-to-equity ratio substantially greater than 100 percent—so the value of an established stock exchange has yet to be realized in Taiwan as a source of capital.

In general, the market has tended to be an extremely volatile and speculative one, with average daily turnover amounting to US$1 billion. In 1990, the TAIEX traded a total of 232.3 billion shares. In the same year, the New York Stock Exchange, which is about 35 times as large in terms of dollar value and has five-and-a-half times as many listed issues, traded a total of 39.6 billion shares. The TAIEX reached an all-time index high of 12,495.34 in February 1990, falling 80 percent to 2,560.47 by October 1990. The exchange's market capitalization rose to a peak of US$170 billion in 1990, and fell by 68 percent to US$63 billion in mid-1993. Between 1985 and mid-1993, the TAIEX delivered total returns of 425 percent in US dollar terms, 255 percent in New Taiwan dollar terms. During the same period, the US stock market rose 198 percent. The TAIEX closed 1993 at 6,070.56, the highest since June 1991, but still 51.4 percent below its 1990 high.

The TAIEX experienced a steep, speculative runup in share prices in 1987 and 1988. During that period, the main market index rose 393 percent, an increase that was followed by an additional 90 percent gain in the first nine months of 1989. This rise would have been even greater had there not been a daily trading range limit of 3 percent. Such a limit still exist, but it has been expanded to 7 percent. The upward trend was fueled largely by excess liquidity, speculation, and a scarcity of alternative investment vehicles. Margin lending by underground financiers also played a significant role.

In early 1990 the market reached an all-time high. Following the establishment of this new benchmark, the TAIEX was caught in a steep downward spiral that saw the market plunge 80 percent in a little over six months. The market has yet to recover fully from this crash.

Unlike the situation in many developed markets worldwide, where institutional investors call the shots, the TAIEX is largely the domain of small investors, who maintain millions of trading accounts and view it more as a casino than as a capital market institution. Although institutional securities holdings are minimal, direct holdings by the government and its agencies are substantial, leading to the potential for market management.

The severe downturn brought financial ruin to many investors during the second half of 1990 and much of 1991. However, the long-term consequences appear to have been positive. Among other things, speculative fever has been dampened, and the public has begun to develop a more sophisticated attitude toward investment. In addition, many stocks are now at levels that more accurately reflect their true value, a development that should serve to bring more long-term investors into the market.

In response to complaints of rampant insider trading and roulette-style investment by TAIEX investors, the SEC has recently instituted a crackdown on some of the more flagrant abuses. In September 1992 authorities arrested a well-known speculator on charges of insider trading, signaling that TAIEX oversight will be intensified. This may help to attract investors who have avoided TAIEX in the past. Despite crackdowns on informal financing, such underground operators continue to offer margin credit as well as other supra-legal informal products, such as options, futures, and trading in unregistered securities.

The dramatic changes that have taken place since the early 1990 have helped to bring about a streamlining of the entire sector. With daily trading volume remaining well below the highs recorded in 1990 and comparatively low-risk investments such as bonds attracting greater interest, the number of securities houses fell from a high of 374 in July 1990 to 351 in October 1991. In the course of this decline, sixteen firms went out of business, and seven merged with others to create stronger successor firms. Further consolidation is expected, a trend that many industry observers believe will serve to enhance efficiency and sharpen the competitiveness of the remaining firms.

Securities Categories There are 271 firms and nearly 300 separate securities listed on the TAIEX. Equities listed on the TAIEX are divided into three categories based on corporate capitalization. Category A consists of the shares of companies with capital of at least NT$400 million—about US$15 million—and income that is at least 10 percent of capital, or a minimum of NT$80 million—about US$3 million—and at least 5 percent of capital. The ratio of net worth to assets must be at least one to three, although there is a wide range of exceptions to this requirement. There must be at least 2,000 shareholders, and at least 1,000 of these shareholders must hold blocks of at least 1,000 shares. Large shareholders must control at least 10 million, or 20 percent of the shares outstanding, whichever is greater.

Category B includes shares of companies with capital of at least NT$200 million—about US$7.5 million—and earnings equal to at least 5 percent of capital over a period of time. There is no requirement for net worth to assets ratios. However, there must be a minimum of 1,000 shareholders, of whom at least 500 must hold blocks of at least 1,000 shares. Large shareholders must control a minimum of 10 million shares or 20 percent of all shares.

Category C covers approved new high-technology companies. Such companies must have a total capitalization of at least NT$200 million—about US$7.5 million—and have products that are ready to go on the market, not just in the development stage. Underwriters must agree to hold at least 50 percent of the issue for their own accounts, and directors, officers, supervisors, and other major shareholders accounting for 10 percent of the shares must agree not to dispose of their holdings within two years of issue.

There are also certain companies whose shares are designated as full delivery shares. This designation means that the companies in question are in financial difficulty and that advance payment and physical delivery of certificates are required in order to complete a trade.

Ongoing Changes The entire Taiwanese securities market is currently in transition owing to government policy initiatives. From its inception, only domestic entities and individuals were eligible to buy or sell securities on the TAIEX. In 1982, foreign investors were allowed to subscribe to beneficiary certificates giving them rights to the underlying assets of listed Taiwanese companies.

To take advantage of the 1982 policy change, four foreign companies entered into joint ventures with Taiwanese firms to provide management services for securities trust funds, the equivalent of open-end mutual funds. At present, these entities are permitted to offer mutual funds that allow nonresidents to invest indirectly in the Taiwan stock market. These funds are registered in Taiwan and regulated by the ROC Securities and Exchange Commission, and they trade on stock exchanges in the United States and the United Kingdom.

In addition to the funds that have been set up specifically to facilitate overseas investment in Taiwan equities, there are also various open-end and closed-end funds on the island that are available to foreign investors subject to certain limitations. The open-end funds may be purchased by foreigners using local currency. Redemptions must also be made in local currency, and ordinary income is subject to taxation. The closed-end funds are listed on the TAIEX, but, in contrast to other stocks, they can be bought and sold by foreigners.

The Securities and Exchange Commission has recently begun to allow foreign brokerage firms meeting certain minimum capital requirements and other qualifications to set up branches in Taiwan. These brokers cannot buy and sell directly for overseas clients. They can buy and sell foreign securities on behalf of Taiwanese clients. Their presence is helping to upgrade the level of expertise in the securities industry on the island. This step, together with the marketing of foreign mutual funds by authorized domestic financial institutions, gives ROC investors access to a more extensive range of overseas securities and related products.

As part of its efforts to enter the General Agreement on Tariffs and Trade (GATT), Taiwan announced further easing of restrictions at the end of 1993. It anticipates that foreigners will be allowed to invest in all types of private financial firms, including securities firms.

Direct Foreign Securities Investment The Taiwanese government has taken limited steps to allow direct investment by foreign institutional investors in ROC equities, while stating that it plans to permit direct investment by foreign individual investors in the future. The limitation of foreign participation to institutional investors, such as pension funds, insurance companies, and banks—none of which are major buyers in developing markets—was designed to eliminate short-term hot money traders who, it was thought, would unsettle the TAIEX, an ironic justification in view of the manic nature of Taiwan's domestic market participation.

Foreign brokerages were excluded from direct participation, although they have been operating in a gray area, often using the authorized institutions as fronts in a procedure that Taiwanese regulators have so far officially ignored. The authorities still require approved foreign securities investors with existing foreign exchange quotas to make separate application for foreign exchange each time they want to bring funds in or out, making operations more tentative and cumbersome.

At the end of 1993 Taiwanese authorities opened up stocks to greater foreign ownership. Foreign institutions were to be allowed to own up to 10 percent of shares in public owned firms, up from 5 percent. Total allowable foreign ownership was increased from 10 percent to between 20 and 30 percent, depending on the type of company. This was disappointing to foreign investors, who had been hoping for elimination of limits.

Eventually, foreign participation should help to reduce market volatility and increase the flow of foreign investment capital into the ROC. However, there remain some serious hurdles to foreigners wishing to invest in Taiwan's securities market. Foreign ownership of Taiwanese securities firms may not cumulatively exceed 40 percent, and no individual foreign entity may own more than 10 percent of such a firm, although these ownership caps are slated to be eliminated. In addition, no foreign investing entity can invest more than a total of US$50 million, and aggregate foreign investment in Taiwanese securities cannot exceed US$2.5 billion. Principal and earnings from foreign securities transactions cannot be remitted from Taiwan until six months after the principal was committed.

The Over-the-Counter Securities Market Taiwan has a budding over-the counter (OTC) securities market. The market began in 1982 to trade bonds and government paper. In 1989 it was expanded to give small companies a place to raise equity capital as well as to serve as a secondary market for such issues. At the end of 1991 only nine of the more than 700 companies with unlisted nominally public shares that were potentially eligible had listed on the new market, and trading was only a skimpy NT$813 million—about US$31.5 million.

This lack of response is at least partially due to restrictive qualifications for inclusion. Listing requirements include capital of at least NT$50 million—about US$1.9 million—and an income of at least 2 percent of capital, if the firm is at least two years old, or NT$100 million—about US$3.8 million—but no income requirement if the firm is new and is at least partly funded through a public offering. There must be at least 100 large shareholders holding blocks of at least 1,000 shares and accounting for at least 10 percent of all shares. Company officials may not trade their shares for two years. In addition, the offering must be recommended by at least two underwriters, and the transfer agent must operate out of the securities association.

Subsidiaries can list if the parent firm is a listed company and the financials of both the parent and the subsidiary meet the established size and income criteria. However, the subsidiary's operations must be separate from those of its parent; the parent must own no more than 50 percent of the shares; and the subsidiary's officials—who must meet certain standards—must deposit a portion of their shares with a custody agent, thereby freezing them. Observers still hope that, despite its slow start, the OTC equities market will take off once the locals become accustomed to it. However, it has a long way to go to reach the minimum threshold necessary for it to operate as a going concern and provide companies with a significant source of funds.

The lack of success of the OTC equities market is at least partially offset by the success of the OTC debt market, which in 1991 traded NT$3.74 trillion—about US$145 billion—of securities, mostly government paper. This OTC bond market was also relatively somnolent until authorities instituted a public auction system in 1991. Since the system started, the CBC has quadrupled the amount of government bonds issued, and lowered the cost of issue because it no longer has to use negotiated private placements. The CBC issued NT$215 billion (about US$8.5 billion)

in fiscal 1993, and it expects to issue NT$150 (US$5.75 billion) in fiscal 1994.

This activity has attracted dozens of new trading firms, and the market has absorbed them as readily as it has the government debt. Spreads are relatively narrow, interest rates have fallen, and there appears to be a substantial amount of liquidity in the market. Secondary market trading was expected to reach NT$12.75 trillion (about US$47.5 billion) in 1993, although the bulk of this activity represents repurchase agreements—short-term borrowings that use holdings as collateral rather than real sales.

No one is exactly saying that the government has crowded out the private sector, but corporate issuers have taken a back seat in the developing bond market. Few have floated medium- to long-term debt, and most would still prefer to sell short-term securities. However, the government has been slow to authorize additional commercial paper. Private issuers are further hampered by the absence of a credit rating agency. At present, even well-established entities must pay banks guarantor fees in order to sell their debt. Some companies are testing the idea of issuing bonds without this guarantee, which can cost up to 1 percent of the face amount.

Pension Funds Pension funds have traditionally been unadventurous, investing in money market and bank short-term interest-bearing instruments, a few bonds, and government paper. Pension funds have not been accustomed even to think in terms of riskier investments. The authorities recently gave the quasi-public Central Trust of China (CTC), which is responsible for the largest cooperative pension fund in the country, worth NT$43 billion (about US$2.75 billion), permission to invest up to 20 percent of its funds on the TAIEX. This move is largely political, designed to shore up the sagging market by involving some more stable investors. The CTC has been slow to respond, grudgingly committing less than 10 percent of the total authorized. Pension funds are not expected to become a significant source of investment funds available to the private economy any time in the foreseeable future.

Linkages with Singapore Preliminary negotiations are under way to establish a network that links the TAIEX with its counterpart in Singapore. This system would help facilitate the exchange of data on stock listings, management, futures, commodities, and options as well as make available information on standards, regulations, and business practices. In addition, the system would provide Taiwan with greater access to Singapore's expertise in international finance and aid in promoting the growth of Taipei as a regional financial center.

The Gold Market

The government has recently liberalized restrictions related to the domestic gold market, which currently ranks among the most active in the world. In 1991 Taiwan's total imports of gold amounted to around 200 metric tons, while domestic per capita purchases averaged approximately 12 grams.

This level of interest is due at least in part to the lifting in 1986 of the long-standing import ban on gold intended for sale to the general public and the legalization of domestic transactions in the metal. The CBC and many jewelry firms are authorized to import and sell gold on the open market. Foreign exchange banks licensed by the central bank are entitled to act as agents for foreign concerns in the sale of gold coins and gold foil.

Exports of gold were authorized in mid-1992. The government is considering the establishment of a formal gold exchange and allowing various government financial institutions to set up a gold deposit system or issue gold certificates. These steps would do a great deal to increase liquidity. In conjunction with the creation of a reliable system of gold appraisal, these changes would also help to foster the development of gold futures trading and the emergence of a better organized spot market.

The Futures Market

The legal status of futures operations remains ambiguous. Futures trading actually began in Taiwan in 1971, when a US futures company set up a branch office in Taipei. Subsequently, three other companies were established, but all four essentially confined their activities to dealing in agricultural futures and hedging.

The liberalization of foreign exchange controls in July 1987 encouraged a number of Hong Kong futures firms to enter into cooperative arrangements with Taiwanese firms. An estimated 300 futures companies of various kinds have begun operations on the island since then. To establish more effective regulation and control over this burgeoning market, the Ministry of Economic Affairs drafted a Foreign Futures Trading Law to regularize and rein in this anarchic activity.

Currency & Foreign Exchange

INTERNATIONAL PAYMENT INSTRUMENTS

Bank-to-bank letters of credit (L/Cs) constitute Taiwan's most important international payments instruments. In 1991, Taiwan imported US$63 billion in goods and services, of which two-thirds, US$42 billion, were financed through L/Cs. On a smaller scale, company-to-company payments are made via open accounts (O/A), documents against payment (D/P), and documents against acceptance (D/A). International exporters can minimize financial risk by requiring their Taiwan trading partners to finance imports through L/Cs. The majority of Taiwan importers use L/Cs valid for up to 180 days. L/Cs are available in Taiwan at all domestic national and foreign banks authorized to handle foreign exchange. (Refer to "International Payments" chapter.)

CURRENCY

Taiwan's currency is the New Taiwan dollar (NT$). Established in 1949, the money is referred to locally as *yuan*, or dollar. It is also known colloquially as *kuai*, meaning "unit of money." Coins are issued by the Central Bank of China (CBC) in denominations of NT$0.5, NT$1, NT$5, and NT$10. CBC notes are issued in denominations of NT$50, NT$100, NT$500, and NT$1,000. The NT$1,000 bill was worth about US$37.50 at the 1993 year-end exchange rate of NT$26.65=US$1.

REMITTANCE AND EXCHANGE CONTROLS

Foreign exchange issues are regulated by the Statute for Governing Foreign Exchange, which is administered by the CBC, the Ministry of Finance, and the Ministry of Economic Affairs. The statute was liberalized in 1987 to allow private sector firms to hold trade-related foreign exchange, codify rules for non-trade related inward and outward flows, and allow licensed foreign exchange banks to set rates according to the market within a range set by the government.

There are technically no foreign exchange limitations on the repatriation of capital and profits from investments in Taiwan provided that the initial investment was approved and registered with Taiwanese authorities. Most other non-trade-related transactions involving outward or inward remittances by foreign or resident individuals or entities have a US$5 million annual limit per account. Remittances of amounts greater than US$1 million require a 10 working day waiting period.

Individuals are limited to carrying a maximum of NT$40,000 in cash—about US$1,500—out of the country. Individuals may import unlimited amounts of currency as long as it is declared on entry. Otherwise, they may take no more than US$5,000 out of the country when they leave. Individual conversions of foreign currency into local currency are limited to a maximum of US$5,000 per transaction.

The CBC and designated banks—including approved foreign institutions—are the only entities legally allowed to process foreign exchange transactions. Exchanges may not take place directly between buyer and seller. Because of the government-monitored bank monopoly on foreign exchange transactions, the rate of exchange does not vary from location to location, as it does in some other places such as Hong Kong. However, different outlets may only change specific items, such as their own traveler's checks or cash, or US dollars but not Hong Kong dollars. Travelers can change money at the airports and at most hotels.

There is a thriving black market for foreign exchange, mostly operated through gold shops in Taipei and other large cities. There is seldom a significant spread between official and black market exchange rates. However, vast sums of money are reportedly exchanged on this black market to evade government controls and accounting. Black market dealers have a reputation for an almost supernatural ability to predict impending rate changes and to make substantial profits from them.

Despite official controls on flows of currency in

Taiwan's Foreign Exchange Rates - Year-End Actual
New Taiwan Dollar (NT$) to United States Dollar (US$)

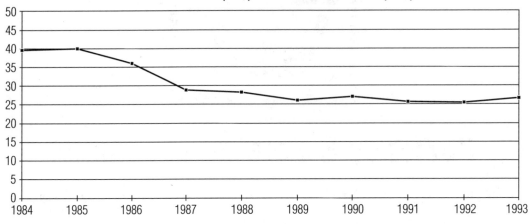

January 1, 1994 US$1 = NT$26.36

and out of Taiwan, hundreds of millions of unregistered New Taiwan dollars have been spirited out of the country in recent years. Much of this capital flight was a response to limitations on interest rates and a lack of internal investment opportunities and the fact that the strong Taiwanese currency had considerably more purchasing power outside the country than it had internally. Such outflows played a major role in the government's decisions to begin opening up the financial system. Although this money has been spread worldwide, much of it has gone into Taiwanese investment projects in mainland China, despite the Taiwanese government's continuing ban on direct investment in the PRC.

FOREIGN EXCHANGE OPERATIONS

Only authorized financial entities are allowed to deal in foreign exchange, and the only transactions allowed are those involving direct commercial exchanges. These include contractual import and export deals; overseas loans; remittance of intangibles, such as royalties, interest payments, and salaries; outward capital investment; and dividend and royalty receipts from abroad. There is no market for speculative activity or other financial transactions, and individuals and businesses cannot hold free foreign exchange balances for their own uses.

Foreign businesses in Taiwan cannot use foreign exchange in domestic transactions. Although firms can hold trade-related balances, they must deposit all foreign exchange in a licensed foreign exchange bank account, from which it must be converted to local currency or sold to the CBC directly or through one of its approved banks. Registered foreign businesses can open local currency accounts. However, only foreign exchange earned from export activities

can be converted for deposit in such accounts.

An interbank foreign exchange call market was set up in August 1989. Transaction currencies were initially limited to the US dollar, but they have since been expanded to include a total of 14 major currencies. In 1991 this market was linked to foreign exchange markets in Singapore and Hong Kong. It also allows currency swaps and margin trading in foreign exchange to a limited degree.

RATES OF EXCHANGE

Since 1989 the New Taiwan dollar has remained fairly stable and traded in a relatively narrow range, with a high of 24.8 in July 1992 and a low of 27.8 in January 1989 relative to the US dollar. In 1989 the NT$-US$ exchange rate averaged 26.4; in 1990 26.9; in 1991 26.8; in 1992 25.2; and for the first five months of 1993 25.8. By year-end 1993, the New Taiwan dollar had fallen to 26.65 to the US dollar. This stability, even in the face of ongoing deregulation, underscores the New Taiwan dollar's underlying strength, buttressed as it is by Taiwan's huge foreign currency reserves and balance of trade surplus.

Taiwan nominally has a controlled floating foreign exchange rate. Prior to 1978, the CBC pegged its currency to the US dollar at a fixed rate of NT$40 to US$1. The CBC no longer pegs the currency directly to US or any other currency, although it does maintain rates within a certain range with reference to the US dollar. This shift has allowed market forces to exercise a somewhat greater influence on exchange rates. Spot rates for NT$-US$ trades move within a narrow range nominally based on weighted average prices from the previous day's trading by five major Taiwanese banks as adjusted at the discretion of the CBC in a process that is not exactly transparent.

Individual banks set their own rates for other currencies. Banks can also set their own rates on forward transactions in any currency based on supply and demand, but they are liable for fulfilling the contracts themselves. The government rescinded buyback agreements designed to protect these banks from adverse moves in forward markets as part of foreign exchange liberalization in 1987. The result has been that the forward market has effectively closed down. In 1993 forward foreign currency transactions accounted for only slightly more than 3 percent of all foreign exchange activities. Such transactions are usually undertaken as an accommodation to clients.

The US government in particular has accused the CBC of manipulating its currency and keeping it artificially low to protect its markets. Nevertheless, the New Taiwan dollar has appreciated by about 60 percent against the US dollar since 1985, moving from its 40 to 1 rate in the late 1970s and early 1980s to its 26 to 1 rate in fall 1993.

FOREIGN RESERVES

Taiwan's foreign exchange reserves have stabilized at about US$84 billion, the highest international reserve level in the world as of mid-1993. The CBC acknowledges that if backlogs from years of trade surpluses, gold—which the IMF excludes from its calculations of international reserves—and dedicated accounts are added in, this figure would rise even higher, to around US$100 billion.

This strong financial position has kept the New Taiwan dollar strong—too strong to suit some in Taiwan—and has proved to be a management headache for the CBC, which is concerned with investing the funds. The CBC used to keep virtually all its reserves in low-yielding US government paper, but over the last few years it has purchased large quantities of gold and diversified its holdings to include other world currencies, primarily the yen and the deutsche mark.

As another measure of Taiwan's financial strength, its current debt servicing ratio is estimated at between 2 and 3 percent, one of the world's lowest.

FURTHER READING

The preceding discussion is provided as a basic guide to money, finances, financial institutions, and financial markets in Taiwan. Those interested in current developments may wish to consult the *Far Eastern Economic Review* and the *Free China Review*, both of which frequently cover economic and financial developments in Taiwan.

Exchange Rates NT$/US$

YEAR	JAN	FEB	MAR	APR	MAY	JUN	JUL	AUG	SEP	OCT	NOV	DEC
1984	40.205	40.236	40.078	39.784	39.716	39.843	39.477	39.092	39.159	39.226	39.419	39.509
1985	39.209	39.228	39.544	39.728	39.906	39.857	40.136	40.501	40.465	40.195	39.981	39.906
1986	39.405	39.239	39.027	38.690	38.461	38.163	38.119	37.422	36.885	36.647	36.438	36.001
1987	35.304	35.056	34.681	33.826	32.354	31.226	31.114	30.290	30.151	30.036	29.813	28.959
1988	28.628	28.665	28.687	28.695	28.666	28.723	28.726	28.693	28.914	28.880	28.170	28.199
1989	27.821	27.716	27.591	26.998	25.788	26.023	25.816	25.685	25.737	25.739	26.029	26.138
1990	26.081	26.117	26.361	26.369	26.961	27.391	27.163	27.291	27.302	27.288	27.245	27.162
1991	27.197	27.109	27.311	27.333	27.282	27.166	26.982	26.730	26.559	26.406	25.975	25.768
1992	25.150	25.049	25.406	25.308	25.016	24.769	24.783	25.120	25.227	25.278	25.404	25.457
1993	25.452	25.837	26.026	25.987	25.978	26.267	26.682	26.950	26.931	26.845	26.620	26.650

Source: US Federal Reserve System

International Payments

International transactions add an additional layer of risk for buyers and sellers that are familiar only with doing business domestically. Currency regulations, foreign exchange risk, political, economic, or social upheaval in the buyer's or seller's country, and different business customs may all contribute to uncertainty. Ultimately, however, the seller wants to make sure he gets paid and the buyer wants to get what he pays for. Choosing the right payment method can be the key to the transaction's feasibility and profitability.

There are four common methods of international payment, each providing the buyer and the seller with varying degrees of protection for getting paid and for guaranteeing shipment. Ranked in order of most security for the supplier to most security for the buyer, they are: Cash in Advance, Documentary Letters of Credit (L/C), Documentary Collections (D/P and D/A Terms), and Open Account (O/A).

Cash in Advance

In cash in advance terms the buyer simply prepays the supplier prior to shipment of goods. Cash in advance terms are generally used in new relationships where transactions are small and the buyer has no choice but to pre-pay. These terms give maximum security to the seller but leave the buyer at great risk. Since the buyer has no guarantee that the goods will be shipped, he must have a high degree of trust in the seller's ability and willingness to follow through. The buyer must also consider the economic, political and social stability of the seller's country, as these conditions may make it impossible for the seller to ship as promised.

Documentary Letters of Credit

A letter of credit is a bank's promise to pay a supplier on behalf of the buyer so long as the supplier meets the terms and conditions stated in the credit. Documents are the key issue in letter of credit transactions. Banks act as intermediaries, and have nothing to do with the goods themselves.

Letters of credit are the most common form of international payment because they provide a high degree of protection for both the seller and the buyer. The buyer specifies the documentation that he requires from the seller before the bank is to make payment, and the seller is given assurance that he will receive payment after shipping his goods so long as the documentation is in order.

Documentary Collections

A documentary collection is like an international cash on delivery (COD), but with a few twists. The exporter ships goods to the importer, but forwards shipping documents (including title document) to his bank for transmission to the buyer's bank. The buyer's bank is instructed not to transfer the documents to the buyer until payment is made (Documents against Payment, D/P) or upon guarantee that payment will be made within a specified period of time (Documents against Acceptance, D/A). Once the buyer has the documentation for the shipment he is able to take possession of the goods.

D/P and D/A terms are commonly used in ongoing business relationships and provide a measure of protection for both parties. The buyer and seller, however, both assume risk in the transaction, ranging from refusal on the part of the buyer to pay for the documents, to the seller's shipping of unacceptable goods.

Open Account

This is an agreement by the buyer to pay for goods within a designated time after their shipment, usually in 30, 60, or 90 days. Open account terms give maximum security to the buyer and greatest risk to the seller. This form of payment is used only when the seller has significant trust and faith in the buyer's ability and willingness to pay once the goods have been shipped. The seller must also consider the economic, political and social stability of the buyer's country as these conditions may make it impossible for the buyer to pay as promised.

DOCUMENTARY COLLECTIONS (D/P, D/A)

Documentary collections focus on the transfer of documents such as bills of lading for the transfer of ownership of goods rather than on the goods themselves. They are easier to use than letters of credit and bank service charges are generally lower.

This form of payment is excellent for buyers who wish to purchase goods without risking prepayment and without having to go through the more cumbersome letter of credit process.

Documentary collection procedures, however, entail risk for the supplier, because payment is not made until after goods are shipped. In addition, the supplier assumes the risk while the goods are in transit and storage until payment/acceptance take place. Banks involved in the transaction do not guarantee payments. A supplier should therefore only agree to a documentary collection procedure if the transaction includes the following characteristics:

- The supplier does not doubt the buyer's ability and willingness to pay for the goods.
- The buyer's country is politically, economically, and legally stable.
- There are no foreign exchange restrictions in the buyer's home country, or unless all necessary licenses for foreign exchange have already been obtained.
- The goods to be shipped are easily marketable.

Types of Collections

The three types of documentary collections are:
1. Documents against Payment (D/P)
2. Documents against Acceptance (D/A)
3. Collection with Acceptance (Acceptance D/P)

All of these collection procedures follow the same general step-by-step process of exchanging documents proving title to goods for either cash or a contracted promise to pay at a later time. The documents are transferred from the supplier (called the remitter) to the buyer (called the drawee) via intermediary banks. When the supplier ships goods, he presents documents such as the bill of lading, invoices, and certificate of origin to his representative bank (the remitting bank), which then forwards them to the buyer's bank (the collecting bank). According to the type of documentary collection, the buyer may then do one of the following:

- With Documents against Payment (D/P), the buyer may only receive the title and other documents after paying for the goods.
- With Documents against Acceptance (D/A), the buyer may receive the title and other documents after signing a time draft promising to pay at a later date.

- With Acceptance Documents against Payment, the buyer signs a time draft for payment at a later date. However, he may only obtain the documents after the time draft reaches maturity. In essence, the goods remain in escrow until payment has been made.

In all cases the buyer may take possession of the goods only by presenting the bill of lading to customs or shipping authorities.

In the event that the prospective buyer cannot or will not pay for the goods shipped, they remain in legal possession of the supplier, but he may be stuck with them in an unfavorable situation. Also, the supplier has no legal basis to file claim against the prospective buyer. At this point the supplier may:

- Have the goods returned and sell them on his domestic market; or
- Sell the goods to another buyer near where the goods are currently held.

If the supplier takes no action the goods will be auctioned or otherwise disposed of by customs.

Documentary Collection Procedure

The documentary collection process has been standardized by a set of rules published by the International Chamber of Commerce (ICC). These rules are called the Uniform Rules for Collections (URC) and are contained in ICC Publication No. 322. (See the last page of this section for ICC addresses and list of available publications.)

The following is the basic set of steps used in a documentary collection. Refer to the illustration on the following page for a graphic representation of the procedure.

(1) The seller (remitter, exporter) ships the goods.
(2) and (3) The seller forwards the agreed upon documents to his bank, the remitting bank, which in turn forwards them to the collecting bank (buyer's bank).
(4) The collecting bank notifies the buyer (drawee, importer) and informs him of the conditions under which he can take possession of the documents.
(5) To take possession of the documents, the buyer makes payment or signs a time deposit.
(6) and (7) If the buyer draws the documents against payment, the collecting bank transfers payment to the remitting bank for credit to the supplier's account. If the buyer draws the documents against acceptance, the collecting bank sends the acceptance to the remitting bank or retains it up to maturity. On maturity, the collecting bank collects the bill and transfers it to the remitting bank for payment to the supplier.

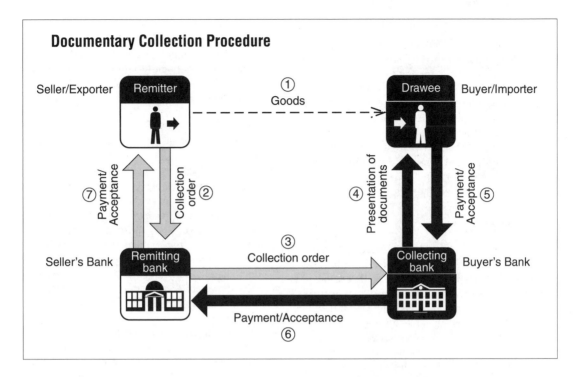

Documentary Collection Procedure

TIPS FOR BUYERS

1. The buyer is generally in a secure position because he does not assume ownership or responsibility for goods until he has paid for the documents or signed a time draft.
2. The buyer may not sample or inspect the goods before accepting and paying for the documents without authorization from the seller. However, the buyer may in advance specify a certificate of inspection as part of the required documentation package.
3. As a special favor, the collecting bank can allow the buyer to inspect the documents before payment. The collecting bank assumes responsibility for the documents until their redemption.
4. In the above case, the buyer should immediately return the entire set of documents to the collecting bank if he cannot meet the agreed payment procedure.
5. The buyer assumes no liability for goods if he refuses to take possession of the documents.
6. Partial payment in exchange for the documents is not allowed unless authorized in the collection order.
7. With documents against acceptance, the buyer may receive the goods and resell them for profit before the time draft matures, thereby using the proceeds of the sale to pay for the goods. The buyer remains responsible for payment, however, even if he cannot sell the goods.

TIPS FOR SUPPLIERS

1. The supplier assumes risk because he ships goods before receiving payment. The buyer is under no legal obligation to pay for or to accept the goods.
2. Before agreeing to a documentary collection, the supplier should check on the buyer's creditworthiness and business reputation.
3. The supplier should make sure the buyer's country is politically and financially stable.
4. The supplier should find out what documents are required for customs clearance in the buyer's country. Consulates may be of help.
5. The supplier should assemble the documents carefully and make sure they are in the required form and endorsed as necessary.
6. As a rule, the remitting bank will not review the documents before forwarding them to the collecting bank. This is the responsibility of the seller.
7. The goods travel and are stored at the risk of the supplier until payment or acceptance.
8. If the buyer refuses acceptance or payment for the documents, the supplier retains ownership. The supplier may have the goods shipped back or try to sell them to another buyer in the region.
9. If the buyer takes no action, customs authorities may seize the goods and auction them off or otherwise dispose of them.
10. Because goods may be refused, the supplier should only ship goods which are readily marketable to other sources.

LETTERS OF CREDIT (L/C)

A letter of credit is a document issued by a bank stating its commitment to pay someone (supplier/exporter/seller) a stated amount of money on behalf of a buyer (importer) so long as the seller meets very specific terms and conditions. Letters of credit are often called documentary letters of credit because the banks handling the transaction deal in documents as opposed to goods. Letters of credit are the most common method of making international payments, because the risks of the transaction are shared by both the buyer and the supplier.

STEPS IN USING AN L/C

The letter of credit process has been standardized by a set of rules published by the International Chamber of Commerce (ICC). These rules are called the Uniform Customs and Practice for Documentary Credits (UCP) and are contained in ICC Publication No. 400. (See the last page of this section for ICC addresses and list of available publications.) The following is the basic set of steps used in a letter of credit transaction. Specific letter of credit transactions follow somewhat different procedures.

- After the buyer and supplier agree on the terms of a sale, the buyer arranges for his bank to open a letter of credit in favor of the supplier.
- The buyer's bank (the issuing bank), prepares the letter of credit, including all of the buyer's instructions to the seller concerning shipment and required documentation.
- The buyer's bank sends the letter of credit to a correspondent bank (the advising bank), in the seller's country. The seller may request that a particular bank be the advising bank, or the domestic bank may select one of its correspondent banks in the seller's country.
- The advising bank forwards the letter of credit to the supplier.
- The supplier carefully reviews all conditions the buyer has stipulated in the letter of credit. If the supplier cannot comply with one or more of the provisions he immediately notifies the buyer and asks that an amendment be made to the letter of credit.
- After final terms are agreed upon, the supplier prepares the goods and arranges for their shipment to the appropriate port.
- The supplier ships the goods, and obtains a bill of lading and other documents as required by the buyer in the letter of credit. Some of these documents may need to be obtained prior to shipment.
- The supplier presents the required documents to the advising bank, indicating full compliance with the terms of the letter of credit. Required documents usually include a bill of lading, commercial invoice, certificate of origin, and possibly an inspection certificate if required by the buyer.
- The advising bank reviews the documents. If they are in order, the documents are forwarded to the issuing bank. If it is an irrevocable, confirmed letter of credit the supplier is guaranteed payment and may be paid immediately by the advising bank.
- Once the issuing bank receives the documents it notifies the buyer who then reviews the documents himself. If the documents are in order the buyer signs off, taking possession of the documents, including the bill of lading, which he uses to take possession of the shipment.
- The issuing bank initiates payment to the advising bank, which pays the supplier.

The transfer of funds from the buyer to his bank, from the buyer's bank to the supplier's bank, and from the supplier's bank to the supplier may be handled at the same time as the exchange of documents, or under terms agreed upon in advance.

Parties to a Letter of Credit Transaction

Buyer/Importer	Buyer	Issuing bank	Buyer's bank
Seller/Supplier/Exporter	Seller	Advising bank	Seller's bank

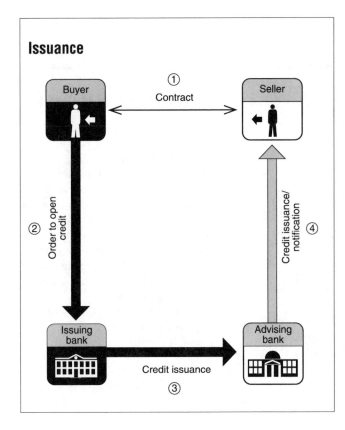

Issuance of a Letter of Credit

① Buyer and seller agree on purchase contract.
② Buyer applies for and opens a letter of credit with issuing ("buyer's") bank.
③ Issuing bank issues the letter of credit, forwarding it to advising ("seller's") bank.
④ Advising bank notifies seller of letter of credit.

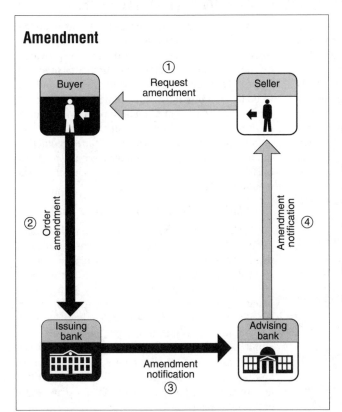

Amendment of a Letter of Credit

① Seller requests (of the buyer) a modification (amendment) of the terms of the letter of credit. Once the terms are agreed upon:
② Buyer issues order to issuing ("buyer's") bank to make an amendment to the terms of the letter of credit.
③ Issuing bank notifies advising ("seller's") bank of amendment.
④ Advising bank notifies seller of amendment.

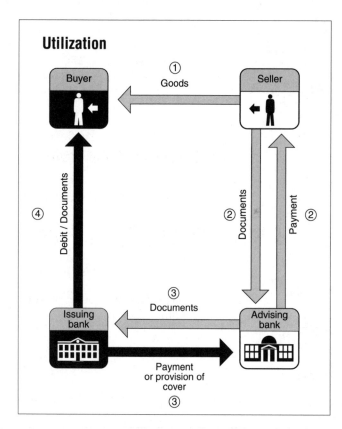

Utilization

①
Goods

Buyer

Seller

④
Debit / Documents

②
Documents

②
Payment

③
Documents

Issuing bank

Advising bank

Payment
or provision of
cover

③

Utilization of a Letter of Credit

(irrevocable, confirmed credit)

① Seller ships goods to buyer.

② Seller forwards all documents (as stipulated in the letter of credit) to advising bank. Once documents are reviewed and accepted, advising bank pays seller for the goods.

③ Advising bank forwards documents to issuing bank. Once documents are reviewed and accepted, issuing bank pays advising bank.

④ Issuing bank forwards documents to buyer. Seller's letter of credit, or account, is debited.

COMMON PROBLEMS IN LETTER OF CREDIT TRANSACTIONS

Most problems with letter of credit transactions have to do with the ability of the supplier to fulfill obligations the buyer establishes in the original letter of credit. The supplier may find the terms of the credit difficult or impossible to fulfill and either tries to do so and fails, or asks the buyer for an amendment to the letter of credit. Observers note that over half of all letters of credit involving parties in East Asia are amended or renegotiated entirely. Since most letters of credit are irrevocable, amendments to the original letter of credit can only be made after further negotiations and agreements between the buyer and the supplier. Suppliers may have one or more of the following problems:

- Shipment schedule stipulated in the letter of credit cannot be met.
- Stipulations concerning freight cost are deemed unacceptable.
- Price is insufficient due to changes in exchange rates.
- Quantity of product ordered is not the expected amount.
- Description of product to be shipped is either insufficient or too detailed.
- Documents stipulated in the letter of credit are difficult or impossible to obtain.

Even when suppliers accept the terms of an letter of credit, problems often arise at the stage where banks review, or negotiate, the documents provided by the supplier against the requirements specified in the letter of credit. If the documents are found not to be in accord with those specified in the letter of credit, the bank's commitment to pay is invalidated. In some cases the supplier can correct the documents and present them within the time specified in the letter of credit. Or, the advising bank may ask the issuing bank for authorization to accept the documents despite the discrepancies found.

Limits on Legal Obligations of Banks

It is important to note once again that banks *deal in documents and not in goods.* Only the wording of the credit is binding on the bank. Banks are not responsible for verifying the authenticity of the documents, nor for the quality or quantity of the goods being shipped. As long as the *documents* comply with the specified terms of the letter of credit, banks may accept them and initiate the payment process as stipulated in the letter of credit. Banks are free from liability for delays in sending messages caused by another party, consequences of Acts of God, or the acts of third parties whom they have instructed to carry out transactions.

TYPES OF LETTERS OF CREDIT

Basic Letters of Credit

There are two basic forms of a letter of credit: the Revocable Credit and the Irrevocable Credit. There are also two types of irrevocable credit: the Irrevocable Credit not Confirmed, and the Irrevocable Confirmed Credit. Each type of credit has advantages and disadvantages for the buyer and for the seller. Also note that the more the banks assume risk by guaranteeing payment, the more they will charge for providing the service.

1. Revocable credit This credit can be changed or canceled by the buyer without prior notice to the supplier. Because it offers little security to the seller revocable credits are generally unacceptable to the seller and are rarely used.

2. Irrevocable credit The irrevocable credit is one which the issuing bank commits itself irrevocably to honor, provided the beneficiary complies with all stipulated conditions. This credit cannot be changed or canceled without the consent of both the buyer and the seller. As a result, this type of credit is the most widely used in international trade. Irrevocable credits are more expensive because of the issuing bank's added liability in guaranteeing the credit. There are two types of irrevocable credits:

a. The Irrevocable Credit not Confirmed by the Advising Bank (Unconfirmed Credit) This means that the buyer's bank which issues the credit is the only party responsible for payment to the supplier, and the supplier's bank is obliged to pay the supplier only after receiving payment from the buyer's bank. The supplier's bank merely acts on behalf of the issuing bank and therefore incurs no risk.

b. The Irrevocable, Confirmed Credit In a confirmed credit, the advising bank adds its guarantee to pay the supplier to that of the issuing bank. If the issuing bank fails to make payment the advising bank will pay. If a supplier is unfamiliar with the buyer's bank which issues the letter of credit, he may insist on an irrevocable confirmed credit. These credits may be used when trade is conducted in a high risk area where there are fears of outbreak of war or social, political, or financial instability. Confirmed credits may also be used by the supplier to enlist the aid of a local bank to extend financing to enable him to fill the order. A confirmed credit costs more because the bank has added liability.

Special Letters of Credit

There are numerous special letters of credit designed to meet specific needs of buyers, suppliers, and intermediaries. Special letters of credit usually involve increased participation by banks, so financing and service charges are higher than those for ba-

sic letters of credit. The following is a brief description of some special letters of credit.

1. Standby Letter of Credit This credit is primarily a payment or performance guarantee. It is used primarily in the United States because US banks are prevented by law from giving certain guarantees. Standby credits are often called non-performing letters of credit because they are only used as a backup payment method if the collection on a primary payment method is past due.

Standby letters of credit can be used, for example, to guarantee the following types of payment and performance:

- repayment of loans;
- fulfillment by subcontractors;
- securing the payment for goods delivered by third parties.

The beneficiary to a standby letter of credit can draw from it on demand, so the buyer assumes added risk.

2. Revolving Letter of Credit This credit is a commitment on the part of the issuing bank to restore the credit to the original amount after it has been used or drawn down. The number of times it can be utilized and the period of validity is stated in the credit. The credit can be cumulative or noncumulative. Cumulative means that unutilized sums can be added to the next installment whereas noncumulative means that partial amounts not utilized in time expire.

3. Deferred Payment Letter of Credit In this credit the buyer takes delivery of the shipped goods by accepting the documents and agreeing to pay his bank after a fixed period of time. This credit gives the buyer a grace period, and ensures that the seller gets payment on the due date.

4. Red Clause Letter of Credit This is used to provide the supplier with some funds prior to shipment to finance production of the goods. The credit may be advanced in part or in full, and the buyer's bank finances the advance payment. The buyer, in essence, extends financing to the seller and incurs ultimate risk for all advanced credits.

5. Transferable Letter of Credit This allows the supplier to transfer all or part of the proceeds of the letter of credit to a second beneficiary, usually the ultimate producer of the goods. This is a common financing tactic for middlemen and is used extensively in the Far East.

6. Back-to-Back Letter of Credit This is a new credit opened on the basis of an already existing, nontransferable credit. It is used by traders to make payment to the ultimate supplier. A trader receives a letter of credit from the buyer and then opens another letter of credit in favor of the supplier. The first letter of credit is used as collateral for the second credit. The second credit makes price adjustments from which come the trader's profit.

OPENING A LETTER OF CREDIT

The wording in a letter of credit should be simple but specific. The more detailed an L/C is, the more likely the supplier will reject it as too difficult to fulfill. At the same time, the buyer will wish to define in detail what he is paying for.

Although the L/C process is designed to ensure the satisfaction of all parties to the transaction, it cannot be considered a substitute for face-to-face agreements on doing business in good faith. It should therefore contain only those stipulations required from the banks involved in the documentary process.

L/Cs used in trade with East Asia are usually either irrevocable unconfirmed credits or irrevocable confirmed credits. In choosing the type of L/C to open in favor of the supplier, the buyer should take into consideration generally accepted payment processes in the supplier's country, the value and demand for the goods to be shipped, and the reputation of the supplier.

In specifying documents necessary from the supplier, it is very important to demand documents that are required for customs clearance and those that reflect the agreement reached between the buyer and the supplier. Required documents usually include the bill of lading, a commercial and/or consular invoice, the bill of exchange, the certificate of origin, and the insurance document. Other documents required may be copies of a cable sent to the buyer with shipping information, a confirmation from the shipping company of the state of its ship, and a confirmation from the forwarder that the goods are accompanied by a certificate of origin. Prices should be stated in the currency of the L/C, and documents should be supplied in the language of the L/C.

THE APPLICATION

The following information should be included on an application form for opening an L/C.

(1) **Beneficiary** The seller's company name and address should be written completely and correctly. Incomplete or incorrect information results in delays and unnecessary additional cost.

(2) **Amount** Is the figure a maximum amount or an approximate amount? If words like "circa," "ca.," "about," etc., are used in connection with the amount of the credit, it means that a difference as high as 10 percent upwards or downwards is permitted. In such a case, the same word should also be used in connection with the quantity.

(3) **Validity Period** The validity and period for presentation of the documents following shipment of the goods should be sufficiently long to allow the exporter time to prepare his documents and ship them to the bank. Under place of validity, state the domicile of either the advising bank or the issuing bank.

(4) **Beneficiary's Bank** If no bank is named, the issuing bank is free to select the correspondent bank.

(5) **Type of Payment Availability** Sight drafts, time drafts, or deferred payment may be used, as previously agreed to by the supplier and buyer.

(6) **Desired Documents** Here the buyer specifies precisely which documents he requires. To obtain effective protection against the supply of poor quality goods, for instance, he can demand the submission of analysis or quality certificates. These are generally issued by specialized inspection companies or laboratories.

(7) **Notify Address** An address is given for notification of the imminent arrival of goods at the port or airport of destination. Damage of goods in shipment is also cause for notification. An agent representing the buyer may be used.

(8) **Description of Goods** Here a short, precise description of the goods is given, along with quantity. If the credit amount carries the notation "ca.," the same notation should appear with the quantity.

(9) **Confirmation Order** It may happen that the foreign beneficiary insists on having the credit confirmed by the bank in his country.

Sample Letter of Credit Application

Sender American Import-Export Co., Inc. 123 Main Street San Francisco, California USA Our reference AB/02	**Instructions to open a Documentary Credit** San Francisco, 30th September 19.. Place / Date

Please open the following [X] irrevocable [ ] revocable documentary credit	**Domestic Bank Corporation** Documentary Credits P.O. Box 1040 San Francisco, California

Beneficiary ① Taiwan Trading Co. 41-3 Fu Chou St. Taipei / Republic of China	Beneficiary's bank (if known) ④ Taiwan Commercial Bank Taipei Main Branch Taipei / Republic of China
Amount ② US\$ 70,200.--	Please advise this bank [ ] by letter [X] by letter, cabling main details in advance [ ] by telex / telegram with full text of credit
Date and place of expiry ③ 25th November 19.. in San Francisco	

Partial shipments	Transhipment	Terms of shipment (FOB, C & F, CIF)
[X] allowed [ ] not allowed	[ ] allowed [X] not allowed	CIF Oakland

Despatch from / Taking in charge at	For transportation to	Latest date of shipment	Documents must be presented not later than
Taiwan	Oakland	10th Nov. 19.. ③ 15	days after date of despatch

Beneficiary may dispose of the credit amount as follows [X] at sight upon presentation of documents ⑤ [ ] after ....days, calculated from date of	[ ] by a draft due .... drawn on [ ] you [ ] your correspondents which you / your correspondents will please accept

against surrender of the following documents ⑥ [X] invoice (....3....copies) Shipping document [X] sea: bill of lading, to order, endorsed in blank [ ] rail: dublicate waybill [ ] air: air consignment note [ ]	[X] insurance policy, certificte (............. copies) covering the following risks: "all risks" including war up to [ ] Additional documents final destination in USA [X] Confirmation of the carrier that the ship is not more than 15 years old [X] packing list (3 copies)

Notify address in bill of lading / goods addressed to American Import-Export Co., ⑦ 123 Main Street San Francisco, California USA	Goods insured by [ ] us [X] seller

Goods ⑧
1,000 "Record players ANC 83 as per proforma invoice
       no. 74/1853 dated 10th September 19.."
 	
       at US\$70.20 per item

Your correspondents to advise beneficiary [ ] adding their confirmation [X] without adding their confirmation ⑨ Payments to be debited to our..US Dollar........................account no 10326679150

NB. The applicable text is marked by [X]

American Import-Export Co.

Signature _____

For mailing please see overleaf

Vertical left margin text: This credit is subject to the «Uniform customs and practice for documentary credits» fixed by the International Chamber of Commerce. It is understood that you do not assume any responsibility neither for the correctness, validity or genuineness of the documents which will be remitted to you nor for the description, quality, quantity and weight of the goods thereby represented.

TIPS FOR PARTIES TO A LETTER OF CREDIT

Buyer

1. Before opening a letter of credit, the buyer should reach agreement with the supplier on all particulars of payment procedures, schedules of shipment, type of goods to be sent, and documents to be supplied by the supplier.
2. When choosing the type of L/C to be used, the buyer should take into account standard payment methods in the country with which he is doing business.
3. When opening a letter of credit, the buyer should keep the details of the purchase short and concise.
4. The buyer should be prepared to amend or renegotiate terms of the L/C with the supplier. This is a common procedure in international trade. On irrevocable L/Cs, the most common type, amendments may be made only if all parties involved in the L/C agree.
5. The buyer can eliminate exchange risk involved with import credits in foreign currencies by purchasing foreign exchange on the forward markets.
6. The buyer should use a bank experienced in foreign trade as the L/C issuing bank.
7. The validation time stated on the L/C should give the supplier ample time to produce the goods or to pull them out of stock.
8. The buyer should be aware that an L/C is not failsafe. Banks are only responsible for the documents exchanged and not the goods shipped. Documents in conformity with L/C specifications cannot be rejected on grounds that the goods were not delivered as specified in the contract. The goods shipped may not in fact be the goods ordered and paid for.
9. Purchase contracts and other agreements pertaining to the sale between the buyer and supplier are not the concern of the issuing bank. Only the terms of the L/C are binding on the bank.
10. Documents specified in the L/C should include those the buyer requires for customs clearance.

Supplier

1. Before signing a contract, the supplier should make inquiries about the buyer's creditworthiness and business practices. The supplier's bank will generally assist in this investigation.
2. The supplier should confirm the good standing of the buyer's bank if the credit is unconfirmed.
3. For confirmed credit, the supplier should determine that his local bank is willing to confirm credits from the buyer and his bank.
4. The supplier should carefully review the L/C to make sure he can meet the specified schedules of shipment, type of goods to be sent, packaging, and documentation. All aspects of the L/C must be in conformance with the terms agreed upon, including the supplier's address, the amount to be paid, and the prescribed transport route.
5. The supplier must comply with every detail of the L/C specifications, otherwise the security given by the credit is lost.
6. The supplier should ensure that the L/C is irrevocable.
7. If conditions of the credit have to be modified, the supplier should contact the buyer immediately so that he can instruct the issuing bank to make the necessary amendments.
8. The supplier should confirm with his insurance company that it can provide the coverage specified in the credit, and that insurance charges in the L/C are correct. Insurance coverage often is for CIF (cost, insurance, freight) value of the goods plus 10 percent.
9. The supplier must ensure that the details of goods being sent comply with the description in the L/C, and that the description on the invoice matches that on the L/C.
10. The supplier should be familiar with foreign exchange limitations in the buyer's country which may hinder payment procedures.

GLOSSARY OF DOCUMENTS IN INTERNATIONAL TRADE

The following is a list and description of some of the more common documents importers and exporters encounter in the course of international trade. For the importer/buyer this serves as a checklist of documents he may require of the seller/exporter in a letter of credit or documents against payment method.

Bill of lading A document issued by a transportation company (such as a shipping line) to the shipper which serves as a receipt for goods shipped, a contract for delivery, and may serve as a title document. The major types are:

Straight (non-negotiable) Bill of Lading Indicates that the shipper will deliver the goods to the consignee. The document itself does not give title to the goods. The consignee need only identify himself to claim the goods. A straight bill of lading is often used when the goods have been paid for in advance.

Order (negotiable or "shippers order") Bill of Lading This is a title document which must be in the possession of the consignee (buyer/importer) in order for him to take possession of the shipped goods. Because this bill of lading is negotiable, it is usually made out "to the order of" the consignor (seller/exporter).

Air Waybill A bill of lading issued for air shipment of goods, which is always made out in straight non-negotiable form. It serves as a receipt for the shipper and needs to be made out to someone who can take possession of the goods upon arrival - without waiting for other documents to arrive.

Overland/Inland Bill of Lading Similar to an Air Waybill, except that it covers ground or water transport.

Certificate of Origin A document which certifies the country of origin of the goods. Because a certificate of origin is often required by customs for entry, a buyer will often stipulate in his letter of credit that a certificate of origin is a required document.

Insurance document A document certifying that goods are insured for shipment.

Invoice/Commercial Invoice A document identifying the seller and buyer of goods or services, identifying numbers such as invoice number, date, shipping date, mode of transport, delivery and payment terms, and a complete listing and description of the goods or services being sold including prices, discounts, and quantities. The commercial invoice is usually used by customs to determine the true cost of goods when assessing duty.

Certificate of manufacture A document in which the producer of goods certifies that production has been completed and that the goods are at the disposal of the buyer.

Consular Invoice An invoice prepared on a special form supplied by the consul of an importing country, in the language of the importing country, and certified by a consular official of the foreign country.

Dock Receipt A document/receipt issued by an ocean carrier when the seller/exporter is not responsible for moving the goods to their final destination, but only to a dock in the exporting country. The document/receipt indicates that the goods were, in fact, delivered and received at the specified dock.

Export License A document, issued by a government agency, giving authorization to export certain commodities to specified countries.

Import License A document, issued by a government agency, giving authorization to import certain commodities.

Inspection Certificate An affidavit signed by the seller/exporter or an independent inspection firm (as required by the buyer/importer), confirming that merchandise meets certain specifications.

Packing List A document listing the merchandise contained in a particular box, crate, or container, plus type, dimensions, and weight of the container.

Phytosanitary (plant health) Inspection Certificate A document certifying that an export shipment has been inspected and is free from pests and plant diseases considered harmful by the importing country.

Shipper's Export Declaration A form prepared by a shipper/exporter indicating the value, weight, destination, and other information about an export shipment.

GLOSSARY OF TERMS OF SALE

The following is a basic glossary of common terms of sale in international trade. Note that issues regarding responsibility for loss and insurance are complex and beyond the scope of this publication. The international standard of trade terms of sale are "Incoterms," published by the International Chamber of Commerce (ICC), 38, Cours Albert Ier, F-75008 Paris, France. Other offices of the ICC are British National Committee of the ICC, Centre Point, 103 New Oxford Street, London WC1A 1QB, England and US Council of the ICC, 1212 Avenue of the Americas, New York, NY 10010 USA.

C&F (Cost and Freight) Named Point of Destination The seller's price includes the cost of the goods and transportation up to a named port of destination, but does not cover insurance. Under these terms insurance is the responsibility of the buyer/importer.

CIF (Cost, Insurance, and Freight) Named Point of Destination The seller's price includes the cost of the goods, insurance, and transportation up to a named port of destination.

Ex Point of Origin ("Ex Works" "Ex Warehouse" etc.) The seller's price includes the cost of the goods and packing, but without any transport. The seller agrees to place the goods at the disposal of the buyer at a specified point of origin, on a specified date, and within a fixed period of time. The buyer is under obligation to take delivery of the goods at the agreed place and bear all costs of freight, transport and insurance.

FAS (Free Alongside Ship) The seller's price includes the cost of the goods and transportation up to the port of shipment alongside the vessel or on a designated dock. Insurance under these terms is usually the responsibility of the buyer.

FOB (Free On Board) The seller's price includes the cost of the goods , transportation to the port of shipment, and loading charges on a vessel. This might be on a ship, railway car, or truck at an inland point of departure. Loss or damage to the shipment is borne by the seller until loaded at the point named and by the buyer after loading at that point.

Ex Dock - Named Port of Importation The seller's price includes the cost of the goods, and all additional charges necessary to put them on the dock at the named port of importation with import duty paid. The seller is obligated to pay for insurance and freight charges.

GLOSSARY OF INTERNATIONAL PAYMENT TERMS

Advice The forwarding of a letter of credit or an amendment to a letter of credit to the seller, or beneficiary of the letter of credit, by the advising bank (seller's bank).

Advising bank The bank (usually the seller's bank) which receives a letter of credit from the issuing bank (the buyer's bank) and handles the transaction from the seller's side. This includes: validating the letter of credit, reviewing it for internal consistency, forwarding it to the seller, forwarding seller's documentation back to the issuing bank, and, in the case of a confirmed letter of credit, guaranteeing payment to the seller if his documents are in order and the terms of the credit are met.

Amendment A change in the terms and conditions of a letter of credit, usually to meet the needs of the seller. The seller requests an amendment of the buyer who, if he agrees, instructs his bank (the issuing bank) to issue the amendment. The issuing bank informs the seller's bank (the advising bank) who then notifies the seller of the amendment. In the case of irrevocable letters of credit, amendments may only be made with the agreement of all parties to the transaction.

Back-to-back Letter of Credit A new letter of credit opened in favor of another beneficiary on the basis of an already existing, nontransferable letter of credit.

Beneficiary The entity to whom credits and payments are made, usually the seller/supplier of goods.

Bill of exchange A written order from one person to another to pay a specified sum of money to a designated person. The following two versions are the most common:

Draft A financial/legal document where one individual (the drawer) instructs another individual (the drawee) to pay a certain amount of money to a named person, usually in payment for the transfer of goods or services. Sight Drafts are payable when presented. Time Drafts (also called usance drafts) are payable at a future fixed (specific) date or determinable (30, 60, 90 days etc.) date. Time drafts are used as a financing tool (as with Documents against Acceptance D/P terms) to give the buyer time to pay for his purchase.

Promissory Note A financial/legal document wherein one individual (the issuer) promises to pay another individual a certain amount.

Collecting bank (also called the presenting bank) In a Documentary Collection, the bank (usually the buyer's bank) that collects payment or a time draft from the buyer to be forwarded to the remitting bank (usually the seller's bank) in exchange for shipping and other documents which enable the buyer to take possession of the goods.

Confirmed letter of credit A letter of credit which contains a guarantee on the part of both the issuing and advising bank of payment to the seller so long as the seller's documentation is in order and terms of the credit are met.

Deferred Payment Letter of Credit A letter of credit where the buyer takes possession of the title documents and the goods by agreeing to pay the issuing bank at a fixed time in the future.

Discrepancy The noncompliance with the terms and conditions of a letter of credit. A discrepancy may be as small as a misspelling, an inconsistency in dates or amounts, or a missing document. Some discrepancies can easily be fixed; others may lead to the eventual invalidation of the letter of credit.

D/A Abbreviation for "Documents against Acceptance."

D/P Abbreviation for "Documents against Payment."

Documents against Acceptance (D/A) *See* Documentary Collection

Documents against Payment (D/P) *See* Documentary Collection

Documentary Collection A method of effecting payment for goods whereby the seller/exporter instructs his bank to collect a certain sum from the buyer/importer in exchange for the transfer of shipping and other documentation enabling the buyer/importer to take possession of the goods. The two main types of Documentary Collection are:

Documents against Payment (D/P) Where the bank releases the documents to the buyer/importer only against a cash payment in a prescribed currency; and

Documents against Acceptance (D/A) Where the bank releases the documents to the buyer/importer against acceptance of a bill of exchange guaranteeing payment at a later date.

Draft *See* Bill of exchange.

Drawee The buyer in a documentary collection.

Forward foreign exchange An agreement to purchase foreign exchange (currency) at a future date at a predetermined rate of exchange. Forward foreign exchange contracts are often purchased by buyers of merchandise who wish to hedge against foreign exchange fluctuations between the time the contract is negotiated and the time payment is made.

Irrevocable credit A letter of credit which cannot be revoked or amended without prior mutual consent of the supplier, the buyer, and all intermediaries.

Issuance The act of the issuing bank (buyer's bank) establishing a letter of credit based on the buyer's application.

Issuing bank The buyer's bank which establishes a letter of credit in favor of the supplier, or beneficiary.

Letter of credit A document stating commitment on the part of a bank to place an agreed upon sum of money at the disposal of a seller on behalf of a buyer under precisely defined conditions.

Negotiation In a letter of credit transaction, the examination of seller's documentation by the (negotiating) bank to determine if they comply with the terms and conditions of the letter of credit.

Open Account The shipping of goods by the supplier to the buyer prior to payment for the goods. The supplier will usually specify expected payment terms of 30, 60, or 90 days from date of shipment.

Red clause Letter of Credit A letter of credit which makes funds available to the seller prior to shipment in order to provide him with funds for production of the goods.

Remitter In a documentary collection, an alternate name given to the seller who forwards documents to the buyer through banks.

Remitting bank In a documentary collection, a bank which acts as an intermediary, forwarding the remitter's documents to, and payments from the collecting bank.

Sight draft *See* Bill of exchange.

Standby Letter of Credit- A letter of credit used as a secondary payment method in the event that the primary payment method cannot be fulfilled.

Time draft *See* Bill of exchange.

Validity The time period for which a letter of credit is valid. After receiving notice of a letter of credit opened on his behalf, the seller/exporter must meet all the requirements of the letter of credit within the period of validity.

Revocable Letter of Credit A letter of credit which may be revoked or amended by the issuer (buyer) without prior notice to other parties in the letter of credit process. It is rarely used.

Revolving Letter of Credit A letter of credit which is automatically restored to its full amount after the completion of each documentary exchange. It is used when there are several shipments to be made over a specified period of time.

FURTHER READING

For more detailed information on international trade payments, refer to the following publications of the International Chamber of Commerce (ICC), Paris, France.

Uniform Rules for Collections This publication describes the conditions governing collections, including those for presentation, payment and acceptance terms. The Articles also specify the responsibility of the bank regarding protest, case of need and actions to protect the merchandise. An indispensable aid to everyday banking operations. (A revised, updated edition will be published in 1995.) ICC Publication No. 322.

Documentary Credits: UCP 500 and 400 Compared This publication was developed to train managers, supervisors, and practitioners of international trade in critical areas of the new UCP 500 Rules. It pays particular attention to those Articles that have been the source of litigation. ICC Publication No. 511.

The New ICC Standard Documentary Credit Forms Standard Documentary Credit Forms are a series of forms designed for bankers, attorneys, importers/exporters, and anyone involved in documentary credit transactions around the world. This comprehensive new edition, prepared by Charles del Busto, Chairman of the ICC Banking Commission, reflects the major changes instituted by the new "UCP 500." ICC Publication No. 516.

The New ICC Guide to Documentary Credit Operations This new Guide is a fully revised and expanded edition of the "Guide to Documentary Credits" (ICC publication No. 415, published in conjunction with the UCP No. 400). The new Guide uses a unique combination of graphs, charts, and sample documents to illustrate the Documentary Credit process. An indispensable tool for import/export traders, bankers, training services, and anyone involved in day-to-day Credit operations. ICC Publication No. 515.

Guide to Incoterms 1990 A companion to "Incoterms," the ICC "Guide to Incoterms 1990" gives detailed comments on the changes to the 1980 edition and indicates why it may be in the interest of a buyer or seller to use one or another trade term. This guide is indispensable for exporters/importers, bankers, insurers, and transporters. ICC Publication No. 461/90

These and other relevant ICC publications may be obtained from the following sources:

ICC Publishing S.A.
International Chamber of Commerce
38, Cours Albert Ier
75008 Paris, France
Tel: [33] (1) 49-53-28-28 Fax: [33] (1) 49-53-28-62
Telex: 650770

International Chamber of Commerce
Borsenstrasse 26
P.O. Box 4138
8022 Zurich, Switzerland

British National Committee of the ICC
Centre Point, New Oxford Street
London WC1A QB, UK

ICC Publishing, Inc.
US Council of the ICC
156 Fifth Avenue, Suite 820
New York, NY 10010, USA
Tel: [1] (212) 206-1150 Fax: [1] (212) 633-6025

Corporate Taxation

AT A GLANCE

Corporate Income Tax Rate (%)	25 (a)
Capital Gains Tax Rate (%)	25 (a) (b)
Branch Tax Rate (%)	25 (a)
Withholding Tax (%)	
Dividends	15/20/35 (c)
Interest	10/20 (d)
Royalties from Patents, Know-how, etc.	15/20 (d)
Branch Remittance Tax	0
Net Operating Losses (Years)	
Carryback	0
Carryforward	5

(a) Maximum rate. For details, see Taxes on Corporate Income and Gains.
(b) Effective January 1, 1990, income taxation of securities transactions was suspended, but a securities transaction tax of 0.6 percent (0.1 percent on bonds and other securities authorized by competent authority) is imposed.
(c) See Taxes on Corporate Income and Gains for details.
(d) The 20 percent rate applies to payments to nonresidents. For the definition of a nonresident corporation, See Taxes on Corporate Income and Gains.

TAXES ON CORPORATE INCOME AND GAINS

Corporate Income Tax

A domestic profit-seeking enterprise is subject to business income tax on all its income, regardless of source. A foreign profit-seeking enterprise is subject to tax on only its income from Republic of China (ROC) sources. All profit-seeking enterprises, including subsidiaries of foreign companies, incorporated under the Company Law of the ROC are considered domestic profit-seeking enterprises. A branch office or a fixed place of business of a foreign profit-seeking enterprise operating in the ROC is treated as a domestic profit-seeking enterprise for tax purposes.

Tax is levied on that portion of income generated in the ROC.

Tax Rates

Corporate income tax rates for 1993 are progressive, as indicated in the following table:

Total Net Income		
Exceeding (NT$)	Not Exceeding (NT$)	Rate (%)
0	50,000	0
50,000	100,000	15
100,000	——	25

Companies limited by shares may obtain tax credits equal to 5 to 20 percent of amounts invested in automation equipment or technology, antipollution equipment or technology, research and development, human resource training or international brand name development. If companies limited by shares meet requirements for minimum capital investment and the number of employees, they qualify for credits equal to 20 percent of amounts invested in less developed areas and in areas deficient in resources. Twenty percent of amounts invested in the stocks of "important technology-based enterprises," "important investment enterprises" and "venture capital investment enterprise" may be credited against income taxes if the stocks are held for more than two years. If not fully used in the current year, these investment credits may be carried forward for four years.

Capital Gains

No preferential rate is available. Capital gains are subject to the same corporate tax rates as other in-

Note: This section is courtesy of and © Ernst & Young from their Worldwide Corporate Tax Guide, 1993 Edition. This material should not be regarded as offering a complete explanation of the taxation matters referred to. Ernst & Young is a leading international professional services firm with offices in 100 countries, including Taiwan. Refer to "Important Addresses" chapter for addresses and phone numbers of Ernst & Young offices in Taiwan.

come. Capital gains of nonresident corporations are subject to tax at a fixed rate of 25 percent. A nonresident corporation is a foreign corporation without a branch office or fixed place of business in Taiwan. Gain on a sale of land is exempt from income tax, but is subject to land value increment tax. Effective January 1, 1990, income taxation of securities transactions is suspended, but a securities transaction tax of 0.6 percent or 0.1 percent is imposed.

Administration

The tax year is normally the calendar year. Permission must be requested to use any other period. An annual tax return must be filed between the twentieth of the second month to the last day of the third month after the close of the tax year. A company that meets certain specified conditions may file a blue return and thus qualify for a higher limit for the deduction of entertainment expenses. With the prior approval of the tax authorities, a profit-seeking enterprise may extend the time for filing for up to one and one-half months. A profit-seeking enterprise may be granted a two-month extension of time to file the return if it is a corporate entity and is filing a return certified by a CPA. Payment of tax after the original due date or payment of additional assessed tax is subject to interest computed from the date immediately following the original due date to the date of payment at the prevailing interest rate provided by the Directorate General of Postal Remittances and Savings Bank.

The late filing penalty is 10 percent of tax due but no less than NT$1,500. The nonfiling penalty is 20 percent of the tax assessed by the authorities, but no less than NT$4,500. Underreporting of taxable income is subject to a penalty of up to two times the underpayment of tax.

A profit-seeking enterprise must pay an interim tax equivalent to 50 percent of the preceding year's tax liability before the last day of the seventh month of the tax year; otherwise, the tax authorities will assess one month's interest based on the prevailing interest rate provided by the Directorate General of Postal Remittances and Savings Bank.

Dividends

The dividend withholding tax is 15 percent for a resident taxpayer and 35 percent for a nonresident taxpayer, which is reduced to 20 percent if the investment is approved by the ROC government pursuant to the Statute for Investment by Foreign Nationals or the Statute for Investment by Overseas Chinese.

Foreign Tax Relief

A tax credit is allowed for foreign income tax paid by a domestic profit-seeking enterprise, but it may not exceed the additional amount of the ROC tax resulting from the inclusion of the foreign-source portion in the profit-seeking enterprise's total income.

DETERMINATION OF TRADING INCOME

General

Income for tax purposes is computed according to generally accepted accounting principles, adjusted for certain statutory provisions. Taxable income, therefore, often does not equal income for financial reporting purposes.

Necessary and ordinary expenses of a profit-seeking enterprise are deductible, provided these are adequately supported. The Assessment Rules for Income Tax Returns of Profit-Seeking Enterprises, promulgated by the Ministry of Finance, provide guidelines for determining deductible business expenses. Transactions must conform to regular business practice; otherwise, tax authorities may assess tax based on industry statistics.

Inventories

Inventories are valued for tax purposes at either cost or the lower of cost or market value. In determining the cost of goods sold, specific identification, FIFO, LIFO, weighted average, moving average, simple average, or any other method prescribed by competent authority may be used. However use of two different cost methods in one fiscal year is not allowed. Furthermore, if the LIFO method is adopted, valuation by lower of cost or market value must not be applied.

Provisions

Provisions for a retirement fund approved by the authorities are deductible in amounts of not more than 15 percent of total payroll. The applicable percentage depends on whether the fund is managed separately from the business entity and whether it conforms to the provisions of the Labor Standards Law.

Allowance for bad debts is limited to 1 percent of the balance of outstanding trade accounts and notes receivable (secured or unsecured) at year-end.

Companies limited by shares may set up provisions for losses on outbound foreign investments equal to 20 percent of the gross amount invested.

Capital Receipts

Capital receipts are excluded from trading income; however, a registration fee is charged at 0.025 percent of original or additional capital contribution.

Tax Depreciation, Depletion and Amortization

A taxpayer can take a depreciation deduction for most property (except land) used in trade or business. If certain criteria are met, companies limited by shares may use an accelerated depreciation method. If a taxpayer does not apply to the tax authorities for a particular method of depreciation, the tax authorities will deem the taxpayer to have chosen the straight-line method.

Depletion of assets in the form of nonreplaceable resources is computed either annually or per unit. This method must be applied consistently from year to year. In addition, a taxpayer can take an amortization deduction for intangibles and organization expenses. Licenses and copyrights are amortized over 10 and 15 years, respectively. Trademarks, patents and franchises should be amortized over the period prescribed by the respective laws governing the granting of these rights. Organization and pre-operating expenses should be amortized over five years or more starting from the first year of operation, except when the total life of the business is less than five years.

Relief for Losses

If certain requirements are met, companies may carry forward approved losses for five years. Carrybacks are not permitted.

Groups of Companies

Associated or related companies in a group are taxed separately for business income tax purposes. There is no concept of group assessment under which losses may be offset with gains within a group of companies.

OTHER SIGNIFICANT TAXES

The table below summarizes other significant taxes.

Nature of Tax	Rate (%)
Business tax or value-added tax on sales, general rate	5
Tax on gross business receipts of other specified businesses	0.1 to 25
Land value increment tax, on unearned increase in the value of land, payable by the seller at the time of ownership transfer	10 to 60
National medical plan, on monthly salary up to NT$28,800 (plan is optional for service enterprises);	
paid by Employer	5.6
Employee	1.4

MISCELLANEOUS MATTERS

Foreign Exchange Controls

Under foreign exchange control regulations, a qualified importer (exporter) may remit out (in) unlimited funds for the import (export) of goods. A registered business entity or a nonbusiness organization may remit out unlimited funds for noncommodity trade expenditures such as freight, insurance premiums, commissions, agency fees, and royalty and technical service fees and remit in unlimited funds for services provided. In addition, an adult legally residing in the ROC or a registered business entity or nonbusiness organization may remit out up to US$5 million yearly for other expenditures, such as repatriation of invested principal, remittance of profits, purchase of foreign real properties, purchase of corporate stocks and bonds, loans to foreign borrowers and donations. However, each outward remittance exceeding US$1 million cannot be made until 10 business days after the date the application is filed with the central bank. An adult legally residing in the ROC may currently bring into the ROC up to US$5 million a year for any reason.

If an investor intends to repatriate invested capital or profits overseas without being subject to exchange control limits, the approval of the outward investment by the Ministry of Economic Affairs is required.

Debt-to-Equity Rules

There is no debt-to-equity ratio restriction in ROC Company Law. However, the debt-to-equity ratio for Taiwan entities that are established by foreign investors with foreign debt may not exceed 3:1. The Ministry of Economic Affairs prescribes minimum capital for different types of companies and by industry.

Controlled Foreign Companies

A subsidiary or a branch of a foreign company is taxed independently according to Income Tax Law. Neither a subsidiary nor a branch is obliged to disclose the results and activities of its home company. However, if a branch office shares the expenses of its head office, audited and duly authenticated financial statements related to the allocation must be provided to the tax authority.

Antiavoidance Legislation

ROC Income Tax Law does not contain specific regulations to prevent the diversion of income and capital gains as long as the underlying transactions are carried out according to regular business practice. However, the general rule is that the tax authorities may ignore transactions which constitute an abuse of legal forms provided by the Civil Code. The same applies to sham transactions or transactions made to conceal the actual facts. Such transactions are not taken into account when taxes are calculated.

TREATY WITHHOLDING TAX RATES

The only country with which the ROC has a tax treaty is the Republic of Singapore. Under this tax treaty, if a shareholder is a Singapore resident and earns dividends in the ROC, the tax withheld will not exceed an amount which, together with the corporate income tax payable on the profits of the invested company, constitutes 40 percent of that part of the taxable income out of which the dividends are declared. In general, under domestic tax law, a 35 percent withholding tax is imposed on dividends paid to nonresidents (*see* Taxes on Corporate Income and Gains for details concerning a reduced 20 percent rate). Under the treaty, the royalty withholding tax rate is reduced from the normal 20 to 15 percent. The interest withholding tax rate is still 20 percent, the same rate levied on residents of countries with which the ROC has no tax treaty.

Personal Taxation

AT A GLANCE—MAXIMUM RATES

Income Tax Rate (%)	40
Capital Gains Tax Rate (%)	40
Net Worth Tax Rate (%)	0
Estate and Gift Tax Rates (%)	60

INCOME TAXES—EMPLOYMENT AND SELF-EMPLOYMENT

Who Is Liable

Consolidated (personal) income tax is levied each calendar year on the earned income of both resident and nonresident individuals from Taiwan [Republic of China (ROC)] sources. Taiwan-source income includes all employment income derived from services performed in Taiwan, regardless of whether the employer is a resident of Taiwan.

Individuals are considered resident in the ROC if they are domiciled and reside in the ROC or, if not domiciled, have resided in the ROC for at least 183 days in a tax year. A resident is subject to consolidated income tax on all ROC-source income and is required to prepare and submit an income tax return for the payment of tax due.

Taxable income of residents is computed by deducting from consolidated income certain allowable exemptions and deductions. Taxpayers and their spouses must file joint returns, but may compute taxes on each spouse's salary income separately. The incomes of a taxpayer's dependents are also included.

For the taxation of nonresidents, *see* Nonresidents.

Taxable Income

An individual's consolidated income is the total of the following categories of ROC-source income:

- business profits including dividends, profits distributed by cooperatives and partnerships, profits from a sole proprietorship and profits from sporadic business transactions; income from professional practice;
- salaries, wages, allowances, stipends, annuities, cash awards, bonuses, pensions, subsidies and premiums paid by an employer for group life insurance policies that offer payment upon maturity;
- interest income;
- rental income and royalties;
- income from self-employment in farming, fishery, animal husbandry, forestry and mining;
- gain from sales of rights and properties other than land;
- cash or payments in kind received as winnings in competitions or lotteries; and
- miscellaneous income.

Income Tax Rates

Personal income tax rates for residents for 1993 are set forth in the following table.

Taxable Income Exceeding NT$	Not Exceeding NT$	Tax on Lower Amount NT$	Rate on Excess %
0	300,000	0	6
300,000	800,000	18,000	13
800,000	1,600,000	83,000	21
1,600,000	3,000,000	251,000	30
3,000,000	—	671,000	40

The tax rate for nonresident individuals is 20 percent.

Note: This section is courtesy of and © Ernst & Young from their Worldwide Personal Tax Guide, 1993 Edition. This material should not be regarded as offering a complete explanation of the taxation matters referred to. Ernst & Young is a leading international professional services firm with offices in 100 countries, including Taiwan. Refer to "Important Addresses" chapter for addresses and phone numbers of Ernst & Young offices in Taiwan.

Deductible Expenses

Itemized deductions and special deductions may be deducted from gross income.

Itemized Deductions

The following itemized deductions are available:

- Contributions and donations: up to 20 percent of gross consolidated income if given to officially registered educational, cultural, public welfare or charitable organizations; in full if given for national defense or troop support or if contributed directly to government agencies.
- Insurance premiums: up to NT$24,000 a person for life insurance, labor insurance and government employee insurance for a taxpayer, his or her spouse, and lineal blood relatives.
- Unreimbursed medical and maternity expenses incurred by a taxpayer, his or her spouse, and dependents in government hospitals; hospitals that have entered into contracts with the government under either the government employee insurance program or the labor insurance program; or hospitals maintaining complete and accurate accounting records as recognized by the Ministry of Finance.
- Uncompensated casualty losses.
- Mortgage interest paid on loans from financial institutions for the purchase of a residence for personal use (limited to one): up to NT$80.000, after subtracting a special deduction for savings and investments claimed for the same tax year.

A taxpayer may claim a standard deduction in lieu of the itemized deductions listed above. The standard deduction is NT$33,000 for a single taxpayer and NT$49,500 for a married taxpayer filing jointly.

Special Deductions

The following special deductions are available:

- Salary and wage earner's special deduction: The lesser of either total salaries and wages earned or NT$45,000 is deductible by each salary and wage earner included in the same return.
- Special deduction for savings and investments: Up to NT$270,000 for each family unit is deductible for income from a savings trust fund; for dividends received from companies listed on the Taiwan Stock Exchange; and for interest income on deposits with financial institutions, as well as treasury bonds, corporate bonds and financial bonds, but excluding interest income from postal savings

accounts (which is not taxable) and short-term commercial paper (which is subject to a final 20 percent withholding tax at source).
- Special deduction for the handicapped: NT$45,000 is deductible for a person meeting the definition of "handicapped person" in the Handicapped Welfare Law.
- Special deduction for property losses: Losses from disposals of property are deductible to the extent of gains from the disposal of property in the same tax year and may be carried forward for three years.

Personal Exemptions

For 1992, a taxpayer is entitled to personal exemptions of NT$60,000 for the taxpayer, his or her spouse, and each dependent. The exemption amount increases annually by a nominal amount. For 1993, the proposed amount is NT$63,000.

DIRECTORS' FEES

Directors' fees are taxable as ordinary income.

INVESTMENT INCOME

Dividend and interest income are subject to personal income tax and are taxed together with other kinds of income. However, interest income from postal savings accounts is excluded from gross income. Furthermore, interest income from short-term commercial paper is subject to 20 percent final withholding at the source and is not included in gross income. Special deductions are available (*see* Deductible Expenses).

Rental income and royalties are included in taxable income and are taxed at the rates set forth in Income Tax Rates.

RELIEF FOR LOSSES

Except for losses from disposal of properties described in Deductible Expenses and Capital Gains and Losses, no loss may be carried forward or back.

CAPITAL GAINS AND LOSSES

There is no separate taxation of capital gains. However, losses from disposal of properties are deductible only to the extent of gains from disposal of properties in the same taxable year. Net losses may be carried forward for three years to the extent of gains from the same years.

Gains from the sale of stocks and corporate bonds are exempt from income tax and losses are not deductible. A securities transaction tax is imposed at a rate of 0.6 percent (0.1 percent for bonds).

ESTATE AND GIFT TAXES

Estate Tax

Estate tax is imposed on the estate of a decedent who was a national of the ROC or had property within the ROC. If the decedent was a Chinese national regularly domiciled in the ROC, tax is levied on all property, wherever located. If the decedent was a Chinese national regularly domiciled outside the territory of the ROC or a foreign national, tax is levied only on property located in the ROC.

The basis for estate tax is the fair market value of property, less legal exclusions, exemptions and other deductions. Land and buildings are valued at an officially assessed value determined by the relevant government agencies. Agricultural land is assessed at 50 percent of its value if the heirs continue to use it for agricultural purposes.

There is an exemption of NT$2 million for each decedent. Other deductions from total taxable property are:

- NT$2 million for the decedent's surviving spouse.
- NT$250,000 for each of the decedent's surviving parents, dependent brothers and sisters, and lineal descendants as well as an additional NT$250,000 for each year by which the age of each lineal descendant and dependent brother and sister is less than 20 years.
- NT$400,000 for funeral expenses.
- Direct and necessary expenses to execute the decedent's will and administer the estate.
- Taxes and penalties owed and debts incurred by the decedent before his or her death. Certain property is not subject to estate tax. Exclusions are allowed for
- Proceeds from life assurance policies with designated beneficiaries.
- Furniture, household equipment and other daily necessities up to NT$450,000.
- Patents and literary and artistic works created by the decedent.
- Donations to government agencies and enterprises and to privately incorporated educational, cultural, social welfare, charitable and religious organizations.
- Property set aside for ancestral worship.

The executor of an estate, or the heir in the absence of an executor, must file an estate tax return with the local tax bureau within six months after the death of the deceased, and the tax bureau must complete the tax assessment within the following two months. Payment of tax is due within two months after receipt of a tax demand notice. When tax is more than NT$300,000, a taxpayer may, subject to prior approval, pay it in two to six installments, at inter-

vals of no more than two months between each installment, or pay the tax in kind. A taxpayer who is not satisfied with an assessment may seek relief through administrative and judicial reviews.

The net estate after exclusions, deductions and exemptions is taxed at the following rates for 1993 (*See* following table.)

Estate Tax

Taxable Net Estate Exceeding NT$	Not Exceeding NT$	Tax on Lower Amount NT$	Rate on Excess %
0	300,000	0	2
300,000	600,000	6,000	3
600,000	1,140,000	15,000	5
1,140,000	1,620,000	42,000	7
1,620,000	2,160,000	75,600	9
2,160,000	2,700,000	124,200	11
2,700,000	3,510,000	183,600	14
3,510,000	4,080,000	297,000	17
4,080,000	5,100,000	393,900	20
5,100,000	7,650,000	597,900	23
7,650,000	10,200,000	1,184,400	26
10,200,000	14,400,000	1,847,400	30
14,400,000	24,000,000	3,107,400	34
24,000,000	33,600,000	6,371,400	38
33,600,000	48,000,000	10,019,400	42
48,000,000	90,000,000	16,067,400	46
90,000,000	160,000,000	35,387,400	52
160,000,000	—	71,787,400	60

Gift Tax

Taxable Net Estate Exceeding NT$	Not Exceeding NT$	Tax on Lower Amount NT$	Rate on Excess %
0	300,000	0	4
300,000	570,000	12,000	5
570,000	1,140,000	25,500	6
1,140,000	1,620,000	59,700	8
1,620,000	2,160,000	98,100	11
2,160,000	2,700,000	157,500	14
2,700,000	3,315,000	233,100	17
3,315,000	4,080,000	337,650	20
4,080,000	5,100,000	490,650	23
5,100,000	7,200,000	725,250	26
7,200,000	9,600,000	1,271,250	30
9,600,000	14,400,000	1,991,250	35
14,400,000	28,800,000	3,671,250	40
28,800,000	45,000,000	9,431,250	45
45,000,000	90,000,000	16,721,250	50
90,000,000	150,000,000	39,221,250	55
50,000,000	—	72,221,250	60

Gift Tax

A tax is imposed on gifts made by a donor who is a national of the ROC or has property within the ROC. If the donor is a Chinese national regularly domiciled in the ROC, the tax is levied on any donated property, wherever located. If the donor is a Chinese national regularly domiciled outside the territory of the ROC or a foreigner, tax is levied only on donated property located in the ROC. The net gift, after exclusions and exemptions, is taxed at the following graduated rates for 1993.

Like estates, gifts are valued at fair market value. Land and buildings are valued at officially assessed values determined by government agencies.

An annual exemption of NT$450,000 is allowed for taxable gifts. Exclusions from total taxable gifts include donations to government agencies and enterprises; to educational, cultural, public welfare and charitable organizations; and property set side for ancestral worship.

A donor must file a gift tax return with the local tax bureau within 30 days of making a gift if total gifts during the calendar year, including the current gift, exceed NT$450,000. The local tax bureau must complete the tax assessment within two months after it receives the return. Payment is due within two months after the receipt of a tax demand notice. When tax is more than NT$300,00, a taxpayer may, subject to prior approval, pay the tax in two to six installments at intervals of no more than two months between each installment, or pay the tax in kind. A taxpayer who is not satisfied with an assessment may seek relief through administrative and judicial reviews.

SOCIAL SECURITY TAXES

No social security taxes are levied in Taiwan.

FILING AND PAYMENT PROCEDURES

The tax year is the calendar year. A taxpayer must file an annual income tax return between February 20 and March 31 following the close of the tax year. With the permission of the local tax bureau, the deadline may be extended to April 30.

The tax payment periods for aliens are different, depending on the length of residence in the ROC.

- For any individual in the ROC not more than 90 days, income tax payable is withheld directly at the time of payment by the payer at the appropriate withholding rate. However, capital gains from property transactions or securities transactions (currently exempt) or interest income should be declared, and any tax paid one week before departure.

- Any individual in the ROC for more than 90 days but less than 183 days must file an income tax return one week before departing or applying for a visa extension or appoint a tax guarantor.
- Any individual staying in the ROC for 183 days or more must file an annual income tax return for the preceding year between February 20 and March 31 of each year. However, any individual who intends to leave the territory of the ROC any time during the year and not come back within the same year must file an income tax return within one week before departure or appoint a tax guarantor.

Taxpayers are required to submit supporting documents issued by their non- resident employers stating the amount of compensation paid. The documents must be attested by the tax office that has jurisdiction over the employer or by a certified public accountant.

NONRESIDENTS

The rate of withholding tax on interest and royalty income of nonresidents is 20 percent. For dividends, the rate is either 20 percent or 35 percent. Nonresidents are subject to 20 percent tax on other income including employment income. Nonresident individuals are deemed to have discharged their income tax liability if tax on ROC-source income subject to withholding has been withheld and if declaration and payment have been made of income tax on other ROC-source income (for example, remuneration received from a nonresident employer for services rendered in the ROC). A nonresident taxpayer is not entitled to personal exemptions or deductions. Income tax is computed on gross income.

A foreign person in the ROC for not more than 90 days during a tax year is not subject to income tax on salary received from a nonresident employer, but is subject to 20 percent withholding tax on salary from a resident employer. A foreign person who has stayed in the ROC for more than 90 days and is therefore subject to ROC income tax is required to file a return declaring salary income, including that from a nonresident employer, or a local branch or subsidiary, for services rendered in the ROC.

See Filing and Payment Procedures.

DOUBLE TAX RELIEF/ DOUBLE TAX TREATIES

The only country with which the ROC has a comprehensive tax treaty is the Republic of Singapore. Under this tax treaty, if a shareholder is a Singapore resident and receives dividends from the ROC, tax withheld on dividends is generally 15 percent, after a gross-up for corporate taxes paid. However, for dividends from foreign investment approved (FIA) companies with or without tax holidays, the maximum withholding tax is 20 percent. The effect for both types of dividends is that the tax withheld, together with corporate income tax payable on the profits, may not exceed 40 percent of that part of the taxable income out of which the dividends are declared. Under the treaty, the royalty withholding tax rate is reduced from the normal 20 to 15 percent. The withholding tax rate for interest remains at 20 percent.

Ports & Airports

The late 1980s and early 1990s have seen a major increase in the amount of air and shipping traffic passing through East Asia. Planners saw this coming some years back, and have been scrambling to expand and improve facilities at ports and airports throughout the region; many are currently at or over capacity. Air cargo traffic has been growing faster in Asia than anywhere else in the world, and passenger traffic has increased by leaps and bounds. However, with all the new facilities opening in the near future, there are estimates that by 1997 airport capacity will actually exceed demand. This may mean that airlines and cargo carriers will schedule more frequent service with smaller aircraft, something which is not currently possible, largely because of the small number of slots available at airport terminals and the many major airports operating with only one runway. Long a major center for shipping, Asia is fast becoming the leader in container port traffic. The largest increases in container traffic worldwide have been at the Asian hub ports, and four of the world's five leading countries in container traffic are located on the western side of the Pacific Rim: Japan, Singapore, Hong Kong and Taiwan are ranked two through five, respectively, with the USA at number one.

of existing facilities, construction begins in 1997 on a new airport in the southwestern county of Tainan county, with the total cost put at US$5.88 billion. By 2020, 22 million passengers are expected to pass through the airport each year.

There are currently 32 air cargo carriers serving Chiang Kai Shek Airport with regular flights, and 14 serving Kaohsiung. Airlines serving both cities include: Taiwan's China Air Lines and Transasia, as well as foreign carriers Continental, Cathay Pacific, Japan-Asia Airways, Malaysia Airlines, Phillipine Airlines, Royal Brunei, and Thai Airways. Other major lines serving only Taipei are: Australia Asia, Canadian, Cargolux, Delta, Federal Express, Garuda Indonesia, KLM, Lufthansa, Singapore Airlines, and United Airlines. Domestic air cargo moving to or from Taipei goes through Sung Shan airport on China Air Lines, Far East Air Transport, Transasia, and Great China. (For address and telephone information, refer to the Airlines section of "Important Addresses" chapter.) Taipei's airport authorities can be contacted at:

Chiang Kai Shek International Airport
PO Box 9
Taoyuan, Taiwan
Tel: [886] (2) 7121212

AIRPORTS

Taiwan has 14 airports, but only two are open to international flights: Chiang Kai Shek International Airport, 40 km (25 miles) west of Taipei, and Kaohsiung International Airport. About 95 percent of the airfreight passing through Taiwan goes through Chiang Kai Shek, and the amount of it is increasing rapidly. In 1992 Chiang Kai Shek handled 723,000 metric tons of air cargo, up 22 percent from 594,669 in 1990. The airport is in the midst of a US$1 billion expansion which includes a second runway and terminal, due to be completed by mid-decade. The government is also spending US$720 million on five other airports around the island. In addition to renovations

PORTS

Taiwan's ports handle approximately 125 million metric tons of cargo annually – only the United States, Japan and Great Britain handle more. The island's main port at Kaohsiung is now the third busiest port in the world, and often considered to be one of the most efficient. The other major Taiwanese port is Keelung, 24 km (15 miles) northeast of the capital city of Taipei. There are three other international ports: Taichung, Hualien, and Suao which together account for approximately 10 percent of Taiwan's cargo shipping. Both Kaohsiung and Keelung rank in the top 10 container ports worldwide, and while Taichung handles far less, it has greatly increased the amount of tonnage handled annually, particularly for container freight, in recent years. The ports of Taiwan are administered by:

Ministry of Transportation and Communications
2 Changsha St.
Sec. 1, Taipei, Taiwan
Tel: [886] (2) 3112661 or 3492900
Fax: [886] (2) 3118587

Kaohsiung

Kaohsiung is Taiwan's principal port, on the island's southwest coast. It currently has 98 wharves and four container terminals, but plans to build two more container terminals in the near future, and eventually will expand to eight terminals. Container Terminal No. 5 will be built in the Ta Jen Commercial Harbor Area, with eight container berths. The Ta Lin Commercial Harbor Area is earmarked for development, with deepwater wharves which will accommodate ships of up to 100,000 dead weight tonnage (dwt). A major air/sea transport hub is also in the planning stages. The port is administered by:

Kaohsiung Harbor Bureau
62 Lin Hai 2nd Road
Kaohsiung, Taiwan
Tel: [886] (7) 5612311 Fax: [886] (7) 5611694

Port facilities:
Transportation Service—Truck, rail and barge.
Cargo Storage—Covered, 328,763 square meters. Open, 73,410 square meters. Refrigerated, 3,823 square meters.
Special Cranes—Heavy lift capacity is 200 metric tons. Container, 20 with 40 metric ton capacity.
Air Cargo—Kaohsiung International Airport is located 15 km from the seaport.
Cargo Handling—Containerized, bulk and general cargo can all be adequately handled by existing port equipment. For specialized handling needs there are available at port 6 ore and bulk cargo terminals, 6 tanker terminals, 3 liquefied gas terminals and 1 Ro-Ro off-loading point. Additionally, there are exclusive wharves for petrochemicals, sugar and grain.
Weather—Temperatures range from 9°C to 34°C and annual rainfall is 160 cm. Typhoon season runs from June to November with the hardest rain in July and August.
Construction—Building continues on container terminal No. 4 and Ta Jen commercial harbor area.

Keelung

Keelung, a natural harbor, is the second largest port in Taiwan. The gateway to Taipei, located 24 km (15 miles) to the southeast, Keelung is a natural harbor. Keelung has 58 berths total and three container terminals, one of which was constructed only in the past two years. Special storage sheds for perishables are available. A 10-year port facility remodeling project is planned, including the new deepwater berths capable of accommodating ships up to 200,000 dwt. The port is administered by:

Keelung Harbor Bureau
Port Building
1 Chung Cheng Road
Keelung, Taiwan

Port facilities:
Transportation Service—Truck, rail and barge.
Cargo Storage—Covered, 145,000 square meters. Open, 225,000 square meters.
Special Cranes—Heavy lift capacity is 250 metric tons. Container, 11 with 35 metric ton capacity maximum.
Air Cargo—Chiang Kai Shek International Airport is located 65 km from port.
Cargo Handling—Containerized, bulk and general cargo can all be handled by existing port equipment. Machineries, raw materials and garments are among Keelung's main imports. One ore and bulk cargo terminal and two tanker terminals provide specialized handling at port.
Weather—Temperatures range from 6°C to 33°C, and annual rainfall is 400 cm. Typhoon season runs from June to November.
Construction—Port improvement strategies include the conversion of 6 break-bulk berths into full container facilities.

Business Dictionary

The transliteration system used in this mini-dictionary is known as **Wade-Giles** (after the two originators) and is the standard Latin-alphabet transliteration system used in Taiwan. The **pin-yin** system is used in Mainland China and now generally in Western countries. No transliteration system is ideal since there are some sounds which cannot be adequately represented using the Latin alphabet. Only through listening to and imitating the pronunciation of native speakers can a truly accurate reproduction of the actual sounds of the language be achieved.

Multi-syllabic Chinese words have been joined by a hyphen to assist reading and pronunciation.

TONES

Each Chinese syllable contains one of four tones or is unstressed. In the **Wade-Giles** system the tones are always marked by the numbers 1, 2, 3, 4, or the syllables are unmarked to signify an unstressed syllable.

1st tone (high level): is spoken high and the voice does not rise or fall.

2nd tone (rising): starts with the voice lower at the entry point, then finishes at the same level as the 1st tone.

3rd tone (falling-rising): starts with the voice lower than the 2nd tone, then dips and rises to a point just lower than the 1st tone.

4th tone (falling): the voice falls from high to low.

Each syllable is pronounced with one of these tones unless it is unstressed. In such cases the tone distinctions are absent and the unstressed syllable is pronounced light and short.

VOWELS

Letter	Approximate pronunciation
a	like **a** in jar (but without the **r**-sound)
e	like **e** in her (but without the **r**-sound)
	like **e** in egg when followed by an **h**
	like **u** in hug when followed by **n** or **ng**
i	like **ee** in fee
	like **i** in hit when followed by an **h**, but sounded at the back of the mouth
o	like **aw** as in paw
u	like **oo** as in moon
	like **oo** in look, when followed by **n** or **ng**
	like **i** as in hit, but sounded at the back of the mouth when following **sz, ts'** or **ts**
ü	similar to German **ü** or **u** in French lune
ou	as in soul
ien	like **yen**
uei	like **way**
ei	like **ay** in pay

In syllables with compound vowels, the pronunciation starts from one vowel and "flows" into the other(s) e.g., **i, ia, iao**.

CONSONANTS

These are pronounced approximately the same as in English. One of the main characteristics of the **Wade-Giles system**, however, is the use of apostrophes to distinguish between voiced and non-voiced consonants. E.g., **p'** is pronounced like **p** in pat, but strongly, with a small puff of breath. Plain **p** without the apostrophe is pronounced more like a **b**.

These can be considered as pairs, e.g., **k'/k, p'/p, t'/t, ch'/ch, ts'/ts,** where the consonants without apostrophes are pronounced respectively, **g, b, d, j, dz.**

h	as the start of a word, like **ch** in Scottish loch. At the end of a syllable, see **i** above.
j	like **r** in English, but the tongue is curled back to touch the roof of the mouth so that it sounds something like the **s** in pleasure.
s	always like **s** in sap
sh	like **sh** in ship but with the tongue curled back to touch the roof of the mouth
hs	like **sh** in ship but well forward in the mouth with the lips spread widely
y	like **y** in yellow

English	Mandarin (ROC)	Transliteration	Pronunciation

GREETINGS AND POLITE EXPRESSIONS

English	Mandarin (ROC)	Transliteration	Pronunciation
Hello	您好	nin2 hao3	nin how
(morning)	早安，您早	tsao3 an1, nin2 hao3	dzow (as in how) ahn, nin dzow
(anytime)	日安，您好	jih4 an1, nin2 hao3	ri (as in rip) ahn, nin how
(evening)	晚安	wan3 an1	wahn ahn
Good-bye	再見	tsai4 chien4	dzy jen
Please	請	ch'ing3	ching
Pleased to meet you.	很高興能認識您	hen3 kao1-hsing4 neng2 jen4-shih nin 2	hun gow-shing nung ren-shi(shi as in ship) nin
Please excuse me.	對不起，抱歉	tui4 pu4 ch'i3, pao4-ch'ien 4	dway boo chee, bow (ow as in how)-chen
Excuse me for a moment. (when leaving a meeting)	對不起，請稍等	tui4 pu4 ch'i3, ch'ing3 shao1 teng3	dway boo chee, ching show (rhymes with how) dung
Congratulations	祝賀您，恭喜您	chu4-ho4 nin2, kung1-hsi3 nin2	jew-her nin, gong-shee nin
Thank you	謝謝，感謝您	hsieh4-hsieh, kan3-hsieh4 nin2	sheh-sheh, gahn-sheh nin
Thank you very much.	非常感謝	fei1-ch'ang2 kan3-hsieh4	fay-chahng gahn-sheh
Thank you for the gift.	謝謝您的禮物	hsieh4-hsieh nin2-te li3-wu4	sheh-sheh nin-duh lee-woo
I am sorry. I don't understand Chinese.	對不起，我不懂中文	tui4 pu4 ch'i3, wo3 pu4 tung3 chung1-wen2	dway boo chee, war boo dong jong-wen
Do you speak English?	你會說英語嗎？	ni3 hui4 shuo1 ying1-yü3 ma?	nee hway shwar ying-yu (French u as in lune) mah?
My name is...	我叫...，我的名字是	wo3 chiao4..., wo3-te ming2-tzu shih4	war jow..., war-duh ming-dzi shi
Is Mr./Ms. ... there? (on the telephone)	...麻煩請找 ...先生/女士	...ma2-fan ch'ing2 chao3... hsien1-sheng/nu3-shih4	...mah-fahn ching-jow... shen-shung/nu (French u)-shi
Can we meet tomorrow?	明天見好嗎？	ming2-t'ien1 chien4 hao3 ma?	ming-tyen jen how mah?
Would you like to have dinner together?	一起吃飯怎麼樣？	i1-ch'i3 ch'ih1-fan4 tsem3-mo yang4?	ee-chee chi(as is chip)-fahn dzem-ma yahng?
Yes	好的	hao3-te	how-duh
No	不行	pu4-hsing2	boo-shing

English	Mandarin (ROC)	Transliteration	Pronunciation

DAY/TIME OF DAY

English	Mandarin (ROC)	Transliteration	Pronunciation
morning	早上，上午	tsao3-shang4, shang4-wu3	dzow shahng, shahng-woo
noon	中午	chung1-wu3	jong-woo
afternoon	下午	hsia4-wu3	shah-woo
evening	傍晚	pang4-wan3	bahng-wahn
night	晚上	wan3-shang4	wahn-shahng
today	今天	chin1-t'ien1	jin-tyen
yesterday	昨天	tso2-t'ien1	dzaw (aw as in draw)-tyen
tomorrow	明天	ming2-t'ien1	ming-tyen
Monday	禮拜一	li3-pai4 i1	lee-buy ee
Tuesday	禮拜二	li3-pai4 erh4	lee-buy err
Wednesday	禮拜三	li3-pai4 san1	lee-buy sahn
Thursday	禮拜四	li3-pai4 szu4	lee-buy si (as in sip)
Friday	禮拜五	li3-pai4 wu3	lee-buy woo
Saturday	禮拜六	li3-pai4 liu4	lee-buy lyoo
Sunday	禮拜日	li3-pai4 jih4	lee-buy ri (as is rip)
holiday	假日	chia4-jih4	jya-ri (as in rip)
New Year's Day	新年，元旦	hsin1 nien2, yuan2 tan4	shin nyen, yuahn dahn
time	時間	shih2-chien1	shi (as in ship)-jen

NUMBERS

English	Mandarin (ROC)	Transliteration	Pronunciation
one	一	i1	ee
two	二	erh4	err
three	三	san1	sahn
four	四	szu4	si (as in sip)
five	五	wu3	woo
six	六	liu4	lyoo
seven	七	ch'i1	chee
eight	八	pa1	bah
nine	九	chiu3	jyoo
ten	十	shih2	shi (as in ship)
eleven	十一	shih2-i1	shi-ee
fifteen	十五	shih2-wu3	shi-woo
twenty	二十	erh4-shih	err-shi
twenty-one	二十一	erh4-shih-i1	err-shi-ee
thirty	三十	san1-shih	sahn-shi
thirty-one	三十一	san1-shih-i1	sahn-shi-ee

English	Mandarin (ROC)	Transliteration	Pronunciation
fifty	五十	wu3-shih	woo-shi
one hundred	一百	i4 pai3	ee-buy
one hundred one	一百零一	i4 pai3 ling2 i1	ee buy ling ee
one thousand	一千	i4 ch'ien1	ee chen
one million	一百萬	i4 pai3 wan4	ee buy wahn
first	第一	ti4-i1	dee-ee
second	第二	ti4-erh4	dee-err
third	第三	ti4-san1	dee-sahn

GETTING AROUND TOWN

English	Mandarin (ROC)	Transliteration	Pronunciation
Where is...?	...在哪裡？	...tsai4 na2-li3 ?	dzy nah-lee?
Does this train go to ...?	這班火車去...嗎？	che4 pan1 huo3-ch'e1 ch'ü4 ...ma?	jay bahn whar-cher chu (French u)...mah?
Please take me to (location)	請送我到...（地點）	ch'ing3 sung4 wo tao4 ...	ching song war dow ...
Where am I?	這是哪裡？	chei4 shi4 na2-li3?	jay shi nah-lee?
airplane	飛機	fei1-chi1	fay-jee
airport	機場	chi1-ch'ang3	jee-chahng
bus (public)	公車	kung1-ch'e1	gong-cher
taxi	計程車	chi4 ch'eng2 ch'e1	jee chung cher
train	火車	huo3-ch'e1	whar (as in war)-cher
train station	火車站	huo3-ch'e1 chan4	whar-cher jahn
ticket	車票	ch'e1-p'iao4	cher-pyow (as in how)
one-way (single) ticket	單程票	tan1-ch'eng2 p'iao4	dahn-chung-pyow
round trip (return) ticket	來回票	lai2-hui2 p'iao4	lie-hway-pyow

PLACES

English	Mandarin (ROC)	Transliteration	Pronunciation
airport	機場	chi1 ch'ang3	jee chahng
bank	銀行	yin2-hang2	yin-hahng
barber shop	理髮店	li3-fa4 tien4	lee-far-dyen
beauty parlor	美容院，髮廊	mei3-jung2 yuan41, fa4-lang2	may-rong ywahn, fah-lahng
business district	商業區	shang1-yeh4 ch'ü1	shahng-ye (as in yet) chu (French u)
chamber of commerce	商會	shang1-hui4	shahng-hway
clothes store	服飾店	fu2-shih4 tien4	foo-shi dyen
exhibition	展覽	chan2-lan3	jahn-lahn
factory	工廠	kung1-ch'ang3	gong-chahng

English	Mandarin (ROC)	Transliteration	Pronunciation
hotel	旅館，賓館	lü2-kuan3, pin1-kuan3	lu (as in French lune)-gwahn, bin-gwahn
hospital	醫院，診所	i1-yuan4, chen2-so3	ee-ywahn, jun-saw
market	市場	shih4-ch'ang3	shi-chahng
post office	郵局	yu2-chu2	yoe (as in Joe)-ju (French u)
restaurant	餐館，餐廳	ts'an1-kuan3, ts'an1-t'ing1	tsahn-gwahn, tsahn-ting
rest room/toilet (W.C.)	盥洗室，衛生間，洗手間，廁所	kuan4-hsi3-shih4, wei4-sheng1-chien1, hsi2-shou3-chien1, ts'e4-so3	gwahn-shee-shi, way-shung-jen, shee-show-jen, tser-saw
sea port	海港，港口，碼頭	hai2-kang3, kang2-k'ou3, ma3-t'ou2	high-gahng, gahng-koe, mah-toe (oe as in Joe)
train station	火車站	huo3-ch'e1 chan4	hwar-cher jahn

At the bank

English	Mandarin (ROC)	Transliteration	Pronunciation
What is the exchange rate?	匯率是多少？	hui4-lü4 shih4 to1 shao3 ?	hway-lu (French u) shi daw show (rhymes with how)?
I want to exchange...	我想換...	wo2 hsiang3 huan4 ...	war shyang hwahn...
Australian dollar	澳幣	ao4 pi4	ow (Rhymes with how)-bee
British pound	英磅	ying1 pang4	ying bahng
Chinese yuan (PRC)	人民幣	jen2-min2 pi4	ren-min bee
French franc	法國法郎	fa4-kuo2 fa4-lang2	far-gwar far-lahng
German mark	德國馬克	te2-kuo2 ma3-k'e4	der-gwaw mah-ker
Hong Kong dollar	港幣	kang3 pi4	gahng bee
Indonesia rupiah	印度尼西亞盧比，印尼盾	yin4-du4-ni2-hsi1-ya4 lu2-pi3, yin4-ni2 tun4	yin-doo-nee-she-ya loo-bee, yin-nee dun (like ou in could)
Japanese yen	日元，日幣	jih4 yuan2, jih4 pi4	ri ywahn, ri bee
Korean won	韓國圓，韓幣	han2-kuo2 yuan2, han2 pi4	hahn-gwar ywahn, hahn bee
Malaysia ringgit	馬來西亞林吉特，馬幣	ma3-lai2-hsi1-ya4 lin2-chi2-t'e4, ma3 pi4	mah-lie-she-ya lin-jee-ter, mah bee
Philippines peso	菲律賓比索	fei1-lu4-pin1 pi2-so3	fay-lu (French u)-bin bee-saw
Singapore dollar	新加坡元	hsin1-chia1-p'o1 yuan2	shin-jar-paw ywahn
New Taiwan dollar (ROC)	新台幣	hsin1 t'ai2 pi4	shin-tie bee
Thailand baht	泰國銖	t'ai4-kuo2 chu1	tie-gwaw joo
U.S. dollar	美元，美金	mei3 yuan2, mei3 chin1	may ywahn, may jin

English	Mandarin (ROC)	Transliteration	Pronunciation
Can you cash a personal check?	可以兌現個人支票嗎？	k'e2-i3 tui4-hsien4 ko4-jen2 chih1-p'iao4 ma?	ker-yee dway-shen ger-ren ji (i as in zip)-pyow mah?
Where should I sign?	我在哪裡簽字？	wo3 tsai4 na2-li3 ch'ien1 tzu4?	war dzy nah-lee chen dzi (i as in zip)?
Traveler check	旅行支票	lü3-hsing2 chih1-p'iao4	lu-(French u) shing ji-pyow
Bank draft	銀行匯票	yin2-hang2 hui4-p'iao4	yin-hahng hway-pyow

At the hotel

I have a reservation.	我已經預訂了房間	wo2 i3-ching1 yü4-ting4 le fang2-chien1	war ee-jing yu (French u) -ding-la fahng-jen
Could you give me a single/ double room?	能給我訂一個單人／雙人房間嗎？	neng2 kei2 wo3 ting4 i2-ko4 tan1-jen2/shuang1-jen2 fang2-chien1 ma?	nung gay waw ding ee-gi (as in give) dahn-ren/ shwahng- ren fahng-jen mah?
Is there...? air-conditioning	有沒有...？空調，冷氣	yu3 mei2 yu3...? k'ung1 t'iao2, leng3 ch'i4	yoe may-yoe...? kong-tyow, lung-chee
heating	暖氣	nuan3 ch'i4	nwahn-chee
private toilet	私人盥洗室	szu1-jen2 kuan4-hsi3 shih4	si(as in sip)-ren gwahn-she shi
hot water	熱水	je4 shui3	rer shway
May I see the room?	我能看一下房間嗎？	wo3 neng2 k'an4 i2-hsia4 fang2-chien1 ma?	waw nung kahn ee-sha fahng-jen mah?
Would you mail this for me please?	您能幫我郵寄這份東西嗎？	nin2 neng2 pang1 wo3 yu2-chi4 che4 fen4 tung1-hsi1 ma?	nin nung bahng waw yoe-jee jay fun dong-she mah?
Do you have any stamps?	您有郵票嗎？	nin2 yu3 yu2-p'iao4 ma?	nin yoe yoe-pyow mah?
May I have my bill?	買單	mai3 tan1	my dahn

At the store

Do you sell...?	這裡有沒有...？	che4-li3 yu3 mei2-yu3...?	jer-lee yoe may-yoe...?
Do you have anything less expensive?	有沒有便宜一點的？	yu3 mei2-yu3 p'ien2-i i4-tien3-te?	yoe may-yoe pyen-ee ee-dyen-duh?
I would like (quantity).	我想要（數量）...	wo2 hsiang3 yao4...	waw shyahng yow...
I'll take it.	我要這件	wo3 yao4 chei4 chien4	waw yow jay jen
I want this one.	我想要這個	wo2 hsiang3-yao4 chei4-ko	waw shyahng-yow jay-guh
When does it open/close?	什麼時候開/關門、打佯？	shem2-mo shih2-hou4 k'ai1/ kuan1 men2, ta3-yang2?	shemma shi-hoe ky/gwahn mun, dah vahng?

English	*Mandarin (ROC)*	*Transliteration*	*Pronunciation*

COUNTRIES

America (USA)	美國	mei3-kuo2	may-gwaw
Australia	澳洲	ao4-chou1	ow-joe
China (PRC)	中國大陸	chung1-kuo2 ta4-lu4	jong-gwaw dah-loo
France	法國	fa4-kuo2	fah-gwaw
Germany	德國	te2-kuo2	der-gwaw
Hong Kong	香港	hsiang1-kang3	shyahng-gahng
Indonesia	印尼	yin4-ni2	yin-nee
Japan	日本	jih4-pen3	ri-bun
Korea	韓國	han2-kuo2	hahn-gwaw
Malaysia	馬來西亞	ma3-lai2-hsi1-ya4	mah-ly-she-yah
Philippines	菲律賓	fei1-lü4-pin1	fay-lu (French u)-bin
Singapore	新加坡	xin1-chia1-p'o1	shin-jyah-paw
Taiwan	台灣 （中華民國）	t'ai2-wan1 (chung1-hua2 min2-guo2)	ty-wahn(jong-hua min-guo)
Thailand	泰國	t'ai4-kuo2	ty-gwaw
United Kingdom	英國	ying1-kuo2	ying-gwaw

EXPRESSIONS IN BUSINESS

1) General business-related terms

accounting	會計	k'uai4-chi4	kwy-jee
additional charge	額外費用	e2-wai4 fei4-yung4	er-wy fay-yong
advertise	登廣告	teng1 kuang3-kao4	dung gwahng-gow (as in how)
advertisement	廣告	kuang3-kao4	gwahng-gow
bankrupt	破產	p'o4-ch'an3	paw-chahn
brand name	商標	shang1-piao1	shahng-byow
business	公司	kung1-szu1	gong-si
buyer	買方	mai3-fang1	my fahng
capital	資金，資本	tzu1-chin1, tzu1-pen3	dzi (as in zip)-jin, dzi-bun
cash	現金	hsien4-chin1	shen-jin
charge	記帳	chi4-chang4	jee-jahng
check	支票	chih1-p'iao4	ji-pwow
claim	索賠	so3-pei2	saw-bay
collect	收帳	shou1-chang4	show-jahng
commission	傭金，回扣	yung1-chin1, hui2-k'ou	yong-jin, hway-co
company	公司	kung1-szu1	gong-si

English	Mandarin (ROC)	Transliteration	Pronunciation
copyright	版權	pan3-ch'uan2	bahn-chwahn
corporation	股份有限公司	ku3-fen4 yu3-hsien4 kung1-szu1	goo-fun yoe-shen gong-si
cost (expense)	費用	fei4-yung4	fay-yoong
currency	貨幣	huo4-pi4	hwaw-bee
customer	客戶	k'o4-hu4	ker-hoo
D/A (documents against acceptance)	承兌交單	ch'eng2-tui4 chiao1-tan1	chung (as in lung)-dway jyow-dahn
D/P (documents against payment)	付款交單	fu4-k'uan3 chiao1-tan1	foo-kwahn jyow-dahn
deferred payment	延期付款	yan2-ch'i1 fu4-k'uan3	yen-chee foo-kwahn
deposit	存款	ts'un2-k'uan3	tsoun (ou as in could)-kwahn
design	設計	she4-chi4	sher-jee
discount	折扣	che2-k'ou4	jer-koe
distribution	分配	fen1-p'ei4	fun-pay
dividends	紅利	hung2-li4	hong-lee
documents	文件	wen2-chien4	wun-jen
due date	到期日	tao4 ch'i1 jih4	dow chee ri
exhibit	展覽	chan2-lan3	jahn-lahn
ex works	工廠交貨	kung1-ch'ang3 chiao1-huo4	gong-chahng jyow-hwaw
facsimile (fax)	傳眞	ch'uan2-chen1	chwahn-jun
finance	財務，金融	ts'ai2-wu4, chin1-jung2	tsy-woo, jin-rong
foreign businessman	外商	wai4 shang1	wy-shahng
foreign capital	外資	wai4 tzu1	wy-dzi
foreign currency	外國貨幣	wai4-guo2 huo4-pi4	wy-gwaw hwaw-bee
foreign trade	對外貿易	tui4-wai4 mao4-i4	dway-wy-mow (rhymes with how)-ee
government	政府	cheng4-fu3	jung-foo
industry	工業	kung1-yeh4	gong-yeh
inspection	檢查	chien3-ch'a2	jen-chah
insurance	保險	pao2-hsien3	bow-shen
interest	利息	li4-hsi1	lee-shee
international	國際的	kuo2-chi4-te	gwaw-jee-duh
joint venture	合資	ho2-tzu1	her-dzi
label:	標籤	piao1-ch'ien1	byow (rhymes with how)-chen

English	Mandarin (ROC)	Transliteration	Pronunciation
letter of credit	信用狀	hsin4-yung4 chuang4	shin-yong jwahng
license	許可，執照	hsü2-k'o3, chih2-chao4	shu (French u)-ker, ji-jow (rhymes with how)
loan	貸款	tai4-k'uan3	dy-kwahn
model (of a product)	產品模型	ch'an2-p'in3 mo2-hsing2	chahn-pin maw-shing
monopoly	壟斷，公賣	lung3-tuan4, kung1-mai4	long-dwahn, gong-my
office	辦公室	pan4-kung1-shih4	bahn-gong-shi
patent	專利	chuan1-li4	jwahn-lee
pay	支付	chih1-fu4	ji-foo
payment for goods	貨款	huo4-k'uan3	hwaw-kwahn
payment by installment	分期付款	fen1-ch'i1 fu4-k'uan3	fun-chee foo-kwahn
permit	執照	chih2-chao4	ji-jow
principal	本金	pen3-chin1	bun-jin
private (not government)	民營（非政府性）	min2-ying2 (fei1 cheng4-fu3-hsing4)	min-ying (fay jung-foo-shing)
product:	產品	ch'an2-p'in3	chahn-pin
profit margin	獲利率	huo4-li4 lü4	hwaw-lee lu (French u)
registration	註冊	chu4-ts'e4	jew-tser
report	報告	pao4-kao4	bow-gow (both as in how)
research and development (R&D)	研究與發展	yen2-chiu1 yü3 fa1-chan3	yen-jew yu (French u) fah-jahn
return (on investment)	回收（投資）	hui2-shou1 (t'ou2-tzu1)	hway-show (as in low) (toe-dzi)
sample	樣品	yang4-p'in3	yahng-pin
seller	賣方	mai4-fang1	my-fahng
settle accounts	結帳	chieh2 chang4	jyeh-jahng
service charge	服務費	fu2-wu4 fei4	foo-woo-fay
sight draft	即期匯票	chi2-ch'i1 hui4-p'iao4	jee-chee hway-pyow
tax	稅	shui4	shway
telephone	電話	tien4-hua4	dyen-hwah
telex	電傳	tien4-ch'uan2	dyen-chwahn
trademark	商標	shang1-piao1	shahng-byow
visa	Visa信用卡，簽帳卡	Visa hsin4-yung4 k'a3, ch'ien1-chang4 k'a3	Visa shin-yong car, chen-jahng car

English	Mandarin (ROC)	Transliteration	Pronunciation
2) Labor			
compensation	薪資	hsin1-tzu1	shin-dzi
employee	職員	chih2-yuan2	ji-yuahn
employer	僱主， 老板	ku4-chu3, 1 ao2-pan3	goo-joo, low (as in how)-bahn
dismiss	解僱	chieh3-ku4	jyeh-goo
foreign worker	外籍勞工	wai4-chi2 lao2-kung1	wy-jee low (as in how)-gong
hire	僱用，聘請	ku4-yung4, p'in4-ch'ing3	gew-yong, pin-ching
immigration	移民	i2-min2	ee-min
interview	面試	mien4-shih4	myen-shi
laborer	勞工	lao2-kung1	low (as in how)-gong
skilled	熟手	shu2-shou3	shew-show (as in low)
unskilled	生手	sheng1-shou3	shung-show
labor force	勞動力	lao2-tung4 li4	low (as in how)-dong lee
labor shortage	勞力短缺	lao2-li4 tuan3-ch'üeh1	low-lee dwahn-chweh
labor stoppage	停工	t'ing2 kung1	ting-gong
labor surplus	勞力過剩	lao2-li4 kuo4-sheng4	low-lee gwor-shung
minimum wage	最低工資	tsui4 ti1 kung1-tzu1	dzway dee gong-dzi
profession/ occupation	專業	chuan1-yeh4	jwahn-yeh
salary	薪資	hsin1-tzu1	shin-dzi
strike	罷工	pa4-kung1	bar-gong
training	在職培訓	tsai4 chih2 p'ei2-hsün4	dzy-ji pay-shun (French u)
union	工會	kung1-hui4	gong-hway
wage	工資	kung1-tzu1	gong-dzi
3) Negotiations (Buying / Selling)			
agreement	協議	hsieh2-i4	shyeh-ee
arbitrate	仲裁	chung4-ts'ai2	jong-tsy
brochure/ pamphlet	手冊，小冊子	shou3-ts'e4, hsiao3 ts'e4-tzu	show-tser, shyow (ow as in how) tser- dzi
buy	買	mai3	my
confirm	確認	ch'ueh4-jen4	chweh-ren
contract	合同，契約	ho2-t'ung2, ch'i4-yueh1	her-tong, cheey-yweh

English	Mandarin (ROC)	Transliteration	Pronunciation
cooperate	合作	ho2-tso4	her-dzwor
cost	價值	chia4-chih2	jyar-ji
counteroffer	還價，出價	huan2-chia4, ch'u1-chia4	hwahn-jyar, chew-jyar
countersign	會簽	hui4 ch'ien1	hway chen
deadline	截止日期	chieh2-chih3 jih4-ch'i1	jyeh-ji ri-chee
demand	要求	yao1-ch'iu2	yow (ow as in how)-chyo (o as in go)
estimate	估計，預計	ku1-chi4, yü4-chi4	gew-jee, yu (French u)-jee
guarantee	保證	pao3-cheng4	bow (ow as in how)-jung
label	標簽	piao1-ch'ien1	byow-chen
license	許可證	hsü2-k'o3 cheng4	shu (French u)-ker jung
market	市場	shih4-ch'ang3	shi (as in ship)-chahng
market price	市價	shih4 chia4	shi-jyah
minimum quantity	最少訂購量	tsui4 shao3 ting4-kou4 liang4	dzway show (as in how) ding-go lyahng
negotiate	談判	t'an2-p'an4	tahn-pahn
negotiate payment	付款談判	fu4-k'uan3 t'an2-p'an4	foo-kwahn tahn-pahn
order	訂單	ting4-tan1	ding-dahn
packaging	包裝	pao1-chuang1	bow (as in how)-jwahng
place an order	發出訂單	fa1-ch'u1 ting4-tan1	fah-choo ding-dahn
price	價格	chia4-ko2	jyah-ger
price list:	價格表，報價表	chia4-ko2 piao3, pao4 chia4 piao3	jyah-ger byow, bow-jyah byow
product features	產品特點	ch'an2-pin3 t'e4 tien3	chahn-pin ter-dyen
product line	產品系列	ch'an2-pin3 hsi4-lieh4	chahn-pin shee-lyeh
quality	質量，品質	chih4-liang4, p'in3-chih4	ji-lyahng, pin-ji
quantity	數量	shu4-liang4	shoo-lyahng
quota	配額	p'ei4-e2	pay-er
quote (offer)	報價	pao4-chia4	bow-jyah
sale	銷售	hsiao1-shou4	shyow (as in how)-show (as in low)
sales confirmation	銷售確認書	hsiao1-shou4 ch'üeh4-jen4-shu1	shyow-show chweh-ren shoo
sell	銷售	hsiao1-shou4	shyow-show
sign	簽署	ch'ien1-shu3	chyen-shoo

English	Mandarin (ROC)	Transliteration	Pronunciation
signature	簽字	ch'ien1-zi4	chyen-dzi
specifications	規格	kuei1-ko2	gway-ger
standard (quality)	標準（質量，品質）	piao1-chun3 (chih4-liang4, p'in3-chih4	byow-jwun (chih-lyahng, pin-ji)
superior (quality)	優質	yu1-chih4	yow (as in low)-ji
trade	貿易	mao4-i4	mow (as in how)-ee
unit price	單價	tan1 chia4	dahn-jyah
value	價值	chia4-chih2	jyah-ji
value added:	增值，加值	tseng1-chih2, chia1-chih2	dzung-ji, jyah-ji
warranty (and services)	保證書（及服務）	pao3-cheng4-shu1 (chi2 fu2-wu4)	bow-jung-shoo (jee foo-woo)
The price is too high.	價錢太高	chia4-ch'ien2 t'ai4 kao1	jyah-chen ty gow
We need a faster delivery.	我們交貨要盡快	wo3-men chiao1-huo4 yao4 chin4 k'uai4	warm'n jyow-hwaw k'uai yow jin- kwy
We need it by...	我們需在...之前收到	wo3-men hsü1 tsai4 ... chih1 ch'ien2 shou1-tao4 shou1-tao4	warm'n dzy...ji-chen show (as in low) -dow (as in how)
We need a better quality.	我們要比這個品質更好的	wo3-men yao4 pi3 che4 ko4 p'in3-zhi4 keng4 hao3 te	warm'n yow (as in how) bee jay-guh pin-ji gung how-duh
We need it to these specifications.	我們要符合這個規格的產品	wo3-men yao4 fu2-ho2 che4 ko4 kuei1 -ke2 tech'an2-p'in3	warm'n yow foo-her jay-ger gway-ger duh chahn-pin
I want to pay less.	我想要少付點	wo2 hsiang3-yao4 shao3 fu4 tie'rh3	war shyahng-yow show (both as in how) foo yee-diahr
I want the price to include	我希望這個價錢包括	wo3 hsi1-wang4 che4-ko chia4-ch'ien2 pao1-k'uo4	war shee-wahng jay-guh jyah-chen bow-kor
Can you guarantee delivery?	您能保證交貨時間嗎？	nin2 neng2 pao3-cheng4 chiao4-huo4 shih2-chien1 ma?	nin nung bow-jung jyow-hwaw shi-jyen mah

4) Products/Industries

English	Mandarin (ROC)	Transliteration	Pronunciation
aluminum	鋁	lü3	lu (French u)
automobile	汽車	ch'i4-ch'e1	chee-cher
automotive accessories	汽車零件	ch'i4-ch'e1 ling2-chien4	chee-cher ling-jen
biotechnology	生物科技學	sheng1-wu4 k'o1-chi4-hsueh2	shung-woo ker-jee-shweh
camera	照相機	chao4-hsiang4-chi1	jow-shyahng-jee

English	Mandarin (ROC)	Transliteration	Pronunciation
carpets	地毯	ti4-t'an3	dee-tahn
cement	水泥	shui3-ni2	shway-nee
ceramics	瓷器	tz'u2-ch'i4	tsi-chee
chemicals	化學品	hua4-hsueh2-p'in3	hwah-shweh-pın
clothing	服裝，服飾	fu2-chuang1, fu2-shih4	foo-jwahng, foo-shi
for women	女裝	nü3-chuang1	nu (French u)-jwahng
for men	男裝	nan2-chuang1	nahn-jwahng
for children	童裝	t'ung2-chuang1	tong-jwahng
coal	煤	mei2	may
computer	電腦	tien4-nao3	dyen-now (as in how)
computer hardware	電腦硬體	tien4-nao3 ying4-t'i3	dyen-now ying tee
computer software	電腦軟體	tien4-nao3 juan2-t'i3	dyen-now rwahn-tee
construction	建築	chien4-chu4	jyen-joo
electrical equipment	電器設備	tien4-ch'i4 she4-pei4	dyen-chee sher-bay
electronics	電子	tien4-tzu3	dyen-dzi
engineering	工程	kung1-ch'eng2	gong-chung
fireworks	鞭炮	pien4-p'ao4	byen-pow
fishery products	漁業產品	yü2-yeh4 ch'an2-pin3	yu (French u)-yeh chahn-pin
food products	食品	shih2-p'in3	shi-pin
footwear	鞋類	hsieh2-lei4	shyeh-lay
forestry products	林業產品	lin2-yeh4 ch'an2-p'in3	lin-yeh chahn-pin
fuel	燃料	jan2-liao4	rahn-lyow
furniture	家俱	chia1-chü4	jyah-ju (French u)
games	遊戲	yu2-hsi4	yoe-shee
gas	瓦斯	wa3-szu1	wah-si
gemstone	寶石	pao3-shih2	bow (as in how)-shi
glass	玻璃	po1-li2	bor-lee
gold	金器	chin1-ch'i4	jin-chee
hardware	五金類	wu3-chin1-lei4	woo-jin-lay
iron	鐵	t'ieh3	tyeh

English	Mandarin (ROC)	Transliteration	Pronunciation
jewelry	珠寶	chu1-pao3	joo-bow (as in how)
lighting fixtures	燈飾	teng1-shih4	dung-shi
leather goods	皮製品	p'i2-chih4-p'in3	pee-ji-pin
machinery	機械	chi1-hsieh4	jee-shyeh
minerals	礦物質	k'uang4-wu4-chih4	kwahng-woo-ji
musical instruments	樂器	yueh4-ch'i4	yweh-chee
paper	紙張	chih3-chang1	ji-jahng
petroleum	石油	shih2-yu2	shi-yoe
pharmaceuticals	藥物	yao4-wu4	yow (as in how)-woo
plastics	塑膠	su4-chiao1	soo-jyow
pottery	陶器	t'ao2-ch'i4	tow-chee
rubber	橡膠	hsiang4-chiao1	shyahng-jyow
silk	絲綢	szu1-ch'ou2	si-choe
silver	銀器	yin2-ch'i4	yin-chee
spare parts	零件，配件	ling2-chien4, p'ei4-chien4	ling-jyen, pay-jyen
sporting goods	運動用品	yün4-tung4 yung4-p'in3	yune (French u)-dong yong-pin
steel	鋼	kang1	gahng
telecommunication equipment	電訊設備	tien4-hsün4 she4-pei4	dyen-shoon sher-bay
television	電視	tien4-shih4	dyen-shi
textiles	紡織品	fang3-chih1-p'in3	fahng-ji-pin
tobacco	煙草	yen1-ts'ao3	yen-tsow (as in how)
tools:	工具	kung1-chü4	gong-ju (French u)
hand (powered)	手動	shou3-tung4	show (as in low)-dong
power	電力	tien4-li4	dyen-lee
tourism	旅遊	lü3-yu2	lu (French u)-yoe
toys	玩具	wan2-chü4	wahn-ju (French u)
watches/clocks	手錶/鐘	shou2-piao3/chung1	show (as in low)-byow (as in how)/jong
wood	木材	mu4-ts'ai2	moo-tsy

English	Mandarin (ROC)	Transliteration	Pronunciation
5) Services			
accounting service	會計服務	k'uai4-chi4 fu2-wu4	kwy-jee foo-woo
advertising agency	廣告商	kuang3-kao4 shang1	gwahng-gow shahng
agent	代理人	tai4-li3-jen2	dy-lee-ren
customs broker	報關行	pao4-kuan1-hang2	bow (as in how)-gwahn-hahng
distributor	經銷商	ching1-hsiao1 shang1	jing-shyow-shahng
employment agency	職業介紹所	chih2-yeh4 chieh4-shao4-so3	ji-yeh jyeh-show(as in how) sore
exporter	出口商	ch'u1-k'ou3-shang1	chew-ko-shahng
freight forwarder	發運代理人	fa1-yün4 tai4-li3-jen2	fah-yun (French u) dy-lee-ren
importer	進口商	chin4-k'ou3-shang1	jin-ko-shahng
manufacturer	製造商	chih4-tsao4-shang1	ji-dzow (as in how) shahng
packing service	包裝服務	pao1-chuang1 fu2-wu4	bow-jwahng foo-woo
printing company	印刷公司	yin4-shua1 kung1-szu1	yin-shwah gong-si
retailer	零售商	ling2-shou4-shang1	ling-show-shahng
service(s)	服務	fu2-wu4	foo-woo
supplier	供應商	kung4-ying4-shang1	gong-ying-shahng
translation services	翻譯服務	fan1-i4 fu2-wu4	fahn-ee foo-woo
wholesaler	批發商	p'i1-fa-shang1	pee-fah-shahng
6) ShippingTransportation			
bill of lading	提單	t'i2-tan1	tee-dahn
cost, insurance, freight (CIF)	到岸價	tao4-an4-chia4	dow-ahn-jyah
customs	海關	hai3-kuan1	high-gwahn
customs duty	關稅	kuan1-shui4	gwahn-shway
date of delivery	交貨日期	chiao1-huo4 jih4-ch'i1	jyow (as in how)-hwor ri-chee
deliver (delivery)	交貨	chiao1-huo4	jyow-hwor
export	出口	ch'u1-k'ou3	choo-kow (rhymes with low)

English	Mandarin (ROC)	Transliteration	Pronunciation
first class mail	第一類郵件	ti4-i1 lei4 yu2-chien4	dee-ee lay yoe-jyen
free on board (F.O.B.)	船上交貨價格（離岸價）	ch'uan2-shang4 chiao1-huo4 chia4-ko2 (li2-an4 chia4)	chwahn-shahng jyow-hwor jyah-ger (lee-ahn jyah)
freight	運費	yün4-fei4	yune-fay
import	進口	chin4-k'ou3	jin-kow (rhymes with low)
in bulk	散裝	san3-chuang1	sahn-jwahng
mail (post)	郵寄	yu2-chi4	yoe-jee
country of origin	原產地	yuan2 ch'an3 ti4	ywahn chahn dee
packing	包裝	pao1-chuang1	bow (rhymes with how)-jwahng
packing list	裝箱單	chuang1-hsiang1-tan1	jwahng-shyahng- dahn
port	港口	kang2-k'ou3	gahng-kow (rhymes with low)
ship (to send):	發貨	fa1-huo4	fah-hwor
by air	空運	k'ung1-yün4	kong-yune
by sea	海運	hai3-yün4	high-yune
by train	火車運輸	huo3-ch'e1 yün4-shu1	hwor-cher yune-shoo
by truck	卡車運輸	k'a3-ch'e1 yün4-shu1	kah-cher yune-shoo

WEIGHTS, MEASURES, AMOUNTS

English	Mandarin (ROC)	Transliteration	Pronunciation
barrel	桶	t'ung3	tung
bushel	蒲士爾	p'u2-shih4-erh3	poo-shi-err
centimeter	厘米，公分	li2-mi3, kung1-fen1	lee-mee, gong-fun
dozen	一打（十二個）	i1-ta2 (shih2-erh4-ko4)	ee-dah (shi-err- guh)
foot	英尺	ying1-ch'ih3	ying-chi
gallon	加侖	chia1-lun2	jar-loun (ou as in would)
gram	公克	kung1-k'o4	gong-ker
gross (144 pieces)	羅	lo2	law
gross weight	毛重	mao2-chung4	mow (rhymes with how)-jong
hectare	公頃	kung1-ch'ing3	gong-ching
hundred (100)	一百	i4-pai3	ee-bye
inch	英寸	ying1-ts'un4	ying-tsoun (ou as in would)

English	Mandarin (ROC)	Transliteration	Pronunciation
kilogram	公斤	kung1-chin1	gong-jin:
kilometer	公里， 千公尺	kung1-li3, ch'ien1 kung1-ch'ih3	gong-lee, chyen gong-chi
meter	米	mi3	mee
net weight	淨重	ching4-chung4	ching-jong
mile (English)	英里	ying1-li3	ying-lee
liter	升	sheng1	shung
ounce	盎司	ang4-szu1	ahng-si
pint	品脫	p'in3-t'uo1	pin-taw (rhymes with saw)
pound (weight measure avoirdupois)	磅（常衡重量）	pang4 (ch'ang2-heng2 chung4-liang4)	bahng (chahng-hung jong-lyahng)
quart (avoirdupois)	夸脫	k'ua4-t'o1	kwah-taw
square meter	平方公尺	p'ing2-fang1 kung1-ch'ih3	ping-fahng gong-chi
square yard	平方碼	p'ing2-fang1 ma3	ping-fahng mah
size	尺寸	ch'ih3-ts'un4	chi-tsoun (ou as in would)
ton	噸	tun1	doun (ou as in would)
yard	碼	ma3	mah
jin (Chinese pound)	斤	chin1	jin
liang (Chinese ounce)	兩	liang3	liahng
ts'un (Chineseinch)	寸	ts'un4	tsoun
ch'ih (Chinese foot)	尺	ch'ih3	chi (as in chip)

TAIWAN-SPECIFIC ORGANIZATIONAL TITLES

board of directors	理事會，董事會	li3-shih4-hui4, tung3-shih4-hui4	lee-shi-hway, dong-shi-hway
chairman	理事長， 董事長	li3-shih4-chang3, tung3-shih4-chang3	lee-shi-jahng, dong-shi-jahng
manager	經理	ching1-li3	jing-lee
(assistant manager)	副經理	fu4-ching1-li3	foo-jing-lee
president	總裁，董事長	tsung3-ts'ai2, tung3-shih4-chang3	dzong-tsy, dong-shi-jahng
vice president	副總裁，副董事長	fu4 tsung3-ts'ai2, fu4 tung3-shih4-chang3	foo-dzong-tsy, foo-dong-shi-jahng

English	*Mandarin (ROC)*	*Transliteration*	*Pronunciation*

TAIWAN-SPECIFIC EXPRESSIONS AND TERMS

You are welcome	不客氣	pu2 k'o4-ch'i4	boo ker-chee
It doesn't matter	沒關係	mei2 kuan1-hsi4	may gwahn-shee
Please do not smoke	請勿抽煙	ch'ing3 wu4 ch'ou1 yen1	ching woo chow (rhymes with grow)-yen
Have a nice trip	旅途愉快	lü3-t'u2 yü2-k'uai4	lu (French u)-too yu (French u)-kwy

COMMON SIGNS

Please do not disturb: (sign to put on the door of hotel room)	請勿打擾	ch'ing3 wu4 ta2-jao3	ching woo dah-row (rhymes with now)
Enter	入口	ju4 k'ou3	roo-kow (rhymes with low)
Exit	出口	ch'u1 k'ou3	choo-kow (as above)
Men	男廁所 （男盥洗室）	nan2 ts'e4-so3 (nan2 kuan4-hsi3-shih4)	nahn tser-sore (nahn gwahn-shee-shi)
Women	女廁所 （女盥洗室）	nü3 ts'e4-so3 (nü3 kuan4-hsi3-shih4)	nu (French u) tser-sore (nu gwahn-shee-shi)
No smoking	禁止吸煙	chin4-chih3 hsi1-yen1	jin-ji shee-yen
Handle with care	小心輕放	hsiao3-hsin1 ch'ing1 fang4	shyow (rhymes with now)-shin ching fahng

Important Addresses

GOVERNMENT

GOVERNMENT AGENCIES

Central Trust of China
49 Wu Chang Street
Section 1, Taipei, Taiwan
TEL [886](2) 311-1151; FAX [886](2) 311-8107

Civil Aeronautics Administration
Sungshan Airport
Taipei
Tel: (2) 5142458 Fax: (2) 7175828

Council for Economic Planning and Development,
Executive Yuan
9/F., 87 Nanking E. Rd.
Sec. 2, Taipei
Tel: (2) 5225300, 5513522 Fax: (2) 5519011
Tlx: 11385

Council for Labor Affairs, Executive Yuan
5/F., 232 Min Shen E. Rd.
Sec. 3, Taipei
Tel: (2) 7182512 Fax: (2) 5149240/2

Council of Agriculture, Executive Yuan
37 Nan Hai Rd.
Taipei
Tel: (2) 3812997 Fax: (2) 3812991

Council of Cultural Planning and Development
102 Aikuo E. Rd.
Taipei
Tel: (2) 3518030 Fax: (2) 3222937

Department of Health
100 Aikuo E. Rd.
Taipei
Tel: (2) 3210151 Fax: (2) 3122907

Directorate General of Budget, Accounting &
Statistics, Executive Yuan
1 Chung Hsiao E. Rd.
Sec. 1, Taipei
Tel: (2) 3915231

Directorate General of Post
55 Chinshan S. Rd.
Sec. 2, Taipei
Tel: (2) 3969111 Fax: (2) 3911209

Directorate General of Telecommunications
31 Aikuo E. Rd.
Taipei
Tel: (2) 3443601 Fax: (2) 3223738

Environmental Protection Administration,
Executive Yuan
1 Hsiang Yang Rd.
Taipei
Tel: (2) 3117722 Fax: (2) 3116071

Fair Trade Commission, Executive Yuan
8-12/F., 150 Tun Hwa N. Rd.
Taipei
Tel: (2) 5455501 Fax: (2) 5450107

Foreigners' Service Center
Taipei Municipal Police Headquarters
96 Yen Ping S. Rd.
Taipei
Tel: (2) 3818341

Government Information Office,
Executive Yuan
2 Tien Chin St.
Taipei
Tel: (2) 3419211, 3228888
Fax: (2) 3920923, 3416252

Hsinchu Science-Based Industrial Park
3 Shing An Rd.
Hsinchu
Tel: (35) 773310 Fax. (35) 776222
Tlx: 32188 NSCSITA

Hualien Harbour Bureau
66 Hai-Ann Rd.
Hualien
Tel: (3) 8325131/8 Fax: (3) 8333757 Tlx: 3609

Inspectorate General of Customs
85 Hsinsheng S. Rd.
Sec. 1, Taipei
Tel: (2) 7413181 Fax: (2) 7114166

International Cooperation Department
15 Foochow St.
Taipei
Tel: (2) 3918198 Fax: (2) 3213275

Kaohsiung City Government
Bureau of Labor Affairs
132 Chung Shang 3rd. Rd.
Kaohsiung
Tel: (7) 3312872 Fax: (7) 3330377

Kaohsiung City Government
Department of Reconstruction
2 Szewei 3rd Rd.
Kaohsiung
Tel: (7) 3368333

Kaohsiung Export Processing Zone
2 Chung 1st Rd.
Kaohsiung
Tel: (7) 8217141/9 Fax: (7) 8310897

Keelung Harbour Bureau
Port Building
Keelung
Tel: (2) 4236911 Fax: (2) 4284811/2

Ministry of Economic Affairs
15 Fu Chou St.
Taipei
Tel: (2) 3212200 Fax: (2) 3919398

Ministry of Economic Affairs
Anti-Counterfeiting Committee
1 Hu Kou St.
Taipei
Tel: (2) 3510271, 3210561 Fax: (2) 3212827
Tlx:- 11434

Ministry of Economic Affairs
Board of Foreign Trade
1 Hu Kou St.
Taipei
Tel: (2) 3510271, 3510286
Fax: (2) 3315387, 3513603, 3517080

Ministry of Economic Affairs
Bureau of Commodity Inspection and Quarantine
4 Tsi Nan Rd.
Sec. 1, Taipei
Tel: (2) 3512141 Fax: (2) 3932324 Tlx: 27247

Ministry of Economic Affairs
Industrial Development and Investment
Commission
10/F., 7 Roosevelt Rd.
Sec.1, Taipei
Tel: (2) 3947213 Fax: (2) 3926835

Ministry of Economic Affairs
Industrial Development Bureau
41-3 Hsin Yi Rd.
Sec. 3, Taipei
Tel: (2) 7541255 Fax: (2) 7030160

Ministry of Economic Affairs
International Corporation Department
15 Fu Chou St.
Taipei
Tel: (2) 3918198 Fax: (2) 3213275

Ministry of Economic Affairs
Investment Commission
8/F., 7 Roosevelt Rd.,
Sec. 1, Taipei
Tel: (2) 3513151 Fax: (2) 3963970

Ministry of Economic Affairs
Kaohsiung Export Processing Zone Administration
600 Chiachang Rd., Nantze
Kaohsiung
Tel: (7) 3611212 Fax: (2) 3614348

Ministry of Economic Affairs
Medium and Small Business Administration
3/F., 368 Fu Hsing N. Rd.
Sec. 1, Taipei
Tel: (2) 7049470 Fax: (2) 7054409

Ministry of Economic Affairs
National Bureau of Standards
3/F., 185 Hsin Hai Rd.
Sec. 2, Taipei
Tel: (2) 7380007

Ministry of Economic Affairs
Taipei Export Processing Zone Administration
7/F., 90 Nan Yang St.
Taipei
Tel: (2) 3310012 Fax: (2) 3314520

Ministry of Education
5 Chungshan S. Rd.
Taipei
Tel: (2) 3513111 Fax: (2) 3966803 Tlx: 10894

Ministry of Finance
2 Ai Kuo W. Rd.
Taipei
Tel: (2) 3228000 Fax: (2) 3965829

Ministry of Finance
Inspectorate General of Customs
4/F., 131 Nanking E. Rd.
Sec. 3 Taipei
Tel: (2) 7169219

Ministry of Finance
National Tax Administration
547 Chung Hsiao E. Rd.
Sec. 4, Taipei
Tel: (2) 7631313 Fax: (2) 7617698, 7644520

Ministry of Finance
Securities & Exchange Commission
12/F., 3 Nan Hai Rd.
Taipei
Tel: (2) 3928572, 3413101
Fax: (2) 3634950, 3948249

Ministry of Foreign Affairs
2 Chieh Shou Rd.
Taipei
Tel: (2) 3119292 Fax: (2) 3144972 Tlx: 11299

Ministry of Justice
130 Chungking S. Rd.
Sec. 1, Taipei 10036
Tel: (2) 3146871 Fax: (2) 3896759

Ministry of the Interior
107 Roosevelt Rd.
Sec. 4, Taipei
Tel: (2) 3625241

Ministry of the Interior
Bureau of Entry & Exit
172-1 Poai Rd.
Taipei
Tel: (2) 3710380

Ministry of the Interior
Copyright Committee
107 Roosevelt Rd.
Sec. 4, Taipei
Tel: (2) 3625241 Fax: (2) 3634950, 3628354

Ministry of Transportation and Communications
2 Changsha St.
Sec. 1, Taipei
Tel: (2) 3112661, 3492900 Fax: (2) 3118587

Ministry of Transportation and Communications
Tourism Bureau
9/F., 280 Chung Hsiao E. Rd.
Sec. 4, Taipei
Tel: (2) 7218541, 7313679 Fax: (2) 7118241

Nantze Export Processing Zone
600 Chia Chang Rd., Nan Tze
Kaohsiung
Tel: (7) 3611212 Fax: (7) 3614348

Overseas Chinese Affairs Commission
30 Kungyuan Rd.
Taipei
Tel: (2) 3810039 Fax: (2) 3313392

Taichung Export Processing Zone
1 Chien Kuo Rd., Tantze Hsiang
Taichung
Tel: (4) 5322113/7 Fax: (4) 5322200

Taichung Harbour Bureau
Harbour Building, Wuchi
Taichung District
Tel: (4) 6562611

Taipei City Government
Bureau of Labor Affairs
8/F., Di Hua Street
Sec. 1, Taipei
Tel: (2) 5210506 Fax: (2) 5429331

Taipei City Government
Department of Reconstruction
39 Chang An W. Rd.
Taipei
Tel: (2) 5413411/9

Taiwan Provincial Government
Department of Labor Affairs
Liming New Village
Taichung
Tel: (4) 25415120

Taiwan Provincial Government
Department of Reconstruction
4 Shen Fu Rd., Chung Hsin Village
Nantou
Tel: (4) 9312954

OVERSEAS DIPLOMATIC MISSIONS OF TAIWAN

See also: CETRA, FETS, MOEA Offices Overseas

Costa Rica
Embassy of the Republic of China
Del I.C.E. de San Pedro
700 Metros Sur Carretera Lateral Izquierda
(Contiguo bar Zapoticos)
San Jose, Costa Rica C.A.
Postal address: Apartado 907-1000, Costa Rica C.A.
Tel: [506] 2481880

Korea
Embassy of the Republic of China
#83, 2-ka, Myung Dong, Chung-gu
Seoul, Rep. of Korea
Tel: [82] (2) 776-4392
Consulate-General (Pusan)
PO Box 736
Pusan, Rep. of Korea
Tel: [82] (51) 246-3617

Panama
Embassy of the Republic of China
Apartado 4285
Panama 5, Rep. of Panama
Tel: [507] 233424

South Africa
Embassy of the Republic of China
1147 Schoeman St.
Hatfield, Pretoria 0083, South Africa
Tel: [27] (12) 437946

Consulate-General (Cape Town)
PO Box 1122
Cape Town 8000, South Africa
Tel: [27] (21) 4181188

Consulate-General (Johannesburg)
10/F., Safren House
19 Ameshhoff St.
Braamfontein
Johannesburg 2001, South Africa
Tel: [27] (11) 3398147

FOREIGN DIPLOMATIC MISSIONS
IN TAIWAN

*See also: Foreign Chambers of Commerce &Business
Organizations*

Costa Rica
Embassy of the Republic of Costa Rica
1/F., 108 Chung Cheng Rd.
Sec. 2, Taipei
Tel: (2) 8712422 Fax: (2) 8711415

Dominican Republic
Embassy of the Dominican Republic
110 Chung Cheng Rd.
Sec. 2, Taipei
Tel: (2) 8717939 Fax: (2) 8722151
Tlx: 19873 EMBAJADOR

Panama
Embassy of the Republic of Panama
5/F., 13 Teh Huei St.
Taipei
Tel: (2) 5968563/4 Fax: (2) 5927145
Tlx: 25738 CONSULPA

South Africa
Embassy of the Republic of South Africa
13/F., 205 Tun Hwa N. Rd.
Taipei
Tel: (2) 7153251 Fax: (2) 7123214 Tlx: 21744

GOVERNMENT RUN CORPORATIONS

Aluminum Corporation [Taiwan]
11, Chengkung 11 Rd.
Kaohsiung
Tel: (7) 3351141

BES Engineering Corporation
4/F., 320 Chunghsiao E. Rd.
Taipei
Tel: (2) 7314901 Fax: (2) 7314901

Chung Hsing Paper Corporation [Taiwan]
10/F., 35 Kuanfu S. Rd.
Taipei
Tel: (2) 7673171 Fax: (2) 7659026

Euro-Asia Trade Organization
4/F., 1 Hsuchou Rd.
Taipei
Tel: (2) 3932115 Fax: (2) 3928393

Fertilizer Co. Ltd. [Taiwan]
6-11/F., 90 Nanking E. Rd.
Sec. 2, Taipei
Tel: (2) 5422231 Fax: (2) 5634597

Kaohsiung Ammonium Sulfate Corporation, Ltd.
100-2 Chungshan 3rd Rd.
Kaohsiung
Tel: (7) 3319369 Fax: (7) 3352346

Machinery Manufacturing Corporation [Taiwan]
3 Taichi Rd., Hsiao-kang
Kaohsiung
Tel: (7) 8020111 Fax: (7) 8022129

Petrochemical Development Corporation [China]
9-10/F., 6 Roosevelt Rd.
Sec. 1, Taipei
Tel: (2) 3923111 Fax: (2) 3517224

Petroleum Corporation [Chinese]
83 Chunghwa Rd.
Sec. 1, Taipei
Tel: (2) 3610221 Fax: (2) 3319645

Power Company [Taiwan]
242 Roosevelt Rd.
Sec. 3, Taipei
Tel: (2) 3561234 Fax: (2) 3561509

Ret-Ser Engineering Agency (VACRS)
207 Sung Chiang Rd.
Taipei
Tel: (2) 5038641 Fax: (2) 5031113

Shipbuilding Corporation [China]
6/F., 20 Pa Teh Rd.
Taipei
Tel: (2) 7710181 Fax: (2) 7715703

Steel Corporation [China]
5/F., 25 Jen Ai Rd.
Sec. 4, Taipei
Tel: (2) 7216411 Fax: (2) 7210393

Sugar Corporation [Taiwan]
25 Paoching Rd.
Taipei
Tel: (2) 3110521 Fax: (2) 3817049

Tang Eng Iron Works, Co. Ltd.
458 Hsinhsing Rd., Hukou
Hsinchu
Tel: (35) 981721 Fax: (35) 981646

Tobacco and Wine Monopoly Bureau [Taiwan]
4 Nanchang St.
Sec. 1, Taipei
Tel: (2) 3214567 Fax: (2) 3972086

TRADE PROMOTION ORGANIZATIONS

WORLD TRADE CENTERS

Taipei World Trade Center Co., Ltd.
4-8/F., CETRA Tower, 333 Keelung Rd.
Sec. 1, Taipei 10548
Tel: (2) 7255200 Fax: (2) 7576653
Tlx: 21676 CETRA

World Trade Center Kaohsiung
Southeast Bldg.
21st Wu-Fu 3rd Rd., 10/F.
Kaohsiung
Direct communications to: Acting Director and US
Representative, WTC Kaohsiung
7188 Cradlerock Way, Ste. 152
Columbia, MD 21045 USA
Tel: [1] (301) 499-8170
Fax: [1] (301) 381-3718

World Trade Center Taichung
60 Tienpao St.
Taichung 40706
Tel: (4) 2542271 Fax: (4) 2542341

GENERAL TRADE ASSOCIATIONS & LOCAL CHAMBERS OF COMMERCE

Chinese Federation of Labor
11/F., 201-18 Tun Hua N. Rd.
Taipei
Tel: (2) 713511 Fax: (2) 7135116

Chinese National Association of Industry and
Commerce
13/F., 390 Fu Hsing S. Rd.
Sec. 1, Taipei
Tel: (2) 7070111 Fax: (2) 7070977

Chinese National Federation of Industries
12/F., 390 Fu Hsing S. Rd.
Sec. 1, Taipei
Tel: (2) 7033500 Fax: (2) 7033982

Chinese Products Promotion Center
6/F., 285 Nan King E. Rd.
Sec. 3, Taipei
Tel: (2) 7155896, 7134821 Fax: (2) 7130115

Chinese Productivity Center
2/F., 340 Tun Hua N. Rd.
Taipei 10592
Tel: (2) 7137731 Fax: (2) 7120650

Committee of International Technical Cooperation
185 Hsinghai Rd.
Sec. 2, Taipei
Tel: (2) 7375647 Fax: (2) 7350736

I-Lan Hsien Industrial Association
26-6 Nau Chung Rd.
I Lan City
Tel: (39) 325747

Import-Export Association of Taipei
5/F., 350 Sung Chiang Rd.
Taipei
Tel: (2) 5813521/7 Fax: (2) 5423704

Industrial Association of Pingtung Country
426 Kung Tung Rd.
Ping Tung City
Tel: (8) 7370304 Fax: (8) 7373590

Nan Tou Hsien Chambers of Trade
24 Min Chuan St.
Nan Tou City, Nan Tou Hsien
Tel: (49) 225151

Taichung Chamber of Industry
8, Shih Fu Rd.
Taichung
Tel: (4) 2263613 Fax: (4) 2297398

Taipei Chamber of Commerce
6/F.-1, 602 Tun Hwa S. Rd.
Taipei
Tel: (2) 7542572

Taipei Industrial Association
10/F., 62 Chung Shan Rd.
Sec. 2, Pan Chiao, Taipei Hsien
Tel: (2) 9559077 Fax: (2) 9559090

Taiwan Chamber of Commerce
4/F., 158 Sung Chiang Rd.
Taipei
Tel: (2) 3113144, 3114152 Fax: (2) 5211980

Taiwan Importers & Exporters Association
14/F., 2 Fu Hsing N. Rd.
Taipei
Tel: (2) 7731155 Fax: (2) 7731159

Taiwan Industrial Association
7/F.-3, 233 Nan Men Rd.
Tainan
Tel: (6) 2279711 Fax: (6) 2229309

Taiwan Manufacturers' Industrial Association
Rm. 905, 100 Chung Hsiao E. Rd.
Sec 2, Taipei
Tel: (2) 3215791 Fax: (2) 3951754

Taiwan Provincial Federation of Labor
11/F., 44, Roosevelt Rd.
Sec. 2, Taipei
Tel: (2) 3916241, 3916243 Fax: (2) 3916243

Taiwan Provincial Industrial Association
8/F.-3, 390 Fu Hsing S. Rd.
Sec. 1, Taipei
Tel: (2) 7074339 Fax: (2) 7074341

FOREIGN CHAMBERS OF COMMERCE & BUSINESS ORGANIZATIONS

Those marked with a (*) also issue passports and visas in the absence of a diplomatic office in Taiwan. However, paperwork is often sent elsewhere and the process make take a few days to a few weeks.

Australia
Australian Commerce & Industry Office*
Rm. 2605, 333 Keelung Rd.
Sec. 1, Taipei
Tel: (2) 7202833 Fax: (2) 7576707

Austria
Austrian Trade Delegation Taipei Office*
Suite 608, 205 Tun Hwa N. Rd.
Taipei
Tel: (2) 7155221 Fax: (2) 7173242
Tlx: 28864 AUTRADEL

Belgium
Belgian Trade Association, Taipei*
Rm. 901, 131 Min Sheng E. Rd.
Sec. 3, Taipei
Tel: (2) 7151215 Fax: (2) 7126258
Tlx: 22004 BELTRADE

Brazil
Brazil's Foreign Trade Association, Taipei Office
10/F., 36 Kuan Chen Rd.
Taipei
Tel: (2) 3319390, 3143730 Fax: (2) 3116100
Tlx: 21721 DANDW

Canada
Canadian Trade Office in Taipei*
13/F., 365 Fu Hsing N. Rd.
Taipei
Tel: (2) 7137268 Fax: (2) 7127244
Tlx: 29484 CANTAI

Chile
Chilean Trade Office Taipei
Rm. 7B-06/7, 5 Hsin Yi Rd.
Sec. 5, Taipei
Tel: (2) 7230329 Fax: (2) 7230318
Tlx: 17866 CHILOF TP

Denmark
Danish Trade Organization, Taipei Office*
4/F., 12, Lane 21, An Ho Rd.
Taipei
Tel: (2) 7213386 Fax: (2) 7315120

Europe
European Council of Commerce & Trade
12/F.-1, 64 Tun Hwa N. Rd.
Taipei
Tel: (2) 7400236 Fax: (2) 7720530

France
Chinese French Industrial, Commercial
and Services Cooperation
10/F., 7 Roosevelt Rd.
Sec. 1, Taipei
Tel: (2) 3123258 Fax: (2) 3123240
Tlx: 16224 OCIFA TW

France-Asia Trade Promotion Association*
Rm. 1401, 205 Tun Hwa N. Rd.
Taipei
Tel: (2) 7133552 Fax: (2) 7171353
Tlx: 27954 FATPA

French Chamberoof Commerce & Industry in Taipei
Rm. 7B-01, 5 Hsin Yi Rd.
Sec. 5, Taipei
Tel: (2) 7232740/2 Fax: (2) 7232743

French Institute in Taipei
15/F., Fu Key Bldg., 99 Jen Ai Rd.
Sec. 2, Taipei
PO Box 3731, Taipei
Tel: (2) 3940849/50 Fax: (2) 3940851
Tlx: 23898 IFTAIPEI

Germany
German Trade Office, Taipei*
(Deutsches Wirtschaftsburo Taipei)
4/F., 4 Min Sheng E. Rd.
Sec. 3, Taipei
Tel: (2) 5069028 Fax: (2) 5068182
Tlx: 26226 GERTRADE

Indonesia
Indonesian Chamber of Commerce to Taipei*
3/F., 46-1 Chung Cheng Rd.
Sec. 2, Shih Lin, Taipei
Tel: (2) 8310451 Fax: (2) 8361844

Ireland
Institute for Trade & Investment of Ireland
Rm. 7B-09, 5 Hsin Yi Rd.
Sec. 5, Taipei
Tel: (2) 7251691 Fax: (2) 7251653

Italy
Italian Trade Promotion Office
Rm. 2C-14, 5 Hsin Yi Rd.
Sec. 5, Taipei
Tel: (2) 7251542 Fax: (2) 7251422

Japan
Chinese/Japanese Interchange Association
Kaohsiung Office
6/F., 81 Chung Hwa 3rd Rd.
Kaohsiung
Tel: (7) 7714008 Tlx: 21695 KOORYUU

Chinese/Japanese Interchange Association
Taipei Office
43 Chi Nan Rd.
Sec. 3, Taipei
Tel: (2) 3517250/4

Jordan
Jordanian Commercial Office
3/F., 425-1 Chung Shan N. Rd.
Sec. 6, Taipei
Tel: (2) 72523434 Fax: (2) 7577240

Korea
Korean Trade Center, Taipei
Rm. 2214, 333 Keelung Rd.
Sec. 1, Taipei
Tel: (2) 7252343 Fax: (2) 7577240

Malaysia
Malaysian Friendship and Trade Center, Taipei*
8/F., Sanho Plastic Bldg.
102 Tun Hwa N. Rd.
Taipei
Tel: (2) 7132626 Fax: (2) 7181877

Those marked with a (*) also issue passports and visas in the absence of a diplomatic office in Taiwan. However, paperwork is often sent elsewhere and the process make take a few days to a few weeks.

Mexico
Mexican Trade Services
Rm. 2602, 333 Keelung Rd.
Sec. 1, Taipei
Tel: (2) 7576526/8 Fax: (2) 7576180

Netherlands
Netherlands Trade & Investment Office*
Rm. B 5/F., 133 Min Sheng E. Rd.
Sec. 3, Taipei
Tel: (2) 7135760 Fax: (2) 7130194

New Zealand
New Zealand Commerce & Industry Office
25/F., 333 Keelung Rd.
Sec. 1, Taipei
Tel: (2) 7577060 Fax: (2) 7576972

Norway
Norwegian Trade Office Taipei
11/F., 148 Sung Chian Rd.
Taipei
Tel: (2) 5435484, 5213436 Fax: (2) 5619044

Philippines
Philippine Trade & Investment Center
Rm. 7B-19, 5 Hsin Yi Rd.
Sec. 5, Taipei
Tel: (2) 7232527/8, 7232024 Fax: (2) 7232025

Saudi Arabia
Saudi Arabian Trade Office
65 Lane 2, Yang Teh Ta Tao
Sec. 2, Shih Lin District, Taipei
Tel: (2) 8818837/8

Singapore
Office of the Singapore Trade
Representative, Taipei
9/F., 85 Jen Ai Rd.
Sec. 4, Taipei
Tel: (2) 7721940 Fax: (2) 7721943
Tlx: 27220 TRADETAI

Spain
Spanish Chamber of Commerce*
7/F.-1, 40 Tun Hwa S. Rd.
Sec. 2, Taipei
Tel: (2) 3256234 Fax: (2) 7542572
Tlx: 13134 OFCOMES

Sweden
Exportrade Taipei, Swedish Trade Council*
Rm. 102, 96 Chung Shan N. Rd.
Sec. 2, Taipei
Tel: (2) 5627601 Fax: (2) 5319504
Tlx: 12434 SITRO

Switzerland
Trade Office of Swiss Industries*
Rm. 1614, 333 Keelung Rd.
Sec. 1., Taipei
Tel: (2) 7201001/3 Fax: (2) 727576984
Tlx: 26926 TOSITPE

Thailand
Thai Airways International Ltd.
Administration Office*
6/F., 150 Fu Hsing N. Rd.
Taipei
Tel: (2) 7121882 Tlx: 21584 THAI

Thai Airways International Ltd.
Thai Trade Office
Rm. 7E-06, 5 Hsin Yi Rd.
Sec. 5, Taipei
Tel: (2) 7231800/2 Fax: (2) 7251314

United Kingdom
Anglo-Taiwan Trade Committee*
9/F., 99 Jen Ai Rd.
Sec. 2, Taipei
Tel: (2) 3224242 Fax: (2) 3948673
Tlx: 11106 ATTIC

United States of America
American Institute in Taiwan (AIT)*
7, Lane 134, Hsin Yi Rd.
Sec. 3, Taipei
Tel: (2) 7092000, 7201550 Fax: (2) 7027675

American Institute in Taiwan
(Commercial Unit)
Rm. 3207, 333 Keelung Rd.
Sec. 1, Taipei
Tel: (2) 7201550 Fax: (2) 7577162

TAIWAN OFFICES OF THE CHINA EXTERNAL TRADE DEVELOPMENT COUNCIL (CETRA)

CETRA Head office
4-8/F., CETRA Tower, 333 Keelung Rd.
Sec. 1, Taipei 10548
Tel: (2) 7255200 Fax: (2) 7576653

CETRA Design Promotion Center
2/F., CETRA Exhibition Hall, Sungshan Airport
340 Tun Hwa N. Rd.
Taipei
Tel: (2) 7151551 Fax: (2) 7168783

CETRA Hsinchu
3 Kuang Fu Rd.
Sec. 2, Hsinchu
Tel: (35) 718033, 722649 Fax: (35) 723063

CETRA International Trade Institute
7/F., CETRA Tower, 333 Keelung Rd.
Sec. 1, Taipei 10548
Tel: (2) 72382345, 7576194
Fax: (2) 7576632, 7576193

CETRA Kaohsiung
8/F., 456 Chung Haiao 1st Rd.
Kaohsiung
Tel: (7) 2016776 Fax: (7) 7168783

CETRA Taichung
1-4/F., 260 Ying Tsai Rd.
Taichung
Tel: (4) 2035933, 2035978 Fax: (4) 2038222

CETRA Tainan
11 Fl., 54 Cheng Kung Rd.
Tainan
Tel: (6) 2296623

CETRA Tung Chan Campus
66 Tung Shan St.
Hsinchu
Tel: (35) 721571/3 Fax: (35) 721434

OVERSEAS REPRESENTATIVE OFFICES OF CETRA, FETS & MINISTRY OF ECONOMIC AFFAIRS

Argentina
Oficina Commercial de Taiwan, Division Economica
av. de Mayo 654, 4 Piso 1084
Casilla de Correo No. 196
1401 Capital Federal
Buenos Aires, Argentina
Tel: [54] (1) 3340653/4, 3345581
Fax: [54] (1) 3345581 Tlx: 23564 CCTROC

Australia
Far East Trading Co., Pty. Ltd. (FETS)
PO Box 148, World Trade Center
Melbourne, Vic. 3005, Australia
Tel: [61] (3) 6112988 Fax: [61] (3) 6112983
Tlx: AA 37248 FETRAM

Far East Trade Service, Inc. (FETS)
Suite 1907, MLC Center
King St.
Sydney N.S.W. 2000, Australia
Tel: [61] (2) 2326626, 2326999
Fax: [61] (2) 2327429

Austria
Far East Trade Service, Inc. (FETS)
Branch Office in Vienna
Stubenring 4-12A
A-1010 Vienna, Austria
Tel: [43] (222) 5131933/4
Fax: [43] (222) 5137632 Tlx: 116286 FETS A

Belgium
Far East Trade Service, Inc. (FETS)
Belgium Branch Office
World Trade Center 1, 16eme etage
Boulevard Emile Jacqmain 162
Boite 33
1210 Brussels, Belgium
Tel: [32] (2) 2185157, 2185197
Fax: [32] (2) 2186835 Tlx: 25343 FETS B

Brazil
Centro Commercial de Taipei do Brasil
Div. de Promocao do Comercio
Alameda Jau 1742, Conj. 101
CEP 01420
Sao Paulo-SP, Brazil
Tel: [55] (11) 2800151, 8810260
Fax: [55] (11) 8837929 Tlx: 1133890 TWTC BR

Canada
Far East Trade Service, Inc. (FETS)
Suite 2108, 1800 McGill College Ave.
Montreal, Quebec H3A 3J6, Canada
Tel: [1] (514) 844-8909
Fax: [1] (514) 844-9246

Taipei Economic and Cultural Office
Economic Division
Suite 3315, 2 Bloor St. East
Toronto, Ontario M4W 1A8, Canada
Tel: [1] (416) 922-2412/3
Fax: [1] (416) 922-2426 Tlx: 28086 TROC TOR

Far East Trade Service, Inc.
#650-409 Granville St.
Vancouver, B.C. V6C 1T2, Canada
Tel: [1] (604) 682-9501
Fax: [1] (604) 682-9775 Tlx: 51162 FETS VCR

Chile
Oficina Comercial del Lejano Oriente
Division Economica
La Gioconda 4222, Las Condes
Casilla 2-T, Correo Tajamar
Santiago, Chile
Tel: [56] (2) 2282919, 2283185
Fax: [56] (2) 2285854 Tlx: 340412

Colombia
Officina Comercial del Lejano Oriente
Division Comercial
Carrera 7 No. 79-75, Oficina 502
Apartado Aereo 75189 Chapinero
Bogota D.E., Colombia
Tel: [57] (1) 2110028, 2126526
Fax: [57] (1) 2554076, 2125794
Tlx: 45892 CEBCA CO

Costa Rica
Oficina Del Agregado Economica
Embajada de la Republica de China
PO Box 324-2010 Zapote
San Jose, Costa Rica
Tel: [506] 248180, 533441 x13, 29
Fax: [506] 340441 Tlx: 2174 MEARO

Denmark
Economic Division
Taipei Economic and Cultural Office
Ny Ostergade 3, 1/F.
DK-1101 Copenhagen K, Denmark
Tel: [45] 33-12-35-05
Fax: [45] 33-93-39-16

Dominican Republic
Oficina Del Agregado Comercial
Embajada de la Republica de China
Apartado 20322
Santo Domingo, Republica Dominicana
Tel: [1] (809) 5671275/6
Fax: [1] (809) 5415207 Tlx: 3264255 ECHINA

Egypt
Far East Trade Service, Inc. (FETS)
16/F., WTC Cairo, 1191 Corniche El-Nil
PO Box 521 Maadi
Cairo, Arab Republic of Egypt
Tel: [20] (2) 748872/9 Fax: [20] (2) 748890

France
Centre Asiatique de Promotion Economique et
Commercial
3, av. Bertie Albrecht, 5ème étage
75008 Paris, France
Tel: [33] (1) 45-63-33-54, 45-63-79-00
Fax: [33] (1) 42-89-10-84 Tlx: 641275 CAPEC

Far East Trade Service, Inc. (FETS)
Succursale a Paris
25-27, rue d'Astorg
75008 Paris, France
Tel: [33] (1) 42-66-05-12, 42-66-05-62
Fax: [33] (1) 42-66-04-31 Tlx: 281744 FETS F

Germany

Taiwan Trade Service, Düsseldorf
5-6/F., Willi-Becker-Allee 11
4000 Düsseldorf 1, Germany
Tel: [49] (211) 78180
Fax: [49] (211) 781839 Tlx: 8582232 FETS D

Far East Trade Service Center (FETS)
Westendstrasse 8
D-6000 Frankfurt/Main 1, Germany
Tel: [49] (69) 727641/2, 727679
Fax: [49] (69) 727553 Tlx: 416777 FETS D

Taipei Trade Office
Hamburg Branch Office
Grosse Bleichen 12
2000 Hamburg 36, Germany
Tel: [49] (40) 351627, 341981
Fax: [49] (40) 346601 Tlx: 403906 FETSHHD

Taipei Trade Center, Hamburg
3/F., Neuer Wall 50
2000 Hamburg 36, Germany
Tel: [49] (40) 360017/0 Fax: [49] (40) 367937

Far East Trade Service Center (FETS)
Stuttgart Branch Office
Rotebuehlplatz 20 C
7000 Stuttgart 1, Germany
Tel: [49] (711) 224085/6
Fax: [49] (711) 224087 Tlx: 722474 FETSS D

Greece

Taipei Economic and Cultural Office
54 Queen Sophia Ave., 4/F.
GR 115 28 Athens, Greece
Tel: [30] (1) 7243107/8 Fax: [30] (1) 7241035
Tlx: 218938 FETC GR

Guatemala

Embajada de la Republica de China
Oficina del Agregado Comercial
7a, Avenida, 1-20, Zona 4
Edificio Torre Cafe
7 Nivel, Of. 730-340
Postal address: PO Box 1834
Guatemala City, Guatemala C.A.
Tel: [502] (2) 318715, 318705
Fax: [502] (2) 315154 Tlx: 5107 MEARO GU

Hong Kong

Far East Trade Service, Inc. (FETS)
80 Gloucester Rd., 2/F.
Hong Kong
Tel: [852] 8655372 Fax: [852] 8562423

Hungary

Taipei Trade Office, Economic Division
Rakoczi UT. 1-3/III em.
H-1088 Budapest, Hungary
Tel: [36] (1) 2512884 Fax: [36] (1) 2514003

CETRA Trade and Investment Center
Taipei Trade Office
Pozsonyi UT 77-79, 1/F.
H-1133 Budapest, Hungary
Tel: [36] (1) 120-3430, 160-2806
Fax: [36] (1) 160-2713 Tlx: 20-2884

Indonesia

Taipei Economic and Trade Office
Wisma Dharmala Sakti
7/F., Jl. Jendral Sudirman No. 32
Jakarta 10220, Indonesia
Tel: [62] (21) 5703047 Fax: [62] (21) 588775
Tlx: 62154 SINOCH IA

Italy

Centre Commercial per l'estremo
Oriente
Via Errico Petrella, 2
20124 Milano, Italy
Tel: [39] (2) 29403319, 29404196
Fax: [39] (2) 2047077 Tlx: 331594 BOFTTF I

Ivory Coast

Abidjan
Far East Trade Service, Inc. (FETS)
01-PO Box 3782
Abidjan-01, Ivory Coast
Tel: [225] 326936, 326939 Fax: [225] 415798
Tlx: 22573 FETS CI

Japan

Far East Trade Service Center (FETS)
9-28, Hakata-ku
Fukuoka 812, Japan
Tel: [81] (92) 472-7461
Fax: [81] (92) 472-7463

Association of East Asian Relations
4/F., Nichiei Building
408, Tosabori 1-chome, Nishi-ku
Osaka 550, Japan
Tel: [81] (6) 443-8481/6 Fax: [81] (6) 443-8577
Tlx: JPOSAOF J64785

Far East Trade Service Center (FETS)
Osaka Office
9/F., Nissei Midosuji Bldg.
2-4, 4-chome, Minami Senba Chuo-ku
Osaka 542, Japan
Tel: [81] (6) 244-9611/4
Fax: [81] (6) 244-9614

Taipei Economic and Cultural Representative
Office in Japan
Tokyo Office, Economic Division
20-2, 5-chome, Siroganedai, Minato-ku
Tokyo, Japan
Tel: [81] (3) 3280-7990/4
Fax: [81] (3) 3280-7928 Tlx: J28511 HANIRY

Far East Trade Service Center (FETS)
Totate International Bldg.
12-19 Shibuya 2-chome, Shibuya-ku
Tokyo 150, Japan
Tel: [81] (3) 3407-9711/4
Fax: [81] (3) 3407-9715

Jordan

Commercial Office of the Republic of China
(Taiwan), Economic Division
PO Box 476
Dahiat Al-Emir Rashed
Amman, Jordan
Tel: [962] (6) 671530, 671536
Fax: [962] (6) 683991 Tlx: 21303 JDEM JON

Korea
Office of Economic Counselor
Embassy of the Republic of China
#83, 2-ka, Myung-dong, Chung-ku
Seoul, Korea
Tel: [82] (2) 776-2889, 757-5567
Fax: [82] (2) 757-3859 Tlx: K27529 MEARO K

Kuwait
Far East Trade Service Inc. (FETS)
PO Box 27574
13136 Safat, Kuwait
Tel: [965] 2418394 Fax: [965] 2448255

Malaysia
Taipei Economic and Cultural Center
in Malaysia, Economic Division
Lot 901, 9/F., Amoda Building 22
Jalan Imbi
55100 Kuala Lumpur, Malaysia
Tel: [60] (3) 2426771, 2425549
Fax: [60] (3) 2423906 Tlx: FETTC MA 30052

Mexico
Far East Trade Service, Inc. (FETS)
Edificio Omega
Campos Eliseos 345, Piso 9
Col. Chapultepec Polanco
11560 Mexico DF, Mexico
Tel: [52] (5) 202-6281, 202-5954
Fax: [52] (5) 202-6317

Netherlands
Far East Trade Service, Inc. (FETS)
Vareseweg 5
3047 AT Rotterdam, Netherlands
Tel: [31] (10) 4053388 Fax: [31] (10) 4625283

Taiwan Trade Center
Vareseweg 5
3047 AT Rotterdam, Netherlands
Tel: [31] (10) 4460300 Fax: [31] (10) 4625265

Taipei Economic and Cultural Office,
Economic Division
Javastraat 482585 AR.
Den Haag, The Netherlands
Tel: [31] (70) 3469552 Fax: [31] (70) 3600105

New Zealand
Taipei Economic and Cultural Office
4/F., Norwich Union Building
Cnr. of Queen & Durham St.
G.PO Box 4018
Auckland, New Zealand
Tel: [64] (9) 303-3903
Fax: [64] (9) 302-3399
Tlx: NZ 60209 EASTRAD

Taipei Economic and Cultural Office,
Economic Division
21/F., Marac House
105-109, The Terrace
Wellington, New Zealand
Tel: [64] (4) 4736474/5, 4993628
Fax: [64] (4) 4991458

Nigeria
Taipei World Trade Center Company
3/F., 24 Campbell St.
P.M.B. 12857 Marina
Lagos, Nigeria
Tel: [234] (1) 632783 Fax: [234] (1) 630615
Tlx: 21030 TWTC NG

Panama
Embajada de la Republica de China,
Oficina del Consejero Economico
Apto Postal 6-2696 (El Dorado)
Panama City, Rep. De Panama
Tel: [507] 694235, 692995, 692929
Fax: [507] 239698 Tlx: 2661

Paraguay
Oficina del Agregado Comercial
Embajada de la Rep. de China
Casilla de Correo 2690
Asuncion, Republica de Paraguay
Tel: [595] (21) 494361, 448573
Fax: [595] (21) 448573
Tlx: 702 PY ECHINA ASUNCION

Peru
Oficina Economica y Cultural de Taipei
Av. Gregorio Escobedo
No. 426 Jesus Maria
Lima 11, Peru
Postal address: PO Box Casilla 18-0170
Lima 18, Peru
Tel: [51] (14) 623544, 639502, 633604
Fax: [51] (14) 631072, 6336034

Philippines
Taipei Economic & Cultural Center,
Economic Division
PO Box 948
Manila, Philippines
Tel: [63] (2) 8177322, 8161920
Fax: [63] (2) 8177321 Tlx: 45346 EDPEC PM

Russia
Taipei World Trade Center Co., Ltd.
PO Box 121019
Moscow 224, Russia
Tel: [7] (95) 2482005, 2482731, 2482743
Fax: [7] (95) 2482692

Saudi Arabia
Taiwan Products Display Center
FETS, Saudi Arabia
PO Box 1138
Dammam 31431, Saudi Arabia
Tel: [966] (3) 8325485 Fax: [966] (3) 8325485

Office of Commercial Attaché
Consulate General of the Republic of China
2/F., Alireza Tower
Madina Rd.
PO Box 580
Jeddah 21421, Saudi Arabia
Tel: [966] (2) 6512264, 6515133
Fax: [966] (2) 6515133

Office of Economic Counselor
Embassy of the Republic of China
PO Box 94377
Riyadh 11693, Saudi Arabia
Tel: [966] (1) 4881605, 4881900
Fax: [966] (1) 4881605

Singapore
Taipei Representative Office
460 Alexandra Rd., #23-00 PSA Bldg.
Singapore 0511
Tel: [65] 2786511 Fax: [65] 2789962
Tlx: RS 25438 SIMISON

Far East Trade Service Inc. (FETS)
Singapore Representative Office
5 Shenton Way, #02-01 UIC Bldg.
Singapore 0106
Tel: [65] 2249433, 2249441 Fax: [65] 2250473
Tlx: RS 28140 FETs

South Africa
Office of the Economic Counselor
Embassy of the Republic of China
Suite 1749, Sanlam Sentrum
Cnr. Jeppe & Von Wielligh Sts.
PO Box 1148
Johannesburg 2000, Rep. of South Africa
Tel: [27] (11) 296335/8 Fax: [27] (11) 232236
Tlx: 89808

Spain
Far East Trade Service S.A. (FETS)
Torres De Colon, Planta 12-B
Torre II
Plaza De Colon No. 2
28046 Madrid, Spain
Tel: [34] (1) 4101414, 4101513
Fax: [34] (1) 4107314 Tlx: 41633 FETSS E

Sweden
Taipei Trade, Tourism & Information Center
Wennergren Center
Sveavagen 166, 4 Tr.
S-113 46 Stockholm, Sweden
Tel: [46] (8) 7298523, 7288573
Fax: [46] (8) 7288584, 315748
Tlx: 15360 SHAMO S

Switzerland
Far East Trade Service, Inc. (FETS)
Sihlquai 306
8005 Zurich, Switzerland
Tel: [41] (1) 2717620 Fax: [41] (1) 2717679

Thailand
Taipei Economic and Trade Center,
Economic Division
10/F., Kian Gwan Bldg.
140 Wit Thayu Rd.
Bangkok 10330, Thailand
Tel: [66] (2) 2519393/6
Fax: [66] (2) 2535251, 2531354
Tlx: 82184 Chinata TH

Turkey
Far East Trade Service, Inc. (FETS)
Yapi Kredi Plaza B Blok
KAT: 9 Buyukdere Cad. 80620
4 Levent
Istanbul, Turkey
Tel: [90] (1) 2686537, 2686217
Fax: [90] (1) 2682499

United Arab Emirates
Far East Trade Service, Inc. (FETS)
Rm. 106, 1/F., Abdul Aziz Mirza Bldg.
PO Box 5852
Dubai, UAE
Tel: [971] (4) 367814/5 Fax: [971] (4) 367768
Tlx: 46717 FETSD EM

United Kingdom
Majestic Trading Co., Ltd.
5/F., Bewlay House
2 Swallow Place
London W1R 7AA, UK
Tel: [44] (71) 629-1516/8 Fax: [44] (71) 499-8730
Tlx: 25397 MAJECO G

Taiwan Products Promotion Co. Ltd.
4/F., Centric House
390/391 Strand
London WC2R OLT, UK
Tel: [44] (71) 379-0765/8 Fax: [44] (71) 379-5962

United States of America
Coordination Council for North American Affairs,
Commercial Division
8/F., 20 North Clark St.
Chicago, IL 60602, USA
Tel: [1] (312) 332-2535/9 Fax: [1] (312) 332-0847
Tlx: 282168 ROCTRADE CGO

Far East Trade Service, Inc. (FETS)
225 North Michigan Ave., Suite 333
Chicago, IL 60601, USA
Tel: [1] (312) 819-7373 Fax: [1] (312) 819-7377

Coordination Council for North American Affairs,
Commercial Division
1360 Post Oak Blvd., Suite 2150
Houston, TX 77056, USA
Tel: [1] (713) 961-9794/6, 961-9785
Fax: [1] (713) 961-9809 Tlx: (650) 3159479 ROCTRA

Coordination Council for North American Affairs,
Commercial Division
3660 Wilshire Blvd., Suite 918
Los Angeles, CA 90010, USA
Tel: [1] (213) 380-3644 Fax: [1] (213) 380-3407
Tlx: 9103214021 ROCTRADE LSA

Coordination Council for North American Affairs,
Commercial Division
801 Brickell Avenue, Suite 2380
Miami, FL 33131, USA
Tel: [1] (305) 371-2860 Fax: [1] (305) 371-2953

Coordination Council for North American Affairs,
Investment and Trade Office
8/F., 126 E. 56th St.
New York, NY 10022, USA
Tel: [1] (212) 532-7055 Fax: [1] (212) 213-4189
Tlx: 426299 CETDC NY

Far East Trade Service, Inc. (FETS)
555 Montgomery St., Suite 603
San Francisco, CA 94111-2564, USA
Tel: [1] (415) 788-4304 Fax: [1] (415) 788-0468

Coordination Council for North American Affairs,
Economic Division
4301 Connecticut Ave. NW, Suite 420
Washington, D.C. 20008, USA
Tel: [1] (202) 686-6400 Fax: [1] (202) 363-6294/5
Tlx: 440292 SINOECO

Venezuela
Oficina Comercial de Taiwan
Apartado 69149, Altamira
Caracas 1062-A, Venezuela
Tel: [58] (2) 310745 Fax: [58] (2) 328673
Tlx: 24619 TAICOM VE

INDUSTRY–SPECIFIC TRADE ORGANIZATIONS IN TAIWAN

Acid & Alkali Industries [Taiwan Regional
Association of]
8/F.-1, 390 Fu Hsing S. Rd.
Sec. 1, Taipei 10640
Tel: (2) 7023910 Fax: (2) 7023910

Adhesive Tape Manufacturers [Taiwan Regional
Association of]
Rm. 4B-14, 5 Hsin Yi Rd.
Sec. 5, Taipei 10509
Tel: (2) 7252217

Agricultural Machinery Manufacturers Association
[Taiwan]
57 Chung Hus Rd.
Sec. 2, Taipei 10731
Tel: (2) 3813789 Fax: (2) 3821409

Automobile Repair Industries Association [Taiwan]
3/F., 4-1 Fu Shun St.
Taipei 10453
Tel: (2) 5966965 Fax: (2) 5966965

Bags Association [Taiwan]
12/F., 22 Ai Kuo E. Rd.
Taipei 10726
Tel: (2) 3925310, 3925305 Fax: (2) 3979253

Bakery Association [Taiwan]
2/F., Lane 96, Kun Ming St.
Taipei
Tel: (2) 3314741 Fax: (2) 3611285

Bankers Association of Taiwan, ROC
21, Fu Chung Rd., Pan Chiao
Taipei Hsien
Tel: (2) 9690555 Fax: (2) 9676416

Barley Industry [Taiwan Association of]
6/F., 6 Tun Hua N. Rd.
Taipei 10390
Tel: (2) 7412093

Brown Sugar Association [Taiwan]
3/F., 62 Hsi Ning N. Rd.
Taipei
Tel: (2) 5522021 Fax: (2) 5522776

Building Materials Association [Taiwan]
Rm. 4, 7/F., 374 Pa Teh Rd.
Sec. 2, Taipei 10558
Tel: (2) 7518834 Fax: (2) 7772101

Canners Association [Taiwan]
7/F., 170 Min Sheng E. Rd.
Sec. 2, Taipei 10444
Tel: (2) 5022660/9 Fax: (2) 5022667

Carpet Manufacturers Association [Taiwan]
Rm. 207, 2/F., 25 Pao Ai Rd.
Taipei 10035
Tel: (2) 3810660 Fax: (2) 3831802

Cement Manufacturers' Association [Taiwan]
8/F.-5, 390, Fu Hsing S. Rd.
Sec. 1, Taipei 10640
Tel: (2) 7015733, 7015756 Fax: (2) 7069951

Cement Products Association [Taiwan]
3/F., 62-1 Kaifeng St.
Sec. 2, Taipei 10011
Tel: (2) 3310687 Fax: (2) 3896351

Ceramic Industries [Taiwan Regional Association
of]
124 Lane 27, Chung Shan N. Rd.
Sec. 2, Taipei 10419
Tel: (2) 5616536, 5712395

Chemical Suppliers Association [Taipei]
3/F., 21 Lane 47, Sinsheng N. Rd.
Sec. 1, Taipei 10422
Tel: (2) 5417531, 5417530 Fax: (2) 5814394

Clock, Watch & Glasses Association [Taipei]
3/F., 210 Chung Hwa Rd.
Sec. 2, Taipei
Tel: (2) 3063634

Clothing Manufacturers Association [Taiwan]
8/F.-3, 202 Nanking E. Rd.
Sec. 5, Taipei 10573
Tel: (2) 7666661/2 Fax: (2) 7625722

CNS Certification Mark Association, ROC
10/F.-3, 321, Fu Hsing S. Rd.
Sec. 1, Taipei
Tel: (2) 7033433 Fax: (2) 7051254

Coal Mining Association [Taiwan]
3/F., 17 Tai Yuan Rd.
Taipei 10208
Tel: (2) 5414111/3 Fax: (2) 5417517

Computer Association [Taipei]
3/F., 2, Pa Teh Rd.
Sec. 3, Taipei
Tel: (2) 7764249 Fax: (2) 7764410

Concrete Industry Association [Taiwan Ready-
Mixed]
Rm. 6, 5/F., 263 Shin Yee Rd.
Sec. 4, Taipei 10657
Tel: (2) 7038287 Fax: (2) 7038287

Confectionery Biscuit and Floury Food Association
[Taiwan]
9/F.-1, 390 Fu Hsing S. Rd.
Sec. 1, Taipei 10640
Tel: (2) 7041662 Fax: (2) 7084429

Corn Industry Association [Taiwan]
B1, 3 Alley 42, lane 78, Fu Hsing S. Rd.
Sec. 2, Taipei
Tel: (2) 7553353 Fax: (2) 7840128

Cotton Spinners Association [Taiwan]
11/F., 22 Ai Kuo E. Rd.
Taipei 10726
Tel: (2) 3916445 Fax: (2) 3916449

Decorative Pottery Exporters Association [Taiwan]
13/F., 25 Min Sheng E. Rd.
Taipei 10448
Tel: (2) 5639171, 5435343 Fax: (2) 5639171

Deep Sea Tuna Boatowners and Exporters
Association [Taiwan]
4/F., 40-42 Chungking S. Rd.
Sec. 3, Taipei 10742
Tel: (2) 3037189, 3016554 Fax: (2) 3095495

Department Stores Association [Taipei]
5/F., 8 Ken Ku St.
Taipei
Tel: (2) 5412313 Fax: (2) 5634339

Dyestuff & Pigment [Taiwan]
Industrial Association
7/F., 137 Fu Hsing S. Rd.
Sec. 1, Taipei
Tel: (2) 7318131, 7412802 Fax: (2) 7318132

Eel Exporters Association [Taiwan]
8/F., 24 Chilin Rd.
Taipei 10424
Tel: (2) 5711254, 5711255 Fax: (2) 5635752

Electric Appliance Manufacturers Association
[Taiwan]
6/F., 6 Chung Hsiao W. Rd.
Sec. 1, Taipei 10012
Tel: (2) 3718371 Fax: (2) 3312917

Electric Engineering Association [Taiwan]
11/F., 76 Sung Chiang Rd.
Taipei 10428
Tel: (2) 5719238/9 Fax: (2) 5232996

Electric Wire & Cable Industries Association.
[Taiwan]
11/F.-1, 2 Fu Chin St.
Taipei
Tel: (2) 7151784/5 Fax: (2) 7182307

Electronics Manufacturers Association [Taiwan
Export Processing Zone]
600-6 Chia Chang Rd., K.E.P.Z.
Kaohsiung 81120
Tel: (7) 3632250 Fax: (7) 3636050

Feather Export Association [Taiwan]
Rm. 711, 7/F., 27 Chung Shan N. Rd.
Sec. 3, Taipei 10451
Tel: (2) 5954983 Fax: (2) 5918702

Feed Industry Association [Taiwan]
Rm. C, 9/F., 368 Fu Hsing S. Rd.
Sec 1, Taipei
Tel: (2) 7028070 Fax: (2) 7028073

Fire Fighting Appliance Manufacturers [Taiwan
Association of]
3/F., 459-1 Chung Hua Rd.
Sec. 2, Taipei 10733
Tel: (2) 3017423 Fax: (2) 3076031

Flour Mills Association [Taiwan]
6/F., 6 Tun Hwa N. Rd.
Taipei
Tel: (2) 7512181 Fax: 7410803

Flower Export Association [Taiwan]
Rm. 901, 41 Chung Hsiao W. Rd.
Sec. 1, Taipei
Tel: (2) 3313146 Fax: (2) 3119336

Food Industrial Association [Taiwan]
6/F., 10 Chungking S. Rd.
Sec. 1, Taipei 10036
Tel: (2) 3719848 Fax: (2) 3817084

Footwear Exporters Association [Taiwan]
13/F., 131 Sung Chiang Rd.
Taipei 10429
Tel: (2) 5066190 Fax: (2) 5081489

Frozen Meat Industry Association [Taiwan]
4/F., 19 Lane 118, An Chu St.
Taipei 10675
Tel: (2) 7339112, 7335351 Fax: (2) 7354155

Frozen Seafood Exporters Association [Taiwan]
3/F., 29 Lane 30, Yung Chi Rd.
Taipei 10541
Tel: (2) 7657157 Fax: (2) 7634259

Frozen Seafood Industries Association [Taiwan]
8/F.-6, 103 Chung Cheng 4th Rd.
Kaohsiung 80-113
Tel: (7) 2411894 Fax: (7) 2519603

Frozen Vegetable & Fruit Manufacturers [Taiwan
Association of]
Rm. 6, 11/F., 103 Chung Cheng 4th Rd.
Kaohsiung
Tel: (7) 2015694, 2517317 Fax: (7) 2210471

Fruit & Vegetable Juice Manufacturers Association
[Taiwan]
3/F., 6 Lane 59, Yi Tung St.
Taipei 10431
Tel: (2) 5070830 Fax: (2) 5080516

Fruit Exporters Association [Taiwan]
12/F.-3, 31-1, Hsin Sheng N. Rd.
Sec. 2, Taipei 10423
Tel: (2) 5715191 Fax: (2) 5628411

Furniture & Handicraft Products Manufacturers
Association [Taiwan Export Processing Zone]
1 West 17th St., K.E.P.Z.
Kaohsiung 80681
Tel: (7) 8319394

Garment Industry Association [Taiwan]
8/F., 22 Ai Kuo E. Rd.
Taipei 10726
Tel: (2) 3919113 Fax: (2) 3919055

Garment Industry Association [Taiwan Export Processing Zone]
3 E. 1st Rd., K.E.P.Z.
Kaohsiung 80681
Tel: (7) 8215066, 8413957 Fax: (7) 8418542

Gas Appliance Manufacturers Association [Taiwan]
5/F., 3 Lane 328, Lang Chiang Rd.
Taipei 10482
Tel: (2) 5038831, 5032704 Fax: (2) 5044842

High Pressure Gas Industry Association [Taiwan]
3/F.-3, 102 Tung Hwa S. Rd.
Taipei
Tel: (2) 7513012, 7717333 Fax: (2) 7112559

Gifts & Housewares Exporters Association [Taiwan]
6/F., 28 Alley 2, Lane 250, Nanking E. Rd.
Sec. 5, Taipei 10571
Tel: (2) 7697303 Fax: (2) 7615942

Glass Industry Association [Taiwan]
12/F.-3, 22 Chungking N. Rd.
Sec. 1, Taipei 10206
Tel: (2) 5376018 Fax: (2) 5376765

Glove Manufacturers Association [Taiwan]
12/F., 22 Ai Kuo E. Rd.
Taipei
Tel: (2) 3918396 Fax: (2) 3951532

Hand Tools Association [Taiwan Regional]
3/F., 687-1 Min Tsu E. Rd.
Taipei 10488
Tel: (2) 7152250, 7130667 Fax: (2) 7152617

Handbags Export Trade Association [Taiwan]
12/F., 22 Ai Kuo E. Rd.
Taipei
Tel: (2) 3925305, 3925310 Fax: (2) 3949253

Handicraft Association [Taipei]
2/F., 18-1 Hsining S. Rd.
Taipei 10448
Tel: (2) 3810306 Fax: (2) 3818605

Hardware Dealers Association [Taipei]
Rm. B, 11/F. 185, Chung Shan N. Rd.
Sec. 2, Taipei
Tel: (2) 5958481, 5958461 Fax: (2) 59281188

Hat Exporters Association [Taiwan]
6/F., 22 Ai Kuo E. Rd.
Taipei 10726
Tel: (2) 3937892, 3937894 Fax: (2) 3963842

Hosiery Manufacturers Association [Taiwan]
6/F., 22 Ai Kuo E. Rd.
Taipei 10726
Tel: (2) 3913709, 3921483 Fax: (2) 3221744

Hotel Business Association [Taiwan]
4/F., 7, Chung Hwa Rd.
Sec. 1, Taichung
Tel: (4) 2244868

Industrial Fasteners Institute [Taiwan]
4/F.-1, 71 Sung Chiang Rd.
Taipei 10428
Tel: (2) 5060918 Fax: (2) 5072429

Instruments Commercial Association [Taipei]
3/F., 20, Lane 16, An Tong St.
Taipei
Tel: (2) 7111300 Fax: (2) 7753434

International Standard Hotels [The Association of Taipei]
8/F.-1, 369 Fu Hsing N. Rd.
Taipei
Tel: (2) 7172155, 7172453 Fax: (2) 7172453

Jewelry Industry Association [Taiwan]
Rm. 11, 6/F., 41 Chung Hsiso W. Rd.
Sec. 1, Taipei 10012
Tel: (2) 3610108 Fax: (2) 3615033

Knitting & Woven Manufacturers Association [Kaohsiung Export Processing Zone]
1 West 17th St., K.E.P.Z.
Kaohsiung 80681
Tel: (7) 8218524, 8216770

Knitting Industry Association [Taiwan]
7/F., 22 Ai Kuo E. Rd.
Taipei 10726
Tel: (2) 3945121 Fax: (2) 3971356

Leather Goods Manufacturers [Taiwan Regional Association of]
6/F.-1, 5-1 Nanking W. Rd.
Taipei 10403
Tel: (2) 5210090 Fax: (2) 5210090

Leather Industries Association [Taiwan Export Processing Zone]
1 West 17th St., K.E.P.Z.
Kaohsiung 80681
Tel: (7) 8216862

Leather Manufacturers Association [Taiwan]
4/F., 7 Chung Hwa Rd.
Sec. 1, Taichung 40302
Tel: (4) 2238725 Fax: (4) 2204904

Machinery Industry [Taiwan Association of]
2/F., 110 Huaning St.
Taipei 11037
Tel: (2) 3813722, 3813724 Fax: (2) 3813711

Man-Made Fiber Industries Association [Taiwan]
9/F., 22 Ai Kuo E. Rd.
Taipei
Tel: (2) 3914151 Fax: (2) 3947327

Marble and Stone Mining Industry Association [Taiwan]
3/F., 301 Tsingtao E. Rd.
Taipei 10022
Tel: (2) 3919300 Fax: (2) 3411881

Margarine Industries Association [Taiwan]
9/F., 390 Fu Hsing S. Rd.
Sec. 1, Taipei 10640
Tel: (2) 7060839 Fax: (2) 7085979

Monosodium Glutamate Manufacturers Association [Taiwan]
4/F., 6 Chang-chun Rd.
Taipei 10413
Tel: (2) 5414313, 5119540 Fax: (2) 5414313

Musical Instrument Association [Taipei]
3/F., 416-2 Ting Chou
Taipei
Tel: (2) 7662710

Newspaper Publishers' Association [Taipei]
260, Pa Teh Rd.
Sec. 2, Taipei
Tel: (2) 7735167 Fax: (2) 7775833

Non-Woven Fabrics Industry Association [Taiwan]
4/F., 51 Min Sheng E. Rd.
Sec. 3, Taipei
Tel: (2) 5019010 Fax: (2) 5059791

Optical & Precision Instrument Industries
Association [Taiwan Export Processing Zone]
18 Chien Kuo Rd., Tantzu Hsiang
Taichung Export Processing Zone
Taichung Hsien
Tel: (4) 5322123, 5322127

Paint Industry Association [Taiwan]
7/F-1, Alley 1, Lane 75, Chung Hua Rd.
Sec. 2, Taipei 10731
Tel: (2) 3814249 Fax: (2) 3754258

Paper Containers Industry Association [Taiwan]
4-1 Lane 6, Ching Tien St.
Taipei 10619
Tel: (2) 3517469 Fax: (2) 3517292

Paper Industry Association [Taiwan]
5/F., 20 Pa Teh Rd.
Sec. 3, Taipei 10560
Tel: (2) 7526352, 7528137 Fax: (2) 7528139

Petrochemical Industry Association [Taiwan]
9/F.-2, 390 Fu Hsing S. Rd.
Sec. 1, Taipei 10640
Tel: (2) 7073018, 7073175 Fax: (2) 7555154

Pharmaceutical Industry Association [Taiwan]
6/F., 8 Cheng Teh Rd.
Sec. 1, Taipei
Tel: (2) 5511671, 5511890 Fax: (2) 5239936

Plastic Bags Exporters Association [Taiwan]
4/F., 140 Chung Hsiao E. Rd.
Sec. 1, Taipei 10023
Tel: (2) 3917604 Fax: (2) 3932714

Plastic Christmas Tree Manufacturers & Exporters
Association [Taiwan]
10/F., 320 Chung Hsiao E. Rd.
Sec. 4, Taipei
Tel: (2) 7312063 Fax: (2) 7711036

Plastics Industry Association [Taiwan]
8/F., 162 Chang An E. Rd.
Sec. 2, Taipei 10406
Tel: (2) 7719111/3 Fax: (2) 7315020

Plywood Manufacturers & Exporters Association
[Taiwan]
9/F., 82 Chung Shan N. Rd.
Sec. 1, Taipei 10417
Tel: (2) 5212548, 5212551 Fax: (2) 5626290

Precious Stones Manufacturing Association
[Taiwan]
Rm. 611, 6/F., 41 Chung Hsiao W. Rd.
Sec. 1, Taipei
Tel: (2) 3610108 Fax: (2) 3615033

Preserved Fruits [Taiwan Regional Association of]
6/F.-4, 36-1 San Ming St., Yuan Lin
Chang Hua Hsien 51001
Tel: (2) 8321006 Fax: (2) 8321280

Printing Industry Association [Taiwan]
Rm. A, 6/F., 71 Jen Ai Rd.
Sec. 2, Taipei 10625
Tel: (2) 3919274, 3942615 Fax: (2) 3919294

Refractory Manufacturers' Association [Taiwan]
120 Chung Yang N. Rd.
Sec. 4, Pei Tou District
Taipei 11268
Tel: (2) 8915906 Fax: (2) 8912765

Refrigerating and Air-conditioning Engineering
Association of ROC [Taiwan]
2/F., Fu-lo Mansion
2 Lane 995, Min Sheng E. Rd.
Taipei 10581
Tel: (2) 7685423/4 Fax: (2) 7685424

Refrigeration Industry Association [Taiwan]
3/F., 29 Lane 30, Yung Chi Rd.
Taipei 10550
Tel: (2) 7657152 Fax: (2) 7634259

Rice & Cereals Association [Taiwan Province]
Rm. 9, 4/F., 18 Chung Cheng N. Rd.
Sanchung City, Taipei Hsien 24103
Tel: (2) 9867375 Fax: (2) 9867375

Rubber Industry [Taiwan Regional Association of]
7 Ning Po E. St.
Taipei 10767
Tel: (2) 3512261 Fax: (2) 3412691

Salt Trade Federation [Taiwan]
297 Chien Kang Rd.
Sec. 1, Tainan 70203
Tel: (6) 2652238

Science-based Industrial Park Manufacturers
Association [Taiwan]
7/F., 2 Hsin An Rd.
Hsinchu City
Tel: (35) 775996

Screw Industrial Association [Taiwan]
4/F.-1, 71 Sung Chiang Rd.
Taipei
Tel: (2) 5060918 Fax: (2) 5072429

Sewing Machine Association [Taipei]
2/F., 46, Chin Hsi St.
Taipei
Tel: (2) 5620687

Sewing Machine Exporters Association [Taiwan]
Rm. 1, 12/F., 185 Ming-chuan Rd.
Taichung 40301
Tel: (4) 2245712 Fax: (4) 2239042

Shipbuilding Association [Taiwan]
9/F., 16 Chung Hua Rd.
Sec. 1, Taipei 10031
Tel: (2) 3122641 Fax: (2) 3119514

Shoe Industry Association [Taiwan]
13/F., 131 Sung Chiang Rd.
Taipei
Tel: (2) 5066191/4 Fax: (2) 5081489

Silk & Filament Weaving Industrial Association
[Taiwan]
6/F., 22 Ai Kuo E. Rd.
Taipei 10736
Tel: (2) 3917815, 3917817 Fax: (2) 3973225

Soap and Detergent Manufacturers' Association
[Taiwan]
64 Kai-feng St.
Sec. 2, Taipei 10011
Tel: (2) 3610611/2

Soy Sauce & Fermenting Industry Association
[Taiwan]
4/F.-3, 24 Peiping E. Rd.
Taipei 10026
Tel: (2) 3410739 Fax: (2) 3518475

Spectacles Industry Association [Taiwan]
2/F., 206 Min Chuan E. Rd.
Sec. 2, Taipei 10462
Tel: (2) 5061541, 5057583 Fax: (2) 5070260

Sporting Goods Manufacturers Association
[Taiwan]
8/F., 22 Teh Huei St.
Taipei 10469
Tel: (2) 5941864 Fax: (2) 5919396

Steel & Iron Industries Association [Taiwan]
10/F., 9 Chang An E. Rd.
Sec. 1, Taipei 10404
Tel: (2) 5427900, 5427903 Fax: (2) 5316708

Steel Wire & Wire Rope Industries Association
[Taiwan]
5/F., 369 Fu Hsing N. Rd.
Taipei 10483
Tel: (2) 7155032 Tlx: 26155

Surgical Dressings & Medical Instruments
Industrial Association [Taiwan]
3/F., 85 Chien Kuo S. Rd.
Sec. 2, Taipei 10633
Tel: (2) 7071856 Fax: (2) 3250286

Sweater Industry Association [Taiwan]
9/F.-1, 22 Ai Kuo E. Rd.
Taipei 10726
Tel: (2) 3945216 Fax: (2) 3945270

Synthetic Leather Industries [Taiwan Regional
Association of]
5/F., 30 Nanking W. Rd.
Taipei 10410
Tel: (2) 5219204 Fax: (2) 5415823

Synthetic Resins Manufacturers Association
[Taiwan]
4/F., 82 Chien Kuo N. Rd.
Sec. 2, Taipei
Tel: (2) 5040883 Fax: (2) 5040883

Synthetic Stretch Yarn [Taiwan Association of]
12/F., 22 Ai Kuo E. Rd.
Taipei 10726
Tel: (2) 3410571 Fax: (2) 3218793

Tableware Manufacturing & Export Association
[Taiwan]
20 Lane 131, Hangchow S. Rd.
Sec. 1, Taipei 10044
Tel: (2) 3419342 Fax: (2) 3948980

Tanneries [Taiwan Regional Association of]
6/F.-1, 5-1 Nanking W. Rd.
Taipei
Tel: (2) 5413472 Fax: (2) 5210090

Tea Manufacturers Association [Taiwan]
Rm. 9, 10/F., 165 Nanking W. Rd.
Taipei 10102
Tel: (2) 5417251 Fax: (2) 5416601

Textile Federation [Taiwan]
22 Ai Kuo E. Rd.
Taipei
Tel: (2) 3417251 Fax: (2) 3923855

Textile Printing Dyeing & Finishing Industrial
Association [Taiwan]
12/F., 22 Ai Kuo E. Rd.
Taipei 10726
Tel: (2) 3211095/7, Fax: (2) 3223522

Thermo-Bottle Industry Association [Taiwan]
10/F., 6 Jen Ai Rd.
Sec. 1, Taipei
Tel: (2) 3917543, 3917533 Fax: (2) 3916955

Tobacco and Wine Industry [Taiwan Provincial
Federation of]
2/F., 1, Nan Chang Rd.
Sec. 1, Taipei
Tel: (2) 3212096

Towel Industry Association [Taiwan]
12/F., 22 Ai Kuo E. Rd.
Taipei 10726
Tel: (2) 3210866, 3410435 Fax: (2) 3410434

Toy Manufacturers Association [Taiwan]
6/F., 42 Min Sheng E. Rd.
Sec. 1, Taipei 10443
Tel: (2) 5711264, 5711266, 5362107 Fax: (2) 5411061

Transportation Vehicle
Manufacturers' Association [Taiwan]
9/F., 390 Fu Hsing S. Rd.
Sec. 1, Taipei
Tel: (2) 7051101 Fax: (2) 7066440

Travel Agents [Taipei Association of]
6/F., 20, Sze Ping St.
Taipei
Tel: (2) 5312191 Fax: (2) 5415825

Umbrella Manufacturers Association [Taiwan]
6/F.-4, 149 Ho Ping W. Rd.
Sec. 2, Taipei 10721
Tel: (2) 3117557 Fax: (2) 3119162

Vegetable Oil Manufacturers Association [Taiwan]
6/F., 27 Chang An E. Rd.
Sec. 1, Taipei 10404
Tel: (2) 5616351 Fax: (2) 5621745

Vegetable Processing Association [Taiwan]
15/F., 125 Nan King E. Rd.
Sec. 2, Taipei
Tel: (2) 5616351 Fax: (2) 5074012

Vegetables Exporters Association [Taiwan]
12/F.-3, 31-1 Hsin Sheng N. Rd.
Sec. 2, Taipei 10473
Tel: (2) 5316517, 5715191

Weaving Industry Association [Taiwan]
10/F., 22 Ai Kuo E. Rd.
Taipei 10726
Tel: (2) 3911318/9/7 Fax: (2) 3929413

Wooden Furniture Industrial Association [Taiwan]
Rm. 905 100 Chung Hsiao E. Rd.
Sec. 2, Taipei
Tel: (2) 3215791, 3215811 Fax: (2) 3951754

Wool Textile Industrial Association [Taiwan]
6/F., 22 Ai Kuo E. Rd.
Taipei
Tel: (2) 3913544 Fax: (2) 3518771

Yacht Industry Association [Taiwan]
14/F.-3, 59 Tun Hwa S. Rd.
Sec. 2, Taipei
Tel: (2) 7038481 Fax: (2) 7541744

Zippers Manufacturers Association [Taiwan]
3/F., 9-3 Lane 174, Pa Teh Rd.
Sec. 2, Taipei 10401
Tel: (2) 7310638, 7400692 Fax: (2) 7401109

FINANCIAL INSTITUTIONS

BANKS

Central Bank

The Central Bank of China
2 Roosevelt Rd.
Sec. 1, Taipei
Tel: (2) 3936161 Fax: (2) 3973750 Tlx: 21532

Commercial Banks

Chang Hwa Commercial Bank Ltd.
57 Chung Shan N. Rd.
Sec. 2, Taipei
Tel: (2) 5362951 Tlx: 11323, 11695, 24604

Hua Nan Commercial Bank Ltd.
38 Chungking S. Rd.
Sec. 1, Taipei
Tel: (2) 3713111 Fax: (2) 3315737
Tlx: 11307, 11592 HUANANBK

Overseas Chinese Commercial Banking
Corporation
8 Hsiang Yang Rd.
Taipei
Tel: (2) 3715181 Fax: (2) 3814056, 3315098
Tlx: 12380

Shanghai Commercial & Savings Bank, Ltd.
16 Jen Ai Rd.
Sec. 2, Taipei
Tel: (2) 3933111 Fax: (2) 3928391
Tlx: 11306, 22507 SCSBANK

Taipei Bank
50 Chung Shan N. Rd.
Sec. 2, Taipei
Tel: (2) 5425656 Fax: (2) 5231235
Tlx: 11722A, 11722B

United World Chinese Commercial Bank
65 Kuan Chien Rd.
Taipei
Tel: (2) 3125555 Fax: (2) 3318263
Tlx: 21378, 26648

Domestic Banks

Bank of Taiwan
120 Chung King S. Rd.
Sec. 1, Taipei 10036
Tel: (2) 3147377/88 Fax: (2) 38114139
Tlx: 11201 TAIWANBK

Export-Import Bank of the Republic of China
8/F., 3 Nan Hai Rd.
Taipei
Tel: (2) 3210511 Fax: (2) 3940630 Tlx: 26044

Farmers Bank of China
85 Nanking E. Rd.
Sec. 2, Taipei
Tel: (2) 5517141 Fax: (2) 5975794
Tlx: 21610, 11841 FARMERBK

First Commercial Bank
30 Chungking S. Rd.
Sec. 1, Taipei
Tel: (2) 3111111, 3613611 Fax: (2) 3315739
Tlx: 11310, 11729, 11740, 11741 FIRSTBK

International Commercial Bank of China
100 Chi Lin Rd.
Taipei 10424
Tel: (2) 5633156 Fax: (2) 5632614

Land Bank of Taiwan
46 Kuan Chien Rd.
Taipei
Tel: (2) 3613020 Fax: (2) 3812066
Tlx: 14564 LABK

Taiwan Co-operative Bank
77 Kuan Chien Rd.
Taipei
Tel: (2) 3118811 Fax: (2) 3316567
Tlx: 23749 COOPBANK

Foreign Banks

Amsterdam-Rotterdam Bank N.V. (Netherlands)
2-3/F., 49-51 Min Sheng E. Rd.
Sec. 3, Taipei
Tel: (2) 5037888 Tlx: 19174

Bank of America N.T. & S. A. (USA)
205 Tun Hwa N. Rd.
Taipei
Postal address: PO Box 127, Taipei
Tel: (2) 7154111 Fax: (2) 7132850
Tlx: 11339, 22378

Banque Nationale de Paris (France)
7/F., 214 Tun Hwa N. Rd.
Taipei
Tel: (2) 7161167 Fax: (2) 7152027 Tlx: 22000

Banque Paribas (France)
11/F., 205 Tun Hwa N. Rd.
Taipei
Tel: (2) 7151980 Fax: (2) 7131182 Tlx: 27004

Chase Manhattan Bank, N.A. (USA)
9/F., 115 Min Sheng E. Rd.
Sec. 3, Taipei
Tel: (2) 5141234 Fax: (2) 5141299 Tlx: 21823

Citibank, N.A. (USA)
52 Min Sheng E. Rd.
Sec. 4, Taipei
Tel: (2) 7155931, 7155949 Fax: (2) 7127388
Tlx: 11277, 23547 CITIBANK

Dai-Ichi Kangyo Bank Ltd. (Japan)
137 Nanking E. Rd.
Sec. 2, Taipei
Tel: (2) 5064371 Fax: (2) 5074387/8
Tlx: 11220

Development Bank of Singapore
9/F., 214 Tun Hwa N. Rd.
Taipei
Tel: (2) 7137711 Fax: (2) 7137774 Tlx: 13066

Dresdner Bank AG (Germany)
19/F., 30 Chungking S. Rd.
Sec. 1, Taipei
Tel: (2) 3619191 Fax: (2) 3619190 Tlx: 19233

Hongkong & Shanghai Banking Corporation Ltd.
(Hong Kong)
13-14/F., International Trade Bldg.
333 Keelung Rd.
Sec. 1, Taipei 10548
Tel: (2) 7230088 Fax: (2) 7576333 Tlx: 10934

Lloyds Bank International Ltd. (UK)
3/F., 87 Sung Chiang Rd.
Taipei
Tel: (2) 5068521 Fax: (2) 5081252 Tlx: 28804

Manufacturers Hanover Trust Co. (USA)
10/F., 62 Tun Hwa N. Rd.
Taipei
Tel: (2) 7213150 Fax: (2) 7310264 Tlx: 28274

Royal Bank of Canada
Union Enterprise Plaza
12/F., 109 Min Sheng E. Rd.
Sec. 3, Taipei
Tel: (2) 7130911 Fax: (2) 7132884 Tlx: 13384

Standard Chartered Bank (UK)
337 Fu Hsing N. Rd.
Taipei
Tel: (2) 7166261 Fax: (2) 7164068 Tlx: 12133

Toronto Dominion Bank (Canada)
2/F., 337 Fu Hsing N. Rd.
Taipei
Tel: (2) 7162160 Fax: (2) 7134816 Tlx: 22503

Wespac Banking Co. (Australia)
15/F., 99 Fu Hsing N. Rd.
Taipei
Tel: (2) 7129133 Fax: (2) 7154207 Tlx: 11048

INSURANCE COMPANIES

Aetna Life Insurance Co., of America
3/F., 658 Tun Hwa S. Rd.
Taipei
Tel: (2) 3259213 Fax: (2) 7556123

Cathay Insurance Co., Ltd.
237 Chien Kuo S. Rd.
Sec. 1, Taipei
Tel: (2) 7067890 Fax: (2) 7042915 Tlx: 11143

Central Insurance Co., Ltd.
6 Chung Hsiao W. Rd.
Sec. 1, Taipei
Tel: (2) 3819910 Fax: (2) 3116901

Central Reinsurance Corp.
12/F., 53 Nanking E. Rd.
Sec. 2, Taipei
Tel: (2) 5115211 Fax: (2) 5235350 Tlx: 11471

China Mariners' Assurance Corporation
62 Hsin Sheng S. Rd.
Sec. 1, Taipei
Tel: (2) 3913201 Fax: (2) 3918372, 3915945

Jardine Insurance Brokers (Taiwan) Ltd.
14/F., World Trade Bldg., 50 Hsin Sheng S. Rd.
Sec. 1, Taipei
Tel: (2) 3954611/4 Fax: (2) 3932233

Kuo Hua Insurance Co., Ltd.
166 Chang An E. Rd.
Sec. 2, TaipeiTel: (2) 7514225 Fax: (2) 7817801

Nan Shan Life Insurance Co., Ltd.
302 Min Chuan E. Rd.
Taipei
Tel: (2) 5013333 Fax: (2) 5012555

Shin Kong Marine Insurance Co.
13 Chien Kuo N. Rd.
Sec. 2, Taipei
Tel: (2) 5075335 Fax: (2) 5063423, 5046312

Tai An Insurance Co., Ltd.
59 Kuan Chien Rd.
Taipei
Tel: (2) 3819678 Fax: (2) 3719668, 3816057

Taiwan Fire & Marine Insurance Co., Ltd.
9/F., 49 Kuan Chien Rd.
Taipei
Tel: (2) 3317261 Fax: (2) 3610859

Union Insurance Co., Ltd.
12/F., 219 Chung Hsiao E. Rd.
Sec. 4, Taipei
Tel: (2) 7765567 Fax: (2) 7317670 Tlx: 27616

STOCK EXCHANGE

Ministry of Finance, Securities and Exchange
Commission
12/F., 3 Nan Hai Rd.
Taipei
Tel: (2) 3928572 Fax: (2) 3948249

Taiwan Stock Exchange Corporation
City Bldg., 10/F., 85 Yen-Ping South Rd.
Taipei 10034
Tel: (2) 3114020 Fax: (2) 3114004 Tlx: 22914

SERVICES

ACCOUNTING FIRMS

Taipei Accountants Association
9/F., 1 Nan Hai Rd.
Taipei
Tel: (2) 3945290 Fax: (2) 3972573

Coopers & Lybrand
12/F., 367 Fu Hsing N. Rd.
Taipei
Tel: (2) 5455678 Fax: (2) 5140248 Tlx: 16573

Diwan, Ernst & Young
17/F., Cathay Chung
Cheng Bldg., 2 Chung Cheng Rd.
Sec. 3, Kaohsiung
Tel: (7) 2240011 Fax: (7) 2220198

Diwan, Ernst & Young
7/F., 239 Min Chuang Rd.
Taichung
Tel: (4) 3235500 Fax: (4) 3235577

Diwan, Ernst & Young
9/F., CETRA Tower
333, Keelung Rd.
Sec. 1, Taipei
Tel: (2) 720-4000 Fax: (2) 7576050

Peat, Marwick, Mitchell & Co.
12/F., 367 Fu Hsing N. Rd.
Taipei
Tel: (2) 7138001, 7138582 Fax: (2) 7150947
Tlx: 23184 PMMTPE

Price Waterhouse
27/F., CETRA Tower
333 Keelung Rd.
Sec. 1, Taipei 110
Tel: (2) 7296666 Fax: (2) 7576371
Tlx: 24241 PWTPE

T.N. Soong & Co. (Arthur Andersen)
12/F., Hung Tai Century Tower
156 Min Sheng E. Rd.
Sec. 3, Taipei
Postal address: PO Box 1539, Taipei
Tel: (2) 5459988 Fax: (2) 5459966

T.N. Soong & Co. (Arthur Andersen)
7/F., Malayan Overseas Insurance Bldg.
168 Chung Cheng 4th Rd.
Kaohsiung
Tel: (7) 2514311/6 Fax: (7) 2412577, 2719017

T.N. Soong & Co. (Arthur Andersen)
28/F., Long Bon World Trade Bldg.
160 Taichun Kan Rd.
Sec. 1, Taichung
Tel: (4) 3280055 Fax: (4) 3280700

ADVERTISING AGENCIES

Taipei Association of Advertising Agencies
2/F. 4-1, Alley 3, Lane 217
Chung Hsiao E. Rd.
Sec. 3, Taipei
Tel: (2) 7523765 Fax: (2) 7417051

ARZ International Co., Ltd.
2/F., 5, Alley 1, Lane 61
Ruei An St.
Taipei
Tel: (2) 7849111 Fax: (2) 7554022, 7556840

Ball Partnership Agency, Ltd.
10/F., 85 Jen Ai Rd.
Sec. 4, Taipei
Tel: (2) 7751950, 7417934 Fax: (2) 7417934

Bozell/CCAA
4/F., No. 26, Nanking E. Rd.
Sec. 3, Taipei
Tel: (2) 5063101 Fax: (2) 5070060

Brain Advertising Co., Ltd.
5-7/F., 208 Nanking E. Rd.
Sec. 3, Taipei
Tel: (2) 7413131 Fax: (2) 7721579

BSB Taiwan Company Limited
6/F., Chant Bldg., 120 Chien Kou N. Rd.
Sec. 2, Taipei
Tel: (2) 5055305 Fax: (2) 5055332

Daiko HWG Advertising Corp.
13/F., No. 89, Nanking E. Rd.
Sec. 5, Taipei
Tel: (2) 7535577

DDB Needham Worldwide Inc.
4/F., Quantas House, #1 Lin Shen S. Rd.
Taipei
Tel: (2) 3951995 Fax: (2) 3951998

Denstu Inc.-Taipei
11/F., 167 Tun Hua N. Rd.
Taipei
Tel: (2) 7191911 Fax: (2) 7120439

Dentsu, Young & Rubicam/Taipei
6/F., 146 Sung Chiang Rd.
Taipei
Tel: (2) 5219322 Fax: (2) 5219249
Tlx: 78513457

Hwa Wei & Grey Advertising Co.
12/F., 180 Nanking E. Rd.
Sec. 4, Taipei
Tel: (2) 7113181 Fax: (2) 7810476

International Advertising Agency Ltd.
4/F., 73 Fu Hsing N. Rd.
Taipei
Tel: (2) 7526211 Fax: (2) 7526210

J. Walter Thompson Limited
18/F., Union Century Bldg., 163 Keelung Rd.
Sec. 1, Taipei
Tel: (2) 7469028 Fax: (2) 7664166

Leo Burnett Co., Inc., Taiwan Branch
7/F., 123 Chung Hsiao E. Rd.
Sec. 2, Taipei
Tel: (2) 3961222 Fax: (2) 3973046 Tlx: 23504

Lintas Taiwan
Rm. 501, Lotus Bldg., 136 Jen Ai Rd.
Sec. 3, Taipei
Tel: (2) 7015299 Fax: (2) 7015129

McCann-Erickson Taiwan Co.
4/F., Ming Tai Bldg., 1 Jen-Ai Rd.
Sec. 4, Taipei 10649
Tel: (2) 7517561 Fax: (2) 7411513

Ogilvy & Mather (Taiwan) Co., Ltd.
8/F., 51 Min Sheng E. Rd.
Sec. 3, Taipei
Tel: (2) 5055789 Fax: (2) 5052334 Tlx: 12490

Saatchi & Saatchi Advertising
10/F., 311 Nanking E. Rd.
Sec. 3, Taipei
Tel: (2) 7135201 Fax: (2) 7150548 Tlx: 21317

Series/DMB&B Tokyu
2/F.-1, No. 8, Alley 3, Lane 303, Nanking E. Rd.
Sec. 3, Taipei
Tel: (2) 7186336 Fax: (2) 7186334

Stentor/BBDO
6/F., LiFung Tower, 1 Nanking E. Rd.
Sec. 4, Taipei 10568
Tel: (2) 7138781 Fax: (2) 7129371

Taiwan Advertising Co., Ltd.
10/F., 91 Nanking E. Rd.
Sec. 3 Taipei
Tel: (2) 5069201 Fax: (2) 5079244

United Advertising Co.
10/F., 83 Chungking S. Rd.
Sec. 1, Taipei
Tel: (2) 3143366 Fax: (2) 3143314

LAW FIRMS

Anglo-American Law Office
12/F., 71 Jen Ai Rd.
Sec. 2, Taipei
Tel: (2) 3921843

Baker & McKenzie
15/F., Hung Tai Center
168 Tun Hwa N. Rd.
Taipei
Tel: (2) 7126151 Fax: (2) 7169250

Cheng Chang & Associates Law Offices
3/F.,-7, 2 Fu Hsing N. Rd.
Taipei
Tel: (2) 7415091 Fax: (2) 7415090 Tlx: 20963

Ding & Ding Law Offices
10/F., 563 Chung Hsiao E. Rd.
Sec. 4, Taipei
Tel: (2) 7534151 Fax: (2) 7647171

Dong & Lee, Attorneys at Law
9/F., 141 Jen Ai Rd.
Sec. 3, Taipei
Tel: (2) 7764612 Fax: (2) 7411686

Far East United Law Office
4/F., 176 Chung Hsiao E. Rd.
Sec. 1, Taipei
Tel: (2) 3928811 Fax: (2) 3214414

Formosa Transnational Attorneys at Law
15/F., 136 Jen Ai Rd.
Sec. 3, Taipei
Tel: (2) 7557366 Fax: (2) 7556486

Howe & Lloyd
8/F.-A, 230 Hsin Yi Rd.
Sec. 2, Taipei
Tel: (2) 3416000 Fax: (2) 3915972

Hua, Kao, Juo & Lin Lawyers
11/F., 296 Kuang Fu S. Rd.
Taipei
Tel: (2) 7764621 Fax: (2) 7764623

Huang & Partners Attorneys and
Counsellors-at-Law
10/F., 683 Min Sheng E. Rd.
Taipei
Tel: (2) 7135172 Fax: (2) 7120480

Jones, Day, Reavis & Pogue
7/F., 2 Tun Hwa S. Rd.
Sec. 2, Taipei
Tel: (2) 7046808/9 Fax: (2) 7046791

Kaplan, Russin, Vecchi & Parker
Rm. 901, 9/F., 205 Tun Hwa N. Rd.
Taipei
Tel: (2) 7128956/7 Fax: (2) 7134711
Tlx: 23775 KAPRUS

Lee & Li, Attorneys-at-Law
7/F., 201 Tun Hwa N. Rd.
Taipei
Tel: (2) 7153300 Fax: (2) 7133966 Tlx: 11651

Liang & Associates Attorneys-at-Law
12/F.-2, 76 Tun Hwa S. Rd.
Sec. 2, Taipei
Tel: (2) 7556595 Fax: (2) 7082946

Michael C. F. Chang Attorney-at-Law
Rm. 402, 58 Fu Hsing N. Rd.
Taipei
Tel: (2) 7732033 Fax: (2) 7725850

Orient Alliance Law Offices
7/F., 53 Nan Chang Rd.
Sec. 2, Taipei
Tel: (2) 3913191/5 Fax: (2) 3949045

Tsar & Tsai Law office
9/F., 249 Tun Hwa S. Rd.
Sec. 1, Taipei
Tel: (2) 7814111 Fax: (2) 7213834, 7315581
Tlx: 22732 TSARTSAI

Tseng, Tsai, Chern & Yang
4/F., 131 Min Sheng E. Rd.
Sec. 3, Taipei
Tel: (2) 7130177 Fax: (2) 7169250

Wang, Sun, Chao & Chen
Attorneys-at-Law
12/F., 96 Chung Hsiao E. Rd.
Sec. 2, Taipei
Tel: (2) 3218448 Fax: (2) 3938767

TRANSLATORS & INTERPRETERS

ABC
1 Fu Shing N. Rd.
Taipei
Tel: (2) 7312483

Business Consultant & Service
PO Box 11394
Taipei
Tel: (2) 8739601 Fax: (2) 8729550

Chung Hua Translation Service
5/F., 60 Po Ai Rd.
Taipei
Tel: (2) 3315297 Fax: (2) 3119784

Presidential Translation Service (Main)
11/F.-6, 1, Fu Hsing N. Rd.
Taipei
Tel: (2) 7312483, 3317077 Fax: (2) 7526464

Pristine Translation & Information Consultants
2/F., 2 Alley 2, Lane 244, Roosevelt Rd.
Sec. 3, Taipei
Tel: (2) 3947670 Fax: (2) 3919023

Pristine Translation & Information Consultants
2/F., 5 Lane 734, Ting Chou Rd.
Taipei
Tel: (2) 3947640

Shakespeare
3/F., 190 Nanking E. Rd.
Sec. 2, Taipei
Tel: (2) 5066401

Today Translation Service
3/F., 186 Nanking E. Rd.
Sec. 2, Taipei
Tel: (2) 5067601 Fax: (2) 5066222

TRANSPORTATION

AIRLINES

Air Associates, Ltd.
11/F., 131 Min Sheng E. Rd.
Sec. 3, Taipei
Tel: (2) 7139858 Fax: (2) 7121690

Air Canada
8/F., 61 Nanking E. Rd.
Taipei
Tel: (2) 5078133

Air France
10/F., 167 Fu Hsing N. Rd.
Taipei
Tel: (2) 7187300

Air India
9/F., 1-341 Chung Hsiao E. Rd.
Sec. 4, Taipei
Tel: (2) 7410163

Air Nauru
2 Min Tzu E. Rd.
Taipei
Tel: (2) 5948116

Air New Zealand
6/F., 98 Nanking E. Rd.
Sec. 2, Taipei
Tel: (2) 5313980, 5418080

Alitalia Airlines
4/F., 169 Chung Hsiao E. Rd.
Sec. 4, Taipei
Tel: (2) 7415161 Fax: (2) 7523048

Asiana Airlines
5/F., 65 Chien Kuo N. Rd.
Sec. 2, Taipei
Tel: (2) 5081114 Fax: (2) 5080960

British Airways
6/F., 98 Nanking E. Rd.
Sec. 2, Taipei
Tel: (2) 5114784

Canadian Airlines International
Taipei Tel: (2) 5034111

Canadian Pacific Airlines
3/F., 90 Chien Kuo N. Rd.
Sec. 2, Taipei
Tel: (2) 5114784

Cathay Pacific Airways, Taiwan Branch
1/F., 65 Nanking E. Rd.
Sec. 3, Taipei
Tel: (2) 7152333, 5077000
Kaohsiung Tel: (7) 2013166

China Air Lines
131 Nanking E. Rd.
Sec. 3, Taipei
Tel: (2) 7151212, 7152626
Kaohsiung Tel: (7) 2826141

Continental Airlines
2/F., 150 Fu Hsing N. Rd.
Taipei
Tel: (2) 7120131

Delta
1/F., 50, Nan King E. Rd.
Sec. 2, Taipei
Tel: (2) 5513656, 5510923 Fax: (2) 5317364

EVA Airways
166 Min Sheng E. Rd.
Sec. 2, Taipei
Tel: (2) 5011999 Fax: (2) 5022599

Far Eastern Air Transport Corp.
5, Alley 123, Lane 405, Tun Hwa N. Rd.
Taipei
Tel: (2) 3615431, 7121555 Fax: (2) 7189724
Kaohsiung Tel: (7) 2411181

Formosa Airlines
11/F., 87 Sung Chiang Rd.
Taipei
Tel: (2) 5074188 Fax: (2) 5065912

Fushing Airlines
2/F., 150 Fu Hsing N. Rd.
Taipei
Tel: (2) 7152766 Fax: (2) 7185658

Garuda Indonesia
1/F., 66, Sung Chiang Rd.
Taipei
Tel: (2) 5612311 Fax: (2) 5238920

Great China Airlines
38 Jen Ai Rd.
Sec. 2, Taipei
Tel: (2) 3568000
Kaohsiung Tel: (7) 8017327

Japan Asia
Taipei Tel: (2) 7765151
Kaohsiung Tel: (7) 2411156

KLM Royal Dutch Airlines
1 Nanking E. Rd.
Sec. 4, Taipei
Tel: (2) 7171000 Fax: (2) 7173767

Korean Air
53 Nanking E. Rd.
Sec. 2, Taipei
Tel: (2) 5214242 Fax: (2) 5611204

Lufthansa German Airlines
3/F., 90 Chien Kuo N. Rd.
Sec. 2, Taipei
Tel: (2) 5034114 Fax: (2) 5095827

Makung Airlines
305, Ho Tune Rd., Chien Chin
Kaohsiung
Tel: (7) 2211175 Fax: (7) 7199204

Malaysian Airline System
102 Tun Hwa N. Rd.
Taipei
Tel: (2) 5147888, 7168388 Fax: (2) 7129312
Kaohsiung Tel: (7) 2229348

Mandarin Airlines
Taipei Tel: (2) 7171230,

Northwest Orient
181 Fu Hsing N. Rd.
Taipei
Tel: (2) 7161555 Fax: (2) 7190237

Olympic Airways
6/F.-2, 125 Roosevelt Rd.
Sec. 3, Taipei
Tel: (2) 3623302

Philippine Airlines
2/F., 90 Chien Kuo N. Rd.
Sec. 2. Taipei
Tel: (2) 5033030 Fax: (2) 5096183

Quantas Airways Ltd.
11/F., 9 Nanking E. Rd.
Sec. 3, Taipei
Tel: (2) 5062311 Fax: (2) 5065006

Royal Brunei
11/F., 9, Nan King E. Rd.
Sec. 3, Taipei
Taipei Tel: (2) 5062236, 5073171 Fax: (2) 5072472

Saudi Arabian Airlines
4/F., 222 Nanking E. Rd.
Sec. 2, Taipei
Tel: (2) 5063171 Fax: (2) 5067288

Scandinavian Airlines System
2/F., 150 Fu Hsing N. Rd.
Taipei
Tel: (2) 7120138 Fax: (2) 7185658

Silkair
Kaohsiung Tel: (7) 2154222

Singapore Airlines Limited.
148 Sun Chiang Rd.
Taipei
Tel: (2) 5516655, 5314232 Fax: (2) 5235955

South African Airways
Rm. 1203, 12/F., Bank Tower Bldg.
205 Tun Hwa N. Rd.
Taipei
Tel: (2) 7136363 Fax: (2) 7139478

Swiss Air Transport Co., Ltd.
8/F., 61 Nanking E. Rd.
Sec. 3, Taipei
Tel: (2) 5078133 Fax: (2) 5075816

Taiwan Airlines
2/F., 306 Jen Ai Rd.
Sec. 4, Taipei
Tel: (2) 7551772
Kaohsiung Tel: (7) 8035077

Taiwan Navigation Corporation
7/F., 17 Hsu Chang St.
Taipei
Tel: (2) 3113882

Thai Airways International
2/F., 150 Fu Hsing N. Rd.
Taipei
Tel: (2) 7154622, 7152766 Fax: (2) 7129801
Kaohsiung Tel: (7) 2514081

Transasia Airways
Taipei Tel: (2) 5579000
Kaohsiung Tel: (7) 2152868

United Air Lines
12/F., 2 Jen Ai Rd.
Sec. 4, Taipei
Tel: (2) 3258868, 7037600 Fax: (2) 7097564

Varig Brazilian Airlines
5/F., 259 Nanking E. Rd.
Sec. 3, Taipei
Tel: (2) 7126892 Fax: (2) 7181057

TRANSPORTATION & CUSTOMS BROKERAGE FIRMS

Companies may offer more services in addition to those listed here. Service information is provided as a guideline and is not intended to be comprehensive.

Air Tiger Express Co., Ltd.
133, Chung Hsiao E. Rd.
Sec. 5, Taipei
Tel: (2) 7643196, 7672145 Fax: (2) 7660224
Airfreight, air cargo agents, customs broker

Airlife Freight (Taiwan) Corp.
PO Box 55-617
Taipei
Tel: (2) 7647711/6 Fax: (2) 7606868
Aircargo agent, customs brokers container, storing & warehouse service, shipping agent

Allport Express Inc.
4//F., 391, Shin Yi Rd.
Sec. 4, Taipei
Tel: (2) 7582108, 7586499 Fax: (2) 7294105
Customs broker, forwarder, shipping agent

American Consolidation Services
7/F., 2 Nan King E. Rd.
Sec. 2, Taipei
Tel: (2) 5378537 Fax: (2) 5611990
Cargo consolidation, documentation,shipping arrangement

American President Lines, Ltd.
5/F., 245 Tun Hwa S. Rd.
Sec. 1, Taipei
Tel: (2) 7764531 Fax: (2) 7772570
Shipping

Anlun Transportation Co.
PO Box 63-142
Taichung
Tel: (4) 2956779 Fax: (4) 2963213
Container, storing & warehouse service, forwarder

Barwil Agencies Inc.
11/F., 148 Sung Chiang Rd.
Taipei
Tel: (2) 5368222 Fax: (2) 5431972
Tlx: 21943 BARWIL
Shipping

Cargolux Airlines International SA
11/F., 131 Min Sheng E. Rd.
Sec. 3, Taipei
Tel: (2) 7139858 Tlx: 21546 LAIFU
International air cargo

Chian Stone Transportation Co., Ltd.
5/F., 51-4, Chang An E. Rd.
Sec. 2, Taipei
Tel: (2) 5215235 Fax: (2) 5215270
Container, storing & warehouse service, customs broker

China Air Lines
131 Nanking E. Rd.
Sec. 3, Taipei
Tel: (2) 7152626 Fax: (2) 7174641
Air cargo

China Trade & Development Corporation
6/F., CUTICO Bldg., 136 Sung Chiang Rd.
Taipei
Tel: (2) 5217272 Fax: (2) 5217055
Shipping

Chinese Maritime Transport Ltd.
8th-10/F., 15 Chi Nan Rd.
Sec. 1, Taipei
Tel: (2) 3212121 Fax: (2) 3411234
Tlx: 11235 OOLINES, 11384 INCSHIP
Container, storing & warehouse service, shipping agent

Crown International Forwarder Co.
4/F.-4, 165 Min Sheng E. Rd.
Sec. 5, Taipei
Tel: (2) 7622500, 7608233 Fax: (2) 7612378, 7467622
Forwarder

Evergreen Marine Corporation
Evergreen Bldg., 166 Min Sheng E. Rd.
Sec. 2, Taipei
Tel: (2) 5057766 Fax: (2) 5371023, 5420585
Tlx: 11476, 21569 EVERMARINE
Air cargo, container, storing & warehouse service, shipping agents

Far Eastern Air Transport Corp.
5, Alley 123, Lane 405, Tun Hwa N. Rd.
Taipei 10592
Tel: (2) 7121555 Fax: (2) 7122428
Air cargo, airline

Federal Express
361 Da Nan Rd., Shih Lin
Taipei
Tel: (2) 7883535 Fax: (2) 9912037
Air cargo, courier

Federal Express Corporation
75 Hsin Chung 2nd Rd.
Kaohsiung 802
Tel: (7) 3361066 Fax: (7) 3361061
Air cargo, courier

Federal Express Corporation
1/F., 770 Pa-Teh Rd.
Sec. 4, Taipei 11510
Tel: (2) 7883636 Fax: (2) 7882503 Tlx: 13974
Air cargo, courier

Formosa Shipping & Enterprise Corp.
7/F., 95 Nanking E. Rd.
Sec. 2, Taipei
Tel: (2) 5612270/3 Fax: (2) 5615161
Shipping

Grand Express International Inc.
(Agent for SPX Div. of DHL Group)
1/F., 82 Chien Kuo N. Rd.
Sec. 2, Taipei
Tel: (2) 5036858 Fax: (2) 5032781
Airfreight, air cargo agent, shipping

Handsome Express Co., Ltd.
8/F., San Yang Chung Hsiao Bldg.
180 Chung Hsiao E. Rd.
Sec. 4, Taipei
Tel: (2) 7518431, 7112151 Fax: (2) 7515872
Shipping

Hapag-Lloyd (Taiwan) Shipping Agencies, Ltd.
11/F., 285 Chung Hsiao E. Rd.
Sec. 4, Taipei
Tel: (2) 7521155 Fax: (2) 7310062
Shipping Agent

Home French Customs Packing & Shipping Co.
PO Box 73-91
Taipei
Tel: (2) 8722111 Fax: (2) 8722115
Customs broker, shipping agent

Jardine, Matheson & Co., Ltd.
13/F., 50 Hsin Sheng S. Rd.
Sec. 1, Taipei
Tel: (2) 3931177 Fax: (2) 3931160, 3920435
Tlx: 11391, 21851 JARDINES
Shipping

Kline Air Service (Taiwan) Ltd.
PO Box 81-193
Taipei
Tel: (2) 7138146 Fax: (2) 7153663
Air cargo agent, customs broker

Kuehne & Nagel (Taiwan) Ltd.
4/F., 219 Nanking E. Rd.
Sec. 3, Taipei
Tel: (2) 7130421 Fax: (2) 7133591
Tlx: 23647 KNTAI
Shipping

Lien Ho Co., Ltd.
9/F., 83 Chungking S. Rd.
Sec. 1, Taipei
Tel: (2) 3111567 Fax: (2) 3149122
Shipping

Maersk Taiwan Ltd. Shipping Agency
4/F., 123 Chung Hsiao, E. Rd.
Sec. 2, Taipei
Tel: (2) 3943521 Fax: (2) 3939483 Tlx: 24086
Shipping

Maritime Transportation Agencies Ltd.
11/F., 285 Chung Hsiao E. Rd.
Sec. 4, Taipei
Tel: (2) 7521155 Fax: (2) 7310062 Tlx: 21822
Shipping

Morrison Express Co., Ltd.
14/F., 186 Nan King E. Rd.
Sec. 4, Taipei
Tel: (2) 7314411 Fax: (2) 7719414
Container, storing & warehouse service,
airfreight, customs broker, shipping agent

MSAS Cargo International Ltd.
Rm. 406, 155 Keelung Rd.
Sec. 1, Taipei
Tel: (2) 7635577 Fax: (2) 7695695, 7603505
Air/sea freight, customs broker, charters, forwarder

Nan Tai Enterprises Co., Ltd.
3/F., 2 Tun Hwa S. Rd.,
Sec. 1, Taipei
Tel: (2) 7768611 Fax: (2) 7514855, 7513577
Shipping

Ocean Pioneer Shipping Co., Ltd.
37 Chi Nan Rd.
Sec. 2, Taipei
Tel: (2) 3218811 Fax: (2) 3414977, 3971320
Tlx: 11098, 21586 OPIONEER
Shipping

Oceanic Trading Corporation
4/F., 210 Nanking E. Rd.
Sec. 3, Taipei
PO Box 1473 Taipei
Tel: (2) 7521133, 7712131 Fax: (2) 7517402
Tlx: 11266
Shipping

Power Air Cargo Co. Ltd.
PO Box 55-788
Taipei
Tel: (2) 5015533 Fax: (2) 5084787
Air cargo export & import forwarder, container,
storing & warehouse service, customs broker,
shipping agent

San Yang Navigation Co., Ltd.
5/F., 71 Nanking E. Rd.
Sec. 2, Taipei
Tel: (2) 5117151 Fax: (2) 5428612
Shipping

Schenker (H.K.) Ltd., Taiwan Branch
4/F., 164 Fu Hsin N. Rd.
Taipei
Tel: (2) 7722333
Air cargo agency, customs broker, international air/
sea forwarder, packing

Schenker (H.K.) Ltd., Tao-Yuan Office
B-11 Aircargo Terminal
CKS International Airport
Tao-Yuan
Tel: (3) 3834361
Air cargo agency, customs broker, international air/
sea forwarder, packing

Sea Shipping Co., Ltd.
Rm. 402, 130 Chung Hsiao E. Rd.
Sec. 2, Taipei
Tel: (2) 3945136 Fax: (2) 3921687
Shipping

Sea-Land Service, Inc.
9/F., 2 Nanking E. Rd.
Sec. 2, Taipei
Tel: (2) 5311122 Fax: (2) 5424237
Shipping agent

Seven Ocean Maritime Transport Co., Ltd.
5/F., 103 Nanking E. Rd.
Sec. 3, Taipei
Tel: (2) 5080808 Fax: (2) 5068664
Shipping

Southward Corporation
7th-10/F., 143-45, Chung Shan N. Rd.
Sec. 1, Taipei
Tel: (2) 5411614 Fax: (2) 5411622
Shipping

Star Shipping & Trading Co., (Taiwan) Ltd.
7th Fl, 219 Nanking E. Rd.
Sec. 3, Taipei
Tel: (2) 7151133 Fax: (2) 7160966 Tlx: 11464
Shipping

Strong Maritime Corporation
6/F., 87 Sung Chiang Rd.
Taipei
Tel: (2) 5091789
Shipping

Super Air Express Co., Ltd.
2/F., 232 Tun Hwa N. Rd.
Taipei
Tel: (2) 7124555 Fax: (2) 7173411, 7176143
Air cargo agents, forwarding

Ta Shin Shipping Co., Ltd.
3/F., 71 Nanking E. Rd.
Sec. 2, Taipei
Tel: (2) 5221144, 5221391 Fax: (2) 5364194
Shipping

Tait & Co., Ltd.
9/F., 320 Chung Hsiao E. Rd.
Sec. 4, Taipei
Tel: (2) 7210000 Fax: (2) 7315347
Shipping

Taiwan Navigation Co., Ltd.
7/F., 17 Hsu Chang St.
Taipei
Tel: (2) 3113882, 3113465, 3614883 Fax: (2) 3316596
Shipping

All addresses and telephone numbers are in Taiwan, Republic of China unless otherwise noted. The country code for Taiwan is [886].

Taiwan Swire Ltd.
John Swire & Sons (H.K.) Ltd.
Taiwan Branch
7/F., 18 Chang An E. Rd.
Sec. 1, Taipei
Tel: (2) 5636011 Fax: (2) 5620731, 5613444
Shipping

Thyssen Haniel Logistics (Taiwan) Ltd.
10/F., 275, Nan King E. Rd.
Sec. 3, Taipei
Postal address: PO Box 81-184
Tel: (2) 7191215 Fax: (2) 7196632, 7196829
Air cargo agents, forwarding, shipping agents

TNT Express Worldwide, Kaohsiung Branch
No. 5, Alley 1, Lane 80, Wu Fu 2nd Rd.
Kaohsiung
Tel: (7) 2270900/1/2 Fax: (7) 2263845
Air cargo, courier

TNT Express Worldwide, Taichung Branch
No. 57, Han Kou Rd.
Sec. 1, Taichung
Tel: (4) 3282099, 3261584 Fax: 3262054
Air cargo, courier

TNT Skypak International, Taipei Branch
3/F., 207 Tun Hua N. Rd.
Taipei
Tel: (2) 7132345, 7127700 (Pick up hotline)
Fax: (2) 7122234 Tlx: 25062 TNTPAC
Air cargo, courier

Uniglory Marine Corporation
6/F., 172 Min Sheng E. Rd.,
Sec. 2, Taipei
Tel: (2) 5016711, 5017211 Fax: (2) 5017592
Shipping Agent

Union Transportation Ltd.
B1-2, 7, Lane 768, Pa Teh Rd.
Sec. 4, Nan Kang, Taipei
Tel: (2) 7866988 Fax: (2) 7861925, 7861956
Air cargo agents, shipping agents

United Agencies Shipping Co., Ltd.
13/F., 50 Hsin Sheng S. Rd.
Sec. 1, Taipei
Tel: (2) 3934261 Fax: (2) 3962379 Tlx: 28395
Shipping

United Shipping Corporation
6/F., 46 Nanking E. Rd.
Sec. 5, Taipei
Tel: (2) 7466700
Shipping

United Terminals Ltd.
14/F., 50 Hsin Sheng S. Rd.
Sec. 1, Taipei
Tel: (2) 3936242 Fax: (2) 3931160, 3920435
Shipping

UPS International Inc., Taiwan Branch
B1, 361 Ta Nan Rd.
Taipei
Tel: (2) 8833868 Fax: (2) 8833890 Tlx: 17669
Air cargo, courier

Wilhelmsen Agencies Inc., Taipei Office
11/F., 148 Sung Chiang Rd.,
Taipei
Tel: (2) 5368222 Fax: (2) 5431972
Shipping

Worldwide Freight Terminal, Inc.
201, Ta Tung Rd.
Sec. 1, Hsi Chih, Taipei Hsien
Tel: (2) 6413111 Fax: (2) 6435750 Tlx: 31163
Container, storing & warehouse service, forwarder, shipping

Yangming Marine Transport Corp.
4/F., 53 Huai Ning St.
Taipei
Tel: (2) 3812911/9 Fax: (2) 3148058
Shipping agent

PUBLICATIONS, MEDIA & INFORMATION SOURCES

DIRECTORIES & YEARBOOKS

Asian Computer Directory
(Monthly)
Washington Plaza
1st Fl., 230 Wanchai Road
Wanchai, Hong Kong
Tel: [852] 8327123 Fax: [852] 8329208

Asian Printing Directory
(Annual; English/Chinese)
Travel & Trade Publishing (Asia)
16th Fl., Capitol Centre
5-19 Jardines Bazaar
Causeway Bay, Hong Kong
Tel: [852] 8903067 Fax: [852] 8952378

Asia Pacific Leather Directory
(Annual)
Asia Pacific Leather Yearbook
(Annual)
Asia Pacific Directories, Ltd.
6/F., Wah Hen Commercial Centre
381 Hennessy Rd.
Hong Kong
Tel: [852] 8936377 Fax: [852] 8935752

Bankers Handbook For Asia
(Annual)
Dataline Asia Pacific Inc.
3rd Fl., Hollywood Center
233 Hollywood Road
Hong Kong
Tel: [852] 8155221 Fax: [852] 8542794

Directory of Manufacturers & Exporters
(Quarterly)
International Trade Association of the R.O.C
8/F., 148 Chung Hsiao E. Rd
Sec. 4, Taipei

Directory of Package Plant Suppliers of Taiwan
(Annual)
Coordination Committee on Package Plant
110 Hwai Ning St
Taipei
Tel: (2) 3831832 Fax: (2) 3813711

Directory of Turn-Key in Taiwan
Taiwan Association of Machinery Industry
2/F., 110 Huaining St
Taipei
Tel: (2) 3813722 Fax: (2) 3813711

Exhibitions 'Round the World
(Annual)
Trade Winds Inc.
PO Box 7-179
Taipei 10602
Tel: (2) 3932718 Fax: (2) 3964022

Financial & Investment Yearbook ROC
(Annual)
China Economic News Service
555 Chunghsiao East Road
Section 4, Taipei
Tel: (2) 7681234 Fax: (2) 7632303

Imports-Exports of the Republic of China
(Annual)
China External Trade Development Council
4-8/F., CETRA Tower, 333 Keelung Rd
Sec. 1, Taipei 10548
Tel: (2) 7255200 Fax: (2) 7576653

International Tax and Duty Free Buyers Index
(Annual)
Pearl & Dean Publishing, Ltd.
9/F., Chung Nam Bldg., 1 Lockhart Rd.
Hong Kong
Tel: [852] 8660395 Fax: [852] 2999810

Kompass Register Of Taiwan Industry And
Commerce
(Annual)
Trade Winds, Inc.
No. 7, Lane 75, Yungkang St.
Taipei
Tel: (2) 3922718 Fax: (2) 3964022

Manufacturers and Traders of Taiwan
Chinese National Export Enterprises Assoc
c/o China Products Color Magazine Assoc
6/F., 285 Nanking E. Rd
Sec. 3, Taipei
Tel: (2) 7122767 Fax: (2) 7130115

Taipei Traders Information System
(Annual)
Import-Export Association of Taipei
5/F., 350 Sung Chiang Rd
Taipei
Tel: (2) 5813521/7 Fax: (2) 5423704

Taiwan Bicycles & Parts Buyer's Guide
(Annual)
Trade Winds, Inc.
No. 7, Lane 75, Yungkang St.
Taipei
Postal address: PO Box 7-179, Taipei
Tel: (2) 3932718 Fax: (2) 3964022 Tlx: 24177

Taiwan Business Directory
(Biennial)
China Credit Information Service Ltd
9/F., 30 Kung Yuan Road
Taipei
Tel: (2) 3810720 Fax: (2) 3310578

Taiwan Buyer's Guide
(Annual)
China Productivity Center
PO Box 769
Taipei
Tel: (2) 7137731 Fax: (2) 7120650 Tlx: 22954

Taiwan Buyer's Guide: Hardware
(Annual)
Trade Winds, Inc.
No. 7, Lane 75, Yungkang St.
Taipei
Postal address: PO Box 7-179, Taipei
Tel: (2) 3932718 Fax: (2) 3964022 Tlx: 24177

Taiwan Exports
(Annual)
Ministry of Economic Affairs
Board of Foreign Trade
1 Hu Kou St
Taipei
Tel: (2) 3510271, 3510286
Fax: (2) 3315387, 3513603, 3517080

Taiwan Gifts & Housewares
(Annual)
Trade Winds, Inc.
No. 7, Lane 75, Yungkang St.
Taipei
Postal address: PO Box 7-179, Taipei
Tel: (2) 3932718 Fax: (2) 3964022 Tlx: 24177

Taiwan Industrial Suppliers : A Buyer's Best
Resource
(Annual)
China Economic News Service
555 Chunghsiao East Road
Section 4, Taipei
Tel: (2) 7681234 Fax: (2) 7632303

Taiwan Machinery
(Semi-annual)
China Economic News Service
555 Chunghsiao East Road
Section 4, Taipei
Tel: (2) 7681234 Fax: (2) 7632303

Taiwan Statistical Data Book
(Annual)
CMC Taipei Liaison Office
PO Box 22048
Taipei 100, Taiwan
Tel: (2) 7529244 Fax: (2)7415432

Taiwan Trade Yellow Pages
(Annual)
Trade Pages Corp.
PO Box 72-50
Taipei
Tel: (2) 3050803 Fax: (2) 3071000

Taiwan Yellow Pages
(Annual)
Taiwan Yellow Pages Corp.
2/F., Chouwoo House
57 Tun Hwa S. Rd
Tel: (2) 7715995 Fax: (2) 7818982

US Firms in Taiwan : Directory
(Annual)
PO Box 68-328
Taipei, Taiwan
Tel: (2) 5942111 Fax: (2) 5923671 Tlx: 21374

Who Makes Machinery in Taiwan
(Annual)
Taiwan Association of Machinery Industry
2/F., 110 Huaining St
Taipei
Tel: (2) 3813722 Fax: (2) 3813711

World Jewelogue
(Annual)
Headway International Publications Co.
907 Great Eagle Center
23 Harbour Rd.
Hong Kong
Tel: [852] 8275121 Fax: [852] 8277064

NEWSPAPERS

Asian Wall Street Journal
Dow Jones Publishing Co. (Asia)
2/F., AIA Bldg., 1 Stubbs Rd.
GPO Box 9825
Hong Kong
Tel: [852] 5737121 Fax: [852] 8345291

Central Daily News
(Chinese)
260 Pa Teh Rd.
Sec. 2, Taipei
Tel: (2) 7763322

China News
11/F., 110 Yen Ping S. Rd.
Taipei
Tel: (2) 3887931 Fax: (2) 3815859

China Post
8 Fu Shun St.
Taipei
Tel: (2) 5943042 Fax: (2) 5957962

China Times
(Chinese)
132 Ta Li St.
Taipei
Tel: (2) 3087111 Fax: (2) 3082745

Economic Daily News
(Chinese)
555 Chung Hsiao E. Rd.
Sec. 4, Taipei
Tel: (2) 7681234 Fax: (2) 7632303

Financial Times
(Chinese)
Rm. 625A, 209 Sung Chiang Rd.
Taipei
Tel: (2) 7310376

International Herald Tribune
7/F., Malaysia Bldg., 50 Gloucester Rd.
Wanchai, Hong Kong
Tel: [852] 8610616 Fax: [852] 8613073

United Daily News
(Chinese)
555 Chung Hsiao E. Rd.
Sec. 4, Taipei
Tel: (2) 7681234

All publications are in English unless otherwise noted.

GENERAL BUSINESS & TRADE PERIODICALS

Asia Business
(Weekly)
PO Box 8-275
Taipei
Tel: (2) 7216769 Fax: (2) 7727466

Asian Business
(Monthly)
Far East Trade Press, Ltd.
2/F Kai Tak Commercial Bldg.
317 Des Voeux Rd.
Central, Hong Kong
Tel: [852] 5457200 Fax: [852] 5446979

Asian Finance
(Monthly)
3rd Fl., Hollywood Center
233 Hollywood Road
Hong Kong
Tel: [852] 8155221 Fax: [852] 8504437

Asian Monetary Monitor
(Bimonthly)
GPO Box 12964
Hong Kong
Tel: [852] 8427200

Asiaweek
(Weekly)
199 Des Voeux Road
Central, Hong Kong
Tel: [852] 8155662 Fax: [852] 8155903

Business News Weekly
(Weekly)
China Economic News Service
United Daily News Building
555 Chungh Siao Rd.
Sec. 4, Taipei 10516
Tel: (2) 6422629 Fax: (2) 6427422

Business Week, Asia Edition
(Weekly)
2405 Dominion Centre
43-59 Queens Rd. E.
Hong Kong
Tel: [852] 3361160 Fax: [852] 5294046

Economic Review
(Bimonthly)
International Commercial Bank of China
100 Chi Lin Rd.
Taipei 10424
Tel: (2) 5633156 Fax: (2) 5632614

The Economist, Asia Edition
(Weekly)
The Economist Newspaper, Ltd.
1329 Charter Rd.
Hong Kong
Tel: [852] 8681425

Far Eastern Economic Review
(Weekly)
Review Publishing Company Ltd
6-7th Fl., 181-185 Gloucester Rd.
Hong Kong
Tel: [852] 8911533

Financial Statistics, Taiwan District
(Monthly)
Central Bank of China
2 Roosevelt Road
Economic Research Department
Sec. 1, Taipei
Tel: (2) 3936161 Fax: (2) 3973750 Tlx: 21532

Monthly Bulletin Of Statistics
The Republic Of China
(Monthly)
Li Ming Cultural Enterprise Company
1 Chung Hsiao East Road
Sec. 1, Taipei
Tel: (2) 3814910

Newsweek International, Asia Edition
(Weekly)
Newsweek, Inc.
47/F., Bank of China Tower
1 Garden Rd.
Central, Hong Kong
Tel: [852] 8104555

Taiwan Enterprise
(Monthly)
Taiwan Enterprise Press Ltd
25 Foo Shou Street
Taipei
Postal address: PO Box 73-4, Taipei
Tel: (2) 8313648

Taiwan Exporters
(Semi-monthly)
Nancy Yu Huang
8 Fu Shun St
Taipei

Taiwan Industrial Panorama
(Monthly)
Ministry of Economic Affairs, Industrial
Development & Investment Center
7 Roosevelt Road
Sec 1., Taipei
Tel: (2) 3947213 Fax: (2) 3926835

Taiwan Trade Opportunities
(Monthly)
China External Trade Development Council
4-8/F., CETRA Tower, 333 Keelung Rd
Sec. 1, Taipei 10548
Tel: (2) 7255200 Fax: (2) 7576653

Time, Asia Edition
(Weekly)
Time, Inc.
31/F., East Tower, Bond Centre
89 Queensway
Hong Kong
Tel: [852] 8446660 Fax: [852] 5108799

Times Enterprise (Shih Tai Chi Yeh)
(Chinese, with some articles in English)
Times Enterprise Corporation
10/F., No 219 Hsi Ning S. Road
Taipei

Trade Monthly
(Monthly)
Import-Export Association of Taipei
5/F., 350 Sung Chiang Rd.
Taipei
Tel: (2) 5813521/7 Fax: (2) 5423704

Trade Winds Weekly : The Asian Weekly for
International Traders
(Weekly)
Trade Winds, Inc.
No. 7, Lane 75, Yungkang St.
Taipei
Postal address: PO Box 7-179, Taipei
Tel: (2) 3932718 Fax: (2) 3964022 Tlx: 24177

World Executives Digest
(Monthly)
3/F., Garden Square Bldg., Greenbelt Drive Cor.
Legaspi Makati
Metro Manila, Philippines
Tel: [63] (2) 8179126

INDUSTRY–SPECIFIC PERIODICALS

Agricultural Association Of China Journal
(Quarterly; in Chinese,with summaries, added
tableoof contents, and some articles in English)
Taiwan Agricultural Research Institute
189 Chungcheng Rd
Wufeng
Taichung, Taiwan
Fax: (4) 3338162

Asia Computer Weekly
(Bimonthly)
Asian Business Press Pte., Ltd.
100 Beach Rd., #26-00 Shaw Towers
Singapore 0718
Tel: [65] 2943366 Fax: [65] 2985534

Asia Labour Monitor
(Bimonthly)
Asia Monitor Resource Center
444-446 Nathan Road, 8th Fl., Flat B
Kowloon, Hong Kong
Tel: [852] 3321346

Asia Pacific Brodcasting & Telecommunications
(Monthly)
Asian Business Press Pte., Ltd.
100 Beach Rd., #26-00 Shaw Towers
Singapore 0718
Tel: [65] 2943366 Fax: [65] 2985534

Asia Pacific Food Industry
(Monthly)
Asia Pacific Food Industry Publications
24 Peck Sea St., #03-00 Nehsons Building
Singapore 0207
Tel: [65] 2223422 Fax: [65] 2225587

Asia Pacific Food Industry Business Report
(Monthly)
Asia Pacific Food Industry Publications
24 Peck Sea St., #03-00 Nehsons Building
Singapore 0207
Tel: [65] 2223422 Fax: [65] 2225587

Asia-Pacific Dental News
(Quarterly)
Adrienne Yo Publishing Ltd.
4th Fl., Vogue Building
67 Wyndham Street
Central, Hong Kong
Tel: [852] 5253133 Fax: [852] 8106512

Asiamac Journal: The Machine-Building and Metal
Working Journal for the Asia Pacific Region
(Quarterly; English, Chinese)
Adsale Publishing Company
21st Fl., Tung Wai Commercial Building
109-111 Gloucester Road
Hong Kong
Tel: [852] 8920511 Fax: [852] 8384119, 8345014
Tlx: 63109 ADSAP HX

Asia Travel Guide
(Monthly)
Interasia Publications, Ltd.
190 Middle Rd., #11-01 Fortune Center
Singapore 0718
Tel: [65] 3397622 Fax: [65] 3398521

Asian And Pacific Council Food And Fertilizer
Technology Center Technical Bulletin
(Semi-monthly)
5/F., 14 Wenchow St
Taipei
Fax: (2) 3620478

Asian Architect And Contractor
(Monthly)
Thompson Press Hong Kong Ltd.
Tai Sang Commercial Building, 19th Fl.
24-34 Hennessy Road
Hong Kong

Asian Aviation
(Monthly)
Asian Aviation Publications
2 Leng Kee Rd., #04-01 Thye Hong Centre
Singapore 0315
Tel: [65] 4747088 Fax: [65] 4796668

Asian Computer Monthly
(Monthly)
Computer Publications Ltd.
Washington Plaza, 1st Fl.
230 Wanchai Road
Wanchai, Hong Kong
Tel: [852] 9327123 Fax: [852] 8329208

Asian Defence Journal
(Monthly)
Syed Hussain Publications (Sdn)
61 A&B Jelan Dato, Haji Eusoff
Damai Complex
PO Box 10836
50726 Kuala Lumpur, Malaysia
Tel: [60] (3) 4420852 Fax: [60] (3) 4427840

Asian Electricity
(11 per year)
Reed Business Publishing Ltd.
5001 Beach Rd., #06-12 Golden Mile Complex
Singapore 0719
Tel: [65] 2913188 Fax: [65] 2913180

Asian Electronics Engineer
(English/Chinese/Korean, Monthly)
Trade Media Ltd.
29 Wong Chuck Hang Rd.
Hong Kong
Tel: [852] 5554777 Fax: [852] 8700816

Asian Hospital
(Quarterly)
Techni-Press Asia Ltd.
PO Box 20494
Hennessy Road
Hong Kong
Tel: [852] 5278682 Fax: [852] 5278399

Asian Hotel: & Catering Times
(Bimonthly)
Thomson Press (HK)
19/F., Tai Sang Commercial Building
23-34 Hennessy Rd.
Hong Kong
Tel: [852] 5283351 Fax: [852] 8650825

Asian Manufacturing
Far East Trade Press Ltd.
2nd Fl., Kai Tak Commercial Building
317 Des Voeux Road
Central, Hong Kong
Tel: [852] 5453028 Fax: [852] 5446979

Asian Medical News
(Bimonthly)
MediMedia Pacific Ltd.
Unit 1216, Seaview Estate
2-8 Watson Rd.
North Point, Hong Kong
Tel: [852] 5700708 Fax: [852] 5705076

Asian Meetings & Incentives
(Monthly)
Travel & Trade Publishing (Asia)
16/F., Capitol Centre
5-19 Jardines Bazaar
Causeway Bay, Hong Kong
Tel: [852] 8903067 Fax: [852] 8952378

Asian Oil & Gas
(Monthly)
Intercontinental Marketing Corp.
PO Box 5056
Tokyo 100-31, Japan
Fax: [81] (3) 3667-9646

Asian Plastic News
(Quarterly)
Reed Asian Publishing Pte., Ltd.
5001 Beach Rd.
#06-12 Golden Mile Complex
Signapore 0719
Tel: [65] 2913188 Fax: [65] 2913180

Asian Printing: The Magazine for the Graphic Arts
Industry
(Monthly)
Travel & Trade Publishing (Asia)
16/F., Capitol Centre
5-19 Jardines Bazaar
Causeway Bay, Hong Kong
Tel: [852] 8903067 Fax: [852] 8952378

Asian Security & Safety Journal
(Bimonthly)
Elgin Consultants, Ltd.
Tungnam Bldg.
Suite 5D, 475 Hennessy Rd.
Causeway Bay, Hong Kong
Tel: [852] 5724427 Fax: [852] 5725731

Asian Shipping
(Monthly)
Asia Trade Journals Ltd.
7th Fl., Sincere Insurance Building
4 Hennessy Road
Wanchai, Hong Kong
Tel: [852] 5278532 Fax: [852] 5278753

Asian Sources: Computer Products
Asian Sources: Electronic Components
Asian Sources: Gifts & Home Products
Asian Sources: Hardware
Asian Sources: Timepieces
(All publications are monthly)
Asian Sources Media Group
22nd Fl., Vita Tower
29 Wong Chuk Hang Road
Wong Chuk Hang, Hong Kong
Tel: [852] 5554777 Fax: [852] 8730488

Asian Water & Sewage
(Quarterly)
Techni-Press Asia, Ltd.
PO Box 20494, Hennessy Rd.
Hong Kong
Fax: [852] 5278399

Asiatechnology
(Monthly)
Review Publishing Company Ltd.
6-7th Fl., 181-185 Gloucester Road
GPO Box 160
Hong Kong
Tel: [852] 8328381 Fax: [852] 8345571

ATA Journal: Journal for Asia on Textile & Apparel
(Bimonthly)
Adsale Publishing Company
Tung Wai Commercial Building, 21st Fl.
109-111 Gloucester Road
Wanchai, Hong Kong
Tel: [852] 8920511 Fax: [852] 8384119

Building & Construction News
(Weekly)
Al Hilal Publishing (FE) Ltd.
50 Jalan Sultan, #20-06, Jalan Sultan Centre
Singapore 0719
Tel: [65] 2939233 Fax: [65] 2970862

Business Traveller Asia-Pacific
(Monthly)
Interasia Publications
200 Lockhart Rd., 13/F.
Wanchai, Hong Kong
Tel: [852] 5749317 Fax: [852] 5726846

Cargo Clan
(Quarterly)
Emphasis (HK), Ltd.
10/F., Wilson House
19-27 Wyndam St.
Central, Hong Kong
Tel: [852] 5215392 Fax: [852] 8106738

Cargonews Asia
(Bimonthly)
Far East Trade Press, Ltd.
2/F. Kai Tak Commercial Bldg.
317 Des Voeux Rd.
Central, Hong Kong
Tel: [852] 5453028 Fax: [852] 5446979

Catering & Hotel News International
(Biweekly)
Al Hilal Publishing (FE) Ltd.
50 Jalan Sultan, #20-26, Jalan Sultan Centre
Singapore 0719
Tel: [852] 2939233 Fax: [852] 2970862

China Sources : Hardware
(Monthly)
Sino Comm Company Ltd
B1K B 5/F Vita TWR
29 Wong Chuk Hang Road
Hong Kong

Chung-Kuo Hai Yun (Maritime China)
(Quarterly)
4306 China Resources Building
26 Harbour Road
Hong Kong
Tel: [852] 5736211

Electronic Business Asia
(Monthly)
Cahners Publishing Company
275 Washington St.

Tel: [1] (617) 964-3030 Fax: [1] (617) 558-4506

Energy Asia
(Monthly)
Petroleum News Southeast Asia Ltd.
6th Fl., 146 Prince Edward Road W
Kowloon, Hong Kong
Tel: [852] 3805294 Fax: [852] 3970959

Far East Health
(10 per year)
Update-Siebert Publications
Reed Asian Publishing Pte
5001 Beach Rd.
#06-12 Golden Mile Complex
Singapore 0719
Tel: [65] 2913188 Fax: [65] 2913180

Information and Computer
(Monthly; Chinese)
116 Nanking E. Rd
Sec. 2, Taipei
Tel: (2) 5422540 Fax: (2) 5310760

International Construction
(Monthly)
Reed Business Publishing, Ltd.
Reed Asian Publishing Pte
5001 Beach Rd.
#06-12 Golden Mile Complex
Singapore 0719
Tel: [65] 2913188 Fax: [65] 2913180

Journal Of The Chinese Chemical Society
(Bimonthly)
Chinese Chemical Society
PO Box 609
Taipei
Tei: (2) 6226149

Lloyd's Maritime Asia
(Monthly)
Lloyd's of London Press (FE)
Rm. 1101 Hollywood Centre
233 Hollywood Rd.
Hong Kong
Tel: [852] 8543222 Fax: [852] 8541538

Media: Asia's Media and Marketing Newspaper
(Biweekly)
Media & Marketing Ltd.
1002 McDonald's Bldg., 46-54 Yee Wo St.
Causeway Bay, Hong Kong
Tel: [852] 5772628 Fax: [852] 5769171

Medicine Digest Asia
(Monthly)
Rm. 1903, Tung Sun Commercial Centre
194-200 Lockhart Rd.
Wanchai, Hong Kong
Tel: [852] 8939303 Fax: [852] 8912591

Oil & Gas News
(Weekly)
Al Hilal Publishing (FE) Ltd.
50 Jalan Sultan, #20-06, Jalan Sultan Centre
Singapore 0719
Tel: [65] 2939233 Fax: [65] 2970862

Petroleum News, Asia's Energy Journal
(Monthly)
Petroleum News Southeast Asia, Ltd.
6/F., 146 Prince Edward Rd. W.
Kowloon, Hong Kong
Tel: [852] 3805294 Fax: [852] 3970959

Shipping & Transport News
(Monthly)
Al Hilal Publishing (FE) Ltd.
50 Jalan Sultan, #20-06, Jalan Sultan Centre
Singapore 0719
Tel: [65] 2939233 Fax: [65] 2970862

Southeast Asia Building Magazine
(Monthly)
Safan Publishing Pte.
510 Thomson Rd.
Block A, #08-01 SLF Complex
Singapore 1129
Tel: [65] 2586988 Fax: [65] 2589945

All publications are in English unless otherwise noted.

Tai-Wan Shui Li
(Quarterly; Chinese and English)
Taiwan Water Conservancy Publishing Commision
11-4 5/F., Tzuen Hsien Street
Taichung 40429
Tel: (4) 2260781/3 Fax: (4) 2202397

Taiwan Computer
(Monthly)
United Pacific International, Inc
PO Box 81-417
Taipei
Tel: (2) 7150751 Fax: (2) 7125591 Tlx: 28784

Taiwan Furniture
(3 per year)
China Economic News Service
555 Chunghsiao East Road
Section 4, Taipei
Tel: (2) 7681234 Fax: (2) 7632303

Taiwan Sugar
(Bimonthly)
Taiwan Sugar Corporation
Rm. 606, 25 Pao Ching Rd
Taipei 100

Target Machinery & Hardware (TMH)
(Monthly)
United Pacific International, Inc
PO Box 81-417
Taipei
Tel: (2) 7150751 Fax: (2) 7169493 Tlx: 28784

Tien Hsin Chi Shu
(Quarterly; Chinese, with summaries in Enlish)
Directorate General of Telecommunications
31 Aikuo East Road
Taipei 106
Tel: (2) 3443601 Fax: (2) 3223738

Trade Winners, Computers & Communications :
Including Electronics & Components Information
(Weekly)
PO Box 7-250
Taipei
Tel: (2) 7333988 Fax: (2) 7333990

Travel News Asia
(Bimonthly)
Far East Trade Press, Ltd.
2/F Kai Tak Commercial Bldg.
317 Des Voeux Rd.
Central, Hong Kong
Tel: [852] 5453028 Fax: [852] 5446979

Travel Trade Gazette Asia
(Weekly)
Asian Business Press Pte., Ltd.
100 Beach Rd., #26-00 Shaw Towers
Singapore 0718
Tel: [65] 2943366 Fax: [65] 2985534

What's New in Computing
(Monthly)
Asian Business Press Pte., Ltd.
100 Beach Rd., #26-00 Shaw Towers
Singapore 0718
Tel: [65] 2943366 Fax: [65] 2985534

RADIO & TELEVISION STATIONS

Broadcasting Corporation of China (BCC)
53 Jen Ai Rd.
Sec. 3, Taipei
Tel: (2) 7710150 Fax: (2) 7113169

China Television Company
120 Chung Yang Rd.
Nankang District
Taipei
Tel: (2) 7838303

Chinese Television System
100 Kuang Fu South Rd.
Taipei
Tel: (2) 7119038 Fax: (2) 7775414

Government Information Office, Executive Yuan
2 Tien Chin St.
Taipei
Tel: (2) 3419211, 3228888 Fax: (2) 3920923, 3416252

Taiwan Television Enterprise
10 Pa Teh Rd.
Sec. 3, Taipei
Tel: (2) 7711515 Fax: (2) 7771419

LIBRARIES

National Central Library
20 Chung Shan S. St.
Taipei, 10040
Tel: (2) 3819132 Fax: (2) 3610144

National Central Library, Taiwan Branch
1 Hsinshen S. Rd., PO Box 106
Sec. 1, Taipei 106
Tel: (2) 7718528

National Taiwan University Library
1 Roosevelt Rd.
Sec. 1, Taipei 10764
Tel: (2) 3510231

Department of Information Library
Ministry of Foreign Affairs
2 Chieh Shou Rd.
Taipei
Tel: (2) 3119292 Fax: (2) 3144972 Tlx: 11299

Index

D

E

O

P

R

W

Y